International HRM

Managing Diversity in the Workplace

Edited by Maryann H. Albrecht

University of Illinois at Chicago

Copyright © Blackwell Publishers Ltd 2001
Editorial matter and organization copyright © Maryann H. Albrecht 2001

First published 2001

2 4 6 8 10 9 7 5 3 1

Blackwell Publishers Ltd
108 Cowley Road
Oxford OX4 1JF
UK

Blackwell Publishers Inc.
350 Main Street
Malden, Massachusetts 02148
USA

British Library Cataloguing in Publication Data

A CIP catalogue record for this book is available from the British Library.

Library of Congress Cataloging-in-Publication Data

International HRM : managing diversity in the workplace / edited by Maryann H. Albrecht.
     p.   cm.
   Includes bibliographical references and index.
   ISBN 0-631-21921-8 (alk. paper) — ISBN 0-631-21922-6 (pb : alk. paper)
     1. Diversity in the workplace. 2. International business enterprises—Management. 3. Diversity in the workplace—Case studies. 4. International business enterprises—Management—Case studies.   I. Albrecht, Maryann H.

HF5549.5.M5 I58 2000
658.3′008—dc21

                                                                                    00-034328

Typeset in 10 on 12 pt Monotype Baskerville
by Ace Filmsetting Ltd, Frome, Somerset
Printed in Great Britain by TJ International, Padstow, Cornwall

This book is printed on acid-free paper.

Contents

Notes on Contributors   xii

Foreword by Fred Luthans   xv

Acknowledgments   xvii

Introduction   1

Part I   Understanding Cultural Diversity in Global Business   **7**

1   Difference and Danger: Cultural Profiles of Nations and Limits to Tolerance   9
Geert Hofstede

- Hofstede presents the dominant values in nation-states around the world, with an emphasis on findings related to tolerance.

2   Key Concepts: Underlying Structures of Culture   24
Edward T. Hall and Mildred Reed Hall

- This summary of classic concepts of culture targets culture as communication in words, material items, and behavior.

3   European Leadership in Globalization   41
Philip R. Harris and Robert T. Moran

- What are the characteristics of successful organizations at the millennium? These are listed, along with the contribution of European leaders to that process and the competencies of different types of global business leaders.

4   The Yin and Yang of Managing in Asia   55
Dean Allen Foster

- Foster compares Western and Asian traditions, management styles, and practices in preparation for emerging markets in the Pacific Rim.

5 *Case*: A Difficult Start   59
Charlotte Butler and Henri-Claude de Bettignies

- This case is set in Thailand and describes the challenges faced by an expatriate manager. It illustrates issues of leadership, communication, cultural differences in management styles, and the impact of culture on expectations and behavior.

6 *Exercise*: The World Wide Web and Cultural Diversity   63
Maryann H. Albrecht

- This exercise provides a selection of websites that allow the searcher to explore global culture and also contact those organizations providing data on countries, organizations, and international business.

Part II   Strategic Human Resource Management   **69**

7 Are We Global Yet?   71
James W. Walker

- This editor's column outlines the emerging trends and concerns in the development and the implementation of global HR strategies.

8 International HR Policy Basics   76
John J. Fadel and Mark Petti

- The authors create a basic framework and the items that need to be included in an international HR policy.

9 Integrated HR Systems Help Develop Global Leaders   79
Linda K. Stroh, Sven Grasshoff, André Rudé, and Nancy Carter

- Information systems are critical for employment in a global context. This article provides an outline for that system and recommendations for its development and implementation.

10 A Contingency Matrix Approach to IHRM   83
Fred Luthans, Paul A. Marsnik, and Kyle W. Luthans

- A consideration of national values and different domains is incorporated into this matrix approach to IHRM.

11 Reaping the Rewards of NAFTA   103
Dick Bottorff

- The North American Free Trade Agreement (NAFTA) provides

opportunities, and this author outlines possibilities and offers
suggestions for successful trade agreements.

12   *Case*: Diversity Management at Hewlett-Packard, Europe   108
Linda Brimm and Mandakini Arora

- What is an effective structure for managing diversity? This case
  discusses the relevance of diversity and the difference between U.S.
  and European management of diversity. The management of
  processes is also an issue, and one that is unique in case presentations –
  most case studies focus only on structures, strategies, and action plans.

13   *Case*: Eurochem Shanghai: Corporate Policy or China Practice?   125
Miles Dodd

- The young new manager confronts an obvious result of running
  roughshod over local practices. An expatriate manager for China
  arbitrates the process of educating the young manager. The case is
  designed to portray diversity issues of training, sensitivity, balance
  of norms, relationships among subsidiaries and the home office, and
  the benefits of diversity.

Part III   Recruitment, Selection, and Placement in a Global Context   131

14   The Boundaryless Organization: Implications for Job Analysis,
Recruitment, and Selection   133
Jodi Barnes Nelson

- "The Boundaryless Organization" lists the issues and offers
  recommendations for practitioners and researchers. Topical focus is
  on recruitment and selection in a global and heterogeneous workforce.

15   Building a Global Workforce Starts With Recruitment   148
Shannon Peters Talbott

- Shannon Peters Talbott tackles the difficult topic of aligning global
  workforce needs to recruitment strategies.

16   Four Faces of Global Culture   152
Peter L. Berger

- Four processes of cultural globalization are related to each other
  and to the cultures they affect. These include a business culture, the
  internationalization of the intelligentsia, the spread of popular
  culture, and a culture of evangelicalism. These cultures are also related
  to work in Latin America and East Asia.

17 European Competencies - Some Guidelines for Companies   160
Bruno Leblanc

   ● What competencies do companies need to develop in Europe in the
     context of a single market? This article reports results from a task force
     made up of HR directors, and develops their ideas.

18 *Case:* Grupo Financiero Inverlat   169
Daniel D. Campbell, Henry W. Lane, and Kathleen E. Slaughter

   ● Managers from a Nova Scotia bank confront the challenge of
     managing a recently acquired Mexican organization. The problems
     of cultural differences and language barriers are tackled in the South
     American setting as managers attempt to restructure the operation.

Part IV   Training and Development   **181**

19 Diversity Training: A Competitive Weapon   183
Jenny C. McCune

   ● This training program includes a four-phase plan that targets the
     planning process and the establishment of priorities, training, and
     outreach to all employees. The author provides examples that
     demonstrate the program's competitive advantage.

20 Training Across Cultures   190
Joyce L. Francis

   ● How do you train those of diverse and strong cultural backgrounds
     within an organization? This article provides guidelines that
     accommodate strong individual differences.

21 Strategy and HRM Initiatives for the '00s Environment: Redefining Roles
and Boundaries, Linking Competencies and Resources   196
Richard M. Hodgetts, Fred Luthans, and John W. Slocum, Jr.

   ● Although emerging from an Australian context, this article provides
     competency units and elements that are useful for managerial
     training in a variety of national and global settings.

22 Global Dual-Career Couple Mentoring: A Phase Model Approach   211
Michael Harvey and Danielle Wiese

   ● Organizations can assist expatriates with partners and families.
     The detailed phase model provides a framework for managers.

23 *Case:* Bhiwar Enterprises   234
Gordon Brannan and Joseph J. DiStefano

- A newly minted MBA who is a nephew of an Indian owner of a wholesale trade firm recommends changes that violate both Indian and African culture. Since the firm has been established in Africa for over 40 years, the issue of what to do is at the forefront of all involved in this family business.

Part V   Employee Relations   243

24 The Multicultural Organization   245
Taylor Cox, Jr.

- Taylor Cox, Jr. provides a description of the characteristics of a multicultural organization, a model of its required features, and a review of tools useful for organizational change.

25 Managing Human Resources in Mexico: A Cultural Understanding   261
Randall S. Schuler, Susan E. Jackson, Ellen Jackofsky, and John W. Slocum, Jr.

- The authors contribute focused and specific suggestions for managing cultural differences in human resources between Mexico and the U.S.

26 New Manufacturing Strategies and Labour in Latin America   271
John Humphrey

- Studies in Argentina, Brazil, Chile, and Mexico create a background for exploring the potential of Japanese-based methods of Just-In-Time (JIT) and Total Quality Management (TQM) in Latin America.

27 Coming to Terms With Local People   287
John Channon and Adam Dakin

- This article examines the challenges and opportunities of HRM as business organizations enter Central and Eastern Europe.

28 Being "a Third Culture Man"   291
Geert J. E. M. Sanders

- What is the perspective provided by an "outsider" to the cultures of a corporation? The author identifies and describes that perspective and its relevance for intercultural cooperation.

29 *Case:* The Evaluation   295
Charlotte Butler and Henri-Claude de Bettignies

- In describing problems associated with performance appraisal in different national cultures, the authors help participants understand the global issues, discuss ways of resolving the issues, and explain the implementation of a program in Asia. The case setting is Thailand, with extensions and examples to the global arena.

30 *Case:* Kentucky Fried Chicken and the Global Fast-Food Industry 301
Jeffrey A. Krug

- This case provides an excellent example of strategic and operational
  change as ownership is transferred and as the firm expands and
  develops a global presence. Much of the analysis is educational, and
  focuses on Mexico and the development of KFC's investment strategy
  in Mexico and Latin America.

Part VI Issues in Global and Cultural Diversity **327**

31 Put Your Ethics to a Global Test 329
Charlene Marmer Solomon

- Charlene Marmer Solomon provides general guidelines and the steps
  needed to develop and implement a global program for ethical
  behavior.

32 Diversity Stress as Morality Stress 336
Rae André

- Coping with the stress of decisions made complex by diversity issues is
  an important and current topic in HR. Rae André enumerates the
  causes of this stress and productive and counterproductive reactions.

33 Remote Control 345
Neil Merrick

- The problems of virtual teams are highlighted in an article that tackles
  Internet communication in multicultural and international firms.

34 Should HR Survive? A Profession at the Crossroads 348
Anthony J. Rucci

- Should HR survive? Here is a suggestion that HRM as a profession
  may eliminate itself, as strategic HR planning becomes a part of
  organizational systems and cultures.

35 Cultural Diversity Programs to Prepare for Work Force 2000: What's Gone
  Wrong? 355
Norma M. Riccucci

- The author examines diversity programs in one nation, their
  shortcomings, and recommendations that can be usefully considered
  by international and multinational organizations.

36 *Case:* Anglo-German Trading Corporation 360
Kenneth E. Roberts

● This case targets environmental issues, communication among international managers, and ethics. The setting is South America, where a general manager must make a decision about a project involving the killing and processing of penguins, a profitable venture for the firm. The conflict between the manager's perception of business values and his personal values is an effective vehicle for group discussion of some ethical issues involved in global business.

37 *Case:* Novell's Global Strategy: "Bytes Are Somewhat Narcotic"   362
Marjorie McEntire, C. Brooklyn Derr, and Chris Meek

● This case shows the importance of a global vision in shaping a swift 17-year rise of Novell from its headquarters to locations in Europe, South America, and Asia. It describes present themes for international growth (the product, entrepreneur, business plan, and competitive challenges).

Index   382

Notes on Contributors

Maryann H. Albrecht   Department of Managerial Studies, University of Illinois at Chicago, Member of the Leadership Group, National Academy of Management, and past President and current Board member, Midwest Academy of Management

Rae André   Organizational Behavior and Theory, Northeastern University

Mandakini Arora   Research Associate, INSEAD

Peter L. Berger   Professor of Sociology and Director, Institute for the Study of Economic Culture, Boston University

Dick Bottorff   Director, International Business Development, National Computer Systems, Inc.

Gordon Brannan   Western Business School, University of Western Ontario

Linda Brimm   Affiliate Professor, INSEAD

Charlotte Butler   Research Associate, INSEAD

Daniel D. Campbell   Richard Ivey School of Business, University of Western Ontario

Nancy Carter   National Director of International HR Consulting Services, KPMG Peat Marwick LLP

John Channon   School of Slavonic and East European Studies (SSEES), University of London

Taylor Cox, Jr.   Professor, School of Business Administration, University of Michigan

Adam Dakin   Director, SSEES-Communicaid

Henri-Claude de Bettignies   Professor of Organizational Behavior, INSEAD

C. Brooklyn Derr   University of Utah

Joseph J. DiStefano   Western Business School, University of Western Ontario

With the exception of case authors, the affiliation of contributors was based on article notes, personal contact, a review of membership lists for national and international organizations, and a review of the *National Faculty Directory*, 30th ed., published in the United States by the Gale Group, 1999. Case authorship is based on the affiliation listed for that case.

Miles Dodd	Regional Director, INSEAD-Euro Asia Centre
John J. Fadel	Senior Manager, International Assignment Services, Deloitte & Touche
Dean Allen Foster	Director, Cross-cultural Training Division, Berlitz International, Inc.
Joyce L. Francis	School of International Service, American University, Washington, DC
Sven Grasshoff	Vice-President, Corporate HR Department-International, Citibank, NA and Past President of the International Personnel Association
Edward T. Hall	Researcher and Consultant in Intercultural Communications
Mildred Reed Hall	Researcher and Consultant in Intercultural Communications
Philip R. Harris	Harris International
Michael Harvey	Puterbaugh Chair in American Free Enterprise, University of Oklahoma
Richard M. Hodgetts	Professor of Strategic Management and International Business, Florida International University
Geert Hofstede	Senior Fellow of the Institute for Research on Intercultural Cooperation
John Humphrey	Institute of Development Studies, University of Sussex
Ellen Jackofsky	Associate Professor of Organizational Behavior and Associate Provost of Academic Affairs, Cox School of Business, Southern Methodist University
Susan E. Jackson	Professor of Management, Stern School of Business, New York University
Jeffrey A. Krug	Department of Business Administration, University of Illinois at Urbana-Champaign
Henry W. Lane	Professor, Richard Ivey School of Business, University of Western Ontario
Bruno Leblanc	EAP, Berlin
Fred Luthans	George Holmes Distinguished Professor of Management, University of Nebraska-Lincoln
Kyle W. Luthans	Bloomsburg University
Paul A. Marsnik	St. John's University-Collegeville, MN
Jenny C. McCune	Bozeman, Montana
Marjorie McEntire	Visiting Assistant Professor, University of Utah
Chris Meek	Associate Professor, Brigham Young University
Neil Merrick	Contributor, *People Management*
Robert T. Moran	Professor of Cross-cultural Communication, American Graduate School of International Management
Jodi Barnes Nelson	University of Georgia
Mark Petti	Manager, International Assignment Services, Deloitte & Touche
Norma M. Riccucci	Public Administration and Policy, Rockefeller College of

	the University at Albany, State University of New York
Kenneth E. Roberts	Staffordshire University (*Emeritus*)
Anthony J. Rucci	Executive Vice-President of Human Resources, Cardinal Health, Inc.
André Rudé	Past President of the International Personnel Associate and Personnel/Expatriate Tax Manager, Hewlett-Packard
Geert J. E. M. Sanders	Associate Professor, School of Management and Organization, University of Groningen, the Netherlands and Professor, Faculty of Economics, University of Bremen, Germany
Randall S. Schuler	Professor of Management, Stern School of Business, New York University
Kathleen E. Slaughter	Professor, Richard Ivey School of Business, University of Western Ontario
John W. Slocum, Jr.	O'Paul Corley Professor of Management, Cox School of Business, Southern Methodist University
Charlene Marmer Solomon	Contributing editor, *Personnel Journal and Workforce*
Linda K. Stroh	Professor, Institute of Human Resources and Industrial Relations and Director, WorkPlace Studies Program, Loyola University, Chicago
Shannon Peters Talbott	Contributor, *Recruitment Staffing Sourcebook* (supplement to *Personnel Journal*)
James W. Walker	Vice-President, Emerging Technologies for Network Solutions, Inc. and Editor, *Human Resource Planning*
Danielle Wiese	University of Oklahoma

Foreword

Finally, we no longer have to preface everything we write and talk about with the over-used line – "In the coming new millennium . . .". The transition to the new millennium and the twenty-first century has been smooth (not even any Y2K glitches), but now the things that we have talked about and predicted have become a sobering reality. We no longer have the excuse, "let off the hook," that this *(fill in the blank)* we should be doing by the next millennium or century. We are now in the new millennium and twenty-first century and must come to grips with the here-and-now: deferring to the year 2000 is no longer possible.

Most would agree that the two biggest '00s environmental realities facing management are technology and globalization. Most of the mass media have focused on the truly revolutionary, paradigmatic change that advanced IT is having on the very nature of organized activity.

Many of us would argue that globalization is having a similar impact as technology, but is receiving relatively less attention. Yet, whereas IT (hardware and software) can be purchased and fairly easily duplicated, the workforce and its leaders may also be pur-chased, but their knowledge, experience, skills, and especially their motivation, attitudes and self-efficacy are *not* easily duplicated. Thus, those of us in the field of organizational behavior and human resource management contend that the real competitive advantage, even in this era of phenomenal information technology, has been, is, and will be acquir-ing, developing, motivating and retaining human resources. Even Bill Gates is on record as stating that his inventory, the *value* of his company, walks out the door every evening.

Managing human resources has always been a very difficult challenge. As Geert Hofstede recently observed in our twenty-first century special issue of *Organizational Dynamics* (Sum-mer, 1999, p. 34), since management is always about people, and human nature has been extremely stable over recorded history, "the essence of management has been and will be equally stable over time." This, of course, is in stark contrast with technology which is highly volatile and changing almost week to week. Yet, even though HRM remains very difficult, globalization has even compounded the problems. Hofstede notes that HRM "differs less from period to period than from part of the world to part of the world, and even from country to country."

Professor Maryann Albrecht has put together an outstanding resource to help students, professors and practicing managers meet the challenges of *International HRM: Managing Diversity in the Workplace*. This text definitely meets her stated criteria of containing articles and cases that include: (1) cultural diversity in both content and the source of material; (2) readability and practicality; (3) real-life case applications; and (4) a traditional HRM framework with a focus on current issues. The Table of Contents and her following Introduction provides details on how these criteria are accomplished. A careful reading of the prepublication material led to my own conclusion that the criteria have indeed not only been met, but greatly exceeded my expectations. Most impressive to me is the comprehensive treatment of IHRM and the relevant, readable articles and cases.

In closing, on a personal note, it has been another pleasure working with Maryann and playing a small part in her continuing efforts to provide us with excellent learning materials for our courses in IHRM and leadership in our professional associations.

Fred Luthans
George Holmes Distinguished
Professor of Management,
University of Nebraska
Editor, *Organizational Dynamics*
Editor-in-Chief, *Journal of World Business*

Acknowledgments

The author wishes to acknowledge the contributions of Lorna Ragonese, my research assistant, who provided a continuing review of the document. I am also grateful for the help of my Department Head. Chemurduri L. Narayana, and Dean Anthony Rucci for their support of a sabbatical leave to complete the project. Dr Elmer Burack, a longtime mentor at UIC, has always shared a concern for diversity and deserves thanks for his continuing and wise advice.

Several classes of MBA and undergraduate students critiqued this text in its successive iterations. I am grateful for their comments and for those of the anonymous reviewers who helped to strengthen the book. I especially appreciate the contribution of Dr Fred Luthans of the University of Nebraska at Lincoln who supported the concept and provided a foreword for this text.

My colleagues in the National Academy of Management and the Midwest Academy of Management who provided encouragement are too numerous to mention. However, Anne Huff, Brian Niehoff, and Deb Dwyer were especially generous with their advice and enthusiasm.

Professional expertise brings a concept to life. Contributors to the book exemplify that excellence. It continues with the editorial expertise of the staff at Blackwell Publishers. The Commissioning Editor, Catriona King, merits special recognition for her insight and guidance. I am also grateful to the staff at Blackwell, especially Bridget Jennings and Joanna Pyke, for their cheerful and competent management of an international production process.

Editors and publishers work with the support of the publishing community. For that reason, they wish to thank the following for permission to use copyright material.

Albrecht, Maryann H., "The World Wide Web and Cultural Diversity," from Maryann H. Albrecht, *Cultural Diversity: Exercises, Cases, Resources*, Stipes Publishing, LLC Champaign, IL, 1997.

André, Rae, "Diversity Stress as Morality Stress," *Journal of Business Ethics* 14, 1995, with kind permission from Kluwer Academic Publishers.

Berger, Peter L., "Four Faces of Global Culture," reprinted with permission. © *The National Interest* 49, Fall, 1997, Washington, DC.

Bottorff, Dick, "Reaping the Rewards of NAFTA," *Management Accounting*, August 1997, courtesy of CIMA.

Case: "A Difficult Start" written by Charlotte Butler, Research Associate, and Henri-Claude de Bettignies, Professor of Organisational Behaviour at INSEAD. It is intended to be used as a basis for classroom discussion rather than to illustrate either effective or ineffective handling of an administrative situation. © 1996 INSEAD-EAC, Fontainebleau, France. All rights reserved.

Case: "Anglo-German Trading Corporation," by Kenneth E. Roberts, University of Staffordshire, 1997. © K. E. Roberts 1997.

Case: "Bhiwar Enterprises," by Gordon Brannan and Joseph J. DiStefano (UWO), 1986. One-time permission to reproduce granted by Ivey Management Services on February 23, 2000.

Case: "Diversity Management at Hewlett-Packard, Europe," written by Linda Brimm, Professor, and Mandakini Arora, Research Associate, at INSEAD. It is intended to be used as a basis for classroom discussion rather than to illustrate either effective or ineffective handling of an administrative situation. © 1996 INSEAD-EAC, Fontainebleau, France. All rights reserved.

Case: "Eurochem Shanghai: Corporate Policy or China Practice?," written by Miles Dodd, Regional Director of INSEAD-Euro Asia Centre. It is intended to be used as a basis for classroom discussion rather than to illustrate either effective or ineffective handling of an administrative situation. © 1998 INSEAD-EAC, Fontainebleau, France. All rights reserved.

Case: "Grupo Financiero Inverlat," by Henry W. Lane and Kathleen E. Slaughter (UWO), 1997. One-time permission to reproduce granted by Ivey Management Services on February 23, 2000.

Case: "Kentucky Fried Chicken and the Global Fast Food Industry," by Jeffrey A. Krug. Copyright © 1997 Ciber, Indiana.

Case: "Novell's Global Strategy: 'Bytes Are Somewhat Narcotic,'" by Marjorie McEntire, C. Brooklyn Derr, and Chris Meek (University of Utah). © 1996 Marjorie McEntire, C. Brooklyn Derr, and Chris Meek.

Case: "The Evaluation" written by Charlotte Butler, Research Associate, and Henri-Claude de Bettignies, Professor of Organisational Behaviour at INSEAD. It is intended to be used as a basis for classroom discussion rather than to illustrate either effective or ineffective handling of an administrative situation. © 1996 INSEAD-EAC, Fontainebleau, France. All rights reserved.

Channon, John and Adam Dakin, "Coming to Terms with Local People," *People Management* 1:12, June, 1995.

Cox, Taylor, Jr., "The Multicultural Organization," *Academy of Management Executive* 5:2, 1991.

Fadel, John J. and Mark Petti, "International HR Policy Basics," *Global Workforce*: supplement to *Workforce*, April, 1997.

Foster, Dean Allen, "The Yin and Yang of Managing in Asia," *HR Magazine* 40:3, March, 1995, courtesy of Society for Human Resource Management.

Francis, Joyce L., "Training Across Cultures," *Human Resources Development Quarterly* 6:1, Spring, 1995, courtesy of Jossey Bass, Inc.

Hall, Edward T. and Mildred Reed Hall, "Key Concepts: Underlying Structures of

Culture," *Understanding Cultural Differences*, Intercultural Press, Inc., Yarmouth, ME, 1995.

Harris, Philip R. and Robert T. Moran, "European Leadership in Globalization," *European Business Review* 96:2, 1996, copyright © 1996, MCB University Press, Bradford.

Harvey, Michael and Danielle Wiese, "Global Dual-Career Couple Mentoring: A Phase Model Approach," *Human Resource Planning* 21:2, 1998, courtesy Human Resources Planning Society.

Hodgetts, Richard M., Fred Luthans, and John W. Slocum, Jr., "Strategy and HRM Initiatives for the '00s Environment: Redefining Roles and Boundaries, Linking Competencies and Resources," reprinted from *Organizational Dynamics*, Autumn, 1999, © 1999 American Management Association International. Reprinted by permission of American Management Association International, New York. All rights reserved. www.amanet.org

Hofstede, Geert, "Differences and Danger: Cultural Profiles of Nations and Limits to Tolerance," *Higher Education in Europe* 21:1, 1996, Taylor & Francis Ltd, PO Box 25, Abingdon, Oxford OX14 3UE.

Humphrey, John, "New Manufacturing Strategies and Labour in Latin America," reprinted by permission from *Asia Pacific Business Review* 2:4, Summer, 1996, published by Frank Cass & Co., 900 Eastern Avenue, Ilford, Essex. Copyright Frank Cass & Co., Ltd.

Leblanc, Bruno, "European Competencies – Some Guidelines for Companies," *Journal of Management Development* 13:2, 1994, copyright © 1994 MCB University Press, Bradford.

Luthans, Fred, Paul A. Marsnik, and Kyle W. Luthans, "A Contingency Matrix Approach to IHRM," *Human Resource Management* 36, Summer, 1997, John Wiley & Sons, Inc.

McCune, Jenny C., "Diversity Training: A Competitive Weapon," reprinted from *Management Review*, June 1996, © 1996 American Management Association International. Reprinted by permission of American Management Association International, New York. All rights reserved. www.amanet.org

Merrick, Neil, "Remote Control," *People Management*, September 26, 1996. © Neil Merrick 1996.

Nelson, Jodi Barnes, "The Boundaryless Organization: Implications for Job Analysis, Recruitment, and Selection," *Human Resource Planning* 20, 1997, courtesy Human Resources Planning Society.

Riccucci, Norma M., "Cultural Diversity Programs to Prepare for Work Force 2000: What's Gone Wrong?," reproduced with permission from *Public Personnel Management* 26:1, Spring, 1997, published by the International Personnel Management Association (IPMA), Alexandria, VA, 703-549-7100, www.ipma-hr.org

Rucci, Anthony J., "Should HR Survive? A Profession at the Crossroads," *Human Resource Management* 36:1, 1997, copyright John Wiley & Sons, Inc.

Sanders, Geert J. E. M., "Being 'a Third Culture Man'," *Cross Cultural Management: An International Journal* 2:1, 1995, courtesy of Barmarick Publications, Hull.

Schuler, Randall S., Susan E. Jackson, Ellen Jackofsky, and John W. Slocum, Jr., "Managing Human Resources in Mexico: A Cultural Understanding," reprinted with permission from *Business Horizons*, May–June, 1996. Copyright © 1996 by the Board of Trustees at Indiana University, Kelley School of Business.

Solomon, Charlene Marmer, "Put Your Ethics to a Global Test," *Personnel Journal* 70, 1996.

Stroh, Linda K., Sven Grasshoff, André Rudé, and Nancy Carter, "Integrated HR Systems Help Develop Global Leaders," *HR Magazine Focus*, April, 1998, courtesy Society for Human Resource Management.

Talbott, Shannon Peters, "Building a Global Workforce Starts With Recruitment," *Recruitment Staffing Sourcebook*, supplement to *Personnel Journal*, March, 1996.

Walker, James W., "Are We Global Yet?," *Human Resource Planning* 21:4, 1998, courtesy Human Resources Planning Society.

Exhibits 30.2, "Leading U.S. Fast-food Chains Ranked by 1996 Sales" and 30.5, "Top U.S. Chicken Chains – Market Share, 1988–97", courtesy *Nations's Restaurant News*.

Exhibit 30.8, "Mexico's Major Trading Partners – % Total Exports and Imports, 1992–6," *Direction of Trade Statistics Yearbook*, 1997, International Monetary Fund.

Exhibit 30.9, "Selected economic data for Canada, the United States, and Mexico," *International Financial Statistics*, 1998, International Monetary Fund.

Table 35.1: "Types and Perceived Effectiveness of Diversity Programs," "SHRM/CCH Survey," Commerce Clearing House, Inc., May 26, 1993.

Introduction

This book focuses on cultural diversity in the global workforce. It is designed to provide the knowledge, skills, and attitudes managers and human resource managers need for success in their international, multinational, and global environments.

Three critical questions relating to diversity form the foundation of the book:

1. What are the trends and current issues in global diversity that affect management and human resource management?
2. What are the solutions?
3. What is needed to implement these solutions?

WHAT IS DIFFERENT ABOUT THIS BOOK?

As organizations have moved from a regional setting to a global arena, there are significant changes in perspectives, structures, systems, and behaviors. These include the:

- integration of cultural and global diversity into the strategic planning of the organization. The functional areas of management and human resource management are now critically related to success in managing cultural diversity;
- increasing use of technology and information systems to monitor and develop business systems; and
- development of skill- and competency-based models for human resource hiring, training, and development in both regional and global contexts.

These changes require a strong, success-oriented, and ethical business culture. How that happens in a global environment with its different perceptions, expectations, and behavior is the concern of all who manage individuals from diverse cultures and subcultures. It is of special concern for those in international, multinational, and global enterprises. How can a book best convey that diversity and solutions for the problems managers encounter?

Several criteria were used to select material from the thousands of articles and hundreds of cases available. These provide a distinct focus for the book and include:

- *Cultural diversity in both the content and the source of material.*
  Great effort was made to seek out information from a variety of cultural perspectives rather than from authors from one nation or continent.
- *Readability and practicality.*
  All articles and cases were evaluated as above average to excellent for readability and for practical application. Evaluations were made by the provider organization and/or by classes of graduate and undergraduate students.
- *Case applications.*
  The cases at the end of each section provide real-life examples of successes and problems in a variety of countries. They highlight national differences and challenge students to provide real-life solutions to the issues managers have confronted in a variety of global settings.
- *A traditional framework with a focus on current issues.*
  While following a sectional outline familiar to managers and human resource professionals, the emphasis is on emerging issues. Core information is provided as a foundation for current topics.

Did it work? Hundreds of articles and cases are not included here but the results of student, practitioner, and reviewer comments indicate the final selections are sound. They highlight important issues and provide solutions applicable to a variety of organizations in a variety of cultural settings. Most importantly, managers and HR managers indicate they learn a great deal by reading articles and cases where cultural diversity is built into authorship, research, and problem solving. For example, many North American students found that an Australian concern for managerial competencies helped them solve problems in their own career. Many Asian managers were impressed by the differences between Mexico and other nations in South America, especially because of the expansion of many Asian multinational firms in that region. All students in graduate and advanced undergraduate classes felt they benefited from the articles and case discussions and the opportunity to use the World Wide Web to explore other cultures.

WHO BENEFITS FROM READING THIS BOOK?

This book is designed for graduate students, managers, and advanced undergraduate students interested in cultural diversity, human resources, and management in a global context. It is especially useful:

- as a major source for MBA and executive courses in cultural diversity, or international human resource management;
- as a supplemental text for courses in human resource management, international management, organizational behavior, and cross-cultural communication.

Because these topics are usually covered in entry-level courses and/or electives, financial, economic, and accounting topics are not included in the material covered in the book.

SUGGESTIONS FOR THE INSTRUCTOR – HOW TO USE CASE STUDIES

Case studies chosen for this book illustrate successful practices and/or issues that need resolution. Some readers will encounter case studies for the first time and need guidance.

For instructors who are relatively new to the process, I offer a few suggestions based on my own experiences.

1. *Emphasize that the cases are "real"*
   Cases are based on real organizations and present the very real circumstances and data challenging a manager.

2. *Encourage an open mind*
   In a complex and competitive world, students seek certainty. The experience of many instructors is that some will try to force a problem and solution based on a sectional reading or their own particular interest and expertise. Others may make strong attempts to get you to identify a problem for them. A balanced approach is to provide a format while encouraging them to apply all their knowledge and insight. A strategy I have used successfully is to encourage students to read the case three times. The first reading is for general understanding, with no attempt to identify issues. That perspective is background for a second reading and a time when they identify problems, prioritize them, and establish causes. Finally, a third reading provides a look at evidence and the information needed for informed decisions.

   When students need a format for their written or oral presentations, I suggest they consider:
   a. the background of the firm (size, industry, products, structure, and the names and position of any individuals mentioned in the case;
   b. issues and evidence for their problem selection(s);
   c. several solutions that match up with the identified problem(s);
   d. development of a plan that solves major problems and that is realistic for the firm. Students also provide a justification for their proposed changes.

3. *Encourage justifications*
   You can see from my suggested format for cases that I've found many students confuse opinions with fact. They often need reminders to present evidence for their judgments. I've found the statement "I can't grade opinions" helps them understand why a factual basis for their selection of problems and solutions is essential.

4. *Save time for class discussion*
   Especially when cases present the issues of diversity, class discussion is useful. It creates a showcase for hard work, provides for different interpretations and is a forum for realistic solutions. I usually allow 20–30 minutes for a full class discussion. When teams are used, I allow 20 minutes for group discussion and 10 minutes for a team report on their problems and solutions.

5. *Performance and recognition in groups*
   There are many successful ways to promote high performance in groups. Based on my own experience, I can provide a few suggestions. For ongoing groups, I ask students to indicate their name, willingness to serve as a manager, and area of functional interest in business. Those who wish to serve as a manager must have prior work experience as a manager or supervisor or provide a strong argument to justify selection as a team manager. I assign managers for groups of five to seven and allow managers to select their own functionally balanced teams. I discourage friends from participating in the same team.

   When teams discuss cases, I ask them to assign a facilitator who will make sure all individuals contribute, and a recorder who will present results. There are a variety of methods to ensure all individuals prepare and participate. I allow class time for discussion and, with established groups, I usually use peer reviews twice during a course. Individuals give their name and group number and use "grades" of A to D (and a reason) to evaluate others on the items of both Quality of Contribution and Quantity of Contribution. Depending on the class time devoted to cases, at least ten percent of their course grade is based on these evaluations. In the rare event a first evaluation is very low, I discuss the problems with a student and negotiate a new beginning either in the same or with a different group.

SELECTED ELEMENTS FOR DIFFERENT COURSES

This book covers core material in global diversity with an emphasis on the knowledge and practices useful for today's managers. All of the material is useful for courses in diversity as well as for those courses in management and human resource management. However, those in charge of half-term courses, or courses in organizational behavior, international management or cross-cultural communication may wish to select items that match up with their own course outlines.

To assist you in course planning, the Table of Contents provides a brief synopsis of each item. For those wishing a case that covers the material, I would suggest using the last case in the book, "Novell's Global Strategy."

Instructors are most aware of the background of class members, their interests, the time available for reading, and the fit with other curriculum material. However, I can offer some suggestions for short courses and related topics. Table 1.1 has article suggestions for half-term courses and for courses where global diversity is an important secondary emphasis. Cases are not ranked in this table but they are listed as a planning tool. In Table 1.1, the letter C denotes a suggestion that the item has a priority as core content and S indicates supplemental material for the courses:

ICD (half-course)	International Cultural Diversity in a half-term format
(I)HRM (half-course)	Human Resource Management or International Human Resource
	Management in a half-term format
OB	Organizational Behavior
IM	International Management
CC	Cross-Cultural Communication.

Table 1.1   Book Items and Their Suggested Selection as Core or Supplemental Material

Book Items	ICD (Half-course)	(I)HRM (Half-course)	OB	IM	CC
Section 1 Understanding Cultural Diversity in Global Business					
1. Difference and Danger	C	C	C	C	C
2. Key Concepts	C	C	C	C	C
3. European Leadership in Globalization	C	C	C	C	C
4. The Yin and Yang of Managing in Asia	C	C	C	C	C
5. *Case*: A Difficult Start					
6. Exercise: The World Wide Web and Cultural Diversity	C	S	S	S	S

Section II   Strategic Human Resource Management

7. Are We Global Yet?	S	S	S	S	S
8. International HR Policy Basics	C	C	C	C	C
9. Integrated HR Systems Help Develop Global Leaders	C	S	S	S	C
10. A Contingency Matrix Approach to IHRM	C	C	C	C	C
11. Reaping the Rewards of NAFTA	S	S	S	C	S
12. *Case*: Diversity Management at Hewlett-Packard, Europe					
13. *Case*: Eurochem Shanghai: Corporate Policy or China Practice?					

Section III   Recruitment, Selection, and Placement in a Global Context

14. The Boundaryless Organization	S	C	C	S	C
15. Building a Global Workforce Starts with Recruitment	S	S	S	C	S
16. Four Faces of Global Culture	C	C	C	C	C
17. European Competencies	C	C	C	C	C
18. *Case*: Group Financiero Inverlat					

Section IV   Training and Development

19. Diversity Training	C	S	S	S	C
20. Training Across Cultures	C	C	S	S	C
21. Strategy and HRM Initiatives for the '00s Environment	C	C	S	S	S
22. Global Dual-Career Couple Mentoring	S	C	C	C	C
23. *Case*: Bhiwar Enterprises					

Section V   Employee Relations

24. The Multicultural Organization	C	C	C	C	C
25. Managing Human Resources in Mexico	C	C	C	C	C
26. New Manufacturing Strategies and Labour in Latin America	S	S	S	C	S
27. Coming to Terms with Local People	S	S	S	S	S
28. Being "a Third Culture Man"	S	S	C	S	C
29. *Case* "The Evaluation"					
30. *Case*: Kentucky Fried Chicken and the Global Fast-Food Industry					

Section VI   Issues in Global and Cultural Diversity

31. Put Your Ethics to a Global Test	C	C	C	C	C
32. Diversity Stress as Morality Stress	S	S	C	S	C
33. Remote Control	S	S	S	S	S
34. Should HR Survive?	C	C	S	C	S
35. Cultural Diversity Programs to Prepare for Work Force 2000	C	C	S	C	C
36. *Case*: Anglo German Trading Corporation					
37. *Case*: Novell's Global Strategy					

Part I

Understanding Cultural Diversity in Global Business

1 Difference and Danger: Cultural Profiles of Nations and
Limits to Tolerance   9
Geert Hofstede

2 Key Concepts: Underlying Structures of Culture   24
Edward T. Hall and Mildred Reed Hall

3 European Leadership in Globalization   41
Philip R. Harris and Robert T. Moran

4 The Yin and Yang of Managing in Asia   55
Dean Allen Foster

5 *Case*: A Difficult Start   59
Charlotte Butler and Henri-Claude de Bettignies

6 *Exercise*: The World Wide Web and Cultural Diversity   63
Maryann H. Albrecht

Chapter 1

Difference and Danger: Cultural Profiles of Nations and Limits to Tolerance

Geert Hofstede

In spite of internal differences, most nation-states display a common mental programming of a majority of their inhabitants. This programming consists of shared symbols, heroes, and rituals that provide a national identity, and shared values that serve to stabilize the national society. Dominant values in nation-states around the world have been classified according to four dimensions. One of these is *Uncertainty Avoidance*, which among other things stands for the degree of tolerance for whatever or whoever is different, for the strength of the feeling that *what is different, is dangerous*. The counselling process is affected by the mental programming of counsellor and client. Effective counselling of persons not sharing the same cultural profile demands special efforts, especially if the level of *Uncertainty Avoidance* for either or both parties is high.

THE CONCEPT OF MENTAL PROGRAMMING

Mental Programming is an informatician's metaphor for the pattern of thinking, feeling, and acting that every person has acquired in childhood and carries along throughout life. Without such mental programmes, the behaviour of people would be unpredictable, and social life, impossible.

A person's mental programming is partly unique, partly shared with others. One can distinguish three levels of uniqueness in mental programmes:

i)   The one furthest from being unique and the most basic is the *universal level* of mental programming which is shared by all, or almost by all, mankind. This level is the biological *operating system* of the human body, which includes a range of expressive behaviours such as laughing and weeping, and kinds of associative and aggressive behaviours which are also found in the higher animals. This level of programming has been popularized by ethologists (biologists specialized in animal behaviour) such as Eibl-Eibesfeldt, who has called one of his books *Der vorprogrammierte Mensch* [Man the Pre-Programmed] (Munich: Deutscher Taschenbuch Verlag, 1976).

ii) The *collective level* of mental programming is shared with some but not with all other people. It is common to people belonging to a certain group or category, but different among people belonging to other groups or categories. The whole area of subjective human culture (as opposed to objective culture that consists of human artifacts; see Triandis, 1972, p. 4) belongs to this level. It includes the language in which people express themselves, the deference they show to their elders, the physical distance from other people they maintain in order to feel comfortable, the way they carry out basic human activities like eating, making love, or toilet behaviour, and the ceremonials surrounding them.

iii) The *individual level* of human programming is the truly unique part. No two people are programmed exactly alike, not even identical twins reared together. This level is that of individual personality, the one providing for a wide range of alternative behaviours within the same collective culture.

The borderlines between the three levels are a matter of debate within the social sciences. To what extent are individual personalities the product of a collective culture? Which behaviours are human universals, and which are culture-dependent?

Mental programmes can be inherited, that is, transferred in our genes, or they can be learned after birth. Of the three levels, the universal level must be entirely inherited. It is part of the genetic information common to the human species. Programming at the individual level should be at least partly inherited, that is, genetically determined. It is otherwise difficult to explain the differences in capabilities and temperament between successive children of the same parents raised in very similar environments. At the middle, collective level, however, all mental programmes are learned. They are shared with people who went through the same learning process, but who do not have the same genes. As an example, one should think of the existence of the people of the United States of America. A mixture of all the world's genetic roots, present-day Americans display a collective mental programming very recognizable to the outsider. They illustrate the force of collective learning.

Mental programming manifests itself in several ways. From the many terms used to describe mental programmes, the following four together cover the total concept rather neatly: *symbols, heroes, rituals,* and *values.* Of these, *symbols* are the most superficial, and *values,* the most profound, with *heroes* and *rituals* in between.

Symbols are words, gestures, pictures, or objects which carry a particular meaning only recognized as such by those who share the mental programme. The words in a language or a jargon belong to this category, as do dress, hairdos, Coca-Cola, flags, and status symbols. Heroes are persons, alive or dead, real or imaginary, who possess characteristics that are highly prized by those sharing the mental programme, and thus serve as models for behaviour. Rituals are collective activities, technically superfluous to reach desired ends, but considered socially essential. They are therefore carried out for their own sake. Ways of greeting and paying respect to others, and social and religious ceremonies are examples of rituals. Symbols, heroes, and rituals together constitute the visible part of mental programmes; elsewhere, they have been subsumed under the term, *practices* (Hofstede, 1991, p. 7).

Values are the invisible part of mental programming. Values can be defined as "broad tendencies to prefer certain states of affairs over others" (Hofstede, 1980, p. 19). They are feelings having a plus and a minus side.

The transfer of collective mental programmes through learning goes on throughout life. The most fundamental elements, the values, are learned first, when the mind is still relatively unprogrammed. A baby learns to distinguish between dirty and clean (hygienic values) and between evil and good, unnatural and natural, abnormal and normal (ethical and moral values). Somewhat later, the child learns to distinguish between ugly and beautiful (aesthetic values), and between paradoxical and logical, irrational and rational (intellectual values). By the age of ten, most children have their basic value system firmly in place, and after that age, changes are difficult to make.

Because they were acquired so early, values as a part of mental programming often remain unconscious to those who hold them. They therefore cannot normally be discussed, nor can they be directly observed by outsiders. They can only be inferred from the way people act under various circumstances.

The transfer of collective mental programmes is a social phenomenon which, according to Durkheim (1937 [1895], p. 107), should be explained socially. Societies, organizations, and groups have ways of conserving and passing on mental programmes from generation to generation with an obstinacy which many people tend to underestimate. The elders programme the minds of the young according to the way they were once programmed themselves. What else can they do, or who else will teach the young? Theories of race, very popular among past generations, were an erroneous genetic explanation for the continuity of mental programmes across generations.

Collective mental programming takes place within the collectivities of which people are a part. Everybody belongs to different categories at the same time; therefore, everybody carries different levels of mental programming.

The most obvious ones are the following:

- a family level, determined by the family or family substitute in which a person grew up;
- a sex-determined level, according to whether a person was born as a girl or as a boy;
- a generational level, according to the decade in which a person was born;
- a social class level, associated with educational opportunities and with a person's occupation or profession;
- a linguistic level, according to the language or languages in which a person was programmed;
- a religious level, according to the religious tradition in which that person was programmed;
- for those who are employed, an organizational or corporate culture level according to the way a person was socialized by his or her work environment;
- an occupational level, representing the shared mental programming, across national borders, of persons within the same type of occupation (like counsellors);
- a nation-state level according to one's country (or countries for people who migrated during their lifetimes);
- within nation-states, possibly a regional and/or ethnic level.

This article will focus on the level associated with the nation-state. It corresponds partly with what was once called *national character*, and later, *national culture*. National characters are intuitively evident, and have been so for hundreds and even thousands of years. However, because of the value elements in national mental programmes, statements about national characters were almost without exception extremely biased. They often contained more information about the person making the statement than about the nation that was the object of the statement.

In order to avoid this bias, only comparative information about differences in nation-state-linked mental programmes that treat the data of every nation-state as equivalent will be used.

NATIONAL CULTURE DIFFERENCES

Human societies as historically and organically developed forms of social organization have existed for at least ten thousand years. Nation-states as political units into which the entire world is divided and to one of which any human being is supposed to belong are a much more recent phenomenon in human history. The concept of a common mental programming applies, strictly speaking, more to societies than to nation-states. Nevertheless, many nation-states do form historically developed wholes even if they are composed of different regions and ethnicities, and even if less integrated minorities live within their borders.

Nation-states contain institutions that standardize mental programmes: a dominant language (sometimes more than one), common mass media, a national education system, a national army, a national political system, national representation in sports events with a strong symbolic and emotional appeal, and a national market for certain skills, products, and services. Today's nation-states do not attain the degree of internal homogeneity of the isolated, usually nonliterate, societies traditionally studied by field anthropologists, but most nation-states are the source of a considerable amount of common mental programming of their citizens.

A popular term at the present time is *national identity*. National identity is part of the mental programming of a national population, but at the conscious level of practices, symbols, heroes, and rituals. There is an increasing tendency for ethnic, linguistic, and religious groups to fight for recognition of their own identity, if not for national independence. Ulster, the republics of the former Yugoslavia, and parts of the former Soviet Union are evident examples. But the groups struggling are not necessarily very different in terms of their deepest level of mental programmes: values. They may struggle on the basis of rather similar values, as has been found to be the case for the Flemish and Walloons in Belgium, and for the Croats and Serbs in former Yugoslavia.

In the first half of the twentieth century, social anthropology developed the conviction that all societies, traditional or modern, faced and still face the same basic problems; only the answers differ. Attempts at identifying these common basic problems used conceptual reasoning, interpretation of field experiences, and statistical analysis of data about societies. In 1954, two Americans, the sociologist Alex Inkeles and the psychologist Daniel Levinson, published a broad survey of the literature in English on what was then still called *national character*. They suggested that the following issues qualify as common basic problems worldwide, with consequences for the functioning of societies, of groups within these societies, and of individuals within these groups:

i) relation to authority;
ii) conception of self, in particular:
 – the relationship between individual and society, and
 – the individual's concept of masculinity and femininity;
iii) ways of dealing with conflicts, including the control of aggression and the expression of feelings (Inkeles and Levinson, 1969 [1954], p. 447).

Twenty years later, the author had the opportunity to study a large body of survey data about the values of people in over fifty countries around the world. These people were working in the local subsidiaries of one large multinational corporation: IBM. At first sight it might seem strange that employees of a multinational corporation – a very special kind of people – could be used to identify differences in *national* value systems. However, a crucial problem in cross-national research is always to sample respondents who are functionally equivalent. The IBM employees represented almost perfectly matched samples. They were similar in all respects except nationality, which made the effects of nationality differences in their answers stand out unusually clearly.

A statistical analysis of the answers to questions about the values of similar IBM employees in different countries revealed common problems, but solutions differing from country to country, in the following areas:

i)   social inequality, including the relationship to authority;

ii)   the relationship between the individual and the group;

iii)   concepts of masculinity and femininity: the social implications of having been born as a boy or as a girl;

iv)   ways of dealing with uncertainty, relating to the control of aggression and the expression of emotions.

These four problem areas could be expressed in four dimensions of national cultures, labelled *Power Distance* (large versus small), *Individualism versus Collectivism*, *Masculinity versus Femininity*, and *Uncertainty Avoidance* (strong versus weak). Every country studied could be located somewhere between the extremes (poles) of each dimension.

These empirical results covered amazingly well the areas predicted by Inkeles and Levinson twenty years earlier. The author only discovered the prediction made by Inkeles and Levinson *after* he had identified the four dimensions in the IBM data. It provided strong support for the theoretical importance of the empirical findings. Problems basic to all human societies should turn up in different studies regardless of the approaches followed.

A dimension associates a number of phenomena in a society that were empirically found to occur in combination; even if at first sight there does not always seem to be a logical necessity for their going together. The logic of societies, however, is not the same as the logic of individuals looking at them.

The IBM research results have been replicated by others on other samples of respondents: on students (Hofstede and Bond, 1984) and on national élites (Hoppe, 1990). These research results correlate significantly with the results of other cross-national studies of values, like the European Value Systems Study (Ester *et al.*, 1993), and the worldwide values surveys by Schwartz (1994).

More recently, a fifth dimension of differences among national cultures was identified, opposing a *Long Term Orientation* in life to a *Short Term Orientation*. East Asian nations tend to score *Long Term*; European countries more *Short Term*. Data allowing for the computation of scores on this dimension have so far only been collected for twenty-three nations.

POWER DISTANCE AND UNCERTAINTY AVOIDANCE

Power Distance has been defined as "the extent to which the less powerful members of institutions within a country expect and accept that power is distributed unequally". It

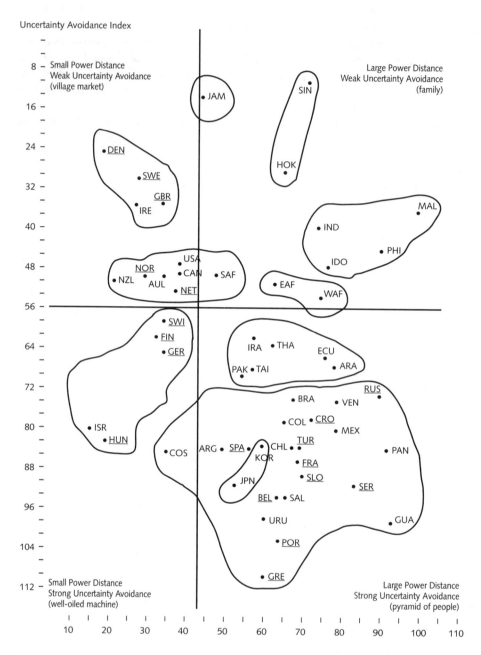

Figure 1.1 The Relative Position of Fifty-four Countries or Regions on the *Power Distance* x *Uncertainty Avoidance* Dimensions (for country name abbreviations, see Figure 1.2)

ARA	Arab-speaking countries (Egypt, Iraq, Kuwait, Lebanon, Libya, Saudi Arabia, United Arab Emirates)	JPN	Japan
		KOR	South Korea
		MAL	Malaysia
ARG	Argentina	MEX	Mexico
AUL	Australia	NET	Netherlands
AUT	Austria	NOR	Norway
BEL	Belgium	NZL	New Zealand
BRA	Brazil	PAK	Pakistan
CAN	Canada	PAN	Panama
CHL	Chile	PER	Peru
COL	Colombia	PHI	Philippines
COS	Costa Rica	POR	Portugal
CRO	Croatia	RUS	Russia
DEN	Denmark	SAF	South Africa
EAF	East Africa (Ethiopia, Kenya, Tanzania, Zambia)	SAL	Salvador
		SER	Serbia
ECU	Ecuador	SIN	Singapore
FIN	Finland	SLO	Slovenia
FRA	France	SPA	Spain
GER	Germany	SWE	Sweden
GBR	Great Britain	SWI	Switzerland
GRE	Greece	TAI	Taiwan
GUA	Guatemala	THA	Thailand
HOK	Hong Kong	TUR	Turkey
HUN	Hungary	URU	Uruguay
IDO	Indonesia	USA	United States
IND	India	VEN	Venezuela
IRA	Iran	WAF	West Africa (Ghana, Nigeria, Sierra Leone)
IRE	Ireland		
ISR	Israel		
ITA	Italy	*Note*: In Figures 1.1 and 1.3, European countries have been underlined.	
JAM	Jamaica		

Figure 1.2 Abbreviations for Country Names

represents the degree of social inequality in the mental programming of people. All societies are unequal, but some are more unequal than others, and this inequality is reflected in the mental programmes of people.

Uncertainty Avoidance has been defined as "the extent to which the members of a culture feel threatened by uncertain or unknown situations". It stands for the need for structure, social conformity, and absolute truths. People in a strongly uncertainty avoiding society have been pre-programmed to be active, anxious, precise, and to dislike the unpredictable. People in weakly uncertainty avoiding societies have been pre-programmed to be passive, relaxed, imprecise, and to dislike the predictable. Obviously, individual personalities within these societies vary in regard to these counts.

Figure 1.1 illustrates the relative positions of the answers by the respondent samples from fifty-four countries and regions on *Power Distance* and *Uncertainty Avoidance*.

The IBM survey data, collected around 1970, did not cover eastern Europe, except for what was then still Yugoslavia. In 1993, the author went back to the old Yugoslavia data, which could be split into data from Croatia, Serbia, and Slovenia. More recent replications on samples more-or-less matched with the IBM employee data samples were collected in Hungary (Varga, 1986) and Russia (Bollinger, 1988). Attempts have been made to collect data with the same questionnaire in other eastern European countries, but the survey populations were poorly matched with the IBM employee population, so that the results are not useful.

The top left quadrant of Figure 1.1 contains six northern and western European countries: Denmark, Sweden, Norway, the Netherlands, Ireland, the United Kingdom, and overseas countries initially populated by British migrants. These combine small *Power Distance* with weak *Uncertainty Avoidance*. In the mental programmes of these people, there is little social inequality and little need for structure.

The bottom left quadrant contains the German-speaking countries of Austria, Switzerland, and Germany, plus Finland, Hungary, and Israel. These combine small *Power Distance* with stronger *Uncertainty Avoidance*. The mental programmes still display little social inequality, but more need for structure.

The two quadrants to the left thus host all Germanic countries, plus Finland and Hungary. In all of these countries, survey respondents scored low on *Power Distance*. The closeness of Austria and Hungary is remarkable: the Austro-Hungarian empire survives in the mind-sets of people.

The top right quadrant (large *Power Distance* but weak *Uncertainty Avoidance*) contains countries in Africa, Asia, and the Caribbean, not populated by Europeans.

The bottom right quadrant contains all Latin European countries studied (including Belgium), all Latin American countries (Costa Rica being an exception), the South and East European countries of Slovenia, Croatia, Serbia, Turkey, Russia, and Greece, plus Japan and Korea, and some other Asian and Muslim countries (Taiwan, Thailand, Iran, Pakistan, and the Arab-speaking countries). In all of these countries, respondents scored high on both *Power Distance* and *Uncertainty Avoidance*.

Power and structure are the key elements in the organizations people build. Other research (described in Hofstede, 1991, p. 140) has suggested that people from different countries tend to hold different mental models regarding what an organization is. People from the Latin quadrant tend to see an organization as a *pyramid of people*, functioning on the basis of both power and structure. Those from the German-speaking quadrant tend to see an organization as a *well-oiled machine*, functioning on the basis of its structure, but without the need for a constant exercise of power. Those from the Anglo-Nordic quadrant tend to see an organization as a *market*, functioning on the basis of permanent negotiation. Those from the African-Asian quadrant tend to see it as a *family*, in which the family head is the master, and there is little formal structure.

The roots of these different mental programmes lie evidently in history. The Latin countries of Europe grew out of the remains of the Roman Empire; the Germanic countries did not. The Latin European countries later on colonized Latin America, the Germanic countries colonized North America. The Roman Empire was the first large and effective state to be established in its part of the world. In the same way as early childhood experiences have a major impact on personality, these early societal experiences must have had a lasting impact on polity, affecting not only all institutions that have followed but also the corresponding mental programmes. One still speaks of the *Latin mentality*.

The Roman Empire combined two principles new to Europe: *i)* authority centralized in Rome, and *ii)* a system of codified laws, applicable to every Roman citizen. The centralized authority principle supports a large *Power Distance*; the codified law principle supports strong *Uncertainty Avoidance*. Of the two principles, the first dominated the second. The supreme power, the emperor, stood over the law. When the Roman Empire disintegrated, the absolute authority of the ruler was maintained by the Germanic invaders of France, who mixed with the country's Romanized Celtic population (Pirenne, 1939, p. 32), but not by the Germanic Anglo-Saxon invaders of Britain who chased the Romanized Celts without mixing with them.

In the Germanic tradition, the power of the king was subordinate to the assembly of freemen. Therefore, an absolutist rule could never take hold in Britain. When the Norman kings attempted to establish it, they were forced to recognize the rights of the people in the Magna Charta of 1215 (Pirenne, 1939, p. 257). In Germany up until the nineteenth century, a central authority could never last, and the country was composed of small principalities. Federal Germany is still much more decentralized than the countries of Latin Europe.

Russia, Greece, and Serbia inherited the Byzantine culture, which in turn was an offspring of Roman culture. We find their scores on the extreme fringe of the Latin quadrant in Figure 1.1, with extreme *Power Distances* in Russia and Serbia and extreme *Uncertainty Avoidance* in Greece. The Byzantine empire seems to have developed and transferred a hypertrophy of Latin mental programming traits.

The Germanic countries in Figure 1.1 are relatively close on *Power Distance* but display a wider spread on *Uncertainty Avoidance*. The countries turned towards the sea avoided uncertainty less than the countries turned towards the land. How, why, and when exactly this split took place is a question best left to historians.

UNCERTAINTY AVOIDANCE AND TOLERANCE

The term *Uncertainty Avoidance* has been borrowed from American organization sociology, in particular from the work of James G. March (e.g., Cyert and March, 1963, p. 118ff). March and his colleagues recognized it in American organizations. Ways of handling uncertainty, however, are part and parcel of any human institution in any country. All human beings have to face the fact that we do not know what will happen tomorrow. The future is uncertain, but one must live with it anyway.

Extreme uncertainty creates intolerable anxiety. Every human society has developed ways to alleviate this anxiety. These ways belong to the domains of technology, law, and religion. Technology, from the most primitive to the most advanced, helps to avoid uncertainties caused by nature. Laws and rules try to prevent uncertainties in the behaviour of other people. Religion is a way of relating to the transcendental forces that are assumed to control the personal future of humankind. Religion helps one to accept the uncertainties against which one cannot defend oneself. Some religions offer the ultimate certainty of a life after death or of victory over one's opponents.

Anthropologists studying traditional societies have devoted a good deal of their attention to technology, law, and religion. They have illustrated the enormous variety of ways in which human societies deal with uncertainty. Modern societies do not vary essentially from traditional societies in this respect. In spite of the availability of the same information virtually anywhere around the globe, technologies, laws, and religions continue to vary. Moreover, there are no signs of spontaneous convergence.

The essence of uncertainty is that it is a subjective experience, a feeling. A lion tamer may feel reasonably comfortable when surrounded by his animals, a situation which would make most people die of fear. Some people may feel reasonably comfortable when driving on a crowded motorway at seventy miles per hour or more, a situation that is statistically about as risky as that of the lion tamer.

Feelings of uncertainty are not only just personal, but may also be partly shared with other members of one's society. Feelings of uncertainty are acquired and learned. Such feelings and ways of coping with them belong to the cultural heritage of societies and are transferred and reinforced through basic institutions like the family, the school, and the state. They are reflected in the collectively held values of the members of a particular society. Their roots are nonrational. They lead to collective patterns of behaviour in one society which may seem aberrant and incomprehensible to members of other societies.

Among the first things a child learns are the distinctions between *clean* and *dirty*, and between *safe* and *dangerous*. What is considered clean and safe, or dirty and dangerous, varies widely from one society to the next, and even among families within a society. The British-American anthropologist, Mary Douglas, has written a book, *Purity and Danger*. Dirt – that which pollutes – is, Douglas argues, a relative concept, which depends entirely on cultural interpretation. Dirt is basically matter that is out-of-place. Dangerous and polluting things are those that do not fit one's usual framework of thinking and normal classifications, from a given point of view. What a child has to learn is to distinguish clean things from dirty things and safe things from dangerous things. And in strongly uncertainty avoiding cultures, classifications with regard to what is dirty and dangerous are tight and absolute.

Dirt and danger are not limited to matter. They also refer to people. Racism is bred in families. Children learn that persons from a particular category are dirty and dangerous. Ideas too can be considered dirty and dangerous. Children in families learn that some ideas are good and others, taboo. In some cultures, the distinction between good and evil ideas is very sharp. There is a concern about Truth with a capital T. Ideas which vary from this Truth are dangerous and polluting. Little room is left for doubt or relativism. Taboos are supposed to be a characteristic of traditional, primitive societies, but modern societies too are full of taboos. The family is the place in which these taboos are transmitted from generation to generation.

Weak *Uncertainty Avoidance* cultures also have their classifications as to dirt and danger, but these are wider and more prepared to give the benefit of the doubt to unknown situations, people, and ideas. Norms are expressed in basic terms, like being honest and being polite, but allowing a range of personal interpretation as to what both concepts mean in given cases. Deviant behaviour is not so easily felt as threatening. Norms as to dress, hair style, and speech are looser, and children are expected to treat other people equally regardless of their appearance.

The strong *Uncertainty Avoidance* sentiment can be expressed by the credo of xenophobia: *What is different is dangerous*. The weak *Uncertainty Avoidance* sentiment on the contrary is: *What is different is curious*. Somewhere in between is the prevailing sentiment in the author's country, the Netherlands (UAI = 53): *What is different is ridiculous.*

Fundamentalisms are more frequent in strongly than in weakly uncertainty avoiding societies. Tolerance, mysticism, and meditation are more characteristic of weakly than of strongly uncertainty avoiding societies. But the relationship between *Uncertainty Avoidance* and religion is even broader. The grouping of countries according to *Uncertainty Avoidance* scores reflects their dominant religion. Orthodox and Roman Catholic Christian countries score high (except the Philippines and Ireland). Judaic and Muslim countries tend to score in the middle. Protestant Christian countries score low. Eastern religions score medium to very low, with Japan as an exception.

The dominant religious affiliation in a country may have been a *result* of previously existing mental programmes as much as a *cause* of such programmes. All of the great religions of the world at some time in their history underwent profound schisms: between Roman Catholics, Eastern Orthodox, and various Protestant groups in Christianity; between Sunni and Shia in Islam; between liberals and various fundamentalist groups in Judaism; and between Hinayana and Mahayana in Buddhism. Differences in mental programming between groups of believers have probably played a major role in these schisms. Religious conversion does not mean a total change in cultural values.

The value complexes described by the dimensions of *Power Distance, Uncertainty Avoidance, Individualism or Collectivism,* and *Masculinity and Femininity* seem to have survived religious conversions. These value complexes are likely to have influenced to what extent a population has been receptive to certain religions, and how the accepted religion has evolved in that country. Indonesian (Javanese) mysticism, for example, implying weak *Uncertainty Avoidance,* has survived Hindu, Buddhist, Muslim, and Christian conversions.

The split between Germanic and Latin countries as portrayed in Figure 1.1 could also be explained as a split by religion: Protestant versus Roman Catholic. According to the Belgian historian, Henri Pirenne (1939, p. 397), the Roman Catholic Church is in many respects a continuation of the Roman Empire; therefore, the influences of old Rome and new Rome are difficult to separate. However, Ireland, predominantly Roman Catholic, but never part of the Empire, scored like the United Kingdom and not like, for example, Italy, a fact that suggests that the crucial factor is the Empire and not the Church. The Reformation in the Christian churches separated almost exactly those European countries once under the Roman Empire from the rest. All the ex-Roman countries (the ones now speaking Romance languages, with the exception of Romania) refuted the Reformation and remained Roman Catholic; most others became Protestant or mixed. Poland and Ireland were never part of the Roman Empire, but in their case, Roman Catholicism provided them with an identity against non-Roman Catholic oppressors.

In establishing a relationship between *Uncertainty Avoidance* and religious belief, it makes sense to distinguish between western and eastern religions. The western religions, Judaism, Christianity, but also Islam, are based on divine revelation, and all three originated from what is now called the Middle East. What distinguishes the western from the eastern religions is their concern with Truth with a capital T. The western revealed religions share the assumption that there is an absolute Truth that humans can possess which excludes all other truths. The difference between strong and weak *Uncertainty Avoidance* societies adhering to these religions lies in the amount of certainty one needs about having this Truth. In strong uncertainty avoiding cultures, the frequently held belief is that *There is only one Truth and we have it. All others do not have it.* Possessing this Truth is the only road to salvation and the main purpose in a person's life. The consequence of the error of others may be an effort to convert them, to avoid them, or to kill them.

Weak *Uncertainty Avoidance* cultures from the west still believe in Truth, but they have less of a need to believe that they alone possess it. *There is only one Truth and we are looking for it. Others are looking for it as well, and we accept as a fact of life that they look in different directions.* Part of this Truth, anyway, is that God wants nobody to be prosecuted for their beliefs.

Eastern religions are less concerned about Truth. The assumption that there is one Truth which man can possess is absent in their thinking. Buddhism instead stresses the acquisition of insight by meditation. Thus in the east, people will easily absorb elements of different religions. Most Japanese perform both Buddhist and Shinto rituals; however, by standards of western logic, the two religious traditions are mutually exclusive.

What applies to religions applies also to political ideologies which are often difficult to separate from religious inspiration. Marxism in many places took on the form of a secular religion. When East Germany was still solidly communist, the façade of the University of Leipzig was decorated with an enormous banner reading *"Der Marxismus ist allmächtig, weil er wahr ist!"* (Marxism is all-powerful because it is True!). In strong *Uncertainty Avoidance* cultures, we find intolerant political ideologies; in weak *Uncertainty Avoidance* cultures, tolerant ones.

The respect of what is commonly called *human rights* assumes a tolerance for people with different political ideas. One reason for violations of human rights in some countries is a strong *Uncertainty Avoidance* in their culture; however, the same strong *Uncertainty Avoidance* may stimulate a careful application of laws that protect human rights.

INDIVIDUALISM/COLLECTIVISM AND MASCULINITY/FEMININITY

Figure 1.3 displays the relative positions of the respondent samples from fifty-six countries and regions, in regard to the two dimensions of *Individualism-Collectivism* and *Masculinity-Femininity* (for these two dimensions no data are available for Hungary).

Individualism stands for a society in which the ties between individuals are loose. Everyone is expected to look only after him- or herself and his or her immediate family. Collectivism stands for a society in which people from birth onwards are integrated into strong, cohesive, in-groups, which throughout their lifetimes continue to protect them in exchange for unquestioning loyalty.

Collectivism is the normal state of mind of agricultural societies. Hunting and gathering societies are more individualist. Modern individualism developed in England, Scotland, and the Netherlands and was taken to North America by the Pilgrim Fathers. Individualism in countries increases with national wealth (increased individualism is an *effect*, not a *cause* of economic growth). Asian nations that have recently become wealthy have also become more individualistic but not as much as western European countries at the same level of wealth.

The scores regarding individualism in Figure 1.3 closely follow the *Per Capita Gross National Product* of the countries. All wealthy western countries are found in the lower part of the diagram. Japan that combines an Asian tradition of collectivism with western-style modernity scores half-way.

Individualist mental programmes are a precondition for political democracy and for a

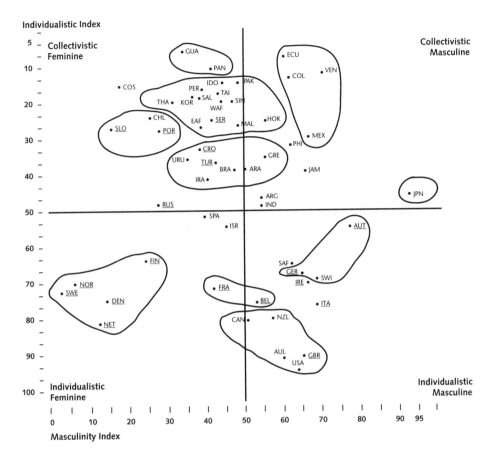

Figure 1.3 The Relative Position of Fifty-four Countries or Regions on the *Individualism* x *Masculinity* Dimensions (for country name abbreviations, see Figure 1.2)

free market economy. One-person-one-vote presupposes that those persons have been programmed to hold personal opinions. The invisible hand of the market economy presupposes that persons will attempt to maximize their individual economic advantage. Both do not apply in nations with collectivist mental programmes and institutions.

Collectivism plays an important role in the ethnic conflicts that regularly erupt in different parts of the world: like those in Bosnia, Somalia, and Burundi. Children in collectivist societies have learned to differentiate between *us* and *them*, to oppose their own in-group to various out-groups. If, in addition, *Uncertainty Avoidance* in these societies has increased under political or ecological threat, the growing feeling that *what is different is dangerous* is projected on the nearest out-groups. The call, *let's hit them first before they hit us*, becomes credible in such situations.

The second dimension in Figure 1.3, *Masculinity*, stands for a society in which social sexual roles are clearly distinct: men are supposed to be assertive, tough, and focused on material success; women are supposed to be more modest, tender, and concerned with the quality of life. *Femininity* stands for a society in which social-sexual roles overlap. Both men and women are supposed to be modest, tender, and concerned with the quality of life.

On the bottom left, the individualistic and feminine side of the diagram, we find a cluster of Nordic countries: Sweden, Norway, Denmark, and Finland, plus the Netherlands. Slightly feminine scores were obtained for France, Spain, and Israel. On the bottom right, individualistic, and masculine side of the diagram, we find the German-speaking countries: Germany, Switzerland, and Austria (moderately individualistic but strongly masculine); the United Kingdom and other Anglo-Saxon countries (very individualistic and fairly masculine), plus some other countries: Italy, Ireland, Belgium, and South Africa (where scores were only based on the white population).

The poorer countries (top half of Figure 1.3) vary in *Masculinity*, from Costa Rica, Slovenia, Russia, Chile, Portugal, and Thailand (quite feminine); to Jamaica, Colombia, Ecuador, Venezuela, and Mexico (quite masculine). (South) Korea distinguishes itself from Japan by a feminine score opposing Japan's extremely high score on *Masculinity*.

Masculine mental programmes lead to personal and political choices in favour of a performance society, sympathy for the strong, and reward according to merit. Feminine mental programmes lead to a welfare society, sympathy for the weak, and reward according to need.

Among the wealthy nations of Europe – the ones in the bottom half of Figure 1.3 – the percentage of their Gross National Product spent on development co-operation with poor countries is strongly negatively correlated with their masculinity scores in the IBM samples. The correlation is over 80. Feminine countries spend much more than masculine ones. The present fashion to reduce development assistance budgets also strikes the masculine countries more than the feminine ones. On the other hand, the percentage of national GNPs spent on armaments is *positively* correlated with the masculinity scores. Politicians in masculine countries tend to favour economic growth over preservation of the ecosystem; those in feminine countries tend to display the opposite preference.

The origins of *Masculinity-Femininity* differences are not immediately evident. The feminine nations concentrated in northwestern Europe (Denmark, Finland, the Netherlands, Norway, and Sweden) share some of the same history. The élites in these countries consisted to a large extent of traders and seafarers. In trading and sailing, maintaining good interpersonal relationships and caring for the ships and the merchandise are competitive advantages. The Hanseatic League (AD 1200–1500) covered all these countries, plus the free cities of Hamburg, Bremen, and Lübeck in northern Germany and the Baltic states. The Hansa was a free association of trading towns and, for the maintenance of such a system, values associated with *Femininity* were functional. Women played an active role in the Hansa trading families. While the Hansa does not explain the origin of North-European *Femininity*, it at least benefited from it and reinforced it.

NATIONAL CULTURE DIFFERENCES AND COUNSELLING

National patterns of culture affect all institutions of a society: its families, its schools, its living communities, its religious communities, its work places, its political bodies, its ways of dealing with health and sickness, birth and death. One cannot understand the *management culture* of a society – as many books on the subject try to do – without understanding the broader culture in which this management culture is embedded. Role patterns are transferred from one institution to another. The role-pair, boss-subordinate, is modelled after the role-pair, teacher-student, and this pair, in turn, after the role-pair, parent-child in a society.

. . .

This article has been given the title, "Difference and Danger", because it was written for a conference labelled *Counselling and Tolerance*. In discussing the four cultural dimensions, special attention has been placed on the dimension of *Uncertainty Avoidance*, on the plus pole associated with *what is different is dangerous*, and on the minus pole, with tolerance of differences. But it is too easy a conclusion that because strongly uncertainty avoiding cultures tend to foster intolerance, counsellors should avoid these cultures. One does not choose one's national cultural context, nor the cultural backgrounds of one's clients. Strong *Uncertainty Avoidance* may be a liability in terms of tolerance, but it is an asset in some other respects, such as precision, attention to detail, and working hard. Weak *Uncertainty Avoidance* cultures may be more tolerant, but their tolerance might also take the form of ignoring the other party's problems; of simply not caring. With a dubious term, such tolerance could be labelled, *repressive*.

opération, 1988.

glewood Cliffs, NJ: Prentice-Hall, 1963.

Universitaires de France, [1895] 1937.

immender Faktor im menschlichen Verhalten.

ociety: Value Change in Europe and North

ork-Related Values. Beverly Hills: Sage

ndon: McGraw-Hill, 1991.

s: An Independent Validation Using 15:4 (1984): 417–33.

ational Differences in Work-Related ment Training and Development", a at Chapel Hill, 1990.

dy of Modal Personality and Socio- *Handbook of Social Psychology*, Vol. 4.

ing Skills: A Practical Guide. Westport,

don: George Allen and Unwin, 1939. ral Dimensions of Values", in U. *ications.* Thousand Oaks, CA: Sage,

ohn Wiley, 1972.

démiai Kiadó, 1986.

Va

Chapter 2

Key Concepts: Underlying Structures of Culture

Edward T. Hall and Mildred Reed Hall

CULTURE IS COMMUNICATION

In physics today, so far as we know, the galaxies that one studies are all controlled by the same laws. This is not entirely true of the worlds created by humans. Each cultural world operates according to its own internal dynamic, its own principles, and its own laws – written and unwritten. Even time and space are unique to each culture. There are, however, some common threads that run through all cultures.

It is possible to say that the world of communication can be divided into three parts: *words, material things*, and *behavior*. Words are the medium of business, politics, and diplomacy. Material things are usually indicators of status and power. Behavior provides feedback on how other people feel and includes techniques for avoiding confrontation.

By studying these three parts of the communication process in our own and other cultures, we can come to recognize and understand a vast unexplored region of human behavior that exists outside the range of people's conscious awareness, a "silent language" that is usually conveyed unconsciously (see Edward T. Hall's *The Silent Language* [New York: Doubleday, 1959]). This silent language includes a broad range of evolutionary concepts, practices, and solutions to problems which have their roots not in the lofty ideas of philosophers but in the shared experiences of ordinary people. In the words of the director of a project on cross-cultural relations, understanding the silent languages "provides insights into *the underlying principles that shape our lives.*" These underlying principles are not only inherently interesting but eminently practical. The readers of this book [*Understanding Cultural Differences*], whether they be German, French, American, or from other countries, should find these principles useful at home and abroad.

Culture can be likened to a giant, extraordinarily complex, subtle computer. Its programs guide the actions and responses of human beings in every walk of life. This process requires attention to everything people do to survive, advance in the world, and gain satisfaction from life. Furthermore, cultural programs will not work if crucial steps are omitted, which happens when people unconsciously apply their own rules to another system.

During the three years we worked on this book [*Understanding Cultural Differences*], we had to learn two different programs for our office computer. The first was quite simple, but mastery did require paying close attention to every detail and several weeks of practice. The second was a much more complex program that required weeks of intensive practice, hours of tutoring, and days of depression and frustration when "the darn thing didn't work." Learning a new cultural program is infinitely more complicated and requires years of practice, yet there are many similarities in the learning process.

Cultural communications are deeper and more complex than spoken or written messages. *The essence of effective cross-cultural communication has more to do with releasing the right responses than with sending the "right" messages.* We offer here some conceptual tools to help our readers decipher the complex, unspoken rules of each culture.

FAST AND SLOW MESSAGES: FINDING THE APPROPRIATE SPEED

The speed with which a particular message can be decoded and acted on is an important characteristic of human communication. There are fast and slow messages. A headline or cartoon, for example, is fast; the meaning that one extracts from books or art is slow. A fast message sent to people who are geared to a slow format will usually miss the target. While the content of the wrong-speed message may be understandable, it will not be received by someone accustomed to or expecting a different speed. The problem is that few people are aware that information can be sent at different speeds.

Examples of Fast and Slow Messages

Fast Messages	*Slow Messages*
Prose	Poetry
Headlines	Books
A communiqué	An ambassador
Propaganda	Art
Cartoons	Etchings
TV commercials	TV documentary
Television	Print
Easy familiarity	Deep relationships
Manners	Culture

Almost everything in life can be placed somewhere along the fast/slow message-speed spectrum. Such things as diplomacy, research, writing books, and creating art are accomplished in the slow mode. Buddha, Confucius, Shakespeare, Goethe, and Rembrandt all produced messages that human beings are still deciphering hundreds of years after the fact. Language is a very slow message; after 4,000 years, human beings are just beginning to discover what language is all about. The same can be said of culture, which incorporates multiple styles of "languages" that only release messages to those who are willing to spend the time to understand them.

In essence a person is a slow message; it takes time to get to know someone well. The message is, of course, slower in some cultures than in others. In the United States it is not too difficult to get to know people quickly in a relatively superficial way, which is all that most Americans want. Foreigners have often commented on how "unbelievably friendly" the Americans are. However, when Edward T. Hall studied the subject for the U.S. State

Department, he discovered a worldwide complaint about Americans: they seem capable of forming only one kind of friendship – the informal, superficial kind that does not involve an exchange of deep confidences.

Conversely, in Europe personal relationships and friendships are highly valued and tend to take a long time to solidify. This is largely a function of the long-lasting, well-established networks of friends and relationships – particularly among the French – that one finds in Europe. Although there are exceptions, as a rule it will take Americans longer than they expect to really get to know Europeans. It is difficult, and at times may even be impossible, for a foreigner to break into these networks. Nevertheless, many businesspeople have found it expedient to take the time and make the effort to develop genuine friends among their business associates.

HIGH AND LOW CONTEXT: HOW MUCH INFORMATION IS ENOUGH?

Context is the information that surrounds an event; it is inextricably bound up with the meaning of that event. The elements that combine to produce a given meaning – events and context – are in different proportions depending on the culture. The cultures of the world can be compared on a scale from high to low context.

> A high context (HC) communication or message is one in which *most* of the information is already in the person, while very little is in the coded, explicit, transmitted part of the message. A low context (LC) communication is just the opposite; that is, the mass of the information is vested in the explicit code. Twins who have grown up together can and do communicate more economically (HC) than two lawyers in a courtroom during a trial (LC), a mathematician programming a computer, two politicians drafting legislation, two administrators writing a regulation. (Edward T. Hall [*Beyond Culture*, New York: Anchor/Doubleday], 1976)

Japanese, Arab, and Mediterranean peoples, who have extensive information networks among family, friends, colleagues, and clients and who are involved in close personal relationships, are high-context. As a result, for most normal transactions in daily life they do not require, nor do they expect, much in-depth, background information. This is because they keep themselves informed about everything having to do with the people who are important in their lives. Low-context people include Americans, Germans, Swiss, Scandinavians, and other northern Europeans; they compartmentalize their personal relationships, their work, and many aspects of day-to-day life. Consequently, each time they interact with others they need detailed background information. The French are much higher on the context scale than either the Germans or the Americans. This difference can affect virtually every situation and every relationship in which the members of these two opposite traditions find themselves.

Within each culture, of course, there are specific individual differences in the need for contexting – the process of filling in background data. But it is helpful to know whether the culture of a particular country falls on the high or low side of the scale since every person is influenced by the level of context.

Contexting performs multiple functions. For example, any shift in the level of context is a communication. The shift can be up the scale, indicating a warning of the relationship, or down the scale (lowering the context), communicating coolness or displeasure – signaling something has gone wrong with a relationship. In the United States, the boss might communicate annoyance to an assistant when he shifts from the high-context, familiar form of address to the low-context, formal form of address. When this happens the boss is telling the subordinate in no uncertain terms that she or he has stepped out of line and incurred disfavor. In Japan moving the direction of the context is a source of daily feedback as to how things are going. The day starts with the use of honorifics, formal forms of address attached to each name. If things are going well the honorifics are dropped as the day progresses. First-naming in the United States is an artificial attempt at high-contexting; it tends to offend Europeans, who view the use of first names as acceptable only between close friends and family. With Europeans, one is always safe using a formal form of address, waiting for the other person to indicate when familiarity is acceptable.

Like their near relations the Germans, many Anglo-Americans (mostly those of northern European heritage) are not only low-context but they also lack extensive, well-developed information networks. American networks are limited in scope and development compared to those of the French, the Spanish, the Italians, and the Japanese. What follows from this is that Americans, unless they are very unsophisticated, will feel the need for contexting, for detailed background information, any time they are asked to make a decision or to do something. The American approach to life is quite segmented and focused on discrete, compartmentalized information; Americans need to know what is going to be in what compartment before they commit themselves. We experienced this in Japan when we were asked on short notice to provide names of well-placed Japanese and Americans to be participants in a small conference. Like most prudent Americans, we were reluctant to provide names until we knew what the conference was about and what the individuals recommended would be expected to do. This seemed logical and reasonable enough to us. Nevertheless, our reluctance was read as obstructionist by our Japanese colleagues and friends responsible for the conference. In Japan the mere presence of certain individuals endows the group and its activities with authority and status, which is far more important than the topic of the conference. It is characteristic of high-context, high-information societies that attendance at functions is as much a matter of the prestige associated with the function as anything else. This in turn means that, quite frequently, invitations to high-level meetings and conferences will be issued on short notice. It is taken for granted that those invited will eschew all previous commitments if the meeting is important enough. As a general rule Americans place greater importance on how long ago a commitment was made, on the agenda, and on the relevance of the expertise of different individuals to the agenda. . . .

Another example of the contrast between how high- and low-context systems work is this: consider a top American executive working in an office and receiving a normal quota of visitors, usually one at a time. Most of the information that is relevant to the job originates from the few people the executive sees in the course of the day, as well as from what she or he reads. This is why the advisors and support personnel who surround the presidents of American enterprises (as well as the president of the United States) are so important. They and they alone control the content and the flow of organizational information to the chief executive.

Contrast this with the office of virtually any business executive in a high-context country such as France or Japan, where information flows freely and from all sides. Not only are people constantly coming and going, both seeking and giving information, but the entire form and function of the organization is centered on gathering, processing, and disseminating information. Everyone stays informed about every aspect of the business and knows who is best informed on what subjects.

In Germany almost everything is low-context and compartmentalized. The executive office is both a refuge and a screen – a refuge for the boss from the distractions of day-to-day office interactions and a screen for the employees from continual supervision. Information communicated in the office is not shared except with a select few – the exact antithesis of the high-information cultures.

High-context people are apt to become impatient and irritated when low-context people insist on giving them information they do not need. Conversely, low-context people are at a loss when high-context people do not provide *enough* information. One of the great communications challenges in life is to find the appropriate level of contexting needed in each situation. Too much information leads people to feel they are being talked down to; too little information can mystify them or make them feel left out. Ordinarily, people make these adjustments automatically in their own country, but in other countries their messages frequently miss the target.

The other side of the coin when considering context level is the apparent paradox that high-context people, such as the French, want to see *everything* when evaluating a *new* enterprise to which they have not been contexted. Annual reports or tax returns are not enough. Furthermore, they will keep asking until they get the information they want. Being high-context, the French are driven to make their own synthesis of the meanings of the figures. Unlike Americans, they feel uncomfortable with someone else's synthesis, someone else's "bottom line."

SPACE

Every living thing has a visible physical boundary – its skin – separating it from its external environment. This visible boundary is surrounded by a series of invisible boundaries that are more difficult to define but are just as real. These other boundaries begin with the individual's personal space and terminate with her or his "territory."

Territoriality

Territoriality, an innate characteristic whose roots lie hundreds of millions of years in the past, is the act of laying claim to and defending a territory and is a vital link in the chain of events necessary for survival. In humans, territoriality is highly developed and strongly influenced by culture. It is particularly well developed in the Germans and the Americans. Americans tend to establish places that they label "mine" – a cook's feeling about a kitchen or a child's view of her or his bedroom. In Germany this same feeling of territoriality is commonly extended to all possessions, including the automobile. If a German's car is touched, it is as though the individual himself has been touched.

Space also communicates power. A corner office suite in the United States is conventionally occupied by "the brass," and a private office in any location has more status than

a desk in the open without walls. In both German and American business, the top floors
are reserved for high-ranking officials and executives. In contrast, important French officials occupy a position in the *middle*, surrounded by subordinates; the emphasis there is on
occupying the central position in an information network, where one can stay informed
and can control what is happening.

Personal space

Personal space is another form of territory. Each person has around him or her an
invisible bubble of space which expands and contracts depending on a number of things:
the relationship to the people nearby, the person's emotional state, cultural background,
and the activity being performed. Few people are allowed to penetrate this bit of mobile
territory and then only for short periods of time. Changes in the bubble brought about by
cramped quarters or crowding cause people to feel uncomfortable or aggressive. In northern Europe, the bubbles are quite large and people keep their distance. In southern
France, Italy, Greece, and Spain, the bubbles get smaller and smaller so that the distance
that is perceived as intimate in the north overlaps normal conversational distance in the
south, all of which means that Mediterranean Europeans "get too close" to the Germans,
the Scandinavians, the English, and those Americans of northern European ancestry. In
northern Europe one does not touch others. Even the brushing of the overcoat sleeve
used to elicit an apology.

The multisensory spatial experience

Few people realize that space is perceived by *all* the senses, not by vision alone. Auditory
space is perceived by the ears, thermal space by the skin, kinesthetic space by the muscles,
and olfactory space by the nose. As one might imagine, there are great cultural differences in the programming of the senses. Americans to some extent and Germans to a
greater extent rely heavily on auditory screening, particularly when they want to concentrate. High-context people reject auditory screening and thrive on being open to interruptions and in tune with what goes on around them. Hence, in French and Italian cities one
is periodically and intrusively bombarded by noise.

Unconscious reactions to spatial differences

Spatial changes give tone to communication, accent it, and at times even override the
spoken word. As people interact, the flow and shift of distance between them is integral to
the communication process. For example, if a stranger does not maintain "normal"
conversational distance and gets too close, our reaction is automatic – we feel uncomfortable, sometimes even offended or threatened and we back up.

Human beings in the course of a lifetime incorporate literally hundreds of spatial cues.
They imbibe the significance of these cues like mother's milk, in the context of their own
culture. Just as a fragrance will trigger a memory, these cues and their associated behaviors
release unconscious responses, regulating the tone, tempo, and mood of human transactions.

Since most people don't think about personal distance as something that is culturally patterned, foreign spatial cues are almost inevitably misinterpreted. This can lead to bad feelings which are then projected onto the people from the other culture in a most personal way. When a foreigner appears aggressive and pushy, or remote and cold, it may mean only that her or his personal distance is different from yours.

Americans have strong feelings about proximity and the attendant rights, responsibilities, and obligations associated with being a neighbor. Neighbors should be friendly and agreeable, cut their lawns, keep their places up, and do their bit for the neighborhood. By contrast, in France and Germany, simply sharing adjacent houses does not necessarily mean that people will interact with each other, particularly if they have not met socially. Proximity requires different behavior in other cultures.

TIME

Life on earth evolved in response to the cycles of day and night and the ebb and flow of the tides. As humans evolved, a multiplicity of internal biological clocks also developed. These biological clocks now regulate most of the physiological functions of our bodies. It is not surprising, therefore, that human concepts of time grew out of the natural rhythms associated with daily, monthly, and annual cycles. From the beginning humans have been tied to growing seasons and were dependent on the forces and rhythms of nature.

Out of this background two time systems evolved – one as an expression of our biological clocks, the other of the solar, lunar, and annual cycles. These systems will be described under the headings "Time as Structure" and "Time as Communication." In the sections that follow, we restrict ourselves to those manifestations of time that have proved to be stumbling blocks at the cultural interface.

Monochronic and polychronic time

There are many kinds of time systems in the world, but two are most important to international business. We call them monochronic and polychronic time. Monochronic time means paying attention to and doing only one thing at a time. Polychronic time means being involved with many things at once. Like oil and water, the two systems do not mix.

In monochronic cultures, time is experienced and used in a linear way – comparable to a road extending from the past into the future. Monochronic time is divided quite naturally into segments; it is scheduled and compartmentalized, making it possible for a person to concentrate on one thing at a time. In a monochronic system, the schedule may take priority above all else and be treated as sacred and unalterable.

Monochronic time is perceived as being almost *tangible*: people talk about it as though it were money, as something that can be "spent," "saved," "wasted," and "lost." It is also used as a classification system for ordering life and setting priorities: "I don't have time to see him." Because monochronic time concentrates on one thing at a time, people who are governed by it don't like to be interrupted. Monochronic time seals people off from one another and, as a result, intensifies some relationships while shortchanging others. Time becomes a room which some people are allowed to enter, while others are excluded.

Monochronic time dominates most business in the United States. While Americans perceive it as almost in the air they breathe, it is nevertheless a learned product of northern European culture and is therefore arbitrary and imposed. Monochronic time is an artifact of the industrial revolution in England; factory life required the labor force to be on hand and in place at an appointed hour. In spite of the fact that it is *learned*, monochronic time now appears to be natural and logical because the great majority of Americans grew up in monochronic time systems with whistles and bells counting off the hours.

Other Western cultures – Switzerland, Germany, and Scandinavia in particular – are dominated by the iron hand of monochronic time as well. German and Swiss cultures represent classic examples of monochronic time. Still, monochronic time is not natural time; in fact, it seems to violate many of humanity's innate rhythms.

In almost every respect, polychronic systems are the antithesis of monochronic systems. Polychronic time is characterized by the simultaneous occurrence of many things and by a *great involvement with people.* There is more emphasis on completing human transactions than on holding to schedules. For example, two polychronic Latins conversing on a street corner would likely opt to be late for their next appointment rather than abruptly termi-nate the conversation before its natural conclusion. Polychronic time is experienced as much less tangible than monochronic time and can better be compared to a single point than to a road.

Proper understanding of the difference between the monochronic and polychronic time systems will be helpful in dealing with the time-flexible Mediterranean peoples. While the generalizations listed below do not apply equally to all cultures, they will help convey a pattern:

Monochronic People	**Polychronic People**
Do one thing at a time	Do many things at once
Concentrate on the job	Are highly distractible and subject to interruptions
Take time commitments (deadlines, schedules) seriously	Consider time commitments an objective to be achieved, if possible
Are low-context and need information	Are high-context and already have information
Are committed to the job	Are committed to people and human relationships
Adhere religiously to plans	Change plans often and easily
Are concerned about not disturbing others; follow rules of privacy and consideration	Are more concerned with those who are closely related (family, friends, close business associates) than with privacy
Show great respect for private property; seldom borrow or lend	Borrow and lend things often and easily
Emphasize promptness	Base promptness on the relationship
Are accustomed to short-term relationships	Have strong tendency to build lifetime relationships

The relation between time and space

In monochronic time cultures, the emphasis is on the compartmentalization of functions and people. Private offices are sound-proof if possible. In polychronic Mediterranean cultures, business offices often have large reception areas where people can wait. Company or government officials may even transact their business by moving about in the reception area, stopping to confer with this group and that one until everyone has been attended to.

Polychronic people feel that private space disrupts the flow of information by shutting people off from one another. In polychronic systems, appointments mean very little and may be shifted around even at the last minute to accommodate someone more important in an individual's hierarchy of family, friends, or associates. Some polychronic people (such as Latin Americans and Arabs) give precedence to their large circle of family members over any business obligation. Polychronic people also have many close friends and good clients with whom they spend a great deal of time. The close links to clients or customers create a reciprocal feeling of obligation and a mutual desire to be helpful.

Polychronic time and information

Polychronic people live in a sea of information. They feel they must be up-to-the-minute about everything and everybody, be it business or personal, and they seldom subordinate personal relationships to the exigencies of schedules or budgets.

It is impossible to know how many millions of dollars have been lost in international business because monochronic and polychronic people do not understand each other or even realize that two such different time systems exist. The following example illustrates how difficult it is for these two types to relate:

> A French salesman working for a French company that had recently been bought by Americans found himself with a new American manager who expected instant results and higher profits immediately. Because of the emphasis on personal relationships, it frequently takes years to develop customers in polychronic France, and, in family-owned firms, relationships with customers may span generations. The American manager, not understanding this, ordered the salesman to develop new customers within three months. The salesman knew this was impossible and had to resign, asserting his legal right to take with him all the loyal customers he had developed over the years. Neither side understood what had happened.

These two opposing views of time and personal relationships often show up during business meetings. In French meetings, the information flow is high, and one is expected to read other people's thoughts, intuit the state of their business, and even garner indirectly what government regulations are in the offing. For the French and other polychronic/high-context people, a tight, fixed agenda can be an encumbrance, even an insult to one's intelligence. Most, if not all, of those present have a pretty good idea of what will be discussed beforehand. The purpose of the meeting is to create consensus. A rigid agenda and consensus represent opposite goals and do not mix. *The importance of this basic dichotomy cannot be overemphasized.*

Past- and future-oriented countries

It is always important to know which segments of the time frame are emphasized. Cultures in countries such as Iran, India, and those of the Far East are past-oriented. Others, such as that of the urban United States, are oriented to the present and short-term future;

still others, such as those of Latin America, are both past- and present-oriented. In Germany, where historical background is very important, every talk, book, or article begins with background information giving a historical perspective. This irritates many foreigners who keep wondering, "Why don't they get on with it? After all, I am educated. Don't the Germans know that?" The Japanese and the French are also steeped in history, but because they are high-context cultures, historical facts are alluded to obliquely. At present, there is no satisfactory explanation for why and how differences of this sort came about.

TIME AS COMMUNICATION

As surely as each culture has its spoken language, each has its own *language of time*; to function effectively in France, Germany, and the United States, it is essential to acquaint oneself with the local language of time. When we take our own time system for granted and project it onto other cultures, we fail to read the hidden messages in the foreign time system and thereby deny ourselves vital feedback.

For Americans, the use of appointment-schedule time reveals how people feel about each other, how significant their business is, and where they rank in the status system. Treatment of time can also convey a powerful form of insult. Furthermore, because the rules are informal, they operate largely out of awareness and, as a consequence, are less subject to conscious manipulation than language.

It is important, therefore, to know how to read the messages associated with time in other cultures. In France almost everything is polychronic whereas in Germany monochronic promptness is even more important than it is in the United States.

Tempo, rhythm, and synchrony

Rhythm is an intangible but important aspect of time. Because nature's cycles are rhythmic, it is understandable that rhythm and tempo are distinguishing features of any culture. Rhythm ties the people of a culture together and can also alienate them from members of other cultures. In some cultures people move very slowly; in others, they move rapidly. When people from two such different cultures meet, they are apt to have difficulty relating because they are not "in sync." This is important because synchrony – the subtle ability to move together – is vital to all collaborative efforts, be they conferring, administering, working together on machines, or buying and selling.

People who move at a fast tempo are often perceived as "tailgating" those who move more slowly, and tailgating doesn't contribute to harmonious interaction – nor does forcing fast-paced people to move too slowly. Americans complain that the Germans take forever to reach decisions. Their time is out of phase with American time and vice versa. One must always be contexted to the local time system. There will be times when everything seems to be at a standstill, but actually a great deal is going on behind the scenes. Then there will be other times when everything moves at lightning speed and it is necessary to stand aside, to get out of the way.

Scheduling and lead time

To conduct business in an orderly manner in other countries, it is essential to know how much or how little lead time is required for each activity: how far ahead to request an appointment or schedule meetings and vacations, and how much time to allow for the preparation of a major report. In both the United States and Germany, schedules are sacred; in France scheduling frequently cannot be initiated until meetings are held with concerned members of the organization to permit essential discussions. This system works well in France, but there are complications whenever overseas partners or participants are involved since they have often scheduled their own activities up to two years in advance.

Lead time varies from culture to culture and is itself a communication as well as an element in organization. For instance, in France, if the relationship is important, desks will be cleared when that person arrives, whether there has been any advance notice or not. Time will be made to work together, up to twenty-four hours a day if necessary. In the United States and to some extent in Germany, on the other hand, the amount of lead time can be read as an index of the relative importance of the business to be conducted, as well as of the status of the individuals concerned. Short lead time means that the business is of little importance; the longer the lead time, the greater the value of the proceedings. In these countries, two weeks is the minimum advance time for requesting appointments. In Arab countries, two weeks may be too long – a date set so far in advance "slides off their minds"; three or four days may be preferable. In Japan, lead time is usually much shorter than in the United States, and it is difficult to say how many conferences on important subjects, attended by all the most competent and prestigious Japanese leaders in their fields, fail to attract suitable counterparts from the United States because of the short lead time. Although misunderstandings are blameless artifacts of the way two very different systems work, accidents of culture are seldom understood for what they are.

Another instance of time as communication is the practice of setting a date to end something. For example, Americans often schedule how long they will stay in a foreign country for a series of meetings, thus creating the psychological pressure of having to arrive at a decision by a certain date. *This is a mistake.* The Japanese and, to a lesser degree, the French are very aware of the American pressure of being "under the gun" and will use it to their advantage during negotiations.

The importance of proper timing

Choosing the correct timing of an important event is crucial. Politicians stake their careers on it. In government and business alike, announcements of major changes or new programs must be carefully timed. The significance of different time segments of the day also must be considered. Certain times of the day, month, or year are reserved for certain activities (vacations, meal times, and so on) and are not ordinarily interchangeable. In general in northern European cultures and in the United States, anything that occurs outside of business hours, very early in the morning or late at night, suggests an emergency. In France, there are times when nothing is expected to happen, such as national holidays and during the month of August, when everything shuts down for *vacances*. Culturally patterned systems are sufficiently complex so that it is wise to seek the advice of local experts.

In the United States, the short business lunch is common and the business dinner rarer; this is not so in France, where the function of the business lunch and dinner is to create the proper atmosphere and get acquainted. Relaxing with business clients during lunch and after work is crucial to building the close rapport that is absolutely necessary if one is to do business.

Appointments

The way in which time is treated by Americans and Germans signals attitude, evaluation of priorities, mood, and status. Since time is highly valued in both Germany and the United States, the messages of time carry more weight than they do in polychronic countries. Waiting time, for example, carries strong messages which work on that part of the brain that mobilizes the emotions (the limbic system). In the United States, only those people with very high status can keep others waiting and get away with it. In general, those individuals are the very ones who know enough of human relations to avoid "insults of time" whenever possible. It is the petty bureaucrat who likes to throw his weight around, the bully who takes pleasure in putting people down, or the insecure executive with an inflated ego who keeps visitors waiting. The waiting-room message is a double-edged sword. Not only does it communicate an attitude towards the visitor, but it reveals a lot about the individual who has kept a visitor waiting. In monochronic cultures such as those in the United States and Germany, keeping others waiting can be a deliberate putdown or a signal that the individual is very disorganized and can't keep to a schedule. In polychronic cultures such as those of France or Hispanic countries, no such message is intended. In other words, one's reading of the message should be tempered by the context, the realities of the situation, and not with an automatic projection of one's own culture.

Clearly, interactions between monochronic and polychronic people can be stressful unless both parties know and can decode the meanings behind each other's language of time. The language of time is much more stable and resistant to change than other cultural systems. We were once involved in a research project in New Mexico, conducting interviews with Hispanics. Our subjects were sixth- and seventh-generation descendants of the original Spanish families who settled in North America in the early seventeenth century. Despite constant contact with Anglo-Saxon Americans for well over a hundred years, most of these Hispanics have remained polychronic. In three summers of interviewing, we never once achieved our scheduled goal of five interviews each week for each interviewer. We were lucky to have two or three. Interviews in Hispanic homes or offices were constantly interrupted when families came to visit or a friend dropped by. The Hispanics seemed to be juggling half a dozen activities simultaneously, even while the interviews were in progress.

Since we are monochronic Anglo-Saxons, this caused us no little concern and considerable distress. It is hard not to respond emotionally when the rules of your own time system are violated. Nor was an intellectual understanding of the problem much help at first. We did recognize, however, that what we were experiencing was a consequence of cultural differences and was, therefore, a part of our data. This led us to a better understanding of the importance as well as the subtleties of information flow and information networks in a polychronic society.

INFORMATION FLOW: IS IT FAST OR SLOW AND WHERE DOES IT GO?

The rate of information flow is measured by how long it takes a message intended to produce an action to travel from one part of an organization to another and for that message to release the desired response. Cultural differences in information flow are often the greatest stumbling blocks to international understanding. Every executive doing business in a foreign land should know how information is handled – where it goes and whether it flows easily through the society and the business organization, or whether it is restricted to narrow channels because of compartmentalization.

In low-context countries, such as the United States, Germany, and Switzerland, information is highly focused, compartmentalized, and controlled, and, therefore, not apt to flow freely. In high-context cultures, such as the French, the Japanese, and the Spanish, information spreads rapidly and moves almost as if it had a life of its own. Those who use information as an instrument of "command and control" and who build their planning on controlling information are in for a rude shock in societies where people live in a sea of information.

In high-context cultures, interpersonal contact takes precedence over everything else; wherever people are spatially involved with each other, information flows freely. In business, executives do not seal themselves off behind secretaries and closed doors; in fact in Japan senior executives may even share offices so that each person knows as much about the entire base of operations as possible, and in France an executive will have ties to a centrally located bureau chief to keep a finger on the pulse of information flow. In these cultures most people are already highly contexted and therefore do not need to be briefed in much detail for each transaction; the emphasis is on stored rather than on transmitted information. Furthermore, channels are seldom overloaded because people stay in constant contact; therefore, the organizational malady of "information overload" is rare. Schedules and screening (as in the use of private offices) are minimized because they interfere with this vital contact. For high-context people, there are two primary expectations: to context everybody in order to open up the information channels and determine whether the group can work together and to appraise the chances of coming to an agreement in the future. The drive to stay in touch and to keep up to date in high-context cultures is very strong. Because these cultures are also characteristically high-information flow cultures, being out of touch means to cease to exist as a viable human being.

Organizations where information flows slowly are familiar to both Americans and northern Europeans because low-flow information is associated with both low-context and monochronic time resulting from the compartmentalization associated with low-context institutions and of taking up one thing at a time. In the United States, information flows slowly because each executive has a private office and a secretary to serve as a guard so that the executive is not distracted by excessive information. Since executive territory is jealously guarded, American executives often do not share information with their staff or with other department heads. We were once hired as consultants to a large government bureaucracy in which there were problems. Our study revealed multiple causes, the most important of which was a bottleneck created by a high-ranking bureaucrat who managed to block practically all the information going from the top down and from the bottom up. Once the problem had been identified, an agency staff director remarked, "I see we have a blockage in information." In a high-context situation every-one would have already known that this was the case. In a low-context system, however, it was necessary to call in outside consultants to make explicit what some people had suspected but were unable or unwilling to identify.

ACTION CHAINS: THE IMPORTANCE OF COMPLETION

An action chain is an established sequence of events in which one or more people participate – and contribute – to achieve a goal. It's like the old-fashioned ritual of courtship with its time-honored developmental stages. If either party rushes things too much, omits an important procedure, or delays too long between steps, the courtship grinds to a halt.

Business is replete with action chains: greeting people, hiring and training personnel, developing an advertising campaign, floating a stock offering, initiating a lawsuit, merging with or taking over other companies, even sinking a golf putt. Many bureaucratic proce-dures are based unconsciously on the action-chain model. Because of the diversity of functions, it may be difficult for some people to link all these activities in their minds, but the common thread of underlying, ordered sequence ties each case to the others.

Because the steps in the chain are either technical (as in floating a stock offering or completing a merger) or else so widely shared and taken for granted that little conscious attention is paid to the details, the need to reexamine the entire pattern has largely gone unrecognized in the overseas setting.

There are important rules governing the structure, though not the content, of action chains. If an important step is left out, the action must begin all over again. Too many meetings and reports, for example, can break the action chains of individual projects, making it difficult for people to complete their work. In fact the breaking of an action chain is one of the most troublesome events with which human beings have to contend in our speeded-up technological twentieth century.

All planning must take into account the elaborate hierarchy of action chains. Monochronic, low-context cultures, with their compartmentalized approach and depend-ence on scheduled activities, are particularly sensitive to interruptions and so are more vulnerable to the breaking of action chains than high-context cultures. Most Americans are brought up with strong drives to complete action chains. High-context people, be-cause of their intense involvement with each other and their extensive, cohesive networks, are more elastic; there is more "give" in their system. Some polychronic peoples will break an action chain simply because they don't like the way things are going or because they think they can "get a better deal." For instance, we once knew a monochronic architect in New York who was designing a building for a polychronic client. The client continually changed the specifications for the building. With each change, the building design had to be revised, even down to alterations in the building's foundations. The architect found this process particularly devastating because designing and constructing a building is an incredibly complex and elaborate collection of action chains. Changing one thing is likely to throw everything else out of gear.

The relationship between action chains and disputes is important. All cultures have built-in safeguards – even though they may not always work – to prevent a dispute from escalating to an out-and-out battle. Keep in mind, however, that these safeguards apply only within the context of one's own culture. In any foreign situation where a dispute appears imminent, it is essential to do two things immediately: proceed slowly, taking every action possible to maintain course and stay on an even keel; and seek the advice of a skillful, tactful interpreter of the culture.

INTERFACING: CREATING THE PROPER FIT

The concept of interfacing can be illustrated by a simple example: it is impossible to interface an American appliance with a European outlet without an adaptor and a transformer. Not only are the voltages different, but the contacts on one are round; on the other, thin and flat. The purpose of this [article] is to serve as an adaptor for business executives operating at the interfaces between American, French, and German cultures.

The problems to be solved when interfacing vary from company to company, but some generalizations are possible.

First, it is more difficult to succeed in a foreign country than at home.

Second, the top management of a foreign subsidiary is crucial to the success of interfacing. Therefore, it is important to send the very best people available, take their advice, and leave them alone. Expect that your foreign manager or representative will start explaining things in terms of the local mentality which may sound alien and strange.

Cultural interfacing follows five basic principles:

1. The higher the context of either the culture or the industry, the more difficult the interface;
2. The greater the complexity of the elements, the more difficult the interface;
3. The greater the cultural distance, the more difficult the interface;
4. The greater the number of levels in the system, the more difficult the interface;
5. Very simple, low-context, highly evolved, mechanical systems tend to produce fewer interface problems than multiple-level systems of great complexity that depend on human talent for their success.

An example of an easy-to-interface business would be the manufacture of small components for microscopes by two divisions, one in Germany, the other in Switzerland. The cultural distance in this case is not great since both cultures are low-context as well as monochronic, and the business operation itself does not involve different levels of complexity.

A difficult-to-interface enterprise would be a newspaper or magazine in two countries that are vastly different, such as France and the United States. Publishing is a high-context enterprise which must be neatly meshed at literally dozens of points, including writing, advertising, and editorial policy. The success of newspapers and magazines depends on writers and editors who understand their audience's culture and know how to reach their readers.

The importance of context and following the rules

The key to being an effective communicator is in knowing the degree of information (contexting) that must be supplied. If you're communicating with a German, remember she or he is low-context and will need lots of information and all the details, in depth. If you're communicating with someone from France, she or he is high-context and won't require as much information. Here are two examples from our interviews:

> One German manager working for a French firm was fired after his first year because he didn't perform as expected. The German manager was stunned. His response was, "But nobody told me what they wanted me to do."

> The opposite problem was encountered by a Frenchman who resigned from a German firm because he was constantly being told what he already knew by his German superior. Both his intelligence and his pride were threatened.

In both situations, the executives were inept at releasing the right response from their subordinates.

One of the factors that determines whether one releases the right response includes observing the rules of the other culture, including the time system. In Germany a salesman can have a very fine presentation, but if he arrives late by even a few minutes, no one will be impressed, no matter how good it is. Indeed, in all probability, the Germans will not even wait around to hear it. In France form is preeminent; without it, no message can release the right response. Americans must take great care not to alienate the French by being casual and informal in their manners; if Americans are not meticulously polite and formal, their message will not get through to the French, and they and their product will suffer.

The importance of the right interpreter

Releasing the right response will also depend on choosing the right interpreter. An interpreter's accent or use of the local dialect can cause a negative reaction. The importance of this facet of communication cannot be overstressed, yet it is one of the most frequent violations of the unwritten laws of communication abroad. For example, if you are trying to communicate with a Japanese executive using an interpreter who is not well educated nor extremely polite and proper, the desired response from the Japanese will not be forthcoming. A well-educated and well-mannered interpreter whose use of the language reflects a good background is also highly desirable in France and Germany.

SUMMARY

Speed of messages, context, space, time, information flow, action chains, and interfacing are all involved in the creation of both national and corporate character. In organizations everything management does communicates; when viewed in the cultural context, all acts, all events, all material things have meaning. Some organizations send strong, consistent messages that are readily grasped by employees and customers alike. Other organizations are less easy to interpret; they do not communicate clearly, or their messages are incongruent. Sometimes one part of the organization communicates one thing and another part communicates something else. The cues around which these corporate and cultural messages are organized are as different as the languages with which they are associated. Most important, their meaning is deeply imbedded and therefore harder for management to change when making the transition from one country to another.

Many messages are implied or have a cultural meaning, and there is a tacit agreement as to the nature of that meaning which is deeply rooted in the context of the communication. There is much that is taken for granted in culture that few people can explain but which every member of the culture accepts as given. Remember that messages come in many forms (most of them not in words) which are imbedded in the context and in the choice of channels.

Within all cultures there are important unstated differences as to what constitutes a proper *releaser*. Our research over the years in choosing the correct releaser has indicated that people cluster around preferences for "words," "numbers," and "pictures." Using the wrong format (sending numbers when words are wanted, words when the recipient only feels comfortable with numbers, or words and/or numbers to the visually oriented person) can only release a negative, frustrated response. The fascinating thing is that the message can be the same in every case. Furthermore, it is quite evident that each culture has its own preferences in this regard.

A television ad that is effective in the United States will have to be translated into a print media message to reach Germans. Germans are print-oriented, which explains in part why there is so little advertising on German TV. Also, Germans are always looking for what is "true" and to them numbers are a way of signaling that a product is exactly as it has been represented. Germans demand facts, facts, and more facts.

It is not uncommon for Americans to experience difficulty getting the French – even those whom they know and have done business with – to reply to inquiries, even urgent ones. This can be exasperating. The reasons are many but most have to do with the importance of immediate human contacts to the French. A solution that succeeds when other methods fail is to use a surrogate to relay messages rather than relying on a letter or a phone call. Why? Because letters and telephone calls aren't personal enough. If you send a properly placed emissary, one whom the individual you are trying to reach likes and trusts and considers important, you add the necessary personal touch to your message and will thereby release the right response.

The French also stress the importance of observing the many rituals of form. If you don't use the right form, the message conveyed is that you are ignorant or ill-mannered or do not care. In any event, the response that is released is almost certain to be negative. Remember that the French deplore casualness and informality. Paying attention to the details and being correct in everything you do is the only tactic that releases the right response in France.

It is not necessary to solve every problem at once, only to show a genuine desire to do so and to take one step at a time, even if it seems to take a lifetime. The rewards are not only material but psychological and mental as well. New frontiers are not only to be found in outer space or in the microworld of science; they are also at the interfaces between cultures.

Chapter 3

European Leadership in Globalization

Philip R. Harris and Robert T. Moran

We are living in an era of change. The perspective is now global. At risk is the survival of the organization and the security of the individual.

What will the successful organization look like in the year 2000? What competencies and qualities will managers and executives need to run these businesses? If change is the constant, can much be said of the future?

In 1994, the Economist Intelligence Unit asked these questions and others to 10,000 senior executives in North America, Europe and Asia. An analysis of responses found:

- management's handling of diversity will be the most significant factor affecting corporate success in North America and Europe;
- senior executives need to possess the attribute of leadership that combines a blend of discipline and flexibility;
- in an era of constant change, corporate culture is a way to bring about organizational change.[1]

For organizations to survive, let alone flourish in the future, their perspective must be global. Pattison states that:

> Global skills and perspectives cannot be viewed as a specialty or segment of business today, they must be an integral part of an enterprise, totally integrated throughout all operations.[2]

Skilful global managers and executives understand the significance of the following six statements. They are convinced of the necessity to manage cultural differences and develop the skills necessary to participate effectively in a global environment:

(1) Japanese culture promotes a sense of group identity. Creating ambiguity is an unconscious cultural process that often leads foreigners to draw false conclusions based on Japanese appearances.
(2) During the first business meeting in Saudi Arabia, one does not conduct business, but uses the time to become acquainted and build trust.
(3) In matters of recruitment and selection, Asian managers interview and often select family and trusted friends to fill positions, while Western managers use more impersonal measures of recruitment.

(4)   When doing business in Indonesia, shaking hands with either gender is acceptable, but using the left hand for taking food or giving a gift is unacceptable; in other cultures, handshakes are avoided, and some form of bow is preferred.

(5)   Los Angeles has a diverse multicultural and multilingual population. Spanish and Korean are the second and third largest foreign-language groups. Cultural sensitivity greatly influences the success or failure of a product or service.

(6)   The Business Council for International Understanding estimates that international personnel who go abroad without cross-cultural preparation have a failure rate much higher than those who had the benefit of such training.

It is our thesis that all management or professional development requires some global intercultural education and skill. Furthermore, we must learn to move beyond the mere coping with cultural differences to creating more synergy and embracing the well-spring of diversity.

Since 1979 the awareness of business and government leaders has risen relative to the importance of the cultural influences on our behaviour. Whether one is concerned about the supervisors of minority employees, the acquisition of a US firm by a foreign owner, joint ventures or strategic alliances, increasing tourism, world trade, or global economic co-operation, culture will impact on the relationships and the operations.

Edgar H. Schein states it profoundly:

> Consider any complex, potentially volatile issue – Arab relations, the problems between Serbs, Croats and Bosnians, corporate decision making, getting control of the US deficit or health care costs, labor/management relations, and so on. At the root of the issue we are likely to find communication failures and cultural misunderstandings that prevent the parties from framing the problem in a common way, and thus make it impossible to deal with the problem constructively.[3]

The challenge is equally formidable for business once the attorneys, financial wizards and globe-trotting negotiators return home to reap the rewards of establishing another joint venture or partnership. The ultimate success or failure will be dependent on those remaining to implement the alliance, and sophisticated and ongoing skills are required of these people who need "to frame problems in a common way".

In identifying the individual competencies required to succeed in today's global marketplace, it is important to distinguish between a person who is sent on a lengthy overseas assignment of two to five years, and those who travel abroad, perhaps many times a year, but only remain in any country for a few days or a few weeks at most:

> The Settler has to deal with a variety of challenges, starting from pre-departure training to the hassles of relocating, transitional challenges to acclimatization, to culture shock to re-entry shock ... As the Settler must receive more in-depth insights into the host country's customs and culture. The language skills must be much more than conversational and a solid knowledge of the country's religion, politics, history, meaning of nature, morals, social structure, education, food and table manners, roles of man and woman, business ethics, negotiation techniques, humor and values is highly important ... The Settler should be extremely open-minded, flexible, friendly and honest ... adaptability is a valuable asset.

The Traveller is a person who leaves his or her country:

On short term assignments, frequently crossing borders in different continents and in time frames of about three to ten weeks, sometimes staying in the host country for no more than two or three days. The Traveller may be a product manager, sales manager, a trainer, advisor or controller.[4]

Different competencies are required of the Settler and the Traveller and different skills are required of individual settlers or travellers depending on their unique responsibilities.

Later we summarize reasons for acquiring cross-cultural understanding and skills. But first, we will begin with the "big picture" of what is happening globally.

ENVIRONMENTAL FORCES INFLUENCING CHANGE

Why must most business organizations, non-governmental organizations (NGOs), and many other institutions become global to survive? In their book, *The Global Challenge: Building the New Worldwide Enterprise*,[5] Moran and Riesenberger identify and describe 12 environmental forces impacting on organizations and influencing change.

The proactive environmental forces are:

(1) *Global sourcing* – organizations are seeking non-domestic sources of raw materials because of cost and quality.
(2) *New and evolving markets* are providing new opportunities for growing business.
(3) *Economies of scale* – today's marketplace requires new approaches, resulting in competitive advantages in price and quality.
(4) *Movement towards homogeneous demand* – globalization is resulting in similar products being required worldwide.
(5) *Lowered transport costs* – the global transport costs of many products have fallen significantly since the 1960s.
(6) *Government tariffs and taxes* – the protectionist tendencies of many governments is declining as evidenced by the North America Free Trade Agreement (NAFTA) and the European Union (EU).
(7) *Telecommunications* – falling prices as a result of privatization and new technologies are impacting on globalization.
(8) *Homogeneous technical standards* – the International Organization for Standardization (ISO) has been successful in developing global standards known as ISO 9000.

The reactive forces are:

(9) *Competition for non-domestic organizations* – new competitive threats are experienced by organizations regularly.
(10) *Risk of volatile exchange rates* – the constant fluctuation of exchange rates in many countries impacts on profits.
(11) *Customers are becoming more global consumers* – globalization is impacting on customers in ways that "local content" in subsidiary produced goods is increasing.
(12) *Global technological change* – technological improvements coming from many areas of the world are requiring organizations to adjust their strategies to survive.

Global Transformations

Too many corporate and government leaders still operate with dated mindsets of the world, and the people in various societies, the nature of work, the worker, and the management process itself. Willis Harman[6] reminds us that we can no longer view our world or culture in terms of industrial-age paradigms, which influence our perceptions, values, and behaviour. Capra and Steindl Rast state:

> Now, in the old paradigm it was also recognized that things are inter-related. But conceptually you first had the things with their properties, and then there were mechanisms and forces that interconnected them. In the new paradigm we say the things themselves do not have intrinsic properties. All the properties flow from their relationships. This is what I mean by understanding the properties of the parts from the dynamics of the whole, because these relationships are dynamic relationships. So the only way to understand the part is to understand its relationship to the whole. This insight occurred in physics in the 1920s and this is also a key insight of ecology. Ecologists think exactly in this way. They say an organism is defined by its relationship to the rest.[7]

Thus, today's leaders are challenged to create new models of management systems. For that to happen, managers and other professionals must become more innovative and recognize the contribution of each individual or unit to the effective workings of the whole.

As Peter Drucker has consistently observed, the art and science of management is in its own revolution, and many of the assumptions on which management practice was based are now becoming obsolete. Thinking managers alter not only their images of their role, but also their managerial style and activities.

Foreign competition and the need to trade more effectively overseas have forced most corporations to become more culturally sensitive and globally minded. Some companies are even investing in university programmes to educate global managers such as the Institute of Management and International Studies at University of Pennsylvania, which was established by Estée Lauder.

The leading business schools, which until recently neglected international and intercultural education, are including this perspective in their curriculum. Managing people from different cultures, whether at home or abroad, is suddenly receiving the attention of business students, as well as those in education or human resource development. Although the market for cross-cultural training in industry and government has generally been premature and soft, it now is gaining strength. In a report from CPC Foundation/ Rand Corporation this perspective is supported. Sponsors of the study include AT&T, Motorola, Deloitte and Touche and universities such as Columbia University and the University of Chicago, among many others. They found corporate and academics alike agreed, in general, on the importance of factors believed to contribute to successful work performance in a global organization. The results:

- Knowledge in one's academic major (domain knowledge) ranks only fifth among the ten factors.
- The three highest-rated factors are ones not generally associated with any specific training: generic cognitive skills, social skills and personal traits.

- Non-academic training and experience (on-the-job training and prior work experience) are as highly rated as is academic knowledge.[8]

Louis Korn, CEO of Korn/Ferry International, an executive recruiting firm, said:

Tomorrow's executives must possess a broad understanding of history, of culture, of technology, and of human relations. They must be as comfortable with cash management, as with history, anthropology, sociology, mathematics, and with the physical and natural sciences.

To that latter list of academic studies, we would add psychology and communications. But Korn wisely added that businesses should develop executive training and promotion practices that reward those who are forward-looking, can deal with different cultures, can manage the results of technological change, and can take the longer view.

A 1989 survey report of 1,500 top managers worldwide revealed that US executives were too parochial and insular in their perspectives.[9] Conducted by Korn/Ferry International and designed by Columbia University's Business School, the findings faulted American managers for minimizing learning foreign languages and cultures, while other multinational executives placed a high priority on multiculturalism. The study indicates that US managerial attitudes towards international business and communications point to a continuation of America's lagging competitiveness. The research projected economic conditions to the year 2000, revealing an expected shortage of talented executives prepared to run global businesses. The following extract from *The Economist* gives some of the highlights in this comparative management analysis:

What does it take to get to the top of a big corporation? Brains, luck and ambition certainly help. But much also depends on the priorities of the big company in question. A recent survey by Korn/Ferry, a headhunter, and Columbia Business School found intriguing variations in what is expected of future chief executives. Americans will read them and weep.

Contrary to recent experience, American bosses think that foreign competition will pose much less of a threat in the twenty-first century than will domestic rivals. Thus today's American chief executives do not expect their successors to need much international experience. Instead they are grooming high-fliers with experience in marketing and finance. And they are hoping to add some grasp of production technology to the skills of tomorrow's chief executives, because they reckon their firms will in the future compete hardest on price.

Japanese and Europeans, in contrast, expect international competition to be intense. Europeans expect more than half of their revenues to come from foreign markets. So international experience will be crucial for tomorrow's Japanese and European bosses. Instead of competing on price, Japanese and Europeans expect to compete on product quality and innovation. Predictably, the Japanese stress products the most. They want chief executives with technical and R&D skills, not marketing. Given the difference in emphasis, whose products do you expect to be buying in ten years?[10]

How do companies foster and create effective global managers? What is a global manager? Many companies establishing worldwide operations are pondering these questions, plus many others, and finding that the human resource element is more limiting at times than the capital investment in globalizing. Bartlett and Ghoshal state:

Clearly, there is no single model for the global manager. Neither the old-line international specialist nor the more recent global generalist can cope with the complexities of cross-border strategies. Indeed, the dynamism of today's marketplace calls for managers with diverse skills. Responsibility for worldwide operations belongs to senior business, country, and functional executives who focus on the intense interchanges and subtle negotiations required. In contrast, those in middle management and front-line jobs need well-defined responsibilities, a clear understanding of their organization's translational mission, and a sense of accountability.[11]

Percy Barnevik, president and CEO of Asea Brown Boveri (ABB), responded when asked if there is such a thing as a global manager:

> Global managers are made, not born. This is not a natural process. We are herd animals. We like people who are like us. But there are many things you can do. Obviously, you rotate people around the world. There is no substitute for line experience in three or four countries to create a global perspective. You also encourage people to work in mixed nationality teams. You *force* them to create personal alliances across borders, which means that sometimes you interfere in hiring decisions.
>
> You also have to acknowledge cultural differences without becoming paralyzed by them. We've done some surveys, as have lots of other companies, and we find interesting differences in perception. For example, a Swede may think a Swiss is not completely frank and open, that he doesn't know exactly where he stands. That is a cultural phenomenon. Swiss culture shuns disagreement. A Swiss might say, "Let's come back to that point later, let me review it with my colleagues." A Swede would prefer to confront the issue directly. How do we undo hundreds of years of upbringing and education? We don't, and we shouldn't try to. But we do need to broaden understanding.[12]

KEY CONCEPTS FOR GLOBAL LEADERSHIP

The following ten concepts contain the underlying message of this article. An awareness of and an application to one's organization of these concepts has direct relevance to the effectiveness of global managers, international lawyers, economic and community development specialists, engineers and technicians, public health officials and ultimately everyone working in today's multicultural environment. An understanding and utilization of these concepts are critical to one's successful global performance.

GLOBAL LEADERSHIP   being capable of operating effectively in a global environment and respectful of cultural diversity. This is an individual who can manage accelerating change and differences. The global leader is open and flexible in approaching others, can cope with situations and people disparate from his or her background, and is willing to re-examine and alter personal attitudes and perceptions.

CROSS-CULTURAL COMMUNICATION   recognizing what is involved in one's image of self and one's role, personal needs, values, standards, expectations, all of which are culturally conditioned. Such a person understands the impact of cultural factors on communication, and is willing to revise and expand such images as part of the process of growth. Furthermore, he or she is aware of verbal and non-verbal differences in communication with persons from another culture. Not only does such a person seek to learn another language, but also he or she is cognizant that, even when people speak the same language, cultural differences can alter communication symbols and meanings and result in misunderstandings. When utilizing the Information Highway, the global leader requires not only computer competency to access the Internet but also cultural sensitivity when interacting with persons from a different cultural context.

CULTURAL SENSITIVITY   integrating the characteristics of culture in general, with experiences in specific organizational, minority, or foreign cultures. Such a person understands the cultural influences on behaviour. This individual translates such cultural awareness into effective relationships with those who are different.

ACCULTURATION   effectively adjusting and adapting to a specific culture, whether that be a subculture within one's own country or abroad. Such a person is alert to the impact of culture shock in successfully managing transitions. Therefore, when operating in an unfamiliar culture or dealing with employees from diverse cultural backgrounds, this person develops the necessary skills and avoids being ethnocentric.

CULTURAL INFLUENCES ON MANAGEMENT   understanding that management philosophies are deeply rooted in culture, and that management practices developed in one culture may not easily transfer to another.

EFFECTIVE INTERCULTURAL PERFORMANCE   applying cultural theory and insight to specific cross-cultural situations that affect people's performance on the job. Such a person makes provisions for the foreign deployment process, overseas adjustment and culture shock and the re-entry of expatriates.

CHANGING INTERNATIONAL BUSINESS   coping with the interdependence of business activity throughout the world, as well as the subculture of the managerial group. There is an emerging universal acceptance of some business technology, computers and management information systems, for example. Yet, the global manager appreciates the effect of cultural differences on standard business practice and principles, such as organizational loyalty.

CULTURAL SYNERGY   building on the very differences in the world's people for mutual growth and accomplishment by co-operation. Cultural synergy through collaboration emphasizes similarities and common concerns and integrates differences to enrich human activities and systems. By combining the best in varied cultures and seeking the widest input, multiple effects and complex solutions can result. Synergy is separate parts functioning together to create a greater whole and to achieve a common goal. For such aggregate action to occur, cross-cultural skills are required.

WORK CULTURE   applying the general characteristics of culture to the specifics of how people work at a point in time and place. In the macro sense, work can be analysed in terms of human stages of development – the work cultures of hunter, farmer, factory worker, and knowledge worker. In the micro sense, work cultures can be studied in terms of specific industries, organizations, or professional groups.

GLOBAL CULTURE   understanding that, while various characteristics of human culture have always been universal, a unique global culture with some common characteristics may be emerging. The influences of mass media, telecommunications, the fax, as well as Cable News Network (CNN) are breaking down some of the traditional barriers among groups of peoples and their diverse cultures. Global managers are alert to serving this commonality in human needs and markets with strategies that are transnational.

CORE CONCEPTS OF CULTURE

Culture is a distinctly human capacity for adapting to circumstances and transmitting this coping skill and knowledge to subsequent generations. Culture gives people a sense of who they are, of belonging, of how they should behave, and of what they should be doing. Culture impacts on behaviour, morale, and productivity at work and includes values and patterns that influence company attitudes and actions. Corporate culture affects how an organization copes with competition and change, whether in terms of technology, economics, or people. Trompenaars states:

> As markets globalise, the need for standardisation in organisational design, systems and procedures increases. Yet managers are also under pressure to adapt their organisation to the local characteristics of the market, the legislation, the fiscal regime, the socio-political system and the cultural system. This balance between consistency and adaptation is essential for corporate success.[13]

Terpstra and David[14] recommend that people in business be triply socialized – to their culture, their business culture, and their corporate culture. When we operate in the global marketplace it is imperative that we be informed about these three cultures of our customers, competitors, venture partners, suppliers, or government officials.

Finally, consider the importance of the ten cultural competencies just described in terms of the observations of the noted author on leadership, James O'Toole:

> Consider just one example of the deep, unprecedented change in the world of business the imminent collapse of recognizable boundaries between nations, between firms, between business units and between functional disciplines. What precedent is there for managing amidst such chaos?
>
> It is now increasingly recognized that the executive's challenge is to pilot through such rolling seas in a purposeful and successful manner, to steer an appropriate organizational course in turbulent conditions. Hence, corporations must not simply change, they must be transformed effectively.[15]

The *Los Angeles Times* (13 January 1996), in a feature on the State of Expatriates, reports that:

(1)   International assignments of personnel have increased by 25 per cent since 1990, with the focus on markets in Asia and former Communist Bloc countries . . .

(2)   A four-year assignment abroad for a single expatriate can cost a company more than $1 million, yet only half of the US expatriates receive training for the overseas posting . . .

(3)   In a recent study of American managers in 12 European countries, Manning, Selvage and Lee discovered that US respondents believe they are better able to adapt to change than

are their European counterparts; but a majority agreed to making changes in US business practices as a result of their European experience . . .

GLOBAL ORGANIZATIONS

In 1994 there were 37,000 transnational corporations with 207,000 affiliates that control one-third of all private sector assets, and have worldwide sales of US$5.5 trillion.

In this century national organizations have evolved into international organizations and now global organizations. In 1974 Barnett and Muller forecast this trend:

> The global corporation is the first institution in human history dedicated to centralized planning on a world scale. Because its primary activity is to organize and to integrate economic activity around the world in such a way as to maximize global profit, it is an organic structure in which each part is expected to serve the whole . . . The rise of such planetary enterprises is producing an organizational revolution as profound for modern man as the Industrial Revolution and the rise of the nation-state itself . . . With their world view, the managers of global corporations are seeking to put into practice a theory of human organization that will profoundly alter the nation-state system around which society has been organized for over four hundred years.[16]

Walter B. Wriston, speaking before the International Industrial Conference in 1974, foretold eloquently the influence of global corporations:

> The role of the world corporation as an agent of change may well be even more important than its demonstrated capacity to raise living standards. The pressure to develop the economy of the world into a real community must come, in part, from an increasing number of multinational firms which see the world as a whole . . . The world corporation has become a new weight in an old balance and must play a constructive role in moving the world toward the freer exchange of both ideas and the means of production so that the people of the world may one day enjoy the fruits of a truly global society.[17]

In discussing the evolution of the various corporations, Moran et al.[18] cite four types of corporations: ethnocentric, polycentric, regiocentric and geocentric.

ETHNOCENTRIC CORPORATIONS. These corporations are home-country-oriented. Ethnocentric managers believe that home-country nationals are more intelligent, reliable, and trustworthy than foreign nationals. All key management positions are centred at the domestic headquarters. Home-country nationals are recruited and trained for all international positions. The ethnocentric approach is fostered by many internal and external influences. The CEO may be limited by the biases of the owners and stockholders. Labour unions may impose intense pressure in favour of domestic employment. Home government policy may force emphasis on the domestic market.

The ethnocentric philosophy is exhibited in many international companies. The standard international company finds great difficulty communicating in different languages and in accepting cultural differences. International strategic alternatives are limited to entry modes such as exporting, licensing, and turnkey operations – because "it works at home it must work overseas".

POLYCENTRIC CORPORATIONS.   These are host-country-oriented corporations. Profit potential is seen in a foreign country, but the foreign market is too hard to understand. The polycentric firm establishes multinational operations on condition that host-country managers "do it their way". The polycentric message is:

> Local people know what is best for them. Let's give them the responsibility and leave them alone as long as they make us a profit.

The polycentric firm is a loosely connected group with quasi-independent subsidiaries as profit centres. Headquarters is staffed by home-country nationals, while local nationals occupy the key positions in their respective local subsidiaries. Host-country nationals have high or absolute sovereignty over the subsidiary's operations. There is no direction from headquarters and the only controls are financially oriented. No foreign national can seriously aspire to a senior position at headquarters.

The polycentric approach often results from great external pressures such as laws in different countries requiring local management participation. Engineering standards may have to be determined locally. The host-country government may be a major customer and therefore influence the ways of doing business.

The polycentric philosophy is often exhibited in multinational corporations. MNCs face a heterogeneous environment where product needs and preferences are diverse. In addition, governmental restrictions may be severe. Strategically, the MNC competes on a market-by-market basis because it believes that "local people know what is best for them".

REGIOCENTRIC CORPORATIONS.   These corporations capitalize on the synergistic benefits of sharing common functions across regions. A regiocentric corporation believes that only regional insiders can effectively co-ordinate functions within the region. For example, a regiocentric organization might select a Japanese subsidiary to manage its Asian operations and a French subsidiary to manage its European operations. The regiocentric message is: "Regional insiders know what neighbouring countries want."

The regiocentric firm is highly interdependent on a regional basis. Regional headquarters organize collaborative efforts among local subsidiaries. The regional headquarters is responsible for the regional plan, local research and development, product innovation, cash management, local executive selection and training, capital expenditure plans, brand policy, and public relations. The world headquarters takes care of world strategy, country analysis, basic research and development, foreign exchange, transfer pricing, intercompany loans, long-term financing, selection of top management, technology transfer, and establishing corporate culture.

GEOCENTRIC CORPORATIONS.   Being world-oriented, a geocentric corporation's ultimate goal is creating an integrated system with a worldwide approach. The geocentric system is highly interdependent. Subsidiaries are no longer satellites and independent city-states. The entire organization is focused on both worldwide and local objectives. Every part of the organization makes a unique contribution using its unique competencies. The geocentric message is:

> All for one and one for all. We will work together to solve problems anywhere in the world.

Geocentrism requires collaboration between headquarters and subsidiaries to establish universal standards with permissible local variations. Diverse regions are integrated through a global systems approach to decision making. Good ideas come from and flow to any country. Resources are allocated on a global basis. Geographical lines are erased and functional and product lines are globalized.

Within legal and political limits, the best people are sought to solve problems. Competence is what counts, not national origin. The reward system motivates managers to surrender national biases and work for worldwide objectives.

The geocentric firm overcomes political barriers by turning its subsidiaries into good citizens of the host nations. It is hoped that the subsidiary will become a leading exporter from the host to the international community. Furthermore, the geocentric organization will provide base countries with an increasing supply of hard currency, new skills, and a knowledge of advanced technology.

CROSS-CULTURAL LEARNING

Nadler[19] suggests that *training* be the focus of the job, while *education* be thought of with reference to the individual, and *development* be reserved for organizational concerns. Whether one is concerned with intercultural training, education, or development, all employees should learn about the influence of culture and be effective cross-cultural communicators if they are to work with minorities within their own society or with foreigners encountered at home or abroad. For example, there has been a significant increase in foreign investments in the USA – millions of Americans now work within the borders of their own country for foreign employers. All along the US–Mexican border, twin plants have emerged that provide for a flow of goods and services between the two countries.

For those executives impressed by "bottom-line" considerations only, factors like these should be considered in strategic planning:

- One out of six US manufacturing jobs is dependent on foreign trade, while four out of five new manufacturing jobs result from international commerce.
- Premature return of an employee and family sent on overseas assignment may cost the company between $50,000 to $200,000 when replacement expenses are included.
- Mistakes of corporate representatives because of language or intercultural incompetence can jeopardize negotiations and undermine customer relations.

Finally, a new reality of the global marketplace is the information highway and its impact on jobs and cross-cultural communications. Many skilled workers in advanced economies are watching their positions migrate overseas where college-educated nationals are doing high-technology tasks for less pay. Consider this:

> Texas Instruments is designing some of its more sophisticated computer chips in India. Motorola Inc. recently set up computer programming and equipment design centers in China, Hong Kong, Singapore, Taiwan and Australia, and it is looking for a site in South America.

Beside computer language, most international exchanges take place with individuals using

English as a second language. While a few corporate representatives will travel abroad, the main communication will occur by means of satellites on the Internet through modems connected to laptop or personal computers. Offshore operations done electronically in developing countries are stimulated by growing software applications that turn skilled tasks into routine work. To stay competitive globally, for example, more and more North American firms are increasing their investments and activities in foreign lands. US engineers can work on a project during the day, then send it electronically to Asia or elsewhere for additional work while they sleep. Such trends represent an enormous challenge for cross-cultural competence.

SUMMARY

Having a sense of culture and its related skills are unique human attributes. Culture is fundamentally a group problem-solving tool for coping in a particular environment. It enables people to create a distinctive world around themselves, to control their own destinies, and to grow. Sharing the legacy of diverse cultures advances our social, economic, technological, and human development. Culture can be analysed in a macro context, such as in terms of national groups, or in a micro sense, such as within a system or organization. Increasingly, we examine culture in a global sense from the perspective of work, leadership or markets.

Because management philosophies and practices are culturally conditioned, it stands to reason that there is much to be gained by including cultural studies in all management or professional development. This is particularly relevant during the global transformation under way. Culturally-skilled leaders are essential for the effective management of emerging global corporations, as well as for the furtherance of mutually beneficial world trade and exchange. In these undertakings, the promotion of cultural synergy by those who are global professionals will help us to capitalize on the differences in people, while ensuring their collaborative action.

In summary, here are parallel reasons why all managers and professionals should advance their culture learning, or why global organizations should include it in their human resource development strategies:

- Culture gives people a sense of identity, whether in nations or corporations, especially in terms of the human behaviour and values to be encouraged. Through it organizational loyalty and performance can be improved.
- Cultural knowledge provides insight into people. The appropriate business protocol can be employed that is in tune with local character, codes, ideology, and standards.
- Cultural awareness and skill can be helpful in influencing organizational culture. Furthermore, subsidiaries, divisions, departments, or specializations have subcultures that can foster or undermine organizational goals and communications.
- Cultural concepts and characteristics are useful for the analysis of work culture in the disappearing industrial and emerging meta-industrial work environments.
- Cultural insights and tools are helpful in the study of comparative management techniques, so that we become less culture-bound in our approach to leadership and management practice.
- Cultural competencies are essential for those in international business and trade.

- Cultural astuteness enables one to comprehend the diversity of market needs, and to improve strategies with minority and ethnic groups at home, or foreign markets abroad.
- Cultural understanding is relevant to all relocation experiences, whether domestic or international. This is valid for individual managers or technicians who are facing a geographic transfer, as well as for their families and subordinates involved in such a cultural change.
- Cultural understanding and skill development should be built into all foreign deployment systems. Acculturation to different environments can improve the overseas experience and productivity, and facilitate re-entry into the home and organizational culture.
- Cultural capabilities can enhance one's participation in international organizations and meetings. This is true whether one merely attends a conference abroad, is a delegate to a regional or foreign association, is a member in a world trade or professional enterprise, or is a meeting planner for transnational events.
- Cultural proficiency can facilitate one's coping with the changes of any transitional experience.
- Cultural diversity is evident not only on this planet, but also in the migration of our species aloft where multicultural crews of astronauts and cosmonauts are creating a new space culture.

Learning to manage cultural differences is a means for all persons to become more global and cosmopolitan in their outlook and behaviour, as well as more effective personally and professionally. When cultural differences are perceived and utilized as a *resource*, then all benefit.

For further information on the subject-matter of this chapter, consult the author's book *Developing the Global Organization* in the MCD Series.

References

1   Mackiewicz, A. and Daniels, N.C., "The successful corporation of the year 2000", *Economist Intelligence Unit*, research report, New York, NY, 1994.
2   Pattison, J.E., *Acquiring the Future*, Dow Jones-Irwin, Homewood, IL, 1990.
3   Schein, E.H., "On dialogue, culture and organizational learning", *Organizational Dynamics*, Vol. 22 No. 2, 1993, pp. 40–51.
4   Bremmer, C., "The global manager – insights in succeeding the challenge", unpublished paper, 1994.
5   Moran, R.T. and Riesenberger, J.R., *The Global Challenge: Building the New Worldwide Enterprise*, McGraw-Hill, London, 1994.
6   Harman, W., *Global Mind Change*, Knowledge Systems, Inc., Indianapolis, IN, 1988.
7   F. Capra and Rast, S., *Belonging in the Universe*, Harper Collins, San Francisco, CA, 1991.
8   "Developing the global work force – insights for colleges and corporations", A College Placement Council (CPC)/Rand Corporation Report, March 1994.
9   *Los Angeles Times*, 15 January 1989, p. 516.
10 *The Economist*, "Myopic high-fliers", 17 June 1989, p. 80.
11 Bartlett, C.A. and Ghoshal, S., "What is a global manager?", *Harvard Business Review*, September/October 1992, p. 131.
12 Taylor, W., "The logic of global business: an interview with ABB's Percy Barnevik", *Harvard Business Review*, March/April 1991, p. 95.
13 Trompenaars, F., *Riding the Waves of Culture*, Economist Books, London, 1993, p. 3.
14 Terpstra, V. and David, K., *The Cultural Environment of International Business*, South-Western Publishing, Cincinnati, OH, 1985.

15 O'Toole, J. *Leading Change – Overcoming the Ideology of Comfort and the Tyranny of Custom*, Jossey-Bass, San Francisco, CA, 1995.

16 Barnett, R.J. and Muller, R.E., *Global Reach: The Power of the Multinational Corporation*, Simon & Schuster, New York, NY, 1974.

17 Wriston, W.B., "The world corporation – new weight in an old balance", *Sloan Management Review*, Winter, 1974.

18 Moran, R.T., Harris, P.R. and Stripp, W.G., *Developing the Global Organization: Strategies for Human Resource Professionals*, Gulf Publishing Co., Houston, TX, 1993.

19 Nadler, L., *The Handbook of Human Resource Development*, John Wiley, New York, NY, 1984.

Further reading

Elashmawi, F. and Harris, P.R., *Multicultural Management – New Skills for Global Success*, Gulf Publishing, Houston, TX, 1993.

Howard, A. (Ed.), *The Changing Nature of Work*, Jossey-Bass, San Francisco, CA, 1995.

Osland, J.S., *The Adventures of Working Abroad – Hero Tales from the Global Frontier*, Jossey-Bass, San Francisco, CA, 1995.

Chapter 4

The Yin and Yang of Managing in Asia

Dean Allen Foster

One quick look at the "shaking" going on today in the Pacific Rim is enough to confirm that Napoleon was right indeed. Economists tell us a staggering 75 percent of the projected growth in international business will come from emerging markets – particularly China and its "baby dragon" neighbors, including Taiwan, Korea, Singapore, Malaysia, Thailand, Indonesia, and Vietnam.

As a result, human resource professionals all over the United States are faced with an unprecedented number of relocations to Asia, while the new expatriates themselves are faced with unprecedented challenges. Just what happens when East meets West?

Business and technology are bringing us closer together. Ironically, that very fact is forcing us to deal with our cultural differences on a magnified scale. To start, it helps if the East and West each see themselves as half of the united, perfect whole they compose when together – like the Taoist symbol of yin and yang. Unless both we and our Asian colleagues value and understand what the other brings to the formula, the mix just won't work.

What, then, are the precise cultural challenges we face when working together in the Pacific Rim? What are the all-too-often uniformed assumptions that underlie behaviors driving each side in its quest for success? How do the expectations of the American work ethic "fit" or "fail" with the Eastern ethos? And most important – what are the implications for HR managers responsible for providing Americans living and working in Asia with the tools necessary for success in the region?

OPPOSITE SIDES OF THE WORLD

A good place to begin bridging the gap is to consider that the United States and Asia lie on opposite sides of the world – literally and culturally. The two regions originate at opposing cultural "poles," each rooted in deep histories that, like two magnets, pull all current activity in opposite philosophical directions.

Without getting too bogged down in philosophy, it does help to consider our relative positions. Western traditions tend to revere constant, unchanging standards, while Eastern traditions accept that changing circumstances can justify changes in behavior. Compare, for example, the Judeo-Christian tradition of the Ten Commandments, with its absolute "thou shalt"s and "thou shalt not"s, with the Confucian and Taoist traditions of the East, which define virtue as exhibiting behaviors appropriate to the circumstances of the moment. Easterners observe the order in the universe and work to perfect, rather than change, their role in it. Their behavior is not governed by Western ideas of abstract universals.

But how does this essential difference between Asians and Americans reveal itself in the workplace? Consider the differences in signing and honoring contracts.

CONTRACTS – WESTERN AND EASTERN STYLE

To Westerners, contracts, once signed, are a cut-and-dry issue. They are relied on to enforce dependable, unchanging behavior over time – regardless of any change in circumstances. In Asia, however, contracts are viewed quite differently.

The Eastern contract is better defined, not as an absolute declaration of the deal, but rather as a statement of principles by which the signers agree to work together as trustworthy partners. Contracts are not expected to guarantee behavior over time, so when circumstances change and new behaviors are required, the partner is expected to be flexible.

Westerners are likely to view such expectations with less than a warm welcome: Americans will all too often view any deviation from an agreement as a breach of understanding and trust. It is important for Western managers to recognize that in Asia the contract is merely the beginning of a negotiation, not the end of it, as Americans usually expect. Expatriate managers who are not sufficiently trained to appreciate these differences may end up costing the company thousands, or even millions, in bungled deals and, perhaps, entirely failed assignments.

THE GROUP VERSUS THE INDIVIDUAL

American management styles, almost universally, presuppose the importance of the individual. We value empowerment, proactive decision making, and ownership of the task. Not surprisingly, this style of management reflects our Western tradition of the power of rational control and the inherent equality of all people.

In contrast, Asian management styles typically subordinate the role of the individual to the greater demands of the group. The power of obligations and relationships and the respect for order are of greater importance in the East. In the West, efficiency and change often equal effectiveness; in the East, passive acceptance of what is, and the ability to perfect one's work with others within the existing conditions, might be a greater virtue – and the way to a smooth-running, successful organization.

Again, unprepared managers from the West may find themselves at a loss to understand the best way to motivate and manage their local teams.

REINVENTING REALITY

In practical terms, then, Westerners doing business abroad simply must rethink their roles, their expectations and the image they present. They must be given the necessary learning environment and details to gain a subtle appreciation of fundamental cultural differences – not simply a brief list of 10 do's and don'ts that will leave them in trouble the minute they face number 11!

The following are some American behaviors that require special attention for managers working in the East.

- **Be "directive," not direct.** American managers need to be more directive, providing detailed, clear and timely information to subordinates. Do not assume that Asian workers will take individual initiative, speak up, question and take risks like their American counterparts often do. More likely than not, until and unless clear information and "green lights" are provided by the manager, subordinates will do nothing. Moreover, directives from Western managers are best given through trusted Asian associates who can function as language and cultural "interpreters."

- **Be careful of the un-Western meeting.** Meetings of Eastern associates are usually not the brainstorming sessions found in the West. In a sense, the manager is required to be all-knowing, make decisions, provide answers and exercise authority – albeit in a concerned and caring way. Most often, meetings begin and end as the leader directs, with discussions guided by the leader throughout. In the face of whatever hierarchy exists at the table, participants will be reticent to volunteer ideas and thoughts, lest they be judged badly by others.

  This is not to say that silent participants in Asia are uninvolved; on the contrary, they may be passionately concerned with the issues on the table – but they are equally concerned about appearing insubordinate. Note, also, that the leader in Asia is traditionally the senior male, precisely because of his age and experience, despite the capabilities and qualifications of other team members.

- **Adopt new communication skills.** To overcome all these differences, Americans need to adopt and practice some necessary communication skills. Consider that in Asia, the person who speaks least often has the most to say, while the person who speaks the most has the least to contribute. In Asia, direct, get-it-done, no-nonsense speech is considered very harsh, and often slams the door shut rather than moving things along. Confronting someone, expressing anger or frustration openly or criticizing in public can end negotiations, at least temporarily.

In contrast, Americans are often surprised by "soft," indirect speech, which can also present a problem. To the U.S. manager, messages can appear qualified, complex, and subtle in meaning beyond comprehension. To manage effectively, then, Americans must work at developing a "context antenna," enabling them to read the context in which the communication occurs – often the key to the real information.

FINAL THOUGHTS

Conflicts that emerge between Asians and Westerners at work often reflect deep, hidden, and consequently, unrecognized fundamental differences in values and beliefs. The first task for human resource managers and their valued employees is to recognize that deep differences do exist, and then identify the areas in the workplace most profoundly affected by those differences.

Next, employees need to be trained in the new skills (management, communication, decision-making, negotiation, etc.) that will help them change their behaviors and be more effective in dealing with Asian colleagues and subordinates. Ideally, there should be cross-cultural training on both sides of the Pacific, thus building a bridge between East and West. Bringing yin and yang together is a challenge not easily met – but it's a task that must be accomplished to form the perfect whole of business success.

Chapter 5

Case: A Difficult Start

Charlotte Butler and Henri-Claude de Bettignies

"As the new managing director, you will begin the job with a certain store of credibility. You can then either add to this store, or lose it altogether." Listening to his site manager, Somchai, describing the problem that had blown up at the plant, Richard Evans recalled these final words of his predecessor on handing over the leadership of the Siam Chemicals Company (SCC) Ltd. a few weeks ago. At least by the calendar it had only been two weeks, although to Richard it seemed more like two months. As he considered what action to take Richard realised that he had already reached his first turning point, from where he could either increase or diminish that precious store of credibility.

Richard had arrived in Bangkok a few weeks ago to take over as managing director of SCC, a subsidiary of Chimique Helvétique Ltd. (CHL), a global Swiss chemicals group headquartered in Basle. He had been working as a business manager with CHL for the last five years, having been recruited from the British chemicals company where he had worked as marketing manager since graduating in English Literature. Richard had been excited by the challenge offered by the SCC appointment but already, only ten days into his three-year stint, he felt overwhelmed by the demands of this new and unfamiliar environment. Whilst he had anticipated the effort required to absorb an enormous amount of information in the brief period allotted for the handover, he had not been prepared for the intense cultural shock of finding himself working and managing in Asia for the first time.

Richard had decided to accept the promotion and move his young family to Thailand on the basis of a four-day visit to SCC, together with his wife, a few months earlier. Now, he wondered what he had got himself into. The books on Thai culture he had so optimistically brought with him would, he had realised, be of little help; in a country that was undergoing a rapid social and economic transformation they were outdated before they were even published. During a conversation with a group of fellow expatriate managers at a welcome party a few days ago, he had learned that only the fittest survived a three-year posting to Asia, and that 60% of expatriate failure was due to family problems. After only a fortnight, he could see why.

His working days were long, but this he had expected. What he had not anticipated was the way his days were lengthened by the three, sometimes four-hour return journey to the industrial site, just outside Bangkok, where SCC was situated. The exhausting heat, the pollution and interminable wait in an unbroken series of traffic jams was quite outside his previous experience. During the first week he had struggled to learn as much as he could about SCC, its history and the evolution of the businesses, the company's most recent results and the strategies currently being implemented. He had also met his exclusively Thai staff, and been relieved to find that his senior managers all spoke reasonable English. His early ambition to learn the Thai language had soon been moderated by the realisation that his free time would be strictly limited.

At the end of his first week, Richard had sorted out his impressions and decided on a list of priorities for the businesses. SCC, which had a workforce of 150 people, operated in three main areas; Polymers, Resins and Speciality Chemicals and Adhesives. All three businesses, it was clear from the latest results and future projections, were doing exceptionally well and were in markets that would remain profitable for the immediate future. The commercial side, then, looked as if it would be fairly straightforward. He decided that he would keep a close eye on the bottom line and let his managers implement the agreed strategy until he was more knowledgeable about the markets and the customer base. Having settled this, he decided that he himself would focus on two main activities: learning how to manage in this new environment and improving safety standards throughout the company.

Learning how to manage here would, Richard realised, be a long process. In the first weeks, communications had been difficult as his ear became attuned to the sometimes stilted English and phrasing of his Thai managers. He was also taken aback by the discovery that his staff really did consider him in the light of the head of the SCC "family", and so treated him with a deference he found rather embarrassing. Their habit of bowing as they walked past so their head would not be taller than his, of opening doors for him and bringing him gifts, the knowledge that his staff watched his every expression to interpret his mood, all this was most disconcerting to someone used to managing in the relatively open and democratic European business environment.

Richard was similarly unprepared for the extent of the power and authority vested in him by his position as MD. Worse, he found that the strict attention to hierarchy that characterised Thai culture put him at an almost insuperable distance from his staff. Their polite way of deferring to him as "the boss", and of evading making any direct judgements, formed a barrier that he found difficult to overcome. Their attitude towards him was summed up by "*Kreng jai*", a phrase that he soon recognised as he heard it several times a day. It meant, his secretary explained, being careful not to put a superior into any sort of difficulty.

As he was fast discovering, this concern for his well-being meant that subordinates were extremely reluctant to give him any bad news, such as the loss of a customer or the resignation of a key manager. In this culture the boss was expected to perceive and know what was happening without having to be told. It was, therefore, hard for Richard to tell when things were going wrong or to estimate the seriousness of a problem, since no one would discuss such things with him directly. It was not that his staff were trying wilfully to deceive him or to cover up mistakes; they were simply obeying their instinct to avoid conflict and make "the boss" feel entirely comfortable. Richard realised that in order to get round these problems, he would have to develop a completely new management style.

With the operators and unskilled workers, Richard had as yet had little chance to communicate. During the first week, he had made daily tours of the site, the operating areas, storerooms, workshops and laboratories and noted several, to him elementary, safety precautions that were being ignored. However, he was relieved to see, judging by the little knot of workmen huddled with their cigarettes in the gatehouse, that the ban on smoking in all parts of the site was strictly observed and that most people wore hard hats and carried masks, even if they did not use them. He was initially pleased to note a member of one work team, engaged in the construction of a new workshop, wearing a safety harness as he hung high above the gantry. Unfortunately, his pleasure had been quickly dissipated by the realisation that the safety harness was not actually attached to anything.

Safety standards, Richard realised, were very poor compared to Europe. This was one area where there was a wide divergence between east and west and, as safety was one of the most heavily emphasised parts of the CHL culture, was something he would have to tighten up. The chemicals industry had a high profile in Europe, where pressure groups were quick to demonise any multinational thought to be neglecting safety or damaging the environment. For all chemicals companies these were potentially highly damaging, and therefore very sensitive, issues. CHL, always extremely nervous about bad publicity, had invested heavily in these areas and built up a strong image as a responsible, environmentally concerned multinational with a good safety record. With this in mind, Richard decided to make it his other priority to encourage the SCC workforce to be more safety conscious. During his time as managing director, he would aim to enforce safety and anti-pollution rules, and raise standards nearer to those of the parent company.

These resolutions came to Richard's mind as he listened to Somchai, who was relaying the phone message he had received from one of the supervisors left in charge at the SCC site. Richard and his top managers were all in central Bangkok, attending a one-day training course. According to the supervisor, in their absence there had been a chlorine leak from one of the chemical storage tanks. However, it was not serious and had not been caused by any major breakdown or crisis.

In fact, it had occurred because an operator, who had been with the company only a few months, had taken a short cut when carrying out a manoeuvre instead of following the procedure laid down in standing instructions. This procedure had recently been altered in order to avoid just such an eventuality, but the operator had ignored the change. Luckily, the state-of the-art western technology installed in the plant had triggered an automatic shutdown at the first sign of trouble. Consequently, of the 15 tons of chlorine stored on the site, only one kilo had leaked out. According to the supervisor on the spot, this low concentration of escaped gas meant that there was absolutely no danger to personnel. Indeed, he believed that everyone present on the site that day had been accounted for. He added that it was the first time anyone remembered such a thing occurring at SCC.

As Somchai noted down the details, Richard rapidly went through a mental checklist of possible danger points. As SCC was situated in an industrial complex, there were no houses in the immediate vicinity, so there was no danger to the ordinary civilian population. What about the local press? Green gas hung over the site at the moment but luckily, observed the supervisor, the favourable wind conditions would ensure that this was quickly dispersed. This meant that, supposing the local media heard about the problem, by the time they reached the plant the gas would have cleared. In the short term, there would be some effect on the vegetation, the foliage would die down and change colour, but it would grow back later.

For those working on the site, the smoke would be an irritant and make breathing difficult. If they were close enough to the source of the leak then this might be potentially hazardous, but the site manager reported that everyone had been evacuated and was being kept well away from the problem area. There had been some panic at first, but calm had now been restored. What about one of the secretaries whom Richard knew to be pregnant? She had proudly told him this when they were first introduced, a new arrival in a Thai family being a very big event. He resolved to arrange for her to go to hospital immediately for a check-up.

Although Richard had enough of a theoretical knowledge of the short term effects of such an incident to work through this checklist, his lack of engineering training meant that he had no direct experience on which to base any further decisions. He therefore found it difficult to judge exactly how serious the situation was, and how he should react in the immediate future.

Meanwhile, Somchai was emphasising that qualified engineers on the site had now taken complete charge, and that all would shortly be well.

Should he leave the course at once and return to the site, or should he stay and leave it to the professionals? In Europe, it was automatically understood that a manager should rely on his professionals to do their job, and not get in their way. "Don't try to do my job for me," would have been their attitude if he had tried to interfere in a similar situation in Basle. But what rule should he apply in Bangkok?

Richard stood up and turned to Somchai, who was preparing to leave and return to the plant. "Shall I come with you?" Richard asked him. "No, please don't worry," replied Somchai. "It was a very small incident and is already under control. I can deal with it." As Richard accompanied him to the door, he still could not decide what to do. Should he leave Somchai to return alone and so demonstrate his confidence in him, or should he himself go and take charge? Was there anything else he could do to help the situation? And how should he manage the follow-up to the incident?

Chapter 6

Exercise: The World Wide Web and Cultural Diversity

Maryann H. Albrecht

If you simply searched on the words "human resource management" or "cultural diversity" on the World Wide Web you'd usually find there are thousands of entries, often concerned with the environment or ecology. These lists save you time and give you the opportunity to learn a great deal about areas of interest to you. There are over a hundred listings that can inform you on topics ranging from the Human Rights Declaration of the United Nations to specific information for human resources professionals or a tour of a culture's ancient or current culture and demographics.

The list begins with instructions and moves on to name other key words you can use with a search engine. The key words or ways to enter a home page are usually given, rather than a specific URL or address, because specific addresses often change over short periods of time. In most cases, educational sites are chosen. Where specific addresses are unlikely to change, as with the United Nations, for example, a specific address is also given. Of course, if you find a site you want to revisit, save it for your own reference. Visit it often and note any change of address.

TOPICS AND LOCATIONS

There are many types of search engine that locate sites of interest, such as Altavista, Lycos, Yahoo, or Infoseek. These sites were researched with Lycos and you can follow this procedure with any search engine of your choice.

1. Begin by going into a network that will give you access to the World Wide Web. Since networks differ on how you instruct them to move to a new location, you will need to ask for instructions if you are not familiar with how to open the location of a search engine. Often you simply type the location and click on a "Go To" symbol.
2. Type the name and location of the search engine you want, for example, http://www.lycos.com/ The search engine will now give you a frame and a way to move to the location you want. For example, if you are interested in information on the culture of the British you could type in the words "The British Page" and the search engine would find the location for you, along with other websites that have those words in them.

The British Page would be "hotlinked," that is, when you placed your mouse on those words, you would see a hand indicating that a click of your mouse would hand you over into the new location. From there you could go to similar links to topics of interest to you. You can also print out pages (if your computer is attached to a printer). At the bottom of most of these pages, there will be hotlinks to send you back to the site's home page, and often hotlinks to related sites. Usually, a button on the top left of your screen will send you back (as often as you use it) until you return to the screen of the search engine or network you used to reach that search engine.

As you can see, you can use either the names of organizations or specific addresses to reach a web location. Given below are the names of places to visit that provide information on regional or international human resource management or on culture specific to a nation or global cultural heritage. Following these, there are listings with specific URL addresses.

SITE NAMES:[1] The names listed below can be typed into a search engine and the search engine will find the link for you. Click onto that hotlink to reach the site.

- African Studies
- Alexandria, Egypt (with links to cultural artifacts of Egypt)
- An Ongoing Voyage (pre- and post-Columbus culture in America)
- Angola
- Archives of African American Museums and Culture
- Asia Ville (with information on other hard-to-locate countries such as Cambodia)
- Asian Voices
- Brasil Web
- British Columbia Human Resources Management Association
- China News Digest
- Council on Employee Benefits
- Cross Cultural Connections
- Cultural Diversity Hotwire
- CultureFinder (links to interesting places)
- Demographic and Population Studies from the Virtual Library
- Disability Resources
- Economic Statistics Briefing Room
- Employee Benefit Research Institute
- Guide to Museums and Cultural Resources on the Web
- Human Resources Professionals Association of Ontario
- Information Resource Management Association of Canada
- International Association for Human Resource Information Management
- International Information Management Congress
- International Institute for Management Development
- International Society of Certified Employee Benefit Specialists
- Irish Literature, Mythology, Folklore
- Italia USA
- Japan Window
- Kona
- Latin World
- Library of Congress Cultural Exhibits
- Megacities

- Museums and Galleries at Southern Utah University
- National Museum of the American Indian
- Nyiregyhaza (a virtual tour of the town)
- Project Genesis (information especially designed for the Jewish College Student)
- Project Hermes (Supreme Court Rulings)
- Society for Human Resource Management
- Tales of Wonder (stories and fables from around the World)
- The Bahai's
- The Beauty of India
- The British Page (information on culture of the British Isles)
- The Fourth World Documentation Project
- The Human Languages Page (an introduction to the languages of the world)
- The World Wide Web of Virtual Library Museums
- U.S. Information Agency
- Voices of Youth: World Summit for Social Development
- Windows on Italy
- World Heritage Test
- World Wide Web of Sports
- Zeus

ADDITIONAL WEBSITES

In addition to the sites listed above, you may want to browse through some of the topics or visit some of the places listed below. These are excellent sources on world culture and several allow you access to information that is difficult to locate, e.g. sites on developing nations. First, the search centers are listed so that you can move quickly to some of the key words listed or enter a key word of your own choice. Of course, you can also enter a specific location by using a complete address. As an example, you could enter a search engine and use the word "Asia" (listed below). This is one of the few places you can find information on the culture and history of Central Asia. For this site, the specific address is also listed, so you could use a browser, such as Netscape, and enter a specific URL (address) which, for Asia, is: http://www.public.adu.edu If the address changes, as they often do, the new address will usually be listed when you enter an address. Of course, using the word with a Search Center will also help you reach the new address.

The search centers:
- **Argus Clearinghouse**
- **A2Z** (Lycos)
- **Internet Public Library**
- **Librarians' Index to the Internet**
- **Look Smart**
- **Magellan**
- **Planet Earth Virtual Library**
- **Point** (Lycos)
- **WebCrawler Select**
- **World Wide Web Virtual Library**
- **Yanoff's Internet Services List**
- **Human Resource Professional's Gateway to the Internet**. A site that links to other

HR locations including other search tools at: http://www.teleport.com/~erwilson/
- **Partnership for Cultural Diversity**. A student organization concerned with diversity and cultural issues.
- **The Ethnic Heritage Council**. A non-profit organization promoting diversity in the Pacific Northwest.
- **University of Maryland's** links to resources on diversity.
- **Yahoo** links using "Society and Culture" which will lead you further into the search engine to topics about cultures, diversity, disabilities, gay resources, and religion.
- **Campus Diversity** (http://www.odfac.usyd.edu). This site has access to training programs as well as a resource center.
- **Saudi Arabian Embassy**
- **Tibetan Cultural and Community Service Center**
- **Guide to Museums and Cultural Resources on the Web**
- **Archives of African American Music and Culture**
- **DBAE and Cultural Diversity**. This site has discipline-based art-educational ideas.
- **Cultural Diversity Seminar**. One group can be found at http://www.mbnet.com/thezone/ seminars/cultdiv.htm
- **National Center for Research on Cultural Diversity and Second Language Learning**
- **The World Wide Web Virtual Libraries.** There's a set of libraries in different topics. You may want to look at what's new in the law library at http://www.law.indiana.edu You can also visit the international division of the virtual library at http://alcazar.com or hunt for an overview at http://www.geocities.com/CollegePark/Library/8419/wbpthfnd.html You can even enter topics, such as "Tibetan," and find information about studies in specific fields.
- **Population and demography.** One good site is at the University of North Carolina at Chapel Hill. You can reach it at http://www.pop.psu.edu/Demography/demography.html
- **National surveys.** One source is Cais at http://www.cais.com Another source you can use is Coombs at http://coombs.anu.edu which provides general resources as well as Asian studies. Coombs also provides a social science virtual library with current information at http://coombs.anu.edu.au/WWWVL-SocSci.html
- **Virtual Book Shop.** A good starting point for difficult to find resources on outstanding works by private presses and first-edition books, especially fiction.
- **Gateway to World History**, which has listings related to research on culture, including a source for Chinese history.
- **Classics and Mediterranean Archaeology**, which will allow you to link to the University of Michigan's exhibits and documents.
- **Thailand.** One source of links to information on Thai culture as well as the country itself is http://www.nectec.or.th/WWW-VL-Thailand.html
- **Virtual Tour of the U.S. Government** at http://www.dreamscape.com/frankvad/us-gov.html
- **Web Art.** The commercial service at http://www.webart.com demonstrates its own work with links to exhibits using its services, including rare works from India and Nepal. The exhibitions provide brief and informative cultural explanations of the use of the art in their cultural context. A link to Emory University (http://emory.edu) can link you to Carlos, an art exhibition maintained by the University.
- **U.S. State Laws.** Emory University also provides a link to laws at federal and local level. See http://emory.edu and move into the home page of the law school.
- **Symbolic.** The French cave paintings, among the oldest known to human civilization, can be visited at http://www.culture.fr Move into the English text and you can visit their most

recent discoveries, art in a Paleolithic cave, and even contrast it with other cultures by linking into *Bibliotheca Universalis*. *Bibliotheca Universalis* is a project to provide access to the major works and artifacts of cultural significance, and you can contrast this by visiting http://www.lacma.org, which will display ancient Islamic art as well as other art sites, or move into the Louvre (http://www.louvre) and explore the artistic expression of a culture over time. For information on architecture as well as art objects, use: http://www.Perseus.tufts.edu and move to the Department of Art and Architecture.

- **Disabilities.** The Integrated Network of Disability Information and Education can be reached at http://www.indie.ca Specialized services can also be reached through the National Rehabilitation Information Center at http://www.cais.net
- **Medical information.** To enter an advanced web site for medical science you can use http://www.uiuc.edu/ph/www/jscole/medembro.html
- **Census/information** on the demography of the United States can be reached through http://www.census.gov, and from here you can also reach information about the U.S. labor force and its composition by using the link to the Department of Labor.
- **The Web Ring**. One way to move around in the Web is to enter and then move to connected web sites, then jumping again to a connected link. The Web Ring is found at http://www.webring.org and you will want to take some time to locate all the sites of interest to you.
- **World facts.** The government is a course of information in itself because it has prepared so much information about other countries. Use http://www.odci.gov and go to CSI, where you can find government publications as well as facts on topics, countries, and regions of the world.
- **Statistics.** The Center of Statistical Resources is located at the University of Michigan and can be reached at http://lib.umich.edu with a full address of http//lib.umich.edu/libhome/Documents.center/stats.html
- **World health**. The World Health Organization tracks health and issues that affect health. Their wealth of information, including any recent outbreaks of disease in a particular location, is found at http://www.who.ch
- **Human rights.** The United Nations is another excellent source of information. You can enter http://un.org and find out a great deal about the United Nations and its Charter and services. The Declaration of Human Rights, an important and thought-provoking document for those interested in multiculturalism, is at http://www.un.org/overview/rights.html
- **Social science links.** You can explore current topics at a high academic level by using the website at http://www.sscl.uwo.ca/explore/socsci.html A clearinghouse of information for science is at http://www.clearinghouse.net
- **Supreme Court rulings**. To find out rulings, by date or by topic, and stay informed on them, go to http://www.ssci.law.cornelledu/supct You can also do research by moving to http://lcweb.loc.gov
- **Chinese poetry and philosophy.** For poetry, look at http://www.chinapage.com/poetry.html There is a discussion of Chinese philosophy at http://www.chinesephilosophy.net
- **Hate groups.** A guide to hate groups on the Internet, for the purpose of keeping track of those who preach intolerance, can be reached through a watch group. Use http://hatewatch.org or move into the law school at Harvard with http://law.harvard.edu/library/guides/hateweb/hate.html
- **Religion.** The facts on almost every religion can be found by entering a World Wide Web virtual library. You can enter a search engine and use the words "Virtual Library" and move on through its links, or enter an online encyclopedia by entering the search words "Encyclopedia" in a search, or move more directly by entering a specific library, such as http://coombs.anu.edu.au/WWWVL-SocSci.html, and then entering the name of a religion. Three

other specific locations which provide information on Catholicism, Buddhism, and Hinduism are http://www.cs.cmu.edu (for Catholicism) http://sfn.saskatoon.sk.ca/rel/bdhism.html (for Buddhism) and http://hindunet.org (for Hinduism). To reach a source for Jewish students, enter a search for Project Genesis.

- **Gender**. Information on research in this area is at http://www.english-www.hss.cmu.edu/gender
- **Asia**. A good source of information can be found at http://www.public.adu.edu and information on Central Asia can be reached at http://greenarrow.com
- **Egypt**. A source complete with pictures of famous archeological treasures can be reached through http://www.memphis.edu with a specific site of http://www.memphis.edu/egypt/egypt.html
- **Japan**. A good source of information is at http://www.ntt.co.jp
- **Cultural exhibits**. The Library of Congress has its own interesting and thorough home page. Use http://lcweb.loc.gov The specific site of the exhibits page is http://lcweb.loc.gov/homepage/exhibits.html
- **World constitutions and laws**. This is an excellent way to examine the ways in which countries view their societies and the behaviors they allow and regulate. Compare documents at http://adi.uan.es
- **The World Heritage Test**. You can test your knowledge at http://cco.cltech.edu with the specific location of http://cco.caltech.edu/~salmon/world.heritage.html
- **The Human Language Page**. Enter a search using "Human Language Page" to have a look at an international language and information on the ways we communicate within and across languages.
- **The British Page**. Enter "The British Page" for a formal look at Britain and information on its culture and interesting archeological exhibits.
- **Handshake Project**. Enter a search using these key words and you will find images of the ways we greet each other in friendship.
- **The Internet Public Library**. Use these words to discover a resource librarians also use to locate material and resource new information.
- **Clearinghouse**. If you want a card catalogue to search engines that will search the whole internet catalogue, use http://www.clear You can also enter through a new address for the Argus Clearinghouse which can pinpoint information sources for you at their new address, http://www.clearinghouse.net/The ARGUS Clearinghouse

Note

1   The advantage of using site names rather than entire location addresses is that it allows you to find the site despite changes in specific address locations. The disadvantage is that you need to go through a search engine, so you may want to save addresses of your favorite sites, visit them often, and note any address changes over time.

Part II

Strategic Human Resource Management

7   Are We Global Yet?   71
         James W. Walker

8   International HR Policy Basics   76
         John J. Fadel and Mark Petti

9   Integrated HR Systems Help Develop Global Leaders   79
         Linda K. Stroh, Sven Grasshoff, André Rudé, and
         Nancy Carter

10 A Contingency Matrix Approach to IHRM   83
         Fred Luthans, Paul A. Marsnik, and Kyle W. Luthans

11 Reaping the Rewards of NAFTA   103
         Dick Bottorff

12 *Case*: Diversity Management at Hewlett-Packard, Europe   108
         Linda Brimm and Mandakini Arora

13 *Case*: Eurochem Shanghai: Corporate Policy or China
         Practice?   125
         Miles Dodd

Chapter 7

Are We Global Yet?

James W. Walker

Globalization of business enterprises has accelerated as opportunities have developed around the world. Leading the way are companies in petroleum and natural resources, aircraft, industrial equipment and construction, pharmaceuticals and chemicals, semiconductors and electronic products, branded consumer goods (e.g., soft drinks, luxury goods), and financial/professional services. These companies no longer just do business in multiple regions or countries, adapting to local market differences. Rather, they are thinking and acting globally and locally – executing integrated strategies and operating in each market in the most effective manner.

As our companies expand globally, the human resource management challenges are great. Our attention in managing people typically focuses on helping employees to understand and effectively handle cultural requirements by building sensitivity to languages, national customs, legal and regulatory environments, and other country and regional differences. We also pay a lot of attention to managing cross-border assignments and to matching individual interests, capabilities, and development needs with business requirements and local circumstances.

However, we give far less attention than we should to the broader strategic challenges of building business that is global and not simply "all over the world." We need to develop the mindset and capabilities among our people so our organizations can extend their influence beyond local and regional boundaries and gain the significant leverage of being global.

GLOBAL MARKET STRATEGIES

Most companies still operate regionally or country by country, emphasizing the differences among them. Often, opportunities addressed are too narrowly defined because of too much "localization," focusing on specific markets and business unit performance.

Increased international trade is critical to economic growth and to growth of business enterprises. In spite of the difficulties in Asia and other regions, largely driven by financial considerations, leading companies are optimistic about their long-term potential as global players. Business strategies for addressing global markets – sourcing, research and development, manufacturing, and, yes, finance – all will continue to be vital over the next decade. Growing competition and unprecedented opportunities are leading many multinational companies to pursue more radical change than ever before. Companies are keeping their sights on aggressive, long-term strategies for development of targeted market opportunities across the world – they are creating advantage on a worldwide scale.

Fundamentally, this requires that our managers and other key employees understand the key trends in the global marketplace and perform within their context.

A global competitive arena is rapidly developing through opening of markets. Instead of local industries locked in national economies, a system of integrated global markets is emerging, involving global players. National borders are becoming less relevant as nations embrace increased international trade as a driver of economic growth. The focus is shifting from the 19 developed countries ($4 trillion GDP) to 68 developing countries ($17 trillion), including populous China, India, and Indonesia. And there is a third set of countries in Asia and Africa awaiting development.

Advances in computing and communications technology are opening up the flow of information and knowledge sharing, which heightens desires and expectations for products and services of global providers. Technology enables company ability to leverage knowledge and talent worldwide.

Global capital markets will continue to develop, with growing scale, mobility, and integration. No longer are companies limited to capital sources and interests within each closed national economy. Capital is available through the private sector across borders to businesses anywhere that can generate attractive returns. At the same time, it is important that common measures and standards of financial performance are being applied globally.

Some companies still see these trends as threats, although the trends represent the greatest opportunities in several generations and the primary business challenge of the 21st century. Other companies still focus nationally, but are gradually adopting approaches to compete globally.

These companies will specialize and become world-class and world-scale or suffer the consequences. Effective companies will pursue long-term commitment, investment, and risk management to achieve results in targeted markets. They will make decisions and implement actions with an understanding of global economics and market potential.

Our challenge is to help our managers and associates understand such global threats and opportunities and engage them in developing effective strategies for addressing them. We must enable everyone to appreciate (and cope with) the uncertainty and rapid change inherent in global businesses.

FLEXIBLE GLOBAL ORGANIZATION

Rapid globalization requires organizational flexibility. Opportunities develop and pass quickly, requiring organizations to seize them through alliances and partnerships. However, many managers and other key employees still feel more comfortable with traditional ownership and control; they have difficulty working within complex network or matrix organizations.

Flexibility is more important because global companies increasingly work with partners around the world. Leading companies effectively establish mergers, acquisitions, joint ventures, and strategic alliances vital in creating opportunities to combine capabilities and apply them across the global marketplace. They are at ease working through partnerships and networks of business relationships.

This flexible organizational approach is vital because it provides a company with:

- Improved knowledge of local markets
- Quicker entry to markets and shorter cycle time for market and product development
- Lower capital requirements
- Leverage of others' capabilities and resources

Within large companies, a network of allied organizations allows business units to be small enough to provide identity with a focused strategy and results, and yet be linked globally. Leading global companies adapt each region and line of business organization to specific requirements. Often we must fight the human tendency to focus locally through strong but insular business units. For example, British Petroleum (recently merged with Amoco) is forging 90 distinct business entities around the world to gain advantage of both global and local focus.

To build flexible organizations, we need to build the capabilities required to operate globally. Managers need to understand the characteristics of flexible organizations and determine the organizational design and capabilities required to achieve business objectives. Because flexible organizations require flexible people, we need to develop capabilities such as:

- Working through varied and changing business relationships
- Working with a tolerance for ambiguity and complexity inherent in multidimensional matrix organizations
- Applying negotiation and collaboration skills
- Understanding and respect for different cultures
- Leveraging diversity and working across borders
- Needed innovation and rapid change
- Integrating global and local perspectives in decisions and actions

Our challenge is to define the capabilities required of leaders to build effective, flexible, global organizations. The capabilities are largely the same as those of all effective leaders; there are the added complexities of multiple cultures and multidimensional organizations. Accordingly, leading companies are investing in the education, job assignments, and other activities that will develop these competencies, not just talking about them. Global development processes and educational programs or "institutes" provide the resources and processes required. Further, development itself helps build flexibility through the "glue technology" provided through development and succession processes (see Paul Evans' article in *Human Resource Planning 15.1*). Leading global companies are known for the excellence of their leadership development.

AN INTEGRATED APPROACH TO ALL MARKETS SERVED

It is hard enough for a company to establish operations in specific markets around the world. It is more difficult to bind it together as a common force with common infrastructure and core competencies. Global companies target investments according to the unique merits and requirements of each regional/local market and operation. However, they also take a broader view, identifying and capitalizing on common characteristics of all markets. Peter Drucker has observed that management is the same all over the world, except that relationships vary with national cultures. Companies too often focus on cultural and other differences, rather than the necessary commonalities. Both are vital.

Local or regional business units and operations are tied to global strategy and organization to achieve world-class quality, sourcing anywhere, world-class costs, shorter cycle time (less time to invent and experiment), and leverage of all available resources to achieve targets. As a result, global companies such as Kodak, Motorola, Otis Elevator, and Merck are rationalizing their operations worldwide, realigning organizations and roles and establishing stronger global or regional "centers" for research, engineering, manufacturing, and distribution.

Units acquire relevant local information and apply it to tailor their organization and priorities to the unique requirements of the markets served. In this way, global companies adapt to the varied requirements of multiple countries and cultures. However, they also challenge conventional wisdom, influence thinking, and initiate changes in business practices in different settings. Leading companies do not merely accept today's rules of competitive behavior as given; they innovate and thereby shape new competitive rules and establish a leadership (market first) advantage.

Global companies sustain this advantage by capturing the inside knowledge gained in each market and sharing the knowledge gained so that it may be used elsewhere. They are simultaneously accessing, assimilating, and leveraging competencies and knowledge from around the world, across industries, locations, and cultures hitherto unrelated, with all the complexity this implies.

One clear characteristic of global companies is a common language, and English is becoming accepted as the standard. In fact, Lionel Jospin, France's Prime Minister, recently suggested that English should "no longer be considered a foreign language" (*The Economist*, 27 June 1998). More broadly, an organizational or business language is required, including terminology and metaphors that are uniformly understood by company associates wherever they work. Companies need to communicate through multiple languages and effective use of frameworks, pictures and graphics, and case examples/stories.

Our challenge is to enable our managers and key employees to think and act both globally and locally. We must help our organizations develop capabilities (people, systems, resources) for worldwide advantage, manage the pitfalls and opportunities for cross-cultural management, and apply information and organizational systems for global knowledge sharing.

SUPERB IMPLEMENTATION EVERYWHERE

The companies that are first into a market often have advantage through initial invest-ment and a unique strategy; however, sustained performance requires superb implemen-tation on a global basis. This requires effective human resource management in several areas.

We must build a workforce with the global business savvy, cross-cultural leadership skills, productivity, and capacity required to achieve results in the more complex global context. We need to attract the best talent worldwide into an inclusive culture (not merely recruit local talent into a national or multinational culture). Global recruiting and selec-tion of talent is important, as is subsequent development through job assignments (career pathing and succession planning).

Through job experience and through education and development, we need to equip individuals to interact with people and build effective organizations in different cultures. We need to help them to gain the sensitivity, flexibility, and knowledge required to work in diverse environments and to work effectively across borders.

We also need to facilitate collaborative work across borders – building and supporting global networks of relationships necessary for collaborative work and knowledge sharing. Effective performance in global organizations requires working in transnational teams, learning from others, bending to the influence of others, and learning to share power. It requires highly developed skills in listening, communicating, debating, negotiating, and managing tensions and differences.

We need to build management processes and practices that work effectively in the complex global business context, and continuously adapt them to changing requirements and feedback. Because of the need for flexibility and rapid change, our emphasis must be on outcomes (e.g., for product innovation, supply-chain performance, customer satisfac-tion). This means focusing on flexible roles, relationships, accountabilities, and competen-cies required (rather than formal job design, responsibilities, decision authorities, etc.)

It is vital that we define accountability for performance. Often in far-reaching compa-nies, greater distance from the corporate headquarters flagpole allows operations to act with greater autonomy and greater differences. In effective global companies, all players are expected to perform according to agreed-upon expectations. Planning and reporting are bottom-up and top-down, so that managers see the larger picture in relation to local results.

Finally, we need to build a capacity to change rapidly. We need to help our organiza-tions assess changing forces affecting business strategies and respond with rapid, effective organizational and business change. As our businesses reach into new markets or develop new products, we need to equip the organization to shift effectively into an implementa-tion mode, coping effectively with inevitable complexity, change, and uncertainty.

This is what I believe it means to be global. It's far more than appreciating differences – it is building an integrated, flexible organization that can effectively seize opportunities wherever they develop.

What is your experience? What are your views?

Chapter 8

International HR Policy Basics

John J. Fadel and Mark Petti

It has finally happened. Your company is venturing out. It opens operations in Belgium in six months, and you're responsible for drafting the international HR policy that will carry the first team of expatriates overseas and back again. You know that to achieve and retain a competitive edge in a world market this policy needs to support your company's global business strategy. You know that it shouldn't be too restrictive or too vague, and that it should reflect local customs of the host country. And *because you know all of this*, you're feeling a little nervous.

But there's no need to worry. When you break down policy development into its basic components, it's less overwhelming. Let's take it step by step. First we'll identify the objectives of a global HR policy.

STATE POLICY OBJECTIVES

Regardless of the corporate business strategy unique to each company that will drive the specifics of an IHR policy, there are certain objectives that any effective IHR policy should aim to accomplish. The policy should attract and motivate employees to accept international assignments. It should provide competitive pay plans to ensure the assignee can maintain his or her accustomed lifestyle. It should promote career succession planning and include guidelines on repatriation and additional overseas assignments. It should facilitate relocation between home and host locations. And finally, it should be cost-effective, understandable and easy to administer.

To meet these objectives, you must have internal or external systems or programs functioning to handle the following six areas.

1. **Candidate identification, assessment and selection.** In addition to the required technical and business skills, key traits to consider include: cultural sensitivity, interpersonal skills and flexibility.
2. **Cost projections.** As the average cost of sending an expat family on an overseas assignment is between three and five times the employee's predeparture salary, quantifying total costs for a global assignment is essential in the budgeting process.

3. **Assignment letters.** Document and formally communicate the assignee's specific job requirements and associated pay in an assignment letter.

4. **Compensation, benefits and tax programs.** Identify the compensation, benefits and tax approach that meets company objectives. Some common approaches to pay include: home balance sheet, destination-based, net-to-net, flexible and lump sum. Tax equalization, tax protection or laissez-faire policies also may be incorporated.

5. **Relocation assistance.** Assist the assignee with disposition or management of home and automobiles, shipment and storage of household goods, visas/work permits and preassignment visits.

6. **Family support.** Provide cultural orientation, language training, spousal support, education assistance, home leave and emergency provisions.

INCLUDE KEY ELEMENTS

When developing an international human resources policy, the following points are usually addressed:

1. Purpose and other general information
2. Relocation preparation
3. Relocation to host location
4. Allowances to maintain standard of living
5. Leaves
6. Education allowance for dependent children
7. Benefit coverages
8. Tax policy
9. Repatriation (or succession plan)
10. Termination agreement.

This is by no means an exhaustive list of items to include. It should be considered the minimum guideline, however, when developing a table of contents.

ADMINISTER THE POLICY

Administration of an IHR policy can be an important determinant of its ultimate success. The proper channels and workflow should be clearly delineated and well-communicated. You need to decide which tasks and activities will be administered internally and which will be outsourced. An assessment of the knowledge, skills and cost required to perform critical functions should be gauged for both internal resources as well as outside service providers. Many multinationals currently outsource certain functions – including relocation, culture/language training, payroll, government reporting, income tax and immigration.

Technology can also facilitate policy administration and should be utilized to help reduce costs, improve efficiencies and improve service quality. In the short term, technology can improve operational efficiency by automating certain manual processes or providing an improved platform for transactions.

Regardless of which feasible solutions you choose, solving specific goals of the company's globalization strategy will be critical. Top priority always must be given to continuing excellence in client service to the international assignees. The ultimate value of a well-designed IHR policy and program is that it allows employees to stay focused on their business priorities and continue contributing to the financial success of the organization.

To retain the value of the human resources function in the ever-changing global business climate, you need to take proactive measures to ensure the growth of your company in this ever-shrinking "small world." It will be the company (regardless of size) that will leverage both knowledge and advanced technology and will take advantage of the overwhelming global business opportunities that await now and in the 21st century.

Chapter 9

Integrated HR Systems Help Develop Global Leaders

Linda K. Stroh, Sven Grasshoff, André Rudé, and Nancy Carter

As corporations strive to expand their global operations, companies with global human resource information systems (HRIS) are likely to be far better positioned to succeed in the highly competitive international market. The tasks of developing global leaders and global HR information systems emerged as the two most important challenges for the global HR function over the next decade in IPA's latest research effort, completed in January. The development of highly sophisticated HR systems should reduce overall HR costs by increasing effectiveness and efficiency. Such systems will also help to simplify the way customers (managers and employees) access and use HR around the globe.

CURRENT CHALLENGES

Multinational companies often discover that, especially in newly emerging markets, local management talent is rarely available to establish and build operations. Consequently, many companies conclude that the only way to start doing business in these markets is to relocate experienced managers from around the globe. Selecting team members for such assignments is no easy task, particularly if the company lacks a database of its worldwide management talent.

Even once established, such a database needs to be constantly reviewed and updated – a time-consuming task for senior management. Compounding the challenge, the managers in the database are constantly moving around the organization on assignments designed to provide opportunities for them to obtain additional skills, with new managers constantly joining the talent pool.

Finally, once an individual has been assessed and selected for a proposed global assignment, the decision to move is far from assured. A number of issues may need to be addressed, including the assignment's impact on family members' careers, education and health. Companies doing work in the international marketplace have discovered that providing predeparture screening and orientation – a potentially lengthy and time-consuming process – is essential to achieving the highest rates of success. An aborted or failed overseas assignment can often cost a company up to $1 million in expenses, as well as result in losing a member of the global talent pool because of resignation or termination.

An HRIS might include data on the potential expatriates' families, training needs, and past technical and cross-cultural experiences. Having such data would enhance the probability not only of selecting the best candidates, but of chances for success on the assignment, thus having a great impact on the future development of global leaders. Because most multinational companies now require international experience in order to move up the corporate hierarchy, tracking information related to international assignments can make a significant contribution to management development.

Value of a Global HRIS

While any multinational corporation needs a database of its global management talent, it should be an integrated HRIS that provides key data on the company's various compensation schemes, benefits, perquisites, and personnel practices and policies, as well as basic demographic data about employees. Such a system is extremely valuable in selecting people for global assignments and managing them while they are abroad. Without a source of accurate, up-to-date information on the labor laws, income tax systems and other employment regulations of countries where corporate managers are doing business, both the global management process and the mobility of employees will be seriously hampered.

An integrated global HRIS assists HR in integrating global issues with local concerns and, consequently, in giving employees who are going abroad information they need to assess the value of the move, both professionally and financially. Information in the system also can help employees address family concerns such as obtaining work permits, appropriate health care, housing, schooling and so forth – all of which can be major stumbling blocks in a manager's decision to accept a global assignment.

As HR strives to become an invaluable business partner, the traditional personnel functions such as staffing, benefits, compensation and training must be managed well in all countries. Otherwise, HR will not have the credibility or the valuable information to help managers decide how to do their jobs better. For this reason, an integrated global HRIS, readily available to all levels of line and HR management, is essential.

What are Companies Doing?

The experiences of several multinational companies that are IPA members provide details on the ways HR information systems can help companies select candidates for global assignments and improve the management of their global operations. Citibank, for example, has a global database that provides basic information on all employees, including their compensation; a talent inventory bank of more than 10,000 managers; and a database on the compensation, benefit and perquisite practices in the 98 countries where Citibank has employees. This last database not only provides information required in making people decisions – especially as they move around the globe – but also helps in furthering understanding and in managing the costs of HR programs.

Many companies are hindered by outdated legacy systems burdened with old technology and lack of flexibility. These systems do not allow HR the global leverage required to meet the needs of global businesses and locations. One approach to information technology used by the Hewlett-Packard Co. has been well accepted. HP's solution was to develop a common information technology infrastructure with networks and communication, centrally managed data centers with common server operating environments, and e-mail-based work-flow services for clients. Hewlett-Packard also recommends that multinational companies move toward using package solutions for software and ensure that information technology operations reporting to business units need to create, develop and connect centralized HR functions to those business units.

In other cases, companies are unsure of what data to include in the global system. According to KPMG Peat Marwick, the types of information required for management purposes from a global HR information system usually fall into these categories:

- Human resource cost information by business unit.
- Personal and performance information on candidates for global assignments.
- Demographics of the candidate pool to meet diversity reporting requirements.
- Benefit plan funding requirements and controls.
- Union membership information.
- Information required for HR if a merger, acquisition or divestiture is expected.
- Data on a global executive-level population for development, promotion and transfer purposes.

The experiences of the companies in the IPA survey indicate that the uses of global HR information systems vary by company. For example, Switzerland-based Asea Brown Boveri Ltd. uses the information it gathers globally only to identify candidates for management-level positions in its locally operated companies. The corporate HR function has as its only global-level responsibility the provision of a list of candidates based on the performance measurement information captured systematically and globally. All other HR information is administered locally and not considered of importance globally.

Other companies are using their global HR information systems to monitor international benefits coverages by requiring the heads of international management teams to submit periodic information on the eligibilities, entitlements and other characteristics of the total worldwide workforce. Still other companies use their systems to manage competitive compensation information. This usually occurs in smaller companies that do not have adequate local HR expertise in salary administration.

BEST PRACTICES AND LESSONS LEARNED

Many questions and concerns arise when a company begins to consider installing a global HRIS. These include how to select the delivery model that best meets the company's articulated needs; whether to administer the system in-house or outsource it; ease in working with the vendor to modify a system so that it is truly global; dealing with reluctance of overseas operations to input still more data for corporate use with no perceived local benefit; the magnitude of the data; the lack of global consistency in input screens and data fields; and legal regulations governing electronic transfer of personal and salary data across geographical borders.

The challenges become even more significant when a corporation tries to link a global

HRIS with a global payroll and benefits delivery system. Many of the companies that have been most successful with such links suggest doing the following:

- Minimize customization.
- Develop strong connections between HR and IT.
- Maintain regular communication between the different geographic IT teams to provide leverage.
- Pay constant attention to the performance of the system.
- Implement the system in phases.
- Provide a common worldwide IT infrastructure, including the PC environment and networks.
- Use automated testing.
- Operate with a focus on the HR function and how it does business, rather than on teaching IT concepts to HR.

Other executives recommend a more decentralized approach, especially if the company has a decentralized management philosophy and culture. Among the advantages are that such an approach eliminates the need to standardize business processes and data across all geographic boundaries, simplifies prioritizing of functions, and ensures that local information technology teams are more responsive to geographic needs and can implement changes rapidly.

Some of the disadvantages of a decentralized system are multiple versions of HR systems increase total costs; leveraging resources and enhancement of systems is more difficult; funding of worldwide initiatives and sharing data worldwide is more difficult; and investment in the system will vary across countries.

There are two major benefits to a centralized approach. It increases access to information by bringing together, for example, a worldwide employee database, an HR Web page, course catalogs and schedules, personnel files, and requisition status, all of which enhance the corporation's global communications. Also, process improvement and automation is possible for some of the following functions; salary planning, resumé searching, college recruiting assessments, affirmative action, planning and reporting, requisition approval, course registration, and employee file updates.

Finally, although the Internet and Web sites have made global HR databases a reality, in many emerging countries – especially the former Soviet bloc and Africa – telephone lines are still inadequate or nonexistent and power supplies are often unreliable, challenging the smooth operation of any global HRIS. Furthermore, given the fluid nature of the HR function, all systems are likely to need constant monitoring, evaluating, and updating. Implementation of an HRIS should therefore be seen as an ongoing process, not a final product. Done well, however, globally integrated HR information systems should have a huge impact on the ability of multinationals to develop leadership in the increasingly competitive global market.

Chapter 10

A Contingency Matrix Approach to IHRM

Fred Luthans, Paul A. Marsnik, and Kyle W. Luthans

INTRODUCTION

A "given" these days is for international human resource management (IHRM) to take the local cultural environment into account when planning and implementing various strategies and techniques. For example, implementing a strategy of empowerment – providing the necessary information and including all employees in the decision making and responsibility of the organization – is successfully being used in a number of United States (U.S.) organizations. The challenge for IHRM is to determine whether this approach will work in other cultures? Diversity training and the development of an organization-wide culture of equity are other currently popular HRM approaches in U.S. companies: however, as Sparrow, Schuler, and Jackson (1994) recently asked, are they appropriate in other cultures? This and other cross-cultural questions may begin to be answered by use of a contingency matrix for IHRM.

What is meant by a contingency matrix approach

Contingency approaches are not new, they can, for example, be found in the classic literature on organization design (Lawrence & Lorsch, 1967; Galbraith, 1973, 1977; Hall, 1991) and leadership (Fiedler, 1967; Evans, 1970; House, 1971). Applied in this article, the contingency matrix is based on "If – Then" relationships that are then used to analyze and provide practical guidelines for effective IHRM (Luthans, 1973, 1976; Luthans & Stewart, 1977). Specifically, the "If" in the contingency matrix is the country or culture and the "Then" is the human resource management concept or technique that will best meet the goals of the multinational corporation (MNC). In strategic management terminology, the contingency matrix approach to IHRM attempts to make the best "fit" between the country/cultural environment and HR concepts and techniques that will strengthen the HR core competency of the MNC.

Table 10.1 shows an example of an IHRM contingency matrix for an MNC involved in four countries. The dimension of "country" is placed along the vertical columns. Other countries could be added or subtracted depending on the MNC's activities. The point is, IHR managers could construct a matrix involving whatever countries are relevant to their

Table 10.1   Contingency Matrix for IHRM

	Japan	Germany	Mexico	China
Recruitment and Selection				
Training				
Compensation				
Labor Relations				
Job Design				

MNC. The horizontal rows simply represent a sample of HR functions; others could be added depending upon the needs for building or strengthening the HR core competency of the MNC.

The ultimate goal of a contingency matrix approach to IHRM would be to have each box filled with reliable and valid information drawn from the results of current relevant research and direct documented experience. Obviously, this ideal will never be fully realized, yet, an incomplete IHRM contingency matrix still seems to be an improvement over the current disorganized jumble of fragmented information available to most IHR managers. The pragmatic value of the contingency matrix is that it could be used to organize the existing body of knowledge and to provide useful guidelines for HR managers who are increasingly trying to deal with diverse cultures.

The cultural ("if") side of the contingency matrix

National cultural dimensions make up the "If" side of the contingency matrix, the vertical columns of Table 10.1. Fortunately, there is some comprehensive research that can be used in diagnosing the cultural dimensions of given countries in constructing the contingency matrix.

By far, the most widely recognized research on the dimensions of national culture comes from the work of Dutch researcher Geert Hofstede (1980). After two questionnaire surveys of over 116,000 employees in IBM subsidiaries located in 70 different countries (making it the largest organizationally based study ever conducted), Hofstede suggested that a country's culture can be depicted along four cultural dimensions which can be summarized as follows:

1. *Power distance* indicates the extent to which a culture accepts that power in institutions and organizations is distributed unequally.
2. *Uncertainty avoidance* indicates the extent to which a culture feels threatened by uncertain or ambiguous situations.
3. *Individualism* refers to a loosely knit social framework in a culture in which people focus on taking care of themselves and their immediate families. *Collectivism*, the opposite end of the continuum from individualism, refers to a tight social framework in which people distinguish between in-groups and out-groups; they expect their in-group (relatives, clans, organizations) to look after them and, in exchange for that, will have loyalty to the group.
4. *Masculinity* refers to the extent to which the dominant values in a culture are assertiveness, money, and things. On the other end of the scale is *femininity*, which refers to the value of caring for others, quality of life, and people.

Countries around the world differ greatly on the above dimensions. For example, Hofstede found the U.S. and Western European countries relatively high on individualism and low on power distance. Asian countries, on the other hand, were found to be collectivistic and have high power distance. Scandinavian countries were found to be feminine and have weak uncertainty avoidance, while Japan was found to be very masculine and have strong uncertainty avoidance. Importantly, however, even within the same regions of the world, Hofstede found major differences. For instance, Singapore was found to have very weak uncertainty avoidance, but Korea had relatively strong uncertainty avoidance, and Italy was relatively individualistic, but Portugal was relatively collectivistic.

Although Hofstede's research findings can still be used as a starting point in diagnosing the culture for a contingency matrix approach to IHRM, his data were gathered in the 1970s and may no longer be as relevant to the dramatically changing world facing today's IHRM. Increasing attention is being given to another Dutch researcher, Fons Trompenaars (1994; and Hampden-Turner & Trompenaars, 1993) who conducted a more recent comprehensive study of about 15,000 managers from 28 countries. Similar to Hofstede, he used individualism and collectivism but also added some new dimensions. Briefly summarized, the Trompenaars' cultural dimensions include:

1. *Individualism vs. collectivism* – the importance of self (U.S., Czechs, Russia, Mexico) versus the group (France, Japan, Southeast Asian countries).

2. *Achievement vs. ascription* – personal status based on what someone does (Austria, U.S., Mexico, Germany) versus who someone is (Venezuela, China, Russia).
3. *Universalism vs. particularism* – rules and truths can be precisely identified and then should be applied everywhere (U.S., Austria, Germany) versus giving attention to personal relationships and treating each situation differently (China, Russia, Venezuela).
4. *Neutral vs. affective* – emotions are held in check and not publicly displayed (Japan, UK, Singapore) versus emotions considered natural and openly displayed (Mexico, Netherlands, Switzerland, China).
5. *Specific vs. diffuse* – outgoing and considerable open public space, but closely guarded and closed private space (Australia, U.S., UK, Switzerland) versus very cool and detached publicly, but when outsiders are allowed to enter private lives, very open (Venezuela, China, Spain, Singapore).

Trompenaars' dimensions seem to go beyond Hofstede's and can provide relevant guidelines for today's IHRM. For example, when a MNC opens a subsidiary in a Western European country, which tends to be high on universalism, a guideline would be that HR policies and labor relations should tend to be relatively legalistic; contracts can be counted on. In newly emerging countries, such as China or Russia, that Trompenaars found to be low on universalism, but high on particularism, the HR focus should be more on building personal relationships: contracts don't mean much.

In some areas of IHRM, Trompenaars' research would agree with Hofstede's earlier work. For example, both sets of research would indicate that team HR techniques and group incentives would work better in collectivistic cultures (Asian countries) than in individualistic cultures (U.S.). Hofstede's work, however, would seem to fall short in addressing important emerging HR concerns such as work–family relationships. Trompenaars' research, on the other hand, would seem to have more relevancy with such issues. For example, Trompenaars found that in diffuse cultures (China, Spain, Singapore) work and private life are closely linked, but in specific cultures (Austria and Switzerland) work tends to be more separate from private life (Hoecklin, 1995).

Because of its recency, the Trompenaars' data reflect some of the important world changes not found in the Hofstede research. For example, Trompenaars includes a sample of eastern European countries in his data set, and some of his findings counter Hofstede's specific results and conventional wisdom. Hofstede (1980) found Mexico to be a collectivist culture in the 1970s, but Trompenaars (1994) found his sample of Mexicans to be relatively individualistic. This could reflect the more democratic form of government and the early 1990s surge in the Mexican economy. Surprisingly, and contrary to conventional wisdom, Trompenaars also found the former communist bloc countries of the CIS (former Soviet Union) and the Czechs to be high on individualism. As MNCs develop HR strategies for eastern European countries, they should be aware of these findings in implementing reward systems or team techniques (Luthans, Patrick, & Luthans, 1995).

The above discussion of the "If" cultural environment provides a point of departure for filling in the cells of the IHRM contingency matrix. The real challenge, however, lies in drawing from the body of relevant research and practical experience in developing the matrix.

The research/experience ("then") side of the contingency matrix

When actually developing a contingency matrix, the question is where to begin. One starting point could be academic journals specializing in international management and/or human resource management. First-hand experiences of IHR practitioners which are sometimes reported in the popular press (*Fortune, The Wall Street Journal*, etc.) can also be valuable. Of course, the highly touted "information highway" is an information gatherer's dream; unfortunately, the "infobaun" can also be an information sorter's nightmare. The challenge is not in finding information for the contingency matrix but rather in devising a systematic mechanism for scanning and screening the mass of available information.

Human resource information systems (HRIS), which are common today in HRM practice, can be used in developing the contingency matrix. The universe of relevant research/experience for the matrix can be found in periodicals, verbal reports, the Internet, various Web sites, and other sources. It is important to note that, practically speaking, not all relevant information will be included in the matrix. The Internet provides an illustrative example of the practical limitations. Anyone familiar with the Internet is aware of the mind-boggling quantity of data available. This database has been compared to the "old west" because there is gold out there, but only a few will find it. The rare gold, in this case, is information relevant to the matrix. The same problems exist in the systematic search for, and categorization of, verbal reports and practical experience.

In contrast to the information available on the Internet or verbal/practical experience, is the relevant data found in periodicals and books. A systematic search for published information found in libraries on virtually any topic is a relatively simple process given today's bibliographic technology. A number of databases are currently available which contain large numbers of academic journals, periodicals, and newspapers. As a demonstration example, we used the Expanded Academic Index (EAI) as a way to systematically search the IHRM literature in building a sample contingency matrix. EAI contains titles, abstracts, and other relevant information on articles published in over 1,500 journals. An important feature of most available library databases (including EAI) is that they enable the searcher to define the parameters by using key words and or subject terms. This search approach is widely used by academics and graduate students but can also be used by IHR professionals in implementing the contingency matrix approach.

In using EAI and other such searching mechanisms to fill in the matrix, the first critical step is the choice of subject terms and time frame. For example, subject terms for compensation may be "gainsharing" or "pay-for-performance" and for job design may be "quality circles" or "work teams." The second step for developing the matrix is to cross-reference each subject term with the selected country or culture. For example, we found 10 articles published after 1991, that were listed under the subject "labor unions" and that had the word Japan or Japanese in the title or abstract. Of course, current technology allows us to see the title, abstract, and often the full text of each of these published works to determine relevancy for the contingency matrix.

A SAMPLE CONTINGENCY MATRIX FOR IHRM

Since most of the existing IHRM research literature to date focuses on Japan, this will best serve to demonstrate the use of the contingency matrix. After a brief literature review of Japanese culture (the "If"), a short list of empirically derived HR recommendations (the "Then") is offered. The intent is not to provide an exhaustive, comprehensive literature review but rather to give a brief overview for demonstrative purposes. Table 10.2 summarizes a sample, filled-in IHRM contingency matrix for Japan, Germany, Mexico, and the People's Republic of China.

The contingency matrix approach to IHRM in Japan

Hofstede (1980) described Japan as being strong in uncertainty avoidance, high on masculinity, above average on collectivism, and above average on power distance. The more recent Trompenaars' (1994) research found that Japan was relatively high on collectivism and had the very highest neutral cultural values (emotions held in check, not publicly displayed). Research by Cole (1989) found that the Japanese cultural norms favor participation and reliance on group decision making. Cole's conclusion supported the earlier research findings of Haire, Ghiselli, and Porter (1966). Kriger and Solomon (1992) found that, consistent with these cultural norms, the Japanese tend toward a decentralized decision making style which reflects a much greater degree both of autonomy and delegation of authority. Several studies have shown that the Japanese tend to place a high value on personal relationships, and they prefer to develop trust, or interpersonal attraction, before making business transactions (Abramson, Lane, Nagai, & Takagi, 1993; Graham, Kim, Lin, & Robinson, 1988; Sullivan & Peterson, 1982). In Japan, taking time to create a relationship is seen as a sign of wisdom and sincerity (Moran, 1987). The Japanese place a premium on long-term relations between customers and suppliers, and they prefer to do business with a minimum of explanation and a maximum of cooperation (Harris & Moran, 1990). Although the Japanese success story in the global economy suffered a setback a few years ago, there is recent evidence that they are once more competitive in world markets (Franco, 1996) and their dedication to continuous improvement is paying off (Henkoff, 1995).

RECRUITMENT AND SELECTION GUIDELINES FOR JAPAN.   The general objective of the HRM function of recruitment is to assess the uncertainties of the labor market and cultural (including legal) customs and policies, and to acquire employees with the desired knowledge, skills, and abilities (Moore & IsHak, 1989). Given Japan's strong emphasis on long-term relationships and trust, it is not surprising to find that large Japanese companies usually recruit at junior levels while senior positions are filled by internal promotion. Even though traditional lifetime employment is declining (Keys, Denton, & Miller, 1994), Japanese companies still place a great deal of emphasis on recruitment and selection because it is assumed that the employees will be with the company for a long time.

The literature is inconsistent concerning the availability of Japanese college graduates for entry-level management positions. For example, an article in *Far Eastern Economic Review*, June 18, 1992, states that

Table 10.2 Sample Information for Selected Countries Using the IHRM Contingency Matrix

	Japan	Germany	Mexico	China
Recruitment & Selection	Prepare for long process Ensure that your firm is "here to stay" Develop trusting relationship with recruit	Obtain skilled labor from government subsidized apprenticeship program	Use expatriates sparingly Recruit Mexican nationals at U.S. colleges	Recent public policy shifts encourage use of sophisticated selection procedures
Training	Make substantial investment in training Use general training & cross training Training as everyone's responsibility	Recognize & utilize apprenticeship programs Be aware of government regulations on training	Use bilingual trainers	Careful observations of existing training programs Utilize team training
Compensation	Use recognition & praise as motivators Avoid pay for performance	Note high labor costs for manufacturing	Consider all aspects of labor costs	Use technical training as reward Recognize egalitarian values Use "more work, more pay" with caution
Labor Relations	Treat unions as partners Allow time for negotiations	Be prepared for high wages & short work week Expect high productivity from unionized workers	Understand changing Mexican labor law Prepare for increasing unionization of labor	Tap large pool of labor in cities Lax labor laws may become more stringent
Job Design	Include participation Incorporate group goal setting Use autonomous work teams Use uniform, formal approaches Encourage co-worker input Empower teams to make decisions	Utilize works councils to enhance worker participation	Approach participation cautiously	Determine employee's motives before implementing participation

in Japan, there are 2.7 white collar jobs for every applicant . . . it is not unusual for a company to send thousands of letters containing a variety of informative materials designed to entice young college graduates. Upon graduation (students) can look forward to jobs with higher salaries, longer holidays, and reduced overtime (p. 33).

A *Business Week* article published only 10 days later (June 29, 1992, p. 51) paints a contrasting, but probably more realistic picture. This news report stated that the soft economy in Japan has dampened the recruiting of college graduates. Although Japanese firms still are offering generous pay packages to recruits, they are trimming expenses by reducing the number of new hires. This situation has helped foreign firms who should find it easier to recruit Japanese college graduates.

Although there is some disagreement over the availability of entry-level Japanese managers, there seems to be consensus concerning the effort required to recruit experienced Japanese executives. In fact, difficulties in recruiting Japanese talent have been a major factor limiting growth for foreign companies in Japan. Japanese employers can put tremendous pressure on employees who they suspect are thinking of leaving. The multinational recruiter must be prepared to spend a great deal of time with prospective Japanese executive recruits. These recruits will want to gather large amounts of information about the parent company before making a decision. This tendency is consistent with Hofstede's high uncertainty avoidance. A critical factor for outside firms in recruiting the Japanese manager is convincing him or her that their company is here to stay. Perhaps the most effective way to reduce anxiety on the part of the Japanese recruit is for the outside firm to have a Japanese manager as its local chief operating officer (Berger, 1990).

The highlighted box which follows each discussed section can be used to summarize the contingency guidelines for that topic concerning the functions of IHRM in Japan. Once again, the intent is simply to demonstrate a sampling of If – Then relationships and not to provide an exhaustive list of doing HRM in Japan.

IF Japan, **THEN** for effective recruitment and selection:

- Be prepared for a lengthy recruitment process.
- Make sure the recruit understands that your company is here to stay.
- Take the time to develop a trusting relationship with the recruit.
- Understand the deliberate, consensus-oriented, decision making style of the recruit.

TRAINING GUIDELINES FOR JAPAN.   In order to design an effective IHRM training program, it is important to understand how different people learn – that is, to understand their learning modes (Fisher, Schoenfeldt, & Shaw, 1993). HRM training, in an international context, is complicated by the fact that people in different cultures tend to have different learning styles. In the case of the Japanese, they tend to favor generalized learning and utilize a "systems" or macro perspective. This Japanese learning style can be contrasted to the Western style which tends to favor specialized learning with a more micro perspective. In addition, Japanese management treats human resources as fixed assets, and employees often consider their employment as lifetime organizational careers.

Consequently, long-term training and development is a critical aspect of the Japanese HR system (Yuen & Kee, 1993).

The Japanese maintain very high standards for education and training. There seems to be a genuine conviction in Japanese management, from top to bottom, that the achievement of high standards of performance is dependent on the existence of a knowledgeable and constantly updated work force. Japanese employees identify with and are committed to organizational and work goals of the group. Training in Japan, in addition to transmitting knowledge and work-related skills, is also part of the communications system, transmitting to employees at all levels the aims and philosophy of the company. All Japanese managers and supervisors have been conditioned to give training, coaching, and counseling to their subordinates, and to extend this to their colleagues in other functions. To be in step with Japanese cultural values, the responsibility for training should be vested in – and accepted by – every individual employee (Brown & Read, 1984). Effective training of Japanese employees is consistent with Hofstede's (1980) and Trompenaars' (1994) collectivism and the Japanese preference for cooperation (Harris & Moran, 1990).

IF Japan, **THEN** for effective training:

- Make a substantial investment in training.
- Use general training and cross-training for long term results.
- Establish training as the responsibility of all employees.

COMPENSATION GUIDELINES FOR JAPAN.   Ideally, an HRM compensation system should align individual objectives with important strategic goals of the organization. Individual objectives will, of course, be at least partially determined by the local culture of the employees. The Japanese compensation system has received considerable attention in the past several years. Media attention has focused on the enormous disparities in pay between U.S. Chief Executive Officers (CEOs) and their subordinates as compared with a much smaller pay disparity in Japan. Since Japan is relatively high on Hofstede's (1980) masculinity cultural dimension, however, high salaries are important because the Japanese value the acquisition of wealth (Hodgetts & Luthans, 1993). Both Hofstede (1980) and Trompenaars (1994) also found Japan to be a collectivist culture, therefore, individually based pay for performance arrangements would not be as effective as group incentive systems, such as gainsharing. In addition, Vance, McClaine, Boje, and Stage (1992) found that collectivist cultures tend to value recognition and praise more than monetary rewards, and Brown and Read (1984) found that money plays only a small and indirect role as a motivator for Japanese employees.

IF Japan, **THEN** for effective compensation systems:

- Use recognition and praise, in addition to money, as motivators.
- Use group incentive systems, such as gainsharing, instead of individually based systems.

LABOR RELATIONS GUIDELINES FOR JAPAN.   The Japanese labor union movement has been shrinking in recent years, and the recent alliance between the Liberal
Democratic Party (LDP) and the Social Democratic Party of Japan further weakens the
movement. The Japanese Trade Union confederation, or Rengo, is also suffering from
declining numbers and a more conservative, less politically active membership (Sakamaki,
1994).

A study by Giorgio Brunello (1992) examined the relationship between unionization
and productivity in Japan. An analysis of data from a sample of 979 union and non-union
Japanese manufacturing firms provided evidence that Japanese unions in the sample
substantially reduced both productivity and profitability as well as regular wages net of
bonuses and fringes (Brunello, 1992).

Effective international labor relations involves knowledge of the local culture and laws
regarding labor relations and collective bargaining. The negotiation process, in particular,
is a problem for managers who are operating in a foreign culture. A recent survey of large
corporations revealed the concern over negotiation skills. Seventy-four percent of the
respondents indicated a need for more negotiation skills with foreign governments and
businesses (Harris & Moran, 1990).

The Japanese negotiation style relies on the development of a smooth, harmonious
relationship that will eventually facilitate consensual decision making (Cattel, Eber, &
Tatsuoka, 1988; Tung, 1984; Moran, 1987). In the initial stages of negotiation, the
Japanese are more concerned with attraction and deference than they are with the exchange of information (Graham, Kim, Lin, & Robinson, 1988). In Japan, a legal contract
is not considered to be an acceptable substitute for interpersonal trust (Hall & Hall, 1987;
Tung, 1984). On the whole, Japanese management and trade unions tend to regard each
other as trustworthy partners, and there is no hint of the assumption which so often
characterizes such relationships in the West – that the interests of companies and trade
unions are, in most respects, fundamentally opposed. The company trade union is one of
the greatest strengths of the Japanese labor relations system, enabling Japanese management to concentrate its attention on the battle with competitors rather than fighting with
their own employees (Brown & Read, 1984).

IF Japan, **THEN** for effective labor relations:

- Treat unions as a partner, not an adversary.
- Allocate substantial time for negotiations.
- Build trust as the first step in negotiations.

JOB DESIGN GUIDELINES FOR JAPAN.   Although job design is not always directly
associated with HRM, it does seem to be especially relevant to effective IHRM. In
particular, the issue of employee participation and the use of work teams is important to
IHRM. The effective use of participation and work teams depends on the culture. In fact,
perhaps more than any other HR area, participation/work teams are dependent on the
ability to understand and respond to cultural differences.

There is research evidence that in Japan job designs involving participative management will be effective. In Japan, Hofstede's high uncertainty avoidance and both Hofstede's and Trompenaars' above average collectivism would support the use of participation as a key feature of job design. The well-known Haire, Ghiselli, and Porter (1966) study used measures of managers' attitudes toward a participative style of management in the international context. They developed a questionnaire which measured four dimensions: (1) the capacity of people for leadership and initiative; (2) sharing information and objectives between leaders and subordinates; (3) the extent to which managers involve their subordinates in the decision-making process; and (4) people's belief in internal versus external control. Using this questionnaire, these researchers studied 3,641 managers in fourteen countries and found that Japanese managers, more than any other group, endorsed group goal setting and mutual influence.

According to Brown and Read (1984), participation, practiced but not legislated, brings to Japanese companies all the benefits which Western theories of industrial democracy are presumed to confer. Joint decision making at the lowest reasonable level enables workers to have a part in managing the environment in which they work. Although it takes a long time to reach decisions by this method, the resulting commitment to carry out the decision is complete. If there is a danger with the use of work teams by multinationals in Japan, it probably lies in the fact that the home country managers know less than the local managers. It would therefore be wise to solicit as much advice from the locals as possible in designing and implementing the work team concept.

A recent study (Smith, 1994) compared the determinants of work team performance in Great Britain, the U.S., and Japan. The results for Japan indicated that Japanese supervisors see teams as more productive if they rely on formal procedure manuals in unfamiliar circumstances and more cooperative if they rely on the manuals in day-to-day circumstances. The Japanese results indicate a uniform formal approach to unfamiliar and day-to-day events, while the Western results suggest that ways of achieving optimal performance are contingent on the type of event encountered. The results also suggest that the most frequent way of handling events in Japan was through co-workers' advice, while in Western countries it was reliance on one's own experience and prior training.

There is evidence that Japanese teams have fewer people but more of an assortment of skills and management levels with decision making authority. There is also evidence that American teams often have far less empowerment than do Japanese teams (*The Economist*, 1992).

IF Japan, **THEN** job design:

- Should include participation.
- Should incorporate group goal setting.
- Should use autonomous work teams.
- Should use uniform, formal approaches in unfamiliar and day-to-day activities.
- Should encourage co-worker input and advice.
- Should empower teams to make decisions.

The contingency approach to IHRM in Germany

Besides Japan, which outside the U.S. has by far the most existing research information to fill in the cells of the contingency matrix, other countries can also be included in this approach to IHRM. For example, in addition to Japan, the MNC may have operations in Germany.

Hofstede did not find German cultural values to be extreme on any dimension, but they were relatively individualist, had small power distance, had strong uncertainty avoidance, and were masculine. Trompenaars' research found the Germans high on universalism (legalistic, universal application of the rules), and achievement, but in the middle of his other cultural dimensions. This cultural profile of the Germans would be considered in applying HRM techniques such as incentive pay (individualism, masculine, and achievement-oriented) and taking a legalistic, contractual approach to labor relations and the use of temporary employees (universalist values).

Although there is considerable information on HRM in the German language (and thus, translators may be a valuable resource in this approach to IHRM), the library search process did not yield much information in the English language about German HRM. The following briefly summarizes a sampling of this information:

1. *Recruitment and selection.* Since business schools do not play much of a role in German higher education (Hofstede, 1993), relatively more emphasis is given to recruiting engineering graduates and skilled labor from government subsidized apprenticeship programs.

2. *Training.* Most of the information on training in Germany focuses on the effectiveness of apprenticeship programs, both on the shop floor and in the office. These programs alternate between practical work and classroom courses. Standards for teaching and training are established, and the skills of trainees are assessed upon completion of the program (Vickers, 1994). A nationally recognized certificate called the "Facharbeiterbrief" is given at the successful completion of the apprenticeship. About two-thirds of the German worker population hold such a certificate, with corresponding occupational pride and self-motivation (Hofstede, 1993). MNCs operating in Germany should recognize the value of apprenticeship programs, however, there is some recent evidence that commitment to such programs is beginning to falter. For example, Von Brachel (1994) notes that German managers, under heavy pressure to reduce expenses, are cutting training, including the vaunted apprenticeship programs.

3. *Compensation.* Germany has the dubious distinction of having the world's highest labor costs and lowest hours worked. For example, workers at IBM Deutschland are receiving $28 per hour and enjoy a 35-hour work week. Although MNCs must be prepared to pay top dollar for German workers, this high price is currently being maligned because of the recession, free trade, and global competition.

4. *Labor relations.* Labor unions in Germany have traditionally been strong, but like those in Japan and the U.S., in recent years they have suffered a reduction in membership and power. For example, IBM Deutschland recently removed 17,500 of its 24,500 workers from the national labor contract with IG Metall, Germany's most powerful labor union. In addition, most new jobs are in smaller, non-union companies and, as a result, unions have been forced to make unwanted concessions ("Out of Service?," 1995). Despite the decline of the labor movement, there is some research evidence that the strong German unions do not stifle productivity and innovation. A study using econometrics models estimated that trade unions do not have a negative impact on innovative activity. This study operationalized

innovative activity as percentage of revenues spent on R&D or the percentage of employees working in R&D (Schnabel, 1992).

5. *Job design.* Perhaps the greatest single factor affecting the design of jobs in Germany is the concept of co-determination. Most German workers are represented by both a union and a work council. While this situation could be viewed as the manifestation of a high degree of worker production, some German managers argue that co-determination undermines their ability to operate efficiently. Research by Scholl (1987) provides evidence that the ability of German managers to make decisions is not hampered by co-determination. Specifically, this study examined both managers and work councils and found that co-determination did not slow down decisions regarding investments or personnel matters.

The contingency matrix approach to IHRM in Mexico

With the advent of the Maquiladora, and the more recent passage of NAFTA, Mexico has received a great deal of attention. MNCs going into Mexico will discover that recruitment and selection, training, compensation, and job design are not simple in this new international business frontier. Flynn (1994) noted that the legal, social, and cultural conditions in Mexico make effective human resource management a significant challenge.

Hofstede found Mexicans to be relatively collectivist and masculine and to be relatively high on both power distance and uncertainty avoidance. By contrast, Trompenaars' more recent findings were that Mexicans were relatively high on individualism and achievement, and had the highest affective cultural values (emotions considered natural and openly displayed). This latter cultural profile probably reflects the new found political and economic freedom experienced in recent years by the Mexican people, especially those who would be employed in an MNC. The following sections discuss a sample of the available information on the management of Mexican human resources.

RECRUITMENT AND SELECTION.   Staffing for low-level positions in Mexico is relatively uncomplicated because the vast majority of the labor pool consists of workers with low-level skills. Staffing of high-level positions is more of a challenge. The extensive use of expatriates is not a viable staffing alternative because Mexican labor law requires that no more than 10 percent of a firm may be non-Mexicans.

MNCs recruiting for high-level positions in Mexico must be cautious about a potential candidate's previous job titles because they may be inflated and not accurately reflect past responsibilities or current abilities (Flynn, 1994). To get around some of these problems, MNCs, such as Nabisco International, have been successfully recruiting at U.S. colleges, such as Texas A&M and the University of Texas, where there are large numbers of excellent Mexican students eager to return to their home country (Flynn, 1994).

TRAINING.   For those MNCs who go to Mexico for its cheap labor, the need for training becomes very important. The bottom line is that cheap labor is not enough. There have to be effective, trained workers in order to compete in today's competitive global marketplace. In a recent Towers Perrin survey of more than 150 Fortune 1,000 CEOs and senior executives, three-fourths said that a skilled work force would be critical to the success of companies in Mexico whose strategies depend on quality or know-how (Flynn, 1994).

Workers at Nissan's Mexican plant were initially resistant to high technology, discipline, and the routine of a manufacturing plant. Nissan was able to overcome this problem by devoting more emphasis to the training of Mexican workers (Ramirez, 1994). Motorola was also able to boost productivity and morale at its Guadalajara, Mexico plant by implementing an Organizational Effectiveness Change model. The steps in this model include instilling a vision or purpose in employees at all levels, developing strategies for reaching company goals, and focusing on appreciation of multiculturalism (Banning, 1991).

In order to maximize the effectiveness of training Mexican workers, it is important that the training be done by trainers who are comfortable with the Spanish language. Bilingual and bi-cultural skills are critical for trainers and upper-level expatriate employees (Flynn, 1994).

COMPENSATION.   Conventional wisdom, backed by wage surveys, indicates that Mexico has low wages, however, on closer analysis, this cheap labor may not be as cheap as it appears. When calculating the real wages of Mexican workers, it is important to note that under Mexican labor law, employees' pay includes compensation for holidays and weekends. It is also important to recognize that cash allowances play a major role in compensation in Mexico. For example, the majority of employers provide one month of pay for a Christmas bonus. If these factors are ignored, Flynn (1994) notes that it is possible to underestimate the cost of Mexican wages by as much as 40 percent.

Performance-based pay can be problematic in Mexican organizations. Traditionally, Mexicans have tended to prefer guaranteed wages and thus may resist pay-for-performance. Conventional wisdom has been that Mexican workers place more emphasis on a congenial working environment than on making more money. This would make a "cultural fit" with Hofstede's profile; however, the Trompenaars data indicating Mexicans to be more individualistic and achievement oriented would counter the traditional assumptions about compensation. Today's Mexican workers may be more interested in pay for performance incentives than in the past.

LABOR RELATIONS.   With increased economic activity and NAFTA, the Mexican union movement has renewed vitality. For example, Mexican labor is receiving assistance from powerful U.S. trade unions to help organize union activities and improve wages and benefits (Alexander, 1994a). Although the Mexican government is still hostile toward independent labor unions, these kinds of labor organizations (such as the Authentic Labor Front and the Federation of Goods and Services Unions) are gaining increasing power in Mexico (Alexander, 1994b). Presently, most manufacturing operations are unionized. MNCs must be aware that labor relations in Mexico may be quite different. For example, when a strike is called in Mexico, the entire plant shuts down until the strike is settled; picket lines are unheard of in Mexico (Flynn, 1994).

JOB DESIGN.   Implementation of participative management programs in Mexican operations must be approached cautiously. Most Mexican line workers have never been involved in participative management programs, so adequate time must be allowed to give them background on what is to be expected of them. Hofstede found Mexicans to have large power distance and strong uncertainty avoidance, so Mexican workers may tend to be more interested in pleasing their immediate boss than in striving for the company as a whole through teams or other participation programs. Since Trompenaars found the Mexicans to have such high affective cultural values, however, they may be very enthusiastic and openly provide input if given the opportunity to participate.

The contingency matrix approach to IHRM in China

Extremely challenging for IHRM are fast-changing countries such as the emerging economic superpower China (PRC). The Chinese are known as being among the toughest negotiators in the world. In addition, China is undoubtedly one of the most difficult countries for an outsider to understand and to which to adapt (Harris & Moran, 1990). One problem for IHRM to overcome in China is that Chinese enterprises have traditionally not had a formal personnel/HR department. Instead, certain managers have been designated or self-selected to carry out the HR functions (Swaak, 1995).

Fortunately, there has been a considerable amount of recent literature on HR issues in China in order to develop the contingency matrix. Although Hofstede's data predated the economic development of China, Trompenaars found the Chinese to be predictably collectivistic and relatively high on particularism (value personal relationships over rules and recognize situational differences), quite affective (openly emotional), very diffuse (cool and detached publicly, but when outsiders allowed to enter private lives, very open), and high on ascription (age, class determines one's status). This cultural profile should greatly affect the implementation of all the HR functions in China.

RECRUITMENT AND SELECTION.   There is still some centralized Chinese government assignment of workers to employers which replaces the traditional recruiting and selection function (Fisher, Schoenfeldt, & Shaw, 1993). As economic reforms proceed in China, however, there is evidence that a more market-driven selection process is well underway (Von Glinow & Chung, 1989). For example, China is currently changing the way employees are selected for public service positions. The implementation of the Provisional Regulations on State Public Servants in China will make it necessary to use a number of assessment instruments when selecting a person for a public service position (Yannian, 1993). In the past, a single appointment system was used. This change in public policy may make it easier for MNCs to use and find acceptance for sophisticated selection procedures, such as valid tests and assessment centers, for hiring Chinese employees at all levels.

TRAINING.   Although there is little research evidence on training techniques in China, there are some practical experiences upon which to draw. For example, McDonald's successfully sent a team of professionals to train their Chinese employees not only on the production of potatoes, beef, and buns, but more importantly they provided training revolving around the company's philosophy of selfless and friendly service (Yannian, 1993). Trompenaars' cultural profile would suggest that training for teams would be accepted and effective for the Chinese.

COMPENSATION/REWARD SYSTEMS.   The contingent application of reward systems can be used in China. Culturally, egalitarianism (collectivism) is still the rule in China, especially with regard to monetary compensation, however, the "duo lao, duo de" or "more work, more pay" (or pay for performance) philosophy is gradually taking hold. Although the era of the "Iron Rice Bowl" (lifetime employment by the state) has been declared to be over, the benefits provided by state enterprises are still far greater than in most other countries. There is evidence that perhaps the most effective reward for Chinese employees is access to training (Von Glinow & Chung, 1989). Training, especially technical training, is highly valued by Chinese employees.

Cash bonuses and other material incentives are possible, but there is currently no effective way to distribute material rewards to "all contributing groups" (e.g., the work group, the department, enterprise, bureaus, ministries) (Von Glinow & Chung, 1989). The new reforms, however, such as the Provisional Regulations may change the perception and the reality of compensation in China. For example. Yannian (1993) notes that under the reforms, promotions, salary increases, and punishment are based on an employee's capabilities. Also, a recent empirical study found, contrary to conventional wisdom, that Chinese employees preferred reward systems based on individual contributions (Chen, 1995). The Chinese employees from state-owned enterprises (a steel maker, petroleum company, and a transportation firm) preferred an unequal distribution of both financial rewards (pay and bonuses) and socioemotional rewards (friendliness, invitation to a party, or display of a photo in the company newsletter). This finding is contrary to what their traditionally assumed collectivist cultural values would predict. These apparent changes, as are occurring in China and the rest of the world, require that the contingency matrix be continually updated and modified.

LABOR RELATIONS.   Effective labor relations in China require that the MNC pay close attention to local regulations. According to a recent article in the *Beijing Review*, most foreign funded enterprises violate Chinese laws as they mistreat local workers. The Chinese government plans to introduce new rules that would strengthen the role of the union and would require employers to provide social insurance, subsidies, and adequate wages to workers. Also, a recent national work conference on trade unions in foreign enterprises, held in Shijiazhuang, was aimed at establishing trade unions in foreign-funded companies to protect the rights of workers.

Millions of Chinese peasants have recently moved from rural areas to the cities in search of employment and the better life that they now are able to see on TV. This large pool of available, cheap labor can be attractive to labor-intensive MNCs. By the same token, conditions in China make labor relations a difficult, and somewhat unpredictable, undertaking. For example, in the city of Shenzhen, the population has surged from 100,000 in 1979 to 2.5 million in 1994. To date, officials in Shenzhen and other similar Chinese cities have been lax in upholding labor laws (Goldstein, 1994), but this can change at any time and greatly affect the MNCs taking advantage of the excess, cheap labor supply.

JOB DESIGN.   A study using World Bank and Chinese Academy of Social Science survey data examined employee participation in management decision making in Chinese local industrial firms. This study argued that it is important to examine employees' reasons for wanting to participate. The study concluded, in a nondemocratic environment, the impact of socioeconomic development on workplace participation is mixed (Tang, 1993). It may, therefore, be advisable to determine the employee's motives for participation before implementing participative management programs in Chinese organizations.

The Trompenaars cultural profile would make a good "fit" with worker participation, and there is some evidence that such programs may be effective in China. For example, a workers congress system, which allows the exercise of a democratic form of worker management has resulted in better corporate policies and improved supervision (Zuying, 1992).

A FINAL WORD

This article has suggested and demonstrated a contingency matrix approach to IHRM. As globalization continues and it becomes increasingly clear that human resources are the real competitive advantage, then effective IHRM becomes critical. As the head of emerging world-class Chrysler noted: "The only way we can beat the competition is with people. That's the only thing anybody has" (Sherman, 1993, p. 96).

The contingency matrix can be an important tool in three major ways in making effective IHRM become a reality: *First*, developing a contingency matrix reminds IHR professionals that there is no "one best way" to conduct human resource management in the transnational, "four any's" (anybody, anywhere, anytime, anyway) environment. *Second*, the contingency matrix can provide IHR professionals with the best prescriptive advice available for conducting HRM across cultures. *Third*, constructing a matrix is realistic, especially in light of user-friendly relevant information search and categorization technology available in most libraries accessible to HR professionals.

The contingency matrix approach suggested here can also aid IHRM scholars by calling attention to areas of potential research. Clearly, the field of HRM has just begun to scratch the surface of international research (filling in the cells of the contingency matrix shown in Table 10.1). At this point it seems that virtually any IHRM topic in any country is a potential contribution. The proposed contingency matrix approach to IHRM can also be of use to scholars as a starting point for theory building. By putting the results of research studies and actual practice into the contingency matrix, a relevant, organized body of knowledge can be made available to IHRM. As was demonstrated in Table 10.2, this contingency matrix can provide specific guidelines for more effective IHRM practice across cultures.

A final caution in using a contingency matrix approach is in order. An important reminder is that in the fast changing transnational environment, *a key challenge will be to keep the matrix up-to-date and to learn from the past*. Obviously, past HR policies and practices, such as lifetime employment in Japan, have and will be changing. The matrix must be continually updated and can be used as a point of departure to anticipate future HRM policies and practices in a learning organization sense (Luthans, Rubach, & Marsnik, 1995). The contingency matrix can systematically categorize and present the best available existing information. However, sustainable competitive advantage in the global economy of tomorrow requires *new* HRM thinking and *innovative* techniques that are implemented across cultures and with the results then fed back into the matrix. This continually updated contingency matrix may help meet the challenge of effective IHRM in an increasingly competitive and complex environment.

References

Abramson, N.R., Lane, H.W., Nagai, H., & Takagi, H. (1993). A comparison of Canadian and Japanese cognitive styles: Implications for management interaction. *Journal of International Business Studies, 24*, 575–87.

Alexander, R. (1994a). The emergence of cross-border labor solidarity. *NACLA Report on the Americas, 28*, 42–7.

Alexander, R. (1994b). Official and independent unions angle for power in Mexico. *NACLA Report on the Americas, 28*, 44–5.

Banning, K. (1991). Motorola turns vision to profits. *Personnel Journal, 70*, 50–5.

Berger, M. (1990). The gentle art of head-hunting. *International Management, December*, 57–9.

Brown, G.F., & Read, A.R. (1984). Personnel and training policies: Some lessons for Western companies. *Long Range Planning, 17*(2), 48–57.

Brunello, G. (1992). The effect of unions on firm performance in Japanese manufacturing. *Industrial and Labor Relations Review, 45*, 471–87.

Cattel, R.B., Eber, H.W., & Tatsuoka, M.M. (1988). *Handbook for the sixteen Personality Factors (16PF) in clinical, educational and research psychology.* Champaign, IL: IPAT.

Chen, C.C. (1995). New trends in reward allocation preference: A Sino–U.S. comparison. *Academy of Management Journal, 38*, 408–28.

Cole, R.E. (1989). *Strategies for learning: Small group activities in American, Japanese, and Swedish industry.* Berkeley: University of California Press.

Evans, M.G. (1970). The effects of supervisory behavior on the path goal relationship. *Organizational Behavior and Human Performance, 5*, 277–98.

Fiedler, F.E. (1967). A theory of leadership effectiveness. New York: McGraw-Hill.

Fisher, C.D., Schoenfeldt, L.F., & Shaw, J.B. (1993). *Human resource management, 2nd ed.* Boston: Houghton Mifflin.

Flynn. G. (1994). HR in Mexico: What you should know. *Personnel Journal, 73*, 34–41.

Franco, L.G. (1996). The Japanese juggernaut rolls on. *Sloan Management Review, 37*(2), 103–19.

Galbraith, J. (1973). *Designing complex organizations.* Reading, MA: Addison-Wesley.

Galbraith, J. (1977). *Organization design.* Reading, MA: Addison-Wesley.

Goldstein, C. (1994). No workers paradise: Labour activists make little headway in Shenzhen. *Far Eastern Economic Review, 157*, 135.

Graham, J.L., Kim, K.K., Lin, C.Y., & Robinson, M. (1988). Buyer–seller negotiations around the Pacific Rim: Differences in fundamental exchange processes. *Journal of Consumer Research, 15*, 48–54.

Haire, M., Ghiselli, E.E. & Porter, L.W. (1966). *Managerial thinking: An international study.* New York: Wiley.

Hall, E.T., & Hall, M.R. (1987). *Hidden differences: Doing business with the Japanese.* Garden City, NY: Anchor Doubleday.

Hall, R.H. (1991). *Organizations, 5th ed.* Englewood Cliffs, NJ: Prentice Hall.

Hampden-Turner, C., & Trompenaars, F. (1993). *The seven cultures of capitalism.* New York: Double Day Currency.

Harris, P.R., & Moran, R.T. (1990). *Managing cultural differences, 3rd ed.* Houston: Gulf.

Henkoff, R. (1995). New management secrets from Japan. *Fortune, November 27*, 135–46.

Hodgetts, R.M., & Luthans, F. (1993). U.S. multi-nationals' compensation strategies for local management: Cross-cultural implications. *Compensation & Benefits Review, March–April*, 42–8.

Hodgetts, R.M., & Luthans, F. (1994). *International management, 2nd ed.* New York: McGraw-Hill.

Hoecklin, L. (1995). *Managing cultural differences: Strategies for competitive advantage.* Wokingham, England: Addison-Wesley Publishing.

Hofstede, G. (1980). *Cultures consequences: International differences in work-related values.* Beverly Hills, CA: Sage.

Hofstede, G. (1993). Cultural constraints in management theories. *Academy of Management Executive,* 7(1), 81–93.

House, R.J. (1971). A path goal theory of leader effectiveness. *Administrative Science Quarterly, 16,* 321–38.

Keys, J.B., Denton, L.T., & Miller, T.R. (1994). The Japanese management theory jungle – Revisited. *Journal of Management, 20,* 373–402.

Kriger, M.P., & Solomon, E.E. (1992). Strategic mindsets and decision-making autonomy in U.S. and Japanese MNCs. *Management International Review, 32,* 327–43.

Lawrence, P.R., & Lorsch, J.W. (1967). *Organization and environment.* Cambridge, MA: Harvard University Press.

Luthans, F. (1973). The contingency theory of management: A path out of the jungle. *Business Horizons, June,* 67–72.

Luthans, F. (1976). *Introduction to management: A contingency approach.* New York: McGraw-Hill.

Luthans, F., Patrick, R., & Luthans, B. (1995). Central and Eastern Europe: Political, economic, and cultural diversity. *Business Horizons, September–October,* 9–16.

Luthans, F., Rubach, M.J., & Marsnik, P. (1995). Going beyond total quality: The characteristics, techniques, and measures of learning organizations. *The International Journal of Organizational Analysis, 3,* 24–44.

Luthans, F., & Stewart, T.I. (1977). A general contingency theory of management. *Academy of Management Review, 2,* 181–95.

Moore, R.W., & IsHak, S.T. (1989). The influence of culture on recruitment and training: Hofstede's cultural consequences as applied to the Asian Pacific and Korea. In Ferris, G.R., & Rowland, K.M. (eds.). *Personnel and human resources management.* Greenwich. CT: JAI Press.

Moran, R.T. (1987). *Getting your yen's worth: How to negotiate with Japan, Inc.* Houston, TX: Gulf.

Out of service? German unions. (1995). *The Economist, February 4,* 59–61.

Ramirez, C.E. (1994). Nissan battles high turnover at Mexican Plant. *Automotive News, July 11,* 24.

Sakamaki, S. (1994). Union blues: Socialist split weakens labor movement. *Far Eastern Economic Review, 157,* 15–16.

Schnabel, C. (1992). Unions and innovative activity in Germany. *Journal of Labor Research, 13,* 393–406.

Scholl, W. (1987). Codetermination and the ability of firms to act in the Federal Republic of Germany. *International Studies of Management and Organization, Summer,* 27–37.

Sharma, B., & Jain, H.C. (1989). Strategies for management of industrial relations in India and Indonesia. *Asian Profile, 17,* 523–31.

Sherman, S. (1993). Are you as good as the best in the world? *Fortune, December 13,* 95–6.

Smith, P.B. (1994). Event management and work team effectiveness in Japan, Britain and USA. *Journal of Occupational and Organizational Psychology, 67,* 33–43.

Sparrow, P., Schuler, R., & Jackson, S. (1994). Convergence or divergence: Human resource practices and policies for competitive advantage worldwide. *International Journal of Human Resource Management, April,* 6–9.

Sullivan, H., & Peterson, R.B. (1982). Factors associated with trust in Japanese–American joint ventures. *Management International Review, 22,* 30–40.

Swaak, R.A. (1995). The role of human resources in China. *Compensation and Benefits Review, September–October,* 39–46.

Tang, W.F. (1993). Workplace participation in Chinese local industries. *American Journal of Political Science, 37,* 920–40.

The team dream. (1992). *The Economist, September 5,* 69.

Trompenaars, F. (1994). *Riding the waves of culture: Understanding diversity in global business.* Burr Ridge,

IL: Irwin Publishing.

Tung, R.L. (1984). *Business negotiations with the Japanese*. Lexington, MA: Lexington.

Vance, C.M., McClaine, S.R., Boje, D.M., & Stage, D. (1992). An examination of the transferability of traditional performance appraisal principles across cultural boundaries. *Management International Review, 32*, 313–26.

Vickers, M. (1994). A new take on-the-job training. *The Vocational Education Journal, 69*, 22–3.

Von Brachel, J. (1994). What price apprenticeships? *Across the Board, 31*, 32.

Von Glinow, M.A., & Chung, B.J. (1989). Comparative human resource management practices in the United States, Japan, Korea, and the People's Republic of China. In Ferris, G.R., & Rowland, K.M. (eds.). *Research in personnel and human resource management*. Greenwich: JAI Press, pp. 153–71.

Yannian, D. (1993). Major reform of personnel management system. *Beijing Review, 36*, 4–5.

Yuen, E.C., & Kee, H.T. (1993). Headquarters, host-culture and organizational influences on HRM policies and practices. *Management International Review, 33*, 361–83.

Zuying, S. (1992). Workers' congress: Active in enterprise management. *Beijing Review, 35*, 28–9.

Chapter 11

Reaping the Rewards of NAFTA

Dick Bottorff

Can your company profit from a direct investment in Mexico? Can its culture withstand the inevitable macroeconomic shocks of devaluation, inflation, or recession? Do you have the right personnel to implement your plan? To answer these questions, examine your company's long-term strategic outlook, and prepare a careful ROI analysis. If your plan gets the go-ahead, sound control during and after the investment will keep your operation on track.

The passage of the North American Free Trade Agreement (NAFTA) has caused many U.S. companies to alter their business approach in North America. So far, attention has focused on Mexico where NAFTA's implementation has brought the most extensive changes. Half of U.S. exports to Mexico began entering duty-free on January 1, 1994. Within five years, two-thirds are scheduled to enter duty-free. Also, Mexican tariffs on all other industrial and most agricultural goods will be eliminated by January 1, 2004.

After the initial rush to invest in Mexico, now many U.S. companies seem to be slowing the pace of their expansion. A tangle of practical problems such as ever-changing regulations, vexing customs delays, and sputtering joint ventures have left the promise of Mexico's huge markets unfulfilled. As if timed to increase uncertainty, the one-third devaluation of the peso, December 20–22, 1994, stunned many companies on both sides of the border. Yet, with careful planning, sound management, and realistic expectations, many U.S. companies have seen a quick return on their investments there. Further, the devalued peso may provide new opportunities for nimble companies to take advantage of the lower dollar cost of Mexican labor and materials. Here's some advice from one U.S. company that has profited from its investment experience.

STRATEGIC ANALYSIS

National Computer Systems (NCS) is a $330 million information services company providing software, services, and systems for the collection, management, and interpretation of data. NCS has a dominant presence in the U.S. education marketplace and a growing international toehold. NCS's business in Mexico historically had been conducted through a local distributor. NAFTA offered NCS further encouragement to invest in a large and promising Mexican market that seemed ready to spend on infrastructure improvements especially in education.

Company culture supported investment in new market development, so a team from the international division, corporate strategic development, human resources, and legal was created to evaluate the options. Our group met from September 1992 to February 1993, shaping a plan to establish a direct presence in Mexico. From the strategic analysis, it appeared that NCS could capitalize on its core competencies in data capture and educational testing in a potentially lucrative market while retaining a strategic focus on significant vertical markets such as education, healthcare, surveys, and commercial data processing. NAFTA had not been approved yet by Congress, but with or without NAFTA approval, there were clear signs that market opportunity and further easing of trade restrictions afforded an attractive opportunity should fundamental investment criteria be met.

THE PAYOFF FROM PLANNING

Our team used conventional ROI analysis to evaluate several courses of action. Once the plan met internal criteria for minimum return on investment and payback, management told the team in February 1993 to proceed with a modest direct investment in a sales and service operation. The approach chosen was evolutionary. The company repurchased distribution rights from the local distributor and set in motion legal steps to form a subsidiary. Future strategic alliances with Mexican companies were not ruled out.

Our team attributes its success to the following steps of thorough planning.

- Start planning early, and devote sufficient time to the process while avoiding a "paralysis of analysis."
- Focus on both qualitative and quantitative goals.
- Evaluate the risks and rewards for the alternatives you are contemplating.
- Have a firm grasp on market demand, the chance of succeeding, and the productivity required to make everything happen.
- Prepare a detailed financial plan with capital investment, ROI, a multiyear profit and projection, expected staffing and personnel cost, and a timetable for implementation.
- Prepare "best case" and "worst case" scenarios.
- Pick leaders with international and company experience early in the planning stage.
- Be flexible as you monitor progress. The unexpected is likely to happen.

ADVICE FROM THE EXPERTS

As NCS was formulating its plan, and during the implementation, it found no shortage of advice. The company warns: Beware of the here-today and gone-tomorrow experts. The quality of seminar advice on NAFTA is inconsistent, perhaps because of the shifting political situation as NAFTA was developed. Details of the agreement were slow to emerge. And it is a long, complex document, which has caused a good deal of difficulty for many lawyers.

The best advice NCS received came from the following sources.

LOCAL LEGAL COUNSEL. NCS was advised to wait for events to unfold before seeking approval for a waiver from balance of payments restrictions on imports into Mexico. Ultimately, the advice proved sound when a new law was passed and NCS was able to obtain a waiver from the requirements. Legal assistance is not cheap, but generally it is worth the money in matters such as incorporation and regulatory advice.

LOCAL CPA. NCS was given sound advice on a number of issues relating to tax payment timetables and mechanics, issuance of tax identification numbers, tax certified invoicing, deductibility of expenses, appropriate documentation, and numerous other issues. Additionally, NCS chose to have the CPA firm, a Big 6 affiliate, prepare the accounting books and taxes during the start-up phase of the subsidiary. U.S. home office publications provided important background information.

U.S. CUSTOMS. A hotline was established to advise companies about duties and other issues. NAFTA timetables are in place for immediate or gradual phase-out of duties on many products, and the U.S. Customs Service can supply this information.

TRADE ASSOCIATIONS. The Minnesota World Trade Center, Minnesota World Trade Association, and similar organizations provide low-cost or free advice that companies should take advantage of because it usually is of high quality.

CUSTOMS BROKER/FREIGHT FORWARDER. NCS received good advice from its customs broker/freight forwarder, a competent source of low-cost or free help, whose business is knowing about the mechanics of international trade.

NCS also found that networking with its business peers about their experiences helped. Many lessons from the international scene parallel those learned domestically. Among the lessons NCS learned are:

- Hire locals, but hire carefully to avoid costly washouts. You may find it to your advantage to work through employment agencies, testing your prospective employees on a temporary basis before you add them to your permanent staff.
- Expect setbacks, but remember that perseverance pays off.
- Allow extra time. Mexico can be a frustratingly slow place in which to do business.
- Avoid *la mordita*, the "bite" or petty bribe. It is fading as practices change and is not necessary to get the job done.
- Provide frequent and strong headquarters support for your venture.
- There will be times when no one will know the answer to a problem that is vexing you. Evaluate the advice, and choose a course redirecting your actions as events transpire. Be flexible.
- Capitalize on what you already have. For example, NCS hired a local sales manager who had left our former distributor several years earlier and who knew the products. And the launching pad of direct subsidiary was provided by a significant order from a trusted U.S.-based customer.
- Beware of a splashy, high-cost entry unless you are very sure of the result. Success is rarely instantaneous in Mexico.
- Small companies – not just large ones – can find profitable markets in Mexico but may need to pursue an entirely different approach due to resource or experience constraints.

THE REWARDS

Mexico is a rapidly developing nation of approximately 86 million with a population that is expanding at a 2.1% rate. Per capita income is expected to rise following a series of setbacks in the 1980s and again in 1995. Inflation fell to under 7% in 1994 although the 1994–95 devaluation brought back substantial inflation. Retail companies such as Wal-Mart, K-Mart, and Radio Shack recently have made substantial investments with the intent of capitalizing on the potential of this growing marketplace. NAFTA has provided the impetus for many companies to follow the *maquiladora* and earlier investment waves that were led by manufacturing companies. But it is not just the retail sector that is attracting attention. With lowered tariffs, the formerly protected markets are now open. The Mexican electricity, petrochemical, gas, and energy service markets are open to U.S. suppliers. NAFTA has opened the Mexican market to U.S. trucking firms, financial services providers, insurance, and telecommunications companies.

THE PITFALLS

Mexico, however, is by no means an easy country in which to operate. Newcomers will be surprised by many things such as the high cost of office space in Mexico City. Rents of $60 per square foot for quality space are not uncommon. Trained professionals are in demand, so be prepared to act fast to hire the right people. Top management can be surprisingly expensive, commanding compensation packages comparable with the United States. In spite of high unemployment, technically qualified employees are difficult to find. You may be disappointed at the slow pace of progress on some of the details such as the pace of contract work on your office, utility installations, and government approvals. Receipt of a tax identification number, for example, a prerequisite for everything from your invoices to your bank account, may take months to obtain. Similarly, negotiating the import thicket can be agonizingly slow and frustrating. Your CPA and local lawyer can help negotiate the governmental hurdles. Experienced nationals can speed your way through the commercial maze. Smaller companies might do well to evaluate partnerships with established Mexican firms. This approach can ease the pain of managing an enterprise hundreds of miles away. In spite of its proximity to the U.S., Mexico will seem very foreign to newcomers.

IMPLEMENTATION

Now that the preferred investment option has been selected, a plan is in place, and the essential marketing decisions of product, price, promotion, and place have been made, decisions about an appropriate support organization, financing, and staffing must be made. Clearly, each company's answers depend on its situation. NCS was able to take proven imaging technology to the Mexican subsidiary of a trusted U.S. customer early on in the establishment of its direct sales and support operation. The repurchase of distribution rights and the attendant base of business developed by its former Mexican distributor meant a quick entry into the market at a modest cost. In June 1993, the first employee was hired to prepare for the market entry. The employee was hired on a contract basis by the parent company because the subsidiary was not legally established yet. A subsidiary was formed and staffed by February 1994 despite some hiring difficulties. Following incorporation, service personnel were the next priority and were on staff of the parent by the fall of 1993. A sales staff was added in January 1994.

During the initial phase of operation and before a tax certification number was received, the Mexican subsidiary operated as a commissioned agent of the U.S. parent, who invoiced the customer. In February 1994, NCS received approval from SECOFI (Secretariat of Trade and Industrial Promotion) to operate without a positive balance of payments. Since that time, NCSi Mexico has been a full buyer and reseller of optical scanning systems and scannable forms to the Mexican data capture market.

Significant management attention has been devoted to the operation. International headquarters personnel have logged some trips to Mexico since the plan was approved. Our financial staff was on site monitoring investment and operational spending and implementing procedures on average one week per month for the first 15 months. Formal management reviews initially were conducted on site every two months. Key local employees have made significant contributions to the start-up. The importance of on-site review, control, and assistance cannot be overemphasized.

Although the full benefits of NAFTA may be years away, NCS has seen quick results from its early entry into this important market. Scanner sales in the first full year of operation ran three times the presubsidiary pace, and important markets for scannable forms and services have been opened. The payback period on the investment was one year. In September 1996, NCS was selected to implement a five-year, $22 million project to handle the opening of Mexico's long-distance telephone market. In all, NCS feels that a local presence, run and staffed by dedicated employees, will afford an excellent opportunity to grow with this expanding, dynamic economy.

Chapter 12

Case: Diversity Management at Hewlett-Packard, Europe

Linda Brimm and Mandakini Arora

The forum room at the sprawling Hewlett-Packard industrial site in Grenoble, set amidst the French Alps, wore a festive look on June 5, 1996. It was the first day of a biannual European diversity and work/life forum that brought together diversity representatives from Hewlett-Packard sites all over Europe. They were there to exchange ideas on managing diversity and to think about a strategy at the European level for the next financial year.

The theme for this forum was "Crossing Bridges" and the metaphor of bridges would recur over the next two days. Helen Wellian, manager – although she sees herself as "facilitator" rather than "manager" – of the European diversity program, in her opening remarks, discussed the choice of theme. She and her colleagues in the room, she said, were "on a bridge, between an HP world that is no longer and an HP world that is not yet." Some of them had found since they had last shared information at a diversity and work/life forum, that "the bridge they were on could, at times, be a very slippery one."

Now, the question underlying the forum discussions and workshops was: "What do we need to stay on this bridge?" in terms of organizational structure, resources, actions, and accountability for diversity.

THE MEANING OF DIVERSITY

"Diversity" has, in the US particularly become a popular term to describe the changing mix of the workforce which is becoming more heterogeneous. A plethora of academic and journalistic articles that have appeared on the subject since the late 1980s, point to diversity as a critical human source issue for the '90s and beyond.

Demographic trends indicate that populations and workforces in developed countries are aging and birth rates are low. By the end of this century, in countries with low proportions of women working, the majority of new entrants into the workforce will be women. Also, with the increased mobility of "human capital," labor will flow from countries where it is in high supply to countries where labor is scarce but job-creation is high.[1]

Changing demographic trends are one reason why organizations, in North America and in Europe, are making efforts to ensure comfortable working environments for older people, women, and minorities. Another reason is that business today is increasingly global. Operations and customer bases cross national borders and cultures.

For businesses, the upshot of these trends is that managers today frequently have to interact with people – as colleagues, employees, suppliers, or customers – who are different from them by nationality, language, religion, gender, or race. Reports of what companies need to do to stay competitive in the '90s and in the 21st century increasingly cite diversity as a strategic and business imperative. Reports on the changing workforce in Europe refer to a "demographic time bomb."

The objective of diversity programs in companies is to draw on skilled people from all groups in society, to create optimal communications between employees in organizations and benefit from their full creative potential and productivity, and to meet the needs of an increasingly diverse and global marketplace.

DIVERSITY AT HEWLETT-PACKARD

A company-wide issue

As a critical business issue for Hewlett-Packard, diversity was given visibility at the corporate level since Lew Platt became CEO of the company in 1992.

There was concern at HP, by the early 1990s, than the company's unique corporate culture – "the HP Way" – was dying. "The HP Way" is, in founder Bill Hewlett's words, "in the last analysis . . . a spirit, a point of view." Managers talk of it as a set of core values: trust, teamwork, respect for the individual, flexibility, and innovation. These values are supposed to be solid and enduring while allowing for change at the level of company practices.

Platt was concerned that employees believed HP to be losing its "human touch" and he hoped to revive the HP Way.[2] In November 1993, he made "Our People," of which workforce diversity is a major part, one of his Hoshins.[3] In his words:

> Our diversity efforts are focused on creating a work environment where all people can contribute to the company and have an opportunity to reach their personal goals. Diversity is much more than a program or a legal requirement at HP, it's a business priority for several compelling reasons. We sell to a diverse, global customer base. We operate in many different countries and cultures, where we need to attract and retain outstanding employees and partners. In addition, a culture that fosters respect for and appreciation of differences among people clearly helps teamwork, productivity, and morale.
>
> Letter to shareholders, *Hewlett-Packard 1994 Annual Report*

The company's *1995 Annual Report* also emphasizes diversity under Hewlett-Packard's role as corporate citizen: "a workforce that benefits from the ideas of women and people of all nationalities, races and lifestyles is necessary to meet the needs of our diverse, global customer base."

Corporate emphasis on diversity as a business issue is partly related to the changing profile of the company. Having started as a test and measurement company in 1939, Hewlett-Packard entered the computing industry in the 1970s. By the 1980s, computer products brought in more revenues than did test and measurement equipment (see Exhib-

Origin: started by Bill Hewlett and David Packard in 1939 in a garage – now marked as "the birthplace of Silicon Valley" – in Palo Alto, California

Businesses (1995): personal computers; UNIX business; test and measurement; hard copy; information storage; medical; components; chemical analysis; service and support

Operations (1995): in 120 countries with just over 100,000 employees (102,300)

Headquarters: Palo Alto, California

Net revenue (1995): $32 billion

Chief Executive Officer: Lewis Platt

Hewlett-Packard, Europe

Origin: Hewlett-Packard started operations in Europe in 1959

Regional headquarters: Geneva

Managing Director, Europe/Africa/Middle East: Franz Nawratil

Employees (1995): 22,000

Net revenue (1995) $11 billion

Exhibit 12.1   Hewlett-Packard: A Profile

its 12.1 and 12.2 respectively for a profile of the company and for orders and revenues by product groups). Today, HP is the world's third largest computer company, after IBM and NEC. This move has necessitated a shift from a product- to a market-orientation. While in the past it relied primarily on the high quality of its technical products, the company is now increasingly stressing the importance of marketing and of understanding its diverse customer base.

An issue linked to diversity is "work/life," or creative work arrangements that allow employees to balance their careers and their personal lives. As HP managers point out, Platt personally has had to deal with the issue of balancing career and family. To quote *The Wall Street Journal*:

> As a former single parent, Mr. Platt knows work–family conflict firsthand. After his first wife died when his daughters were eight and ten, he found it "extraordinarily difficult" to meet family responsibilities and do the travel required by the job, he says.
>
> May 31, 1995

For the years ended October 31 (in millions)	1995	1994	1993
Orders			
Computer products, service and support	$25,815	$19,882	$15,903
Electronic test and measurement instrumentation, systems and service	3,488	2,759	2,335
Medical electronic equipment and service	1,399	1,170	1,196
Chemical analysis and service	844	777	721
Electronic components	964	762	617
Total	$32,510	$25,350	$20,772
Net revenue			
Computer products, service and support	$25,269	$19,632	$15,572
Electronic test and measurement instrumentation, systems and service	3,288	2,722	2,318
Medical electronic equipment and service	1,300	1,141	1,149
Chemical analysis and service	806	754	704
Electronic components	856	742	574
Total	$31,519	$24,991	$20,317

The table above provides supplemental information showing orders and net revenue by groupings of similar products and services. The groupings are as follows:

Computer products, service and support   Computer equipment and systems (hardware and software), networking products, printers, scanners, disk and tape drives, terminals and handheld calculators; support and maintenance services, parts and supplies.

Electronic test and measurement instrumentation, systems and service   Instruments and measurement systems used for design, production and maintenance of electronic equipment; support and maintenance services.

Medical electronic equipment and service   Patient monitoring, cardiology and ultrasound imaging equipment used for clinical diagnosis and care; hospital and healthcare information systems, systems integration and application software; support and maintenance services; medical supplies.

Chemical analysis and service   Gas and liquid chromatographs, mass spectrometers and spectrophotometers used to analyze chemical compounds; laboratory data and information management systems; support, supplies and maintenance services.

Electronic components   Microwave semiconductor and optoelectronic devices that are sold primarily to manufacturers for incorporation into electronic products.

Source: Hewlett-Packard 1995 Annual Report.

Exhibit 12.2   Hewlett-Packard: Orders and Net Revenue by Groupings of Similar Products and Services, 1993–1995

As CEO, Lew Platt's commitment to diversity goes beyond words. In popular diversity management palance, he "walks the talk." In 1993, Platt participated in an executive diversity workshop with his top management team. In 1995, a Diversity Leadership Council, co-chaired by Emily Duncan, head of Corporate Workforce Diversity, and Bob Walker from Corporate Information Systems, was formed. The council is a team of 13 senior managers who represent HP's businesses, geographic regions, personnel, and diversity staff.

In January 1996, the Diversity Leadership Council sponsored a world-wide dialogue of general managers on diversity. Twenty-five sessions were held simultaneously to collect data from senior management on: their organization's success on diversity, what/who the influential contributors to their progress on diversity were; challenges in creating an inclusive environment, and how managers should be accountable for fostering diversity. The Diversity Leadership Council will use the database created from the dialogue sessions to develop action plans.

In the US, Hewlett-Packard has, since the late 1980s, actively sought to enhance the diversity of its workforce. Every business organization and function has a person or a "resource" working on diversity as part of his/her job. In 1993, Hewlett-Packard US was awarded the Personnel Journal Optimas Award, General Excellence Category, for "demonstrating excellence in human resources management and strategy," an important part of which is diversity.

Diversity at Hewlett-Packard, Europe

Organizational structure

In HP, Europe, a program for managing diversity at a company-wide level is relatively new. The position of Diversity Manager, HP, Europe, was created in March 1994. The position was offered to Helen Wellian, a Finance and Administration manager at the company headquarters in Geneva, who had taken an initiative by organizing an off-site conference in 1993 in response to Lew Platt's statements on the importance of diversity. She decided to take it on part-time (75% time) to meet her own work/life balance needs. Soon after accepting the position, Wellian moved to Vienna with her husband, who also works for HP, and "took the job" with her.

One of Wellian's early challenges was to make a case for diversity at a meeting of the European general managers in summer, 1994. In her presentation, she asked every general manager to recommend one person from his (at the time all the general managers were men) entity[4] who could be a diversity representative for the site.

Some people volunteered to be representatives while others were asked by the general managers or personnel managers at their entities. Initially, all the diversity representatives were women. However, given that the company defines diversity broadly (see Exhibit 12.3 for HP, Europe's definition of diversity) and as involving all employees, it was felt that men should also be involved in the diversity effort. Subsequently, there are a few men who work as diversity representatives for their countries or divisions.

A *formal* organizational chart for diversity management at HP, Europe would currently have only Helen Wellian on it as Diversity Manager. There is a European diversity

1. What is diversity?

Everyone is different – in age, gender, nationality, ways of thinking . . . These differences are a source of strength.

Diversity is about recognizing these differences and ensuring they are the causes of – rather than road blocks to – our business success.

Diversity is about creating an all-inclusive work environment that values and benefits from different human attributes, experiences and skills at all levels and enables all employees to develop and contribute to their full potential.

Dimensions of diversity

Age	Sexual orientation
Nationality/Ethnicity	Culture
Gender	Religion
Physical abilities	Language
Economic status	Race
Ways of thinking	

"I believe the word 'diverse' includes not only different genders and races, but also different cultures, lifestyles and ways of thinking."

Lew Platt
CEO and Chairman
HP Company

Exhibit 12.3 From "Mapping out the HP Europe Road to Diversity"

taskforce of five managers from Communications, Management Education, Finance and Administration, and Personnel who work with Wellian to co-ordinate Europe-wide policy on diversity. Wellian is, under Hewlett-Packard's matrix organization, responsible to Heinz Fischer, European Personnel Director in Geneva, and to Emily Duncan in Palo Alto, California. In August 1996, when Wellian goes on maternity leave, someone will be appointed to replace her and will continue to work with her when she returns. Franz Nawratil, Senior Vice President and Managing Director, Europe, "sponsors" the diversity program. He is on the Diversity Leadership Council. In this capacity, he says, his job is to be a spokesperson for Europe's diversity representatives at the corporate level. "Our People" has been one of Nawratil's Hoshins since November 1994.

The managers who work as diversity representatives in different European sites and divisions are not an official diversity staff. This means that they generally work on diversity in addition to their regular jobs, unless they are from Personnel Departments, in which case diversity management might be a part of their job description. They have taskforces, also composed of volunteers from their entities, to work with them.

Initially, there was no budget for diversity management in HP, Europe, apart from a salary for Wellian and funding for two diversity and work/life forums a year, that Heinz Fischer had sanctioned. Since 1995, Wellian says, when she put in a project application for diversity that was approved by HP's European Management Team, she has had an annual budget.

Early grass-roots initiatives on diversity and work/life

While the issues of diversity and work/life were emphasized by Lew Platt and given new visibility through corporate support, this support did not come in a void. In HP, Europe, there had long been pockets of activity and initiatives in these areas at different entities. One area in which there were early initiatives was work/life balance. In 1967, for example, flextime was introduced in HP Boeblingen, West Germany. The scheme was then introduced in the US by HP in 1972.

Other targets of early initiatives were gender and race diversity, either through the formation of employee networks – like a women's lunch-time speaker series in the HP UK sales region in the early 1980s – or through the efforts of managers in Personnel or Training and Development Departments in particular entities. For example, in HP Bristol, diversity awareness training was introduced in 1992, at the initiative of the local Personnel manager, following comments by a few minority employees to the general manager that the work environment was not very inclusive. The Personnel manager, who comments that having a supportive general manager was crucial to her taking initiatives at the site, attended a training course with an American consulting group and, subsequently, asked them to come to Bristol where the session they gave was a success. Training courses by this group are now offered at other HP sites in Europe.

At another European entity, a diversity representative from Training and Development who has been officially working on diversity for only one year, had started special communication training for women at the site three years ago. She says that when diversity management became official, the meaning of diversity was broadened for her to go beyond just gender to age, nationality, language, etc.

People whose efforts at creating an inclusive environment at HP predated the corporate emphasis on diversity were motivated by different factors. One motivating factor, for some, was the personal resonance that the issue of diversity had for them. As one manager says:

> Being a person of color or a woman in an engineering environment sets you apart. There aren't many people like you who graduate from engineering schools in Europe.

Another factor that was, in some cases, central to taking action on diversity, was communication with American managers and an exposure to the diversity issues that HP was dealing with in the US.

The implementation of a company-wide initiative in 1994 gave legitimacy and recognition to what were sometimes isolated efforts to implement change in different entities. One manager who was always personally interested in diversity, commenting on the coalescence of corporate interest and grassroots activity, says:

> It is important that the emphasis on diversity came from the top because this means that, ultimately, people will be evaluated for their performance on diversity.

Also, in entities where there had been no interest in diversity because it was felt that an issue did not exist, there is now pressure to, at the very least, give it serious thought. As Heinz Fischer says, there is now an attempt, through sharing information and best practices across entities, to "create pools of movement on diversity where there were none before. We approach the issue from the top down but try and impel action on it from the bottom up."

THE PROCESS OF DIVERSITY MANAGEMENT AT HEWLETT-PACKARD, EUROPE

Approaching the issue

After her appointment as Diversity Manager in 1994, Wellian went through a diversity training program with an outside European consultant. At the diversity and work/life forum in November 1994, all diversity representatives participated in a one-day training session.

One of the first challenges for the diversity representatives was to spread an awareness, at their entities, of what diversity meant. Most of them were personally convinced of its importance; they now had to convince their colleagues that the company could only benefit from hiring a diverse mix of employees and from valuing differences between employees. They needed to dispel misconceptions that diversity is a "zero-sum game" that would give some groups of people a larger share of the managerial pie at the expense of others.

If, as one manager remarks wryly, "HP senior managers had, traditionally, been tall, white, married men with engineering degrees who speak fluent English," the challenge was to ensure that managers who did *not* fit this description would still be comfortable working in the company and would have equal chances of being promoted to senior positions. The objective is "not to change the world but to change HP" so that it reflects the world it operates in. It is also to respect differences between individuals, whether based on age, gender, class, educational background, language abilities, skin color, sexual orientation (to name only some of the ways in which people are different), for the purpose of creating an organization to which all employees feel they belong. People can differ from each other along different dimensions which means that broad categories like "white men," "women of color," etc., are not necessarily homogeneous and can be misleading.

In trying to spread awareness of what diversity is and why it is important for business, diversity representatives emphasize good communications, that is, getting a message across in a compelling yet non-threatening way to all employees. HP Zurich used a series of cartoons, posted over six months in its offices, in a campaign to draw people's attention to diversity. In Bristol, a team of professional actors was hired to produce a short film which presented the subject in a comic and light-hearted vein. As one diversity representative points out:

> One has to be careful of how one puts one's vision across. Characterizing "white men" as the dominant power group, if done carelessly, will alienate them. They are part of the solution and *not* part of the problem. We have to guard against presenting diversity as a women's issue and painting white men into a corner. Inclusiveness is critical.

Some managers in Europe feel that in American companies, diversity management has often been dominated by quotas, affirmative action, and, consequently, litigation involving companies. They point to the need for caution against transplanting, in entirety, measures developed in the US to Europe:

> – A lot of people tend to say that the message is good but they are put off by the packaging – the style – which they find "too aggressive" or "too naive" or simply "too American."

> – While there is still much to be done in Europe, in the US there is already a backlash with white men feeling that they are being discriminated against . . . We have to be careful to ensure that whatever we do, we do it because it's in the corporation's best interest, and not to meet numerical quotas.

On the one hand managers working for HP in Europe – especially if they work in company headquarters in Geneva – are already in a multicultural environment where they are used to working with people from different national backgrounds. The issues in Europe are often different. For example, there is no clear race issue as there is in the US.

On the other hand, some managers in Europe believe that they have much to learn from the process of diversity management in the US. Here, the risk of not having legal requirements is that "people can hide behind their cultural diversity" and can insist that there is no need for a diversity program at their particular site:

> Even, *even* in HP, we have people who don't want to hear the message, who don't want to say "yes, gay people are okay and people of color are okay," and that's why it's going to take ages here.

> – I agree that one can't have diversity awareness sessions in the same "bare-the-chest" fashion that one would in the US. One has to be more subtle here but subtlety can be taken to the point where there is sometimes denial that an issue even exists.

So it is often a challenge for diversity representatives to convince managers in Europe that "diversity" is not an "American gimmick" and that it has relevance for HP employees around the world. As Fischer puts it, "diversity is no longer an 'American topic' but an 'HP topic'."

Initiatives

Key issues in Europe

The issues that diversity representatives focus on vary by country. In some countries, the question of language is important. For example, in Belgium, following comments by customers, a survey found that women and French speakers were minorities at HP. So, given that the company is also trying to recruit people from a variety of educational backgrounds rather than just technical backgrounds, an FFU (French, Female, University) program was set up. The focus has been on recruitment since, as the Belgian diversity representative puts it, "hiring is the point at which diversity starts." In Spain, some employees felt that Catalan was not being used enough while others, often Americans working at the Barcelona site, felt that English should be used for meetings and internal communications, so the local taskforce is looking into this.

Managers' opinions about language diversity within HP, Europe vary. One senior manager in Geneva says:

> If a customer requests that we speak a particular language, we have to accept this because the customer determines who wins in the marketplace. But . . . one needs a common language throughout the company for communication. The higher up you are in management, the more you have to turn to a common language to communicate. I respect language diversity . . . but one has to accept English as the common company language.

Another focus in some entities is age diversity. In Grenoble, for instance, the diversity taskforce is considering the question of whether company ads and the interviewing process at HP encourage relatively older people to apply to the company for jobs. When older people, especially those who have not been working for a period of time, are hired by HP in Grenoble, the company gives them special training to reintegrate them in the workplace. "Small diversity events" organized every three months, like a workshop or a communications campaign, aim to increase recruitment of older people, as well as of other groups perceived to be underrepresented in the workforce such as women, people with non-technical educational degrees, people with disabilities, etc. Age is also an issue at HP Barcelona where the diversity taskforce is working to increase the number of people with "more experience." The average age at the Barcelona site is 29. In the production line, most people are between 26 and 32 years old, so "they all have children around the same time and need leave around the same time."

A major thrust of diversity initiatives in most entities is to increase the numbers of women who are recruited and to ensure that their chances of promotion within the company are fair.

Efforts to ensure that the company gets a diverse mix of applicants at the recruitment level go beyond the confines of the company to local universities. In Grenoble, for example, there is a company representative who works on communications at the university to encourage women to apply to HP. Outreach efforts also include collaboration with university administration and faculty to influence the subjects that particular groups of people choose to specialize in.

In Belgium, HP launched an ad campaign encouraging women as well as men to apply to HP for jobs, and the diversity taskforce in Brussels collaborates with a Belgian university to study the impact of the ad. Applications from women with technical degrees went up by 40% almost overnight, dispelling the myth, as one manager points out, that "there just aren't enough technically qualified women around."

Subsequently, HP Barcelona also used the ad in Spanish. In Switzerland too, an ad campaign was introduced to encourage women to apply to HP. In journal ads globally, the company is trying to change its image as a purely information technology company by emphasizing that it is a communications company.

Determined not to set quotas or numerical targets in hiring, diversity representatives do, nonetheless, work to "monitor trends" and they review hiring processes to ensure that these do not work to discourage certain groups of people from applying to and being accepted by HP. In Belgium, managers were asked to try to identify one woman as a potential candidate each time they were hiring, even internally. This was done not to oblige them to hire a woman every time but to think about it and possibly identify women with talent in their departments who might otherwise have been ignored. "There were no quotas, but just a monitoring of trends." In HP Switzerland, the diversity taskforce works with the Personnel Department to review hiring decisions and processes, and its goal is to have one women on every professional team in the company by the end of 1996. This goal, as the Swiss diversity representative notes, "has been well-received by managers because it isn't really a quota – it's not as if women have to comprise half of each team."

In Zurich, "Infomarkets" for men and women serve as opportunities for personal career-assessment. Internal networks, in Zurich, also provide support groups for women employees.

In 1995, HP Austria won the "Glass Slipper Award" from among 50 or 60 companies that participated in the questionnaire-based competition. The award is given by the Austrian government to the most women- and family-friendly company in Austria.

In Bristol, LAGER, a gay and lesbian group, was invited to make a presentation to HP employees. Many diversity representatives in Europe believe that sexual orientation is the next big issue they will be dealing with here. In California, there is an active network of gay and lesbian HP employees (GLEN) and, in May 1996, Hewlett-Packard decided that it would offer health care benefits to employees' "domestic partners" of the same or opposite sex. For the moment, this policy will apply only in the US although HP sites in Europe are free to introduce it if they so wish. In Europe, as one HP manager says, "we've barely touched the tip of the iceberg on the issue of sexual orientation."

The issue of work/life is considered to be connected to diversity in that it helps create an inclusive environment. While Hewlett-Packard, Europe pairs the issues of diversity and work/life balance, some managers believe that the two should be kept separate. As one diversity representative from a European division puts it:

> Diversity is a big enough project on its own. You can't mix work/life into this. If you start talking about work/life, you're making an assumption about a solution. Flextime, and other related measures, do not mean that the problem has been solved when the problem is, in fact, one of attitudes, opportunities, a whole syndrome associated with the way in which this organization has been structured.

The agents of change

In March 1995, HP Personnel staff from all over Europe participated in a diversity training program and, in May 1995, joint training was offered for diversity representatives and general managers. Wellian says that this was a key turning point in gaining the commitment of senior management to diversity efforts.

In the belief that managers are the "change agents" without whose support diversity efforts cannot succeed, most entities are working to provide diversity awareness training for all managers. In Bristol, for example, all functional managers have been through an in-depth diversity training session done by the American consultancy group. One of the training modules on "Men and Women Working Together" is, as one manager who has done the program says, "really much more than just men and women working together. It's an intense three-day workshop that can get very emotional as people's values are challenged and they are forced to think about stereotypes and prejudices in general."

In Brussels, all HP Belgium managers were invited by the general manager to a half-day diversity awareness conference in March, 1996. Following a presentation by the local diversity representative and the general manager on why diversity was important for business, an external European consultant did a session on men and women working together and on interaction between junior and senior managers. The latter issue is important in Belgium, where the average age at HP is 37 and senior managers are disproportionately represented at the site. Other sites like Zurich and Vienna have also had diversity training or awareness sessions for managers and supervisors.

Managers are never obliged to attend diversity education programs and many diversity representatives believe that participation in a program often depends on whether the invitation to it comes from senior managers, especially the general manager, at the site. As one diversity representative from Bristol notes,

> Here we've never had to fight battles for diversity because our general manager and functional managers have been very supportive. These are the people who have the power and the ability to mobilize resources for initiatives – like the training sessions. At other sites, the picture might be quite different – a lack of senior and middle management support and a paucity of funds can be major barriers to effecting change, no matter how enthusiastic about and committed to diversity one is.

Strategy at the European level

In her role as facilitator of diversity management in Europe, Wellian, working with the European diversity taskforce of five managers, uses inputs and feedback from diversity representatives and senior managers to formulate strategy and implementation plans for Europe. These are divided into four key areas: education; diversity initiatives; work/life initiatives; and communication and information.

For education, a three-tier diversity education program has been developed. The first level is a one-day "general awareness" session with the European consultant for up to 150 employees at a time. The next level is an "in-depth training" session for a manager and his/her staff. The third level is a three-and-a-half day program for diversity representatives and "champions" of diversity, that addresses the role they play as "agents of change."

All entities in Europe can draw on this education program, or use local equivalents in different languages if these exist.

In the area of communications, there is now a centralized source of information on diversity initiatives. In April 1996, a monthly newsletter – *The Difference* (the title translates better than "diversity" into European languages) – was launched. This goes out electronically to all interested employees. The newsletter provides a forum for news and viewpoints on diversity actions in different entities and aims to foster dialogue between managers and employees. It also reviews relevant publications on diversity. There is also a diversity brochure, explaining what diversity is all about, which diversity representatives can distribute to all employees in their entities (see Exhibit 12.4 for Franz Nawratil's introduction to the brochure).

MEASURING PROGRESS

From the start, it had been decided to run the diversity program "with a European flavor" and not lay down narrow guidelines or quotas. Local diversity representatives would decide, with their general manager and his staff, which issues were important and become champions for those. Not only would they define the issues, they would also define progress. Wellian, when she made her first presentation to the general managers in 1994, expected that the issues and approaches to diversity would vary by country but says it was clear that "a local approach to diversity should not become an excuse for inaction on any site."

There is a tension in diversity efforts between giving each entity the autonomy to define important issues and track progress, and having some way to measure success across the company in Europe. After having initially emphasized a local approach to diversity management, Wellian, Fischer, and Nawratil had to later confront the issue of how to measure progress in HP, Europe overall.

It was decided to focus on gender, that is, to measure the proportion of women being hired or promoted, or leaving the company. The issue of gender diversity is one that is common to almost all HP, Europe sites and, as such, provides one consistent vehicle by which to measure progress. One prominent exception, as European managers point out, is HP Turkey where, since 1995, the general manager has been a woman and men and women are equally represented at all levels of employment.

In 1994, of HP, Europe's top 400 managers, 11 or 2.5% were women. This proportion has increased to approximately 5% in 1996. In 1995, HP, Europe appointed its first ever woman general manager and, in 1996, a second.

As one HP, Europe manager says:

> There is a focus on gender diversity but every country has a different group, a different issue which should be dealt with locally. The broad goal is clear – drawing on skilled people from all of society. In Germany there is a big program for people with disabilities. We should let local initiatives happen and not put the brakes on. For Europe, we had to choose something that was universal just to get this thing off the ground and that was gender.

In Barcelona, for example, the local diversity taskforce decided to focus initially on basic, tangible issues, like increasing the number of women in Research and Development. In

Diversity in HP Europe

Dear colleague,

More and more people are talking about diversity in HP and elsewhere. This brochure sets out to encourage dialogue on diversity while acknowledging that we all have something to learn from it.

Diversity means valuing everyone's different experience, outlook and approach in our business life. Diversity is reflecting the real world in our workforce, business practices and corporate objectives – not only because it is right to do so, but because it makes sound business sense.

Diversity helps remove the obstacles keeping people from reaching their full potential. It is inclusive, not divisive. It has nothing to do with positive discrimination. Diversity is not about championing one set of ideas over another, but rather about valuing all ideas. It is also about ensuring new and better ways of doing business by recognizing everyone's unique contribution.

In many ways, people in HP Europe already practice diversity. We operate in multicultural teams and can see the advantages of working together. We can build on these strengths by including everyone's ideas in our teams. Only if each individual fulfills his or her potential can the company reach its full potential.

As your representative on the world-wide Diversity Leadership Council, I work with a team of managers from all business sectors and geographic operations to create awareness, initiate action and foster accountability for results on diversity throughout HP. I encourage you to share your ideas and thoughts with your colleagues and your HP diversity representative . . .

Franz Nawratil
President and Managing Director
HP Europe

Exhibit 12.4   From "Mapping out the HP Europe Road to Diversity"

other sites too, diversity programs "got off the ground" by focusing on women.

Franz Nawratil points to three measurement systems or "metrics" that the company uses. The most basic is to look at numbers of women being hired and promoted, not for the purpose of imposing quotas but to discern trends. Another is to measure "attrition." There are five bands in the performance scale and attrition, particularly of women, is tracked, especially in the two highest-performing bands to see who leaves the company and why. Exit interviews are done with people leaving HP. This measures reasons for leaving at a personal level. Finally, at a more general level, there is the "openline" or employee survey that is done every two years on each site to gauge employee satisfaction with the workplace. In 1994, six questions on diversity were added to the survey (see Exhibit 12.5).

VISIBLE CHANGE?

HP managers who are working towards building a more diverse company in Europe are cautious in their approach to change. They recognize that it goes against the grain at HP to tell managers that they are obliged to do something and feel that change will not be effective if the ground has not been prepared for it. One diversity representative says she "keeps her ears to the ground" and finds out who, among senior and top management, is sympathetic. Another says she always "tests the waters" before launching an initiative. She finds out what managers are ready to hear and puts her messages across in as non-threatening a way as possible.

Overall, diversity representatives feel that while change is slow and the work can often be frustrating, it is true that diversity is now a visible issue in the company. There is less personal risk associated with working on it and funding for diversity programs is now easier to justify.

Since a program for managing diversity is relatively new, it would be premature to judge where the numbers are going. Instead, diversity representatives talk of a perceptible change in attitudes. Senior management is committed but many diversity representatives do feel the need for spreading awareness through the ranks of middle management.

As one diversity representative says:

> The general manager at my site is genuinely committed to diversity but this is not true of other managers who still need to be persuaded of its importance. Even if they voice support for it, this doesn't mean that they actively encourage it by, for example, providing funding for training sessions. For most managers, "diversity" is still something abstract and far-removed from markets and customers. We need to work on the businesses in Europe, primarily at the field level.

1. Is the management of the entity committed to diversity as a critical business issue?

2. Does the entity management clearly communicate the importance of workforce diversity?

3. Is the entity a good place for women to work?

4. Is the entity a good place for minorities to work?

5. Is the entity a good place for people with disabilities to work?

6. Is the environment free of harassment?

Exhibit 12.5 Questions on Diversity in Hewlett-Packard's Employee Survey (Added January 1994)

The question of accountability has also come up. Most diversity representatives work on diversity in addition to their regular jobs. As one of them says:

> I do this over and above my regular job and had no idea, when I started, just how time-consuming it would be. I find I spend about a third of my time working on it. When I had my performance review recently, my boss reminded me that I am also a functional manager.

Another representative, who is an engineer in one of HP, Europe's business organizations, says, on the other hand:

> Change is slow and can sometimes be frustrating but at least now diversity is on my planning table of objectives for the year. This means it's a "legitimate" issue and will count towards my performance evaluation.

STAYING ON THE BRIDGE

As the forum in Grenoble drew to a close on June 7, 1996, Wellian and Duncan discussed the many questions that had arisen over the past three days. Now was the time to take stock of HP, Europe's progress on diversity and to ask what it would take, in concrete terms, to stay on the bridge that Wellian and her colleagues had worked hard to build.

They had come a long way in a short time in making an issue of diversity and in familiarizing managers with what it meant. At the same time, while the very top levels of management were aware of the importance of diversity, inroads had not really been made into middle management and Wellian believed that future efforts would have to be aimed at middle managers.

Also, following a presentation by Duncan, the issue had been raised of what the organizational structure for managing diversity should be. The important question was how to embed diversity into the company. About half the participants in the forum were from Personnel Departments. Many participants felt that their roles and responsibilities were not clearly defined. There was some confusion between the roles of: "sponsors" of diversity (who had the power in the organization and the resources to implement change); "champions" (who came from any part of the organization, cared about the issues, and wanted to be a part of the change process); and "specialists" (who had the organizational responsibility, skills, and know-how to be able to implement "a major culture change process").

In addition, they knew they could not expect an increase in resources for diversity management. The highly competitive nature of the computer industry would continue to bring heavy pressure to bear on people and costs. Given these circumstances, how could Wellian ensure that diversity management was successfully embedded into the organizational structure of HP, Europe?

Notes

1 These trends were highlighted and analyzed in *Workforce 2000*, a report published by the Hudson Institute in 1987.

2   This case draws on material from *Human resources at Hewlett-Packard (A)* by Gregory Rogers and
    Michael Beer, Harvard Business School, 9-495-051, 1995.
3   The Hoshin planning system was adopted from Japan by Hewlett-Packard in the 1980s; man-
    agers set Hoshins or "breakthrough objectives" for themselves for the year. Some other compa-
    nies that use the Hoshin system are: Procter and Gamble, Intel, Texas Instruments, Zytec, and
    Florida Power & Light.
4   The term "entity" at HP refers to country/area or division.

Chapter 13

Case: Eurochem Shanghai: Corporate Policy or China Practice?

Miles Dodd

Paul Paus had worked in Eurochem head office in Antwerp for four years since joining the company in 1993 with an MBA. He had only just turned thirty, but had already established himself as one of the young "high flyers," and was now on his way to the Eurochem office for China in Shanghai. He was about to move into the international environment which had always been his objective.

The plane from Hong Kong, where he had spent a day on his way from Europe, passed over the lights of Shanghai before landing smoothly. After passing through the immigration and custom formalities, Paus found himself faced with a mass of people all waiting to meet passengers from the many flights arriving at that time of the evening.

He was relieved finally to notice a young man holding a "Eurochem" sign. It was a driver from the Eurochem office. A letter from the branch manager welcomed him, and told him to expect to be picked up at 8.45 at his hotel the following morning and brought to the office.

It was early July, and Shanghai was hot and humid. A typhoon was hovering off the coast some distance away, and there were heavy bursts of rain as the car struggled through the evening traffic to Paus' hotel.

At 9.00 the following morning a Mr Wu of the marketing department called Paus in his hotel room, and said that he was waiting downstairs to take him to the office. It had been a long journey from Europe, and Paus was still tired, however he finished his breakfast, packed his briefcase, and went down to the lobby just after 9.15 to meet Wu.

It took more than an hour to drive to the Eurochem office. The humidity and heat were uncomfortably oppressive, and the rain was still heavy. Hordes of cyclists cowered under ragged inadequate waterproofs. The traffic was very congested and the streets were dirty and flooded where garbage had accumulated to block the drains. Paus felt sticky and hot and wondered whether his move to Shanghai had been as wise as he first thought.

The head of the China subsidiary, Mr Olsen, had been called away to urgent business in Wuhan, so on his arrival, Wu took Paus to the office of Mr Li, the deputy manager. Li did not look very pleased, he was offended by Paus' arrival at the office over one hour late. He greeted Paus briefly, then took him to his new office and introduced him to a secretary, Miss Wang, who had been assigned to him.

Paus set about discovering more about the office, from which the whole China activity of Eurochem was managed.

Olsen was the general manager. He was not originally a Eurochem man. He had studied Chinese for several years and then worked for ten years based in Hong Kong covering the Chinese market for a Swiss chemical company. From there he had been recruited to the Eurochem position. The Eurochem board had little knowledge of China, but knew that it was a market they could not ignore.

The normal Eurochem practice was to appoint managers from within the company to operate overseas branches, but no one had been willing to go to China. The only person with any experience of the country was the international development director who had joined two trade missions to China and identified a number of business opportunities. Olsen was employed through a Hong Kong based head-hunter, and two months later Eurochem gave notice to the trading firm through whom they had been selling their products up to that time. Since his appointment, Olsen had patiently built up a good client base. With Li's help he had carefully developed relationships with customers so that they had come to trust him, and this had enabled him to establish a sound Chinese business for Eurochem. He negotiated a manufacturing joint venture which had earned him the respect of the Eurochem head office, and was now working hard on a second one.

Olsen worked closely with Li and they had managed the branch together since it was opened in 1992.

Li was in his early fifties. He had been an interpreter in his younger days, but had lived through very difficult times. He had joined Eurochem from the Shanghai branch of the Swiss company for which Olsen had previously worked, and they were good business colleagues, although they had little contact outside the office. Li had formerly worked on the marketing side before taking charge of the administration of the office. He still had many friends and contacts amongst the companies buying Eurochem's products.

There were 60 staff of whom 35 were on the engineering side, heavily involved in building a plant at Pudong, a joint venture with a state-owned Chinese company. There were five European engineers in this group. A further 10 people were in the marketing department, which Paus had been appointed to manage, and the remainder were in the accounts department and the management team. Paus was the only expatriate in the marketing team.

Until Paus' arrival, Olsen himself had covered the marketing activity, ably assisted by Wu, who had studied marketing in Hong Kong, and who spoke excellent English. However Olsen was now heavily involved in negotiations for another new plant in Sichuan province, and had no time to deal with the marketing function. He would have been very happy to put Wu in charge of the marketing operation, although he was only 34 years old. However after some discussion between Olsen and Mr Vandenbergh, the director of marketing, head office in Belgium had decided to give the task to Paus, who had been very successful in the European market. Paus assured Eurochem that he would faithfully apply the company systems in China to bring it in line with the rest of the world. Wu thus now reported to Paus.

Paus soon found that the Eurochem Shanghai office was not following head office practice at all. For example it was allowing longer credit to buyers than the head office guidelines indicated. Wu explained that he had carried out his own investigations into the credit worthiness of the companies to whom they were giving credit, and that he had every reason to trust them. He had discussed each case with Olsen, who had thus approved the credit decisions. Up till now, there had been only one default.

Further, Paus noticed that the Eurochem salesmen seemed to spend a lot of time visiting customers who were already well established Eurochem clients. The amounts purchased by these customers remained more or less stable, and Paus felt that the salesmen should be spending more time developing new customers than drinking tea with existing ones. Overall sales of Eurochem products had risen steadily by 8% per year since the office had been opened. This was lower than some competitors had achieved, but the specialised nature of Eurochem's products made direct comparison difficult. Li had told Olsen that an old friend of his working with Eurochem's most direct competitor, Nippo Kasei, reported that Nippo was finding it difficult to maintain its market share. Nevertheless, the marketing director in Antwerp, Mr Vandenbergh, had heard from his contacts in the general chemical industry that "8% in China is nothing" and he had asked Paus to see how he could introduce stricter adherence to Eurochem practices, which Vandenbergh was sure would improve the subsidiary's performance.

Two months after his arrival, Paus called Wu to his office, and announced that he had decided to change the marketing system in order to comply more strictly with the world wide Eurochem system.

He explained that the head office expected the China office to introduce the marketing systems which had proven successful in Europe and the US. Instead of salesmen visiting their own group of customers, they were to form new product teams in which they would concentrate on a particular product throughout the client base. He said that travelling to visit customers took too much time and was inefficient, and was certainly not something which they did very much in Europe. He expected Wu and his team to spend much more time on the telephone to customers instead of going out to visit them. Paus told Wu that the excellent quality of Eurochem products was well known, and that Wu and his salesmen should persuade customers to visit the Eurochem office rather than to expect that the Eurochem staff would visit them. He wanted to see more market data produced and to see more frequent reports of competitors' activities. Paus also declared that he intended to limit the budget for entertaining customers. In addition, he said that Eurochem would no longer permit customers ninety days credit, they should now be limited to thirty days.

Wu was not sure what to think about his new boss. While studying in Hong Kong, he had been introduced to the latest US marketing theories and he could see that many of the practices in China were still based on the old, "guanxi" networks which he privately felt to be a little old-fashioned. For the time being he decided to follow his new boss's instructions, but he felt quite uneasy.

From the beginning, Paus had treated Li as an old-timer, out of touch with the demands of modern business. He had not been outwardly rude, but he made it plain that he did not consider that Li had anything to contribute to the new marketing plan. He had not mentioned his new ideas to Li, and had only hinted to Olsen that he thought that changes should be made as head office had directed – Olsen had told him to discuss any changes with Wu before implementing them.

About three months later, Olsen returned late one afternoon from a visit to Chongqing to find a worried Li awaiting him. His old friend Mr Leung of Shanghai Batteries had called Li angrily to say that, from now on, he would buy his chemicals from Nippo and that he was finished with Eurochem. Li tried to find out the reasons for Leung's unhappiness, but Leung rang off before he could ask.

Next morning Olsen asked Paus to come to his office, and asked him what he knew about the Shanghai Batteries complaint. Paus said that Leung had been very demanding, making some complaints about quality which he had telephoned to Wu and which Paus had judged to be unfounded. He had also complained about the new credit rules imposed by Eurochem. Paus told Olsen that Eurochem practice should be enforced – he showed him a fax from the marketing director in head office fully supporting his efforts to bring discipline to the Chinese market.

Olsen knew Leung of Shanghai Batteries – he was a difficult old man, but had always honoured agreements, and had paid within the terms fixed. He decided to hear what Li and Wu had to say before talking again to Paus.

Paus' cool attitude to Li had continued, frequently offending the elder man by his obvious lack of respect. Since Leung's call, Li had carefully contacted a number of his old friends, and it was soon clear to him that the old networks he, Olsen, and Wu had created were beginning to break down. Another important customer, Mr Deng of Wuzhou Plastics, told Li that he would order his next supply of chemicals from Nippo. Li told Olsen that he thought that the new marketing policy, about which he had heard from Wu, was likely to have a serious negative impact on Eurochem's sales. The latest monthly figures already showed a significant drop – Wu said that Paus had dismissed them as a result of the transition to the new approach and had assured Wu that they would quickly recover.

When Olsen discussed the problem with Wu he found Wu less pessimistic than Li, but still unhappy. Wu said that Paus seldom discussed matters with him, but repeated the head office policy, in Europe and the US. Paus' opinion was that this policy had worked well elsewhere, and the Chinese market should therefore accept them. Wu said that he had asked Paus to visit all the important customers with him soon after his arrival which was considered important in China, but that Paus had not yet found time to do so.

Olsen had talked to Paus on several occasions in an effort to introduce him to the China market, and had suggested several times that he talk to Li and Wu and seek their help and advice. He now knew that his advice had not been followed and felt that Paus was determined to apply the head office practices in China without any modification or adaptation to local practice.

Olsen knew that he must act quickly and decisively to prevent further deterioration in Eurochem's business. He was worried that Paus' connections with the marketing people in Head Office might prove stronger than his own, and thought that it would require several months of repeated falling sales to convince them, by which time it would be too late. He telephoned Vandenbergh, the marketing director, but did not receive much help. Vandenbergh again expressed his full confidence in Paus, but did agree with Olsen that Eurochem Shanghai had performed reasonably so far, and conceded that there were sound technical reasons why Eurochem's 8% growth rate had been good in the particular market circumstances for their products. He also accepted Olsen's important point that Eurochem's main objective was to create relationships with companies such as Jilin Industries, Wuzhou Plastics, and Shanghai Batteries who were already building new facilities which would sharply increase their need for Eurochem products. Vandenbergh was aware that he would have difficulty in justifying his position should Olsen prove to be correct in his judgment of the situation, and thus accepted reluctantly that there might possibly be special circumstances prevailing in China which could not be ignored.

After some consideration, Olsen decided to discuss his worries with the President of Eurochem who was visiting China in connection with the Chongqing project. The President was sympathetic, and encouraged Olsen to take whatever steps he considered appropriate.

Olsen recognized Paus' good qualities, he was young, intelligent, committed to the company, and a determined character. He also knew that China was changing rapidly, and that many of the old practices would eventually disappear.

He had spent many hours in discussion with old Li, and had learned to value his judgement and advice. It had been tough in the early days of Eurochem's Shanghai operations, and the partnership that had grown between them had been the basis of their success.

He had been attracted by Wu's enthusiasm at the employment interview, and had not regretted selecting him from the several hundred applicants for the job. He was bright and open, and keen to apply the skills he had learned in Hong Kong. Olsen felt he represented a new generation of Chinese managers on whom the company would have to rely to run its Chinese business in future.

As he sat at home after enjoying a rare evening with his family, he discussed the dilemma and the personalities involved with his wife. She knew Paus, Li, and Wu — and gave him some valuable ideas. He made up his mind — and decided to talk separately to Paus, Li, and Wu the following morning.

Part III

Recruitment, Selection, and Placement in a Global Context

14 The Boundaryless Organization: Implications for Job Analysis, Recruitment, and Selection 133
Jodi Barnes Nelson

15 Building a Global Workforce Starts With Recruitment 148
Shannon Peters Talbott

16 Four Faces of Global Culture 152
Peter L. Berger

17 European Competencies – Some Guidelines for Companies 160
Bruno Leblanc

18 *Case*: Grupo Financiero Inverlat 169
Daniel D. Campbell, Henry W. Lane, and Kathleen E. Slaughter

Chapter 14

The Boundaryless Organization: Implications for Job Analysis, Recruitment, and Selection

Jodi Barnes Nelson

The boundaryless organization is a paradigm shift that recognizes the limitations inherent in separating people, tasks, processes, and places, and emphasizes the benefits of moving ideas, information, decisions, talent, and actions where they are most needed (Ashkenas, Ulrich, Jick, & Kerr, 1995). This article proposes that some job analysis techniques and recruitment and selection practices are incongruous with the principles of the boundaryless organization. However, existing worker-oriented approaches to job analysis, recruitment based on person-organization value congruence, and selection based on both skills and traits are consistent with the tenets of the boundaryless organization. Limitations of workforce homogeneity are also discussed. Finally, recommendations for researchers and practitioners are offered.

Reengineering, restructuring, even rethinking approaches to organizational design have proliferated in recent management literature (Keidel, 1994). Purported to underlie hundreds of these and other innovative approaches is a fundamental paradigmatic shift called the boundaryless organization. A boundaryless organization is one that focuses on permeating all internal and external boundaries (e.g., those between functions, the organization and its suppliers, even between nations) with free movement of ideas, information, decisions, talent, rewards, and action (Ashkenas et al., 1995).

At the same time, cogent arguments have been made to bury our long-standing conceptualization of the job and, instead, to recognize a post-job society where the norm of payrolled, full-time employees performing narrow duties in particular departments is history (Bridges, 1994). In fact, "work" has been described as undergoing such a fundamental transformation that we must necessarily question and perhaps replace the body of knowledge underlying the psychology of work behavior (Howard, 1995). This literature advocates radical departures from the ways in which we view what are organizations' most important tasks; where, when, and how work is done; and who decides these issues.

While organizational design and strategic management solutions have been proposed for the boundaryless organization (e.g., Ashkenas et al., 1995; Davis, 1995), relatively little has been discussed in terms of the human resource practices and processes to best support it. In other words, how specific human resources practices "fit" or become consonant with boundaryless organizational principles is not clear.

One reason for the lack of clarity surrounding human resources' role in the context of the boundaryless organization is due to the field's traditional dependence on the job as the fundamental unit of the organization. Indeed, job analysis provides the basis for virtually all human resource functions (i.e., recruitment, selection, compensation, training); thus, much of human resource technology is grounded in the notion of individuals holding jobs (Lawler, 1994). However, viewing the job as the fundamental organizational unit has been criticized as outmoded and ineffective (Bridges, 1994; Lawler, 1994). This apparent conflict between the idea of jobs being the central focus of human resources and recent literature proposing that the job is no longer a useful way to organize and manage work is the motivation behind this research.

The purpose of this paper is to examine implications of the boundaryless paradigm for three areas of human resources: job analysis, recruitment, and selection. Due to its centrality to both recruitment and selection, job analysis will be examined first. Two major approaches to job analysis will be evaluated based on boundaryless principles. Recruitment and selection practices will then be similarly evaluated.

The intended goal of this paper is to challenge human resource practitioners and researchers to view job analysis, recruitment, and selection as boundaryless functions. Specifically, it will be argued that one major job analysis method, as well as some existing recruitment and selection practices, can benefit the boundaryless organization. Because one of human resource management's strategic roles is to find the best potential match between the organization and the individual, the importance of organizational culture, and person-organization value congruence in particular is discussed. Finally, general propositions for both practitioners and researchers are provided.

THE BOUNDARYLESS PARADIGM

Underlying the rise of various forms of "new organization" to which have been ascribed the terms virtual organization, empowered organization, high-performing work teams, and process reengineered organization is "a single, deeper paradigm shift that we call the emergence of the boundaryless organization," (p. 2; Ashkenas et al., 1995). This shift recognizes the limitations of the following four types of organizational boundaries: vertical (between levels and ranks of people), horizontal (between functions and disciplines), external (between the organization and its suppliers, customers, and regulators), and geographic (between nations, cultures, and markets). In the boundaryless organization, these boundaries are not used to separate people, tasks, processes and places; rather, the focus is on how to move ideas, information, talent, and decisions where they are most necessary (Ashkenas et al., 1995). Somewhat similarly, Miner and Robinson (1994) define a boundaryless organization as one in which rules regarding membership, departmental identity, and job responsibility are ambiguous. Organization membership rules refer to the blurring of organizational boundaries (e.g., increase in outsourcing of activities, contingent employment arrangements); department identity rules refer to decentralization, cross-functional coordination, and teams which blur functional boundaries; and job responsibility rules refer to a movement toward more general job descriptions, emphasizing important values instead of specific, predetermined duties (Miner & Robinson, 1994; Souder, 1987). Indeed, other researchers have noted increased organizational fluidity over the past decade, particularly in the area of jobs (Belous, 1989).

Conversely, a boundary mindset assumption is that knowledge, skills, and abilities (KSAs) are found in abundance at the top of the organizational pyramid, whereas lower-level workers have narrow technical skills, mostly used to produce services or products (Ashkenas et al., 1995). Thus, every worker in a boundary mindset hierarchy has a clearly defined role. In the boundaryless organization, competencies reside and are recognized throughout the workplace. When an individual has the skill to do a task, he or she is encouraged to do it, regardless of title or position (Ashkenas et al., 1995). Similarly, Lawler (1994) challenges what he calls the job-based approach to organizing and managing (i.e. jobs are the basic building blocks of complex organizations) and calls for a paradigmatic shift to the competency-based organization, which focuses on the individual's needed skills to accomplish organizational goals.

Although virtually all human resource technology is grounded in the notion of individuals holding jobs, there is evidence to suggest that this notion is no longer the best way to think about organizing and managing individuals (Lawler, 1994). In fact, Bridges (1994) posits that while the amount of work in organizations continues to grow, the "familiar envelopes" we call jobs are becoming extinct. First, an increasing number of jobs are in constant flux and job descriptions cannot be rewritten every week. Further when organizations reduce head count, the very jobs that are represented by boxes on an organizational chart encourage hiring because managers are bestowed power according to the number of turf areas they oversee. Finally, jobs are rewarded on the basis of doing the jobs, not for accomplishing the necessary work. Thus, personal accountability for the work is discouraged at the expense of accountability for the job (Bridges, 1994; Bowen & Lawler, 1992).

Bridges (1994) further asserts that most organizations lack effective ways to manage in "de-jobbed" environments which consist of significant numbers of temporary workers, part-timers, consultants, and contract workers. His solution, in part, is a project-based organizational structure whereby job descriptions and supervisors' orders are replaced by evolving demands of a project. The reality is that the "post-job" worker will be far more independent and self-directed than was the job-based worker (Bridges, 1994).

BOUNDARYLESS EMPLOYMENT ARRANGEMENTS

An increase in nontraditional employment contracts between the worker and the organization is cited as an example of blurred organizational boundaries (Miner & Robinson, 1994), as well as evidence of a post-job society (Bridges, 1994). The term contract denotes the different forms employment is taking in the 1990s: temporary, part-time, job-sharing, consulting, contracting, and leasing. Although some employees have little choice but to accept one of these forms of employment, many employees welcome these options for more flexible hours and more control over where they work, how they work, and which projects they would most prefer (Belous, 1989).

The collective contingency of non-traditional U.S. workers numbered over 30 million in 1988 – about one-quarter of the workforce (Belous, 1989). It is now estimated that this contingency represents almost one-half (Halal, 1994) of all employed U.S. workers. Moreover, many companies are not only accepting but encouraging telecommuting among their employees (Charbuck & Young, 1992). Escalating overhead costs coupled with technological advancements such as workflow systems, teleconferencing, videoconferencing, and electronic mail have made working off-site a mutually beneficial option for many workers and organizations.

In sum, boundaryless organization research prescribes permeable structures at all organizational levels. In addition, the growth of diverse employment arrangements provides information about worker mobility and the increasingly flexible nature of employment. Given what we know about the boundaryless organization and the boundaryless worker, what are the important implications for human resources? What, for instance, constitutes effective employee recruitment and selection in such an environment? Because effective recruitment and selection practices are based on some form of job analysis (Gatewood & Feild, 1994), a discussion of analysis and an examination of its role in the boundaryless organization follows.

BOUNDARYLESS JOB ANALYSIS

Given that the job itself may be an increasingly unreliable way to characterize what workers do (Bridges, 1994; Lawler, 1994; Ashkenas et al., 1995), where, if anywhere, does job analysis fit in the boundaryless organization? Job analysis is the measurement of tasks and/or worker attributes for a given job; thus, job analysis techniques can be classified as work-oriented or worker-oriented (Gatewood & Feild, 1994). Work-oriented methods involve specific descriptions of the various tasks performed on a job, whereas worker-oriented methods examine broad human behaviors involved in work activities.

Whether work- or worker-oriented, job analysis methods allow for the inference of worker KSAs and other characteristics (Gatewood & Feild, 1994). KSAs include job-related information and the necessary human abilities to perform certain job activities. The importance of valid KSAs cannot be overstated, as the relationship between them and individual performance in the organization is well-established (Davis, 1995; Gatewood & Feild, 1994).

Although job analysis is considered the virtual cornerstone of human resources practices, it has recently been criticized as inflexible and legalistic (Drucker, 1987); its traditional conception has been called obsolete (Sanchez, 1994). These criticisms parallel other arguments that focus on creating boundaryless conditions between functions, disciplines, and levels of workers (Ashkenas et al., 1995) and those aimed at thriving in a de-jobbed society (Bridges, 1994). In essence, these arguments posit that the job is too myopic, too restrictive, and too inflexible for the success of both the organization and its workers.

The "job" in job analysis, however, need not imply that this systematic process of discovering work-related information is merely useful for a narrow scope of tasks or easily defined duties. Job analysis is a tool to systematically gather data (i.e., tasks and behaviors leading to KSAs) about virtually any kind of work activity (Gatewood & Feild, 1994). Thus, a plausible argument can be made that job analysis would be more important in the boundaryless organization, where work activities are created and evolve more quickly, than in more traditionally structured organizations, where jobs are static for longer time periods.

Contrary to criticisms of the inadequacies of job analysis, it is proposed here that job analysis is capable of examining both diverse and changing occupations. Not all job analysis approaches are equal, however. In general, the worker-oriented approach is proposed as more appropriate than the work-oriented approach because the former possesses the flexibility needed in the boundaryless organization.

Consider a work-oriented method such as the Functional Job Analysis, or FJA (Fine & Wiley, 1977). The FJA assesses specific job outputs, identifies job tasks in terms of task statements (e.g., who does the task, what action is performed, immediate result, tools/equipment used, instructions followed), measures worker involvement with people, data, and things (worker functions scales), and also measures numerous other qualifications and specifications. The main problem with the FJA, and the work approach in general (e.g., identifying what a worker does and how each task is performed), is that it provides limited utility due to the changing nature of the job.

The Position Analysis Questionnaire, or PAQ (McCormick, Jeanneret, & Mecham, 1972), on the other hand, focuses on general worker behaviors instead of tasks. This worker-oriented method includes information about worker input, mental processes, work output, and relationships with others. Worker-oriented methods provide a standardized means for collecting quantitative data across a wide spectrum of jobs and yield helpful information in formulating employee specifications (Gatewood & Feild, 1994). Further, the worker-oriented approach has been called one of the most useful methods of work description developed to date, one that allows "meaningful comparisons" to be made between jobs that are highly dissimilar at the task level (Harvey, Friedman, Hakel, & Cornelius, 1988, p. 639).

Whereas some worker-oriented methods have been criticized for their lack of structure and absence of task data (Gatewood & Feild, 1994), these "limitations" may become less important or even prove useful in the boundaryless organization. For instance, worker-oriented methods do not cover actual task activities, a requirement for job description development. Given that job descriptions are becoming less important for boundaryless organizations (Ashkenas et al., 1995; Miner & Robinson, 1994), however, the worker-oriented approach may have few, if any, limitations.

One criticism that has been aimed specifically at the PAQ is its required reading level, estimated at post-college or higher (Ash & Edgell, 1975). However, another worker-oriented job analysis method modeled after the PAQ, the Job Element Inventory, or JEI (Cornelius & Hakel, 1978), requires a 10th-grade reading level. The JEI has been found to possess a factor analytic structure parallel to that of the PAQ (Harvey et al., 1988). Thus, the JEI's use poses few problems for job incumbents and supervisors who may serve as job analysis raters.

While work- and worker-oriented job analysis methods have not been directly compared by incumbent workers, research shows that workers have criticized the use of a point-factor job analysis questionnaire based on widely used job evaluation scales (Taber & Peters, 1991). Taber and Peters (1991) found the most frequent comment made by hundreds of administrative, technical, and clerical workers was that their jobs could not be described by the job analysis questionnaire. The next most frequent comment was that the questionnaire did not assess some personal attributes brought by the employee to the job (e.g., "Personality, attitude are very important," and "Creativity is not mentioned"). Other comments included (in order): "Interpersonal contacts are inadequately assessed;"

"The job has been revised or is evolving;" and "Job tasks are too diverse to be captured in questionnaire form."

According to Taber and Peters (1991), it is likely that any existing job evaluation procedure cannot comprehensively evaluate jobs which are highly interdependent, continuously evolving, unpredictable, or that involve a diverse set of important but infrequent tasks. Indeed, these very types of "jobs" describe what workers do in a boundaryless organization. Although job analysis and job evaluation serve different (yet related) functions, the Taber and Peters (1991) study implies that workers who are only asked work-oriented information such as major tasks, how much time they spend performing each one, the importance of each task, its complexity, equipment used, etc., perceive these data as inadequate measures of what they do.

SKILLS EMPHASIS AND WORK ANALYSIS

Given that functional boundaries will continue to blur (Ashkenas et al., 1995; Miner & Robinson, 1994), boundaryless organizations may eventually collapse "jobs" into more comprehensive skill- or work-related categories. Not only would this type of integration make the administrative task of job analysis less cumbersome; it could contribute to a culture wherein workers are afforded more freedom and opportunity to engage in different work activities.

For example, Woodsworth, Maylone, and Sywak (1992) found a sufficiently strong relationship between some computing and library jobs to warrant the creation of a single information job family in classification systems. The commonality between jobs was attributed to the jobs' reliance on various information technologies. As information technologies become more interconnected between jobs, functions, and departments, it is plausible that the KSAs which related to these technologies will become more transferable and less job-specific.

However, a big question is which KSAs will be required for future technologies, and thus, future jobs. Arvey, Salas, and Gialluca (1992) have demonstrated that some existing tasks and skills-abilities correlations can help predict future skill requirements for jobs when only a limited number of tasks is known. The authors caution, however, that this technique assumes current tasks and abilities are representative and inclusive of the kinds of skills and abilities that would be forecasted. Moreover, any changes in job structures that would affect existing covariance patterns would diminish the accuracy of skills forecasting results (Arvey et al., 1992).

Recently, work analysis has been advocated to replace the traditional notion of job analysis (Sanchez, 1994). Few guidelines exist as to how to combine tasks into broader units, but Sanchez (1994) proposes that both employees and management examine tasks and KSAs "to group previous job titles into cross-functional, challenging occupational classifications." Although the idea of work analysis may be intuitively appealing, concrete procedures for work analysis are missing. Only general propositions and recommendations (e.g., "analyze work activities to identify workflow, so that new occupational classifications can be based on workflow rather than functional area," Sanchez, 1994) have been stated.

An important question for practitioners and researchers alike is whether existing job analysis methods such as the PAQ and the JEI, or a broader notion such as work analysis, can be used to capture the flexibility, interdependency, and diversity of work in the boundaryless organization. Because the boundaryless organization does not accommodate stable tasks, work-oriented approaches to job analysis may be both cumbersome and ineffective. On the other hand, gathering information about KSAs which ultimately encompass what workers can do, their values, and how these match the organization's culture and operational needs seems the niche that job (or work) analysis should be filling. Somewhat along these lines, Davis (1995) has called for adequate methods to determine "organizational KSAs," a term he likens to unique organizational competencies and assumedly different from a compilation of individual worker KSAs. A job or work analysis method that taps organizational KSAs, work-relevant KSAs, and other worker characteristics that can be tied to the organization, the work, or both, would seem to enhance the success of several human resource functions, especially recruitment and selection.

BOUNDARYLESS RECRUITMENT

Gaining competent employees at all levels of the organization is more than a matter of training; it stems from changes in recruitment and selection philosophy (Ashkenas et al., 1995). Specifically, the boundaryless organization emphasizes the development of a shared mindset among all of its employees and the continuous support of this collective culture. Although Ashkenas et al. (1995) don't describe specific recruiting approaches that aid in achieving this cohesive culture, they state the importance of thoroughly screening applicants, sometimes with the help of customers, based on skills and personality traits that match the technical and cultural needs of the organization.

It makes sense that an organization's culture would be reflected, to some degree, in its recruitment efforts. However, most research suggests that this is not the case. Bretz, Rynes, and Gerhart (1993) found that despite the recent emphasis on unique organizational values, strategies, or cultures in the person-organization fit literature, recruiters continue to emphasize job-related course work or experience and broad personal characteristics (e.g., articulation, personal appearance, general communication skills). In other words, the immediate job fit dominated the recruiting exchange, whereas the organization's culture and values were relatively absent. Similarly, Adkins, Russell, and Werbel (1994) found that recruiters' perceptions of congruence between the applicant and the organization were not related to the recruiters' judgments of employability.

There may be several reasons why person-organization fit is not assessed or emphasized during recruitment. First, many organizations may be unaware of their cultures (Schein, 1985) despite the recent emphasis on unique organizational values, strategies, or cultures in discussions of fit (Bretz et al., 1993). Second, recruiters may not utilize person-organization fit information for different reasons. For instance, recruiters may lack knowledge about the organization's culture, or they may not have the ability to process knowledge about organizational culture into questions intended to measure person-organization fit. Furthermore, they may not know how to weigh person-organization fit measures with traditional job-related KSAs.

Moving toward realistic work cultures

A recruitment technique that is theoretically derived from an individual need-organiza-tion culture matching process is the realistic job preview, or RJP (Wanous, 1992). An RJP presents the candidate with negative and positive aspects about a particular job so that the degree of match between the candidate's wants (derived from individual needs) and the organization's climate (derived from its culture) can be assessed (Wanous, 1992). The more positive and negative information a candidate receives about the job, the more realistic the individual's expectations, and the less likely voluntary turnover is to happen within the first stages of socialization (Meglino, DeNisi, Youngblood, & Williams, 1988). Lawler (1994) notes that RJPs are likely the best approach to selection in the competency-based organization versus the job-based organization.

Given, however, the boundaryless organization's de-emphasis on both hierarchical struc-ture and the job itself, an RJP may not provide enough information to determine the most valid individual-organization match. Specifically, it is suggested that recruiters attempt to communicate, as directly as possible, the culture of their organizations – not just a particu-lar job and its immediate environment – to candidates. Recruiters should provide candi-dates with previews of organizational culture for several reasons. First, the traditional job description (i.e., a thorough listing of specific duties and responsibilities) will become less used by organizations due to the blurring of job rules and functional domains. Instead of workers focusing on "who does what," the values, norms, and beliefs which underlie all of the work in the organization will become increasingly salient to workers. Indeed, many firms have moved to more general job descriptions, emphasizing important values, instead of precise, predetermined duties (Miner & Robinson, 1994; Souder, 1987).

Second, because work is becoming "structured" in a less hierarchical fashion and more according to the requirements of the project (Bridges, 1994; Lawler, 1994), the nature of coworker interactions and communicating different work processes will play more vital roles in the boundaryless organization. Devanna and Tichy (1990) describe creating a culture that allows all levels of the workforce to contribute to business strategy formula-tion, resulting in a fluid power structure. In fact, it has been proposed that every challenge facing the boundaryless organization deals with people management, "with issues of how things get done, not what gets done" (Devanna & Tichy, 1990).

Third, an inferred temporal distinction exists between organizational culture and or-ganizational climate. Traditional RJPs tend to mirror organizational climate. Climate refers to currently shared perceptions of "the way things are around here" (Wanous, 1992), and many times has a specific referent such as a safety climate (Zohar, 1980), a sexual harassment climate (Bill, 1994), or service, cooperation, or rewards/punishments climates (Schneider, 1975).

Culture, on the other hand, refers to subconscious assumptions, shared meanings, and ways of interpreting things that pervade the whole organization (Reichers & Schneider, 1990). Because culture is more fundamental than climate (Wanous, 1992) and less transient than specific work environments (i.e., climates) which are subject to change, it is proposed that applicants and organizations alike would benefit from the exchange of information about the assumptions and values underlying these particular work environments. Whereas "the way things are around here" will change within the organization over time, the as-sumptions, values, and beliefs that are shared among organizational members are more stable, yet not static (Schein, 1985), organizational attributes. These assumptions, values and beliefs can then be used by the candidate to make a relatively stable assessment regarding how well his or her wants and needs can be matched by those of the organization.

Finally, the use of values to convey cultural information is consonant with the person-organization fit literature. The degree of cultural (i.e. values) fit between workers and their organizations has been shown to significantly affect several important work outcomes, including organizational commitment, job satisfaction, and employee turnover (O'Reilly, Chatman, & Caldwell, 1991). The O'Reilly et al. (1991) study demonstrated that the factor analytic structure underlying individual cultural preferences was comparable to the structure underlying organizational culture in several firms. Also, individual variations in preferences for different organizational cultures were associated with interpretable differences in personality characteristics. Thus, the organization may benefit from selecting people who fit a given situation given some combination of task and cultural (values) requirements (O'Reilly et al., 1991; Ashkenas, 1995).

Sources of cultural information

In addition to revealing a deeper layer of organizational information to the candidate, it is proposed that the source of this information will become an increasingly important consideration. Communicating a realistic work culture should include the shared mindsets (Phillips, 1994) of organizational members. As Wanous (1992) advocates, candidates greatly benefit from conversations with incumbent employees. It is further proposed, however, that whenever possible, candidates receive information from employees who share similar group memberships (e.g., race, gender, age, family responsibilities, employment arrangements). This communication exchange should serve to optimize the matching process. If a candidate volunteers information about his single-father role, for example, conversational opportunities with other single fathers or mothers in the organization should be offered to the candidate. Similarly, those who speak English as a second language or have cultural backgrounds that differ from most coworkers should have commensurate opportunities.

In summary, instead of RJPs that focus virtually all of the candidate's attention on the current job and its immediate climate, we need to broaden the RJP, in practice, to encompass realistic work cultures. In addition, the source of this information should ideally include at least one organizational member who shares one or more of the candidate's cultural and/or social group characteristics. Because there are fewer skilled workers (Kessler, 1990) and yet their diversity continues to increase, tomorrow's employees will be able to choose the environments which appear to suit them best (Thomas, 1991).

BOUNDARYLESS SELECTION

As discussed earlier, the importance of job analysis and derived KSAs for the purpose of valid selection practices has been well-established (Gatewood & Feild, 1994). Within the boundaryless organization, however, it is proposed that managers may more effectively attract, select, and retain qualified workers by looking for broad sets of KSAs that may encompass several "jobs," and personality traits reflective of the organization's culture (e.g., O'Reilly et al., 1991; Devanna & Tichy, 1990).

Generally, cognitive ability tests have the reputation as the best predictors of job performance across virtually all types of jobs (Schmidt & Hunter, 1981). Thus, there is no reason to assume that cognitive ability will not continue to be a valid predictor of performance within a boundaryless context. However, it is proposed that increased emphasis will be placed on traits such as adaptability and flexibility (Ashkenas et al., 1995). Indeed, Devanna and Tichy (1990) state that while the boundaryless organization will continue to select workers with the appropriate technical mix, selection will also depend on facilitation skills to create and maintain social networks, the ability to motivate with influence versus power, and the ability as well as willingness to teach others what they have learned.

The main idea here is that predicting individual performance in a boundaryless organization will no longer be a matter of studying the same particulars within a job content domain. For most jobs, the domain will change too quickly (Bridges, 1994). However, as long as the individual's aptitude (e.g., cognitive ability) and/or other validated KSAs exist, increasingly important predictors of performance will include traits such as flexibility, adaptability, or attitude toward training and learning in this changing environment.

A number of studies on personality and job performance have demonstrated personality measures' incremental validity over cognitive ability tests (Gellatly, Paunonen, Meyer. Jackson, & Goffin, 1991; Ferris, Bergin, & Gilmore 1986). Moreover, Day and Silverman (1989) found that personality variables can account for more job performance variance than that predicted by cognitive ability.

The Big Five personality dimensions, which include emotional stability, extroversion, openness to experience, agreeableness, and conscientiousness, are widely used in organizational behavior literature (Wagner & Hollenbeck, 1995), have good psychometric qualities, and are especially attractive due to their demonstrated relationship with job performance (Barrick & Mount, 1991). For instance, conscientiousness has been related to both hirability and counterproductivity (Dunn, Mount, Barrick, & Ones, 1995), as well as several job performance criteria for five occupational groups (Barrick & Mount, 1991).

The Big Five could be especially useful in boundaryless selection. Some research indicates that certain personality dimensions are related to worker traits and ways of working that seem characteristic of the boundaryless organization. For instance, extroversion, agreeableness, and conscientiousness have been reported as significantly related to self-efficacy for self-managed work group participation (Thoms, Moore, & Scott, 1996). Also, the predictive validity of conscientiousness and extroversion is greater for managers in jobs high in autonomy compared with those in jobs low in autonomy (Barrick & Mount, 1993). Expectations of self-management and autonomy are increasing for tomorrow's worker (e.g., Ashkenas et al., 1995: Bridges, 1994).

Another potentially helpful selection tool in the boundary organization is biodata. Biodata is the use of life history data that entails a sophisticated understanding of values, attitudes, motivational forces, and experiential bases (Landy, Shankster-Cawley, & Moran, 1995). Theoretically, people seek opportunities and experiences to maximize long-term adaptation to their environment; and given satisfactory outcomes, people will actively seek out similar situations in the future, resulting in coherent patterns of behavior (Mumford, Stokes, & Owens, 1990). Evidence of construct validity and theory underlying biodata predictors has proliferated in the last decade (Landy et al., 1995).

Dilemma of boundaryless recruitment and selection: too much of a good thing

Ashkenas et al. (1995) emphasize the importance of achieving a shared mindset among employees as early as possible or hiring individuals with shared values. A dilemma regarding a high degree of person-organization culture fit surfaces: What about the potentially negative consequences of attracting and selecting too many like-minded individuals? For instance, Schneider (1987) has suggested that organizational dysfunction and eventual demise can be traced to an overabundance of homogeneous worker characteristics. As a corollary, some diversity of worker attributes may be necessary to respond to environmental threats and opportunities, ultimately ensuring the viability of the organization.

Another caveat to consider is the possibility of adverse impact. Any employment test which results in different acceptance/pass rates for individuals belonging to different groups must be validated and its continued use demonstrated as necessary (e.g., no other test possesses its prediction power). If a disproportionate number of females, for instance, are judged to be a good fit for the organization based on the Big Five, male candidates may have cause for grievance or litigation.

Thus, the very homogeneity of employee values proposed as necessary for the success of the boundaryless organization may lead to two serious problems: decreased organizational performance and adverse impact. Approximately how much and what kinds of cultural parity between worker and organization are necessary for a productive mindset? Approximately how much and what kinds of cultural (i.e. values) similarity between worker and organization lead to litigation and/or poor organizational adaptability?

Because the work and how it is accomplished are based on flexibility to move ideas, information, talent, and decisions where they are most necessary (Ashkenas et al., 1995), the boundaryless organization may be less likely to realize organizational adaptability and performance problems compared to other organizations. The possibility of adverse impact seems a more likely threat. However, if employees are chosen on the basis of the organization's core values which reflect pivotal norms (Schein, 1980), and not on the basis of all possible organizational values and norms, the chance for worker trait homogeneity is lessened.

It may be that just as the organization needs different skill sets to accomplish a unified performance goal, organizations need different traits and worker characteristics to accomplish the longer-term goal of survival (Schneider, 1987). However, worker heterogeneity does not necessarily preclude the selection of homogeneous traits that primarily serve to reinforce core values and pivotal norms. More research is needed to build theory and enhance practitioner success in recruiting and selecting workers for boundaryless organizations.

SUMMARY AND RECOMMENDATIONS

A boundaryless organization presents a challenge to some forms of job analysis, and traditional recruitment and selection practices that center around a job to be analyzed in terms of relatively stable tasks. There now exists evidence to suggest the job, as a structure within the organization, is no longer stable enough to use as a basis for making strategic human resources decisions. Although the scope of this paper was limited to job analysis, recruitment, and selection, boundaryless implications for compensation, training and performance management are certainly as important (Lawler, 1994).

The importance of rethinking and developing job analysis and recruitment and selection strategies which consider the realities of the boundaryless organization, contemporary employment arrangements, and the importance of person-organization fit has been the focus of this paper. Recent work in the area of person-organization fit suggests that value congruency may significantly affect employment satisfaction, organizational commitment, likelihood to quit, and actual turnover (O'Reilly et al., 1991). Thus, value congruency might also be used to help predict employee performance across jobs within an organization. On the other hand, a perfectly value-congruent workforce may present a different set of problems, namely poor adaptability to change (Schneider, 1987) and adverse impact. The boundaryless organization's focus is on reducing unnecessary structures so it can be highly adaptable to change. More research is needed to determine how much value congruence is necessary for optimal organizational adaptability and performance without adverse impact.

RECOMMENDATIONS

1. Some method of analyzing what workers do (i.e., job analysis) is necessary in the boundaryless organization. Worker-oriented job analysis approaches such as the PAQ and the JEI allow more flexibility in the boundaryless organization because they focus on worker behaviors instead of specific tasks. Additionally, worker-oriented approaches provide a standardized way of collecting data across many "jobs." Newer approaches like work analysis, based on workflow, should be pursued.
2. An organization's understanding of its culture and its ability to communicate its cultural attributes (i.e., organizational values) to recruits will benefit both the organization and the recruit more than the conveyance of a job and its immediate climate, leading to a better person-organization match.
3. Recruits who receive cultural information from those employees who share similar group memberships (e.g., race, gender, age, family responsibilities) will be able to make better "matches" between themselves and the organization.
4. Understanding its own culture will enable the organization to articulate core values which can then be translated into traits and non-technical abilities to be validated as selection measures, ultimately enhancing organizational and individual outcomes (e.g., commitment, satisfaction, turnover).
5. Attracting and selecting candidates whose traits highly "match" the organization's cultural profile may result in two problems: organizational dysfunction and adverse impact on different social groups. It is possible that if the boundaryless organization selects employees based on its core values, and affords employees creative individualism in the area of its peripheral values, adverse impact and poor organizational adaptability will be less likely. Research is needed to determine the relationship between worker trait homogeneity and these potential threats.

Rethinking the role of the job in a boundaryless organizational context has tremendous implications for human resource researchers and practitioners alike. Such implications necessitate an examination of how human resources can best fulfill its strategic roles in an environment of fewer vertical, functional, external, and geographical boundaries.

References

Adkins, C.L., Russell, C.J., and Werbel, J.D. "Judgments of Fit in the Selection Process: The Role of Work Value Congruence." *Personnel Psychology*, 47 (1994): 605–23.

Arvey, R.D., Salas, E., and Gialluca, K.A. "Using Task Inventories to Forecast Skills and Abilities." *Human Performance*, 5 (1992): 171–90.

Ash, R.A., and Edgell, S.L. "A Note on the Readability of the Position Analysis Questionnaire (PAQ)." *Journal of Applied Psychology*, 60 (1975): 765–6.

Ashkenas, R., Ulrich, D., Jick, T., and Kerr, S. *The Boundaryless Organization: Breaking the Chains of Organizational Structure.* San Francisco: Jossey-Bass, 1995.

Barrick, M.R., and Mount, M.K. "The Big Five Personality Dimensions: A Meta-analysis." *Personnel Psychology*, 44 (1991): 1–26.

Barrick, M.R., and Mount, M.K. "Autonomy as a Moderator of the Relationships Between the Big Five Personality Dimensions and Job Performance." *Journal of Applied Psychology*, 78 (1993): 111–18.

Belous, R.S. *The Contingent Economy: The Growth of the Temporary, Part-time and Subcontracted Workforce (Report No. 239).* Washington, D.C.: National Planning Association, 1989.

Bill, J.B. "Sexual Harassment as a Work Climate: Moving Beyond the Reasonable Gender Approach." Paper presented at the annual meeting of the Academy of Management. Dallas, 1994 (August).

Bowen, D.E., and Lawler, E.E., III. "Total Quality-oriented Human Resources Management." *Organizational Dynamics*, 20 (1992): 29–41.

Bretz, R.D. Jr., Rynes, S.L., and Gerhart, B. "Recruiter Perceptions of Applicant Fit: Implications for Individual Career Preparation and Job Search Behavior." *Journal of Vocational Behavior*, 43 (1993): 310–27.

Bridges, W. *JobShift.* Reading, MA: Addison-Wesley, 1994.

Charbuck, D.C., and Young, J.S. *The Virtual Workplace*, Forbes, 1992 (November): 184–90.

Cornelius, E.T., and Hakel, M.D. "A Study to Develop an Improved Enlisted Performance Evaluation System for the U.S. Coast Guard." Washington, DC: Department of Transportation, United States Coast Guard, 1978.

Davis, D.D. "Form, Function, and Strategy in Boundaryless Organizations." In A. Howard, (ed.), *The Changing Nature of Work.* San Francisco: Jossey-Bass, 1995.

Day, D.V., and Silverman, S.B. "Personality and Job Performance: Evidence of Incremental Validity." *Personnel Psychology*, 42 (1989): 25–36.

Devanna, M.A., and Tichy, N. "Creating the Competitive Organization of the 21st Century: The Boundaryless Corporation." *Human Resource Management*, 29 (1990): 455–71.

Drucker, P.F. "Workers' Hands Bound by Tradition." *Wall Street Journal* (August 2) (1987): 18.

Dunn, W.S., Mount, M.K., Barrick, M.R., and Ones, D.S. "Relative Importance of Personality and General Mental Ability in Managers' Judgments of Applicant Qualifications." *Journal of Applied Psychology*, 80 (1995): 500–9.

Ferris, G.R., Bergin, T.G., and Gilmore, D.C. "Personality and Ability Predictors of Training Performance for Flight Attendants." *Group and Organization Studies*, 11 (1986): 419–35.

Fine, S.A., and Wiley, W.W. *An Introduction to Functional Job Analysis: A Scaling of Selected Tasks from the Social Welfare Field.* Kalamazoo, MI: W.E. Upjohn Institute for Employment Research, 1977.

Gatewood, R.D., and Feild, H. *Human Resource Selection (3rd ed.).* Fort Worth: Harcourt Brace, 1994.

Gellatly, I.R., Paunonen, S.V., Meyer, J.P., Jackson, D.N., and Goffin, R.D. "Personality, Vocational Interest, and Cognitive Predictors of Managerial Job Performance and Satisfaction." *Personality and Individual Differences*, 12 (1991): 221–31.

Halal, W.E. "From Hierarchy to Enterprise: Internal Markets Are the New Foundation of Management." *The Academy of Management Executive*, 8 (1994): 69–83.

Harvey, R.J., Freidman, L., Hakel, M.D., and Cornelius, E.T. "Dimensionality of the Job Element Inventory, a Simplified Worker-oriented Job Analysis Questionnaire." *Journal of Applied Psychology*, 73 (1988): 639–46.

Howard, A. *The Changing Nature of Work*. A. Howard (Ed.) San Francisco: Jossey-Bass, 1995.

Keidel, R.W. "Rethinking Organizational Design." *The Academy of Management Executive*, 8 (1994): 12–30.

Kessler, L.L. *Managing Diversity in an Equal Opportunity Workplace: A Primer for Today's Manager*. Washington D.C.: National Foundation for the Study of Employment Policy, 1990.

Landy, F.J., Shankster-Cawley, L., and Moran, S.K. "Advancing Personnel Selection and Placement Methods." In A. Howard (ed.) *The Changing Nature of Work*. San Francisco: Jossey-Bass, 1995.

Lawler, E.E. III. "From Job-based to Competency-based Organizations." *Journal of Organizational Behavior*, 15 (1994): 3–15.

McCormick, E.J., Jeanneret, P.R., and Mecham, R.C. "A Study of Characteristics and Job Dimensions as Based on the Position Analysis Questionnaire (PAQ)." *Journal of Applied Psychology*, 56 (1972): 347–68.

Meglino, B.M., DeNisi, A.S., Youngblood, S.A., and Williams, K.J. "Effects of Realistic Job Previews: A Comparison Using an Enhancement and a Reduction Preview." *Journal of Applied Psychology*, 73 (1988): 259–66.

Miner, A.S., and Robinson, D.F. "Organizational and Population Level Learning as Engines for Career Transitions." *Journal of Organizational Behavior*, 15 (1994): 345–64.

Mumford, M.D., Stokes, G.S., and Owens, W.A. *Patterns of Life Adaptation: The Ecology of Human Individuality*. Hillsdale, NJ: Erlbaum, 1990.

O'Reilly, C.A. III, Chatman, J., and Caldwell, D.F. "People and Organizational Culture: A Profile Comparison Approach to Assessing Person-organization Fit." *Academy of Management Journal*, 34 (1991): 487–516.

Phillips, M.E. "Industry Mindsets: Exploring the Cultures of Two Macro-organizational Settings." *Organization Science*, 5 (1994): 384–402.

Reichers, A.E., and Schneider, B. "Climate and Culture: An Evolution of Concepts." In B. Schneider (ed.), *Organizational Climate and Culture*. San Francisco: Jossey-Bass, 1990.

Sanchez, J.I. "From Documentation to Innovation: Reshaping Job Analysis to Meet Emerging Business Needs." *Human Resource Management Review*, 4 (1994): 51–74.

Schein, E.H. *Organizational Psychology, (3rd ed.)*. Englewood Cliffs, NJ: Prentice Hall, 1980.

Schein, E.H. *Organizational Culture and Leadership: A Dynamic View*. San Francisco: Jossey-Bass, 1985.

Schmidt, F.L., and Hunter, J.E. "Employment Testing: Old Theories and New Research Findings." *American Psychologist*, 36 (1981): 1128–37.

Schneider, B. "Organizational Climates: An Essay." *Personnel Psychology*, 28 (1975): 447–81.

Schneider, B. "The People Make the Place." *Personnel Psychology*, 40 (1987): 437–54.

Souder, W.E. *Managing New Product Innovations*. Massachusetts: D.C. Heath and Co., 1987.

Taber, T.D., and Peters, T.D. "Assessing the Completeness of a Job Analysis Procedure." *Journal of Organizational Behavior*, 12 (1991): 581–93.

Thomas, R.R., Jr., *Beyond Race and Gender: Unleashing the Power of Your Total Workforce by Managing Diversity*. New York: American Management Association, 1991.

Thoms, P., Moore, K.S., and Scott, K.S. "The Relationship Between Self-efficacy for Participating in Self-managed Work Groups and the Big Five Personality Dimensions." *Journal of Organizational Behavior*, 17 (1996): 349–62.

Wagner, J.A., and Hollenbeck, J.R. *Management of Organizational Behavior, (2nd ed.)*. Englewood Cliffs, NJ: Prentice Hall, 1995.

Wanous, J.P. *Organizational Entry (2nd ed.)*. Reading, MA: Addison Wesley, 1992.

Woodsworth, A., Maylone, T., and Sywak, M. "The Information Job Family: Results of an Exploratory Study." *Library Trends*, 41 (1992): 250–68.

Zohar, D. "Safety Climate in Industrial Organizations: Theoretical and Applied Implications." *Journal of Applied Psychology*, 65 (1980): 96–102.

Chapter 15

Building a Global Workforce Starts With Recruitment

Shannon Peters Talbott

If you're an HR professional in an international corporation, which members of your workforce are global employees? U.S. citizens living abroad? Japanese employees working in the United States? Swedish managers who are helping to set up operations in Portugal? Or every single member of your workforce?

Without hesitation, most HR professionals would include the first three categories of employees in their answer. Expatriates, usually defined as those living and working outside their home countries, are obviously global: They're key to the success or failure of international business, whether they remain abroad long term or work short stints while operations are being established. Selecting the right people for these assignments is a matter of great concern, as early return or failure is costly and can be damaging to business relations with international partners or customers.

But, where do you find these expats? Do you go out and hire them for the job, or do you select them from among your workforce? Most often, expatriates are selected from within the corporation. Why? Current employees usually are more in sync with a company's organizational culture, and they also have the skills necessary to do the job.

As many HR professionals are learning, however, employees need more than technical expertise to succeed. And, unless every member of an organization is looked upon as a global employee, it may be difficult to find people who have the skills necessary to perform well in the international environment. By keeping long-term goals in sight during recruitment efforts, multinational firms can build a globally aware workforce – one composed of talented members who support the company's global philosophy, have expat potential and can propel the business into the 21st century.

MAKE EVERY HIRE A GLOBAL EFFORT

Every year, hundreds of companies expand their operations into the global marketplace. At the same time, corporations that are established in the international sphere redefine their business to maintain a competitive edge. For organizations in both categories, recruitment and international assignment are key determinants of long-term success.

For many corporations, international recruitment is synonymous with expatriate selection. Within this area, significant progress has been made to ensure candidates are screened for global competency, which – according to most experts – includes such qualities as flexibility, open-mindedness, technical expertise, multiple language proficiency and the willingness to take risks. Says Shirley Gaufin, vice president of HR for Bechtel Group Inc. in San Francisco: "Global awareness is a subtle characteristic, but it's absolutely essential for expatriate success. It's part of someone being a good leader, part of someone being flexible and adaptable."

Today, HR professionals in progressive global companies are discovering that it isn't enough just to look for these skills among members of the expatriate community. Rather, every employee needs to have a certain level of global awareness, and many companies are finding that screening must begin at recruitment. Take, for example, Tetra Pak Inc., a multinational corporation based in Lund, Sweden. At the company's U.S. headquarters in Chicago, personnel manager Barbara Shimkus looks for expat potential every time she makes a hire. "We don't often go out and search for someone to go abroad next year. Expatriates are selected from within the company," Shimkus says. "But when we recruit, we always look for candidates who have global potential. We're interested in people who eventually could relocate internationally and handle that adjustment well."

Overall, Shimkus says candidates with international backgrounds are best suited for careers with the company. She says: "Business is changing, and companies can no longer seek out employees who have limited themselves to a domestic view of the world. Employees who will lead us into the future are those who understand business in the international arena."

Gaufin agrees. At Bechtel, she works with approximately 25,000 people who are handling diverse projects in more than 70 countries worldwide. Recently, Bechtel went through a major restructuring, giving its international regions more autonomy. Instead of ruling from above, the company is focusing on multinational awareness and cultivation of its global talent. Gaufin explains: "In the past, we were more of a U.S. firm doing business internationally. We are now becoming more 'global.' As part of that, we're working to develop a stronger global workforce." What does this mean for recruitment? Bechtel is placing more emphasis than ever before on global competencies, assuring that every member can contribute to future multinational growth.

As Gaufin and Shimkus note, it's to every company's best advantage to consider the future and hire those who can support upcoming needs. But in addition to recruiting for expatriate potential, HR professionals are finding that employees who have international experience and language proficiency help the company function on a day-to-day basis. To see why this is true, just look at the operations of an average global company. Managers must understand differing cultural norms to perform well on business trips and short-term assignments in other parts of the world. HR professionals need to be aware of legal differences surrounding benefits and compensation, as well as local norms regarding vacation and child care. Receptionists and other staff members must answer daily phone calls and correspondence from overseas.

At Tetra Pak, global interaction is common, and employees with multiple-language skills are in high demand. "It seems like every day we're searching the office for someone who speaks Swedish or German or Spanish to translate a fax or interpret a phone call," says Shimkus. Bechtel's internal communications staff are regularly reminded that their employee newsletter reaches an international audience: "We're very careful to avoid mention of the seasons, for example, because they differ with the hemispheres," Gaufin says. This type of awareness is needed by every employee. "Every day, our employees have to consider the fact that they're working within a global framework. There are time changes, cultural variations – small differences that matter."

Gaufin says the more capable employees are at understanding these everyday differences, the more successful the business will be on a global level. "Every employee needs to have a global state of mind, whether it's someone who works overseas or in the United States," Gaufin says. "Employees have to be able to look at the company – and our business – in a global way."

REALIGN YOUR RECRUITMENT STRATEGIES

Identifying the need for these employees is just one-half of the battle: Finding them is the other. Not all applicants have the flexible personalities needed to perform well in a global environment – and even fewer have any sort of international training. In fact, according to the American Institute for Foreign Study, just 5% of college graduates are proficient in a foreign language, and less than half of all students studying business take a course that's internationally focused. Without a recruitment effort that's designed to attract those with global competencies, HR professionals are unlikely to find top talent.

John Amato, former manager of global assignments for St. Louis-based Monsanto Corporation, says that small changes to recruitment advertising can help companies identify global potential. "In writing job descriptions, get away from focusing only on the job's technical skills," Amato says. "Of course, technical expertise is important. But recruitment advertising can tell the applicants a lot more about future potential of the position when you describe behavioral traits needed for the job."

Changes of this type can help companies get a more globally qualified pool of applicants for every hire. This is especially true when recruiters combine the new job criteria with expanded international networking efforts and targeted recruitment campaigns. As Amato recommends: "Network among the global community. Attend conferences where you can meet other specialists. This can help you expand your global applicant pool." Amato also says to look among the college ranks, especially at schools that specialize in international education. Shimkus agrees. "When we recruit from these colleges, it gives us confidence we're identifying people who have a global foundation and a wider understanding of the world," she says.

Identification of global talent is essential to Mary Scelba's recruitment efforts. As assistant vice president of strategic staffing and planning for Warren, New Jersey-based Chubb & Son Inc., she looks for international competency during every recruitment effort. With more than 15% of the company's employees outside of the United States – and rapid overseas growth – Chubb & Son considers global awareness a must-have criterion for every new hire. "An ideal employee is one who is open to other cultures, someone who has multiple-language skills, someone who's flexible and adaptable to meet our changing business needs," Scelba explains.

No positions are more vital to Chubb's global development than the company's international branch managers. To be assured of the highest quality employees in these positions, Chubb recruits globally minded people to participate in the company's international trainee program. After an extensive training in Chubb's practices and standards, these employees move into management slots.

Recruitment efforts for trainees are initially conducted locally, using traditional methods – local campus recruiting, newspaper advertisements and employee referrals. However, Scelba frequently supplements the branches' efforts by identifying potential within the United States. She says that universities offer a concentration of qualified applicants: "We attend international career consortiums that are held specifically for international students. The attendees are ideal applicants." Why? Chubb is looking for people who have just completed master's degrees and who also have three to five years experience working in their home countries. Because the attendees have studied in the United States, they offer additional benefits to the U.S.-based company: "Most are fluent in English and understand U.S. culture. They're bilingual, globally minded and already have international experience to build upon," Scelba says. "But many of them are planning to return to their home countries to work. We source them here, interview them, then refer them to our overseas branches for potential hire."

MAKE RECRUITMENT A FIRST STEP

Whatever your methods for identifying talent, efforts to build your company's international potential must continue long term. Recruitment is just a first step in developing a global workforce, a first stage in cultivating global leadership and supporting your international business. For employees who are already on board, multicultural training and international exposure can strengthen global competencies that already exist. Career planning and internal networking can help top-potential employees excel. And, when overseas assignments are necessary, expats can perform most successfully with a comprehensive expatriation and repatriation program. But, the whole process begins with early identification of potential. "Employees who have strong global skills are a requirement – not only for expatriate positions, but to support immediate needs," says Amato. "Selection of the right people is crucial to the success of international business."

The global business environment is growing so rapidly, you can't afford not to recruit people with global mindsets. If it isn't crucial to your company today – it probably will be tomorrow.

Chapter 16

Four Faces of Global Culture

Peter L. Berger

The term "globalization" has become somewhat of a cliché. It serves to explain every-thing from the woes of the German coal industry to the sexual habits of Japanese teenag-ers. Most clichés have a degree of factual validity; so does this one. There can be no doubt about the fact of an ever more interconnected global economy, with vast social and political implications, and there is no shortage of thoughtful, if inconclusive, reflection about this great transformation. It has also been noted that there is a cultural dimension, the obvious result of an immense increase in worldwide communication. If there is eco-nomic globalization, there is also cultural globalization. To say this, however, is only to raise the question of what such a phenomenon amounts to.

Again, there can be no doubt about some of the facts. One can watch CNN in an African safari lodge. German investors converse in English with Chinese apparatchiks. Peruvian social workers spout the rhetoric of American feminism. Protestant preachers are active in India, while missionaries of the Hare Krishna movement return the compli-ment in Middle America. Both hope and fear attach to these facts.

The hope is that a putative global culture will help to create a more peaceful world. If a global culture is in the making, then perhaps a global civil society might come into being. Ever since John Locke re-emerged from Eastern Europe speaking with a Polish accent, a great amount of hope has been invested in the notion of civil society, that agglomerate of intermediate institutions that Tocqueville saw as the foundation of a vital democracy. Civil society depends on a consensus on civic virtues, and that, after all, is what a culture is supposed to supply. The French sociologist Danièle Hervieu-Léger (in her contribution to the forthcoming volume *The Limits of Social Cohesion*, edited by me) speaks of an "ecumenism of human rights." The same idea is conveyed in a much cruder form by the advertisements of the Benetton company. Whether the idea is couched in sophisticated or crude terms, it too has an evident factual basis. It is also reasonable to hope that a world in which there would be a greater consensus on human rights would also be a more peaceful world.

But there is also fear attached to the prospect of cultural globalization, fear of a worldwide "airport culture" in which the rich diversity of human civilizations will be homogenized and vulgarized. This fear has been vocalized in the rhetoric of "Asian values" that has attained a certain political significance in recent years, as well as in the rhetoric of the various movements of Islamic resurgence. Similar fear, in less virulent form, can be observed elsewhere, for example in the worries about cultural homogenization among Euroskeptics. One of the arguments made by those who opposed Austria's joining the European Union was that Austrians would no longer be able to refer to potatoes as *Erdäpfel*, a homey word that was suddenly imbued with the genius of Austrian identity, but would have to use the High German word *Kartoffeln*. Of course this was silly. But the desire to preserve distinct cultural traditions and a distinct cultural identity in the intense economic and political pressure cooker of the new Europe is not silly at all. The fear, like the hope, is not without foundation.

A more nuanced understanding of cultural globalization will have to take account of both the homogenizing forces and the resistances to them. Benjamin Barber made a move toward such an understanding in his book *Jihad vs. McWorld* (1995). Most recently, and in a more subtle way, Samuel Huntington has discussed the same issues in his *Clash of Civilizations and the Remaking of World Order* (1996), a book to which the present observations are greatly indebted. Huntington, whose view of the contemporary world cannot be accused of being overly optimistic, ends his book with a call to search for commonalities between the contending civilizations, a dialogue of cultures. One need not agree with every aspect of his analysis to agree with his conclusion. A dialogue between cultures, however, presupposes a clearer understanding of all the processes at work, both those of cultural globalization and of resistance to it. It is proposed here that there are at least four distinct processes of cultural globalization going on simultaneously, relating in complex ways both to each other and to the many indigenous cultures on which they impinge.

DAVOS: FROM BOARDROOM TO BEDROOM

First is what Huntington nicely calls the "Davos culture" (after the annual World Economic Summit that meets in that Swiss luxury resort). This culture is globalized as a direct accompaniment of global economic processes. Its carrier is international business. It has obvious behavioral aspects that are directly functional in economic terms, behaviour dictated by the accoutrements of contemporary business. Participants in this culture know how to deal with computers, cellular phones, airline schedules, currency exchange, and the like. But they also dress alike, exhibit the same amicable informality, relieve tensions by similar attempts at humor, and of course most of them interact in English. Since most of these cultural traits are of Western (and mostly American) provenance, individuals coming from different backgrounds must go through a process of socialization that will allow them to engage in this behavior with seemingly effortless spontaneity. This is not always easy. A growing number of consultants in "diversity management" are making a good living advising corporations on how to affect this sort of socialization as smoothly as possible.

But it would be a mistake to think that the "Davos culture" operates only in the offices, boardrooms, and hotel suites in which international business is transacted. It carries over into the lifestyles and presumably also the values of those who participate in it. Thus, for example, the frenetic pace of contemporary business is carried over into the leisure activities and the family life of business people. There is a yuppie style in the corporation, but also in the body-building studio and in the bedroom. And notions of costs, benefits, and maximization spill over from work into private life.

The "Davos culture" is a culture of the elite and (by way of what sociologists call "anticipatory socialization") of those aspiring to join the elite. Its principal social location is in the business world, but since elites intermingle, it also affects at least the political elites. There is, as it were, a yuppie *internationale*. Some years ago, while the apartheid regime was still in power in South Africa, a friend of mine had lunch with a representative of the African National Congress at the United Nations. To my friend's surprise, this individual spent most of the lunch talking about apartment costs in Manhattan. While this yuppification of a representative of what then still understood itself as an anti-capitalist revolutionary movement might have had an ironic aspect, it was a cultural trait that turned out to be very useful a few years later. A number of people from both sides have reported how, when they first met, young ANC exiles and young Afrikaners were surprised by their similar lifestyle preferences and personal values. These were certainly not derived from their respective historical traditions, rather, they were, precisely, commonalities rooted in the "Davos culture." There have been similar reports about the first meetings between young Israelis and Palestinians leading up to the Oslo agreements. Whether one is edified by this spectacle or not, it may be that commonalities in taste make it easier to find common ground politically.

While cultural globalization facilitates interaction between elites, it creates difficulties between these elites and the non-elite populations with whom they must deal. Many moral and ideological conflicts in contemporary societies pit an elite culture against a resentful mass of culturally accredited and economically underprivileged people. As Huntington points out, these resentments may lead to the emergence of a nationalist or religious counter-elite. Also, individuals who participate in the "Davos culture" with reasonable success vary in their ability to balance this participation with other parts of their lives. While some, as previously pointed out, may allow yuppie behavior and values to inundate their private lives, others seek more complicated compromises. On my last visit to Hong Kong I happened to stray into a Buddhist temple and came upon a truly graphic vignette: In front of an altar, facing a large statue of the Buddha, stood a middle-aged man wearing a dark business suit over stocking feet. He was burning incense and at the same time talking on his cellular phone.

FACULTY CLUB INTERNATIONAL

Both critics and advocates of contemporary global capitalism mainly think in terms of the "Davos culture" and its ramifications in popular culture ("Davos" in interaction with "McWorld"). Yet there are at least two other quite different types of cultural globalization going on. One of these is what one might call the "faculty club culture." Essentially, this is the internationalization of the Western intelligentsia, its values and ideologies. To put it graphically, if the "Davos culture" tries to sell computer systems in India, the "faculty club culture" tries to promote feminism or environmentalism there – a rather different agenda.

While this culture has also penetrated the business world (and in turn has been penetrated by it), its principal carrier is not business. Rather, it is carried by foundations, academic networks, non-governmental organizations, and some governmental and multi-national agencies (such as development agencies with social and cultural missions). It too is primarily an elite culture, though here again there are those who aspire to it from the lower echelons of cultural enterprises (say, schoolteachers or social workers who read the books and periodicals that reflect the views emanating from the great cultural centers).

More importantly, the "faculty club culture" spreads its beliefs and values through the educational system, the legal system, various therapeutic institutions, think tanks, and at least some of the media of mass communication. If this culture internationalizes the Western intelligentsia, it also internationalizes the conflicts in which this intelligentsia has been engaged on its home territories. James Hunter has written very insightfully about the American "culture wars" (first in his 1991 book with that title). These conflicts can now be observed worldwide, though always of course subject to local modifications.

A good example of this second process of cultural globalization is the anti-smoking movement, arguably one of the most successful movements in developed societies over the last twenty years or so. Before then it was a small, marginal sect, hardly noticed in public discourse; today, especially in North America and Western Europe, it has largely achieved the goal proclaimed early on by one of its spokesmen – to make smoking an activity engaged in privately by consenting adults. The reasons for this stunning success need not concern us here. The point is that this movement, clearly a product of Western intellectuals, was disseminated worldwide by an alliance of governmental and non-governmental organizations. In a series of conferences, the World Health Organization propagated the anti-smoking cause internationally. At one of the early conferences the travel expenses of all participants from developing societies were paid by the Scandinavian development agencies (the conference was held in Stockholm). These participants, mostly from health and education ministries, came from countries with horrendous health problems and the campaign against smoking was not high on their list of priorities. As was to be expected, they re-ordered their priorities given the incentives to do so. Ironically, the concepts of neo-Marxist dependency theory, which have not been very good at interpreting the transformations of advanced capitalism, fit rather well in the globalization of the "faculty club culture." Here there is overwhelming "dependency," with an indigenous "comprador class" carrying out the agendas devised in the cultural centers of the "metropolis."

There are obvious tensions between the first and second processes of cultural globalization. Clearly, the anti-smoking movement collides with the interests of the tobacco industry. More generally, both feminism and environmentalism collide with notions of economic efficiency held by the international economic elite. At this time, the most visible conflict is between the "ecumenism of human rights," carried out by a multitude of non-governmental organizations, and the belief of the "Davos culture" that all good things, including human rights, will eventually result from the global establishment of successful market economies. And of course there are also tensions between the "faculty club culture" and various indigenous movements of cultural revitalization. The recent women's conference in Beijing pitted mostly Western feminists against an odd alliance of Islamists and the Vatican. Most significant politically, the Western-centered human rights community is meeting with strong opposition in a sizable number of non-Western countries.

THE McWORLD CULTURE

Third, of course, is popular culture. Here Barber's term "McWorld" fits best. And it is this culture that is most credibly subsumed under the category of Westernization, since virtually all of it is of Western, and more specifically American, provenance. Young people throughout the world dance to American music, wiggling their behinds in American jeans and wearing T-shirts with messages (often misspelled) about American universities and other consumer items. Older people watch American sitcoms on television and go to American movies. Everyone, young and old, grows taller and fatter on American fast foods. Here indeed is a case of cultural hegemony, and it is not surprising that others, such as French ministers of culture and Iranian mullahs (not to mention the now defunct Soviet Komsomol functionaries), greatly resent the fact.

These critics of "cultural imperialism" also understand that the diffusion of popular culture is not just a matter of outward behavior. It carries a significant freight of beliefs and values. Take the case of rock music. Its attraction is not just due to a particular preference for loud, rhythmic sound and dangerously athletic dancing. Rock music also symbolizes a whole cluster of cultural values – concerning self-expression, spontaneity, released sexuality, and, perhaps most importantly, defiance of the alleged stodginess of tradition. The consumption of American popular culture has, as it were, sacramental character. Paraphrasing the Book of Common Prayer, these items of consumption are visible signs of an invisible grace – or curse. The hegemony becomes clear by the asymmetry of consumption. Mexicans eat *bamburguesas*, Americans eat tacos. But the Mexicans are consuming whole chunks of American values "in, with, and under" the American hamburgers; the Americans are certainly *not* absorbing non-culinary aspects of Mexican culture by eating tacos.

A couple of years ago, I met a representative of Hallmark greeting cards for the Chinese province of Guandong (a market of some sixty million people). He was happy to report that his product was selling very well. When asked which greeting cards were most popular, he said Valentine cards. "You see, young Chinese men are quite shy with members of the opposite sex. It is difficult for them to express their feelings. It is much easier to send a Valentine card." I did not know what to say to this and mumbled something about how there must be a lot of work translating the texts into Chinese. "Oh no," he said, "they want the cards to be in English."

The people in charge of the globalization of popular culture are, of course, members or aspiring members of the "Davos" elite. The aforementioned Hallmark representative evinced all the characteristics of a successful, with-it yuppie. But the consumers of these cultural exports are a vastly broader population. The indigenous reactions once again vary from complete acceptance to complete rejection, with many degrees of compromise in between. Complete acceptance generally leads to a conflict between the generations, and presumably an important motive for such acceptance among young people is to outrage one's parents. Complete rejection is difficult, even under repressive regimes (the Komsomol functionaries, after trying repression, finally had to compromise by inventing something they would call "Soviet rock"). There are many and complex degrees of compromise, some of them puzzling to the outsider.

A few years ago I visited the Meiji Grand Shrine in Tokyo. I was in the company of my hosts, who were pious adherents of Shinto. When inviting me to go to the Shrine with them, they asked me solicitously whether my religious feelings would be offended by their venerating the Meiji Emperor; I replied courteously (and perhaps rashly) that this would be quite all right. I then stood with them, holding incense sticks in my hands and bowing to the deafening accompaniment of drums being beaten by a row of Shinto priests lined up behind us. I re-emerged from the Shrine somewhat dazed, reflecting that I had just been praying to a dead Japanese potentate. Outside the Shrine was a large park filled with hundreds of young people, fervently dancing to rock music blaring from numerous portable radios. I had noticed some young people inside the Shrine and wondered whether they were now joining the crowd in the park. I asked my hosts whether they saw any contradiction between what was going on inside and outside the Shrine. They were actually puzzled by my question. Certainly not, they replied after a moment of reflection, "Japanese culture has always been successful in integrating elements coming from abroad." One of the most interesting questions about contemporary Japan is whether my hosts were correct in their sanguine view about the absorptive capacity of Japanese culture.

Evangelical Protestantism

Fourthly (though perhaps not finally), a distinctive process of globalization is provided by Evangelical Protestantism, especially in its Pentecostal version (which accounts for something like 80 percent of its worldwide growth). Its globalizing force is best seen by comparing it with the other dynamic religious phenomenon of our time, that of the Islamic resurgence. While the latter has been limited to countries that have always been Muslim and to Muslim diaspora communities, Evangelical Protestantism has been exploding in parts of the world to which this religious tradition has always been alien, indeed, mostly unknown. The most dramatic explosion has occurred in Latin America (it was magisterially described in David Martin's 1990 book, *Tongues of Fire*). But the same variety of Protestantism has been rapidly growing in East Asia (with the notable exception of Japan), in all the Chinese societies (including, despite repression, the People's Republic), in the Philippines, the South Pacific, and throughout sub-Saharan Africa. There are recent, as yet vague, accounts of an incipient growth in Eastern Europe. And while the origins of this religion are in the United States (the "metropolis"), its new incarnations are thoroughly indigenized and independent of foreign missionaries or financial support.

Evangelical Protestantism brings about a cultural revolution in its new territories (in that respect it is very different from its social function on its American homeground). It brings about radical changes in the relations between men and women, in the upbringing and education of children, in the attitudes toward traditional hierarchies. Most importantly, it inculcates precisely that "Protestant ethic" that Max Weber analyzed as an important ingredient in the genesis of modern capitalism – a disciplined, frugal, and rationally oriented approach to work. Thus, despite its indigenization (converts in Mexico and Guatemala sing American gospel songs in Mayan translation), Evangelical Protestantism is the carrier of a pluralistic and modernizing culture whose original location is in the North Atlantic societies.

It is not clear at this point how this startlingly new phenomenon relates to the previously enumerated processes of cultural globalization. It certainly enters into conflicts with indigenous cultures. Most of the persecution of Christians recently publicized by human rights organizations – notably in China, in the Islamic world, and (sporadically) in Latin America – has been directed against Evangelical Protestants. What is clear is that this type of Protestantism is creating a new international culture, increasingly self-conscious as such (here the relation to American Evangelicals *is* relevant), with vast social, economic, and political ramifications. While the new Protestantism should not be misunderstood as a movement of social protest or reform (its motives are overwhelmingly personal and religious), it has large and unintended consequences. These are decidedly favorable to pluralism, to the market economy, and to democracy. It should be observed here that there may be other globalizing popular movements, but Evangelicalism is clearly the most dynamic.

Four faces of globalization: each is distinctive, each relates to the other three in complex ways. Yet they have important common features. The two perhaps most important features have already been mentioned – their Western, principally American, provenance, and related to this, their relation to the English language.

The Western provenance of these processes has given credibility to the frequent charge that they are part and parcel of Western imperialism, with the United States being the core of this malevolent phenomenon. The charge will not hold up. The "Davos culture" is today fully internationalized. It is centered as much in Tokyo and Singapore as it is in New York and London. One could more plausibly speak of an imperialism of the global capitalist system, but that is simply to attach a pejorative term to the fact of an immensely powerful global reality. The concepts of neo-Marxist theory simply do not fit it. As already mentioned, those concepts are somewhat more apt in describing the globalization of the "faculty club culture." Feminist or environmentalist agitators in Bangladesh can indeed be described as agents of a Western-based "cultural imperialism," but it is difficult to see how their activity benefits global capitalism. Multinational corporations do indeed make large profits from the distribution of popular culture, but there is no coercion involved in their success. No one is forcing Japanese teenagers to enjoy rock music or young men in China to express their emotions in terms derived from American romanticism.

Claudio Véliz (in his 1994 book *The New World of the Gothic Fox*) has made this point very tellingly in his description of the collapse of Latin American tradition before the onslaught of "Anglo-Saxon" values and lifestyles, notably those connected with a pluralistic society. He has used a good metaphor to denote this process, proposing that "Anglo-Saxon" culture is now in its "Hellenistic" phase. That is, it is no longer diffused by means of imperial power, British or American; rather, it has become a cultural force in itself, with large numbers of people clamoring to share it. As to Evangelical Protestantism, both leftist intellectuals and Roman Catholic bishops have portrayed it as a gigantic CIA plot, especially in Latin America, but a look at the empirical evidence presents a very different picture, one of a vital, autonomous movement no longer dependent on support from the outside.

If cultural globalization today represents the "Hellenistic" phase of a civilization originating in the northern parts of Europe and America, the English language is its *koiné* (the "basic Greek" that served as the lingua franca of late classical antiquity and that, among other things, became the language of the New Testament). We live, as Véliz puts it, in "a world made in English," and he points out that no other language appears to be a viable successor to English in the foreseeable future. By now there are very straightforward practical reasons for this hegemony of the English language. However much this may enrage intellectuals in certain places (France, for example, or Quebec), English has become *the* medium of international economic, technological, and scientific communication. The millions of people learning English all over the world do so in order to participate in this global communication, not (with few exceptions) because they want to read Shakespeare or Melville in the original. However, one does not use a language innocently. Every language carries a freight of values, of sensibilities, of approaches to reality, all of which insinuate themselves into the consciousness of those who speak it. It makes sense to assume that the attractiveness of English, especially in its American form, is due at least in part to its capacity to express the sensibilities of a dynamic, pluralistic, and rationally innovative world. This is even true of Evangelical Protestantism, which mostly expresses itself in languages other than English, but whose leaders and young people learn English in order to be in touch with the Evangelical centers in the United States. In doing so, they may get more than they bargained for. The road from the Christian Broadcasting Network to Oprah Winfrey is disturbingly straight.

The picture I have sketched is huge and exceedingly complex. There are many aspects of it that are not yet fully understood. There is a very large research agenda here. But one conclusion can be ventured: If one is to heed Huntington's call for a dialogue between cultures, one must pay as much attention to the manner in which the different processes of cultural globalization relate to each other as to their relation with many indigenous cultures. This then will not just be a dialogue between "the West and the rest," but a considerably more complicated enterprise.

Chapter 17

European Competencies – Some Guidelines for Companies

Bruno Leblanc

In 1991, a small group of European executives, all of whom were directors of human resources at an international, European or group level in their companies, joined up, with the present author, into a task force to identify the specific competencies required for companies to develop in Europe in the context of the Single Market. The task force was an off-shoot of a European club of companies. A major objective of the club was to help the member companies increase their understanding of the implications of the emerging Single Market on the development and management of their human resources.[1]

The task force met in Paris for eight one-day sessions and produced a number of conclusions and recommendations. The present text is a further development of those issues.

ORIGINS AND OBJECTIVES OF THE TASK FORCE

The task force was set up to help clarify what specific competencies companies and their managers need in order to respond successfully to the demands of the emerging Single European Market (SEM).

A number of member companies of the club felt that people talk a great deal about these competencies, but that they have never been clearly defined. Also, that they are not easily distinguishable from the more general set of skills and capabilities considered necessary for international development outside Europe. This was partly explained by the fact that many companies do not find it necessary to separate out their specific goals and objectives in Europe from their broader international ambitions.

We also wanted to distinguish between the individual skills needed by, say, expatriate managers, and the more collective corporate competencies required to develop and implement international strategies and policies. The ability of an international manager to operate effectively within a given foreign culture seemed to us distinct from his or her ability to manage pluri-national/pluri-cultural teams. And both of these abilities are different from a company's corporate ability to introduce and develop policies of staff recruitment on a European level, to integrate staff from different European countries, including into its domestic operations, or to develop new transnational modes of corporate organization (e.g. allocating Europe-wide product line management or other Europe-wide responsibility along with traditional country/national subsidiary responsibilities).

Task force members quickly realized that their companies had reached quite different stages of international and European development, and therefore had very different mid-term priorities in this area. So we decided to develop a general framework to help characterize the different stages of European and international development. The framework would include tasks a company has to accomplish at each stage and the competencies needed to do this successfully. We saw this framework as a tool that could help companies identify where they were in the internationalization process and, subsequently, the specific range of competencies that were likely to be of greatest relevance to them.

STAGES IN THE ORGANIZATION PROCESS

Taking the companies represented in the task force as a working sample, we first identified three broad stages in the internationalization process. We found that each one also corresponds to a strategic choice of how to develop in Europe.

(1) *"First landing" stage*: A national company with a strong national base expands its interests into Europe for the first time through a series of acquisitions in different European countries. The main focus of concern is to be successful in preparing, implementing and managing the "foreign" acquisitions.

(2) *"Go native" stage*: A company which has become well-established in Europe through a network of branches and subsidiaries, in which each national subsidiary has gradually been granted autonomy for the day-to-day management of its operations and marketing activities. Human resource policies reinforce the percentage of national managers in each subsidiary: the expatriate general manager of the subsidiary is responsible for the medium and long-term career development of the high calibre members of his/her local staff.

(3) *Integration stage*: A company which is truly European because it has manufacturing facilities and a commercial presence throughout Europe. It now considers that national boundaries must give way to the European perspective and seeks to organize and pursue its development on a continental rather than national basis. It gradually develops a pan-European strategy, within a global strategy, generates awareness of that policy within the company and finds practical ways of implementing it.[2]

DIFFERENTIATION AND INTEGRATION SKILLS

We identified two types of business and management skills as essential in these stages, although they vary in importance depending on the stage of European development a company is at. We called the first set, most relevant to the "landing stage" and "going native" stages, "differentiation skills", and the second set, essential to the "integration stage", "integration skills".

Foreign subsidiaries in the "first landing" and "go native" stages, for example, are very often involved only with the production and/or sale of goods and services locally, not with any export or re-export activities. These foreign subsidiaries are then viewed as so many local units of a "multi-domestic" company, rather than as fully integrated members of an international ensemble, in which *each* geographic territory can have international roles and responsibilities. They need to be sure their expatriate managers have the differentiation skills needed to adjust to a foreign environment.

Differentiation skills

These skills are essential to successful "local" management, and include:

- recognizing the diversity of Europe;
- accepting differences between countries as a fact;
- adjusting to these differences effectively.

They imply the following abilities to:

- obtain and interpret information about foreign national contexts (local institutions, legislations, practices, market specificities, etc.);
- inform, and communicate effectively with a foreign environment about the home company's policies;
- negotiate contracts, partnerships, etc. in a foreign environment;
- be accepted as a foreign representative of one's company abroad;
- manage local operations and personnel abroad effectively;
- tolerate and adjust to local conditions personally (tolerance of expatriation/foreign posting); and
- cope in the long term with a large variety of foreign contexts.

We considered that essential to this group of competencies is the corporate ability, and indeed the willingness, to *import* foreign practices and choices into the home environment of the company when this is a condition for success abroad. For example the ability to:

- identify and accept adjustments to basic product specifications in order to meet the needs of the foreign market, and ability to persuade the company at home to make the necessary changes;
- recruit foreign managers into both the foreign operations and the home environment, integrate them and manage their career development.

The "integration stage" involves setting up and promoting novel, complex, multilateral relationships among the different geographic units of the same company. These relationships can even include allocating strategic or developmental responsibilities to different – domestic or foreign – subsidiaries of the company. Indeed, the very notions of "domestic" and "foreign" units and systems tend to become irrelevant and counter-productive to achieving cohesive international development.

The ability to implement this type of development, which has been called "getting rid of the headquarters mentality" and "decomposing the centre" into equally important and legitimate co-operating territorial units,[3] obviously requires extensive changes of attitudes in the parent company as well as in its subsidiaries. It will be an important factor in the successful emergence of truly pan-European companies.

Integration skills

These skills provide a company with the ability to build a European perspective and European policies from the diversity of national considerations and viewpoints. They include the ability to:

- view Europe as a single region, within which traditional (national) or new (sub-regional) differentiations must be accepted or developed (e.g. new market segmentations);
- develop elements of a common framework for company strategies, policies and operations at a European level (e.g. ability to develop a common company culture);
- build commonalities, at both company and functional levels (common procedures, product specifications, standards, policies, etc.) with a view to achieving economies of scale or minimizing the cost of company development at a European level;
- organize co-operation at a European level (e.g. ability to manage international/pluri-cultural teams and develop international projects).

Thus, a corporate skill that is essential in the process of European development and integration is for the parent company to accept that the best, or most realistic solutions at a European level, are not necessarily those which it has traditionally adopted in its national environment. This implies an ability to acknowledge that in a European perspective, each country's "home" practices are only a special case among other special cases, *and that this includes the head office.*

The task force members agreed that the skills most relevant to meeting the challenges of the emerging Single Market are integration skills, and that there is probably need for more work in this area. However, we believe that differentiation skills are very important to many companies, especially those in the first two stages of internationalization.

THE COMPETENCIES – STAGE BY STAGE

After having identified the different stages of European development and the types of skills needed, the task force looked more closely at the managerial and organizational competencies for each stage.

"First Landing"

For the first landing stage the task force was especially interested in the behavioural and general managerial qualities which managers would need to operate effectively in a foreign environment. We looked at behaviours (personal, interpersonal, managerial), which we believe can serve as a general check-list for the recruitment, guidance and evaluation of expatriate managers (see table 17.1).

All members of the task force agreed that the amount of cultural information and knowledge specific to a particular country, which a manager needs in order to adopt locally effective behaviours, should never be underestimated. Our recommendation is that companies organize exposure to the country or special preparation for their managers before the foreign assignments.

Our discussions revealed that, failing this, serious mistakes are likely despite the best of intentions. Task force members spoke of managers having difficulties interpreting local situations, events and behaviours, as well as in responding to local expectations. Local ideas about proper behaviour and acceptable business and management practice could simply not be guessed at! The result was often failure to meet company objectives and, more generally, an inability to make the most of local business opportunities. Nor did these unprepared managers obtain the confidence of local employees or business partners.

Our group agreed that in order to learn to accept cultural differences between countries, a manager has to consider him/herself as initially "blind and deaf" to local realities and insist on getting properly briefed. We also agreed that it takes time to develop this ability, and that it is possibly one of the most valuable characteristics of an experienced international manager. A manager who has performed well in his/her own home environment will not necessarily find it easy to cope with the intellectual and psychological adjustments necessary in a foreign context.

All this also meant that companies and, more specifically, human resource managers, with international, or European, ambitions, have the difficult responsibility of identifying, preparing and then supporting their expatriate managers. We decided it was also their role to promote attitudes of open-mindedness towards and knowledgeability about the cultures of the company's business partners abroad. This task was likely to become even more important as increasingly large proportions of people in companies became, directly or indirectly, involved in cross-border activities, if only for short periods of time.

Go native stage

In this stage, the general managers of foreign subsidiaries have larger areas of responsibility and their activities take on a more international dimension. Additional skills become necessary, for which they have not necessarily received specific training. For example:

Table 17.1 Major Tasks of Company Managers during the Three Stages of European Development

Responsibility	First landing	Go native	Integration
Commercial	Open up new national market abroad	Increase market share Optimize results in national context	Develop Euro-brands Pricing policy in Single Market
Industrial	Build or acquire production facilities	Improve productivity and quality performance	Rationalize capacity across boundaries
Human resources	Recruit and train new teams Design compensation	Industrial relations Management development	Euro social legislation Pan-Euro IR Multi-cultural team building

- Management skills concerning career management of the better qualified, locally employed staff. This involves knowing how to identify those high calibre staff members capable for an international career, and building an international team of managers among the local staff.
- Analysis and reporting skills on such local factors as new opportunities for take-overs and mergers and the activities of their competitors.
- Product development skills: extending the product or service range locally to respond to, or anticipate, new local competition, by introducing innovations possibly developed by the company in its other territories of operation.

On the corporate level, this requires an increased ability to organize the systematic dissemination of information about international competitive trends and about its own new products and services to all its local managers, at home and abroad. This promotes fruitful cross-fertilization of different subsidiaries Europe-wide (or worldwide), even if the final objective is still a "multi-domestic" model and not a full international, or European, integration of its activities.

The stage of integration

Companies which pursue the integration strategy have to reconcile several objectives and sources of competitive advantage simultaneously, which are always partly contradictory. They are seeking to:

- achieve the maximum benefits from economies of scale, and generate a unique capacity for innovation thanks to rationalizing and consolidating a number of their activities (e.g. R & D, product development, manufacturing, sourcing of materials, components, finance, etc.), on the one hand;
- respond rapidly to local markets and situations in a way that matches more decentralized "local companies" on the other; and also
- organize and foster the effective transfer of learning from any geographic point of the company to any other, so as to maximize the overall rate of innovation of the company in all its markets and operations.

There can be many reasons for engaging the integration process, for example to:

- Satisfy the needs of an emerging "European customer". For instance as automobile companies become increasingly international, it is virtually impossible to have different pricing policies on a national basis. In addition, the development of trans-European fleet operations within the Single Market will gradually lead to integration in the replacement market.
- Take full advantage of Single Market opportunities.
- Revitalize European operations, which may be old and entrenched in national traditions and need to be modernized and streamlined in order to face fierce worldwide competition.
- Organize or rationalize their European activities.
- Remain a player in Europe, the major "playing field" for most of their international business opportunities.

The members of our task force felt that the problems are more cultural and motivational than technical. The issues revolve around how to achieve the best result for Europe as a whole (the team) as opposed to what might appear best for a national manager (the individual player). The balancing act involves how to:

- Centralize some decision making without taking responsibility away from the national managers?
- Get the national managers in partnership with each other while still developing their competitive national spirit?
- Push a "European solution" while remaining sensitive to national culture, tradition, pride in performance, and local social legislation?

We agreed that a simple or rigid organizational answer will only defeat the business objectives of the company. These issues of centralization (Europeanization) versus decentralization ("localization") of decision making must be accepted as permanently live and uneasy ones, needing on-going flexibility and adaptation.

Most importantly, we stressed that the European identity can never be the private domain of the central team, but must be equally shared and developed by everyone in Europe. All general managers of the company have to learn how to learn from each other and develop a measure of "dual membership and loyalty". They have to be equally committed members of their national team and of a European/International group. This is a new and unusual mind-set requirement for many managers, and has sometimes been referred to as an ability to "hold the matrix (of the organization) in one's mind". It means constantly introducing European perspectives into their respective areas of responsibility (see table 17.1). This ability, central to success in the future development of European companies does not easily cohabit with the more traditional notions of a single command structure.

This means that when it comes to real integration, European competencies of individual managers are not enough. The company needs to integrate European competencies at its different levels, and in its different areas of activity.

CONCLUSIONS – IMPLICATIONS FOR TRAINING AND DEVELOPMENT

Top management's responsibility in advocating and pushing through European goals and objectives and the role of the human resources function in developing the corresponding competencies are critical. The tasks include:

Recruitment

- Develop a European recruitment policy.
- Favour mobile, multilingual candidates.
- Develop selection procedures which identify European integration skills and behaviours.

Career Management

- Systematically build expatriate experience into career development programmes.
- Centralize career planning information.
- Give national personnel functions European responsibilities in this area.

Communication

- Communicate the European integration message.
- Explain the importance of mobility for the company to achieve its integration goal.

It is disconcerting that a number of surveys, carried out in different European countries in the last few years by professional organizations or consulting firms, show that in many companies, including large international ones, the personnel and human resources functions lag behind other management functions (such as sales, production or finance), in developing a European perspective and agenda. The members felt that by implementing the following recommendations, human resources would better contribute to successful Europeanization:

(1) The skills and capabilities requirements of companies differ according to the stage of European development. They also differ according to the mode of European development – ownership of foreign subsidiaries or alliances, partnerships, joint ventures, etc.

(2) The task force found that there is a real need to develop training programmes focused around the following topics:

- Discovering the diversity of a company's national environments (economic, social, cultural, etc.) and developing the ability to tolerate and take into account that diversity in fulfilling individual company responsibilities.
- Understanding the meaning and implications of developing and managing from a (pan)-European perspective rather than on a nation-by-nation basis.
- Organizing for transnational/Europe-wide work and co-operation: managing pluricultural teams, developing Euro-strategies and organizations.

Training groups should include participants of different nationalities and teaching staff from different countries. This also holds for one-on-one or on-the-job programmes developed internally.

(3) There is a clear need to re-define the organization of the human resources function within companies at a European level. Discussions between companies with similar development objectives would be useful in moving this process forward.

Notes and Reference

1 Regular members of the task force included: Alan Duke (Michelin), Mike Donogan (Dalgety Plc). Michel Durier (Ciments Français), Carmelo Florez Cosio (Banco Bilbao & Vizcaya, Jean-Pierre de Hochepied (Banque Nationale de Paris). The present author, who chaired the discussions and wrote the final report, was also at that time European Director of a management school (EAP), with institutions in France, Germany, Spain and the UK.

Several members of the task force contributed very valuable position papers, which provided the initial basis of the discussions. None of them, however, bears any responsibility for the present text, given that they have not had an opportunity to comment on it in any way. Nor can the viewpoints expressed here be taken to represent the policies of their companies in any way.

2 Notwithstanding the relevance of the model to our large organizations, we also recognize its limitations. Our companies have created or acquired their own operations abroad. As a result, our model does not consider the problems which can arise from attempts to develop and manage other types of close association with partners abroad (e.g. joint ventures, strategic

alliances, etc.) Nor did we really consider the problems of companies developing their presence abroad through independent local distributors. This is an important limitation, since many medium- and small-size companies can only hope to expand quickly into other European markets on the basis of such co-operative arrangements.

The ability to enter into and manage such arrangements effectively is crucial to their future European development. It is, of course, also important for larger companies forming joint ventures; the problems of properly managing such joint ventures and maintaining satisfactory relationships with one's foreign partner(s) can be formidable and a source of considerable frustration for many companies. Indeed, specialists working in this area have documented the fact that the rate of failure of cross-border joint ventures founded by European companies in Europe tends to be very high (over 60 per cent after three years of life together). A better understanding of the specific skills and competencies of joint venture management will therefore be increasingly important as the European economies become more integrated.

3   Ohmae, K. *The Borderless World*, 1990.

Chapter 18

Case: Grupo Financiero Inverlat

Daniel D. Campbell, Henry W. Lane, and Kathleen E. Slaughter

By October 1996, it had been four months since management at the Bank of Nova Scotia (BNS) increased its stake in the Mexican bank, Grupo Financiero Inverlat (Inverlat), from 8.1 per cent, to an equity and convertible debt package that represented 54 per cent ownership of the bank. A team of Canadian managers had been sent to Mexico to assume management of the ailing financial institution immediately after the deal was struck. Jim O'Donnell, now Director General Adjunto (DGA)[1] of the retail bank at Inverlat, had been there from the beginning.

Jim was a member of the original group that performed the due diligence to analyze Inverlat's finances before negotiations could begin. Later, he and his wife Anne-Marie (also an executive with the bank) were the first Canadians to arrive in Mexico in May 1996. Since then, 14 additional Canadian managers had arrived, and restructured the four most senior levels within Inverlat. The pace of change had been overwhelming. Jim now wondered how successful his early efforts had been and what could be done to facilitate the remaining restructuring.

A BRIEF INVERLAT HISTORY

In 1982, in his last days as leader of the Mexican Republic, President Lopez Portillo announced the nationalization of Mexico's banks. They would remain government institutions for the next 8 to 10 years. Managers characterized the years under government control as a period of stagnation in which the structure of the Mexican financial institutions remained constant despite substantial innovations in technology and practice in the banking industry internationally.

Many Inverlat managers claimed that their bank had generally deteriorated more than the rest of the banking sector in Mexico. Managers believed that there was no overall strategy or leadership. Lacking a strong central management structure, each of the bank's geographic regions began to function independently, resulting in a system of control one manager described as "feudal". The eight regions developed such a level of autonomy that managers commonly referred to Inverlat not as a bank, but as eight small banks. The fragmented structure made new product development almost impossible. When the central corporate offices developed a new product, they had no guarantee that it would be implemented in the regions and ultimately, the branches. The power struggle within the regions demanded such loyalty that employees often had to say: "I cannot support you (in some initiative) because my boss told me not to."

In 1990, an amendment to the Mexican constitution allowed majority private sector ownership of Mexican commercial banks. Between 1990 and 1992, eighteen banks were privatized by the Mexican government including Inverlat. BNS, looking to expand its interests in Latin America, purchased 8 per cent of the company in 1992 for C$154 million.

Under the structure of the newly privatized bank, there were three corporate cultures: that of the original bank: that of the Casa de Bolsa, the bank's brokerage house; and that of the new chair of the bank, an executive from Banamex, Mexico's largest financial institution. Many senior Banamex executives were invited to join Inverlat, some even came out of retirement to do so. The Banamex culture soon dominated the organization, as senior management tried to create a "Little Banamex". Inverlat managers without a history in Banamex said that the strategy could never function because Inverlat did not have the clients, technology, or financial resources of Banamex.

Inverlat's leaders did recognize, however, that the years of stagnation under nationalization had created a bank that had failed to create a new generation of bankers to reflect the changing times. They realized that the bank required a rejuvenation, but the managers did not have the knowledge or the capacity to effect the change.

Nowhere was the lack of development more prominent, and ultimately more devastating, than in the credit assessment function. The banks pursued a growth strategy dependent on increased lending but, unfamiliar with the challenges of lending to the private sector, failed to collateralize their loans properly or to ensure that covenants were being maintained. In early 1995, following a severe devaluation of the Mexican peso, Mexico's credit environment collapsed; so did the bank. The Mexican government assumed responsibility for the bank, and BNS was forced to write down its original investment by almost 95 per cent to C$10 million.

NEGOTIATIONS WITH BNS

Management at BNS chose to view the loss in value of their investment as a further buying opportunity and, in early 1996, they began negotiations with the Mexican government. BNS contributed C$50 million for 16 per cent of new stock in the bank and C$125 million in bonds convertible on March 31, in the year 2000 for an additional 39 per cent of equity. If, in the year 2000, BNS decided not to assume ownership of the bank, they could walk away without converting the debt and retain a much smaller portion of ownership.

As the majority shareholder until the year 2000, the Mexican government contracted BNS to manage the bank. A maximum of 20 BNS managers would be paid by the Mexican government to manage Inverlat on the government's behalf. If BNS wanted more Canadian managers to work in the bank, BNS would have to pay for them. It was intended that the Canadian managers would remain at Inverlat only until the Mexican managers developed the skills to manage the bank effectively on their own.

With the exception of a handful of the most senior officers in the bank, employees at Inverlat had no direct means of receiving information about the progression of the nego-tiations with BNS. Instead, they were forced to rely on often inaccurate reports from the Mexican media. As the negotiation progressed, support among Inverlat employees for a deal with BNS was very strong. Inverlat employees did not want to become government bureaucrats and viewed BNS as a savior that would bring money, technology and exper-tise.

EMPLOYEE EXPECTATIONS

Soon after the deal was completed with BNS, however, the general euphoria was gradu-ally replaced by the fear of actions the Canadians were likely to take as they assumed their management role. Senior managers were worried that they would be replaced by some-one younger, who spoke English and had an MBA. Rumors, supported by inaccurate reports in local newspapers, ran rampant. One newspaper reported that as many as 180 senior level managers would be imported to Inverlat from BNS in Canada.

Anxiety mounted as speculation increased about the magnitude of downsizing that BNS would implement as it restructured the bank in its turnaround. Although BNS had purchased banks in other Latin American countries, few Inverlat employees, including the most senior management, had any knowledge about the strategies that BNS manage-ment had used. Inverlat managers felt that their employees viewed BNS as a "gringo" corporation, and expected them to take the same actions other U.S. companies had taken as they restructured companies they had purchased in Mexico. Most believed that if any foreign bank purchased Inverlat, most of the senior management team would be dis-placed and up to half of the bank staff would be let go. Similarly, very few managers knew the details of the contract that limited the number of managers that could come to the bank from Canada.

Very few of the Mexican employees had had any significant contact with Canadian managers, but the majority expected behavior similar to that of U.S. managers. Only a handful of senior level managers had been in contact during the due diligence and the Canadians realized that they required greater insight into the Mexican culture if they were to manage effectively. As a result, the members of the senior team that were going to manage the Mexican bank arrived in Mexico one month in advance to study Spanish. The Canadian managers studied in an intensive program in Cuernavaca, a small city

80 km southwest of Mexico City. During the three-week course, lectures were available on the Mexican culture. Mexican managers were extremely impressed by this attempt by the Canadians to gain a better understanding of the situation they were entering and thought the consideration was very respectful. One manager commented that:

> At the first meeting, the Canadians apologized because it would be in English, but promised that the next would be in Spanish. The fact is, some are still in English, but the approach and the attempt were very important.

Four months later, the Canadian team was still undergoing intense tutorial sessions in Spanish on a daily basis with varying levels of success.

Canadian managers said they were trying to guard against putting people into positions simply because they were bilingual. A Canadian manager, expressing his commitment to function in Spanish, commented that:

> There are 16 Canadians down here and 10,000 Mexicans. Surely to God, the 16 Canadians can learn Spanish rather than trying to teach the 10,000 Mexicans English or having people feel that they are being left out of promotions or opportunities just because they don't speak English. This is a Spanish-speaking country and the customers speak Spanish.

INVERLAT AND BNS CULTURES

In Canada, BNS was considered the bank with the most stringent financial control systems of the country's largest banks. Stringent, not only in deciding not to spend money in non-essential areas, but also in maintaining a tough system of policies and controls that ensured that managers held to their budgets.

Inverlat executives, on the other hand, were accustomed to almost complete autonomy with little or no control imposed on their spending. Very little analysis was done to allocate resources to a project, and adherence to budget was not monitored. Mexican managers believed that greater controls such as the ones used by BNS should be implemented in Inverlat, but they also felt that conflicts would arise.

An early example experienced in the bank was a new policy implemented by BNS management to control gifts received by managers from clients. BNS managers imposed a limit of 500 pesos[2] for the maximum value of a gift that could be received by an executive. Gifts of larger value could be accepted, but were then raffled off to all employees of the bank at Christmas. Some Mexican managers took offence at the imposition of an arbitrary limit. They felt that it was an indication that BNS did not trust their judgement. Managers thought that it would be better if the bank communicated the need for the use of good judgement when accepting gifts and then trusted their managers to act appropriately.

MANDATE OF BNS

Two months after the arrival of the Canadian executive team, the new bank chairman, Bill Sutton gave an address to 175 senior executives within Inverlat. The purpose of the address was threefold: to outline management's main objectives in the short term; to unveil the new organizational structure of senior level managers; and to reassure employees that no staff reductions would be undertaken for the first year.

The primary objectives, later printed in a special company-wide bulletin were the following:

1. Identify all non-performing loans of the bank.
2. Develop an organization focussed on the client.
3. Improve the productivity and efficiency of all operations and activities.
4. Improve the profitability of the 315 branches.
5. Develop a liability strategy.
6. Improve the integrity of the financial information.

These objectives were generally well received by the Mexican managers. Some criticized them as being too intangible and difficult to measure. Most, however, believed that the general nature of the objectives was more practical, given the type of changes that were being made in the first year. They did agree that the goals would need to be adjusted as planning became more focussed during the 1997 budget planning process.

The new management structure differed sharply from the existing structure of the bank. The original eight geographic regions were reduced to four. Managers were pleased to see that the head of each of these divisions was Mexican and it was generally viewed as a promotion for the managers.

The second change was the nature in which the Canadians were added to the management structure. The senior Canadian managers became "Directores Generales Adjuntos (DGAs)" or senior vice presidents of several key areas, displacing Mexican managers. The Mexican DGAs not directly replaced by Canadians would now report to one or more of the Canadian DGAs, but this was not reflected in the organization chart (see Exhibit 18.1). Mexican DGAs retained their titles and formally remained at the same level as their Canadian counterparts.

Mexican managers later reported mixed feelings by employees about whether or not they worked under a Canadian or Mexican DGA. Many felt that a Mexican DGA and his (there were no female DGAs working within the bank) employees were more "vulnerable" than a Canadian; however, senior managers also felt that they had an opportunity to ascend to the DGA position when it was being held by a Mexican. Many felt that Canadian managers would always hold the key positions in the bank and that certain authority would never be relinquished to a Mexican. This was not the message that BNS management wanted to convey. One of Jim O'Donnell's first comments to his employees was that he would only be in Mexico until one of them felt confident that they could fill his shoes.

The last message was the new management's commitment not to reduce staff levels. A policy of "no hires, no fires" was put in place. Employees were able to breathe a sigh of relief. Many had expected the Canadian management team to reduce staff by 3000 to 5000 employees during the first several months after their arrival.

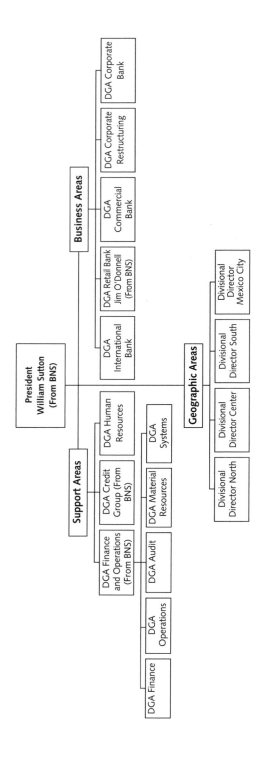

Exhibit 18.1 Grupo Financiero Inverlat Organizational Chart (Post-Re-organization)

THE COMMUNICATION CHALLENGE

Canadian and Mexican managers already experienced many of the difficulties that the two different languages could present. Many of the most senior Mexican managers spoke English, but the remaining managers required translators when speaking with the Canadians. Even when managers reporting directly to them spoke English, Canadians felt frustration at not being able to speak directly to the next level below. One manager commented that "sometimes, I feel like a bloody dictator" referring to the need to communicate decisions to his department via his most senior officers.

Meetings

Even when all managers at a meeting spoke English, the risk of mis-communication was high. A Mexican manager recalled one of the early meetings in English attended by several Mexicans. Each of the Mexican managers left the meeting with little doubt about what had been decided during the meeting. It was only later, when the Mexicans spoke of the proceedings in Spanish, that they realized they each had a different interpretation about what had transpired. What they found even more alarming was that each manager had heard what he had wanted to hear, clearly demonstrating to themselves the effect of their biases on their perception of events.

This problem might have been exacerbated by the way some of the Canadians chose to conduct meetings. Mexican managers were accustomed to a flexible atmosphere in which they were free to leave the room or carry on side-conversations as they saw fit. Canadian managers became frustrated and changed the meeting style to a more structured, controlled atmosphere similar to what they used in Canada. The Mexican managers were told that breaks would be scheduled every two hours and that only then should they get up from the table or leave the room.

Canadian managers believed that the original conduct of the Mexican managers during meetings was due to a lack of discipline and that the new conduct would lead to higher productivity. The Canadians did not recognize the negative impact that could result from the elimination of the informal interactions that had occurred in the original style.

Beyond language

Despite the cross cultural training received in Cuernavaca, some Canadians still felt they had a lot to learn about the cultural nuances that could create major pitfalls. Jim O'Donnell recalled a meeting at which he and several Mexican managers were having difficulty with some material developed by another Mexican not present at the meeting. Jim requested that this manager join them to provide further explanation. Several minutes later, as this person entered the room, Jim said jokingly, "OK, HERE's the guy that screwed it all up." The manager was noticeably upset. It was not until later, after some explaining, that Jim's comment was understood to be a joke. Jim said it brought home the fact that, in the Mexican culture, it was unacceptable, even in jest, to be critical of someone in front of other people.

This was easier said than done. Often, what the Canadians considered a minor differ-ence of opinion could appear as criticism that Mexican managers would prefer be made behind closed doors when coming from a more senior manager. One Mexican manager commented on the risks of disagreeing with an employee when others were present:

> When someone's boss is not in agreement, or critical of actions taken by an employee and says something during a meeting with other employees present, other managers will use it as an opportunity to also say bad things about the manager. Instead, when a disagreement arises in an open meeting, the senior manager should say "see me later, and we will discuss it".

To the contrary, the Canadian managers were trying to encourage an environment in which all managers participated in meetings and positive criticism was offered and ac-cepted.

Mexican communication style

On verbal communication, one of the original Inverlat managers commented:

> In Mexico, interactions between individuals are extremely polite. Because Mexicans will make every effort not to offend the person they are dealing with, they are careful to "sugar-coat" almost everything they say. Requests are always accompanied by "por favor", no matter how insignificant the request.
>
> Mexicans often speak the diminutive form. For example: *Esperame* means *Wait for me*. *Esperame un rato* means *Wait for me a moment*. A Mexican would more often say *Esperame un ratito*. "Ratito" is the diminutive form meaning "a very short moment". It is not as direct.
>
> This politeness is extended into other interactions. Every time a Mexican meets a coworker or subordinate, a greeting such as "Hello, how are you?" is appropriate, even if it is the fourth or fifth time that day that they have met. If you don't do this, the other person will think you are angry with him or her or that you are poorly educated.

One Canadian manager explained that some of the Mexican managers he dealt with went to great lengths to avoid confrontation. He was frustrated when the Mexicans would "tell him what he wanted to hear". Often these managers would consent to something that they could or would not do, simply to avoid a confrontation at the time.

Other messages: intended or otherwise

Due to the high level of anxiety, Mexican managers were very sensitive to messages they read into the actions taken by the Canadians. This process began before the Canadians made any significant changes.

As the Canadians began to plan the new organizational structure, they conducted a series of interviews with the senior Mexican managers. The Canadians decided who they would talk to based on areas where they believed they required more information. Unfor-tunately, many managers believed that if they were not spoken to, then they were not considered of importance to the Canadians and should fear for their positions. Even after the organizational structure was revealed and many Mexican managers found themselves in good positions, they still retained hard feelings, believing that they had not been considered important enough to provide input into the new structure.

Similarly, at lower levels in the bank, because of the lack of activity in the economy as a whole, many employees were left with time on their hands. Because many employees feared staff reductions at some point, they believed that those with the most work or those being offered new work were the ones that would retain their jobs.

Communications as an on-going process

When Jim held his first meeting with the nine senior managers reporting to him, he began by saying that none of them would have their jobs in two months. Realizing the level of anxiety at that point, he quickly added that he meant they would all be shuffled around to other areas of the retail bank. Jim explained that this would give them an opportunity to learn about other areas of the bank and the interdependencies that needed to be considered when making decisions.

Jim stuck to his word, and within two months, all but one of the managers had been moved. Some, however, had experienced anxiety about the method by which they were moved. Typically, Jim would meet with an employee and tell him that in two or three days he would report to a new area (generally, Mexican managers gave at least a month's notice). When that day arrived, Jim would talk to them for 30 to 45 minutes about their new responsibilities and goals, and then he would send them on their way.

For many of the Mexicans, this means of communication was too abrupt. Many wondered if they had been moved from their past jobs because of poor performance. More senior Mexican managers explained that often these managers would come to them and ask why Jim had decided to move them. Most of the Mexicans felt that more communication was required about why things were happening the way they were.

Accountability

Early on, the Canadian managers identified an almost complete lack of accountability within the bank. Senior managers had rarely made decisions outside the anonymity of a committee and when resources were committed to a project, it was equally rare for someone to check back to see what results were attained. As a result, very little analysis was done before a new project was approved and undertaken.

The first initiative taken by the Canadians to improve the level of analysis, and later implementation, was the use of what they called the "business case". The case represented a cost benefit analysis that would be approved and reviewed by senior managers. Initially, it was difficult to explain to the Mexican managers how to provide the elements of analysis that the Canadians required. The Mexicans were given a framework, but they initially returned cases that adhered too rigidly to the outline. Similarly, managers would submit business cases of 140 pages for a $35,000 project.

Cases required multiple revisions to a point of frustration on both sides, but it was only when an analysis could be prepared that satisfied the Canadians and was understood by both parties, that it could be certain that they all had the same perception of what they were talking about.

Some of the Mexican managers found the business case method overly cumbersome and felt that many good ideas would be missed because of the disincentive created by the business case. One manager commented that "It is a bit discouraging. Some people around here feel like you need to do a business case to go to the bathroom."

Most agreed that a positive element of the business case was the need it created to talk with other areas of the bank. To do a complete analysis, it was often necessary to contact other branches of the bank for information because their business would be affected. This was the first time that efforts across functional areas of the bank would be coordinated. To reinforce this notion, often Canadian managers required that senior managers from several areas of the bank grant their approval before a project in a business case could move forward.

Matrix responsibility

Changes in the organizational structure further complicated the implementation of a system of accountability. Senior management had recognized a duplication of services across the different functional areas of the bank. For example, each product group had its own marketing and systems departments. These functions were stripped away and consolidated into central groups that would service all areas of the organization.

Similarly, product groups had been responsible for the development and delivery of their products. Performance was evaluated based on the sales levels each product group could attain. Under the initial restructuring, the product groups would no longer be responsible for the sale of their products, only for their design. Instead, the branches would become a delivery network that would be responsible for almost all contact with the client. As a result, managers in product groups, who were still responsible for ensuring the sales levels, felt that they were now being measured against criteria over which they had no direct control. The Canadian management team was finding it very difficult to explain to the Mexicans that they now had to "influence" instead of "control". Product managers were being given the role of "coaches" who would help the branch delivery network to offer their product most effectively.

As adjustments were made to the structure, the Mexican manager's perception of his status also had to be considered. In the management hierarchy, the Mexican manager's relationships were with the people in the various positions that they dealt with, not with the positions themselves. When a person was moved, subordinates felt loyalty to that individual. As a result, Mexican managers moving within an organization (or even to another organization) often did so with a small entourage of employees who accompanied them.

STAFF REDUCTIONS

As services within the bank were consolidated, it was obvious that staff reductions would be required. Inverlat staff were comforted by the bank's commitment to retain all staff for the first year, particularly when considering the poor state of the economy and the banking sector; but, even at lower levels of the organization, the need for reductions was apparent. Some managers complained that the restructuring process was being slowed considerably by the need to find places for personnel who were clearly no longer required.

Motivations for retaining staffing levels were twofold. First, BNS did not want to tarnish the image of its foreign investment in Mexico with massive reductions at the outset. When the Spanish bank, Banco Bilbao Viscaya (BBV), purchased Banca Cremi the previous year, they began the restructuring process with a staff reduction of over 2000 employees. BNS executives thought that this action had not been well received by the Mexican government or marketplace.

The second reason BNS management felt compelled to wait for staff reductions was that they wanted adequate time to identify which employees were productive and would fit into the new organizational culture, and which employees would not add significant value. The problem was, quality employees were not sure if they would have a job in a year, and many managers thought that employees would begin to look for secure positions in other organizations. One Canadian manager commented that even some employees who were performing well in their current positions would ultimately lose their jobs. Many thought action needed to be taken sooner than later. A senior Mexican manager explained the situation:

> Take the worst case scenario, blind guessing. At least then, you will be correct 50% of the time and retain some good people. If you wait, people within the organization will begin to look for other jobs and the market will choose who it wants. But as the market hires away your people, it will be correct at 90% of the time and you will be left with the rest.

Until that point, not many managers had been hired away from the bank. Many felt that this was due to the poor condition of the banking sector. As the economy improved, however, many believed that the talented managers would begin to leave the bank if job security could not be improved.

Jim felt that something was needed to communicate a sense of security to the talented managers they could already identify, but he was not certain how to proceed.

CONCLUSION

Jim felt that the Canadian team had been relatively successful in the early months. Many managers referred to the period as the "Honeymoon Stage". It was generally felt that the situation would intensify as managers looked for results from the restructured organization and as staff reductions became a reality. Jim then wondered how he could best prepare for the months ahead. Much of the communication with employees to date had been on an ad hoc basis. Jim did not feel they could take the risk of starting reductions without laying out a plan. The negative rumors would cause the bank to lose many of its most valued Mexican managers.

Notes

1 Director General Adjunto is the Mexican equivalent of an Executive Vice President.
2 In late 1996, one Mexican peso was valued at approximately US$0.0128.

Part IV

Training and Development

19 Diversity Training: A Competitive Weapon   183
        Jenny C. McCune
20 Training Across Cultures   190
        Joyce L. Francis
21 Strategy and HRM Initiatives for the '00s Environment:
        Redefining Roles and Boundaries, Linking
        Competencies and Resources   196
        *Richard M. Hodgetts, Fred Luthans, and John W.
        Slocum, Jr.*
22 Global Dual-Career Couple Mentoring: A Phase Model
        Approach   211
        Michael Harvey and Danielle Wiese
23 *Case*: Bhiwar Enterprises   234
        Gordon Brannan and Joseph J. DiStefano

Chapter 19

Diversity Training: A Competitive Weapon

Jenny C. McCune

Melting pot. Glorious mosaic. Multiculturalism. Whatever you call it, the United States, always a nation of immigrants, is becoming more diverse, and not just racially so. Differences in gender, age, sexual orientation and color are redefining the face of the nation.

Companies are reacting by instituting workplace diversity programs. Approximately a third of the Fortune 500 had workplace diversity programs in place last year with another third planning to do so in the next five years, according to Earl Hill, a professor of organization management at Emory University's Goizueta Business School in Atlanta.

Until recently, most companies tackled diversity as a way to comply with government Equal Employment Opportunity and affirmative action regulations. "Now businesses see such programs as methods for gaining an edge over competitors. The number of companies implementing diversity programs is increasing because of the belief that it constitutes a competitive advantage due to [reduced] costs, resource acquisition, marketing, creativity, problem solving and system flexibility," Hill says.

Companies that have slashed their payrolls want to do more with fewer workers, which means that employees from wide-ranging backgrounds must be able to work together. And since their customers and global marketplace are more diverse, employees must help them respond.

"The biggest change is that companies are coming to understand that workplace diversity is a strategic business initiative, it's not just a nice thing to do," says John Kirksey, diversity practice leader at Towers Perrin in New York. "They believe the future of their companies is going to hinge on how they handle diversity."

Because of its growing importance, companies are integrating diversity management into how they conduct business rather than having stand-alone programs. That's why one of Kirksey's clients has its vice president of sales in charge of diversity. It stresses its importance and it's also a way to weave its diversity programs throughout the entire corporate fabric. "It's strategic and something that the company must address from all directions," Kirksey says.

Kirksey, who had been in business for 25 years, says, "I am quite heartened by what I'm seeing. Corporate America is taking this seriously and considers managing workplace diversity as crucial for themselves and for the entire nation." Here are the tales of four companies and their quest to manage diversity.

Texaco: Work in Progress

"We have a workforce diversity strategy, not a program," stresses Edward Gadsden, manager of U.S. workforce diversity and EEO compliance for Texaco Inc. in White Plains, N.Y. Why is Gadsden so into semantics? "A program implies something sitting off in a corner gathering dust; our approach is an organizational change approach. Workplace diversity is part of and tied into company issues and values," he explains.

Texaco's strategy started to take shape two years ago when Gadsden came on board. According to the diversity manager, the impetus stemmed from a number of sources: changing demographics in the workplace and Texaco's customer base, the oil company's quest to be a top-tier company, and the need to fully utilize every member of an organization that over the past five years has shrunk from approximately 27,000 to 19,300 employees.

"To be quite honest, it was a recognition that in order for us to be competitive and in the top tier, we needed to be more efficient and have everyone work together," Gadsden says.

Through focus groups and a national survey of more than 3,000 of its workers, Texaco learned how employees felt about the oil company in general, its training and development, its promotion policies and compensation, and whether Texaco and its managers valued a diverse workforce.

The survey results? In general, workers felt good about Texaco, but did point to the need to improve promotion of minorities. They also wanted managers to be held more accountable on managing diversity and better educated on how to communicate with employees of differing backgrounds.

Based on those findings, Gadsden put together a four-phased plan, what in essence is Texaco's diversity strategy.

STAGE ONE: Form a cross-function team to look at the promotion process and find ways to improve it. The team's members hailed from different departments as well as cut across geographical, gender and race lines. The team discovered that employees wanted a streamlined application process and more feedback on the outcome of promotion requests.

STAGE TWO: Act on the team's findings. The cross-function team published a brochure to educate workers on how to get promoted. Texaco redesigned how it posted job openings. For example, at employees' request, the company instituted a feedback session so employees would be told how they fared in an interview. The company also increased the number of job vacancies that are posted internally and changed the application process. Employees now have to tell their immediate supervisor about going after a new job only after they have made the first cut and have been selected for an interview. Previously workers had to get permission from their bosses before applying for a new position.

STAGE THREE: Develop a diversity training component. Gadsden worked with a team of Texaco HR professionals and an outside consultant to develop what became the

Texaco Diversity Learning Experience. It comes in three flavors – a two-day workshop for executives, a two-day workshop for managers and supervisors, and a one-day affair for employees. The program is an interactive workshop with exercises completed by the participants in addition to lectures and videos. "It's designed to help them understand how it feels to be different in an organization," the diversity manager says. In addition to the general overview, the workshop includes information about how to communicate with people of different backgrounds and experiences.

Texaco started at the top with its Diversity Learning Experience. Its highest-level executives, 75 in total including the CEO, chairman of the board and vice chairman, were the first to take the course. "The leadership drives the behavior of the rest of the corporation," Gadsden says. "Our managers would not buy into it if they didn't see that the heads of [the] corporation believed and were acting upon this."

STAGE FOUR: Bring diversity training to all employees. Currently, the next level of management – 2,800 managers and supervisors – are going through the process, which should be completed in 1997, when the program will be rolled out to the rank and file.

One of the more difficult aspects of workplace diversity is finding the funding for it. Gadsden has succeeded in part by being frugal. He worked with a group of 14 independent consultants rather than handing the contract over to one big firm. He bargained and haggled with his vendors, getting them to reduce fees in return for a guaranteed amount of work. While he uses outside facilitators for his workshops, he also employs internal staff to save money, plus the employees learn by running the programs. Gadsden estimates his cost at $224 a person versus what Gadsden calls a company average of about $1,379 per person.

Like any workplace diversity program, Texaco's is a work in progress. But Gadsden firmly believes his program will be successful and its success will be measurable. He'll compare post-workshop promotion rates for women and minorities at Texaco with the previous internal rate as well as benchmark them against industry averages.

Gadsden also believes he has enough anecdotal data in hand to show that he's on the right track. "We have a manager in one of our plants, in Bakersfield [Calif.]. This was one of our lowest production operations two years ago. This manager implemented a number of team-based initiatives including diversity . . . Today that plant is having its best year ever."

UNUM: VISIBLE DIVERSITY

Portland, Maine, where UNUM Life Insurance Company of America is based, may not be as ethnically diverse as New York or Los Angeles, but that doesn't keep the disability insurer from taking workplace diversity seriously.

Prior to 1989, UNUM, a $13 billion disability and special risk insurance company, viewed workplace diversity like many other larger corporations did: as a matter of complying with the EEO and affirmative action laws.

"We were in compliance mode, doing affirmative action, and trying to bring women and minorities into the company," recalls Sandy Bishop, manager of UNUM's diversity programs. However, UNUM was experiencing high turnover among the very minority workers it was trying so hard to recruit.

The insurer began looking inward. Was it company culture that was driving women and people of color away? UNUM decided that having a diverse workforce was critical. "We built a business case for it," Bishop says. "We wanted our business environment to mirror our world, the people we were insuring."

Its proactive program began simply enough with its HR staff developing a diversity philosophy. In addition, the HR department brokered meetings between senior executives, the majority of whom were white males, and representatives of minority groups. "They would come and talk to senior management and tell them what it was like being a minority and working in this corporation," Bishop says.

The meetings opened UNUM's eyes. "[Senior managers] didn't have a clue what these nondominant groups were experiencing," Bishop says. "What we found was that members of these nondominant groups were spending more time trying to hide in the organization. They were editing their words, trying to be invisible." That was a drain on productivity, plus many valuable contributions were left unmade, the diversity manager says.

Like Texaco, UNUM began with an internal audit of what needed to be done. Through Dialogues on Diversity, people of various ethnic persuasions would come together to talk about issues: how people were treated at UNUM, what programs and plans should be instituted to help raise awareness. In 1992, 18 Dialogues on Diversity were held involving 227 employees.

Out of that came a three-day diversity workshop designed to build "cultural competence." Attendance has increased from 100 people the first year to 250 the third year. It is voluntary and open to all employees.

In its effort to integrate the diversity debate with other business issues, UNUM has an informal diversity structure. There's just Sandy Bishop who acts as a facilitator, but most departments play some role, and the idea is for employees to come forth with plans and ideas.

Corporate communications, for example, publishes a newsletter addressing diversity issues. Last year UNUM founded a Diversity Board made up of members from the five affinity groups that it has identified (people of color, women, people with disabilities, gays/lesbians, older workers). Bishop heads up the Diversity Board, which also includes Stephen B. Center, UNUM's president. The board meets monthly to look at "systematic changes within the organization" to encourage diversity. It's also looking at how the program should be developed from now into the next century.

UNUM also has an education committee that set up "Lunch and Learn" talks on diversity. For example, the company invited John Jenkins, mayor of a nearby town who has also sat on the U.S. Department of Labor's Glass Ceiling Commission, to speak.

How many UNUM employees have participated? Bishop says it's hard to gauge, but last year she received more than 500 surveys from employees on UNUM's various diversity activities.

UNUM also discovered that to manage diversity means moving beyond the workplace. Its minority workers had no social net to turn to outside of the company. Their children were picked on at school because they were different. Minority employees couldn't find places to worship.

As part of its outreach activities, the company has also launched community programs that deal in diversity. "We provide financial support as well as real hands-on training," Bishop says. There's a UNUM mentoring program for local high school students, Students for whom English is a second language are paired off with UNUM employees. The insurance company also holds panels at local schools on dealing with discrimination. For example, UNUM might sponsor a gathering where older employees would speak with students and open a dialogue between the generations, Bishop says.

While UNUM's earlier efforts were restricted to company headquarters, the disability insurer this year is extending its diversity programs to its branch offices. And of the five diversity seminars that UNUM will hold this year, three of them will be in remote locations.

Success is difficult to measure, however. Bishop says that some of UNUM's customers have asked if they can "copy" UNUM's diversity programs, and she views this as a sign of success. She's also gotten a lot of positive feedback from employees. Finally, she sees UNUM's employees taking on her role, for example asking whether it was appropriate to play Christmas music on the phone lines since Christmas isn't a holiday that all religious groups celebrate. "My goal is to do such a good job that I'll eliminate the need for my job," she says.

GTE: Mutual Respect

Telecommunications giant GTE got serious about diversity in the early 1990s for two reasons, says Randy MacDonald, the company's senior vice president of human resources and administration. "First was a recognition of the changing workplace . . . more spouses working and more immigration. Second, and this is still evolving, is that while we're U.S.-based, the workplace is becoming global and we need to address marketplace diversity."

For example, the company staffs its Southern California offices with bilingual employees who speak English and Spanish. As GTE expands around the globe, "it will require bilingual, trilingual employees," MacDonald says. Therefore, hiring people with different backgrounds and skills is imperative.

GTE combines its workplace diversity efforts with its work/family programs (telecommuting, flextime, seminars on balancing work and family). The diversity end consists of minority recruitment, employee career advancement, training on managing and being part of a diverse workforce, as well as multicultural awareness events that celebrate diversity.

The telecommunications company has made a conscious effort to recruit minorities on college campuses, although, as MacDonald points out, "Diversity is an important element, but we're looking for the best person for the job."

Once a person is on board, he or she is eligible for career advancement training, regardless of ethnic background. GTE prides itself on job training for its entire workforce, not just its minority employees. For example, the company regularly holds seminars on the subject and is scheduling a "How to Manage Your Career" Saturday teleconference for later on this year.

The company does offer some specialized educational programs for minorities. For example, its 18-month GTE Associate Development Program gives "high-potential" individuals exposure to line and management positions and then a chance to interview for appropriate positions within GTE.

In fact, MacDonald shies away from such terms as "minority development." As far as

GTE is concerned, dealing with a diverse employee population includes advising parents with high-school-age children how to plan for college expenses or how to plan for retirement. Attendance at all training sessions is voluntary, although some employees are advised by their managers when particular subject matter may be useful to them.

The cornerstone of the Stamford-Conn.-based company's managing diversity program is training. GTE annually spends in excess of $160 million on employee education. "We have hundreds of training courses with 30 to 40 management-type training programs and at least 30 to 40 percent have some sort of diversity complaints," MacDonald says. For example, the company regularly sponsors a two-day seminar, "Managing Personnel Diversity," which is open to all managers. In addition, several GTE regional operations have developed or are in the process of designing similar training seminars for hourly workers.

The goal of such programs? "That people recognize that diversity exists and that while not everyone will agree on issues, there's a need to treat each other with respect," MacDonald says.

Through its actions, the company has increased minority and female representation among its managers. As of last year, roughly 45 percent of new management recruits were women, and 35 percent were minority.

MacDonald says he measures success not by quotas or percentage of minorities employed, but by employee satisfaction. The company annually surveys its employees. Last year, the company received an 80 percent approval rating.

GANNETT: TOTAL INTEGRATION

Gannett Corp. Inc. may well have the granddaddy of diversity programs. The media conglomerate first embarked on managing diversity in 1980.

The publisher of *USA Today* and many small-town papers, as well as the owner of numerous radio and television stations, Gannett wanted to be an industry leader in minority recruitment and retention. It also saw a need to better mirror its audience in terms of the composition of its workforce. Finally, Gannett wanted not only to publish all the news, but to act as a force for change in communities in which it was based and it saw a diverse workforce as the means toward that end.

After 16 years, it looks like the Arlington, Va.-based firm has succeeded in diversifying its employee ranks. Total minority employment was 12 percent in 1980; today it's 26 percent. In terms of managerial positions, minorities took up 9 percent of the job slots when Gannett began focusing on diversity. At the end of last year that figure had jumped to 21 percent. The company has also worked to diversify its board of directors. "Thirty-one percent of our board is minority . . . You have to diversify the ranks of people that run the business," says José Berrios, vice president of diversity and personnel.

While minority recruitment was first emphasized by Gannett, the media company has expanded into career advancement training. "We now handle diversity across the board," Berrios says. "We're training and developing up through the management pipeline."

The company also publishes an in-house newsletter devoted to the topic and sponsors noon seminars, for example on different cultural communications techniques, how communication between members of different genders works, and so on. These lunchtime workshops are open to all employees.

In addition, some of Gannett's regional locations have set up mentoring programs for minorities, but "the newspaper, TV station or radio station have done this on their own. There is not a formal companywide mentoring program," Berrios says.

According to the diversity manager, what has made Gannett's program work is the fact that it is closely aligned with overall business aims. "You have to understand the business tie-in," Berrios says. "It's not an HR program, it's a business objective."

Finally, like any other business venture, a company needs to have goals for a diversity program and the ability to measure results. "You have to have accountability to make it work," Berrios says. "After 16 years, our program is a part of the culture. It's part of everything that we do."

Chapter 20

Training Across Cultures

Joyce L. Francis

The Hudson Institute's landmark study of the future U.S. labor force, *Workforce 2000: Work and Workers for the 21st Century* (Johnston and Packer, 1987), captured wide attention and stimulated a lively debate about the rapidly changing U.S. demographics. Among their conclusions is the remarkable prediction that, due to the "baby bust" of the 1970s and large waves of immigration from Asia and Latin America during the 1980s, 22 percent of the new entrants into the U.S. work force will be immigrant men and women. It is anticipated that 600,000 people are expected to immigrate to the United States every year for the balance of the century, and two-thirds of working-age immigrants are expected to join the labor force. This means that, by the year 2000, nearly 10 percent of the total work force will be composed of immigrants (Johnston and Packer, 1987). In urban areas, the percentage will be far higher.

This increasing cultural diversity in the workplace has significant implications for human resource management and development programs and leads to an important question: Does this mass movement across national borders mean that, when we work and live together, cultural differences will diminish or even disappear? Put another way, will the supposed "melting pot" absorb our differences, sending us forth as members of a new and blended culture? Laurent (1983), of the European Institute of Business Administration, found that the answer is an unambiguous no. In fact, he found quite the opposite. He studied the philosophies and behaviors of managers in nine Western European and two Asian countries, as well as the United States, and came to some surprising conclusions.

Laurent found cultural differences more pronounced among foreign employees working within the same multinational organization than among employees working for organizations in their native lands. When they are working outside their native land, it seems that Germans become more German, Japanese become more Japanese, and so on. He concluded that organizational culture, rather than creating homogeneity over time, is in fact a catalyst for increasing cultural differences. Why this might be so remains unanswered. Adler (1986) has argued that the conforming pressure of the organizational culture brings out employees' resistance, causing them to cling more firmly to their own national identities. Whatever the reason, the evidence makes it clear that employees maintain or even enhance their cultural identity and behavioral patterns when working in a foreign culture.

The implications of this cultural diversity in the workplace for HRD are already being felt. Attempts to come to terms with this phenomenon have resulted in a plethora of training programs under such titles as "Valuing Diversity" or "Managing Diversity" (Geber, 1990). While such programs with a cultural awareness *content* are important in addressing this demographic shift in the workplace, it is equally critical that training professionals concern themselves with the *process* of training for this changing clientele. As training environments become more culturally diverse, are trainers responding to the demographic shift with respect to instructional design? All too often, it is merely assumed that, by learning a new language and joining a new learning environment, participants will naturally adapt to new learning styles.

This article challenges the reader to reconsider. It addresses two questions: Will the training techniques that have been developed and proved effective with a largely homogeneous clientele continue to be appropriate in the culturally diverse work force of the future? If not, what guidelines can training professionals utilize to determine what techniques might be more appropriate and effective?

Is Adult Learning Theory Culture-Bound?

Most HRD professionals would likely describe themselves as *experiential* trainers, subscribing to the adult learning theories of John Dewey (1938), Kurt Lewin (1951), Malcolm Knowles (1970), and others. The underlying assumptions behind experiential training are worth investigating to begin determining the universality or cultural relativity of the field's mainstream methodologies. Holvino (1982) found experiential learning to be

- Active and participatory
- Learning how to learn
- Based on interdependence or independence
- Based on learner's internal direction
- Shared responsibility for learning
- Built on experience and knowledge of learners
- Shared access to power and knowledge
- Focused on problem identification and solution
- Information seeking and sharing

If we can agree that these assumptions do indeed underlie adult or experiential learning theory, then let us look to studies of cultural differences for some indication of their universality.

In the late sixties and early seventies, IBM compiled a remarkable data bank of employee attitudes, surveying over 116,000 employees from seventy-two countries in ten different languages. About 60 of their 105 questions were designed to elicit information on the employees' basic values and beliefs. Geert Hofstede, a Dutch industrial psychologist and cross-cultural researcher, analyzed these cultural data and published his findings (1980, 1986, 1991). Hofstede determined that cultures differed along four work-related value dimensions. He developed an index of relative scores for each dimension with about one hundred points between the lowest- and highest-scoring country. These indexed scores are available for fifty countries and three regions. Two of Hofstede's cultural dimensions are particularly relevant for HRD. The other two dimensions, individualism-collectivism and masculinity-femininity, also affect trainee preferences (see Hofstede, 1986), though I do not believe they are as important for the training environment as the two dimensions discussed here.

Power Distance measures the extent to which the *less* powerful members of a society accept an unequal distribution of power. Inequality exists in all cultures, but the degree to which it occurs and is tolerated varies between one culture and another. In organizations, the level of Power Distance is related to the degree of centralization of authority and the degree of autocratic leadership. A centralized, autocratic organization has a high level of Power Distance; a decentralized, participative organization has a low level.

In a training situation, the Power Distance dimension would describe the degree to which participants are self-directed or trainer-directed. Cultures with small Power Distance value learner-centered learning, placing a premium on trainee initiative. The effectiveness of training in these cultures is related to the amount of communication between trainer and participants as well as among participants. Knowledge can be gained from any competent person. Cultures with large Power Distance, on the other hand, value trainer-centered learning, placing a premium on order. Training effectiveness is considered a product of the knowledge and expertise of the trainer, and knowledge is to be obtained from the trainer (Hofstede, 1986).

Uncertainty Avoidance measures the extent to which members of a society feel threatened by unstructured, unpredictable situations and the extent to which they try to avoid these situations. Societies (and organizations) with strong Uncertainty Avoidance seek to avoid ambiguity and provide greater structure by establishing more formal rules, rejecting deviant ideas and behavior and accepting the possibility of absolute truths.

In a training situation, the Uncertainty Avoidance dimension would describe the degree to which participants seek to structure information and avoid ambiguity through generalized principles and a search for absolute truth. In cultures with weak Uncertainty Avoidance, trainers are allowed to say, "I don't know," and participants are comfortable with unanswered questions. Trainees are encouraged to seek innovative approaches to problem solving, and intellectual disagreements are viewed as stimulating. Cultures with strong Uncertainty Avoidance, on the other hand, expect the trainer to have all the answers. Trainers are considered experts; therefore, intellectual disagreements are considered disrespectful. In these cultures, participants are rewarded for accuracy in problem solving and conformity with trainer-established principles (Hofstede, 1986).

What can be learned by applying the concepts of Power Distance and Uncertainty Avoidance to the assumptions underlying adult learning theory? In experiential training, learning is expected to take place independent of the trainer. Participants learn from one another. Power, responsibility, and knowledge are shared by the participants and the trainer. There is little difference between the power of the trainer and the power of the participants, suggesting a *low Power Distance* value orientation.

In experiential training, the focus is on problem solving and learning how to learn, rather than on absolute truths. The outcomes are not predictable but grow out of the interaction of the participants, requiring periods of considerable ambiguity. Experiential training techniques assume tolerance for ambiguity and, in Hofstede's framework, a *weak Uncertainty Avoidance* value orientation.

In the absence of more complete data on learning environments, let us assume that these two dimensions, Power Distance and Uncertainty Avoidance, have an equal impact

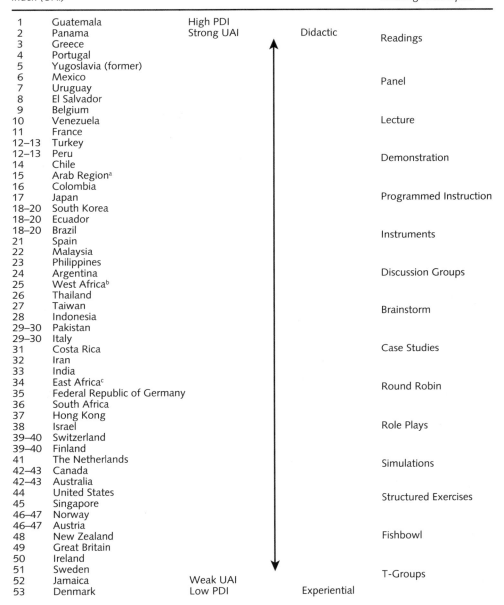

Rank Ordering of Power Distance Index (PDI) plus Uncertainty Avoidance Index (UAI)			Training Techniques
1	Guatemala	High PDI	
2	Panama	Strong UAI	Didactic	Readings
3	Greece		
4	Portugal		
5	Yugoslavia (former)		
6	Mexico		Panel
7	Uruguay		
8	El Salvador		
9	Belgium		
10	Venezuela		Lecture
11	France		
12–13	Turkey		
12–13	Peru		
14	Chile		Demonstration
15	Arab Region[a]		
16	Colombia		
17	Japan		Programmed Instruction
18–20	South Korea		
18–20	Ecuador		
18–20	Brazil		
21	Spain		Instruments
22	Malaysia		
23	Philippines		
24	Argentina		Discussion Groups
25	West Africa[b]		
26	Thailand		
27	Taiwan		
28	Indonesia		Brainstorm
29–30	Pakistan		
29–30	Italy		
31	Costa Rica		Case Studies
32	Iran		
33	India		
34	East Africa[c]		Round Robin
35	Federal Republic of Germany		
36	South Africa		
37	Hong Kong		
38	Israel		Role Plays
39–40	Switzerland		
39–40	Finland		
41	The Netherlands		Simulations
42–43	Canada		
42–43	Australia		
44	United States		Structured Exercises
45	Singapore		
46–47	Norway		
46–47	Austria		
48	New Zealand		Fishbowl
49	Great Britain		
50	Ireland		
51	Sweden		T-Groups
52	Jamaica	Weak UAI	
53	Denmark	Low PDI	Experiential	

Notes: [a] Egypt, Iraq, Kuwait, Lebanon, Libya, Saudi Arabia, United Arab Emirates.
[b] Nigeria, Ghana, Sierra Leone.
[c] Kenya, Ethiopia, Zambia.
Source: Adapted from Hofstede, 1991, pp. 26, 113, and Pfeiffer and Jones, 1983, p. 2.

Figure 20.1 The Cultural Relativity of Training Techniques

on the learning situation. By averaging the country and regional indexes of Uncertainty Avoidance and Power Distance, we can develop a continuum from countries or regions of low Power Distance and weak Uncertainty Avoidance to countries or regions of high Power Distance and strong Uncertainty Avoidance (see Figure 20.1, left side). Similar cultures appear to cluster together. Notice, for example, that many Latin cultures are toward the top of the spectrum, Asian cultures fall in the middle, and the United States, Canada, and most northern European countries are toward the bottom of the list.

The Cultural Relativity of Training Techniques

Hofstede has provided a means of placing cultures along a spectrum of value dimensions relevant to the training situation. What is needed for our purposes is a similar method for comparing training methodologies. Training techniques are commonly characterized as falling along a spectrum from *Didactic* (trainer-centered, low-risk, content-oriented) to *Experiential* (learner-centered, high-risk, process-oriented). In Hofstede's terminology, Didactic techniques can be considered to have a high Power Distance and strong Uncertainty Avoidance value orientation, while experiential techniques can be considered to have a low Power Distance and weak Uncertainty Avoidance value orientation. Pfeiffer and Jones (1983) provide a framework for placing commonly used training techniques along this spectrum of Didactic to Experiential techniques (see Figure 20.1, right side). While the framework is theirs, I have added some techniques to the spectrum, based upon my estimation of their place on the continuum.

By juxtaposing Hofstede's cultural value spectrum with this training technique spectrum, we create a guideline for predicting the relative appropriateness of different training techniques for different cultural groups. If we compare the two sides of Figure 20.1, we can predict which techniques might be appropriate for a given cultural group. *Appropriate* techniques are those that might most effectively challenge the participants without eliciting a high level of resistance. A trainer who has attempted to use a fishbowl exercise in a Latin culture has likely met with some resistance and withdrawal. Conversely, while living and working in Denmark, I often observed that lectures quickly turned into discussion groups as participants readily challenged the lecturer.

Application

This application of cultural values to training methodologies is meant to be only a guideline. Individuals differ widely within each culture and may have learning technique preferences that are quite foreign to their own culture. Moreover, the distinction of cultural differences is limited to national cultures, excluding cultural variations within nations. This is not because these domestic variations do not matter, but because there is too little information from which to draw finer distinctions within foreign cultures. In working across cultures, indeed, in any well-designed training program, alternate techniques should be planned in case participants show resistance, or, conversely, develop group trust more quickly than anticipated. In a multicultural group, it may be necessary to divide the participants into groups and offer more than one type of learning technique in particular modules.

It is also important for a trainer to consider her or his own values and beliefs in deciding on techniques. Many HRD professionals strongly believe in the effectiveness of experiential learning, and our own learning has most likely been greatly enhanced by involving both an affective and a cognitive dimension. Participants do indeed come to the learning environment with valuable knowledge and experience that the trainer may not possess. It must, however, be acknowledged that these beliefs and experiences are not universally shared. Therefore, trainers are faced with a dilemma. When training participants from cultures in which experiential techniques are foreign and at odds with cultural values, we have three choices: (1) to *discard* our own values and preferred techniques, (2) to *impose* our own values and preferred techniques, or (3) to *compromise and improvise*.

Over the years, I have undoubtedly done all three, though I like to think I am more consistently choosing the third path. As a trainer of intercultural skills, I will usually begin with U.S.-born participants by using a simulation. In training a largely Latin American group, however, I will begin by choosing techniques at the Didactic end of the spectrum. As some trust is established, I will explain my beliefs to the group and try to nudge them toward more experiential activities over time.

Moreover, techniques can be improvised to reduce the risk level. A fishbowl, for example, might become a whole-group activity that is videotaped and played back to the whole group to review and discuss, allowing all participants to feel equal risk. A simulation can be rewritten as a case study with small, voluntary role plays.

Training across cultures is both a challenge and an opportunity. HRD professionals are challenged to attend to the participants' cultural values and beliefs as well as their own in establishing learning environments and selecting training techniques. Through utilizing guidelines such as those offered here, we are given an opportunity to expand our repertoire of skills and apply our creativity to improvising on well-used techniques. The unambiguous conclusion is that these challenges and opportunities will expand as the cultural diversity of the training environment increases.

References

Adler, N.J. (1986). *International Dimensions of Organizational Behavior.* Boston: Kent.

Dewey, J. (1938). *Experience and Education.* New York: Macmillan.

Geber, B. (1990). Managing diversity. *Training, 27* (7), 23–30.

Hofstede, G. (1980). *Culture's Consequences: International Differences in Work-Related Values.* Newbury Park, CA: Sage.

Hofstede, G. (1986). Cultural differences in teaching and learning. *International Journal of Intercultural Relations, 10* (3), 301–20.

Hofstede, G. (1991). *Cultures and Organizations: Software of the Mind.* New York: McGraw-Hill.

Holvino, E. (1982). *Training of Trainers Manual.* Brattleboro, VT: Experiment in International Living.

Johnston, W.B., & Packer, A.E. (1987). *Workforce 2000: Work and Workers for the 21st Century.* Indianapolis, IN: Hudson Institute.

Knowles, M.S. (1970). *The Modern Practice of Adult Education: Andragogy vs. Pedagogy.* New York: Association Press.

Laurent, A. (1983). The cultural diversity of Western conceptions of management. *International Studies of Management and Organization, 13* (1), 75–96.

Lewin, K. (1951). *Field Theory in Social Sciences.* New York: HarperCollins.

Pfeiffer, J.W., & Jones, J.E. (1983). *Reference Guide to Handbooks and Annuals.* San Diego: University Associates.

Chapter 21

Strategy and HRM Initiatives for the '00s Environment: Redefining Roles and Boundaries, Linking Competencies and Resources

Richard M. Hodgetts, Fred Luthans, and John W. Slocum, Jr.

The year 2000 and beyond is no longer in the realm of fantasy and science fiction. The new millennium is a sobering reality facing today's managers and their organizations. According to Al Casey, former CEO of American Airlines, "The pace of change will accelerate, and it can't be managed unless it is anticipated and managers constantly reprioritize their goals." The purpose of this article is, first, to identify some of the major characteristics of this '00s environment and, second, to present two of the most important managerial initiatives for organizations to consider in order to compete successfully: the rules and conventional wisdom of strategic thinking and the role and techniques of human resource management.

THE NEW ENVIRONMENT

Obviously, there are a number of new, dramatic dimensions that characterize the '00s environment. In fact, Peter Drucker recently declared that "we are in one of those great historical periods that occur every 200 or 300 years when people don't understand the world anymore, and the past is not sufficient to explain the future." We consider the three most challenging and pragmatic parts of this environment for today's management to be, however, dealing with bigger, stronger and more agile competition, coping with mixed economic growth, and remaining on the cutting edge of e-commerce.

MNCs: BIGGER AND GEOGRAPHICALLY CONCENTRATED

The United Nations has reported that there are more than 45,000 industrial multinational corporations (MNCs) worldwide. The largest 500 of these account for about 80 percent of the world's foreign direct investment. Of these 500 firms, 443 are from the triad countries of the United States, the European Union (EU), and Japan. The breakdown, on a national basis, shows that 162 of these firms are from the United States, 155 are from the EU, and the remaining 126 are from Japan. This overall number of 443 is approximately the same as it was a decade ago, although the composition has changed slightly: American and EU firms have gained at the expense of the Japanese.

The economic power of the 500 MNCs is enormous. Collectively, small, entrepreneurial firms are important and continue to be so in the new millennium, but the largest 500 MNCs have annual revenues in excess of $11 trillion and employ over 35 million people. Additionally, these giant firms extend into a wide range of industries – from autos, chemicals, computers, and consumer goods to industrial equipment, oil, and steel production. Clearly, the large industrial MNCs have a significant impact on international business and the world economy. Unilever, for instance, controls nearly 50 percent of the detergent market in India, Nestlé 80 percent of the Chinese coffee market, and Colgate-Palmolive 75 percent of the Brazilian toothpaste market. The same is true for non-industrial MNCs. Simply put, the major multinationals are big and getting bigger. This is going to present a major challenge for managers in both small and large organizations that want to penetrate these markets in the years ahead.

A second characteristic of MNCs is that they are concentrated in specific geographic regions. Industrialized nations have invested the largest amounts of their foreign direct investment (FDI) in other industrialized nations. Developed countries have put relatively much smaller amounts in less developed countries (LDCs), such as those in Eastern Europe, in industrialized countries that have emerged in the last three decades (like Hong Kong, South Korea, and Singapore), and in newly emerging economies such as China. Specifically, most of the world's FDI is in the United States, the EU, and Japan.

The most economically advanced countries are leading the way in globalization, and companies that want to meet the coming international challenges are going to find themselves confronting strong competition in the most lucrative and well developed of markets. This will be particularly true in the EU, which is the world's largest trading bloc. Today, approximately 38 percent of all world imports and exports are attributable to the EU, while Japan and the rest of Asia generate around 20 percent of the world's total, and North America adds approximately the same. What is particularly significant about these relative percentages is that they have changed little over the last decade, even though world trade has more than doubled during this time period. The dominant countries and companies in world trade have largely been able to maintain both their presence and their position.

MIXED ECONOMIC GROWTH

While the large MNCs in the triad are dominating world trade, they may not be positioned to avoid international economic and political risks. In fact, over the last few years the turbulence of the international economic environment has presented managers with a myriad of new challenges. The U.S. economy continues to flourish, but other countries around the world have problems. In particular, Japan continues in a sustained economic decline in real gross domestic product (GDP). Southeast Asia's economic woes would seem to have bottomed out, but Germany is still languishing. China, the newest and most important country to enter the world stage in the last decade, has seen its GDP grow at a rate well below its target. In Russia, investor confidence continues to be very low, and predictions for this year are that its GDP will continue to decline; some economists are even predicting a collapse. The other former Soviet Union transitionary economies are experiencing similar economic problems.

In the short run, Finland, Ireland, Portugal, and Spain appear headed for better times, but economic growth in the EU as a whole is slowing up. The seemingly never-ending conflict in the Balkans is adding to the uncertainty in all of Europe. The South America economies continue to face problems. In some, such as Colombia, there is economic decline. Mexico, however, appears to be doing moderately well. These mixed world economic developments point to the need for international managers to remain cautious in their strategic planning. The '00s environment is going to be increasingly competitive and much riskier for direct foreign investment.

While there is a natural tendency for multinationals to build upon what made them successful in their core markets, these practices routinely get them into trouble. Consumer goods companies cannot export their business models, products, and marketing formulas and expect them to automatically work in India, Turkey, or Mexico. Emerging markets differ in their governmental policies, regulations, and macroeconomic behaviors; in the structure of their consumer markets; distribution systems; and competitors. For example, when Coca-Cola re-entered the India market several years ago, it invested heavily behind the Coke brand, using its typical global positioning. Yet Coke lost market share to Pepsi with this approach. Recognizing its mistake, Coke re-emphasized a popular local cola brand (Thumbs Up) and refocused its Coke brand advertising to be more relevant to the local Indian consumer. Once Coke pursued this strategy, its market share and profitability rapidly increased.

EVER-ADVANCING INFORMATION TECHNOLOGY

Another dimension of the new millennium environment especially relevant to management is the information revolution, which is taking a variety of different forms. A technology-driven global convergence among computers, television, telephone (including wireless communications), and Internet service providers is resulting in a technology paradox where the quality of information is increasing sharply but the price of its use is plummeting. In Europe, for example, international long distance rates, responding to deregulation and regional and global consolidation, are dropping sharply. Over the past year, they have declined by 30 percent in the Netherlands, 25 percent in France, and over 10 percent in Luxembourg, Greece, Portugal, Denmark, and Ireland.

At the same time, companies are beginning to form strategic alliance agreements to link personal computers and consumer electronic devices, thus moving closer to the creation of technology standards for digital television and other consumer products. For example, Microsoft and Sony have endorsed a technology for connecting videocassette recorders, camcorders, personal computers, and other electronic devices. Microsoft intends to license the software and use it with versions of an operating system to create a standard for non-PC products. Meanwhile, Lucent and Philips are engaged in a joint effort to produce phones for the global market.

These are all significant developments. But by far the biggest and most pervasive IT development will be e-commerce because of its ability to help firms create new international networks that cut expenses, speed delivery time, and open new markets. For example, e-commerce technology is helping to develop temporary networks of outsourcers who work on a contract basis, providing specific goods and services to meet the needs of enterprises. In many ways, e-commerce is changing the fundamental way managers think about creating and delivering value to customers. Bill Gates in his book *Business @ the Speed of Thought* argues that e-commerce should not be limited to just web sites or transactions. He states, "I'm trying to show that it's not just the transaction, it's the customer service, it's the collaboration at a distance, it's the decision about what skills you need inside your company vs. what things you can go out now on the web to take advantage of."

Cisco Systems, Intel, and General Electric, among other manufacturing firms, are utilizing the Internet to link their operations and marketing activities directly with their customers. At Cisco Systems, it's part of the business strategy to become a virtual organization by connecting relevant parts of the business and outside partners using standard Internet protocols. Such protocols connect Cisco with its web of suppliers and manufacturers, making one company. Via the company's Intranet, outside vendors directly monitor orders from Cisco customers and ship the assembled hardware to buyers later in the day, often without Cisco even touching an order.

E-commerce enables organizations to establish direct links to almost anybody, anywhere and to deliver new products and services at very low cost. The major challenge that e-commerce poses to established organizations (e.g., Merrill Lynch and Barnes and Noble) is that it enables innovative upstart firms, such as E*TRADE, Amazon.com, and Priceline.com, to circumvent previous barriers to entry. Using the Internet's portals (e.g., Yahoo and Lycos) that directly relay customers to its Web site, Amazon.com provides a direct link to customers and suppliers to perform transactions on a real-time basis. The Internet has increased price competition between firms since customers can now make price comparisons on-line. Barnes and Noble and its strategic alliance partner, the Bertelsmann Group, have countered Amazon.com's aggressive cyberspace-based promotions by enabling customers to use its web site as a direct on-line ordering system. Customers who do not want to wait for a book to be delivered from Amazon.com can go to the nearest Barnes and Noble location to pick up the book.

E-commerce firms also have the ability to adjust to customers' needs quickly. The result is that product development cycles are becoming much shorter in some industries.

E-commerce will enable firms to become quicker in how they gather, synthesize, utilize, and disseminate information. Firms that learn the fastest and are willing to experiment with new product and service offerings will become the best equipped to compete in the world of e-commerce.

NEW STRATEGIC INITIATIVES

A major initiative that must be undertaken to be successful in the '00s environment is review of corporate strategies. The approaches that were successful in the past must be radically altered in many cases. GE's Jack Welch has observed, "Anytime there is change, there is opportunity." We feel that three ways to take advantage of the change are:

First, move toward formulating and implementing strategies that go beyond current management thinking;

Second, deal with radical technologies that threaten the profitability of established firms and industries:

Third, become more entrepreneurial.

COMPETING ON THE EDGE

During the 1980s there was a wide variety of models that emerged to help explain how to formulate and implement strategy. One of the most popular was Michael Porter's five-forces model. In essence, this model suggested that strategists needed to consider five forces when examining the nature of the current environment in which they competed: new entrants, suppliers, buyers, substitutes, and competitors. More recently, Hamel and Prahalad have suggested that, instead of focusing on industry conditions, management strategists should concentrate on their companies' core competencies and use these skills, processes, and technologies to fashion a sustainable competitive advantage in their value-chain. They argue that only by building and nurturing core competencies can top management sustain the competitive advantage for their organization. Using a tree as a metaphor, the core competencies are the "roots" and the individual products/services are the "fruit."

At Motorola, fast cycle-time in production (minimizing the time between an order and the fulfillment of the order) is a core competency. This core competency rests upon a broad range of underlying skills, including design disciplines that maximize commonality across a product line, flexible manufacturing, sophisticated order-entry systems, inventory management, and supplier management. Motorola's core competency has led to the development of various products in the telecommunications industry, including pagers and cell-phones.

We believe that strategy formulation by top managers in the '00s environment must be far more flexible. Top managers must realize change is not only desirable but necessary. Companies need to be able to compete in an anywhere-anytime-anyplace-any volume-anything environment in which the assumptions and the rules of the game continually change. In their recent book *Competing on the Edge*, Brown and Eisenhardt suggest that companies in the new millennium will have to adopt new ways of thinking that will enable them to live with change and accept the fact that today's distinctive core competencies may be of little value in tomorrow's markets. Among other things, they note that managers must remember that in the '00s strategic advantage will be temporary. Strategy is not a single simple approach but rather a collection of moves that are loosely linked in a semi-coherent strategic direction; reinvention of the business will be the name of the game.

How, then, will enterprises need to organize and operate? Brown and Eisenhardt suggest that in terms of organization design, companies will live in the present by using a structure that has few strict rules and minimal bureaucracy. They also recommend that firms reach into the future by expanding their time horizons, launching more experimental products and services, creating strategic alliances with a focus on newly emerging markets and technologies, and thinking continuously futuristically. The virtual and net-

	Porter's Five Forces Model (1980s)	Hamel & Prahalad's Core Competency Model (1990s)	Brown & Eisenhardt's Competing on the Edge Model (2000s)
Perspective	Sees the industry as having a stable structure	Sees the firm as a bundle of competencies	Views the industry as in rapid, unpredictable change
Goal	Develop a defensible position	Develop a sustainable advantage	Deal with the continuous flow of advantages and opportunities
Driver	Industry structure dominates the situation	Unique firm competencies are the key to success	The ability to change is the most critical factor
Strategy	Pick an industry; pick a strategic position; fit the firm into it	Create a vision; build and then exploit competencies to realize this vision	Gain the edge through a carefully paced and implemented strategy and shape a "semi-coherent" strategic vision that people can follow
Success measure	Profits	Long-term dominance	Continual reinvention

Exhibit 21.1   Changing Models of Strategy

work forms of organization design that focus on sharing authority, responsibility, and resources among people and divisions that must cooperate frequently to achieve common goals will begin to replace traditional hierarchical structures. For example, Corning, Inc. uses 23 strategic alliances to compete in a variety of high-technology markets.

By adopting the new designs, managers will be able to change their strategies, continually realigning their organizations with emerging opportunities, then articulating the new strategies to partners so that everyone in the enterprise knows what the organization is doing. In contrast to the five forces and core competency models as shown in Exhibit 21.1, this new way of thinking meets one of the major strategic initiatives needed for the 21st century: the need to proactively and continually adjust to an ever-changing environment.

GOING BEYOND BEING CUSTOMER-LED

Many of the basic principles of strategy that have helped companies become competitive are now under attack. Firms that have dominated their industry for decades are now finding themselves reeling from the competition. One reason is that markets are changing. Organizations are finding that the old ways of doing things are not sufficient to sustain competitive advantage. In many cases, upstart or second-tier firms are replacing the leaders. For example, for years Chrysler almost always found itself the third member of the Big Three automakers. Then, in the 1980s, the company decided to begin manufacturing minivans. The firm's research proved that customers wanted this product; many of its competitors, after conducting marketing research of their own, concluded that there was not much demand for minivans. They were wrong, and Chrysler wound up ahead of the other automakers. It eventually became an attractive global partner for a new global alliance: DaimlerChrysler.

Similar stories like that of Chrysler abound in other industries. In the rigid disk-drive industry, Seagate Technology introduced a 5.25-inch disk drive. The unit's capacity of 5–10 megabytes (MB) was of no interest to major minicomputer manufacturers that continued to demand 8-inch disk drives of 40–60 MB for their current customers. There seemed to be no market for a 5.25-inch disk drive until Seagate found that emerging personal computer makers could use them for their new desktop PCs. The conclusion: A new market was created and those disk-drive manufacturers that continued producing 8-inch drives eventually were driven from the market. Since then, this story has repeated itself as new upstart firms introduced 3.5-inch drives and supplanted the 5.25-inch manufacturers. Such disruptive technologies will be more common in the future.

At first, such technologies will tend to be used in new markets or for new applications (see Exhibit 21.1). Consider Sony's early transistor for radios. They sacrificed sound fidelity but created a new market for portable radios, offering customers a new and different package of attributes – small size, light weight, and portability.

While these examples would seem to be merely evidence of the need to remain on the cutting edge, they reflect more than the need to keep up. Each of the firms that was eventually displaced had been successful in its own right and was carefully focused on its own customers' base. The problem was that customers were pleased with what the company was currently providing, not interested in changing to a new product. Many outstanding companies, such as IBM, Montgomery Ward, and Digital Equipment, have fallen prey to the "Icarus Paradox." The fabled Icarus of Greek mythology is said to have flown so high, so close to the sun, that his artificial wax wings melted and he plunged to his death in the Aegean Sea. The power of Icarus' wings gave rise to the abandon that doomed him. We believe that the same paradox applies to many successful companies today: Their market share and financial success often seduce them into the excesses that cause their downfall. Success leads to specialization, complacency, dogma, and ritual. The company's management is unwilling to forgo a currently profitable product for one that offers only potentially greater promise. The firm is blinded by both its customers' current needs and its own management's low tolerance to "thinking-out-of-the-box."

Nor is it necessary to focus only on technology-driven products to prove our point. When Wal-Mart first began expanding its operations in the 1970s, the company offered products that were lower-priced and not very appealing to those who shopped at Sears and J.C. Penney. However, as Wal-Mart's quality improved and its prices declined, it began attracting customers from these competitors. Customers began to feel that their current store was not meeting their needs as well as they wanted, and that they could get more value for their money by shopping at Wal-Mart. This strategy has been so successful that today Wal-Mart has greater annual sales than Sears and J.C. Penney combined.

In this new environment, managers must avoid being blindsided by competitors that offer new goods and services to a customer base that may not have yet materialized or is still quite small. What will organizations have to do to prevent falling into this trap? There are two important steps in this strategic imperative that need to be taken. First, top

Traditional Manager	Entrepreneurial Manager
Tries to avoid mistakes	Is willing to make mistakes in order to learn
Postpones recognizing failure	Admits mistakes and moves on
Agrees with those in power	Gets those in power to be committed to what should be done
Wants to please top management	Wants to please customers, sponsor, and self
Likes the system and sees it as nurturing and protective	Dislikes the system and learns how to manipulate it
Works out problems by working within the system	Works out problems by learning how to bypass the system
Utilizes the hierarchy as a basic power differentiation between levels	Uses the hierarchy as only a tool for getting things done more efficiently

Exhibit 21.2   The Traditional versus the Entrepreneurial Manager

managers will have to continually monitor their environment and assess new developments *not* as threats but as learning opportunities. Second, they will have to realize that their present customers, stakeholders (owners, employees, suppliers, and communities), and the current state of their technology can be limiting or inhibiting factors in determining future action. Quite often existing stakeholders and technology encourage a continuation of the status quo, thus effectively blocking management from taking bold new steps needed to effectively compete in the new environment.

THE ROLE OF ENTREPRENEURSHIP

Although the world economic scene is dominated by the very large MNCs as the opening comments indicated, much of the recent economic growth of countries around the world can be directly attributed to entrepreneurship either by smaller start-up firms or by internal venture teams in established enterprises. Such entrepreneurial strategic initiatives will continue to play a major role in the new century. Although entrepreneurial start-ups will continue to be important, the role of entrepreneurship in existing firms, such as the use of venture teams and focus on newly emerging markets as opposed to newly emerging technologies, should play a critical part in the '00s environment.

VENTURE TEAMS

Venture teams are a way to promote the spirit and practice of entrepreneurship in existing firms. These teams typically are made up of two or more people who formally create and share ownership of a new organization within an existing organization. They have the authority to operate with a great degree of freedom and autonomy; structure and formal rules and procedures are held to a minimum. This allows them to formulate their own objectives and, drawing upon their own independent budgets, decide how to proceed.

Venture teams operate quite differently from project teams. Venture team members, too, have philosophies and values sharply different from traditional managers. These differences are spotlighted in Exhibit 21.2.

One reason that entrepreneurial venture teams will be important in the new environment is that they are effective in helping enterprises deal with change. Because their managers are not part of the status quo, they are able to think "out of the box." For example, enterprises that attempt to undermine competition from upstart firms by offering goods and services to newly emerging consumer groups can benefit greatly from venture teams. The primary reason is that companies focused on meeting the needs of a particular market niche are often reluctant to fund new efforts to meet the emerging needs of other niches. However, as we observed in the previous section, if a firm does not address the needs of a newly emerging customer group, it can find itself under serious attack.

How, then, can organizations meet the needs of current customers and also address those in emerging markets? In his book *The Innovator's Dilemma*, Christensen suggests that the creation of a separate type of venture group may be the answer. In this way the company can divide its efforts: Use its current strategy or bundle of core competencies to address the needs of current customers while it employs the venture group to address the newly emerging market. In the process, the venture team focuses on the needs of emerging and future customers and not on existing technology and organization design. This type of approach is heralding a new form of entrepreneurial thinking that may well spell the difference between success and failure for many firms in the new millennium.

NEW ENTREPRENEURIAL THINKING

Besides creating venture teams, our strategic initiative calls for entrepreneurial thinking. Managers need to look at their old approaches, modify them, and sometimes start from scratch to meet new competitive demands. In doing so, they are going to find it necessary to adhere to three entrepreneurially based strategies that admittedly fly in the face of traditionally accepted managerial thinking but can offer great promise in the new environment.

First, many organizations tailor-make their offerings to the exact requirements of their customers. For example, Mattel which is in the fiercely competitive toy industry is attempting to let customers custom-design their own dolls (e.g., Barbie and Ken) through choices of clothing, hair color, skin texture, and other desired attributes. Mattel's ability to mix and match different components and product features will enable it to achieve this customization without costly retooling or extensive modification. Dell Computer also generates tremendous revenue and profits from its ability to mix and match personal computer components according to what each individual customer wants. By maintaining very flexible supply and manufacturing systems, Dell can custom-build each computer and price it accordingly. A few suppliers that design parts according to computer industry standards make all of Dell's standardized components. These standards allow for full interchangeability across manufacturers and user applications.

Second, significant money should be allocated for emerging markets. Traditional thinking would give successful products/markets the lion's share of a company's budget because resource allocation is driven by return on investment (ROI) forecasts. But as a result emerging markets are underestimated in terms of ROI or ignored by senior-level management because they are more concerned with earning profits in a market they currently dominate than in one that they truly do not understand.

Third, organizations tend to be very effective in taking successful technologies and products and penetrating existing markets with these, but they are far less effective in taking new technologies and products into new markets. The demands that are made on them by the unfamiliar markets are challenging. Extending products in a new market often requires continual, incremental improvements in key factors, such as product performance, reliability, price, and distribution channels. For example, in Brazil, approximately 20 percent of all cosmetics are sold through "sack ladies" who sell door-to-door in poorer neighborhoods. In the U.S, the majority of cosmetics are typically sold through direct sales forces. As a result, multinationals such as Revlon Inc. that rely on traditional mass channels are at a distinct disadvantage. In creating dominance in a new market, however, it is often important to be a first-mover because a small number of firms will typically end up with the lion's share of the market and latecomers will lose out. For example, Frito-Lay has been able to sustain its first-mover strategy in Brazil by investing large sums to have local farmers plant higher quality potatoes than normally grown in Brazil in order to insure a quality advantage for its leading brands, like Ruffles. Simultaneously, Frito-Lay has dominated advertising spending. As a consequence, it has grown market share despite a host of local competitors whose pricing is half of Frito-Lay's.

These three points can be illustrated by Global Fleet Graphics, a division of 3M. This division makes premium durable graphic-marking systems for buildings, signs, vehicles, corporate logos, etc. Fleet Graphics has three major competitors: AmericanGraphics, GraphDesign, and FleetGlobal. All three sell products similar to Global Fleet Graphics but at a lower price. Without radical changes, top managers at 3M believed that their division would not be profitable. Rather than focus on saving incremental process changes that would produce short-term market share increases, they rethought the entire way they produced graphics. Contacting R&D people in other 3M divisions resulted in a radical plan for a new low-cost graphics production system that would store graphics digitally. These images would be able to be sent anywhere in the world and Global Fleet Graphics would act as a central repository. Such a system drastically reduced inventory and enabled Global Fleet Graphics to respond to customers' requests in as little as three hours instead of four weeks. Further, working with people in 3M's adhesive division, Global Fleet Graphics addressed customers' need for graphics that can be applied to nontraditional surfaces, such as canvas sides of trucks in Europe. Such adhesives can be easily applied, saving as much as 30 percent on a customer's installation costs.

These examples of entrepreneurial management are in direct conflict with many of the operating approaches used in today's hierarchically designed organizations. Yet the ideas are on target; they account for the success of a growing number of enterprises, from Wal-Mart to Intel to Amazon.com. Organizations that hope to succeed in the '00s environment will have to implement these types of strategic initiatives or they will lose out to competitors that are doing so.

THE ROLE OF HUMAN RESOURCE MANAGEMENT

The strategic initiatives discussed so far provide some of the answers to help meet the environmental challenges facing management in the new millennium. Another, somewhat separate but related initiative, deals with the human resources of today's and tomorrow's organizations. In particular, we feel that human resources techniques can help align the needed strategic initiatives. However, the impression often given by both management experts and the general public is that an organization's human resources will play a diminishing role in the '00s environment. Their reasoning is that information technology will increasingly replace people in the production and service processes of organizations. We would argue the opposite. For example, even those who run Dell's business-to-business e-commerce feel that human resources will become relatively more important. IT tools such as their Premier Pages (small Web pages, linked to large customers' intranets, that let approved employees configure their PCs on-line, pay for them, and track the delivery status) can greatly cut costs and ordering errors, but they also free up Dell sales representatives to do more and better customer service and serious selling.

Like Dell, we believe human resources, and how they are managed, will play an even more important role in the new century. The articles in the Summer 1999 issue of *Organizational Dynamics* on management in the 21st century, and the book *The Human Equation* by Jeff Pfeffer, make a strong case that human resources can provide the competitive advantage in the years ahead.

The latest technology can be purchased and copied by anyone. In most industries, it simply levels the playing field for competitive battles. The skills, ideas, efforts, and behaviors of people are inimitable. It is the people who manage and operate the technology and who interact with and serve the customers. At Dell, the Premier Pages help prevent sales representatives from getting distracted and allow more important direct interaction time with customers. Although the nature and use of human capital will certainly change as at Dell, human resources' relative importance will increase rather than decrease. The question is, "*What* HRM techniques are available to best meet the challenges ahead?"

Although there are a number of high-performance work practices that have been shown to have a very positive impact, we have selected two specific techniques that we believe are most important to the new role of HRM: multirater (360-degree) feedback and pay for performance. We believe that these practices have the greatest potential for meeting the challenges that lie ahead.

MULTIRATER FEEDBACK

Multirater or 360-degree feedback for managers, from subordinates, peers, supervisors managers and sometimes customers, has emerged in recent years as a major performance appraisal tool and, even more important, a human resource development tool. Comparing one's self-rating with others' ratings of us, we can see gaps that give us useful information for personal development purposes. The anonymous information coming from multiple sources provides rich feedback. The recipient of feedback from only one source (the boss in traditional performance appraisals) may not be believed, or negative information may be rationalized away by the recipient. Pooling data from multiple sources (subordinates, peers, managers, customers) provides credibility and validity to the data received. Feedback to the employee explaining how other people view him or her and action plans for how to improve the employee's competencies are critical. At UPS, supervisors and managers agree that multirater feedback improves the performance appraisal process. More than 70 percent of UPS employees said that the feedback from multiple sources was more useful than the insight that they would have received from their managers alone.

An increasing number of firms are using 360 degree feedback. Widely recognized corporations, such as AT&T, Bank of America, Exxon, General Electric, Caterpillar, and Chrysler, have been using this HRM technique for a number of years. Wilson Learning, The Center for Creative Leadership, and Personnel Decisions Inc. are among the largest firms providing multirater competency models for organizations. In general, organizations and human resource professionals are supportive of 360 degree feedback on individual and organizational outcomes. However, there has been concern about the complexities of the 360 degree approach in terms of the psychometric (measurement) properties and implications of the ratings, especially the relationship between self and other ratings, for compensation and promotional issues. Similarly, managers must be trained to accept feedback from others. There may be industry differences in the application of 360 ratings, especially from peers. For example, research has shown that peers tend to be more lenient in public-sector organizations than in private-sector organizations.

There is growing literature on how to successfully implement a 360 degree feedback performance appraisal system in organizations. In a previous *Organizational Dynamics* article, Antonioni emphasized the need to pay attention to the inputs (e.g., purpose, development of the form, and selection and training of the appraisers and appraisees), process (e.g., self-appraisals, coaching steps, and action goals and plans), and outputs (e.g., increased awareness, improved behaviors and performance, and learning). Based on the GE experience reported in the *Boundaryless Organization* and our own practices, we offer the following guidelines for effective application of 360 degree feedback systems:

- Make sure everyone knows how the data will be used (e.g. developmental, career movements, or salary adjustments).
- Define the behaviors (competencies) to be appraised.
- Involve customers and suppliers.
- Relate the feedback data to employee performance and action plans.
- Track personnel decisions made from these data over time.

If properly implemented, multirater feedback systems seem to be the type of HRM initiative to help meet the people challenges in the new environment.

PAY FOR PERFORMANCE, BUT ALSO HAVE "FUN"

All managers know that compensation matters help establish a company's culture by reinforcing behaviors and values that executives hold dear. By signaling what and who in the organization is valued, pay determines an organization's culture. If managers talk about teamwork and cooperation and then do not have a group-based component in their compensation system, employees will ignore such rhetoric and fight for themselves. As managers try to make decisions about pay, they must do so in shifting landscape while being bombarded with advice from consulting companies about which pay system works best for them. According to David Norwood, vice president at Holmes Murphy, 60 percent of companies have made major changes to their performance-management plans in the last two years as they have experimented with different ways to tie pay to performance.

At the turn of last century, paying workers based on their performance was the backbone of Taylor's scientific management movement. For years, many companies rewarded employees, including managers, for their individual performance. Behind this action is the view that behavior is rational and that people take jobs and perform according to how much effort they expect to have to expend for a financial return. If pay is not contingent on performance, individuals will not devote sufficient attention and energy to their jobs, and their performance will suffer. This and other economic models portray work as aversive, implying that the only way people can be induced to work is through some combination of rewards and sanctions.

Notwithstanding, a survey of pay practices of the *Fortune* 1,000 reported a rise from 38 to 50 percent in the number of organizations that use individual as opposed to team-based incentives during the last part of this century. In the retail sector, the number of salespeople that were paid solely on commission (no salary) rose 14 percent. Despite the popularity of this practice, the problems with individual merit pay are numerous and well documented. *Fortune* reported that almost 50 percent of the employees found such systems neither fair nor sensible, and an equal percentage believed that this system provided little value to the company. It has been shown to undermine teamwork, encourage employees to focus on the short term, and lead people to believe that their political skills and ingratiating personality are what drive performance. Columbia Health Care Systems eliminated individual bonuses for physicians and administrators when such a system encouraged employees to meet quotas and earn bonuses by "up-coding" the severity of a patient's medical conditions to claim higher reimbursements from Medicare and other insurers. Highland Superstores, an electronics and appliance retailer, also eliminated commissions when customers complained that salespeople were too aggressive. W. Edwards Deming and other quality experts strongly advise against using such compensation plans because they believe that such plans absorb vast amounts of management time and resources and make almost everybody unhappy.

In the '00s environment, this view of pay for performance is much too narrow. With the increased emphasis on customers, leadership, and associates' knowledge, skill and competency, the traditional view is no longer sufficient. The so-called new pay for performance calls for paying not only for traditional productivity or sales revenue but also for measured improvements in customer satisfaction, employee satisfaction, cycle time, quality, and acquired/demonstrated skills, and competencies. One of the major challenges for organizations is to measure the results for actions taken that are under the control of a manager. Also, the traditional individually oriented pay for performance may be balanced by pay for team performance. At General Mills, half of a manager's annual bonus is linked to business unit results and half to individual performance. Such a reward system addresses not only the team's performance but also individual accountability.

We believe that monetary rewards do impact an employee's behavior and performance, but those organizations that will "win" the recruitment, retention and motivation battles of the next century will also be those that create a fun work environment. Sun Microsystems, The Men's Wearhouse, SAS, and Southwest Airlines, among others, have employees who would rather work there than accept another job elsewhere because the work is fun. Sun Microsystems CEO Scott McNealy wears a Java "decoder" ring that has the motto "Kick butt and have fun." On April Fool's Day, engineers play elaborate pranks on senior managers. One year they built a golf course hole in McNealy's office, complete with green and water hazard. He frequently plays in an intramural squirt gun war with engineers. At Southwest Airlines, Herb Kelleher, its CEO, shows up at departmental meetings and on holidays in a variety of costumes, including the Easter Bunny.

Fun means working in a place where people can use their competencies and can work in an atmosphere of mutual respect and fairness. Fun doesn't translate to easy work; it energizes people. Such companies work very hard at keeping turnover low. By doing so, these companies save directly on replacement costs and untold amounts on experience-based knowledge and customer relations. People don't make decisions in a vacuum, but friends and the quality of social relationships they have with their peers influence them. Social influence can have a potent influence on the quality and quantity of work produced by employees.

Summary

In traditional organizations, managers had time to craft and implement their business strategies knowing what actions competitors might take. In the next millennium, we believe that intellectual or knowledge resources will redefine managers' roles and erode traditional boundaries that separate people and organizations. The principal role of the management of the future will be to link competencies and resources that the organization possesses to create a sustainable competitive advantage. The Internet and e-commerce have created a global market for ideas and exchange of information.

In this article, we argued that in the '00s knowledge-driven economy, managers must go beyond traditional thinking in order to tap the knowledge and creativity of their employees. New strategic initiatives that permit competing on the edge, foster entrepreneurship, and develop employees through multisource feedback and reward risk taking and innovation, promoting fun at the same time, increase the chances for success and can turn change into opportunity in the 21st century.

Selected Bibliography

For insightful articles on the future, see T.W. Malone and R.J. Laubacker, "The Dawn of the E-Lance Economy," *Harvard Business Review*, September–October 1998, pp. 144–52; Eryn Brown, "9 Ways to Win on the Web," *Fortune*, May 24, 1999, pp. 112–25; C.V. Callahan and B.A. Pasternack, "Corporate Strategy in the Digital Age," *Strategy and Business*, Second Quarter, 1999, pp. 10–15; J.A. Gingrich, "Five Rules for Winning Emerging Market Consumers," *Strategy and Business*, Second Quarter, 1999, 19–34; J.L. Bower and C.M. Christensen, "Disruptive Technologies: Catching the Wave," *Harvard Business Review*, January–February, 1995, pp. 43–53.

For a very comprehensive research study supporting the positive contribution that HRM techniques can make to the performance of organizations, see M.A. Huselid, "The Impact of Human Resource Management Practices on Turnover, Productivity, and Corporate Financial Performance," *Academy of Management Journal*, 1995, Vol. 38, pp. 635–72. For a comprehensive treatment of 360-degree feedback, see M. London, *Job Feedback: Giving, Seeking, Using Feedback for Performance Improvement*. (Hillsdale, N.J.: 1997).

For a comprehensive analysis of the positive impact of rewards on performance, see J. Cameron and W.D. Pierce, "Reinforcement, Reward and Intrinsic Motivation: A Meta-Analysis," *Review of Education Research*, 1994, Vol. 64, pp. 363–423; R. Eisenberger and J. Cameron, "Detrimental Effects of Reward: Reality or Myth?" *American Psychologist*, 1996, Vol. 51, pp. 1153–66; and L. Hatcher and T. Ross, "From Individual Incentives to an Organization-Wide Gainsharing Plan: Effects on Teamwork and Product Quality," *Journal of Organizational Behavior*, May 1991, pp. 169–78. For recent theory, research, and practice on pay for performance, see F. Luthans and A.D. Stajkovic articles "Reinforce for Performance: The Need to Go Beyond Pay or Even Rewards," *Academy of Management Executive*, 1999, Vol. 13(2), pp. 49–57, and "A Meta-Analysis of the Effects of Organizational Behavior Modification on Task Performance," *Academy of Management Journal*, 1997, Vol. 47, pp. 1122–49; J. Pfeffer, "Six Dangerous Myths About Pay," *Harvard Business Review*, May–June 1998, pp. 108–21; J. Pfeffer and J.F. Veiga, "Putting People First for Organizational Success," *The Academy of Management Executive*, 1999, Vol. 13(2), pp. 37–48; J. Pfeffer, *The Human Equation: Building Profits by Putting People First* (Boston, MA: Harvard Business School Press, 1998); R. Askenas, D. Ulrich, T. Jick, and S. Kerr, *The Boundaryless Organization* (San Francisco, CA: Jossey-Bass, 1995).

For arguments focusing on the design of new millennium organizations, see David Lei, John Slocum, Jr., and Robert Pitts, "Designing Organizations for Competitive Advantage: The Power of Unlearning and Learning," *Organizational Dynamics*, Winter 1999, pp. 24–38; Jean Lipman-Blumen and Harold Leavitt, "Hot Groups with Attitude," *Organizational Dynamics*, Spring 1999, pp. 63–73; Gregory Dess and Joseph Picken, *Beyond Productivity* (New York: AMACOM, 1999); D.A. Nadler and M.L. Tushman, "The Organization of the Future: Principles of Design for the 21st Century," *Organizational Dynamics*, Summer 1999.

Chapter 22

Global Dual-Career Couple Mentoring: A Phase Model Approach

Michael Harvey and Danielle Wiese

Expatriation is a common practice among U.S.-based multinational corporations (MNCs). However, a number of investigators have demonstrated that there is a high failure rate among expatriates because neither they nor their families are prepared to deal with the level of uncertainty associated with the process. Expatriation is even more stressful for dual-career couples. One method that domestic organizations use to aid the adjustment of their employees is mentoring. Thus, we propose that MNCs incorporate a global mentoring program in order to assist in the organizational socialization of the expatriate and provide some social support to the expatriate and trailing spouse during the expatriation process. This mentoring needs to occur pre-expatriation, during expatriation, and during repatriation. The potential returns to the organization in the form of reduced explicit and implicit costs of expatriation should far outweigh the difficulty associated with establishing the system.

With globalization comes expatriation. Multinational corporations (MNCs) have visions of sending their most talented technical and administrative expertise overseas. They frequently select managers with strong track records and high expectations for their futures within the organization. Certainly, these individuals ought to be excited about an opportunity to go abroad, be successful in their mission, and return to a prosperous career within the company. Unfortunately, this is often not the case. Refusal rates are rising primarily because of dual-career issues (Crendall, Dwyer & Duncan, 1990; Reynolds & Bennett, 1991; Pascoe, 1992; Feldman & Thompson, 1993; Noe & Barber, 1993: Windham International 1994; Harvey, 1995).

Researchers estimate that between 16 and 40 percent of all American expatriates fail to complete their assignments (Mendenhall, Dunbar & Oddou, 1987; Mendenhall & Oddou, 1988; Wederspahn, 1992; Dowling, Schuler & Welch, 1994), a number that is expected to escalate in the near future due to the projected increase in female expatriates and dual-career couples (Harvey, 1996, 1997a, 1997b). Of those American expatriates who do complete their assignments, 30 to 50 percent are considered ineffective or marginally effective by their companies (Copeland & Griggs, 1985; Dowling, Schuler & Welch,

1994). Unsuccessful expatriate managers and the resulting reduced effectiveness of the overseas assignments have direct costs, such as training, moving, and housing expenses, as well as indirect costs, such as declining service levels and lost customers (Wederspahn, 1992). In addition to these expenses, international human resource executives must be concerned with finding suitable replacements for expatriates who fail.

International relocations involve a number of stressors that affect various members of the family differently. This is particularly evident in non-traditional family configurations such as dual-career couples. Everyone faces the disorientation of culture shock and must go through the process of adjusting to the host country culture and general environment (Copeland & Griggs, 1985; Black, Mendenhall & Oddou, 1991). At the same time, the expatriate must also adjust to a new organizational culture (Black, Mendenhall & Oddou, 1991). This dual adjustment makes the expatriate particularly susceptible to confusion about his/her assignment within the organization. This in turn induces inordinately high stress for the expatriate, which can be transferred to the family unit. On the other hand, the trailing spouse experiences stress related to reestablishing the family in the new country (Harvey, 1985). With the increasing number of dual-career couples, many trailing spouses must also absorb the stress associated with relocating their careers to a foreign country during their spouses' expatriation assignment (Statistical, 1992; Collidge & D'Angelo, 1994).

These stressful situations during foreign assignments are heightened by the lack of social support that was generally provided by family and friends in the home country. The stress associated with the trailing spouse's job search in an unfamiliar country and the potential for unemployment or underemployment may spill over into the performance of the expatriate (Greenhaus & Parasuraman, 1986; Gutelle, Reperri & Silver, 1988; Bolger, DeLongis, Kessler & Wetherington, 1989; Lambert, 1990; Jones & Fletcher, 1993; Williams & Alger, 1994). When stress is not properly addressed, the potential dysfunctional consequences to the expatriate and his/her family members may create additional stressors. The resulting increase in tension needs to be proactively addressed by professionals through a reconstructed social support system for the dual-career couple. One potential way to create this restructured social support for expatriated dual-career couples is to provide a mentoring program for the expatriate as well as for the trailing spouse.

The purpose of this article is to: 1) examine the literature on mentoring and to adapt these concepts to increase their applicability to international assignments for dual-career couples; 2) assess the psychological and social stress associated with relocation of dual-career couples prior to, during, and after expatriation; 3) develop an expatriate mentoring model; and 4) examine the cost of implementing a global mentoring program.

THE MENTORING LITERATURE

Researchers have defined mentoring as a one-to-one relationship between a mentor with advanced experience and knowledge and a protégé with less experience and knowledge (Levinson, Darrow, Klein, Levinson & McKee, 1978; Roche, 1979; Hunt & Michael, 1983; Kram, 1985; Hurley, 1988; Mullen, 1994). According to Kram (1985), this relationship typically goes through four distinct stages regardless of the type of mentoring:

1) initiation (six to 12 months), which is defined by the development and clarification of expectations of both mentor and protégé: 2) cultivation (two to five years), during which time career development and psychosocial functions are established within the dyad: 3) separation when the protégé experiences independence and autonomy: and 4) redefinition as the relationship is severed or becomes more of a peer relationship. Mentors are expected to provide upward organizational mobility and personal growth for their protégés (mentee) through coaching, support, and guidance in developing technical, interpersonal, and political skills (Levinson, Darrow, Klein, Levinson & McKee, 1978: Roche, 1979; Hunt & Michael, 1983; Kram, 1983, 1985; Mullen, 1994). The outcome of mentoring varies depending on the needs of the mentee and the ability of the mentor to provide assistance (see Exhibit 22.1). The mentor may provide ongoing assistance to the mentee over an extended period of time in which the role of the mentor evolves into a complex social relationship.

A classical or primary mentoring relationship is an intense development one-on-one relationship of relatively long duration (Levinson, Darrow, Klein, Levinson & McKee, 1978: Clawson, 1980; Kram, 1985), whereas a secondary mentoring relationship is a shorter, less intense, less inclusive developmental process involving multiple mentors, each offering specialized developmental functions to the individual receiving the mentoring (Phillips-Jones, 1982; Zey, 1984; Whitely, Dougherty & Dreher, 1991). Secondary mentorships are more likely to focus on career development functions. In primary mentorships, the mentor protégé dyad is vertical or a fixed-time format hierarchical relationship between senior mentor and junior protégé. This relationship has fixed organizational boundaries, such as the same technical specialty or a complementary area within the organization. Secondary mentorships may contain vertical and horizontal relationships, such as peer-to-peer, individual-level professional (friend/colleague/spouse), and professional association (networking) relationships (Kram & Isabella, 1985; Lankau, 1996; Scandura & Von Glinow, 1997). These protégés may use a "board of mentors" (group) which may be internal as well as external to the organization and at different levels in the organization (McDonald, 1995), where mentors are viewed as trusted confidantes and coaches.

The issues associated with mentoring in an international context have not received much attention (Scandura & Von Glinow, 1997). But, what has been established by domestic studies is that newcomers to an organization are less likely to receive a mentor or acceptance to the extent that they are dissimilar (i.e., diversity) to those in the organization (Jackson, Stone & Alvarez, 1993). This situation is typical of an expatriate entering a host country organization. The trailing spouse of the expatriate also will exhibit diversity when compared to the local culture and when searching for professional opportunities in the host country. The role of a mentor, therefore, becomes paramount in reducing stress and accelerating adjustment for expatriated dual-career couples.

EXPATRIATED DUAL-CAREER COUPLES AND THE COMPOUNDING OF STRESS

Members of an expatriate family experience stress caused by work and family issues that are accentuated in dual-career families. Expatriates generally have a high level of work involvement, meaning that their self-image is strongly tied to their work (Lodahl & Kehner,

Mentoring is Associated with the Mentee:	Supporting Literature
Receiving more promotions	Dreher & Ash, 1990
	Scandura, 1992
	Bachman & Gregory, 1993
Having higher incomes	Dreher & Ash, 1990
	Whitely, Dougherty & Dreher, 1991
	Chao, Walz & Gardner, 1992
Reporting more career satisfaction	Fagenson, 1988
	Chao, Walz & Gardner 1992
	Koberg, Boss, Chappell & Ringer 1994
Having more career mobility	Scandura, 1992
Alleviating some job/role stress and "burnout"	Ford & Wells, 1985
Alleviating work alienation	Koberg, Boss, Chappell & Ringer, 1994
Alleviating turnover intentions	Scandura & Viator, 1994
Accelerating organizational socialization	Chao, Walz & Gardner, 1992
	Ostroff & Kozlowski, 1993
Increasing career commitment	Bachman & Gregory, 1993
Providing positional power, access to important people, and influence over organizational policy	Fagenson, 1988
Providing "reflected power"	Kanter, 1977

Exhibit 22.1 The Impact of Mentoring on the Mentee

1965; Yogev & Brett, 1985). Additionally, a great deal of pressure is placed on expatriates in that the MNC selected them as opposed to host country nationals, causing expectations among those in the organization to frequently be higher than for local managers. Expatriation to a foreign corporate environment is likely to lead to profound role ambiguity, role conflict, and role overload. All of these factors combine to form work conflict, to the extent that an individual experiences incompatible pressures within the work domain (Kahn, Wolfe, Quinn, Snoek & Rosenthal, 1964; Billings & Moos, 1982; Burke, 1988). In addition, these expatriates also experience family conflict, derived from family expectations that may not be met because of time conflicts, role conflicts, and role ambiguity. This situation is most acute in dual-career couples that are expatriated (Harvey, 1995; 1996; 1997a; 1997b and forthcoming a and b). Individuals in dual-career relationships must balance the conflicting pressures of their own career, their spouse's career, and their family responsibilities. Additionally, they must manage the stress "spillover" from their new expatriate position into the family domain.

This inter-role conflict, in which the role pressures from the work and family domains are incompatible and in which the role pressures from the work domain spill over into the family domain and vice versa, is called work-family conflict (Kahn, Wolfe, Quinn, Snoek & Rosenthal, 1964; Frankenhaueser, Lundberg, Frederikson, Belin, Tuomisto & Myrsten, 1989; Lambert, 1990). For an expatriate, fulfillment of expectations in the work role is made more difficult by virtue of participation in the family role and vice versa. This is related to the "spillover" model, which suggests that work and non-work experiences are positively related (Evans & Bartolome, 1984). This model posits that satisfaction and stimulation at work translates into high levels of energy and satisfaction at home, while problems and conflict at work drain and preoccupy the individual, making it difficult to participate adequately in family life. The impact of work conflict on family conflict is well documented (Piotrkowski, 1979; Pleck, 1979; Greenhaus & Kopelman, 1981; Kelly & Voydanoff 1985; Burke & McKeen, 1988; Gutelle, Reperri & Silver, 1988; Nieva, 1988; Bolger, DeLongis, Kessler & Wetherington, 1989; Crouter, Perry-Jenkins, Huston & Crawford, 1989; Frankenhaueser, Lundberg, Frederikson, Belin, Tuomisto & Myrsten, 1989; Lambert, 1990; Higgins, Duxbury & Irving, 1992).

Work-family conflict has been linked to increased health risks for employed parents, poorer performance in the parenting role, decreased productivity at work, marital dissatisfaction between partners, and reduced life expectancy and life satisfaction (Near, Rice & Hunt, 1978; Pleck, Staines & Long, 1980; Greenhaus & Beutell, 1985; Kelly & Voydanoff, 1985; Pleck, 1985; Voydanoff, 1987; Fletcher, 1988). To facilitate better understanding of the stress associated with the expatriation of dual-career couples (Fletcher, 1991; Harvey, 1995), stress may be depicted in the following manner:

Stress Level =
(Demands + Constraints) − Support
where:

Demands = the degree to which the environment contains stimuli that peremptorily require the individual's attention.
Constraints = the degree to which the environment prevents or deters the individual from surviving or coping.
Support = the degree to which the environment has intellectual, technical, social, and financial resources.

To gain insight into the complexities associated with dual-career expatriation, both work and family stress levels must be calculated for each spouse. These two elements affect life satisfaction, which in turn affects absenteeism, turnover, marital discord, family breakdowns, productivity, and morale (Greenhaus & Beutell, 1985; Voydanoff, 1988; Fletcher, 1988; Higgins, Duxbury & Irving, 1992). Providing mentors for both the expatriate and the trailing spouse would appear to be one method of reducing stress by increasing the level of professional support in both the family and work domains, and thereby increasing the likelihood of successful expatriation for the dual-career couple (Harvey, forthcoming a).

If stress was placed solely on the expatriate, the MNC could be more proactive in reducing some of the sources of stress. However, each member of the family must cope with numerous stressors in the new environment. This creates conflict, tension, and negative consequences for everyone in the family. When the expatriate experiences stress at work, "spillover" into the family domain causes the spouse to feel that stress as well in what is called stress crossover. Bolger, DeLongis, Kessler, and Wetherington (1989) found that individuals' feelings of overload at work increased their spouses' feelings of overload at home the following day. Other researchers have found that individuals' reports of negative marital and family relations have been associated with their spouses' stress, role overload, and poor social climate at work (Billings & Moos, 1982; Reperri, 1987). With the dissatisfaction of trailing spouses as the number one reason for expatriate attrition

(*Wall Street Journal*, 1997; Harvey, 1997a, 1997b), it would appear to be appropriate for international human resource management in MNCs to develop means such as mentoring to alleviate some of the stress of an international relocation for both the expatriate and the trailing spouse.

DUAL-CAREER COUPLE ADJUSTMENT TO EXPATRIATION

In adjusting to expatriation, dual-career couples progress through an anticipatory stage, an encounter stage, and finally, role management (Fisher, 1986). During the anticipatory stage, the dual-career couple forms expectations about the job, the organizational culture, the host country nationals, the general culture, and daily life in the host country (Brislin, 1981; Bochner, 1982; Black, 1988). The more complete and accurate the anticipatory stage, the greater the ease and speed of adjustment to the new organization and culture (Black, Mendenhall & Oddou, 1991). Therefore, as part of the pre-departure cross-cultural training (Black & Mendenhall, 1990), the expatriates, as well as their families, should be introduced to repatriated managers and their families, who can provide information that reduces uncertainty and facilitates the formation of accurate expectations of the host country.

Once the dual-career couple has relocated, the key to adjustment is reducing uncertainty. Expatriates will adjust faster to the organization if they have accurate expectations, role clarity (Nicholson, 1984; Pinder & Schroeder, 1987; Black, 1988), role discretion (Brett, 1980; Dawis & Lofquist, 1984; Nicholson, 1984), and low role conflict (Black, Mendenhall & Oddou, 1991). Additionally, the trailing spouse will accelerate adjustment if logistical support – regarding such things as housing, schools, and grocery stores – as well as social support are provided for the family (Copeland & Griggs, 1985; Tung, 1988). Therefore, new expatriates and their trailing spouses could benefit from being mentored by expatriates who have preceded the newly relocated dual-career couple and their families. Host country nationals may also provide insight and information about the host culture and feedback concerning others' expectations of the expatriates, thereby helping the dual-career couple to culturally adjust to the host country.

Both organizational socialization and social support are necessary for healthy adjustment to the host country by dual-career couples.

Organizational socialization

Organizational socialization is the process by which an expatriate is inculcated with the values, expected behaviors, social knowledge, and other important features of the host country organizational setting (Louis, 1980; Ashford & Taylor, 1990). Generally, newcomers progress through four stages of adjustment: 1) group processes (social integration) – sensitivity to group norms and values, understanding of formal and informal work relationships, awareness of which people are more knowledgeable and powerful than others, and knowing how to relate and fit in: 2) task mastery (performance proficiency) – learning the tasks involved in the job (knowledge, skills, abilities): important duties, assignments, and priorities; how to handle routine problems; and how to obtain necessary information; 3) work roles (role clarification) – understanding of boundaries of authority and responsibility and appropriate behaviors: 4) organizational attributes (acculturation) – appreciation of politics, power, goals, and value premises of the organization; knowledge of the organization's mission, special languages, key legends, myths, stories, and management's leadership and motivational style (Feldman, 1981; Ostroff & Kozlowski, 1993; Chao, O'Leary-Kelly, Wolf, Klein & Gardner, 1994).

Organizational socialization may occur through formal organizational programs as well as individual efforts that indoctrinate expatriates to the processes and procedures in the host country organization. Researchers have shown that institutionalized socialization tactics, especially investiture, tend to engender higher levels of organizational commitment for newcomers as well as reduced turnover (Jones, 1986; Allen & Meyer, 1993).

The purpose of organizational socialization is to make sense of the new environment, thereby reducing the level of uncertainty and providing the expatriate with guidance about what to do and how to behave in an acceptable manner, given the cultural context of the foreign organization. On a person-to-person basis, interaction with old-timers (mentor programs) facilitates sense-making, situational identification, and acculturation among newcomers (Louis, 1980; 1990). Thus, mentors may hasten socialization by providing protégés with information about the inner workings of the organization and feedback as to appropriate behavior (Ostroff & Kozlowski, 1993). By providing expatriates with access to mentors, the MNC is demonstrating a willingness to support the expatriate during the overseas assignment.

Social support

Adjustment to an international relocation is frequently dependent on the type and amount of social support received. Social support has been positively linked with the physical and mental health of individuals, making them less vulnerable to stressors (Wallston, Alagna, DeVellis & DeVellis, 1983; Schumaker & Brownell, 1984; Ladewig & McGee, 1986; Suchet & Barling, 1986; Rudd & McKenry, 1986). Providing social support to expatriates assists them in mitigating the negative effects of a relocation, such as loneliness, isolation, culture shock, and frustration, by meeting affiliative needs and providing feedback regarding appropriate behavior in ambiguous or stressful situations in the host country (Mitchell, Billings & Moos, 1982; Wallston, Alagna, DeVellis & DeVellis, 1983; Schumaker & Brownell, 1984).

Before expatriates relocate, social support may be used to 1) ease adjustment by providing verbal information about expatriation, 2) model emotional and behavioral coping strategies, 3) refer appropriate professional services agencies, 4) offer encouragement to seek assistance, and 5) provide problem-solving techniques (Lazarus & Launier, 1978). During the encounter stage of adjustment, social support may be used to provide information about unfamiliar situations and methods for regaining control over the expatriate's life (Taylor, 1983). In order for the expatriation to be successful, the organization must provide adequate social support for the expatriate to reduce stress and the possible spillover of dysfunctional tension to the trailing spouse and other family members (Harvey, forthcoming a).

Social support may be affected by the environment, the resources exchanged, and the perceptions of the exchange (Schumaker & Brownell, 1984). Four types of social support must be provided: 1) emotional – providing trust, empathy, attention, and affection: 2)

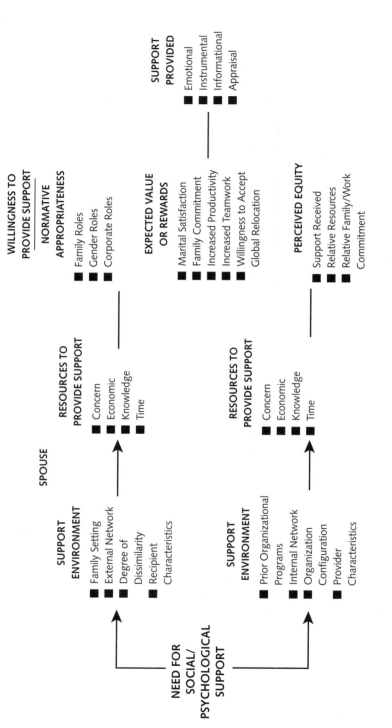

Exhibit 22.2 A Theoretical Model of Social/Psychological Support for the Expatriated Dual-Career Family

Source: Adapted from Schumaker & Brownell, 1984; Perlin, 1985; Granrose, Parasuraman, & Greenhaus, 1992.

instrumental – providing time, resources, or skills: 3) informational – providing facts, opinions, and advice; and 4) appraisal – providing evaluation and feedback on performance (Schuler, Fulkerson & Dowling, 1991; Gomez-Mejia & Wilbourne, 1991; Black, Gregersen & Mendenhall, 1992; Dowling, Schuler & Welch, 1994). This support should be provided by both the spouse and the organization for which the expatriate works (see Exhibit 22.2).

An external support network may consist of a varying number and quality of relationships beyond family that provide social support to family members (i.e., neighbors, friends, and social institutions). Smaller, more dense external social support networks enhance the quality and level of reinforcement during relocation (Tausig & Michello, 1988).

In order to replicate the domestic social support system, expatriate managers and their trailing spouses will attempt to assemble a local social support network. But dual-career couples' characteristics will affect the social support received in the host country. Some of the characteristics that influence the development of social support are the type of coping strategies selected, the ability to communicate the need for social support, and the amount of support he/she is willing to accept (Granrose, Parasuraman & Greenhaus, 1992). Additionally, in order for the support to be provided, the support provider must believe in the legitimacy and reasonableness of the request (Perlin, 1985). In a host country, each of these elements are culture-bound, and therefore willingness to support an expatriate is contingent on the cultural compatibility of the expatriate and the local national.

The resource categories of economic, knowledge, and time support are mainly material or tangible assistance. This includes behavioral assistance, feedback, guidance, information, comfort, intimacy, money, services, and lay referrals (Granrose, Parasuraman & Greenhaus, 1992). The fourth resource, concern, is the emotional sustenance one spouse provides the other or the organization provides the expatriate. Highly concerned spouses (organizations) will provide more support, while spouses (organizations) who are not concerned with the well-being of the family members will provide little support. The

TYPES OF MENTORS BEFORE EXPATRIATION

Expatriate's Mentors	*Trailing Spouse's Mentors*
• Repatriated company managers	• Trailing spouses of repatriated company managers, of suppliers, of channel-of-distribution members, etc.

MENTOR'S ACTIVITIES BEFORE EXPATRIATION

Expatriate's Mentors	*Trailing Spouse's Mentors*
• Establish a bond by providing information	• Identify career orientation
• Establish a mechanism for communication	• Assess career "sabbatical" options
• Define role of mentor	• Review realistic relocation options
• Discuss repatriation	• Establish informal communication links

amount or level of concern determines the amount of support deemed appropriate to give based on the degree of stress and dissatisfaction of the spouse.

The expected values received by the MNC include increased productivity, reduced turnover, and willingness to accept the global relocation. Our model of social support for expatriate families detailed below provides an infrastructure to develop specific programs that address the unique aspects of international relocation.

Before expatriation, mentors may be used to help individuals manage expectations by providing information and possible coping strategies. Mentors may also be used to provide familial support during the expatriation, reducing the strain on the expatriate, who will not have to provide all of the support, and on the spouse, who will still receive the necessary social support. Additionally, mentors may help dual-career couples manage their expectations and provide spouses with expert information on how to take control of their lives during the relocation.

GLOBAL EXPATRIATION MENTORING MODEL TO PROVIDE SOCIAL SUPPORT TO DUAL-CAREER COUPLES

One issue that needs to be addressed is, "How could an expatriation mentoring program facilitate the adjustment, acceptance, and power position of expatriated managers?" To more effectively address the organizational and social support needed by both members of dual-career couples, a three-phase model is being proposed (see Exhibit 22.3). This approach entails providing realistic relocation reviews to both the expatriate and the trailing spouse before, during, and after expatriation.

Phase one: before expatriation

For both members of the expatriate dual-career couple, predeparture mentoring should provide a realistic relocation review underscoring any potential problems relative to their international relocation. In this initial phase, the mentors should come from a pool of managers who have already had an expatriation experience, and who should provide specific information about the difficulties of adjusting to the host country organization. The mentors for the trailing spouse should consist of the trailing spouses of repatriated company managers, of suppliers, of channel-of-distribution members, and the like. These mentors should assist with apprehensions associated with the family's adjustment to the new culture.

PRIMARY SUPPORT   Primary support is directed toward the expatriate manager. The mentors basically have four ways to prepare the manager.

1) Reaffirm the organization's commitment – The mentors should discuss organization, personnel, and strategic situations in the domestic operation and in the host country organization. By establishing this bond with the manager, the mentors provide an "anchor" to the organization. This discussion takes place in all three phases: before, during, and after expatriation. By highlighting the internal similarities and differences in the organization, the mentors also provide a realistic position preview prior to departure. The mentors should also heighten the mentee's awareness of and preparation for culture shock.

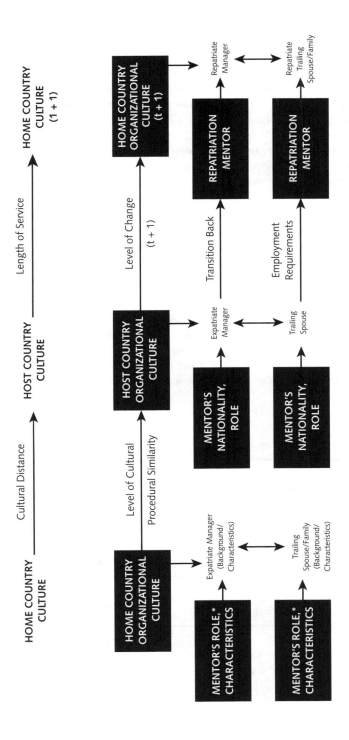

Exhibit 22.3 Expatriate Mentoring Model

Note: *Mentoring Role = Task Mentoring, Career Mentoring, Psycho-Social Mentoring, Role Model Mentoring.

2) Formalize a communication channel – Mentors should develop a mechanism for updating the mentee on shifts in organization, personnel, and strategic operations in the home country. This mechanism should provide both formal and informal communication on a regular and routine basis. The mentors as well as other key individuals should be included in this mechanism.

3) Define expectations/role of mentor during expatriation – The expatriate manager should be assured that the mentors will act as informal arbitrators and spokespersons relative to compensation, appraisal, allowances, and other issues that could create hardships for the expatriate.

4) Discuss advanced planning for repatriation – The mentors should make the manager aware of repatriation plans that need to be taken care of in the home country even before the expatriation occurs.

SECONDARY SUPPORT   Secondary support is directed toward the trailing spouse. The career goals of the trailing spouse during the expatriation of the spouse should provide insights into the nature of the mentoring relationship. It should not be construed that the needs of the trailing spouse are any less important than those of the expatriate. The mentors for the trailing spouse need not be employees but should be people with international experience. The trailing spouse's mentors should undertake the following activities.

1) Identify trailing spouse's career orientation – The mentors should assess career aspirations and options given the trailing spouse's career life cycle and the location of the expatriate's assignment. The mentors should make a realistic assessment of the impediments to continued employment during the foreign assignment well in advance of the couple's departure. Frequently, there are permits and other legal formalities to comply with in order to allow the trailing spouse to be employed once they are in the host country.

TYPES OF MENTORS DURING EXPATRIATION

Expatriate's Mentors	*Trailing Spouse's Mentors*
• Continued communication with original mentors or their replacements	• Continued communication with original mentors or their replacements
• Host country mentors either host country nationals or experienced expatriates	• If sanctioned by the host country, spouses of host country nationals
	• Members of profession or industry association relocation options

MENTORS' ACTIVITIES DURING EXPATRIATION

Expatriate's Mentors	*Trailing Spouse's Mentors*
• Inculcate expatriate in new culture	• Facilitate reestablishment of the household
• Inculcate expatriate in new organization	• Assist in reestablishing career or alternate activities

2) Assess career "sabbatical" options – Mentors should explore alternatives to the trailing spouse's continued career. This analysis should present logical options to the spouse's career. For example, the mentors could point out educational opportunities as an alternative to career placement. The mentors could be an objective third party to give the needed insights into the advantages of gaining an advanced degree during the expatriation assignment of the spouse. The trailing spouse could have improved employment opportunities with an advanced degree upon repatriation.

3) Review realistic relocation options – The mentors should offer insights into the role ambiguity and stress created when altering the family unit roles. Because the dual-career couple's extended family is now so far away, the family situation could become more stressful for the trailing spouse due to modification of the support systems that are frequently well-developed in the home country. If the trailing spouse is not aware of the modification, the international relocation can produce an inordinate amount of stress. Family-related stress is compounded by the stress associated with the "unplanned" change in the trailing spouse's career.

4) Establish informal communication links – A support communication link between the trailing spouse and his/her mentors is very important. This communication "hot line" could provide a support safety net when the trailing spouse is confronted with unanticipated problems. The mentors should serve as resources to resolve the problems encountered in the domestic environment as well as for sending needed materials and supplies to the expatriates in their new international environment.

Phase two: during expatriation

Once the couple has relocated overseas, there should be more than one set of mentors. The original mentors at "headquarters" should continue to provide information on the activities taking place in the home country and organization. At the same time, a new set of mentors for the couple should be provided to facilitate in-country adjustment. If the host country supports the concept of mentoring, host country nationals might accelerate the couple's adjustment by providing the appropriate cultural context. If host country mentors are not available, more experienced expatriates could serve as mentors. While the mentoring provided by host country nationals and expatriates may not be the same, there are a number of services and supports that are essential regardless of which type of mentor is selected.

In addition to the original mentors and the newly assigned mentors, the trailing spouse would benefit from the experience of mentors from the trailing spouse's profession or industry. For example, if the trailing spouse is a CPA, the host organization should make every attempt to link the trailing spouse with individuals in local CPA associations. It is important to note that the connections to the association must be with an individual or group of individuals who are willing to participate in a mentoring relationship. Simply identifying an association or trade group is not enough. The mentors must undertake extensive development of contacts within the group to insure commitment to a mentoring program. While mentors might not directly participate in the reward(s), they recognize the benefits to their group. To obtain such commitment, the individuals in the association or trade group must perceive a tangible benefit to their organization.

TYPES OF MENTORS AFTER EXPATRIATION

Expatriate's Mentors	*Trailing Spouse's Mentors*
● Original mentors or their replacements	● Original mentors or their replacements
● Mentors familiar with the community	● Mentors familiar with the community
	● Mentors familiar with the spouse's career

MENTORS' ACTIVITIES AFTER EXPATRIATION

Expatriate's Mentors	*Trailing Spouse's Mentors*
● Facilitate finding a new position in the organization	● Assist in reestablishing career
● Provide updates on organizational changes	● Consult on resettlement of household
● Provide updates on changes in the work/ home communities	● Encourage participation in mentoring program
● Encourage participation in mentoring program	

PRIMARY SUPPORT   The original, domestic mentors should continue to keep the expatriate informed and follow through with the functions described in the first phase.

The mentors in the new country should provide the following support.

1) Inculcate expatriate in host country's culture – A host country national would be best suited to perform this mentoring function. Expatriates assigned to a boundary-spanning position, such as marketing or sales, require a high level of cultural awareness and sophistication. A host country national mentor could provide these cultural insights. If the mentor is a more experienced expatriate, however, he/she can still provide information in an attempt to accelerate the new manager's understanding of the host country. Ragins and Sundstrom (1989) found that the ultimate benefit of an expatriate mentor is the power conferred on the mentee and the resulting resources that are made available for adjustment to the host country organizational culture.

2) Inculcate expatriate in host country's organization – A host country national mentor is at a slight disadvantage in performing this function. While the host country national can only explain the policies, procedures, and power structures of the foreign organization, an expatriate mentor can point out differences between the host country organization and the domestic organization. Both types of mentors should help the expatriate develop a sensemaking framework that will elevate the individual's self-efficacy as rapidly as possible (Bandura, 1995).

SECONDARY SUPPORT   The mentors' main concern should be to facilitate the adjustment cycle for the trailing spouse and the family, the goal being to encourage intercultural learning and to establish intercultural competence to allow the dual-career couple to effectively relate to those in the host country (Hammer, Gudykunst & Wiseman, 1978; Dinges, 1983; Ruben, 1989; Taylor, 1983). It has been well documented that difficulties in the adjustment of the family unit have a direct impact on the expatriate's performance and the consequent likelihood of premature departure from the international assignment (Lambert, 1990; Jones & Fletcher, 1993; *Wall Street Journal*, 1997). The trailing spouse's mentors should undertake the following activities.

1) Facilitate in reestablishment of the household – The trailing spouse's mentors should provide the cultural context for adjusting to the new environment. This encompasses household activities as well as professional services such as doctors, dentists, and lawyers.

2) Assist in reestablishing career or alternate activities – Frequently, the dual-career trailing spouse will need assistance in establishing his/her career or professional activities in the host country. The host country mentor (either a host country national or an experienced expatriate) can facilitate these activities. Frequently, work permits, certification, and personal interviews are required in order to gain employment in many host countries. A host country national mentor could provide invaluable insight on how to effectively interface with the governmental bureaucracy found in many countries. However, even an experienced expatriate mentor could offer some suggestions. Employment problems are more acute in developing nations where employment opportunities are limited (Joerges & Czarniawska 1998; Stening & Hammer, 1992; Bandura, 1993, 1995; Harrison, Chadwick & Scales, 1996).

In the event that the trailing spouse is not able to continue in his/her profession, the mentors could introduce some alternatives, such as employment at cultural, geographic, and historic sites. Also, the mentors should suggest education, training, and volunteer activities to enhance the trailing spouse's skill set. All of these would help to advance his/her career.

Phase three: after expatriation

It has been well documented that expatriates, and one would assume their trailing spouses, will encounter difficulties upon repatriating to their home country (Kendall, 1981; Harvey, 1982, 1989; Black & Gregersen, 1991; Napier & Peterson, 1991). The home country organization can greatly facilitate the reentry process through increased communication with the expatriates. In some cases, the original mentors who participated in the first phase, before expatriation, will still be in a position to fulfill this need in phase three. In the event the original mentors are unavailable, new mentors should be identified.

PRIMARY SUPPORT   Primary support should revolve around preparation for the expatriate's return to professional as well as personal and family activities. Therefore, it may be necessary to have both organizational and community mentors. The following activities should accelerate the reentry process.

1) Facilitate Finding a New Position in the Organization – The main concern of the expatriate frequently centers on whether or not the company has a position open that fits his/her logical career progression (Harvey, 1989). The mentors should provide insights into possible positions and their relative merits and serve as an informal advocate among various managers who are not personally familiar with the expatriate. This becomes a concern at least six months prior to the return (Kendall, 1981; Harvey, 1982;

Napier & Peterson, 1991). Consequently, the frequency, strength, and depth of communication need to increase six to nine months in advance of repatriation.

2) Provide Updates on Organizational Changes – Returning managers perceive the political consequences of not knowing the present power base and relationships among key managers to be inordinately important (Harvey, 1989). One of the most stressful parts of repatriation is dealing with the dynamic nature of the organization's cultural setting. Mentors should provide a "political" update beginning six to nine months before the expatriate's return.

3) Provide Updates on Changes in the Community – If the local community has undergone significant change, the mentors should provide assistance and information regarding such issues as where to purchase a home, schooling opportunities, and medical facilities. Without this assistance and information, there is a heightened potential for a "spillover" from the manager's personal life that could impact his/her professional repatriation (Greenhaus & Parasuraman, 1986; Lambert, 1990; Jones & Fletcher, 1993).

4) Encourage Participation in Mentoring Program – By entering the mentoring program during any one of the three phases, the repatriated dual-career couple can most effectively update the database of expatriate experience.

SECONDARY SUPPORT   The trailing spouse's mentors have two equally important activities: reestablishing the trailing spouse's career and accommodating the reentry of the family.

1) Assist in Reestablishing Career – The stress from the expatriate manager's professional reentry can compound problems for the trailing spouse in establishing his/her own career (Zedeck, Maslach, Mosien & Skitka, 1989; Blair, 1993). The mentors should provide professional career insights and act as a surrogate for the trailing spouse during the preliminary stages of the search process. To be most effective, six to nine months prior to reentry, the mentors should develop an understanding of the trailing spouse's career aspirations and how the expatriate experience can be positioned as a positive and enriching career activity.

2) Consult on Resettlement of Household in Home Country – Because of the reinitiation of the professional dimension of the dual-career couple's lives, family resettlement is more complicated. Due to the limited time the trailing spouse may have for these more traditional aspects of his/her role, the mentor's information on the relative merits of locations within a city becomes more important.

3) Encourage Participation in Mentoring Program – By entering the mentoring program during any one of the three phases, the repatriated dual-career couple can most effectively update the database of expatriate experience.

JUSTIFYING THE GLOBAL DUAL-CAREER COUPLE MENTORING PROGRAM

It would not be coming to a rash conclusion to ask, "How can such a complex mentoring system be justified?" The process of expatriating managers has been studied for several decades and there are still those experts who contend that a significant percentage of expatriates fail (Mendenhall, Dunbar & Oddou, 1987; Wederspahn, 1992; Dowling, Schuler & Welch, 1994). These authors would underline the explicit cost of those failures by determining the sunk costs associated with: (1) recruiting; (2) assessment; (3) training and development; (4) compensation and benefits; and (5) relocation of expatriate and family. The individual manager's cost associated with a failed expatriate assignment is estimated between $100,000 and $300,000, with a total cost per year for U.S.-based MNCs at approximately $2 billion (Wederspahn, 1992).

While the cost of expatriate failures warrants attention, the more significant impact of a large percentage of expatriates failing may be harder to measure. The implicit or hidden cost of expatriates performing below expectations when compared to their counterparts from other countries may have the greatest impact. The following implicit costs have been identified with expatriates not fulfilling performance expectations: 1) "wasting" the best talent in the organization – the managers who are selected to serve overseas are typically the "best" and the "brightest" executives that the company has. If the failure rate remains high, executives are lost due to not properly preparing managers for overseas assignments; 2) increased refusal rates – when other high-potential managers learn of the failures of their fellow managers during expatriation, they will be reluctant to accept an overseas assignment (Noe & Barber, 1993; Windham International, 1994, Harvey, 1995); 3) loss of mission control – expatriates are used to represent the home country organization in the host country. The dissemination of the corporate culture through expatriate emissaries or the "carrying-the-flag mission" has been identified as a primary reason for using expatriates. If expatriates are not successful in transposing corporate culture, the ability to maintain control is reduced; 4) disruption in key contacts – the constant "shuffling" of expatriate managers reduces the confidence of customers, channel-of-distribution members, government officials, and the like in the host country; and 5) lower quality of relations with host country nationals – the host country nationals employed by the MNC may lose confidence in expatriate managers if they are constantly being replaced and not meeting performance standards. The failure of expatriate managers can have extensive repercussions inside the host country organization as well as with outside constituents.

The proposed global mentoring program is complex and may be difficult to implement, but the explicit costs are minimal. The primary cost of mentoring is the recognition or building of the social capital of the mentors in the organization (Burt, 1997). Social capital is a quasi indicator of the returns (rewards) to the mentors. It helps to elevate the mentors' location in the social structure of the organization (Friedman & Krackhardt, 1997). This would appear to be an insignificant cost relative to the explicit/implicit costs associated with expatriate failures. The system could be difficult to initiate and to effectively implement in the home and host countries. But, if the system were operationalized, the new expatriates who were mentored could help to sustain the program in the future by becoming mentors themselves.

Other than the operational aspects of the expatriate mentoring program, the most troublesome aspect might be in identifying qualified mentors to participate in the program. A mentoring training program might be needed to highlight the critical dimensions of the mentoring process. This developmental aspect of expatriation management would have to be programmed into the training of managers who interface with potential expatriates. In addition, these individuals must be willing volunteers to participate in the expatriate mentoring program or the goals of the mentoring will not be accomplished (Clawson, 1980; Kram & Isabella, 1985; Kram, 1985; Ostroff & Kozlowski, 1993). To reduce the operational issues associated with the expatriate mentoring program, the process could be phased in over an extended period of time. Initially, the expatriates could receive pre-expatriation mentoring, and once that aspect of the program was implemented, the second phase in the host country could be undertaken. Repatriation could be managed by the same mentor who participated in the pre-expatriation phase, and once the number of mentors had increased, a new manager could undertake the responsibilities of mentoring reentry.

SUMMARY AND CONCLUSIONS

The success of expatriate managers is contingent on adjusting to their new corporate and country cultures as rapidly as possible. Frequently, this adjustment process is strongly influenced by his/her spouse and family members. Their lack of social support and preparation for the international relocation creates stress in the family unit, which spills over into the expatriate's professional life. While this family/professional interaction has been well documented, what has not been factored into the assessment of expatriate relocations is the potential impact of dual-career couples relocating overseas.

What is envisioned to facilitate the expatriation dual-career couple's adjustment is a three-stage mentoring program that addresses critical issues of expatriation before, during, and after the relocation. While the mentoring process is complex and would be difficult to implement, the direct cost of such a program would be negligible compared to the cost of expatriate failures. Mentoring by experienced international executives could accelerate the adjustment cycle for both expatriate and the trailing spouse. Developing self-efficacy for an expatriate is the basis of the adjustment process. Mentoring could help to stimulate this process. In addition, the current expatriates could provide the replacements and additions to the mentoring co-ops in the future.

The dual-career couple presents a unique challenge to international human resource managers. Without creative insights into the process of relocating these couples overseas, the frequency of refusal to relocate, failure, and low performance during the assignment will continue to grow. The future competitiveness of MNCs based in the United States may hinge on finding a solution to the dual-career couple's relocation problem. The three-phase global mentoring model is one means for addressing this vexing social issue.

References

Allen, N. and Meyer, J. "Organizational Commitment: Evidence of Career Stage Effects?" *Journal of Business Research*, 26 (1993): 49–61.

Ashford, S. and Taylor, M. "Adaptations to Work Transitions: An Integrative Approach." In K. Rowland and G. Ferris (eds.) *Research in Personnel & Human Resources*. Greenwich, CT: JAI Press, 1990.

Bachman, S. I. and Gregory, K. "Mentor and Protégé Gender. Effects on Mentoring Roles and Outcomes." Paper presented at the Society for Industrial and Organizational Psychology conference. San Francisco: April, 1993.

Bandura, A. *Exercise of Personal and Collective Efficacy in Changing Societies*. Cambridge University Press: New York, 1995.

———"Perceived Self-Efficiency in Cognitive Development and Functioning." *Educational Psychologist*, 28 (1993): 117–48.

Billings, A. and Moos, R. (1982). "Work Stress and the Stress-Buffering Roles of Work and Family Resources." *Journal of Occupational Behavior*, 3 (1993): 215–32.

Black, J. S. and Gregersen, H. "When Yankee Comes Home: Factors Related to Expatriate and Spouse Repatriation Adjustment." *Journal of International Business Studies*, 22(4) (1991): 671–94.

Black, J. S. and Mendenhall, M. "Cross-Cultural Training Effectiveness: A Review and Theoretical Framework for Future Research." *Academy of Management Review*, 15 (1990): 113–36.

Black, S. "Workrole Transitions: A Study of American Expatriate Managers in Japan." *Journal of International Business Studies*, 15 (1988): 113–36.

Black, S. Gregersen, H., and Mendenhall, M. *Global Assignments.* San Francisco, CA: Jossey-Bass Publishers, 1992.

Black, S., Mendenhall, M., and Oddou, G. "Toward a Comprehensive Model of International Adjustment: An Integration of Multiple Theoretical Perspectives." *Academy of Management Review*, 16(2) (1991): 292–310.

Blair, S. "Employment, Family and Perceptions of Marital Quality among Husbands and Wives." *Journal of Family Issues*, 14(2) (1993): 189–212.

Bochner, S. "Cultures in Contact: Studies in Cross-Cultural Interaction." New York: Pergamon Press, 1982.

Bolger, N., DeLongis, A., Kessler, R. C., and Wetherington, E. "The Contagion of Stress Across Multiple Roles," *Journal of Marriage and the Family*, 51 (1989): 175–83.

Brett, J.M. "The Effect of Job Transfers on Employees and Their Families." In C.L. Cooper and R. Payne (eds.) *Current Concerns in Occupational Stress.* New York: Wiley, 1980.

Brislin, R.W. *Cross-Cultural Encounters.* New York: Pergamon Press, 1981.

Burke, R. "Some Antecedents and Consequences of Work-Family Conflict." *Journal of Social Behavior and Personality*, 34 (1988): 287–302.

Burke, R. and McKeen, C. "Work and Family: What We Know and What We Need to Know." *Canadian Journal of Administrative Sciences*, 5 (1988): 30–40.

Burt, R. "The Contingent Value of Social Capital." *Administrative Science Quarterly*, 42 (1997): 339–65.

Chao, G.T., O'Leary-Kelly, A.M., Wolf, S., Klein, H. J., and Gardner, P.D. "Organizational Socialization: Its Content and Consequences." *Journal of Applied Psychology*, 79(5) (1994): 730–43.

Chao, G.T., Walz, P.M., and Gardner, P.D. "Formal and Informal Mentorships: A Comparison on Mentoring Functions and Contrast with Nonmentored Counterparts." *Personnel Psychology*, 45 (1992): 619–36.

Clawson, J. G. "Mentoring in Managerial Careers." In C.B. Deer (ed.), *Work. Family and the Career.* New York: Praeger, 1980.

Coolidge, L. and D'Angelo, D. "Family Issues to Shape the Professional's Future." *The CPA Journal*, May (1994): 16–21.

Copeland, L. and Griggs, L. *Going International: How to Make Friends and Deal Effectively in the Global Marketplace.* New York: Random House, 1985.

Crendall, L., Dwyer, J., and Duncan, R. "Recruitment and Retention of Rural Physicians: Issues for the 1990s." *The Journal of Rural Health*, 6(1) (1990): 19–38.

Crouter, A. C., Perry-Jenkins, M. Huston, T. L. and Crawford, D.W. "The Influence of Work-Induced Psychological States on Behavior at Home." *Basic and Applied Social Psychology*, 10 (1989): 273–92.

Dawis, R. V. and Lofquist, L. H. *A Psychological Theory of Work Adjustment.* Minneapolis: University of Minnesota Press, 1984.

Dinges, N. "Intercultural Competence." In D. Landis and R. Brislin (eds.), *Handbook of Intercultural Training.* New York: Pergamon Press, 1983.

Dowling, P., Schuler, R., and Welch, D. *International Dimensions of Human Resource Management (Second Edition).* Belmont, CA: Wadsworth Publishing Company, 1994.

Dreher, G. F. and Ash, R. A. "A Comparative Study of Mentoring among Men and Women in

Managerial, Professional, and Technical Positions." *Journal of Applied Psychology*, 75 (1990): 539–46.

Evans, P. and Bartolome, F. "The Changing Picture of the Relationship between Career and the Family." *Journal of Occupational Behavior*, 5 (1984): 9–21.

Fagenson, E.A. "The Power of a Mentor." *Group and Organization Studies*, 13 (1988): 182–94.

Feldman, B. "The Dynamics of Ethnic Diversity in Organizations: Toward Integrative Models." In K. Kelley (ed.), *Issues, Theory and Research in Industrial/Organizational Psychology*. Amsterdam: North Holland, 1992.

Feldman, D.C. "The Multiple Socialization of Organization Members." *Academy of Management Review*, 6 (1981): 309–19.

Feldman and Thompson. "Expatriation, Repatriation, and Domestic Relocation: An Empirical Investigation of Adjustment to New Job Assignments." *Journal of International Business Studies*, 24(3) (1993): 507–29.

Fisher, C. "Organizational Socialization: An Integrative Review." *Research in Personnel and Human Resource Management*, 4 (1986): 101–45. Greenwich, CT: JAI Press.

Fletcher, B. "Occupation, Marriage and Disease-Specific Mortality Concordance." *Social Science and Medicine*, 27 (1988): 615–22.

——*Work, Stress, Disease and Life Expectancy*. New York: Wiley and Sons, 1991.

Ford, D. L. and Wells, L. "Upward Mobility Factors among Black Public Administrators: The role of Mentors." *Centerboard*, 3 (1985): 38–48.

Frankenhaueser, M., Lundberg, U., Frederikson, M., Belin, B., Tuomisto, M., and Myrsten, A. "Stress On and Off the Job as Related to Sex and Occupational States in White Collar Workers." *Journal of Occupational Behavior*, 10 (1989): 321–46.

Friedman, R. and Krackhardt, D. "Social Capital and Career Mobility." *Journal of Applied Behavioral Science*, 33(3) (1997): 316–34.

Gomez-Mejia, L. and Wilbourne, T. "Compensation Strategies in a Global Context." *Human Resource Planning*, 14(1) (1991): 29–41.

Granrose, C., Parasuraman, S., and Greenhaus, J. "A Proposed Model of Support Provided by Two-Career Couples." *Human Relations*, 45 (1992): 1367–93.

Greenhaus, J. and Beutell, N. "Sources of Conflict between Work and Family Roles." *Academy of Management Review*, 10 (1985): 76–88.

Greenhaus, J. H. and Kopelman, R. E. "Conflict Between Work and Non-Work Roles: Implications for the Career Planning Process." *Human Resource Planning*, 4(1) (1981): 1–10.

Greenhaus, J. and Parasuraman, S. "A Work-Nonwork Interactive Perspective of Stress and Its Consequences." *Journal of Organizational Behavior Management*, 8 (1986): 37–60.

Gutelle, B., Reperri, R.L., and Silver, D.L. "Nonwork Roles and Stress at Work." In C.L. Cooper and R. Payne (eds.), *Causes, Coping and Consequences of Stress at Work*. Chichester, U.K.: Wiley, 1988.

Hammer, M., Gudykunst, W., and Wiseman, W. "Dimensions of Intercultural Effectiveness: An Exploratory Study." *International Journal of Intercultural Relations*, 2 (1978): 382–93.

Harrison, J.K., Chadwick, M., and Scales, M. "The Relationship between Cross-Cultural Adjustment and Personality Variables of Self-Efficacy and Self-Monitoring." *International Journal of Intercultural Relations*, 20(2) (1996): 167–88.

Harvey, M. "The Other Side of Foreign Assignments: Dealing with the Repatriation Dilemma." *The Columbia Journal of World Business*, 17(1) (1982).

——"The Executive Family: An Overlooked Variable in International Assignments." *The Columbia Journal of World Business*, Summer (1985): 84–93.

——"Repatriation of Corporate Executives: An Empirical Study." *Journal of International Business Studies*, 20(1) (1989): 131–44.

——"The Impact of Dual-Career Families on International Relocations." *Human Resource Management Review*, 5(3) (1995): 223–34.

——"Dual-Career Couples: The Selection Dilemma." *International Journal of Selection and Assessment*,

4(4) (1996a).

——"Addressing the Dual-Career Expatriation Dilemma." *Human Resource Planning*, 19(4) (1996b).

——"Dual-Career Expatriates: Expectations. Adjustment, and Satisfaction with International Relocation." *Journal of International Business Studies*, 28(3) (1997a).

——"The Impact of the Dual-Career Expatriate on International Human Resource Management." *Journal of International Management*, 3(3) (1997b).

——"Dual-Career Couples during International Relocation: The Trailing Spouse." *International Journal of Human Resource Management*, (forthcoming a).

——, Harvey, M. and Buckley, M.R. "The Development Process for Programs Addressing Dual-Career Families Being Relocated Internationally." *Human Resource Management Review*, (forthcoming b).

Higgins, C., Duxbury, L., and Irving, R. "Work-Family Conflict in the Dual-Career Family." *Organizational Behavior and Human Decision Processes*, 51 (1992): 51–75.

Hunt, D.M. and Michael, C. "Mentorship: A Career Training and Development Tool." *Academy of Management Review*, 8 (1983): 475–85.

Hurley, D. "The Mentor Mystique." *Psychology Today*, May (1988): 41–3.

Jackson, S.E., Stone, V.K. and Alvarez, E.B. "Socialization Amidst Diversity: The Impact of Demographics on Work Team Oldtimers and Newcomers." *Research in Organizational Behavior*, 15 (1993): 45–109.

Joerges, B. and Czarniawska, B. "The Question of Technology or How Organizations Inscribe the World." *Organization Studies* 19(3) (1998): 363.

Jones, F. and Fletcher, B. "An Empirical Study of Occupational Stress Transmission in Working Couples." *Human Relations*, 46(7) (1993): 881–903.

Jones, G.R. "Socialization Tactics, Self-Efficacy, and Newcomers' Adjustments to Organizations." *Academy of Management Journal*, 29 (1986): 262–79.

Kahn, R.L., Wolfe, D.M., Quinn, R., Snoek, J.D., and Rosenthal, R. A. "Organizational Stress: Studies in Role Conflict and Ambiguity." New York: Wiley, 1964.

Kanter, R.M. *Men and Women of the Corporation.* New York: Basic Books, Inc., 1977.

Kelly, R. and Voydanoff, P. "Work Family Role Strain among Employed Parents." *Family Relations*, 34 (1985): 367–74.

Kendall, D. "Repatriation: An Ending and a Beginning." *Business Horizons*, November–December (1981): 21–5.

Koberg, C.S., Boss, W., Chappell, D., and Ringer, R.C. "An Investigation of the Antecedents and Outcomes of Mentoring." Paper presented at the annual meeting of the Academy of Management, Las Vegas, 1994.

Kram, K.E. "Phases of the Mentor Relationship." *Academy of Management Journal*, 6 (1983): 608–25.

Kram, K. E. *Mentoring at Work: Development Relationships in Organizational Life.* Glenview, IL: Scott, Foresman, 1985.

Kram, K.E. and Isabella, L. "Mentoring Alternatives: The Role of Peer Relationships in Career Development." *Academy of Management Journal*, 28 (1985): 110–32.

Ladewig, B.H. and McGee, G.W. "Occupational Commitment, a Supportive Family Environment, and Marital Adjustment: Development and Estimation of a Model." *Journal of Marriage and the Family*, 48 (1986): 821–9.

Lambert, S. "Processing Linking Work and Family: A Critical View and Research Agenda." *Human Relations*, 43(4) (1990): 239–57.

Lankau, M.J. "An Examination and Comparison of Mentoring and Peer Development Relationships in the Context of Project Teams." Unpublished Doctoral Dissertation, University of Miami, 1996.

Lazarus, R.S. and Launier, E. "Stress-Related Transactions between Person and Environment." In L.A. Pervin and M. Lewis (eds.), *Perspectives in Interactional Psychology*, New York: Plenum, 1978.

Levinson, D.J., Darrow, C.N., Klein, E.B., Levinson, M.H., and McKee, B. *The Seasons of a Man's*

Life. New York: Knopf, 1978.

Lodhal, T.M. and Kehner, N. "The Definition and Measurement of Job Involvement." *Journal of Applied Psychology*, 49 (1965): 24–33.

Louis, M.R. "Surprise and Sense-Making: What Newcomers Experience in Entering Unfamiliar Organizational Settings." *Administrative Science Quarterly*, 25 (1980): 226–51.

Louis, M.R. "Newcomers as Lay Ethnographers: Acculturation during Socialization." In B. Schneider (ed.), *Organizational Climates and Cultures*. San Francisco: Jossey-Bass, 1990.

McDonald, K.S. "The New Mentoring." *Fortune*, November 27 (1995): 213.

Mendenhall, M., Dunbar, E., and Oddou, G. "Expatriate Selection, Training, and Career Pathing: A Review Critique." *Human Resource Management*, 26(3) (1987): 331–45.

Mendenhall, M. and Oddou, G. "The Overseas Assignment: A Practical Look." *Business Horizons*, Sept–Oct (1988): 78–84.

Mitchell, R.E., Billings, A.G., and Moos, R.H. "Social Support and Well-Being: Implications for Prevention Programs." *Journal of Primary Prevention*, 3(2) (1982): 77–98.

Mullen, E. "Framing the Mentoring Relationship as an Information Exchange." *Human Resource Management Review*, 4(3) (1994): 257–81.

Napier, N. and Peterson, R. "Expatriation Re-entry: What Do Expatriates Have to Say?" *Human Resource Planning*, 14(1) (1991): 19–28.

Near, J. P., Rice, R. W., and Hunt, R.G. "Work and Extrawork Correlates of Life and Job Satisfaction." *Academy of Management Journal*, 21 (1978): 248–64.

Nicholson, N. "A Theory of Work Role Transitions." *Administrative Science Quarterly*, 29 (1984): 172–91.

Nieva, V. "Work and Family Linkages." In B. Gutek, A. Stromber, and L. Larwood (eds.), *Women and Work*, New York: Sage, 1988.

Noe, R. and Barber, A. "Willingness to Accept Mobility Opportunities: Destination Makes a Difference." *Journal of Organizational Behavior*, 14 (1993): 159–75.

Ostroff, C. and Kozlowski, S.W.J. "The Role of Mentoring in the Information Gathering Processes of Newcomers during Early Organizational Socialization." *Journal of Vocational Behavior*, 42 (1993): 170–3.

Pascoe, R. "Employers Ignore Expatriate Wives at Their Own Peril." *Wall Street Journal*, March 2 (1992): A20(w), A12(e), col. 3.

Perlin, L. "Social Structure and Processes of Social Support." In S. Cohen and S. Syme (eds.), *Social Support and Health*. New York: Academic Press, 1985.

Phillips-Jones, L.L. *Mentoring and Protégés*. New York: Arbor House, 1982.

Pinder, C.C. and Schroeder, K.G. "Time to Proficiency Following Transfers." *Academy of Management Journal*, 30 (1987): 336–53.

Piotrkowski, C.S. *Work and the Family System*. New York: Macmillan, 1979.

Pleck, J.H. "Men's Family Work: Three Perspectives and Some New Data." *The Family Coordinator*, 28 (1979): 481–7.

Pleck, J.H. *Working Wives/Working Husbands*. Beverly Hills, CA: Sage, 1985.

Pleck, J.H., Staines, G.L., and Long, L. (1980). Conflicts between work and family life. *Monthly Labor Review*, 103(3): 29–32.

Ragins, S.B. "Diversity, power, and mentorship in organizations: A cultural, structural, and behavioral perspective." In M. Chemers, M. Coslorzo and S. Skap (eds.), *Diversity in Organizations: New Perspectives for a Changing Workplace*. Newberry Park, CA: Sage, 1995.

Ragins, B. and E. Sundstrom. "Gender and Power in Organizations: A Longitudinal Perspective." *Psychological Bulletin*, 105 (1989): 51–88.

Reperri, R.L. "Family and Occupational Roles and Women's Mental Health." In R.M. Schwartz (ed.), *Women at Work*. Los Angeles, CA: Institute of Industrial Relations, UCLA, 1987.

Reynolds, C. and Bennett, R. "The Career Couple Challenge." *Personnel Journal*, March (1991): 48.

Roche, G. R. "Much Ado about Mentors." *Harvard Business Review*, 57(1) (1979): 14–31.

Ruben, B. "The Study of Cross-Cultural Competence: Traditions and Contemporary Issues." *International Journal of Intercultural Relations*, 13 (1989): 229–40.

Rudd, N. M. and McKenry, P. C. "Family Influences on Job Satisfaction of Employed Mothers." *Psychology of Women Quarterly*, 10 (1986): 363–72.

Scandura, T.A. "Mentorship and Career Mobility: An Empirical Investigation." *Journal of Organizational Behavior*, 13 (1992): 169–74.

Scandura, T. A. and Viator, R. E. "Mentoring in Public Accounting Firms: An analysis of Mentor-Protégé Relationships, Mentoring Functions and Protégé Turnover Intentions." *Accounting Organizations and Society*, 19 (1994): 717–34.

Scandura, T. A. and Von Glinow, M. A. "Development of the International Manager: The Role of Mentoring." *Business and the Contemporary World*, 9(1) (1997): 95–115.

Schein, E. *Organizational Culture and Leadership*. San Francisco: Jossey-Bass, 1985.

Schuler, R., Fulkerson, J., and Dowling, P. "Strategic Performance Measurement and Management in Multinational Corporations." *The Columbia Journal of World Business*, 28 (1991): 56–72.

Schumaker, S. and Brownell, A. "Toward a Theory of Social Support: Closing Conceptual Gaps." *Journal of Social Issues*, 4 (1984): 11–36.

Schumaker, S. and Jackson, J. "The Adverse Effects of Nonreciprocated Benefits." *Social Psychology Quarterly*, 42(2) (1979): 148–58.

Statistical Abstract of the United States. 1992 United States Bureau of the Census, Washington, D.C.: U.S. Government Printing Office.

Stening, B. and Hammer, M. "Cultural Baggage and the Adoption of American and Japanese Managers." *Management International Review*, 32 (1992): 77–89.

Suchet, M. and Barling, J. "Employed Mothers: Inter-role Conflict. Spouse Support, and Marital Functioning." *Journal of Occupational Behavior*, 7 (1986): 167–78.

Tausig, M. and Michello, J. "Seeking Social Support." In J. E. Singer (ed.), *Basic and Applied Social Psychology*, 9(1) (1988): 1–12.

Taylor, S. E. "Adjustment to Threatening Events: A Theory of Cognitive Adaptation." *American Psychologist*, 38(11) (1983): 1161–73.

Tung, R. *The New Expatriates: Managing Human Resources Abroad*. Cambridge, MA: Ballinger, 1988.

Voydanoff, P. *Work and Family Life*. Beverly Hills: Sage, 1987.

Voydanoff, P. "Work and Family: A Review and Expanded Conceptualization." *Journal of Social Behavior and Personality*, 3(4) (1988): 1–22.

Wallston, B.S., Alagna, S.W., DeVellis, B.M. and DeVellis, R.F. "Social Support and Physical Health." *Health Psychology*, 2(4) (1983): 367–91.

"The No. 1 Reason Overseas Assignments Fail: The Spouse Hates It." *The Wall Street Journal*, January 7 (1997): 1A.

Wederspahn, G. "Costing Failures in Expatriate Human Resource Management." *Human Resource Planning*, 15(3) (1992): 27–35.

Whitely, W., Dougherty, T.W. and Dreher, G. F. "Correlates of Career-Oriented Mentoring for Early Career Managers and Professionals." *Journal of Organizational Behavior*, 13 (1991): 141–54.

Williams, K. and Alger, G. "Role Stressors, Mood Spillover, and Perceptions of Work-Family Conflict in Employed Parents." *Academy of Management Journal*, 37 (4) (1994): 837–68.

Windham International and the National Foreign Trade Council (NFTC). *Global Relocation Trends 1994 Survey Report*: 1994.

Yogev, S. and Brett, J. "Perceptions of the Division of Housework and Child Care and Marital Satisfaction." *Journal of Marriage and the Family*, 47 (1985): 609–18.

Zedeck, S., Maslach, C., Mosien, K., and Skitka, K. "Affective Response to Work and Quality of Life." In E. Goldsmith (ed.), *Work and Family: Theory, Rewards, and Applications*. Newberry Park, CA: Sage, 1989.

Zey, M.G. *The Mentor Connection*. Homewood, IL: Dow Jones-Irwin, 1984.

Chapter 23

Case: Bhiwar Enterprises

Gordon Brannan and Joseph J. DiStefano

Pratap Bhiwar had been working as a consultant to the family business between the two years of his M.B.A. program. Near the end of his summer's efforts, he had prepared a report for his cousin who was Managing Director of the Rori Company, one of several businesses owned and operated by the Bhiwar family. His recommendations were intended to rationalize company operations to increase effectiveness and efficiency. Instead, they seemed to have stimulated a rash of arguments among his cousins and uncles that threatened to destroy forty years of solidarity and business success. As the time drew near to return to North America, Pratap wondered what he could do to resolve the problems his report had generated.

HISTORY OF THE BHIWAR FAMILY IN AFRICA

Mohan Bhiwar emigrated from India with his wife and family to avoid starvation and to start a new life in the British colony of Kenya. However, in Kenya Mohan could not farm as his family had done in India. Agriculture, especially the cultivation of cash crops, was a white man's monopoly. Africans and Asians[1] were prohibited from farming by the colonial government. Mohan, therefore, became a retail peddler in the area around the village in which he had settled.

For twenty years Mohan rose daily at 4:00 a.m. and rode his bicycle into the country-

IVEY Gordon Brannan prepared this case under the supervision of Professor Joseph J. DiStefano solely to provide material for class discussion. The authors do not intend to illustrate either effective or ineffective handling of a managerial situation. The authors may have disguised certain names and other identifying information to protect confidentiality.

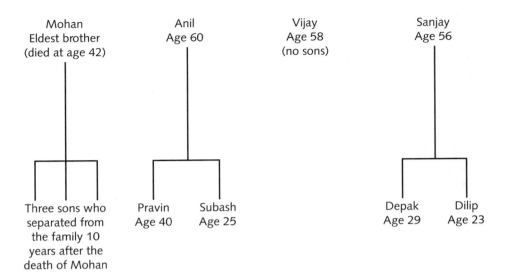

Note: None of the four senior brothers had a formal education. All started working at about the ages of 12 or 13. Each of the older surviving brothers became a millionaire. Pravin, the elder son of Anil, completed high school in Kenya. His brother Subash went to Europe to study business administration before joining the Rori Company. Depak, Sanjay's older son, completed high school in Europe, and his younger brother Dilip finished high school in Kenya.

Exhibit 23.1   Bhiwar Family Structure

side, where he purchased surplus fruit and vegetables from Africans. Mohan brought the produce back to his village and sold it. Then he purchased hardware and cloth, which he sold in the more rural villages.

After a few years Mohan was able to afford to bring over from India his three younger brothers – Anil, Vijay, and Sanjay – and their families. Together the brothers expanded the retail operation and assured themselves of economic survival in their adopted country. The family relationships are shown in Exhibit 23.1.

All four brothers and their families lived together under one roof. In addition to the economic benefits, this arrangement was also a form of social security. For example, in the case of accident or sickness, other members of the family were available to help. This role of the extended family was particularly important in Kenya where no state welfare structure existed. Living together was also culturally acceptable in the Asian community.[2]

For years the brothers continued their retail peddling and saved a little money from the business every year. Eventually the family bought its first car, and three years later they purchased their first truck. When Mohan died of a heart attack, the family leadership passed to Anil, the oldest surviving brother.

The year Mohan died was also the year the fortunes of the family business picked up. In October, a group of African freedom fighters (or terrorists according to the colonists) began a campaign to end colonial rule and white domination in Kenya. The colonial government, which represented white interests in the colony, responded to the terrorism by declaring a state of martial law. As part of its response, the government constructed large prison camps in which to confine captured rebels. These camps had to be supplied with food, clothing, and other provisions. Competitive bids were invited from various firms for the monopoly of supplying the camps. Through an elaborate system of bribery, a common practice in the colony, the Bhiwar brothers successfully obtained the contract.

Their business dealings, however, were not confined to the government. The rebels needed materials for the manufacture of weapons that the brothers were able to supply. The Bhiwars did not consider these activities treasonable. As Asians, they identified with neither the Europeans nor the Africans. They saw the relationship as merely buyer–seller. In their dealings with both the rebels and the government, the brothers were able to name their own prices since their services were in such high demand.

Because of their success during the rebellion and the fact that the brothers had established valuable contacts, they were in a favourable position to buy up surplus agricultural produce to sell to European wholesalers in Kenya. The surpluses resulted from improved agricultural techniques introduced after the rebellion had ended. The techniques were part of an economic revitalization program to reduce inequalities which had been central in originally bringing about the conflict. However, although many farmers were able to produce a surplus, few had the transportation facilities necessary to move their goods to market. The Bhiwar brothers, on the other hand, had both equipment and capital. They were, therefore, able to take advantage of this unusual opportunity.

FAMILY BREAKUP AND A NEW COMPANY

Five years after the rebellion had ended, the older generation of brothers – Anil, Vijay, and Sanjay – decided to retire from active participation in the business. According to tradition, the leadership of the family should have passed to Mohan's oldest son. However, since Anil had been the head of the family unit, his influence and guidance were powerful forces in the transition of leadership. Furthermore, only two of the three sons of Mohan were involved in the business, and both of these were located some distance from the head office where Anil's sons operated.

As the health of the older generation declined, Pravin showed increasing initiative. In addition, he received recognition and credit for the steady success of the business by virtue of his physical location, position in the firm, and family status as Anil's older son. As the gradual transition in leadership occurred, it became clear that Pravin would succeed his father. Mohan's sons, resentful of being deprived of a right they saw as belonging to their oldest brother, refused to work in the family business any longer. Their feelings of bitterness were heightened by their judgment that the surviving uncles had not done a conscientious job of looking after them (one was expected to protect the sons of a deceased brother). The result was the breaking away of Mohan's widow and sons from the main body of the Bhiwar family. To some extent, this was encouraged by the mother who, according to the Bhiwars, never had liked her brothers-in-law.

The breakup of the family was psychologically traumatic for all parties concerned. Such an event was unusual and discouraged in the Asian community. Socially, it was considered a sign of deterioration in the stability of the family. Personally, it diminished the reputations of all the individuals involved. Within the family, it left a great deal of bad feeling between the parties.

After the breakup, Pravin, on the advice of his father and uncles, bought a food processing business (Rori Company) from another Asian family. There were two reasons for this acquisition. First, the Bhiwar brothers felt that they could process food cheaply and add to their revenues. Secondly, the purchase of Rori would provide the sons of Anil and Sanjay with an opportunity to develop a business of their own.

Two years after the acquisition, Depak, Sanjay's older son, was made Managing Director of the Rori Company when he returned from finishing his education in Europe. Over the next decade, he expanded the business primarily through his successful marketing efforts in the United States and Canada. But, in spite of this success, Depak was not entirely satisfied, because his cousin Pravin would not permit him to have full control over operations. All changes proposed by Depak had to be reviewed and ratified by Pravin before being implemented. An organization chart for the company is shown in Exhibit 23.2.

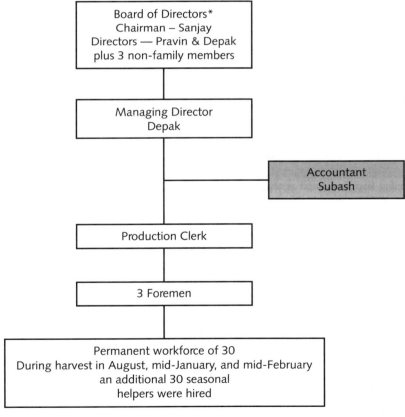

Note: * The Board of Directors never met.

Exhibit 23.2   The Organization of Rori Company

The situation worsened when Pravin's younger brother, Subash, returned to Kenya following completion of his education and was made accountant of the Rori Company. Subash used his position to spy on Depak for his brother Pravin, whose interference in the business and ultimate control of all financial allocations in the family business kept Depak from operating autonomously and efficiently in his own sphere of responsibility. The situation was exacerbated by the fact that personal relations between Depak and the two brothers were strained. Further, it appeared that Pravin was to some extent envious of Depak's ability to work hard and make a success of his operation.

A NEPHEW AS CONSULTANT

Pratap Bhiwar, a nephew through marriage to the older generation (Anil, Vijay, and Sanjay), was home in Kenya for a vacation. He was currently an M.B.A. student in a North American university. While he was visiting with his uncle Sanjay, his cousin Depak arrived and asked him how his studies were going. As the two men began to talk about business in general and the operations of the Rori Company in particular, it occurred to Pratap that he might be able to help Depak with some of the problems he was having in the business. He suggested to Depak that he be hired to do consulting work while he was home for the vacation. Depak was delighted and consulted with his father, Sanjay. The older man also thought the idea had merit, but said that it would be necessary to check with Pravin, who after all was the head of the family interests now that the older generation of men had retired. Pravin made some remarks about outside interference in the affairs of the family, but did not attempt to stop Pratap from helping.

As Pratap started the consulting job, he approached his work using the tough-minded framework of analysis that he was being taught in North America. He viewed the consulting assignment as an opportunity to implement rigorous North American management practices. He decided that any inefficiencies in the operation would be uprooted. He would recommend the firing of poor performers.

After making some preliminary investigations of the operation, Pratap concluded that although the marketing system that Depak had set up was good, the company's costing system was sloppy. In addition, the production setup of the plant was not well-integrated with the rest of the operation because of poor planning and haphazard expansion. However, Pratap told Depak, in order to proceed further, it would now be necessary to analyze in some detail the past financial statements of the company. Depak told him that would be difficult since he did not have the data. In fact, he continued, he had never seen any of the financial statements of the Rori Company. He told Pratap that Pravin kept all the statements to himself. Pratap then asked Depak how, as Managing Director of Rori Company, he made his financial decisions. Depak replied that it was simple. Whenever it was necessary to make an expenditure, he relayed his request for money through Subash who then made the representation to his older brother on Depak's behalf. Pravin would then make a decision and tell Subash what it was; Subash would, in turn, inform Depak.

A little amazed by this system, but quite prepared to work within its constraints for the time being, Pratap approached Subash and asked him to obtain the financial statements. Subash, however, misrepresented Pratap to Pravin, who refused to issue the statements. Pratap then approached his uncle Sanjay to help him. Sanjay went to Pravin and persuaded him to hand over the statements. Pravin, however, was not happy about the whole affair. While reluctantly parting with the financial data, he insinuated that Pratap was simply out to make trouble.

After Pratap had analyzed the financial statements, he discovered that a substantial amount of money had disappeared. When asked, Depak said he didn't know anything about it, since he had no control over expenditures. Pratap told Depak that, as Managing Director of Rori, it was his responsibility to know how and where money was spent. Depak agreed and went to see Pravin. But when he asked Pravin about the money, Pravin exploded in anger and told Depak that he was inefficient as a Managing Director, knew nothing of the business, and had wasted his last six years in the firm. Depak retorted that Pravin had never helped him with the business, so how could he expect him to learn? He added heatedly that whenever he asked Pravin a few questions, he never received any answers. As usual, the meeting ended without Pravin answering any of Depak's questions, and bad feelings continued to exist between the two men.

In these circumstances, Pratap felt that the quarrel over the missing money was not worth further straining the family relationships. He told Depak that he would be able to complete his report with the information he had available.

PRATAP'S REPORT

Several days later, Pratap finished the report. He had come to two major conclusions. First, the capital acquisition policy of the Rori Company was poor and bore no relation to the overall profit objectives of the firm. He felt that the reason was Pravin's absolute financial control. Depak was unable to make necessary capital acquisitions because he could not obtain the money or approval from Pravin. Secondly, Pratap found that Subash was incompetent as an accountant. In failing to gather and to analyze properly the cost data essential to the business, Subash had proven useless to Depak. In short, Pratap concluded that the Rori Company could function neither efficiently nor effectively. The power to make critical financial decisions was in the hands of a man who for all practical purposes was an absentee landlord who refused to listen to his manager.

It was clear to Pratap that he should make two recommendations:

1. Pravin should give Depak control of the financial statements and decisions related to Rori.
2. The incompetent Subash should be removed.

When Pratap showed his report to Depak, Depak said it should be hidden. He felt that the recommendations to rationalize the operations were unacceptable and would result in family conflict. Pratap admitted that he knew it to be true, but was interested in approaching the business problems rigorously and pushing through to logical conclusions. Agreeing that there were some parts of the report that could be implemented without disturbing the family, both men were willing to let the full report "die" in Depak's office.

However, the matter was not resolved so easily. Sanjay kept inquiring about the progress of the report and told Pratap that he would like to see it when it was completed. Eventually, under continual pressure from Sanjay, Pratap brought the report to his uncle. But since Sanjay could not read English, Pratap read the report aloud to him. When Pratap finished, Sanjay agreed with his nephew's conclusions and asked for his recommendations.

Pratap answered that, in his opinion, the Rori Company should be separated from the Bhiwar Enterprises and placed under the complete control of Depak. He said Depak should be totally responsible for profits and free from outside interference. He also stated that Subash should be fired, since he was incapable of doing his job.

Sanjay listened to the recommendations quietly, but told Pratap that they were unacceptable. If Subash were fired, Sanjay continued, Anil would ask why his son had been discharged. If told that his son was incompetent, he would most certainly become angry, and conflict among the elder brothers would inevitably result. Besides, in the eyes of the Asian community in Kenya, Subash was a big executive. What would they think of the solidarity of the Bhiwar family if he were fired from the family business? Sanjay asked if it would be worth breaking up a close partnership between the brothers that had lasted for forty years just for the sake of more efficiency. Was it really worth all this trouble, Sanjay concluded, for a few thousand dollars of inefficiency?

Although Pratap said that he understood his uncle's point of view, he asked the older man if it was worth sacrificing Depak's future in a business where he was going to be constantly constrained. Pratap argued that Depak would eventually become fed up with the whole situation. In fact, he was fed up now. But as the elder son with the burden of responsibility for the Sanjay household in the Bhiwar family he was unlikely to rebel against a situation that helped preserve the stability of the extended family as a strongly integrated social unit. Pratap concluded that Depak would likely leave Rori in frustration. Sanjay replied that he understood all this, but could not really accept the solution proposed by Pratap.

Another factor in the situation was Dilip, the younger brother of Depak. Unlike Depak, he had gone into business on his own, although he worked out of the premises of the Rori Company. Dilip was disgusted with watching his older brother being dominated by Pravin and Subash. He felt so strongly, he stated, that if his father did not resolve the problem soon, he was going to tell Sanjay that he would not speak to him again until he broke away from Anil.

Pratap felt partially responsible for the state of near-crisis in the Bhiwar family and business, since his report had brought to the surface these problems that had previously remained suppressed. Furthermore, he knew that any additional action by him would have to be taken soon, since he had to return to North America shortly. As the time to make flight reservations drew near, Pratap wondered what he should do.

APPENDIX A

A NOTE ON ASIANS AMONG AFRICANS AND EUROPEANS IN KENYA

When the English colonists originally came to Kenya, they came to farm fertile land. Although the native Africans were displaced from their land by the whites in the early days before World War I, the small numbers involved had minimal effects, especially since there was plenty of land. As time passed, however, the whites took more and more land – mainly through the legislative mechanism of the colonial government, which favoured the powerful, agricultural white minority. The African majority in the colony helplessly watched this encroachment and stealing of the land for which they received no remuneration. The Africans were generally regarded as savages by the whites, and, in the colony, had no significant political or economic rights. For the most part, Africans were forced either to farm noncash crops on poor land (cash crops were a white monopoly) or to find work in the towns that sprang up in Kenya as the century progressed.

In this social system of inequality, the Asian community formed a third group. Many Asians had first come to the colony as contracted labour before World War I, primarily to build the railway. After their contracts had expired, many chose to remain in the colony rather than return to India and be faced with poor land and widespread starvation. In the colony, however, Asians, like Africans, were prohibited from farming cash crops. Consequently, many Asians met the growing demand for civil servants, merchants, and professionals. The Asians proved to be brilliant commercial entrepreneurs and, by the 1930s, virtually monopolized the commercial life of Kenya – principally as retail merchants in the towns.

However, although they were a successful commercial community, they were politically less powerful than the whites. During the first half of the twentieth century, they constantly fought for equal rights in Kenya. At the same time, as a community, they remained socially aloof from both the whites and the Africans, identifying strongly with their traditional Indian background. Many hoped one day to return to India after they had become financially successful. Because of this orientation to their homeland, their involvement and identity with the colony were limited to those areas they regarded as being in their interest for political and economic survival.

Their aloofness, economic success, and constant battle for political recognition endeared them neither to the Europeans nor to the Africans. The whites saw them as a threat to their political and economic dominance, while the Africans coveted the Asian commercial success and advancement in the professions and civil service, which many Africans regarded as rightfully belonging to them.

During the colonial period, therefore, the Asians were discriminated against by white legislation which denied them equal access to the political arena. After independence, which followed the rebellion, the new black majority government sought to weaken Asian privileges in the colony by taking over Asian enterprises and giving them to African entrepreneurs. Although there currently are many Africans involved in business, the Asian community has remained an important part of commerce and industry in Kenya. Out of economic necessity, the government of Kenya tolerates Asian businesses and merchants. The number of Africans capable of running commercial operations has been growing constantly so that the position of the Asians remains insecure. Intense nationalism among some African governments also has weakened the status of Asians, as the unilateral expulsion of Asians from Uganda in 1972 illustrated. Taking all these factors together, Asians in Kenya today face a dramatically different situation from the colonial period when, at least in the retail sector, their economic survival was certain.

Appendix B

The Extended Family System

Traditionally, the Asian communities in Kenya were organized according to the extended family system. This consisted of all the brothers of a generation and their sons living together either under one roof or in close proximity. By staying together in this way, the males of one family were able to maintain a powerful social unit. In the case of marriage, the wives lived with their husbands' family.

This tightly knit kinship structure was closely bound up with the commercial enterprises of the families. For example, the structure of the business organization was based less on the ability of the various personnel in the firm than on the family relationships of the personnel to each other. Given this type of organization, it was possible for a family containing a great deal of business talent to be a very unified and powerful force in commercial affairs.

Within the extended family, the leadership traditionally lay with the eldest brother of the oldest generation still in power. In the case of the Bhiwar brothers, this power originally was in Mohan's hands. When he died, the power stayed in his generation and was passed to Anil. When the older brothers retired, tradition dictated that the family leadership be passed to the oldest son of the oldest brother. Note that this does not read "oldest son of the oldest *surviving* brother," which was the rule of succession used by the Bhiwars and resulted in the first family breakup. As head of the household, the oldest man of any generation holding power was the ultimate authority on all matters relating to the family. This power was exercised in many areas, including marriage decisions.

Recently, the extended family structure has been challenged. Although not yet widespread, there is a growing tendency for some Asians to break from the traditional extended family and adopt the North American nuclear form consisting of a father and mother and their children. Sometimes this breaking away can be done in a way that leaves the parties on amicable terms. More often, however, it is accompanied by considerable trauma, since it is not a practice widely accepted by the Asian community at present.

Notes

Names of people, places, and companies have been disguised.

1   In this country blacks are referred to as Africans. Asian is a term that refers to people of East Indian origin, and European is the term used for Caucasians. See Appendix A for a brief discussion of the Asian experience in this multiracial milieu.

2   Appendix B contains a description of some elements of the extended family system.

Part V

Employee Relations

24 The Multicultural Organization 245
Taylor Cox, Jr.

25 Managing Human Resources in Mexico: A Cultural
Understanding 261
*Randall S. Schuler, Susan E. Jackson, Ellen Jackofsky,
and John W. Slocum, Jr.*

26 New Manufacturing Strategies and Labour in Latin
America 271
John Humphrey

27 Coming to Terms With Local People 287
John Channon and Adam Dakin

28 Being "a Third Culture Man" 291
Geert J. E. M. Sanders

29 *Case:* The Evaluation 295
Charlotte Butler and Henri-Claude de Bettignies

30 *Case:* Kentucky Fried Chicken and the Global Fast-Food
Industry 301
Jeffrey A. Krug

Chapter 24

The Multicultural Organization

Taylor Cox, Jr.

EXECUTIVE OVERVIEW

Organizations are becoming increasingly diverse in terms of gender, race, ethnicity, and nationality. This diversity brings substantial potential benefits such as better decision making, greater creativity and innovation, and more successful marketing to different types of customers. But, increased cultural differences within a workforce also bring potential costs in higher turnover, interpersonal conflict, and communication breakdowns.

To capitalize on the benefits of diversity while minimizing the potential costs, leaders are being advised to oversee change processes toward creating "multicultural" organizations. What are the characteristics of such an organization and how do they differ from those of the past? What mechanisms are available to facilitate such a change?

This article addresses these questions. It also describes a model for understanding the required features of a multicultural organization and reviews tools that pioneering companies have found useful in changing organizations toward the multicultural model.

As we begin the 1990s, a combination of workforce demographic trends and increasing globalization of business has placed the management of cultural differences on the agenda of most corporate leaders. Organizations' workforces will be increasingly heterogeneous on dimensions such as gender, race, ethnicity and nationality. Potential benefits of this diversity include better decision making, higher creativity and innovation, greater success in marketing to foreign and ethnic minority communities, and a better distribution of economic opportunity. Conversely, cultural differences can also increase costs through higher turnover rates, interpersonal conflict, and communication breakdowns.

To capitalize on the benefits and minimize the costs of worker diversity, organizations of the '90s must be quite different from the typical organization of the past. Specifically, consultants have advised organizations to become "multicultural."[1] The term refers to the degree to which an organization values cultural diversity and is willing to utilize and encourage it.[2]

Leaders are being charged to create the multicultural organization, but what does such an organization look like, and what are the specific ways in which it differs from the traditional organization? Further, what tools and techniques are available to assist organizations in making the transition from the old to the new?

This article addresses these questions. I have used an adaptation of the societal-integration model developed by Milton Gordon, as well as available information on the early experience of American organizations with managing diversity initiatives, to construct a model of the multicultural organization.

CONCEPTUAL FRAMEWORK

In his classic work on assimilation in the United States, Milton Gordon argued that there are seven dimensions along which the integration of persons from different ethnic backgrounds into a host society should be analyzed.[3] I use "integration" to mean the coming together and mixing of people from different cultural identity groups in one organization. A cultural identity group is a group of people who (on average) share certain values and norms distinct from those of other groups. Although the boundaries of these groups may be defined along many dimensions, I am primarily concerned with gender, race, ethnicity, and national origin. Gordon's seven dimensions are:

1.   Form of acculturation
2.   Degree of structural assimilation
3.   Degree of intergroup marriage
4.   Degree of prejudice
5.   Degree of discrimination
6.   Degree of identification with the dominant group of the host society
7.   Degree of intergroup conflict (especially over the balance of power)

Although Gordon's interest was in societal-level integration, I believe his model can be easily and usefully adapted for analysis of cultural integration for organizations. Therefore, an adaptation of his seven-point framework is used here as a basis for describing organizational models for integrating culturally divergent groups. Exhibit 24.1 shows my proposed six-dimensional adaptation of the Gordon framework along with definitions of each term.

Acculturation is the method by which cultural differences between the dominant (host) culture and any minority culture groups are resolved or treated. There are several alternatives, the most prominent being: 1. a unilateral process by which minority culture members adopt the norms and values of the dominant group in the organization (assimilation); 2. a process by which both minority and majority culture members adopt some norms of the other group (pluralism); and 3. a situation where there is little adaptation on either side (cultural separatism).[4] Pluralism also means that minority culture members are encouraged to enact behaviors from their alternative culture as well as from the majority culture. They are therefore able to retain a sense of identity with their minority-culture group. Acculturation is concerned with the cultural (norms of behavior) aspect of integration of diverse groups, as opposed to simply their physical presence in the same location.

Dimension	Definition
1. Acculturation	Modes by which two groups adapt to each other and resolve cultural differences
2. Structural Integration	Cultural profiles of organization members including hiring, job-placement, and job status profiles.
3. Informal Integration	Inclusion of minority-culture members in informal networks and activities outside of normal working hours
4. Cultural Bias	Prejudice and discrimination
5. Organizational Identification	Feelings of belonging, loyalty and commitment to the organization
6. Inter-group Conflict	Friction, tension and power struggles between cultural groups.

Exhibit 24.1 A Conceptual Framework for Analysis of Organizational Capability for Effective Integration of Culturally Diverse Personnel

Structural integration refers to the presence of persons from different cultural groups in a single organization. Workforce profile data has typically been monitored under traditional equal opportunity and affirmative action guidelines. However, to get a proper understanding of structural integration it is important to look beyond organization-wide profile data, and examine cultural mix by function, level, and individual work group. This is because, it is commonplace in American companies for gaps of fifteen to thirty percentage points to exist between the proportion of minority members in the overall labor force of a firm, and their proportion at middle and higher levels of management.[5]

Even within levels of an organization, individual work groups may still be highly segregated. For example, a senior human resource manager for a Fortune 500 firm who is often cited as a leader in managing diversity efforts, recently told me that there are still many "white-male bastions" in his company. As an assistant vice-president with responsibility for equal opportunity, he indicated that breaking down this kind of segregation was a focal point of his current job.

The informal integration dimension recognizes that important work-related contacts are often made outside of normal working hours and in various social activities and organizations. This item looks at levels of inclusion of minority-culture members in lunch and dinner meetings, golf and other athletic outings, and social clubs frequented by organization leaders. It also addresses mentoring and other informal developmental relationships in organizations.

Cultural bias has two components. Prejudice refers to negative attitudes toward an organization member based on his/her culture group identity, and discrimination refers to observable adverse behavior for the same reason. Discrimination, in turn, may be either personal or institutional. The latter refers to ways that organizational culture and management practices may inadvertently disadvantage members of minority groups. An example is the adverse effect that emphasizing aggressiveness and self-promotion has on many Asians. Many managers that I have talked to are sensitive to the fact that prejudice is a cognitive phenomenon and therefore much more difficult than discrimination for organization managers to change. Nevertheless, most acknowledge the importance of reducing prejudice for long-range, sustained change.

Prejudice may occur among minority-culture members as well as among dominant-culture members. Putting the debate over whether rates of prejudice differ for different groups aside, it must be emphasized that the practical impact of prejudice by majority-culture members is far greater than that of minority-culture members because of their far greater decision-making power (except under extraordinary conditions, such as those of South Africa).

Organizational identification refers to the extent to which a person personally identifies with, and tends to define himself or herself as a member in the employing organization. Levels of organizational identification have historically been lower in the United States than in other countries (notably Japan). Indications are that recent changes in organizational design (downsizing and de-layering) have reduced organizational identification even further. Although levels of organizational identification may be low in general in the U.S. workforce, we are concerned here with comparative levels of identification for members of different cultural identity groups.

Finally, inter-group conflict refers to levels of culture-group-based tension and interpersonal friction. Research on demographic heterogeneity among group members suggests that communication and cohesiveness may decline as members of groups become dissimilar.[6] Also, in the specific context of integrating minority-group members into organizations, concerns have been raised about backlash from white males who may feel threatened by these developments. It is therefore important to examine levels of inter-group conflict in diverse workgroups.

Types of Organizations

This six-factor framework will now be employed to characterize organizations in terms of stages of development on cultural diversity.[7] Three organization types will be discussed: the monolithic organization, the plural organization, and the multicultural organization. The application of the six-factor conceptual framework to describe the three organization types appears in Exhibit 24.2.

The monolithic organization

The most important single fact about the monolithic organization is that the amount of structural integration is minimal. The organization is highly homogeneous. In the United States, this commonly represents an organization characterized by substantial white male majorities in the overall employee population with few women and minority men in management jobs. In addition, these organizations feature extremely high levels of occupational segregation with women and racioethnic minority men (racially and/or culturally different from the majority) concentrated in low-status jobs such as secretary and maintenance. Thus, the distribution of persons from minority-cultural backgrounds is highly skewed on all three components of function, level, and workgroup.

Dimension of Integration	Monolithic	Plural	Multicultural
Form of Acculturation	Assimilation	Assimilation	Pluralism
Degree of Structural Integration	Minimal	Partial	Full
Integration into Informal Organization	Virtually none	Limited	Full
Degree of Cultural Bias	Both prejudice and discrimination against minority-culture groups is prevalent	Progress on both prejudice & discrimination but both continue to exist especially institutional discrimination	Both prejudice and discrimination are eliminated
Levels of Organizational Identification*	Large majority-minority gap	Medium to large majority-minority gap	No majority-minority gap
Degree of Intergroup Conflict	Low	High	Low

Note: * Defined as difference between organizational identification levels between minorities and majorities.

Exhibit 24.2 Organizational Types

To a large extent, the specifications on the frameworks' other five dimensions follow from the structural exclusion of people from different cultural backgrounds. Women, racioethnic minority men, and foreign nationals who do enter the organization must adopt the existing organizational norms, framed by the white male majority, as a matter of organizational survival.

Ethnocentrism and other prejudices cause little, if any, adoption of minority-culture norms by majority group members. Thus, a unilateral acculturation process prevails. The exclusionary practices of the dominant culture also apply to informal activities. The severe limitations on career opportunities for minority-culture members creates alienation, and thus the extent to which they identify with the organization can be expected to be low compared to the more fully enfranchised majority group.

One positive note is that intergroup conflict based on culture-group identity is minimized by the relative homogeneity of the workforce. Finally, because this organization type places little importance on the integration of cultural minority group members, discrimination, as well as prejudice, are prevalent.

While the white-male dominated organization is clearly the prototypical one for the monolithic organization, at least some of its characteristics are likely to occur in organizations where another identity group is dominant. Examples include minority-owned businesses, predominantly Black and predominantly Hispanic colleges, and foreign companies operating in the United States.

Aside from the rather obvious downside implications of the monolithic model in terms of under-utilization of human resources and social equality, the monolithic organization is not a realistic option for most large employers in the 1990s. To a significant degree, large U.S. organizations made a transition away from this model during the '60s and '70s. This transition was spurred by a number of societal forces, most notably the civil-rights and feminists movements, and the beginnings of changes in workforce demographics, especially in the incidence of career-oriented women. Many organizations responded to these forces by creating the plural organization.

The plural organization

The plural organization differs from the monolithic organization in several important respects. In general, it has a more heterogeneous membership than the monolithic organization and takes steps to be more inclusive of persons from cultural backgrounds that differ from the dominant group. These steps include hiring and promotion policies that sometimes give preference to persons from minority-culture groups, manager training on equal opportunity issues (such as civil rights law, sexual harassment, and reducing prejudice), and audits of compensation systems to ensure against discrimination against minority group members. As a result, the plural organization achieves a much higher level of structural integration than the monolithic organization.

The problem of skewed integration across functions, levels, and work groups, typical in the monolithic organization, is also present in the plural organization. For example, in many large U.S. organizations racioethnic minorities now make up twenty percent or more of the total workforce. Examples include General Motors, Chrysler, Stroh Brewery, Phillip Morris, Coca-Cola, and Anheuser-Busch. However, the representations of non-whites in management in these same companies averages less than twelve percent.[8] A similar picture exists in workgroups. For example, while more than twenty percent of the clerical and office staffs at General Motors are minorities, they represent only about twelve percent of technicians and thirteen percent of sales workers. Thus, the plural organization features partial structural integration.

Because of the greater structural integration and the efforts (cited previously) which brought it about, the plural organization is also characterized by some integration of minority-group members into the informal network, substantial reductions in discrimination, and some moderation of prejudicial attitudes. The improvement in employment opportunities should also create greater identification with the organization among minority-group members.

The plural organization represents a marked improvement over the monolithic organization in effective management of employees of different racioethnic, gender, and nationality backgrounds. The plural organization form has been prevalent in the U.S. since the late 1960s, and in my judgment, represents the typical large firm as we enter the 1990s. These organizations emphasize an affirmative action approach to managing diversity. During the 1980s increased evidence of resentment toward this approach among white males began to surface. They argue that such policies, in effect, discriminate against white males and therefore perpetuate the practice of using racioethnicity, nationality, or gender as a basis for making personnel decisions. In addition, they believe that it is not fair that contemporary whites be disadvantaged to compensate for management errors made in the past. This backlash effect, coupled with the increased number of minorities in the organization, often creates greater inter-group conflict in the plural organization than was present in the monolithic organization.

While the plural organization achieves a measure of structural integration, it continues the assimilation approach to acculturation which is characteristic of the monolithic organization. The failure to address cultural aspects of integration is a major shortcoming of the plural organization form, and is a major point distinguishing it from the multicultural organization.

The multicultural organization

In discussing cultural integration aspects of mergers and acquisitions, Sales and Mirvis argued that an organization which simply contains many different cultural groups is a plural organization, but considered to be multicultural only if the organization values this diversity.[9] The same labels and definitional distinction is applied here. The meaning of the distinction between containing diversity and valuing it follows from an understanding of the shortcomings of the plural organization as outlined previously. The multicultural organization has overcome these shortcomings. Referring again to Exhibit 24.2, we see that the multicultural organization is characterized by:

1. Pluralism
2. Full structural integration
3. Full integration of the informal networks
4. An absence of prejudice and discrimination
5. No gap in organizational identification based on cultural identity group
6. Low levels of intergroup conflict

I submit that while few, if any, organizations have achieved these features, it should be the model for organizations in the 1990s and beyond.

Creating the multicultural organization

As I have discussed issues of managing diversity with senior managers from various industries during the past year, I have observed that their philosophical viewpoints cover all three of the organizational models of Exhibit 24.2. The few who are holding on to the monolithic model often cite geographic or size factors as isolating their organizations from the pressures of change.

Some even maintain that because American white males will continue to be the single largest gender/race identity group in the U.S. workforce for many years, the monolithic organization is still viable today. I think this view is misguided. By understanding the generic implications of managing diversity (that is, skill at managing work groups which include members who are culturally distinct from the organization's dominant group), it becomes clear that virtually all organizations need to improve capabilities to manage diverse workforces.

Further, focusing too much attention on external pressures as impetus for change, misses the fact that gross under-utilization of human resources and failure to capitalize on the opportunities of workforce diversity, represent unaffordable economic costs.

Fortunately, the monolithic defenders, at least among middle and senior managers, seem to represent a minority view. Based on my observations, the majority of managers today are in plural organizations, and many are already convinced that the multicultural model is the way of the future. What these managers want to know is how to transform the plural organization into the multicultural organization. Although progress on such transformations is at an early stage, information on the tools that have been successfully used by pioneering American organizations to make this transformation is beginning to accumulate.

Exhibit 24.3 provides a list of tools that organizations have used to promote organization change toward a multicultural organization. The exhibit is organized to illustrate my analysis of which tools are most helpful for each of the six dimensions specified in Exhibit 24.1.

Creating pluralism

Exhibit 24.3 identifies seven specific tools for changing organizational acculturation from a unilateral process to a reciprocal one in which both minority-culture and majority-culture members are influential in creating the behavioral norms, values, and policies of the organization. Examples of each tool are given below.

TRAINING AND ORIENTATION PROGRAMS. The most widely used tool among leading organizations is managing or valuing cultural diversity training. Two types of training are most popular: awareness and skill-building. The former introduces the topic of managing diversity and generally includes information on workforce demographics, the meaning of diversity, and exercises to get participants thinking about relevant issues and raising their own self-awareness. The skill-building training provides more specific information on cultural norms of different groups and how they may affect work behavior. Often, these two types of training are combined. Such training promotes reciprocal learning and acceptance between groups by improving understanding of the cultural mix in the organization.

Among the many companies who have made extensive use of such training are McDonnell Douglas, Hewlett Packard, and Ortho Pharmaceuticals. McDonnell Douglas has a program ("Woman-Wise and Business Savvy") focusing on gender differences in work-related behaviors. It uses same-gender group meetings and mixed-gender role-plays. At its manufacturing plant in San Diego, Hewlett Packard conducted training on cultural differences between American-Anglos and Mexican, Indochinese, and Filipinos. Much of the content focused on cultural differences in communication styles. In one of the most thorough training efforts to date, Ortho Pharmaceuticals started its three-day training with small groups (ten to twelve) of senior managers and eventually trained managers at every level of the company.

Specific data on the effectiveness of these training efforts is hard to collect, but a study of seventy-five Canadian consultants found that people exposed to even the most rudimentary form of training on cultural diversity are significantly more likely to recognize the impact of cultural diversity on work behavior and to identify the potential advantages of cultural heterogeneity in organizations.[10]

In addition, anecdotal evidence from managers of many companies indicates that valuing and managing diversity training represents a crucial first step for organization change efforts.

Model Dimension	Tools
I. Pluralism *Objective/s*: – create a two-way socialization process – ensure influence of minority culture perspectives on core organization norms and values	1. Managing/valuing diversity (MVD) training 2. New member orientation programs 3. Language training 4. Diversity in key committees 5. Explicit treatment of diversity in mission statements 6. Advisory groups to senior management 7. Create flexibility in norm systems
II. Full Structural Integration *Objective/s* – no correlation between culture-group identity and job status	1. Education programs 2. Affirmative action programs 3. Targeted career development programs 4. Changes in manager performance appraisal and reward systems 5. HR policy and benefit changes
III. Integration in Informal Networks *Objective/s* – eliminate barriers to entry and participation	1. Mentoring programs 2. Company sponsored social events
IV. Cultural Bias *Objective/s* – eliminate discrimination – eliminate prejudice	1. Equal opportunity seminars 2. Focus groups 3. Bias reduction training 4. Research 5. Task forces
V. Organizational Identification – no correlation between identity group and levels of organization identification	1. All items from the other five dimensions apply here
VI. Intergroup Conflict *Objective/s* – minimize interpersonal conflict based on group-identity – minimize backlash by dominant-group members	1. Survey feedback 2. Conflict management training 3. MVD training 4. Focus groups

Exhibit 24.3 Creating the Multicultural Organization: Tools for Organization Change

New member orientation programs are basic in the hiring processes of many organizations. Some companies are developing special orientations as part of its managing diversity initiatives. Proctor and Gamble's "On Boarding" program, which features special components for women and minority hires and their managers is one example.

LANGUAGE TRAINING   is important for companies hiring American Asians, Hispanics, and foreign nationals. To promote pluralism, it is helpful to offer second language training to Anglos as well as the minority-culture employees, and take other steps to communicate that languages other than English are valued. Leaders in this area include Esprit De Corp, Economy Color Card, and Pace Foods. For many years, the women's clothier Esprit De Corp has offered courses in Italian and Japanese. At Economy Color Card, work rules are printed in both Spanish and English. Pace Foods, where thirty-five percent of employees are Hispanic, goes a step farther by printing company policies and also conducting staff meetings in Spanish and English. Motorola is a leader in the more traditional training for English as a second language where classes are conducted at company expense and on company time.

INSURING MINORITY-GROUP INPUT AND ACCEPTANCE. The most direct and effective way to promote influence of minority-culture norms on organizational decision making is to achieve cultural diversity at all organization levels. However, an important supplemental method is through ensuring diversity on key committees. An example is the insistence of USA Today President Nancy Woodhull on having gender, racioethnic, educational, and geographic diversity represented in all daily news meetings. She attributes much of the company's success to this action.

Another technique is explicitly mentioning the importance of diversity to the organization in statements of mission and strategy. By doing this, organizations foster the mindset that increased diversity is an opportunity and not a problem. Examples of organizations that have done this are The University of Michigan and the Careers Division of the National Academy of Management. The latter group has fostered research addressing the impact of diversity on organizations by explicitly citing this as part of its interest.

Another way to increase the influence of minority-group members on organizational culture and policy is by providing specially composed minority advisory groups direct access to the most senior executives of the company. Organizations which have done this include Avon, Equitable Life Assurance, Intel, and U.S. West. At Equitable, committees of women, Blacks and Hispanics (called "Business Resource Groups") meet with the CEO to discuss important group issues and make recommendations on how the organizational environment might be improved. CEO John Carver often assigns a senior manager to be accountable for following up on the recommendations. U.S. West has a thirty-three-member "Pluralism Council" which advises senior management on plans for improving the company's response to increased workforce diversity.

Finally, a more complex, but I believe potentially powerful, tool for promoting change toward pluralism is the development of flexible, highly tolerant climates that encourage diverse approaches to problems among all employees. Such an environment is useful to workers regardless of group identity, but is especially beneficial to people from nontraditional cultural backgrounds because their approaches to problems are more likely to be different from past norms. A company often cited for such a work environment is Hewlett Packard. Among the operating norms of the company which should promote pluralism are: 1. Encouragement of informality and unstructured work; 2. Flexible work schedules and loose supervision; 3. Setting objectives in broad terms with lots of individual employee discretion over how they are achieved; 4. A policy that researchers should spend at least ten percent of company time exploring personal ideas. I would suggest that item four be extended to all management and professional employees.

Creating full structural integration

EDUCATION EFFORTS.   The objective of creating an organization where there is no correlation between one's culture-identity group and one's job status implies that minority-group members are well represented at all levels, in all functions, and in all work groups. Achievement of this goal requires that skill and education levels be evenly distributed. Education statistics indicate that the most serious problems occur with Blacks and Hispanics.[11]

A number of organizations have become more actively involved in various kinds of education programs. The Aetna Life Insurance Company is a leader. It has initiated a number of programs including jobs in exchange for customized education taught by community agencies and private schools, and its own in-house basic education programs. The company has created an Institute for Corporate Education with a full-time director. Other companies participating in various new education initiatives include PrimAmerica, Quaker Oats, Chase Manhattan Bank, Eastman Kodak, and Digital Equipment. In Minnesota, a project headed by Cray Research and General Mills allows businesses to create schools of its own design. I believe that business community involvement in joint efforts with educational institutions and community leaders to promote equal achievement in education is critical to the future competitiveness of U.S. business. Business leaders should insist that economic support be tied to substantive programs which are jointly planned and evaluated by corporate representatives and educators.

AFFIRMATIVE ACTION.   In my opinion, the mainstay of efforts to create full structural integration in the foreseeable future, will continue to be affirmative action programs. While most large organizations have some kind of program already, the efforts of Xerox and Pepsico are among the standouts.

The Xerox effort, called "The Balanced Workforce Strategy," is noteworthy for several reasons including: an especially fast timetable for moving minorities up; tracking representation by function and operating unit as well as by level; and national networks for minority-group members (supported by the company) to provide various types of career support. Recently published data indicating that Xerox is well ahead of both national and industry averages in moving minorities into management and professional jobs, suggests that these efforts have paid off (*Wall Street Journal*, November 5, 1989).

Two features of Pepsico's efforts which are somewhat unusual are the use of a "Black Managers Association" as a supplemental source of nominees for promotion to management jobs, and the practice of hiring qualified minorities directly into managerial and professional jobs.

CAREER DEVELOPMENT.   A number of companies including Mobil Oil, IBM, and McDonald's have also initiated special career development efforts for minority personnel. IBM's long-standing "Executive Resource System" is designed to identify and develop minority talent for senior management positions. McDonald's "Black Career Development Program" provides career enhancement advice, and fast-track career paths for minorities. Company officials have stated that the program potentially cuts a fifteen-year career path to regional manager by fifty percent.

REVAMPING REWARD SYSTEMS. An absolutely essential tool for creating structural integration is to ensure that the organization's performance appraisal and reward systems reinforce the importance of effective diversity management. Companies that have taken steps in this direction include the Federal National Mortgage Association (Fannie Mae), Baxter Health Care, Amtrak, Exxon, Coca-Cola, and Merck. Fannie Mae, Baxter, Coca-Cola, and Merck all tie compensation to manager performance on diversity management efforts. At Amtrak, manager promotion and compensation are tied to performance on affirmative action objectives, and at Exxon, evaluations of division managers must include a review of career development plans for at least ten women and minority men employees.

For this tool to be effective, it needs to go beyond simply including effective management of diversity among the evaluation and reward criteria. Attention must also be given to the amount of weight given to this criterion compared to other dimensions of job performance. How performance is measured is also important. For example, in addition to work-group profile statistics, subordinate evaluations of managers might be useful. When coded by cultural group, differences in perceptions based on group identity can be noted and used in forming performance ratings on this dimension.

BENEFITS AND WORK SCHEDULES. Structural integration of women, Hispanics, and Blacks is facilitated by changes in human resource policies and benefit plans that make it easier for employees to balance work and family role demands. Many companies have made such changes in areas like child care, work schedules, and parental leave. North Carolina National Bank, Arthur Anderson, Levi Strauss, and IBM are examples of companies that have gone farther than most. NCNB's "select time" project allows even officers and professionals in the company to work part-time for several years and still be considered for advancement. Arthur Anderson has taken a similar step by allowing part-time accountants to stay "on-track" for partnership promotions. Levi Strauss has one of the most comprehensive work–family programs in the country covering everything from paternity leave to part-time work with preservation of benefits. These companies are leaders in this area because attention is paid to the impact on advancement opportunities and fringe-benefits when employees take advantage of scheduling flexibility and longer leaves of absence. This kind of accommodation will make it easier to hire and retain both men and women in the '90s as parents struggle to balance work and home time demands. It is especially important for women, Hispanics, and Blacks because cultural traditions put great emphasis on family responsibilities. Organization change in this area will promote full structural integration by keeping more racioethnic minorities and white women in the pipeline.

Creating integration in informal networks

MENTORING AND SOCIAL EVENTS. One tool for including minorities in the informal networks of organizations is company-initiated mentoring programs that target minorities. A recent research project in which a colleague and I surveyed 800 MBAs indicated that racioethnic minorities report significantly less access to mentors than whites. If company-specific research shows a similar pattern, this data can be used to justify and bolster support among majority-group employees for targeted mentoring programs. Examples of companies which have established such targeted mentoring programs are Chemical Bank and General Foods.

A second technique for facilitating informal network integration is company-sponsored social events. In planning such events, multiculturalism is fostered by selecting both activities and locations with a sensitivity to the diversity of the workforce.

SUPPORT GROUPS. In many companies, minority groups have formed their own professional associations and organizations to promote information exchange and social support. There is little question that these groups have provided emotional and career support for members who traditionally have not been welcomed in the majority's informal groups. A somewhat controversial issue is whether these groups hinder the objective of informal-network integration. Many believe that they harm integration by fostering a "we-versus-they" mentality and reducing incentives for minorities to seek inclusion in informal activities of majority-group members. Others deny these effects. I am not aware of any hard evidence on this point. There is a dilemma here in that integration in the informal networks is at best a long-term process and there is widespread skepticism among minorities as to its eventual achievement. Even if abolishing the minority-group associations would eventually promote full integration, the absence of a support network of any kind in the interim could be a devastating loss to minority-group members. Therefore, my conclusion is that these groups are more helpful than harmful to the overall multiculturalism effort.

CREATING A BIAS-FREE ORGANIZATION. Equal opportunity seminars, focus groups, bias-reduction training, research, and task forces are methods that organizations have found useful in reducing culture-group bias and discrimination. Unlike prejudice, discrimination is a behavior and therefore more amenable to direct control or influence by the organization. At the same time, the underlying cause of discrimination is prejudice. Ideally, efforts should have at least indirect effects on the thought processes and attitudes of organization members. All of the tools listed, with the possible exception of task forces, should reduce prejudice as well as discrimination.

Most plural organizations have used equal opportunity seminars for many years. These include sexual harassment workshops, training on civil rights legislation, and workshops on sexism and racism.

FOCUS GROUPS. More recently, organizations like Digital Equipment have used "focus groups" as an in-house, on-going mechanism to explicitly examine attitudes, beliefs, and feelings about culture-group differences and their effects on behavior at work. At Digital, the center piece of its "valuing differences" effort is the use of small groups (called Core Groups) to discuss four major objectives: 1. stripping away stereotypes; 2. examining underlying assumptions about outgroups; 3. building significant relationships with people one regards as different; 4. raising levels of personal empowerment. Digital's experience suggests that a breakthrough for many organizations will be achieved by the simple mechanism of bringing discussion about group differences out in the open. Progress is made as people become more comfortable directly dealing with the issues.

BIAS-REDUCTION TRAINING. Another technique for reducing bias is through training specifically designed to create attitude change. An example is Northern Telecom's 16-hour program designed to help employees identify and begin to modify negative attitudes toward people from different cultural backgrounds. Eastman Kodak's training conference for its recruiters is designed to eliminate racism and sexism from the hiring process. This type of training often features exercises that expose stereotypes of various groups which are prevalent but rarely made explicit and may be subconscious. Many academics and consultants have also developed bias-reduction training. An example is the "Race Relations Competence Workshop," a program developed by Clay Alderfer and Robert Tucker of Yale University. They have found that participants completing the workshop have more positive attitudes toward Blacks and inter-race relations.

LEVERAGING INTERNAL RESEARCH.   A very powerful tool for reducing discrimination and (to a smaller extent) prejudice, is to conduct and act on internal research on employment experience by cultural group. Time Inc. conducts an annual evaluation of men and women in the same jobs to ensure comparable pay and equal treatment. A second example comes from a large utility company which discovered that minority managers were consistently under-represented in lists submitted by line managers for bonus recommendations. As a result of the research, the company put pressure on the managers to increase the inclusion of minority managers. When that failed, the vice president of human resources announced that he would no longer approve the recommendations unless minorities were adequately represented. The keys to the organization change were, first obtaining the data identifying the problem and then acting on it. My experience suggests that this type of research-based approach is underutilized by organizations.

TASK FORCES.   A final tool for creating bias-free organizations is to form task forces that monitor organizational policy and practices for evidence of unfairness. An example of what I consider to be a well-designed committee is the affirmative action committee used by Phillip Morris which is composed of senior managers and minority employees. This composition combines the power of senior executives with the insight into needed changes that the minority representatives can provide. Of course, minority culture-group members who are also senior managers are ideal but, unfortunately, such individuals are rare in most organizations.

Minimizing intergroup conflict

Experts on conflict management have noted that a certain amount of interpersonal conflict is inevitable and perhaps even healthy in organizations.[12] However, conflict becomes destructive when it is excessive, not well managed, or rooted in struggles for power rather than the differentiation of ideas. We are concerned here with these more destructive forms of conflict which may be present with diverse workforces due to language barriers, cultural clash, or resentment by majority-group members of what they may perceive as preferential, and unwarranted treatment of minority-group members.

SURVEY FEEDBACK.   Probably the most effective tool for avoiding intergroup conflict (especially the backlash form that often accompanies new initiatives targeting minority-groups of the organization) is the use of survey feedback. I will give three examples. As one of the most aggressive affirmative action companies of the past decade, Xerox has found that being very open with all employees about the specific features of the initiative as well the reasons for it, was helpful in diffusing backlash by whites. This strategy is exemplified by the high profile which Chairman David Kearns has taken on the company's diversity efforts.

A second example is Proctor and Gamble's use of data on the average time needed for new hires of various culture groups to become fully integrated into the organization. They found that "join-up" time varied by race and gender with white males becoming acclimated most quickly, and black females taking the longest of any group. This research led to the development of their "on-boarding program" referred to earlier.

A final example is Corning Glass Works' strategy of fighting white-male resistance to change with data showing that the promotion rate of their group was indeed much higher than that of other groups. This strategy has also been used by U.S. West which recently reported on a 1987 study showing that promotion rates for white men were seven times higher than white women and sixteen times higher than non-white women.

The beauty of this tool is that it provides the double benefit of a knowledge base for planning change, and leverage to win employee commitment to implement the needed changes.

CONFLICT-RESOLUTION TRAINING.   A second tool for minimizing intergroup conflict is management training in conflict resolution techniques. Conflict management experts can assist managers in learning and developing skill in applying alternative conflict management techniques such as mediation and superordinate goals. This is a general management skill which is made more crucial by the greater diversity of workforces in the '90s.

Finally, the managing and valuing diversity training and focus group tools discussed previously are also applicable here. AT&T is among the organizations which have explicitly identified stress and conflict reduction as central objectives of its training and focus group efforts.

CONCLUSION

Increased diversity presents challenges to business leaders who must maximize the opportunities that it presents while minimizing its costs. To accomplish this, organizations must be transformed from monolithic or plural organizations to a multicultural model. The multicultural organization is characterized by pluralism, full integration of minority-culture members both formally and informally, an absence of prejudice and discrimination, and low levels of inter-group conflict; all of which should reduce alienation and build organizational identity among minority group members. The organization that achieves these conditions will create an environment in which all members can contribute to their maximum potential, and in which the "value in diversity" can be fully realized.

Notes

1   See, for example, Lennie Copeland, "Valuing Workplace Diversity," *Personnel Administrator*, November 1988; Badi Foster et al., "Workforce Diversity and Business," *Training And Development Journal*, April 1988, 38–42; and R. Roosevelt Thomas, "From Affirmative Action to Affirming Diversity," *Harvard Business Review*, Vol. 2, 1990, 107–17.

2   This definition has been suggested by Afsavch Nahavandi and Ali Malekzadeh, "Acculturation in Mergers and Acquisitions," *Academy of Management Review*, Vol. 13, 83.

3   In his book, *Assimilation in American Life* (New York; Oxford University Press, 1964), Gordon uses the term assimilation rather than integration. However, because the term assimilation has been defined in so many different ways, and has come to have very unfavorable connotations in recent years for many minorities, I will employ the term integration here.

4   These definitions are loosely based on J. W. Berry, "Acculturation: A Comparative Analysis of Alternative Forms," in R. J. Samuda and S. L. Woods, *Perspectives in Immigrant and Minority Education*, 1983, 66–77.

5   This conclusion is based on data from nearly 100 large organizations as cited in "Best Places for Blacks to Work," *Black Enterprise*, February 1986 and February 1989 and in Zeitz and Dusky, *Best Companies for Women*, 1988.

6   Examples of this research include: Harry Triandis, "Some Determinants of Interpersonal Communication," *Human Relations*, Vol. 13, 1960, 279–87 and J. R. Lincoln and J. Miller, "Work and Friendship Ties in Organizations," *Administrative Science Quarterly*, Vol. 24, 1979, 181–99.

7   The concept of stages of development toward the multicultural organization has been suggested in an unpublished paper titled "Toward the Multicultural Organization" written by Dan Reigle and Jarrow Merenivitch of the Proctor and Gamble Company. I credit them with helping me to recognize the evolutionary nature of organizational responses to workforce diversity.

8   See note 5.

9   A. L. Sales and P. H. Mirvis. "When Cultures Collide: Issues of Acquisitions," in J. R. Kimberly and R. E. Quinn, *Managing Organizational Transition*, 1984, 107–33.

10 For details on this study see Nancy J. Adler, *International Dimensions of Organizational Behavior* (Kent Publishing Co., 1986), 77–83.

11 For example, see the book by William Julius Wilson which reviews data on educational achievement by Blacks and Hispanics in Chicago: *The Truly Disadvantaged: Inner City, the Underclass and Public Policy* (University of Chicago Press, 1987). Among the facts cited is that less than half of all Blacks and Hispanics in inner city schools graduate within four years of high school enrollment and only four in ten of those who do graduate read at the eleventh grade level or above.

12 For example, see Gregory Northcraft and Margaret Neale, *Organization Behavior: Conflict in Organizations* (The Dryden Press, 1990), 221.

Chapter 25

Managing Human Resources in Mexico: A Cultural Understanding

Randall S. Schuler, Susan E. Jackson, Ellen Jackofsky, and John W. Slocum, Jr.

Already, the North American Free Trade Agreement (NAFTA) appears to be a big hit. Exports are surging and U.S. job loss appears to be minimal. NAFTA's proponents indicate that the agreement should ease U.S. world trade deficits by making American goods more attractive. And as Mexico strives to modernize its businesses, U.S. investments will keep pouring into the country to help with the process. A survey of more than 1,000 senior executives by KPMG Peat Marwick found that 25 percent have formed alliances with Mexican companies, while 40 percent plan to recruit or have already hired people fluent in Spanish to help them enter the Mexican market.

As U.S. firms set up operations in Mexico, they are confronted with the same challenge as in the United States: How can they most effectively manage their human resources – the people upon whom they depend for success? They realize that being competitive takes more than low cost; it also requires high quality. Because a key ingredient in producing high-quality goods is a company's human resources, mismanaging these resources could result in: (1) a loss of skilled workers; (2) an increase in wages; (3) a reluctance to train new workers; (4) a consequential decline in quality; and (5) an eventual loss of competitive position.

All this can be avoided by an informed approach to managing human resources in Mexico. Such an approach is based on an understanding of the cultural differences between Mexico and the United States. Although it does not provide all the answers, it can maximize the potential benefits resulting from an understanding between the two countries. It can also offer an explanation for what exists in Mexico today and for what may or may not work as the competition for skilled human resources heats up.

CULTURAL VALUES

The differences between Mexican and American human resource management practices can be traced partly to the underlying differences in values between the two countries. In his seminal work on cultural values, Geert Hofstede proposed a framework to study the impact of societal culture on employees. This framework, widely accepted and used by

Power Distance

High	*Low*
• Focus on order	• Focus on equity, fairness
• Well-defined, stable hierarchies	• Flat organizations
• Managers are gods, but paternal	• Democratic managers, use of exchange
• Centralized decision making	relations

Individualism

High	*Low*
• Emphasis on the person	• Emphasis on the group
• Creative person valued	• Creative person disruptive
• Initiative valued	• Conformity valued

Uncertainty Avoidance

High	*Low*
• Focus on security	• Open to the unknown
• Uncomfortable with risk	• Risk equals opportunity
• Defined roles	• Flexible roles
• Focus on information sharing	• Often quick decisions
• Focus on trust	
• Focus on rules (often informal)	

Masculinity

High	*Low*
• Clear sex roles: men dominant	• Flexible sex roles: "fuzzy"
• Survival requires aggressiveness	• Focus on quality of life, nurturing the
	environment
• High performers receive high	• High performers receive recognition
monetary rewards	

Source: Geert Hofstede, "Cultural Constraints in Management Theories," *Academy of Management Executive,* 7 (1993): 81–94.

Figure 25.1 Characteristic Extremes of the Four Cultural Dimensions

managers to understand differences between cultures, consists of four cultural dimensions along which societies can be classified:

Power Distance: the degree to which unequal distribution of power is accepted (such as between manager and workers).

Individualism: the degree to which individual decision making is valued.

Uncertainty Avoidance: the degree to which uncertainty is tolerated (such as regarding job security or work role behaviors).

Masculinity: the degree to which society values assertiveness, performance, ambition, achievement, and material possessions.

More than 50 countries have been classified as being low, medium, or high along these four cultural dimensions. Descriptions of these extremes are provided in figure 25.1. The results comparing the United States and Mexico show minimal differences in masculinity, but significant differences in power distance, individualism, and uncertainty avoidance:

	U.S.	Mexico
Power Distance	40	81
Individualism	91	30
Uncertainty Avoidance	46	82
Masculinity	62	69

Thus, in comparison with the U.S., Mexico's culture is more group- or family-oriented, places more importance on well-defined power and authority structures in organizations, and prefers more certainty and predictability. An analysis of managerial practices in the U.S. and Mexico implies substantial differences in these three cultural dimensions. Applying these differences to managing human resources can be instrumental for U.S. firms desiring to operate in Mexico as effectively as possible with both expatriates and local country nationals on the payroll.

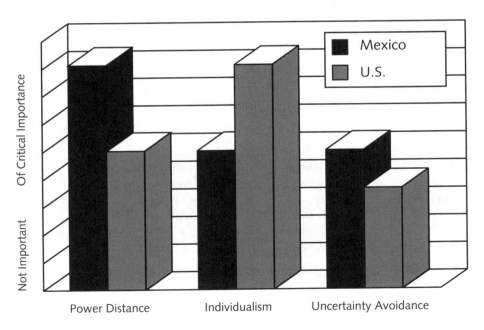

Figure 25.2 Importance of Human Resource Practices: the United States versus Mexico

To explore the differences between U.S. and Mexican firms, we conducted secondary analyses on data obtained as part of a larger international survey conducted in 1991. This was a worldwide study of human resource policies and practices conducted by IBM and Towers Perrin. The survey data that form the basis of the analysis in this article have been published in *Priorities for Competitive Advantage: A Worldwide Human Resources Study* (IBM/Towers Perrin, 1992). In developing the survey questionnaire, some of the authors of this article were invited to incorporate policies and practices and then write survey items that represented the academic and practitioner research and literature through 1990. These items were reviewed for representation and agreement by a series of other academics and practitioners identified by the IBM corporation.

A major topic addressed in one section of the questionnaire was "human resource concepts and practices for gaining competitive advantage." In this section, respondents were asked to indicate the degree of importance they attached to each time in their firm's attempt to gain competitive advantage through human resource policies and practices. They indicated this for the current year (1991) and for the year 2000. For the purposes of this study, we have analyzed the data for the year 2000. This allows us to consider the extent to which future plans and expectations within the firms surveyed are likely to converge.

The specific firms included were those identified jointly by IBM and Towers Perrin as being the most effective in highly competitive environments in each of several countries. Details of the sample, though the names of firms are anonymous, are provided by Towers Perrin (1992). The respondents included the chief operating officers and the senior human resource officers. In total, there were 67 respondents from Mexico and 1,174 from the United States. The several case studies were conducted by Gillian Flynn. The companies used in those case studies are cited in this article. The original study is found in "HR in Mexico: What You Should Know," *Personnel Journal*, August 1994, pp. 34–44.

Figure 25.3   HR Survey

Because our focus is on aiding U.S. firms that do business in Mexico and employ Mexican workers, the general descriptions provided below are based on the results of several case studies of large U.S. firms operating in Mexico. The studies are supplemented by a recent survey of human resource managers in the two countries. These managers were asked to describe specific practices in their organizations, such as benefits, career planning, decision-making, and socialization tactics, and relate which practices would be most applicable and important for a firm to be competitive as it moves forward. Not surprisingly, their comments are rather consistent with the details of the four dimensions shown in figure 25.1 As seen in figure 25.2, the evaluation of these human resource practices are in line with Hofstede's findings. Details of the study are provided in figure 25.3.

POWER DISTANCE

The degree to which the unequal distribution of power is accepted, such as that between manager and workers, is considerably higher in Mexico than in the United States. It can be measured in terms of hierarchical structures, formal or informal relations between them, and the personalization of rules and regulations.

Hierarchy

Mexican organizations reflect the hierarchical structures of church and government. That is, most firms have a bureaucratic structure with power vested at the top. The director general or the *presidente* of the firm has often achieved that position through favors and friendships nurtured over years. Senior managers reporting to the director general are expected to show him proper respect, and usually have the authority to make decisions pertaining to their division.

Employees below these levels have little authority. Because of this, most employees desire that the authority over them be wielded in a kind and sensitive manner. Mexican employees appreciate managers who show a true personal interest and communicate respect for them. If they are told what to do, they try hard to do it. Power is based on trust between worker and supervisor that flows from the top down. Through this paternalistic management system, good labor and community relations are established. In Mexico, workers are rewarded for being loyal and following directions from the person in charge.

Formality

Mexicans tend to prefer a more distant relationship between workers and managers than what is typically found in a society that ranks low on power distance, such as the United States. In low-power-distance societies, status differences between workers and managers are minimized. In walking through Mexican manufacturing plants and construction sites, one rarely sees a Mexican manager getting his hands dirty. Instead, supervisors are told what to do, then pass along these instructions to workers. In contrast, American managers can often be seen walking through the plant, informally chatting with workers and getting their hands dirty when appropriate. Similarly, Mexican managers are typically attired in business suits that reflect their status in the organization, whereas in many U.S. plants managers wear jeans and sport shirts and "look" like workers.

Mexican workers expect managers to keep their distance rather than to be close, and to be formal rather than informal. Calling workers by their first names is not common in Mexico because it would violate status differences between managers and workers. Elderly or eminent people in Mexican organizations are usually referred to as Don and Doña. Nevertheless, despite this need for distance and formality, Mexicans value working conditions in which supervisors are understanding. They look up to bosses who treat them in a warm but dignified manner. Managers who occasionally appear in the company cafeteria, walk through the shop floor, and mingle with them on May Day (Mexican Labor Day) are respected by the workers.

Personalization

In contrast to the people in the U.S., people in Mexico take a more casual approach to rules and regulations. Rules tend to be a loosely applied set of guidelines that indicate what ought to be done, but not what necessarily *is* done. For example, stop signs and no-parking signs are routinely ignored, and one-way streets have traffic in both directions. Few Mexican drivers, it seems, feel obliged to follow "normal" traffic laws. Likewise, Mexican workers may permit themselves to be guided by their own "inner clock" rather than the "clock on the wall." Consequently, many U.S. firms provide buses to pick up workers at various locations so as to avoid uncertain arrival times as well as complications due to traffic problems.

In Mexican organizations, formal rules and regulations are not adhered to unless someone of authority is present. Managers are more likely to be obeyed than a rule because of who they are and the authority they exercise. Without a strong emotional bond between people, rules tend to be ignored. On the other hand, U.S. managers believe that rules establish a system of justice that emphasizes fairness, and thus should be applied impersonally.

Suggestions for Managers

Results of our study corroborated the reality of status differences in managing human resources. We found that tactics promoting equality, employee involvement in decision making, open communication channels, and employee ownership were generally not regarded as necessary or desirable for gaining a competitive advantage in Mexico. Thus, given that Mexican society is high in power distance, we suggest that U.S. firms that use such practices should modify them in working with the Mexican culture. In other words, it is probably unnecessary for senior Mexican managers to involve employees in decision making. A manager should rarely explain why something is to be done, lest workers perceive this as a sign of weakness. Communication channels should follow the hierarchical structure of the organization.

We also found that as firms seek to manage the most out of workers, they are turning their attentions to developing employees with multiple skills that cross functional departments. In cultures with high power distance, such as Mexico, employees rely on a strong hierarchical structure, with those in power demonstrating care and concern for their subordinates. Power flows from the top down, so whatever a supervisor tells a worker to do has been authorized by his boss. Mexican employees expect management to be paternalistic and watch out for them, rather than being dictatorial. Again, unless there is a strong emotional force or bond, employees in Mexican plants tend not to obey rules and regulations. The manager's ability to create such bonding is instrumental in motivating and directing the career paths of subordinates.

INDIVIDUALISM

Individualism has come to be seen as practically the defining characteristic of American society. Not so in Mexico; the degree to which individual decision making is valued is much lower. This can be seen in terms of caring for workers and their families, establishing workplace harmony, and exhibiting paternalism toward employees.

Family and Responsibility to Care

Workers generally do not place high priority on organizations in which self-determination is encouraged. Employees have significant responsibility for the conduct and improvement of workers' lives in the Mexican organization. Having a job is viewed as a social right. In other words, Mexicans grow up assuming that society owes them a job. Consequently, having a job is far more than just an exchange of money for labor.

Mexican law and history reflect the Mexican view that the employer has a moral and family responsibility for all employees, even when there is a union. The Mexican employee is not just working for a paycheck. Workers tend to expect to be treated as the "extended family" of the boss, and to receive a wider range of services and benefits than what is provided north of the border. Examples of these benefits include food baskets and medical attention for themselves and their families (apart from social security). Medical benefits are not considered "an extra" or discretionary; to the Mexican worker, they simply fulfill the employer's role and responsibilities.

Because the cost of newspapers makes help wanted advertisements useless, recruitment is done primarily by approaching people and asking them to apply. So it is common to find many family members working at the same plant. Another significant aspect of employee retention and recruitment involves the need for workers to feel they are part of the operation. The plant will be populated by people oriented to traditional Mexican values and social structure. To achieve this, employers make certain to celebrate numerous holidays, and it is common for companies to throw parties for a variety of events.

Corresponding to this practice is the Mexican view that employees have a reciprocal obligation to be loyal, work hard, and be willing to do whatever is requested of them. American managers who accept the Mexican sense that a job is more than a paycheck and who try to fulfill their part of the "bargain" can reap the benefits of employee loyalty, including a willingness to come to work every day and to work conscientiously.

Harmony

Just like a family that encourages its members to work together by doing their share according to their roles, the Mexican organization encourages and values harmony, rather than conflict. Compared to the United States, there is a low tolerance for adversarial relations in Mexican organizations. This even permeates union/management relations. Under Mexican labor law, union and management both strive to maintain a posture whereby the union is accountable to the workers while management directs the day-to-day business affairs of the firm. Management that directly addresses the workers is welcomed by the unions as a way to foster good relations and minimize grievances. The union disciplines workers who violate the rules; managers are expected to discipline supervisors.

Mexican employees value peaceful relations between union and management. Though such relations could cause American workers to feel they are being coopted by management, in the case of Mexico harmonious relations are seen as normal. Employees are selected because they have demonstrated an ability to get along with others and work cooperatively with those in authority. Obedience and respect are in contrast to the value

American workers place on independence and confrontation. Meetings are forums for people to receive orders, not for discussion and debate.

This characteristic of harmony affects the compensation system as well. Mexican workers prefer to receive compensation as soon as possible after work is completed. Therefore, *daily* incentive systems with automatic payouts for exceeding production quotas, as well as monthly attendance quotas, can be used effectively to motivate workers to higher levels of production.

These incentive pay programs, however, need to be used with care because they may ruffle a few feathers in Mexico, especially among workers. Why? Workers receiving more pay could be viewed as having connections to the higher echelons. Variable pay-for-performance creates social distance among employees. "It's much more important for a Mexican person to have a congenial working environment than it is to make more money," says Alejandro Palma, intercultural business specialist for Clarke Consulting Group. "There have been cases where very good workers, ones who have performed well and received [monetary] recognition for that, have left the company because they felt ostracized by their coworkers."

Instead, Palma suggests other reward strategies, such as making the outstanding worker a team leader. This plays into their desire for respect without isolating individual workers. Says Palma, "Employees-of-the-month programs – where it's on a rotating basis, not permanent like salary compensation – seem to be OK, because everyone has a chance." Other incentives include family days or other activities that include workers' relatives.

The need to keep wages low to maintain a competitive edge leads many employers to add small benefits, such as food baskets, free bus service, and free meals for the workers. These benefits, which are not considered wages, are given personally to the worker. One reason for this system is that under Mexican labor law, a worker's salary cannot be reduced when his job is downgraded. Because these bonuses are paid based on performance, they do not fall under the law and may be withdrawn when the worker's performance suffers. Benefits such as offices, cars, and the like are offered only to managers and accentuate the differences between levels in the managerial hierarchy.

Paternalism

In the United States and other individualistic cultures, people are expected to take care of themselves, and are rewarded for being masters of their own fate. People frequently change jobs and organizations in an effort to improve themselves. Most employees believe that their corporation is no longer responsible for their welfare and that they must manage their career as best they can. Similarly, organizations often downsize or reorganize in an attempt to improve their cost position with little or no regard for the human consequences. There is a sense of independence between the worker and the organization. At times, this leads to adversarial relations.

In contrast, as mentioned earlier, Mexican companies have a significant responsibility under Mexican labor law for the life, health, and dignity of their workers. Organizations take on a paternalistic obligation to their workers. Managers tend to ignore workers who criticize others or who take their complaints to the union because these workers do not exhibit the spirit of cooperation that Mexican society rewards. Mexican workers rally around emotionally charged management speeches that extol them to improve their group's performance rather than management programs that stress competition with others.

Paternalism also influences the labor relations system. The Mexican Federal Labor Law governs all labor matters, and the state labor boards, made up of representatives from the government, unions, and management, oversee the enforcement of the law. After hiring, an employer has 28 days to evaluate the employee's work ethics. After that period, the employer is expected to assume responsibility for the worker; job security is granted and termination becomes expensive. For example, an employer that decides to fire a worker who has been with the company for six months could be charged for an additional six weeks, plus vacation pay and bonuses. Workers may be dismissed only for causes specifically set out in the Mexican Federal Labor Law. These include falsifying employment documents and committing dishonest or violent acts during working hours. Therefore, it is important to screen employees before hiring.

UNCERTAINTY AVOIDANCE

The third cultural value to be considered here, uncertainty avoidance, refers to the extent to which people of a society feel threatened by unstable and ambiguous situations and try to avoid them. In Mexico, a high uncertainty avoidance society, workers typically desire close supervision rather than being left alone. They try hard to follow directions and do what they are being asked to do.

Compensation systems emphasize consistency and certainty, and they are based on rules and regulations. Thus, companies attempting to use incentive pay need to be careful. Arturo Fisher, a consultant for Hewitt Associates who specializes in Latin America, knows of pay plans that have worked, but he expresses concern at their use. "[Mexicans] are more oriented to guaranteed situations, guaranteed pay," says Fisher. "So, pay at risk is OK, but you have to communicate it a little bit more." Workers have assigned roles and are rewarded for following them efficiently. Job security is also highly valued. In low uncertainty avoidance cultures, such as the U.S., managers' and workers' tasks are less structured. Employees are encouraged to take risks and tend to rely more heavily on their own initiative and ingenuity to get things done.

In our study, we found that staffing practices are ways in which companies can influence the amount of uncertainty in the organization. Managers in Mexico tend to follow consistent, though not necessarily equitable, recruiting and training practices. Employees who have long tenure in the system are prized because they have embraced the values of the organization and have demonstrated that they can uphold its traditions.

Success in managing people across the Mexican border is a matter of being able to translate an understanding of relevant cultural differences into action. The job of the human resource manager is not only to understand these differences, but to adjust the relationship between the organization and its workers to be in line with the cultural values of Mexico. It should then be more naturally possible for managerial actions to be in line with the beliefs of that society. From this report, the context of work in Mexico versus common U.S. managerial practices should take into account the differences in the strengths of hierarchical relationships and risk avoidance as well as the collective nature of Mexican society.

Certainly Mexico will continue to become a more important trading partner for the United States in the twenty-first century. Most assuredly it will also continue to be a key location for U.S. companies setting up shop. But as in the United States, doing business effectively involves using all resources wisely. And the most important of these resources is the people – the human assets.

In managing human assets effectively, it pays to "think globally, but act locally." U.S. firms operating abroad have mostly paid attention to local conditions, particularly laws and regulations. These tend to be more obvious, explicit features of doing business in another country. Less obvious and less explicit are the social customs and patterns of behavior that are acceptable to the population. The experiences of many firms, such as Motorola, Nabisco, Ford, General Electric, and General Motors, in selecting, motivating, training, and retaining employees in Mexico indicates that these less obvious and less explicit aspects of a country are neither unimportant in doing business effectively nor the same as in the United States. Their experiences are certainly consistent with the researchers who have argued for years that it is important to heed the admonition, "When in Rome, do as the Romans do."

It might be tempting to suggest that differences between Mexico and the United States are due more to legal and economic factors than to culture. But those studying cultures might suggest that legal and economic differences are preceded by cultural differences. Economics surely have an impact on the management of human resources, particularly through compensation levels, but this is also true when one compares compensation levels in Kentucky versus New York. Many managers are already factoring in some aspects of country characteristics when managing human resource assets. What we are suggesting is that companies extend this factoring to include aspects of national culture. We hope that some of our review has shed light on exactly how the cultural differences of Mexico and the United States affect the management of human resources in these two important countries.

This article, however, is by no means exhaustive. Considering all the topics and activities in human resource practices, such as staffing, appraising, training/leadership, and work design, the existing data and that from our study permitted us to review and describe only some of them. Using Hofstede's cultural classification, however, we could offer some further suggestions and propositions that the manager could consider in crafting a package of human resource management practices to use in setting up operations in Mexico.

By way of review, Mexico is high on power distance, low on individualism, high on uncertainty avoidance, and high on masculinity; and the United States is low on power distance, high on individualism, low on uncertainty avoidance, and high on masculinity. The reader, however, is justified in saying that things could – indeed do – change. The reader is also justified in saying that even within the United States there are cultural differences that also affect how human resources are managed. This of course confirms our major premise: that a systematic understanding of the relationship between dimensions of culture and consistent ways of managing human resources can be used to one's advantage in crafting a set of human resource practices.

Chapter 26

New Manufacturing Strategies and Labour in Latin America

John Humphrey

INTRODUCTION

In the past few years, considerable interest in "Japanese" production management and the reorganization of work has been evident in Latin America. The liberalization of the Latin American economies, involving both an opening-up of previously protected economies to imports of manufactured goods and an increased emphasis on manufacturing exports, has forced companies to recognize that many products have not been meeting the standards of price, quality, delivery, variability and innovation required for international markets, and that even where success has been achieved in export markets, this has often been achieved through cross-subsidization from domestic sales. In this context, "quality mania", or more generally an interest in Japanese methods, is sweeping the continent. While talk is always easier than practice, there are signs that some significant shifts are taking place in parts of Latin American manufacturing.

This article considers the implications of such changes for labour. It considers whether or not the development of industrial production based on Just-in-Time and Total Quality Management (JIT/TQM) is likely to lead to an improvement in labour–management relations at plant level and also to changes in relations between companies and unions. Given the history of authoritarian management and conflictual labour relations in Latin America, will the possible spread of JIT/TQM have a liberalizing effect? Information will be taken from studies on Argentina, Brazil, Chile and Mexico. I attempt not only to provide answers to the questions posed above, but also to discuss the extent to which it is not possible to provide clear answers at the present time.

The article contains three further sections. Section Two outlines what is meant by "Japanese methods" and why they might be expected to change relations between capital and labour. Section Three examines changing patterns of production organization and labour use in Latin America. Section Four considers how these changes are affecting capital–labour relations.

JAPANESE MANAGEMENT AND LABOUR

Three particular aspects of Japanese management are important for the consideration of changing relations between management and labour.

- Improving the flow of products. Just-in-Time can be defined abstractly as production of the right quantity with the right quality at the precise moment it is required. The ideal factory is one where the product undergoes a continual process of transformation from the moment its component elements enter the plant until the point at which it is dispatched to the customer. Factories may be divided up into "mini-factories" specializing in particular product lines or in particular components or sub-assemblies. Within these mini-factories, cellular layouts may be adopted. These arrangements may require multi-tasking and flexible deployment of labour (workers doing different production jobs and moving between them as required) and polyvalence (workers carrying out quality control and routine maintenance work in addition to production jobs), as well as increased emphasis on the reliability of both the quantity and quality of work performed. If cells and low stocks put a premium on producing at the right time, increased emphasis will be placed on routine maintenance, which may be carried out by the workers operating the machinery and equipment. This shift is usually referred to as Total Productive Maintenance (TPM). It may be coupled with the allocation of workers responsible for major and corrective maintenance directly to the production departments where they work.

- The definition of JIT just given already includes a reference to quality. JIT will not work if quality is poor. TQM is an approach to quality which seeks to trace quality defects back to their source and to continuously monitor quality in production. Part of this process involves control of quality by the operator. If the aim of the Japanese system is to produce "right first time", then the role of quality control is modified. Checks are still made, but increasing responsibility is put on to workers to produce correctly the first time and monitor the results of their own work. At the same time, managements put much greater emphasis on the tracing back of quality problems to their source and the correction of factors which give rise to poor quality. Increased pressure on workers to produce right first time is reinforced by the use of cells, internal clients and reduced stocks. Quality problems are noticed more quickly and are more easily attributable to those responsible for them.[1] The responsibility given to the worker can take many forms: visual inspection, 100 per cent testing by means of fixed gauges or measurement, as well as the possible use of Statistical Process Control.

- Trial-and-Error. JIT/TQM involves a continual search for improvement, *kaizen*. Part of this improvement is found through practical experimentation on the shop floor. Engineers work closely with those on the shop floor, and workers and supervisors are involved in resolving problems and searching for ways of improving methods. Pressure to do this is applied systematically by the use of targets for quality and productivity improvement. Management retains responsibility for making major improvements, but the search for quality improvements, stock reductions and more rapid throughput of parts and products is never-ending, and involves attention to detail and continuous minor improvements. In many cases, these minor improvements can only be located by the direct production workers, as only they know the work they do in sufficient detail. The understanding is mobilized through small groups, with names such as quality circles, improvement groups, *kaizen* groups. The continual transformation of production and the activities of small groups may put a premium on team working and/or rotation of jobs. Workers who are familiar with a range of jobs can both adapt to changes in work practices and contribute better to small group activities.[2]

In some accounts of Japanese production management, emphasis is placed on the rupture between JIT/TQM and "traditional" Fordist principles. Other accounts have questioned this contrast, arguing that "Fordism" and "Japanization" are idealized constructs which overemphasize both the unity of each and the contrasts between the two (Elger and Smith, 1994). In this article, the three aspects of the Japanese model outlined above are seen as tendencies which alter the way production is organized, which may be adopted to a greater or lesser extent in different plants.

The new demands placed on labour by these principles put a new emphasis on human resource development. For Japanese management to work it appears to be the case that labour has to be capable of performing a wider range of tasks, more able to take responsibility and initiatives, have a broader understanding of the production process and work together with other workers in teams. Nothing, apparently, could be in greater contrast to Taylor's account of Schmidt, the handler of pig-iron, whose only virtue was his willingness to do exactly as Taylor instructed him (Braverman, 1975: 102–6). Labour under JIT/TQM has to be trained and motivated. Labour, it is argued, is a key factor in competitiveness. Firms which can direct labour's efforts to the needs of the company, unleash its potential and obtain its involvement will be in a stronger position than those that cannot. Instead of control and discipline, the key words are now motivation, involvement, commitment and participation. A committed labour force can help to keep quality high, improve existing processes and more quickly introduce new ones, leading to better productivity, quality, flexibility and speed of innovation. The point is summarized by Mertens:

> The new beliefs [of management] start from the idea that it is workers who know best the problems arising in production, for which they can provide elements for improving both product and process. This requires the establishment of relations of confidence and co-operation, based on a system of values and reciprocity in terms of effort. The transformation of management culture has consequences for the content of labour relations, which will tend to be directed by concepts such as involvement, trust, values and reciprocity (1992: 30–1).

These changes appear to imply shifts in labour relations and, possibly, union relations. According to Gitahy and Rabelo:

> In addition to retraining programmes, firms are also making progress towards more rigorous recruitment systems, in which schooling becomes a key variable, and in the direction of a new pattern of labour management based on more democratic and participative systems (1991: 3).

For the analysis of Latin America this seems to imply two possibilities: either companies transform their labour–management relations as a precondition for successful JIT/TQM, or they continue in the old, authoritarian style and fail to implement JIT/TQM, with dire consequences for competitiveness. The situation in Latin America is, in fact, considerably more complex than this, as will be shown below.

ARE LATIN AMERICAN FIRMS USING JIT/TQM?

Big shifts in the economic policy have been responsible for the current wave of interest in quality and productivity in Latin America. Latin American economies have become more integrated into the world economy and more open to international standards of performance. In the four economies considered here – Argentina, Brazil, Chile and Mexico – the process of liberalization has been very different. In Argentina, a radical shift in policy by the Menem government has caused considerable dislocation of industry. In Brazil, a more gradual liberalization has taken place, while in Chile liberalization was abrupt, brutal and much earlier than elsewhere in the continent, and the interest in quality and productivity comes in the context of a revival in manufacturing industry and improved performance relative to imports in the domestic market and in export markets. In Mexico, NAFTA has delayed the full impact of liberalization on the non-border economy for some time, but in the past decade new, export-oriented industries have grown up in the North, creating a pronounced heterogeneity in industrial structure.

The ideal model of JIT/TQM associates the introduction of Japanese-style management with improved conditions for labour. Production labour should be more competent in a broader range of more demanding tasks. The polyvalent, multi-skilled, responsible and problem-solving workers have to have more skills and be motivated in a different way to the semi-skilled worker typical of Fordism. There is case study material which points to both increased training and multi-skilling, and, at least in the initial period of manufacturing, better relations between labour and management. In terms of multi-skilling, the example of Ford-Hermosillo is perhaps extreme. The plant's organization of work is summarized by Shaiken as follows:

> The plant employs many Japanese-style techniques – work teams, continuous improvement (*kaizen*) groups, job rotation, and a few classifications . . . At [the plant] all workers – skilled and production – fit into a single classification in which all jobs pay the same wage. Groups of 10–25 workers form teams to elect facilitators to co-ordinate production for two-month terms, after which they return to the line (the teams may no longer elect facilitators, according to reports from the plant in the summer of 1993). The actual tasks workers perform are similar to those in a conventional plant, but workers are expected to learn all the jobs on a team and normally rotate through them (1994: 59)

Ford-Hermosillo, for example, has been much studied, along with other auto plants in the North of Mexico (Carrillo, 1990; Shaiken, 1990), but other cases can be found in Latin America. Fleury and Humphrey (1993) describe a number of cases of firms which have developed broad-ranging restructuring along JIT/TQM lines, partly in response to liberalization and the threat of import competition.

One of the firms studied by Fleury and Humphrey was a Brazilian-owned manufacturer of components for cars and trucks. The plant had been restructured into cells, and in many cases this involved teams of 3–4 workers operating a set of 6–8 machines arranged in a U-shape. The workers in each cell were responsible for production, quality control, machine setting and adjustment and routine maintenance. In order to reflect these developments the company had introduced a new occupational structure, as shown in Figure 26.1.[3] There are now six occupations for production workers. Access to each

```
┌─────────────────────────────────────────────────────────────┐
│ Grade One: Operator                                          │
│ Integration                                                   │
│ Training for QC                                               │
│ Kanban and Cells                              Two days        │
│ Safety                                                        │
│ Total Quality Philosophy                                      │
│ Cleanliness and Tidiness                                      │
│ On-the-job Training                           6 months        │
└─────────────────────────────────────────────────────────────┘
```

```
┌─────────────────────────────────────────────────────────────┐
│ Grade Two: Semi-Skilled Operator                             │
│ Product Knowledge                             8 hours         │
│ Measurement                                   20 hours        │
│ On-the-job Training                           6 months        │
└─────────────────────────────────────────────────────────────┘
```

```
┌─────────────────────────────────────────────────────────────┐
│ Grade Three: Skilled Worker                                  │
│ Reading and Interpretation of Designs         40 hours        │
│ Basic Statistics                              8 hours         │
│ Total Quality                                 8 hours         │
│ On-the-job Training                           12 months       │
└─────────────────────────────────────────────────────────────┘
```

Grade Four (3 options):

Operator Setter		Quality Assurance Worker		Zero Defect Worker	
Machine		Statistical Process		Minor Machine	
Preparation	8 hours	Control	8 hours	Maintenance	8 hours
Lubrification	8 hours	Graphs and Charts	12 hours	Care of Tools	6 hours
Basic Pneumatics	40 hours	Quality systems	4 hours	Lubrification	8 hours
				Tool and Equipment	
				Maintenance	8 hours
				Basic Hydraulics	40 hours
				Basic Electrics	40 hours
				Basic Pneumatics	40 hours
On-the-job		On-the-job		On-the-job	
Training	12 months	Training	12 months	Training	12 months

```
┌─────────────────────────────────────────────────────────────┐
│ Grade Five:                                                  │
│ Any two of the Grade Four skills.                            │
└─────────────────────────────────────────────────────────────┘
```

```
┌─────────────────────────────────────────────────────────────┐
│ Grade Six:                                                   │
│ All three of the Grade Four skills.                          │
└─────────────────────────────────────────────────────────────┘
```

Source: Company documents and interviews.

Figure 26.1 Worker Development Plan, Firm Two

depends on a mixture of training on-the-job and formal training in the company's training centre. While the initial two days of training is largely motivational and introduces new workers to concepts such as Quality Control Circles, kanban and total quality, the content becomes increasingly technical. An operator/setter, for example, has to be able to prepare all the machines in the cell and be capable of carrying out routine maintenance on them. This involves courses in basic hydraulics and pneumatics, as well as extensive on-the-job training. The firm had originally expressed the ambitious aim of having all its workers on Grade Six by 1996. The level of pay for this grade is equivalent to that of an experienced toolmaker. In practice, by mid-1995 one third of the labour force had reached Grade Four, and just 6.5 per cent had reached Grade Five. However, it is clear that the logic of cellular manufacturing had led this firm towards the aim of having all workers able to perform a range of complex functions in one or more cells. A new occupational structure was then created to provide the structure and incentives needed to make polyvalence work.

In order to provide the training required in-house, the company expanded its Educational Centre built in 1983. This is now housed in a purpose-built building in the middle of the plant site. It has a number of tutors, and it also has recourse to the Industrial Training Agency, the Serviço Nacional de Aprendizagem Industrial, SENAI, where more advanced courses are provided for skilled workers, but much of the training is carried out by the plant's own staff. An instructor is attached to each manager, and workers are trained to teach other workers. The aim of the plant was to have more than 100 hours off-the-job training per employee in 1993. This compares with levels found in Japanese auto plants (OTA, 1992: 15).[4] This kind of commitment to improving educational standards and training is probably a key indicator of a radical shift in work organization along the lines discussed in the previous section.

Such changes by themselves may imply important shifts in labour–management relations. A commitment to training in the case of Brazil, for example, makes hire-and-fire policies uneconomic. Expecting workers to take initiative and responsibility must curtail some of the more authoritarian labour practices found in factories. At a basic level, the introduction of new manufacturing strategies can provide real improvements for labour in situations where labour–management relations have been authoritarian and labour has been too weakly organized at plant level to resist oppression. Leite quotes a woman worker at a Brazilian plant:

> The [supervisors] are, I would say, more human now. They talk to you. They say "Look, why did this happen. Let's try and improve it a little. Let's make sure it doesn't happen again." So now they talk to us normally, just like I'm talking to you. Before you were shouted at enough to make you cry, right in front of you. (1993: 16–17).

Other informants cited by Leite describe how their opinions count for more and they are encouraged to make suggestions rather than ordered to keep quiet and do as they are told. Such a basic change does clearly indicate how bad conditions were in the plant – although quite typical for Brazilian industry – and how important it is for workers that such basic shifts in attitude take place. This does not mean, of course, that firms using new production methods no longer exercise control, but they do so in a more careful and orderly manner, and they lay more emphasis on "self-control" (*auto controle*), by motivating the individual and mobilizing peer group pressure, as will be shown below.

Table 26.1 Indicators of Reorganization, Metalworking Industry. Four Countries (% of Firms Responding "Yes")

	Argentina	Brazil	Chile	Mexico
Programmes Adopted 1990–2:				
Maintenance tasks transferred	10	42	13	16
Inspection/quality tasks transferred	29	53	50	48
SPC	0	43	0	36
Work teams	19	26	30	38
Programmes Planned 1993–5:				
Maintenance tasks transferred	12	43	27	36
Inspection/quality tasks transferred	48	72	57	68
SPC	6	55	20	54
Work teams	23	57	40	44
Workers' aptitudes:				
Difficulties in assuming responsibilities	70	94	83	83
Difficulties in taking initiatives	63	84	79	67
Basic Education Issues:				
Workers unable to concentrate	66	65	64	63
Lack of capacity for abstraction	54	49	41	54
Cannot learn new skills and abilities	42	69	64	56
Difficulties in reading and writing	33	65	39	51
Limited verbal skills	30	54	45	44
Skill:				
Poor middle management	58	77	70	78
Workers cannot operate new equipment	42	60	53	57
Scarcity of skilled production labour	78	67	79	76
Scarcity of technical and professional staff	33	75	68	69
No. of companies surveyed	52	53	30	50

Source: Abramo (1993).

For every case of broad adoption of JIT/TQM principles, however, there are many cases of failures to adopt JIT/TQM, or more importantly, the use of specific and limited JIT/TQM techniques in response to the crisis caused by liberalization (Roldán, 1993). This is the limitation of the case study approach. Case studies provide little idea of the extent of JIT/TQM use. They show that it is impossible for some firms in Latin America to restructure internally, and that even changes in supplier relations are possible. But the results of case studies are so varied they do not allow an overall picture to emerge. Worse still, firms themselves change so rapidly that what was true at one point in time no longer holds a year or so later. Some of the most characteristic features of Ford-Hermosillo described by Shaiken (1990), such as rotation of workers between production and maintenance tasks and the election of team leaders, did not last into the 1990s.

In this situation, more general assessments of the spread of JIT/TQM in Latin America are of great use, whatever their shortcomings. A study of 185 firms in the metalworking industries of four countries by the Programa Regional del Empleo para America Latina y el Caribe, PREALC, provides important information, and some of the results are presented in table 26.1. The survey considered the use of techniques which change the work performed by labour – SPC, teamworking, and the integration of inspection and maintenance tasks with production work. It shows, firstly, that there are considerable variations in the use of JIT/TQM techniques within countries, between countries and between techniques. Brazilian firms claim the greatest use of such techniques, followed by Mexico. Overall, in all of the countries, a minority of firms were using most of the techniques, even though one would expect larger firms in the metalworking industries to be among the first users of JIT/TQM. The transfer of inspection tasks to production workers was most common among the firms studied, but the use of other techniques varied considerably from country to country. As might be expected, in all four countries, firms are expected to do more in the future than in the past, although expectations in Argentina lag considerably behind those of other countries.

This use of programmes altering the nature of production work which are commonly associated with JIT/TQM is, however, combined with considerable doubts about workers' aptitudes, basic educational standards and skills. Most firms complain that workers have difficulties in taking responsibility and initiative. The kinds of abilities which a basic education might be expected to provide, such as the ability to concentrate, a capacity for abstraction, capacity to learn new skills, the ability to read and write and verbal skills, are all deficient. In addition, firms face problems with labour supply at all levels.

It is clear that use of JIT/TQM techniques is not necessarily blocked by these labour supply problems. Brazil, which has the worst indicators for basic education, also has the highest use of programmes which extend the activities of production workers. What does this imply for the spread of JIT/TQM?

Firstly, problems with educational standards are not a barrier to the use of JIT/TQM, but firms may have to invest heavily in education and training to improve labour's skills and capacities. This is evident in Brazil. Firms developing JIT/TQM have often developed adult education programmes for their labour forces, literacy and numeracy programmes, and intensive training programmes, not only in technical skills but also in such basic skills as communication and group discussion.[5] This means that smaller firms which may lack the infrastructure and resources to invest in education programmes, and which may not be able to pay higher-than-average wages to secure the better-educated labour, will be at a severe disadvantage.

Secondly, there is a clear risk that firms will adapt their work organization to the characteristics of their labour forces. Instead of making heavy investments to make JIT/TQM possible, they will instead opt for production practices which need less input from labour. Firms become locked into cycles of labour capacities and work organization which reinforce each other. Poorly-trained and educated labour is confined to tasks which do not develop capacities. Carvalho (1994) has expressed concerns about work organization and education in the Brazilian petrochemical industry.

This does not mean that firms will not adopt JIT/TQM at all. It will affect the nature of this adoption. As was argued in the previous section, firms operating processes such as assembly of simple parts can develop low-stock, high flow, high quality production without using systematic job rotation, team-working or multi-skilling. Beyond this, however, it is possible that firms using more complex operations will use variants of them which do not require increased skills and responsibilities compared to more traditional work organization. Leite provides an example of this. She describes how management at a large North American transnational in Brazil adopted a production system developed by Goldtratt, which required less of a revolution in factory organization and culture than kanban and less inputs from workers (1993: 4–8).

Kaplinsky, who distinguishes between techniques and system:

> The various elements of production organization introduced by the Japanese in recent decades can be seen in either the limited context of a specific production technique – potentially applicable across a range of production systems – or as an integral component of the new production system itself. For example, specific techniques have been developed to reduce inventories (Just-in-Time, JIT) and to ensure better quality procedures (Total Quality Control, TQC). These can be implemented as stand-alone changes in procedure, often within the context of large-batch production of standardized products; alternatively, their introduction can be co-ordinated and be linked to the use of a battery of additional techniques to enable the flexible production of diversified, high quality products. To operate effectively and to approach the levels of achievement attained by many Japanese firms (and some Western imitators), there is little doubt that these JMTs must be adopted as part of a wider, co-ordinated package of measures. Nevertheless, even when introduced in a fragmented manner, the competitive returns can often be high (1995: 58).

Firms which do not develop education and training policies to overcome the problems outlined in table 26.1 will not go on to develop other areas such as *kaizen* activities or multi-skilling. They may obtain significant improvements in performance in the short term, but they will not develop continuous improvement. One of the limitations of studies like that of PREALC is precisely that it cannot distinguish easily between systemic and non-systemic uses of JIT/TQM.

Low levels of schooling and training are one important factor which limits the spread of JIT/TQM, operating as an obstacle which can only be surmounted by the larger and better-organized firms. However, four other factors may also inhibit the spread of the kinds of labour practices which might transform labour–management relations, and they will be mentioned briefly:

- Firms may simply not have the managerial competence needed to develop JIT/TQM. They introduce specific techniques such as cellular production or kanban in limited parts of their plants because they do not have the technical or organizational capabilities for wholesale change. Roldán (1993) analyses cases of limited adoption in the Argentine case.
- In sectors with limited competition, established manufacturing strategies will continue to be viable. While it is now clear that the principles of JIT/TQM are widely applicable in manufacturing industry, and in other sectors (banks, telecommunications), the pressure to adopt new manufacturing strategies is very uneven.
- In plants using simple production processes, the principles of production flow and quality-at-source may be achieved without resort to methods such as team-working or multi-skilling. In North America, organization by team-working or job rotation are found much more extensively in Japanese transplants in the auto industry than in the electrical industry (Kenney and Florida, 1992b). A similar pattern can be seen in the case of Northern Mexico. While quite extensive use of JIT/TQM is apparent in the motor industry (Ramirez, 1993), the same is not true for the electrical industry, particularly in the maquiladora plants. Kenney and Florida find little evidence of "Japanese" practices in Japanese maquiladoras, and they

attribute this to the fact that working practices are very standard, educational levels are low and turnover is high (Kenney and Florida, 1992a: 21–2). Shaiken and Browne's study of 13 Japanese plants also finds limited use of "Japanese" techniques, such as team-working, quality circles, multi-tasking, low stock production and *kaizen* (Shaiken and Browne, 1991). The plants are competitive, providing good quality and productivity and gaining market access (ibid: 48), so the organization of work does not appear to be a problem. Attention to design and the detail of manufacturing processes, combined with intensive use of traditional quality control and some linked *kaizen* practices may be a recipe for success.

- A very different problem is apparent in Mexican auto plants. Managements may wish to introduce JIT/TQM along the lines of Hermosillo in their plants in central Mexico, but labour conflicts prevent them from doing so. Carrillo's (1995) study of the contrast between Ford's Hermosillo and Cuautitlán plants shows clearly how management was unable to make rapid changes in the latter plant, situated in Central Mexico. Similarly, the work of Abo and his team on hybridization shows a large difference in the use of Japanese work organization in Nissan's plants in Northern and in Central Mexico.[6] The implications of this point will be considered below.

For many reasons, JIT/TQM use is likely to be very patchy in Latin America. But it is still legitimate to ask what might be the impact of JIT/TQM on labour in the plants which do adopt it. The question has been put clearly by Leite:

> Are Brazilian industrialists really opting for systemic modernization based on job enrichment and more democratic labour relations? Up to what point will the position taken by the managements found in the studies by Gitahy and Rabelo and Fleury and Humphrey be extended to at least a significant part of Brazilian industry (if not the whole of it), or will it be restricted to a small number of technologically advanced firms? Is the current stage of research sufficient to allow us to talk of a new tendency among firms in relation to the management of labour? And, finally, if we assume that firms are in fact more inclined to adopt systemic modernization . . . it is necessary to ask to what extent these transformations are leading to more substantial changes in labour relations, particularly in terms of the adoption of a more democratic and participatory model of industrial relations (1992: 21).

The remainder of this contribution will attempt to answer this last question.

New Manufacturing Strategies and Labour Relations

Better treatment for workers at plant level, and the emergence of less authoritarian labour relations has led to some expectation in Latin America that a new "modern" and less authoritarian era in relations between companies and unions might also emerge. So far there is little sign of this. On the contrary, three tendencies, none of them favourable to the union, can be perceived: the continued marginalization of weak unions, an attack on the rights of established unions, and the creation of a new, weakened unionism in new regions of production. None of this is unfamiliar to those with a knowledge of unionism in Japan. Toyota, for example, smashed a combative union in the early 1950s and replaced it with a subordinate, company union. Japanese transplants abroad, too, have become less and less willing to recognize unions. Costa and Garanto (1993: 107) show that in Europe, the rate of recognition of unions in Japanese plants established in the early 1970s was about 80 per cent. For plants established in the late 1980s, this rate had fallen to under 40 per cent. When unions are recognized, they are subject to restrictive conditions. Oliver and Wilkinson refer to no-strike deals, binding arbitration and agreements on flexibility (1992: 288–96).

The first situation mentioned above was continued marginalization. Briefly, unions in Brazil and Mexico have continued to find it difficult to develop constructive relations with managements, even when they show themselves willing to cooperate and to accept, even support, new manufacturing practices. Managements still fear the unions and do not want to risk involvement. Firms see the new manufacturing practices as a means of marginalizing the union threat further. Better working conditions and better and more direct relations between management and labour on the shop floor is seen as a means of making the union redundant. Clearly, however, the marginalization of the union is a key element in labour control. In Brazil, the development of profit-sharing schemes to motivate and reward workers is markedly different in plants with strong and weak unions. In plants with weak unions, bonuses are tied to individual or sectional performance, according to highly specific performance criteria and personal appraisal. The bonus scheme is part of a sophisticated and personalized system of control. In the strongly-unionized periphery of São Paulo, the unions have negotiated plant-wide schemes linked to general performance indicators (production, quality and absenteeism), and also successfully fought for a lump-sum bonus, which is more valuable to low-paid workers.

Where unions have been strong, firms developing new manufacturing strategies have often tended to seek to undermine union power, and for obvious reasons. Union power has often been constructed around negotiated "rigidities" which protect workers from arbitrary managerial power and give workers a firm basis from which to negotiate. Managements wish to sweep these rigidities away. Strong unionism in Latin America has, in addition, been constructed behind protective trade barriers, and as these are dismantled, companies wish to make wholesale changes in production.

At the national level, formerly strong labour systems have been under attack. In both Argentina and Mexico, legislation has undermined previously held union rights (Catalano and Novick, 1992; Garza, 1993). At plant level, there have been many well-publicized attempts to smash union power. In Argentina, management at the Acinder steel plant:

> declared a lock-out, decided to dismiss all the personnel and re-hire them, obliging each worker to accept the new work methods. At the same time, the firm de-recognized the local union leadership as its interlocutor . . . and attempted to begin negotiations with the national leadership of the UOM, which refused the invitation. As the workers at the plant united behind the union, the firm began mass recruitment of new workers among the unemployed in southern Rosario (Novick and Palomino, 1993: 324).

In this case, organized resistance from workers and the union forced the company to retreat. In the case of the Ford plant at Cuautitlán in Central Mexico, management succeeded in sacking the plant's workers en masse during a strike in 1987 and then selectively re-hiring them under quite a different labour contract. In this case, the company had some support from the national union (Carrillo, 1995). There have been other cases of open conflict between management and organized labour at plants in Central Mexico, as firms seek to redefine work methods and labour–management relations.[7]

Forcing through radical changes in working practices might be expected to engender conflict between management and labour and opposition from unions. However, it is also clear that in new plants, managements have tried to either marginalize or subordinate unions. Once again, this is seen most clearly in the North of Mexico, where in the maquiladoras, unions are hardly recognized at all, and in the new non-maquila auto plants, the unions are in a greatly weakened position compared to Central Mexico (in the past at least). Garza (1993: 156–7) lists a number of areas in which contracts at Ford Hermosillo, GM Ramos Arizpe and the electrical maquilas give great freedom to the companies, including defining work methods, hiring of temporary workers, recruitment, overtime and internal mobility of labour. In the past, the union would have had a say in these issues. Similarly, Carrillo (1995) outlines the efforts Ford has made to establish new contracts in its Northern plants, separate them from the Central plants and define a wide degree of discretion for management. According to Carrillo:

> The Hermosillo agreement was a development of one first tried out by Ford at its Chihuahua engine plant, and it allowed the company a wide degree of freedom in plant organization. The firm carefully restricted the union's role at Hermosillo, so that the free operation of the principles of responsible autonomy might be achieved. The union was left with practically no powers to interfere in production because work teams had wide powers to resolve day-to-day conflicts and interpret plant regulations. The result was that the local union representatives at Hermosillo never enjoyed the autonomy and influence which had once been enjoyed by representatives in Central Mexico, because of a structural lack of power to negotiate changes in the workplace. The company retained exclusive decision-making powers over such issues as the level of employment in the plant, recruitment and the content of training (1995: 92–3)

Carrillo links the company's attitude to the union and the form of contract it negotiated with the CTM to the flexibility in work organization desired by the company. This flexibility concerns not only the right to reorganize work and encourage team-working, which unions might find acceptable. The application of JIT/TQM and *kaizen* also contains a spirit of continuing pressure and ceaseless demands for improvements in performance which are much less acceptable to unions. Work in JIT/TQM plants may be more interesting and varied, and workers may find that it is more meaningful, but it is also more stressful. Berggren sums up the experience of Japanese auto transplants in the United States as follows:

> High quality products produced by a high quality workforce under a dedicated management offering job security and equal treatment, while at the same time demanding virtually unlimited performance, excessive working hours and the subjection to harsh conduct and discipline codes – the work experience of the transplants really seems to be a contradictory one (1993: 31).

Work is more meaningful and more stressful. On balance, workers may prefer it like this, and there is little to suggest that given the choice workers would wish to return to the Fordist management style. However, the balance of meaning and stress is one which can be negotiated. Managements will push for more until they meet with sufficient resistance for them to stop. This resistance may be collective (stoppages, strikes, negotiations) or individual (poor quality, turnover). Not having a union helps management to impose a tough bargain.

Some of the apparently more attractive aspects of JIT/TQM can be used to this end. Team-working is a good example. Shaiken's description of work organization at Ford Hermosillo highlights this point:

> The [plant's] teams are structured both to capture the loyalty and good spirits of people who work together and to generate peer pressure to improve production when necessary. The work group makes many decisions normally taken by managers in a traditional plant, such as when to rotate jobs or who to send to training classes. In addition, the teams mete out discipline for absenteeism. If a member is absent, a facilitator may have to work on the line or other members may have to be pulled out of training classes, hence considerable peer pressure can exist for people not to miss work (1994: 60).

The control over individuals is exercised by the team, which in turn, is subject to performance targets. Küsel (1990) describes a similar pattern of team pressure in the General Motors plant in Ramos Arizpe in Northern Mexico.

Similar patterns can be observed elsewhere. In Brazil a firm had built a sophisticated plant on a greenfield site, well away from the strong union with which it had been in conflict at the company's main site. The plant was technically advanced, and work was organized around teams. The plant offered job rotation and also promotion based on the systematic acquisition of skills and experiences. In principle all workers could be promoted from the bottom rungs of the ladder to the highest positions in the factory. As part of the process, the firm had introduced annual assessments of performance based on three items: the training courses workers had taken, the development of their operational skills and their attitude and behaviour (such as contributions to the suggestions scheme, effort, absenteeism and team spirit). A very good score meant promotion, but a poor score led to dismissal. At the same time, the firm was considering devolving responsibility to teams for accepting new team members and dismissing team members whose performance was not satisfactory. If management were to go ahead with the scheme, team members would be free to expel a worker from the team, with the consequence that this would mean the worker would be dismissed from the firm. This was in a context where the team itself was set clear targets for quality and productivity, and in which the team suffered sanctions being applied for failing to meet them. Management talked of intervention in a team which failed to meet its targets. "Intervention" was also used in Brazil to denote the suspension of an elected trade union leadership by the Ministry of Labour and its replacement by Ministry appointees. The pressure placed on team members by their peers could be intense. Individualized appraisal and rewards, combined with group responsibility and pressure, can be a powerful means of control.

The success of JIT/TQM depends in part on combining new and more efficient working practices with increasing intensity. For inefficient companies, using new manufacturing strategies can lead to great improvements in efficiency without increasing intensity of work. For many Latin American companies, *any* attention to manufacturing will produce big dividends because they have been such inefficient producers in the past. However, in order to reach international standards of competitiveness, intensity of work is also required. Work is both smarter and harder.

For this reason, firms may make great efforts to deal with worker grievances as a means of nipping discontent in the bud and preventing unions from organizing in plants. This strategy is very clear in Brazil. As Leite (1993) has observed, managements seek to anticipate the union as a means of marginalizing it. In Brazil, managements fear the unions because they cannot be excluded completely from the scene. The Brazilian labour system still guarantees unions formal rights of representation and gives unions a role in collective bargaining. Managements associate union activity with militancy and opposition to change. Therefore, they try to pre-empt union demands by offering wages and conditions which are attractive to workers. In fact, one of the motivations for management adoption of Quality Circles, Improvement Groups, better and more open relations between management and labour ("open-door" access to senior management, "morning coffee with the boss", registers of workers' state of spirit, collective gymnastics) is precisely to catch worker discontent before the unions can mobilize around it.

This is why one sees what are apparently open and co-operative relations between management and labour within plants and a strongly hostile attitude to the union. Most of all management want to relate to workers as individuals, or as teams which are oriented towards the management problematic, not as a collectivity with the right to express different interests. This combination of, on the one hand, valuing workers through practices such as openness to individual grievances, recognition of the contributions workers can make to efficiency and investment in training, and on the other, intensified control, individualized appraisal and reward and hostility to collective organization is new in Latin America. There is the risk that the initial attractions of JIT/TQM will allow firms to marginalize collective organization and develop strong control systems, leaving workers defenceless in the face of demands for increasing intensity of work. In this context, the need for a countervailing power and organization is more necessary than ever, and unions will continue to have an important role in protecting workers from the worst excesses of management power.

Notes

1   It should be noted that, while the focus here is on direct production workers, all of the innovations described here will only work well if considerable attention is paid to such factors as design for manufacturability, simplification of layouts and increasing the reliability of production processes. In fact, changing labour–management relations is only part of the process of introducing JIT/TQM. Firms should also change management structures, improve engineering capabilities improve design, etc. and these non-labour issues are just as important for overall performance.

2   The importance of small group activities does not in any way diminish the role and efforts of managements in seeking improvement. Most commentators agree that workers are involved in making minor changes, which frees management to plan major innovations.

3   Toolroom and maintenance workers are not included in this scheme.

4   Because training is so important for promotion in Firm Two, access to it must be transparent. The courses already taken by workers and plans for the coming year were on public display in each cell's meeting area.

5   See Fleury and Humphrey (1993), Gitahy and Rabelo (1991) and Posthuma (1991).

6   Information from a presentation at the 2nd Gerpisa meeting in Paris, June 1994. More generally, see Abo (1994).

7   See, for example, Pries (1992) for the case of VW at Puebla. One exception to this tendency might appear to be the agreement between unions and firms in the auto industry (Cardoso and Comin, 1993). But in this case the agreement focuses mainly on output, prices and employment, and not on the internal regulation of the plants.

References

Abo, Tetsuo, 1994. *The Hybrid Factory*. New York, Oxford University Press.

Abramo, Lais, 1993. "Las transformaciones en el mundo del trabajo, escolaridad y calificación en un contexto de cambio tecnólogico", paper presented to 5th Workshop on Planning Policy and Education Management, Santiago, October.

Braverman, Harry, 1975. *Labour and Monopoly Capital*. New York, Monthly Review.

Berggren, Christian, 1993, "Lean Production – The End of History?" in *Des Realités du Toyotisme*, Actes du Gerpisa, No.6.

Cardoso, A., and A. Comin, 1993. "Câmaras setoriais, modernização produtiva e democratização das relações de trabalho no brasil", paper presented to 1st Latin American Congress on the Sociology of Work, Mexico City, November.

Carrillo, Jorge (ed.), 1990. *La Nueva Era de la Industria Automotriz en México*. Tijuana, COLEF.

Carrillo, Jorge, 1995. "Flexible production in the auto sector: industrial reorganization at Ford-Mexico", *World Development*, Vol. 23, No. 1.

Carvalho, Ruy de Quadros, 1994. "Capacitacão tecnológico limitada e uso do trabalho na indústria brasileira", *São Paulo em Perspectiva*, Vol. 8, No. 1.

Catalano, Ana, and Marta Novick, 1992. "Relaciones laborales y sociología del trabajo: a la búsqueda de una confluencia", *Sociedad*, 1(1) (Buenos Aires).

Costa, Isabel da, and Annie Garanto, 1993. "Entreprises japonaises et syndicalisme en Europe", *Le Mouvement Social*, No. 162.

Elger, Tony, and Chris Smith, 1994. "Introduction", in T. Elger and C. Smith (eds), *Global Japanisation?* London, Routledge.

Fleury, Afonso, and John Humphrey, 1993. "Human resources and the diffusion and adaptation of new quality methods in Brazilian manufacturing", Research Report 24. Brighton, Institute of Development Studies.

Garza, Enrique de la, 1993. *Reestructuración productiva y respuesta sindical en México*. Mexico City, UNAM/UAM.

Gitahy, Leda, and Flávio Rabelo, 1991. "Educação e Desenvolvimento Tecnológico: o caso da indústria de autopeças". DPCT/IG/UNICAMP, Textos para Discussão, No. 11.

Kaplinsky, R., 1995. "Technique and system: the spread of Japanese management techniques to developing countries", *World Development*, Vol. 23, No. 1.

Kenney, Martin and Richard Florida, 1992a. "Japanese Maquiladoras", University of California Davis, Program in East Asian Business and Development, Working Paper, No. 44.

Kenney, Martin and Richard Florida, 1992b. "Japanese styles of management in three U.S. transplant industries: autos, steel and electronics", paper presented at workshop on Japanese Management Styles: an international comparative perspective, Cardiff, Business School, September.

Küsel, C., 1990. "'La Calidade Tiene Prioridad Número I.' Restruturación del proceso de trabajo e introducción de conceptos japoneses de organización en la industria automotriz mexicana", in J. Carrillo (ed.) *La Nueva Era de la Industria Automotriz en México*, Tijuana, El Colégio de la Frontera Norte.

Leite, Márcia, 1992. "Modernização Tecnológica e Relaçõ es de Trabalho no Brasil: notas para uma discussão", paper presented to Seminar "Work and Education", São Paulo, Fundação Carlos Chagas.

Leite, Márcia, 1993. "Cambio tecnológico y mercado de trabalho." Projeto Regional PREALC/OIT/ACDI, Relatório Final.

Mertens, Leonard, 1992. "El desafio de las relaciones laborales en la nueva competividad," *Critica & Communicación*, Vol. 8 (Lima).

Novick, Marta, and Héctor Palomino, 1993. "Estrategias empresariales frente a la reestructuración económica y respuesta sindical: un caso Argentino", *Economia & Trabajo*, Vol. 1, No. 2.

OTA, 1992. "Worker training: competing in the new international economy". Washington, DC, Congress of the United States, Office of Technology Assessment.

Oliver, N., and B. Wilkinson, 1992. *The Japanisation of British Industry*, 2nd edition, Oxford: Blackwell.

Posthuma, Anne, 1991. "Changing production practices and competitive strategies in the Brazilian auto components industry", unpublished D. Phil. dissertation, University of Sussex.

Pries, Ludger, 1992. "Contexto estructural y dinámica de acción del conflicto en la Volkswagen de México en 1992". Mimeo, El Colégio de Puebla.

Ramirez, José Carlos, 1993. "Recent transformations in the Mexican motor industry", *IDS Bulletin*, Vol. 24, No. 2.

Roldán, Martha, 1993. "Industrial restructuring, deregulation and new JIT labour processes in Argentina: towards a gender-aware perspective", *IDS Bulletin*. Vol. 24, No. 2.

Shaiken, Harley, 1990. *Mexico in the Global Economy: high technology and work organization in export industries*. University of California, San Diego, Centre for U.S.-Mexican Studies. Monograph Series 33.

Shaiken, Harley, 1994. "Advanced manufacturing in Mexico: a new international division of labour?", *Latin American Research Review*, Vol. 29, No. 2.

Shaiken, Harley, and Harry Browne, 1991. "Japanese work organization in Mexico", in G. Székely (ed.), *Manufacturing Across Oceans and Borders*, University of California San Diego, Center for U.S.-Mexican Studies. Monograph Series No. 36.

Chapter 27

Coming to Terms With Local People

John Channon and Adam Dakin

"Like trying to saddle a cow," was Stalin's memorable description of his attempts to impose his version of communism on a reluctant Poland. Many companies establishing operations in Central and Eastern Europe over the last few years may have found the welcome warmer, but the cultural challenges are no less daunting.

The view that personnel problems were more acute in Eastern Europe than any other region emerged from a small survey conducted recently by SSEES-Communicaid, a partnership between the School of Slavonic and East European Studies (SSEES) at London University and a corporate language training company, Communicaid. Almost all the HR directors and managers of 30 British and multinational companies questioned agreed that western companies had generally underestimated cultural differences and their impact on the establishment of operations and the nature of the local workforce.

The academic work of SSEES and Communicaid's experience over the past two years confirms the finding that understanding and responding sympathetically to cultural issues has been one of the major hurdles for companies establishing themselves in Central and Eastern Europe. The limited experience and market information on which companies could draw before going into the region magnified the personnel problems they encountered, for both expatriate and local staff. This meant that, at least initially, each company has had to find its own solutions to staffing problems, although networks and benchmarking groups are now growing up.

The special conditions in Central and Eastern Europe have meant companies are looking at strategies that may be different to their other international operations. While in some countries companies may be happy to maintain a dominant expatriate presence, they have found that, in this region, the dangers of what might be seen as the "colonial" approach are too great.

Over 70 per cent of the companies interviewed for the survey had adopted what we have termed a "standard strategy" when setting up a greenfield operation. In almost all cases they were aiming for 99–100 per cent local staffing in the long term, as most felt local staff would have a better understanding of the local market. An expatriate presence was usual in the initial stages to set up the operation and oversee a transitional period, during which local staff could be trained to take over in management and support positions.

Companies that did not adopt the standard strategy were those that had a rigid company culture they wanted to implant, or those that were investing only for the short term.

Local staff therefore have a vital role to play in company strategy. But this has raised its own issues, not least resulting from the special characteristics of the workforce: generally high levels of technical skill and good English, but a need for training in modern management techniques and commercial skills such as accountancy, marketing and service principles – including even such basic skills as answering the telephone properly.

Equipping local staff to integrate fully into free-market culture requires substantial training. Concepts such as profit and loss, responsibility and the need for strategic thinking are alien – the most immediate legacy of the communist period – and it will take time for these to become accepted.

The communist economic system has been the most profound and immediate influence on the nature of the workforce across the region. The command economy, dominated by the military-industrial complex and quota-based production targets, was inherently inflexible and unable to respond to consumer demand. Quantity, not quality, was the priority – a principle that is perhaps reflected by the rather over-enthusiastic embracing of capitalism in some quarters, and the "quick buck" attitude of its exponents: making as much money as they can without the accompanying responsibility of customer service.

Hierarchical command structures restricted the ability of individuals to show initiative, although some improvisation was necessary to find the resources to meet production quotas. Although strong in the field of technology, inflexible bureaucracy often stifled development potential and left the typical communist economy little room to adapt or modernise.

The culture gap applies across the region, but is most acute in Russia and least so in what may be considered the "emerged" markets of Central Europe. The strongest evidence of this is the variation in the estimated time it takes to complete the transitional stage of operations. Most companies expect the transition to local staffing to take about 18 months in the four major markets of Central Europe (the Czech Republic, Slovakia, Poland and Hungary) and over 36 months in Russia and the Commonwealth of Independent States (CIS), which formed out of the former non-Russian Soviet Union states. In the Balkans, which some companies treat as a separate area, there is so little investment it is impossible to generalise.

Part of the problem is that "western" countries have for so long referred to the countries of Central and Eastern Europe as the "Soviet bloc" or the "eastern bloc". Such terms conjure images of granite-faced masses and Soviet military might, so that the cultural and linguistic diversity and the multifarious traditions of the individual countries have been frequently overlooked. Myriad peoples, cultures and languages encompass the vast geographical mass that makes up the lands east of the former Iron Curtain. Some have rich democratic traditions and a history of close relations with the West; some have known only conflict and dictatorship and view the West with more suspicion. All these countries share the common experience of emerging from communism, but their individual responses to the process have varied widely. In general, the region can be broken down into three distinct areas:

- Central Europe – the Czech Republic, Poland, Slovakia, Hungary and Slovenia. Here we would also include the Baltic states.

- Russia and the former Soviet Union.
- South central region (the Balkans), Romania, Bulgaria, Albania and the former Yugoslavia.

In Central Europe, communism was in place for 45 years and was less hardline. These countries also have pre-communist intellectual, economic and political traditions which are close to those of Western Europe, and now see themselves restored to their rightful status as Central European countries.

In the former Soviet Union, communism is more deep-rooted, not only because it was in place for 70 years but because in many respects it adapted itself to local Slavonic, particularly Russian, traditions. Historically, the area was more isolated from Western Europe. There was autocratic government and a peasant culture, with a strong tradition of collectivism and mutual support or patronage mechanisms in the face of a harsh external climate. This is a far more difficult culture in which to establish an operation, because there are no deep-seated traditions of private enterprise or private property.

A problem that companies have commented on, and which has often been overlooked, is that of nationalism and national tensions. This is particularly the case in the Balkans, where the instability associated with the region is the direct result of political nationalism in its most dangerous form.

One consumer goods company found it had underestimated the problems of nationalist tension when it tried to organise a training session for its central south-east region operation, which includes the former Yugoslavia, Bulgaria, Romania, Greece and Moldova. The session was a failure. Following this, it sees one of its priorities as "corporatising" staff so they can rise above national loyalties to become "company people".

Young people are generally more accepting than the older generation, in whom the "psychological baggage" of the communist period is more deeply ingrained. However, in many societies age is deeply respected and a young person will not necessarily be considered competent, no matter how experienced, merely because of their age.

Companies have also found this problem with expatriate employees, many of whom are young and single purely because of the difficulty of placing families in what can be a harsh environment. It can take time for a young manager to be accepted, particularly away from the more developed business centres, where attitudes remain more traditional. Patience and proof of competence is the key. As far as local staff are concerned, one experienced regional manager described the ideal candidate as "a 25-year-old who speaks English, is self-motivated, attracted to the West, with a well-connected father".

A group of managers who have experience of setting up in-country operations also mentioned the need for a local "fixer": someone who can smooth the way through the local bureaucracy and literally "get the electricity switched on in the office". This person will usually be from the older generation, with good contacts at all levels.

But beware of old-style patronage systems. It may be hard to dismiss a local employee if they have a patron higher up in the company – as a financial services company in Moscow was recently reminded, politely. It attempted to get rid of someone and had to withdraw the notice of dismissal because the individual was protected by an influential patron.

The investment required in training staff and the shortage of people with the necessary corporate skills make poaching of local staff at all levels the most serious problem that established operations now face. Companies are increasingly finding they have to offer incentives to retain key staff, including higher wages, long-term career development and training, and long-service bonus schemes.

The problem is that for many local staff, particularly in countries which are less stable, the priority is not necessarily their long-term career path but their ability to exist on a day-to-day basis. They may be the breadwinner for a large, extended family, and will take advantage of any chance to improve their wages.

Incentives may be one way to insure against the loss of staff, but building trust with the local community should also be an important element of the process. Trust will help to allay fears that western companies are around merely to make a quick buck.

Respect for local culture and experience is vital, as is an understanding for the culture and the historical background of the situation. Some effort to speak the local language also goes a long way. But companies must be wary of appearing patronizing, and should remember that western solutions are not always appropriate.

After the Berlin Wall came down, and after Boris Yeltsin's rise to power in Russia, many western companies piled in with their textbooks, expecting to implement a prede-termined management model. The plan was to put their own managers in for a long period and to pull them out only when the joint venture, or local office, had absorbed the western parent company's way of working.

Many now realize that the situation is far more sensitive and that there are aspects of Central and East European culture which can be built on. For example, collectivism is a strong trait throughout the region, but needs to be harnessed in creative teamworking towards a common goal, rather than being used defensively against authority. Hence the trend towards establishing a local management cadre which can develop its own solu-tions. If companies accept the collectivist tradition and work within it, they will make greater progress towards persuading people to work in a "western" way.

The fact is that we have as much to learn from Central and Eastern Europe as it does from us. There is a tremendous enthusiasm and energy to be tapped, particularly among the younger people, and there is every reason to believe that they will be able to rebuild their economies to compete with ours. Working in the right way, western companies can be part of that upturn.

Chapter 28

Being "a Third Culture Man"

Geert J. E. M. Sanders

Imagination is more important than knowledge. To raise new questions, new possibilities, to regard old problems from a new angle, requires creative imagination and marks real advance in science.

Albert Einstein

Some years ago I met a Japanese colleague describing himself as "a third culture man". Originating from Japan, he went to an American university to study social anthropology. Re-entering Japanese society after seven years, he realized that he could no longer join his former circles of associates. His compatriots looked upon him as an outsider. Having missed some crucial transitions experienced by his contemporaries, he could not see an opportunity to take up the thread. He decided to take advantage of his unusual course of life. He was appointed to a special chair in Social Anthropology at one of the top ten universities in Tokyo. Most of his time now he is involved in field research on the Philippine Islands. With his two contrasting backgrounds, he has a unique viewpoint at his disposal. In a colourful and contagious way he introduced me into his professional world which is permeated by his sensitive observations and analyses.

GERSDAM CASE

I had a similar experience with the third culture phenomenon when I coached one of my Dutch students during his practical work in Gersdam (a fictitious name for a city near Berlin in the former German Democratic Republic) in the course of 1990 and 1991. After the Berlin wall was pulled down in November 1989, many West German companies wanted to establish joint ventures with East German firms and vice versa.

In this case, a reputable West German waste processing company had found a candidate in the Gersdam refuse department. It is a municipal department with two hundred employees. In the preparatory period, mutual exchanges of managers took place. East German managers became acquainted with managerial and technical practices in West Germany; some West German managers took office in Gersdam, introducing the most advanced technical tools and being alert to opportunities for reorganization. At that time the West German company invited my Dutch student, whose father was working for this company, to chart the start-up of the co-operation systematically. After all, the board of directors was very aware of the many failures in co-operation between Western and Eastern companies, due to different collective mental programmings and, as a consequence of that, communication breakdowns.

My student revealed himself to be a (corporate) anthropologist. From the beginning of his assignment he lived in an apartment building in the midst of former GDR citizens. In order to obtain the inside view, he adopted the role of an apprentice who is eager to learn.

What about his experiences within the organization? After having been formally introduced into the refuse department, he started with extensive participant observation. In the first weeks he concentrated his attention on the daily practices of the blue-collar workers. Following this initial period, he studied the other parts of the organization.

Characteristics of his approach were his open-mindedness and his refusal to judge or condemn. This enabled him to be surprised by his experiences, especially in the initial period. He asked the employees to help him to understand their working practices. How did they develop them? What were the problems they had? What did they need to solve their problems and how did they want to influence their situation?

He discovered that they initially adopted a very reserved attitude towards him. Rumours were circulating that he was acting as a spy for the West Germans. Why did he want to know all these things? In the past, before the changes (*die Wende*) in 1989, nobody was at all interested in their ideas or opinions. After the changes, they felt themselves neglected again: so many West German experts had already given their negative evaluation of East German methods. After a while, this suspicious attitude gave way to a gradually emerging astonishment. The researcher really wanted to gain insights into their perception of their working environment. He was then invited to take the backstage view. He met motivated insiders who helped him to clarify his observations. As a consequence of joint exploration insights could be found.

As the familiarity between the employees and the researcher increased, the employees began to question him about his most significant discoveries.

I will limit myself to describing the characterization of the prevailing mental condition of the members of the refuse department in his report.

LOCUS OF CONTROL

The condition refers to the locus of control, a psychological construct, described by Rotter (1966). Rotter distinguishes two forms of locus of control. On the one hand, some people believe that they are autonomous; that is, that they are masters of their own fates and hence bear personal responsibility for what happens to them. They see the controlling force of their lives as coming from inside themselves. Rotter calls these people internalizers.

On the other hand, Rotter proposes that many people believe that they are helpless pawns of fate, that they are controlled by outside forces over which they have little if any influence. Such people believe that their locus of control is external rather than internal. These people are called externalizers.

In general the members of the refuse department could be characterized as externalizers. This can be attributed to the past, centrally steered German Democratic Republic (e.g.

Niethammer et al., 1991). In that system, everybody had a relatively guaranteed life as long as they complied with the rules. The predominant orientation was towards an apathetic attitude instead of one of taking initiatives.

In this enterprise, there were many managerial levels. Being a loyal member of the Socialist Party was an essential criterion for becoming a manager; professional skill was of secondary importance. Conformity in behaviour of subordinates was something positively evaluated by superiors. On the surface, the members did their work in "the right communal sense"; below the surface, feelings of alienation and frustration pervaded the organizational practices. These feelings were not only caused by mental pressures, but also by the lack of good quality work materials.

I will give one specific example of the effects of the locus of external control on the daily practices in the refuse department. It concerns the internally oriented punctuality of the workers in their working hours, the absence of market-orientedness and the functioning of the departments as fortresses. The employees started in the morning with the daily round of the garbage truck and finished in the afternoon, exactly on time. They adhered punctually to breaks too, interrupting their tours and returning to the central workstation. Efficient planning of the tours did not exist: the lorry-drivers organized their days as was convenient for them. The citizens were always in uncertainty as to the removal of their waste.

Inside the refuse department, the different sections like Technical Service, Production, Administration, Personnel and Finance operated in complete isolation from each other. In this context, Technical Service dominated Production, being in a position to determine the scheduling of its own work processes. Because of the separation between Production and Administration, Production did not have the slightest idea about the results it periodically achieved.

After six months, when the researcher fed back his results to the members of the organization, they apparently experienced some cause for reflection and discussion. In retrospect, his stay at the company proved to be a worthwhile episode for starting and stimulating a better mutual understanding between the different parties concerned; for example, the East and West German managers in relation to each other, the departments with regard to each other, the relation between the organization and the civic environment. He enabled the different parties to take a step backwards and to look critically at themselves and the others. As a result of his presence and findings the members of the organization started to create a mutually shared meaning of the different ways in which they constructed their organizational realities and of their different cultural backgrounds. His "third culture position" turned him into an unsuspected witness. Recently a West German colleague told me that she regarded the Gersdam case as an exceptional study; she was not acquainted with a similar situation of an East–West German joint venture where a *West German* researcher had gained admittance to the more intimate layers of the organization.

LEARNING ATTITUDE

What is, in my opinion, the relevance of the "third culture perspective" for cross-cultural management?

During recent years, an increase of mergers, takeovers, and joint ventures across na-tional borders has been observed. Usually these initiatives are motivated by thorough financial considerations. Proportionately, the cultural aspects are neglected. In her an-thropological study *American Enterprise in Japan*, Tomoko Hamada (1991) describes how both partners in an American–Japanese joint venture managed to stir up a hornets' nest. Each side was subject to ethnocentrism: an exaggerated tendency to think the character-istics of one's own group or "race" superior to those of others. This fact, combined with a lack of or inadequate command of each other's language, caused a series of conflicts. This concerned areas such as personnel policies, product quality, marketing and sales, and financial reports. Over the course of many years, both companies learned to co-operate interculturally the hard way. Playfulness and creativity could not be found. What was lacking is, in terms of Morgan (1993), *imaginization*, an invitation to develop new ways of thinking about organization and management, an invitation to re-imagine ourselves and what we do.

The more the environment of organizations becomes dynamic and unpredictable, the more the organizations have to be strong reflections of such an environment. Peters (1992) elaborates this as follows: "when things are stable, stable firms that do 'it' as they did it yesterday, only a tiny bit better, have an advantage. When things are unstable, those who find dramatically new ways to do it (regardless of what 'it' is) have a major advantage".

It is my experience that the best performing companies look for – and celebrate – diversity; this orientation characterizes the collective mental programming of their mem-bers. A third culture perspective is an inseparable part of it.

References and Further Reading

Fortuin, M. (1991), *Von VEB zur GMBH*, Internal Publication School of Management and Organi-zation, University of Groningen.

Hamada, T. (1991), *American Enterprise in Japan*, State University of New York Press, Albany, NY.

Hofstede, G., Neuijen, J.A., Ohayv, D.D. and Sanders, G.J.E.M. (1990), "Measuring organizational cultures: a qualitative and quantitative study across twenty cases", *Administrative Science Quarterly*, June, pp. 286–316.

Morgan, G. (1993), *Imaginization: The Art of Creative Management*, Sage Publications, Newbury Park, CA.

Niethammer, L., Von Plato, A. and Wierling, D. (1991), *Die Volkseigene Erfahrung: Eine Archäologie des Lebens in der Industrieprovinz der DDR*, Rowohlt, Berlin.

Peters, T. (1992), *Liberation Management: Necessary Disorganization for the Nanosecond Nineties*, Alfred A. Knopf, New York, NY.

Rotter, J.B. (1966), "Generalized expectancies for internal versus external control of reinforce-ment", *Psychological Monographs*, Vol. 80, whole of No. 1.

Chapter 29

Case: The Evaluation

Charlotte Butler and Henri-Claude de Bettignies

"Why?" To Richard Evans, Managing Director of the Siam Chemicals Company (SCC) the single word, written in the margin of the company evaluation form, seemed to stare accusingly up at him. The form was densely written, filled out with comments under all the headings that made up the annual assessment process, yet for him, this one word obliterated all the carefully thought out phrases he had composed. For that single word represented a spontaneous and quite uncharacteristic outburst from the subject of the evaluation of Mr Somsak, one of his Thai business managers. For Richard Evans it meant that he would now have to take a critical decision which could affect both his authority in the company, and the future standards by which his local managers would be judged.

The ringing of the phone interrupted his thoughts. He picked it up and his secretary, Wilai, put through James Brown, a colleague based in the Singapore office of their mutual parent company, Chimique Helvétique Ltd. (CHL), a Swiss chemicals group headquartered in Basle.

"Dick," James's voice echoed down the line. "I just got a copy of Somsak's evaluation. I was absolutely amazed when I read it. I gave the guy an 'A' but you've only given him an overall 'C'. What's going on? As you know, he's worked with me for the last three years in the polymers side of the business. I know he reports to you as his direct line manager for his activities as a senior manager in SCC, but I am his boss when it comes to his operating performance and his work for us has been outstanding. He has way surpassed all his commercial and financial objectives – moved more product and at higher prices. We consider him exceptional. So what are you trying to do to the guy? Make him quit? You know how sensitive the Thai locals are to the slightest hint of a negative remark, let alone anything as direct and public as this. I told him when we had our assessment interview how pleased I was with his performance. Now, when he sees this he's going to be devastated. This is just a slap in the face. You know the problem we had when you first took over. This will finish things off, for sure. What's going on?"

Evans did indeed remember the problem. He had flown out from Geneva to take over as MD of the company with very little preparation or briefing. Newly promoted to his present grade it was his first time in Asia, and the cultural shock had been enormous. He still remembered those first weeks with a shudder. It had been a nightmare of trying to note all the advice his predecessor, who had stayed on for a few days, was giving him, to absorb the details of the company's businesses in the local market and master the details of its past and current performance, then meeting his exclusively local staff and, at the same time as all this, settling in his unhappy family.

Richard, an Englishman, had joined CHL five years ago, having been recruited from the British chemicals group he had joined straight after graduating. He and his wife, Mary, had welcomed the move to Switzerland and spent four happy years in Basle, their three children well settled in the international school and all of them enjoying the novelty of being able to spend weekends skiing in the mountains. To be then so suddenly up-rooted and put down in a strange new world where they spoke not a word of the language or had any notion of its customs, was a terrible and unwelcome shock, especially to his wife. In Bangkok, there were no pavements along which she could take the baby out in its pram, shopping for food was a major expedition and, with the elder children leaving at 7 am for the long bus journey to school, she was thrown on her own resources for the 12, 13 or even 14 hours a day her husband was absent. Coping with their new life imposed a considerable strain on all of them.

It was on one of those exhausting and confusing first days that Somsak, considered one of the senior and longer established mainstays of the company after three years in the job, had resigned. It had happened after a meeting during which Somsak had mentioned that he did not always find the CHL matrix system easy to understand. Thai people, he explained to Richard, found the concept of two bosses impossible to reconcile with their strong sense of hierarchy. They preferred to know exactly who was their senior manager, the man whose approval they should seek. Richard had seized on the opportunity to demonstrate his qualities as the new MD by, as he saw it, helping Somsak function better within the system. In what he considered a constructive way, one that had always previously been successful in dealing with European managers, he had tried to coach Somsak in how to approach his dual responsibilities more effectively. He had been stunned when Somsak had reacted with the words, "I realise from what you have said that I am not doing a good job. I am not suitable for my post and so the only thing I can do is to resign." Only the strenuous efforts of Somsak's other boss, Brown, to whom he owed a strong sense of allegiance, had persuaded Somsak to stay.

In the 18 months since this early setback, Evans had undergone an intensive and often tough course in cross-cultural management. His experiences had led him to conclude that some issues were not important enough to bring out in the open and risk undermining the harmony of the company and that more often than not, discretion was indeed the better part of valour. However, the evaluation issue was one that he judged would have to be tackled head-on. Unfortunately, it seemed likely that the first casualty of this intention would be Somsak.

During the last 18 months, Somsak had maintained a very polite and correct but by no means warm attitude towards his MD. For his part, Evans had come to appreciate that Somsak was a hard working and meticulous manager. He was willing to work every hour of the day, was highly intelligent and spoke excellent English, having been dealing with European companies for many years. Richard had made every effort to convey his appreciation of Somsak's efforts and recently, had been heartened by signs of a more trusting, comfortable relationship between them. Now, the evaluation question threatened all the gains Richard had so painstakingly made.

Name   Job Title

Division   Company

Age   Years in Service   Years on the Job

1. EXECUTIVE PERFORMANCE REVIEW
a. Review is to be done by the Reviewer and discussed with the Employee.
b. Complete Sections 2, 3, 4, 5 and 6 before completing this section.
c. Highlight most noteworthy areas of performance after taking into consideration achievements against objectives, work-related dimensions and external/other factors. Indicate both achievements and areas for improvement.

OVERALL PERFORMANCE RATING
A   Excellent   Reviewer's Name
B   Superior
C   Competent   Reviewer's Position
D   Marginal
E   Poor   Reviewer's Signature   Date

RATING DEFINITIONS
To arrive at the overall rating, an 80:20 weighting between objectives and work related dimensions is recommended.

Excellent   (A) – Performance that consistently delivers very high quality results, far exceeding expectations.
Superior   (B) – A high quality performance where results exceed expectations.
Competent   (C) – Satisfactory performance that effectively meets expectations.
Marginal   (D) – Performance that often falls short of expectations.
Poor   (E) – Totally unsatisfactory performance that does not meet expectations.

Source: Company documents.

Exhibit 29.1   Chimique Helvétique Ltd., Executive Performance Review

The annual evaluation process was imposed on all the CHL group's subsidiaries and had been in use in Thailand ever since the company's foundation, seven years ago. The same format was used company-wide for all management grades, employees in supervisory grades and below being evaluated by a much simpler, numerical form. The process was designed to measure an individual's input and output, competencies and results (Exhibit 29.1). The basis for performance appraisal was a set of six to seven key, previously agreed objectives to be achieved by a certain point in time. Objectives could be weighted to show their relative importance, and all were judged according to a grading system ranging from A to E.

The actual process was carried out during two, one-to-one interviews. During the first, a manager's past year's performance was reviewed. The senior manager would encourage his or her subordinate to talk about his performance, go through last year's objectives, and assess how well they had been achieved. In Europe, individuals did this without hesitation, enjoying the opportunity to debate their performance as equals and quick to argue their case forcefully if they disagreed at any point.

Such frankness was impossible in Thailand where, as it quickly became clear to Richard, his managers expected to be told how well they had done. It was not for them to make any judgement about their performance; what else was the boss there for? They were not disposed to talk about themselves at all. Moreover, the discomfort with any hint of criticism made the whole meeting a minefield. So instead of a dialogue, Richard found himself spending an hour in which he did most of the talking. He tried in vain to provoke some response, posing open, detached questions such as what did they want out of their job, were they happy or not. The reply was always polite, brief and invariably non-controversial except for any issue concerning their staff or the overall business performance. Their perceived role as middlemen for their staff would prompt them to talk about pay and whether or not it was up to market rates, or about parity between jobs. But to talk about themselves was something they resolutely refused to do.

A second meeting set objectives for the coming year. In the west, managers usually set their own objectives and Evans had had some success in instituting this evolutionary procedure with some of his direct reports. But it was a difficult process more characterised by verbal suggestions from himself that his managers would go away and write up. If their English was poor, they would return and ask him to write it up for them.

Richard knew that his local managers found the very idea of sitting down with their boss to appraise their performance a threatening and alien concept. Even the most senior, who had a good command of English and had been with the company for some time, found it difficult both to meet Richard for their own assessment, and also to carry out the process with their own staff.

The most contentious part concerned the overall performance rating. The group used a standard A–E grading in which according to a normal distribution, an "A" grade would apply only to the top 3–4% of outstanding managers. These would not necessarily be the most senior, but those who had displayed real leadership qualities, for example, had perhaps innovated a certain way of doing things, and whose performance was above and beyond the average.

A "B" grade was awarded to those whose performance was judged to be excellent in all respects, and who had added to the overall improvement of the company (perhaps by serving on one of the committees for safety or an Action team). A "C" grade, into which category 60–70% of managers usually fell, implied a good, standard performance with all requirements fulfilled. A "D" grade implied that there was scope for improvement and an "E" grade that there was a real problem.

Looking through the record of previous evaluations, it was clear to Richard that his predecessors had decided it was better not to rock the boat by insisting on adhering to European standards. Over 90% of managers had been awarded an "A" grade, although some MDs had tried to indicate nuances by giving A−, A+, A++, etc. Richard also had a shrewd suspicion that in interviews with their subordinates, his managers had similarly glossed over any potentially controversial issues. A query he had once made about an "A" grade awarded to someone who was clearly not pulling his weight had been met with the assurance "Oh, it is OK, we all work round him."

His suspicions were endorsed when he checked the previous year's results. Then, 95% of those evaluated had been given an "A" grade, with a very few clearly reluctantly given "B" grades. In part, he had come to realise, the local attitude was associated with the Thai school marking system where a "B" meant "could try harder" and a "C" meant trouble. Only an "A" grade, therefore, was psychologically acceptable.

This year, however, Richard had decided that he would tackle the issue directly by imposing the norm for the performance rating, and so align SCC with standards in the rest of the group. He himself would make sure that the norm was respected in his own direct reports and, where there were discrepancies in those of other managers, he himself would change the grades.

In part, he was motivated by wider strategic considerations. SCC had been established in Thailand for eight years. The last three years had seen rapid growth and good results. The company was considering implanting itself in other parts of the region, and would expect its successful Thai offshoot, staffed by experienced people familiar with the parent company's organisation and trained to the high standards of safety and quality that were a key part of its culture, to provide managers for the new subsidiaries.

This project coincided with a move, initiated by the group human resources director, to identify an international cadre of managers that could be moved between countries in support of CHL's global ambitions. However, this required a common standard in grading job performance and career potential between different parts of the group. Richard therefore decided that this year, he would implement the system as intended by headquarters, and award grades so that anyone looking at the results would be able to make judgements about an individual's potential based on a common language.

Not greatly to his surprise, the whole process had brought nothing but trouble. Faced by this latest problem, Richard was almost tempted to give up and award everyone the "A" grade they were accustomed to and the same salary increase. However, he knew this would only be a short-term respite that would not be good for SCC in the long run. It would not give recognition for an exceptional performance and so effective SCC managers would probably vote with their feet, confident that in the hectic Thai job market they could walk into another probably better paid job the same or, at the latest, the next day.

With this in mind, Richard had to decide what to do about Somsak. In his own mind, an overall "C" grade was the correct judgement. For despite his outstanding work for his Singapore boss, Somsak had failed to meet three out of the four objectives Richard had set for him in his wider role as a senior manager in SCC. These had been concerned with building up communications between his polymers business and the rest of the company, and supporting the key safety and quality assurance initiatives.

In the last year, Somsak had put a huge effort into building up his own team but ironically, instead of building bridges he had only succeeded in forming an isolated clique whose behaviour was having a divisive effect on the rest of SCC. The team acted like a family centred on Somsak. Whilst the shared strong identity and bonds made them all work well for each other, it meant they rejected all those outside the group. Consequently, working relations between the polymers team and the rest of the company were very strained. Again, this mirrored Thai society, where the family formed the core that owed no allegiance to anyone outside it. All the energy expended on fostering the inner circle was countered by an attitude of total selfishness towards everyone else.

During the interview, Richard had spent considerable time talking to Somsak about the evaluation process in a bid to explain what he was trying to achieve by introducing the new approach. Going through the four objectives and where he felt they had not been achieved, he had explained that his notion of leadership in a senior manager like Somsak was to help lead the company by building bridges. He had also emphasised that in the wider CHL group, "C" was considered a good grade.

Later, after much heart searching, Richard had given Somsak a "C" grade overall, not the "A" grade he had so obviously expected. In reaching this decision, Richard felt he had made a big effort to be fair. He believed that he now understood some of the conflict that Somsak felt, the permanent tension caused by trying to please two bosses and the consequences of failure in terms of loss of face. So he had ignored the things Somsak had not done and given him credit for those that he had. After working together for the past 18 months, he felt that he was finally able to communicate with Somsak and that therefore he would understand, and accept the decision in the spirit it was meant.

The reaction had been far worse than his expectations. A visibly hurt and uncomprehending Somsak had asked "But where did I go wrong?" As far as he was concerned, he had worked incredibly hard for 12 months and at the end had been awarded a disgraceful "C" grade. He had returned that day and given back the form on which he had written his single comment. His injured pride and sense of injustice was affecting all his team, and Richard could see only problems ahead.

As he looked through the report one more time, Richard Evans knew he had to make an important decision. Should he compromise his principles and upgrade Somsak, or stick to his guns and risk losing him? Sticking to his principles, it was clear, would make life difficult with his Singapore colleague who would resent the loss of such an effective manager. And after all, he wondered, was it fair to inflict western standards on Asian managers who worked hard, and did everything right according to their own cultural norms? Whatever the outcome, Richard was determined to find some way of avoiding a recurrence next year, Which raised the question of how?

Chapter 30

Case: Kentucky Fried Chicken and the Global Fast-Food Industry

Jeffrey A. Krug

Kentucky Fried Chicken Corporation (KFC) was the world's largest chicken restaurant chain and third largest fast-food chain. KFC held over 55 percent of the U.S. market in terms of sales and operated over 10,200 restaurants worldwide in 1998. It opened 376 new restaurants in 1997 (more than one restaurant a day) and operated in 79 countries. One of the first fast-food chains to go international during the late 1960s, KFC has developed one of the world's most recognizable brands.

Japan, Australia, and the United Kingdom accounted for the greatest share of KFC's international expansion during the 1970s and 1980s. During the 1990s, KFC turned its attention to other international markets that offered significant opportunities for growth. China, with a population of over one billion, and Europe, with a population roughly equal to the United States, offered such opportunities. Latin America also offered a unique opportunity because of the size of its markets, its common language and culture, and its geographical proximity to the United States. Mexico was of particular interest because of the North American Free Trade Agreement (NAFTA), a free trade zone between Canada, the United States, and Mexico that went into effect in 1994.

Prior to 1990, KFC expanded into Latin America primarily through company-owned restaurants in Mexico and Puerto Rico. Company-owned restaurants gave KFC greater control over its operations than franchised or licensed restaurants. By 1995, KFC had also established company-owned restaurants in Venezuela and Brazil. In addition, it had established franchised units in several Caribbean countries. During the early 1990s, KFC shifted to a two-tier strategy in Latin America. First, it established 29 franchised restaurants in Mexico following enactment of Mexico's new franchise law in 1990. This allowed KFC to expand outside of its company restaurant base in Mexico City, Guadalajara, and Monterrey. KFC was only one of many U.S. fast-food, retail, and hotel chains to begin franchising in Mexico following the new franchise law. Second, KFC began an aggressive franchise building program in South America. By 1998, it was operating franchised restaurants in 32 Latin American countries. Much of this growth was in Brazil, Chile, Colombia, Ecuador, and Peru.

COMPANY HISTORY

Fast-food franchising was still in its infancy in 1952 when Harland Sanders began his travels across the United States to speak with prospective franchisees about his "Colonel Sanders Recipe Kentucky Fried Chicken." By 1960, "Colonel" Sanders had granted KFC franchises to over 200 take-home retail outlets and restaurants across the United States. He had also succeeded in establishing a number of franchises in Canada. By 1963, the number of KFC franchises had risen to over 300 and revenues had reached $500 million.

By 1964, at the age of 74, the Colonel had tired of running the day-to-day operations of his business and was eager to concentrate on public relations issues. Therefore, he sought out potential buyers, eventually deciding to sell the business to two Louisville businessmen – Jack Massey and John Young Brown Jr. – for $2 million. The Colonel stayed on as a public relations man and goodwill ambassador for the company.

During the next five years, Massey and Brown concentrated on growing KFC's franchise system across the United States. In 1966, they took KFC public and the company was listed on the New York Stock Exchange. By the late 1960s, a strong foothold had been established in the United States, and Massey and Brown turned their attention to international markets. In 1969, a joint venture was signed with Mitsuoishi Shoji Kaisha, Ltd. in Japan, and the rights to operate 14 existing KFC franchises in England were acquired. Subsidiaries were also established in Hong Kong, South Africa, Australia, New Zealand, and Mexico. By 1971, KFC had 2,450 franchises and 600 company-owned restaurants worldwide, and was operating in 48 countries.

Heublein, Inc.

In 1971, KFC entered negotiations with Heublein, Inc. to discuss a possible merger. The decision to seek a merger candidate was partially driven by Brown's desire to pursue other interests, including a political career (Brown was elected Governor of Kentucky in 1977). Several months later, Heublein acquired KFC. Heublein was in the business of producing vodka, mixed cocktails, dry gin, cordials, beer, and other alcoholic beverages. However, Heublein had little experience in the restaurant business. Conflicts quickly erupted between Colonel Sanders, who continued to act in a public relations capacity, and Heublein management. Colonel Sanders became increasingly distraught over quality control issues and restaurant cleanliness. By 1977, new restaurant openings had slowed to about twenty per year. Few restaurants were being remodelled and service quality had declined.

In 1977, Heublein sent in a new management team to redirect KFC's strategy. A "back-to-the-basics" strategy was immediately implemented. New unit construction was discontinued until existing restaurants could be upgraded and operating problems eliminated. Restaurants were refurbished, an emphasis was placed on cleanliness and service, marginal products were eliminated, and product consistency was reestablished. By 1982, KFC had succeeded in establishing a successful strategic focus and was again aggressively building new units.

R. J. Reynolds Industries, Inc.

In 1982, R. J. Reynolds Industries, Inc. (RJR) merged Heublein into a wholly owned subsidiary. The merger with Heublein represented part of RJR's overall corporate strategy of diversifying into unrelated businesses, including energy, transportation, food, and restaurants. RJR's objective was to reduce its dependence on the tobacco industry, which had driven RJR sales since its founding in North Carolina in 1875. Sales of cigarettes and tobacco products, while profitable, were declining because of reduced consumption in the United States. This was mainly the result of an increased awareness among Americans about the negative health consequences of smoking.

RJR had no more experience in the restaurant business than did Heublein. However, it decided to take a hands-off approach to managing KFC. Whereas Heublein had installed its own top management at KFC headquarters, RJR left KFC management largely intact, believing that existing KFC managers were better qualified to operate KFC's businesses than were its own managers. In doing so, RJR avoided many of the operating problems that plagued Heublein. This strategy paid off for RJR as KFC continued to expand aggressively and profitably under RJR ownership. In 1985, RJR acquired Nabisco Corporation for $4.9 billion. Nabisco sold a variety of well-known cookies, crackers, cereals, confectioneries, snacks, and other grocery products. The merger with Nabisco represented a decision by RJR to concentrate its diversification efforts on the consumer foods industry. It subsequently divested many of its non-consumer food businesses. RJR sold KFC to PepsiCo, Inc. one year later.

PEPSICO, INC.

Corporate strategy

PepsiCo, Inc. was formed in 1965 with the merger of the Pepsi-Cola Co. and Frito-Lay Inc. The merger of these companies created one of the largest consumer products companies in the United States. Pepsi-Cola's traditional business was the sale of soft drink concentrates to licensed independent and company-owned bottlers that manufactured, sold, and distributed Pepsi-Cola soft drinks. Pepsi-Cola's best known trademarks were Pepsi-Cola, Diet Pepsi, Mountain Dew, and Slice. Frito-Lay manufactured and sold a variety of snack foods, including Fritos Corn Chips, Lay's Potato Chips, Ruffles Potato Chips, Doritos, Tostitos Tortilla Chips, and Chee-tos Cheese Flavored Snacks. PepsiCo quickly embarked on an aggressive acquisition program similar to that pursued by RJR during the 1980s, buying a number of companies in areas unrelated to its major businesses. Acquisitions included North American Van Lines, Wilson Sporting Goods, and Lee Way Motor Freight. However, success in operating these businesses failed to live up to expectations, mainly because the management skills required to operate these businesses lay outside of PepsiCo's area of expertise.

Poor performance in these businesses led then-chairman and chief executive officer Don Kendall to restructure PepsiCo's operations in 1984. First, businesses that did not support PepsiCo's consumer product orientation, such as North American Van Lines, Wilson Sporting Goods, and Lee Way Motor Freight were divested. Second, PepsiCo's foreign bottling operations were sold to local business people who better understood the culture and business environment in their respective countries. Third, Kendall reorganized PepsiCo along three lines: soft drinks, snack foods, and restaurants.

Restaurant business and acquisition of Kentucky Fried Chicken

PepsiCo first entered the restaurant business in 1977 when it acquired Pizza Hut's 3,200-unit restaurant system. Taco Bell was merged into a division of PepsiCo in 1978. The restaurant business complemented PepsiCo's consumer product orientation. The marketing of fast-food followed many of the same patterns as the marketing of soft drinks and snack foods. Therefore, PepsiCo believed that its management skills could be easily transferred among its three business segments. This was compatible with PepsiCo's practice of frequently moving managers among its business units as a way of developing future top executives. PepsiCo's restaurant chains also provided an additional outlet for the sale of Pepsi soft drinks. Pepsi-Cola soft drinks and fast-food products could also be marketed together in the same television and radio segments, thereby providing higher returns for each advertising dollar. To complete its diversification into the restaurant segment, PepsiCo acquired Kentucky Fried Chicken Corporation from RJR-Nabisco for $841 million in 1986. The acquisition of KFC gave PepsiCo the leading market share in chicken (KFC), pizza (Pizza Hut), and Mexican food (Taco Bell), three of the four largest and fastest-growing segments within the U.S. fast-food industry.

Management

Following the acquisition by PepsiCo, KFC's relationship with its parent company underwent dramatic changes. RJR had operated KFC as a semi-autonomous unit, satisfied that KFC management understood the fast-food business better than they did. In contrast, PepsiCo acquired KFC in order to complement its already strong presence in the fast-food market. Rather than allowing KFC to operate autonomously, PepsiCo undertook sweeping changes. These changes included negotiating a new franchise contract to give PepsiCo more control over its franchisees, reducing staff in order to cut costs, and replacing KFC managers with its own. In 1987, a rumor spread through KFC's headquarters in Louisville that the new personnel manager, who had just relocated from PepsiCo's headquarters in New York, was overheard saying that "There will be no more home grown tomatoes in this organization."

Such statements by PepsiCo personnel, uncertainties created by several restructurings that led to layoffs throughout the KFC organization, the replacement of KFC personnel with PepsiCo managers, and conflicts between KFC and PepsiCo's corporate cultures created a morale problem within KFC. KFC's culture was built largely on Colonel Sanders' laid-back approach to management. Employees enjoyed relatively good employment stability and security. Over the years, a strong loyalty had been created among KFC employees and franchisees, mainly because of the efforts of Colonel Sanders to provide for his employees' benefits, pension, and other non-income needs. In addition, the Southern environment of Louisville resulted in a friendly, relaxed atmosphere at

KFC's corporate offices. This corporate culture was left essentially unchanged during the Heublein and RJR years.

In stark contrast to KFC, PepsiCo's culture was characterized by a strong emphasis on performance. Top performers expected to move up through the ranks quickly. PepsiCo used its KFC, Pizza Hut, Taco Bell, Frito Lay, and Pepsi-Cola divisions as training grounds for its top managers, rotating its best managers through its five divisions on average every two years. This practice created immense pressure on managers to continuously demonstrate their managerial prowess within short periods, in order to maximize their potential for promotion. This practice also left many KFC managers with the feeling that they had few career opportunities with the new company. One PepsiCo manager commented that "You may have performed well last year, but if you don't perform well this year, you're gone, and there are 100 ambitious guys with Ivy League MBAs at PepsiCo who would love to take your position." An unwanted effect of this performance driven culture was that employee loyalty was often lost and turnover tended to be higher than in other companies.

Kyle Craig, president of KFC's U.S. operations, was asked about KFC's relationship with its corporate parent. He commented:

> The KFC culture is an interesting one because I think it was dominated by a lot of KFC folks, many of whom have been around since the days of the Colonel. Many of those people were very intimidated by the PepsiCo culture, which is a very high performance, high accountability, and highly driven culture. People were concerned about whether they would succeed in the new culture. Like many companies, we have had a couple of downsizings, which further made people nervous. Today, there are fewer old KFC people around and I think to some degree people have seen that the PepsiCo culture can drive some pretty positive results. I also think the PepsiCo people who have worked with KFC have modified their cultural values somewhat and they can see that there were a lot of benefits in the old KFC culture.
>
> PepsiCo pushes their companies to perform strongly, but whenever there is a slip in performance, it increases the culture gap between PepsiCo and KFC. I have been involved in two downsizings over which I have been the chief architect. They have been probably the two most gut-wrenching experiences of my career. Because you know you're dealing with peoples' lives and their families, these changes can be emotional if you care about the people in your organization. However, I do fundamentally believe that your first obligation is to the entire organization.

A second problem for PepsiCo was its poor relationship with KFC franchisees. A month after becoming president and chief executive officer in 1989, John Cranor addressed KFC's franchisees in Louisville, in order to explain the details of the new franchise contract. This was the first contract change in thirteen years. It gave PepsiCo greater power to take over weak franchises, relocate restaurants, and make changes in existing restaurants. In addition, restaurants would no longer be protected from competition from new KFC units and it gave PepsiCo the right to raise royalty fees on existing restaurants as contracts came up for renewal. After Cranor finished his address, there was an uproar among the attending franchisees, who jumped to their feet to protest the changes. The franchisees had long been accustomed to relatively little interference from management in their day-to-day operations (a tradition begun by Colonel Sanders). This type of interference, of course, was a strong part of PepsiCo's philosophy of demanding change. KFC's franchise association later sued PepsiCo over the new contract. The contract remained unresolved until 1996, when the most objectionable parts of the contract were removed by KFC's new president and CEO, David Novak. A new contract was ratified by KFC's franchisees in 1997.

PepsiCo's divestiture of KFC, Pizza Hut, and Taco Bell

PepsiCo's strategy of diversifying into three distinct but related markets – soft drinks, snack foods, and fast-food restaurants – created one of the world's largest consumer products companies and a portfolio of some of the world's most recognizable brands. Between 1990 and 1996, PepsiCo grew at an annual rate of over 10 percent, surpassing $31 billion in sales in 1996. However, PepsiCo's sales growth masked troubles in its fast-food businesses. Operating margins (profit as a percent of sales) at Pepsi-Cola and Frito Lay averaged 12 and 17 percent between 1990 and 1996, respectively. During the same period, margins at KFC, Pizza Hut, and Taco Bell fell from an average of over 8 percent in 1990 to a little more than 4 percent in 1996. Declining margins in the fast-food chains reflected increasing maturity in the U.S. fast-food industry, more intense competition among U.S. fast-food competitors, and the aging of KFC and Pizza Hut's restaurant base.

As a result, PepsiCo's restaurant chains absorbed nearly one-half of PepsiCo's annual capital spending during the 1990s. However, they generated less than one-third of PepsiCo's cash flows. Therefore, cash was diverted from PepsiCo's soft drink and snack food businesses to its restaurant businesses. This reduced PepsiCo's return on assets, made it more difficult to compete effectively with Coca-Cola, and hurt its stock price. In 1997, PepsiCo spun off its restaurant businesses into a new company called Tricon Global Restaurants, Inc. (see Exhibit 30.1). The new company was based in KFC's headquarters in Louisville, Kentucky. PepsiCo's objective was to reposition itself as a packaged goods company, to strengthen its balance sheet, and to create more consistent earning growth. PepsiCo received a one-time distribution from Tricon of $4.7 billion, $3.7 billion of which was used to pay off short-term debt. The balance was earmarked for stock repurchases.

FAST-FOOD INDUSTRY

According to the National Restaurant Association (NRA), food-service sales topped $320 billion in 1997 for the approximately 500,000 restaurants and other food outlets making up the U.S. restaurant industry. The NRA estimated that sales in the fast-food segment of the food service industry grew 5.2 percent to 104 billion in 1997, up from $98 billion in 1996. This marked the fourth consecutive year that fast-food sales have either matched or exceeded sales in full-service restaurants, which grew 4.1 percent to $104 billion in 1997. The growth in fast-food sales reflected the long, gradual change in the restaurant industry from an industry once dominated by independently operated sit-down restaurants to an industry fast becoming dominated by fast-food restaurant chains. The U.S. restaurant industry as a whole grew by approximately 4.2 percent in 1997.

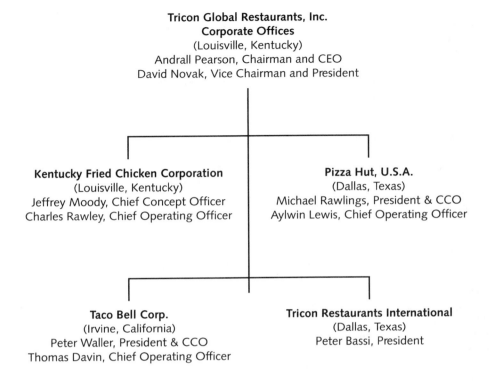

Exhibit 30.1   Tricon Global Restaurants, Inc., Organizational Chart (1998)

Major fast-food segments

Six major business segments made up the fast-food segment of the food service industry. Sales data for the leading restaurant chains in each segment are shown in Exhibit 30.2. Most striking is the dominance of McDonald's, which had sales of over $16 billion in 1996. This represented 16.6 percent of U.S. fast-food sales, or nearly 22 percent of sales among the nation's top 30 fast-food chains. Sales at McDonald's restaurants averaged $1.3 million per year, compared to about $820,000 for the average U.S. fast-food restaurant. Tricon Global Restaurants (KFC, Pizza Hut, and Taco Bell) had U.S. sales of $13.4 billion in 1996. This represented 13.6 percent of U.S. fast-food sales and 17.9 percent of the top 30 fast-food chains.

Sandwich chains made up the largest segment of the fast-food market. McDonald's controlled 35 percent of the sandwich segment, while Burger King ran a distant second with a 15.6 percent market share. Competition had become particularly intense within the sandwich segment as the U.S. fast-food market became more saturated. In order to increase sales, chains turned to new products to win customers away from other sandwich chains, introduced products traditionally offered by non-sandwich chains (such as pizzas,

Sandwich Chains	Sales	Share	Family Restaurants	Sales	Share
McDonald's	16,370	35.0%	Denny's	1,850	21.2%
Burger King	7,300	15.6%	Shoney's	1,220	14.0%
Taco Bell	4,575	9.8%	Big Boy	945	10.8%
Wendy's	4,360	9.3%	Int'l House of Pancakes	797	9.1%
Hardee's	3,055	6.5%	Cracker Barrel	734	8.4%
Subway	2,700	5.8%	Perkins	678	7.8%
Arby's	1,867	4.0%	Friendly's	597	6.8%
Dairy Queen	1,225	2.6%	Bob Evans	575	6.6%
Jack in the Box	1,207	2.6%	Waffle House	525	6.0%
Sonic Drive-In	985	2.1%	Coco's	278	3.2%
Carl's Jr.	648	1.4%	Steak'n Shake	275	3.2%
Other Chains	*2,454*	*5.2%*	Village Inn	246	2.8%
Total	46,745	100.0%	Total	8,719	100.0%

Dinner Houses	Sales	Share	Pizza Chains	Sales	Share
Red Lobster	1,810	15.7%	Pizza Hut	4,927	46.4%
Applebee's	1,523	13.2%	Domino's Pizza	2,300	21.7%
Olive Garden	1,280	11.1%	Little Caesar's	1,425	13.4%
Chili's	1,242	10.7%	Papa John's	619	5.8%
Outback Steakhouse	1,017	8.8%	Sbarros	400	3.8%
T.G.I. Friday's	935	8.1%	Round Table Pizza	385	3.6%
Ruby Tuesday	545	4.7%	Chuck E. Cheese's	293	2.8%
Lone Star Steakhouse	460	4.0%	Godfather's Pizza	266	2.5%
Bennigan's	458	4.0%	Total	10,614	100.0%
Romano's Macaroni Grill	344	3.0%			
Other Dinner Houses	*1,942*	*16.8%*			
Total	11,557	100.0%			

Grilled Buffet Chains	Sales	Share	Chicken Chains	Sales	Share
Golden Corral	711	22.8%	KFC	3,900	57.1%
Ponderosa	680	21.8%	Boston Market	1,167	17.1%
Ryan's	604	19.4%	Popeye's Chicken	666	9.7%
Sizzler	540	17.3%	Chick-fil-A	570	8.3%
Western Sizzlin'	332	10.3%	Church's Chicken	529	7.7%
Quincy's	259	8.3%	Total	6,832	100.0%
Total	3,116	100.0%			

Source: Nation's Restaurant News.

Exhibit 30.2   Leading U.S. Fast-food Chains Ranked by 1996 Sales ($000s)

fried chicken, and tacos), streamlined their menus, and upgraded product quality. Burger King recently introduced its "Big King," a direct clone of the Big Mac. McDonald's quickly retaliated by introducing its "Big 'n Tasty," a direct clone of the Whopper. Wendy's introduced chicken pita sandwiches and Taco Bell introduced sandwiches called "wraps," breads stuffed with various fillings. Hardee's successfully introduced fried chicken in most of its restaurants. In addition to new products, chains lowered pricing, improved customer service, co-branded with other fast-food chains and established restaurants in non-traditional locations (e.g., McDonald's has installed restaurants in Wal-Mart stores across the country) to beef up sales.

The second largest fast-food segment was dinner houses, dominated by Red Lobster, Applebee's, Olive Garden, and Chili's. Between 1988 and 1996, dinner houses increased their share of the fast-food market from eight to over 13 percent. This increase came mainly at the expense of grilled buffet chains, such as Ponderosa, Sizzler, and Western Sizzlin'. The market share of steak houses fell from six percent in 1988 to under four percent in 1996. The rise of dinner houses during the 1990s was partially the result of an aging and wealthier population that increasingly demanded higher quality food in more upscale settings. However, rapid construction of new restaurants, especially among relative newcomers, such as Romano's Macaroni Grill, Lone Star Steakhouse, and Outback Steakhouse, resulted in overcapacity within the dinner house segment. This reduced per restaurant sales and further intensified competition. Eight of the sixteen largest dinner houses posted growth rates in excess of 10 percent in 1996. Romano's Macaroni Grill, Lone Star Steakhouse, Chili's, Outback Steakhouse, Applebee's, Red Robin, Fuddruckers, and Ruby Tuesday grew at rates of 82, 41, 32, 27, 23, 14, 11, and 10 percent, respectively.

The third largest fast-food segment was pizza, long dominated by Pizza Hut. While Pizza Hut controlled over 46 percent of the pizza segment in 1996, its market share has slowly eroded because of intense competition and its aging restaurant base. Domino's Pizza and Papa John's Pizza have been particularly successful. Little Caesar's is the only pizza chain to remain predominately a take-out chain, though it recently began home delivery. However, its policy of charging customers $1 per delivery damaged its perception among consumers as a high-value pizza chain. Home delivery, successfully introduced by Domino's and Pizza Hut, was a driving force for success among the market leaders during the 1970s and 1980s. However, the success of home delivery drove competitors to look for new methods of increasing their customer bases. Pizza chains diversified into non-pizza items (e.g., chicken wings at Domino's, Italian cheese bread at Little Caesar's, and stuffed-crust pizza at Pizza Hut), developed non-traditional units (e.g., airport kiosks and college campuses), offered special promotions, and offered new pizza variations with an emphasis on high quality ingredients (e.g., "Roma Herb" and "Garlic Crunch" pizza at Domino's and "Buffalo Chicken Pizza" at Round Table Pizza).

Chicken segment

KFC continued to dominate the chicken segment, with 1997 sales of $4 billion (see Exhibit 30.3). Its nearest competitor, Boston Market, was second with sales of $1.2 billion. In 1998, KFC operated 5,120 restaurants in the United States, eight fewer restaurants than in 1993. Rather than building new restaurants in the already saturated U.S. market, KFC focused on building restaurants abroad. In the United States, KFC focused on closing unprofitable restaurants, upgrading existing restaurants with new exterior signage, and improving product quality. The strategy has paid off. While overall U.S. sales during the last ten years remained flat, annual sales per unit increased steadily in eight of the last nine years.

Sales ($m)	1992	1993	1994	1995	1996	1997	Growth Rate (%)
KFC	3,400	3,400	3,500	3,700	3,900	4,000	3.3
Boston Market	43	147	371	754	1,100	1,197	94.5
Popeye's	545	569	614	660	677	727	5.9
Chick-fil-A	356	396	451	502	570	671	11.9
Church's	414	440	465	501	526	574	6.8
Total	4,758	4,952	5,401	6,118	6,772	7,170	8.5
U.S. Restaurants							
KFC	5,089	5,128	5,149	5,142	5,108	5,120	0.1
Boston Market	83	217	534	829	1,087	1,166	69.6
Popeye's	769	769	853	889	894	949	4.3
Chick-fil-A	487	545	534	825	717	762	9.0
Church's	944	932	937	953	9,890	1,070	2.5
Total	7,372	7,591	8,007	8,638	8,795	9,067	4.2
Sales per unit ($'000s)							
KFC	668	663	680	720	764	781	3.2
Boston Market	518	677	695	910	1,012	1,027	14.7
Popeye's	709	740	720	743	757	767	1.6
Chick-fil-A	731	727	845	608	795	881	3.8
Church's	439	472	496	526	531	537	4.1
Total	645	782	782	782	782	782	3.9

Source: Tricon Global Restaurants, Inc., *1997 Annual Report*; Boston Chicken, Inc., *1997 Annual Report*; Chick-fil-A, corporate headquarters, Atlanta; AFC Enterprises, Inc., *1997 Annual Report*.

Exhibit 30.3 Top U.S. Chicken Chains, 1992–7

Despite KFC's continued dominance within the chicken segment, it has lost market share to Boston Market, a new restaurant chain emphasizing roasted rather than fried chicken. Boston Market has successfully created the image of an upscale deli offering healthy, "home-style" alternatives to fried chicken and other "fast-foods." It has broadened its menu beyond rotisserie chicken to include ham, turkey, meat loaf, chicken pot pie, and deli sandwiches. In order to minimize its image as a "fast-food" restaurant, it has refused to put drive-thrus in its restaurants and has established most of its units in outside shopping malls rather than in free-standing units at intersections so characteristic of other fast-food restaurants.

In 1993, KFC introduced its own rotisserie chicken, called "Rotisserie Gold," to combat Boston Market. However, it quickly learned that its customer base was considerably different from that of Boston Market's. KFC's customers liked KFC chicken despite the fact that it was fried. In addition, customers did not respond well to the concept of buying whole chickens for take-out. They preferred instead to buy chicken by the piece. KFC withdrew its rotisserie chicken in 1996 and introduced a new line of roasted chicken called "Tender Roast," which could be sold by the piece and mixed with its Original Recipe and Extra Crispy Chicken.

Other major competitors within the chicken segment included Popeye's Famous Fried Chicken and Church's Chicken (both subsidiaries of AFC Enterprises in Atlanta), Chick-fil-A, Bojangle's, El Pollo Loco, Grandy's, Kenny Rogers Roasters, Mrs. Winner's, and Pudgie's. Both Church's and Popeye's had similar strategies – to compete head-on with other "fried chicken" chains. Unlike KFC, neither chain offered rotisserie chicken and non-fried chicken products were limited. Chick-fil-A focused exclusively on pressure-cooked and char-grilled skinless chicken breast sandwiches, which it served to customers in sit-down restaurants located predominately in shopping malls. As many malls added food courts, often consisting of up to fifteen fast-food units competing side-by-side, shopping malls became less enthusiastic about allocating separate store space to food chains. Therefore, in order to complement its existing restaurant base in shopping malls, Chick-fil-A began to open smaller units in shopping mall food courts, hospitals, and colleges. It also opened free-standing units in selected locations.

Demographic trends

A number of demographic and societal trends contributed to increased demand for food prepared away from home. Because of the high divorce rate in the United States and the fact that people married later in life, single-person households represented about 25 percent of all U.S. households, up from 17 percent in 1970. This increased the number of individuals choosing to eat out rather than eat at home. The number of married women working outside of the home has also increased dramatically during the last twenty-five years. About 59 percent of all married women have careers. According to the Conference Board, 64 percent of all married households will be double-income families by 2000. About 80 percent of households headed by individuals between the ages of 25 and 44 (both married and unmarried) will be double-income. Greater numbers of working women increased family incomes. According to *Restaurants & Institutions* magazine, more than one-third of all households had incomes of at least $50,000 in 1996. About eight percent of all households had annual incomes over $100,000. The combination of higher numbers of dual-career families and rising incomes meant that fewer families had time to prepare food at home. According to Standard & Poor's Industry Surveys, Americans spent 55 percent of their food dollars at restaurants in 1995, up from 34 percent in 1970.

Fast-food restaurant chains met these demographic and societal changes by expanding their restaurant bases. However, by the early 1990s, the growth of traditional free-standing restaurants slowed as the U.S. market became saturated. The major exception was dinner houses, which continued to proliferate in response to Americans' increased passion for beef. Since 1990, the U.S. population has grown at an average annual rate of about one percent and reached 270 million people in 1997. Rising immigration since 1990 dramatically altered the ethnic makeup of the U.S. population. According to the Bureau of the Census, Americans born outside of the United States made up ten percent of the population in 1997. About 40 percent were Hispanic, while 24 percent were Asian. Nearly 30 percent of Americans born outside of the United States arrived since 1990. As a result of these trends, restaurant chains expanded their menus to appeal to the different ethnic tastes of consumers, expanded into non-traditional locations such as department stores and airports, and made food more available through home delivery and take-out service.

Industry consolidation and mergers and acquisitions

Lower growth in the U.S. fast-food market intensified competition for market share among restaurant chains and led to consolidation, primarily through mergers and acquisitions, during the mid-1990s. Many restaurant chains found that market share could be increased more quickly and cheaply by acquiring an existing company rather than building new units. In addition, fixed costs could be spread across a larger number of restaurants. This raised operating margins and gave companies an opportunity to build market share by lowering prices. An expanded restaurant base also gave companies greater purchasing power over suppliers. In 1990, Grand Metropolitan, a British company, purchased Pillsbury Co. for $5.7 billion. Included in the purchase was Pillsbury's Burger King chain. Grand Met strengthened the franchise by upgrading existing restaurants and eliminated several levels of management in order to cut costs. This gave Burger King a long-needed boost in improving its position against McDonald's, its largest competitor. In 1988, Grand Met had purchased Wienerwald, a West German chicken chain, and the Spaghetti Factory, a Swiss chain.

Perhaps most important to KFC was Hardee's acquisition of 600 Roy Rogers restaurants from Marriott Corporation in 1990. Hardee's converted a large number of these restaurants to Hardee's units and introduced "Roy Rogers" fried chicken to its menu. By 1993, Hardee's had introduced fried chicken into most of its U.S. restaurants. Hardee's was unlikely to destroy the customer loyalty that KFC long enjoyed. However, it did cut into KFC's sales, because it was able to offer consumers a widened menu selection that appealed to a variety of family eating preferences. In 1997, Hardee's parent company, Imasco Ltd., sold Hardee's to CKE Restaurants, Inc. CKE owned Carl's Jr., Rally's Hamburgers, and Checker's Drive-In. Boston Chicken, Inc. acquired Harry's Farmers Market, an Atlanta grocer that sold fresh quality prepared meals, in 1997. The acquisition was designed to help Boston Chicken develop distribution beyond its Boston Market restaurants. Also in 1997, AFC Enterprises, which operated Popeye's and Church's, acquired Chesapeake Bagel Bakery of McLean, Virginia, in order to diversify away from fried chicken and to strengthen its balance sheet.

The effect of these and other recent mergers and acquisitions on the industry was powerful. The top ten restaurant companies controlled almost 60 percent of fast-food sales in the United States. The consolidation of a number of fast-food chains within larger, financially more powerful parent companies gave restaurant chains strong financial and managerial resources that could be used to compete against smaller chains in the industry.

International quick-service market

Because of the aggressive pace of new restaurant construction in the United States during the 1970s and 1980s, opportunities to expand domestically through new restaurant construction in the 1990s were limited. Restaurant chains that did build new restaurants found that the higher cost of purchasing prime locations resulted in immense pressure to increase annual per restaurant sales, in order to cover higher initial investment costs. Many restaurants began to expand into international markets as an alternative to the United States. In contrast to the U.S. market, international markets offered large customer bases with comparatively little competition. However, only a few U.S. restaurant chains had defined aggressive strategies for penetrating international markets by 1998.

Three restaurant chains that had established aggressive international strategies were McDonald's, KFC, and Pizza Hut. McDonald's operated the largest number of restaurants. In 1998, it operated 23,132 restaurants in 109 countries (10,409 restaurants were located outside of the USA). In comparison, KFC, Pizza Hut, and Taco Bell together operated 29,712 restaurants in 79, 88, and 17 countries, respectively (9,126 restaurants were located outside of the United States). Of these four chains, KFC operated the greatest percentage of its restaurants (50 percent) outside of the United States. McDonald's, Pizza Hut, and Taco Bell operated 45, 31, and two percent of their units outside of the U.S.A. KFC opened its first restaurant outside of the United States in the late 1950s. By the time PepsiCo acquired KFC in 1986, KFC was already operating restaurants in 55 countries. KFC's early expansion abroad, its strong brand name, and managerial experience in international markets gave it a strong competitive advantage vis-à-vis other fast-food chains that were investing abroad for the first time.

Exhibit 30.4 shows *Hotels'* 1994 list of the world's thirty largest fast-food restaurant chains (*Hotels* discontinued reporting these data after 1994). Seventeen of the thirty largest restaurant chains (ranked by number of units) were headquartered in the United States. There were a number of possible explanations for the relative scarcity of fast-food restaurant chains outside of the U.S.A. First, the United States represented the largest consumer market in the world, accounting for over one-fifth of the world's gross domestic product (GDP). Therefore, the United States was the strategic focus of the largest restaurant chains. Second, Americans were more quick to accept the fast-food concept. Many other cultures had strong culinary traditions that were difficult to break down. Europeans for example, had histories of frequenting more mid-scale restaurants, where they spent several hours in a formal setting enjoying native dishes and beverages. While KFC was again building restaurants in Germany by the late 1980s, it previously failed to penetrate the German market, because Germans were not accustomed to take-out food or to ordering food over the counter. McDonald's had greater success penetrating the German market, because it made a number of changes in its menu and operating procedures, in order to better appeal to German culture. For example, German beer was served in all of McDonald's German restaurants. KFC had more success in Asia and Latin America, where chicken was a traditional dish.

Aside from cultural factors, international business carried risks not present in the U.S. market. Long distances between headquarters and foreign franchises often made it difficult to control the quality of individual restaurants. Large distances also caused servicing and support problems. Transportation and other resource costs were higher than in the domestic market. In addition, time, cultural, and language differences increased communication and operational problems. Therefore, it was reasonable to expect U.S. restaurant chains to expand domestically as long as they achieved corporate profit and growth objectives. As the U.S. market became saturated, and companies gained expertise in international markets, more companies turned to profitable international markets as a means of expanding restaurant bases and increasing sales, profits, and market share.

Franchise	Location	Units	Countries
1 Pizza Hut	Dallas, Texas	10,433	80
2 McDonald's	Oakbrook, Illinois	23,132	70
3 KFC	Louisville, Kentucky	9,033	68
4 Burger King	Miami, Florida	7,121	50
5 Baskin Robbins	Glendale, California	3,557	49
6 Wendy's	Dublin, Ohio	4,168	38
7 Domino's Pizza	Ann Arbor, Michigan	5,238	36
8 TCBY	Little Rock, Arkansas	7,474	22
9 Dairy Queen	Minneapolis, Minnesota	5,471	21
10 Dunkin' Donuts	Randolph, Massachusetts	3,691	21
11 Taco Bell	Irvine, California	4,921	20
12 Arby's	Fort Lauderdale, Florida	2,670	18
13 Subway Sandwiches	Milford, Connecticut	8,477	15
14 Sizzler International	Los Angeles, California	681	14
15 Hardee's	Rocky Mount, North Carolina	4,060	12
16 Little Caesar's	Detroit, Michigan	4,600	12
17 Popeye's Chicken	Atlanta, Georgia	813	12
18 Denny's	Spartanburg, South Carolina	1,515	10
19 A&W Restaurants	Livonia, Michigan	707	9
20 T.G.I. Friday's	Minneapolis, Minnesota	273	8
21 Orange Julius	Minneapolis, Minnesota	480	7
22 Church's Fried Chicken	Atlanta, Georgia	1,079	6
23 Long John Silver's	Lexington, Kentucky	1,464	5
24 Carl's Jr.	Anaheim, California	649	4
25 Loterria	Tokyo, Japan	795	4
26 Mos Burger	Tokyo, Japan	1,263	4
27 Skylark	Tokyo, Japan	1,000	4
28 Jack in the Box	San Diego, California	1,172	3
29 Quick Restaurants	Berchem, Belgium	876	3
30 Taco Time	Eugene, Oregon	300	3

Source: Hotels, May 1994; PepsiCo, Inc. 1994 Annual Report.

Exhibit 30.4 The World's 30 Largest Fast-Food Chains, Year-end 1993, Ranked by Number of Countries

KENTUCKY FRIED CHICKEN CORPORATION

KFC's worldwide sales, which included sales of both company-owned and franchised restaurants, grew to $8.0 billion in 1997. U.S. sales grew 2.6 percent over 1996 and accounted for about one-half of KFC's sales worldwide. KFC's U.S. share of the chicken segment fell 1.8 points to 55.8 percent in 1997 (see Exhibit 30.5). This marked the sixth consecutive year that KFC sustained a decline in market share. Market share fell from

	KFC	Boston Market	Popeye's	Chick-fil-A	Church's	Total
1988	72.1	0.0	12.0	5.8	10.1	100
1989	70.8	0.0	12.0	6.2	11.0	100
1990	71.3	0.0	12.3	6.6	9.8	100
1991	72.7	0.0	11.4	7.0	8.9	100
1992	71.5	0.9	11.4	7.5	8.7	100
1993	68.7	3.0	11.4	8.0	8.9	100
1994	64.8	6.9	11.3	8.4	8.6	100
1995	60.5	12.3	10.8	8.2	8.2	100
1996	57.6	16.2	10.0	8.4	7.8	100
1997	55.8	16.7	10.1	9.4	8.0	100
Change	−16.3	16.7	−1.9	3.6	−2.1	0

Source: Nation's Restaurant News.

Exhibit 30.5   Top U.S. Chicken Chains, Market Share, 1988–97 (%)

72.1 percent of the market in 1988 to 55.8 percent in 1997, a total market share loss of 16.3 points. Boston Market, which established its first restaurant in 1992, increased its market share from zero to 16.7 percent over the same period. On the surface, it appeared as though Boston Market's market share gain was achieved by taking customers away from KFC. However, KFC's sales growth remained fairly stable and constant over the last ten years. Boston Market's success was largely a function of its appeal to consumers who did not regularly patronize KFC or other chicken chains that sold fried chicken. By appealing to a market niche that was previously unsatisfied, Boston Market was able to expand the existing consumer base within the chicken segment of the fast-food industry.

Refranchising strategy

The relatively low growth rate in sales in KFC's domestic restaurants during the 1992–7 period was largely the result of KFC's decision in 1993 to begin selling company-owned restaurants to franchisees. When Colonel Sanders began to expand the Kentucky Fried Chicken system in the late 1950s, he established KFC as a system of independent franchisees. This was done in order to minimize his involvement in the operations of individual restaurants and to concentrate on the things he enjoyed the most – cooking, product development, and public relations. This resulted in a fiercely loyal and independent group of franchises. PepsiCo's strategy when it acquired KFC in 1986 was to integrate KFC's operations into the PepsiCo system, in order to take advantage of operational, financial, and marketing synergies. However, such a strategy demanded that PepsiCo become more involved in decisions over franchise operations, menu offerings, restaurant management, finance, and marketing. This was met by resistance by KFC franchises, who fiercely opposed increased control by the corporate parent. One method for PepsiCo to deal with the conflict with KFC franchises was to expand through company-owned restaurants

	Company-owned	% Total	Franchised/Licensed	% Total	Total
1986	1,246	26.4	3,474	73.6	4,720
1987	1,250	26.0	3,564	74.0	4,814
1988	1,262	25.8	3,637	74.2	4,899
1989	1,364	27.5	3,597	72.5	4,961
1990	1,389	27.7	3,617	72.3	5,006
1991	1,836	36.6	3,186	63.4	5,022
1992	1,960	38.8	3,095	61.2	5,055
1993	2,014	39.5	3,080	60.5	5,094
1994	2,005	39.2	3,110	60.8	5,115
1995	2,026	39.4	3,111	60.6	5,137
1996	1,932	37.8	3,176	62.2	5,108
1997	1,850	36.1	3,270	63.9	5,120
1986–93 Compounded Annual Growth Rate					
	7.1%		−1.7%		1.1%
1993–97 Compounded Annual Growth Rate					
	−2.1%		1.5%		0.1%

Source: Tricon Global Restaurants, Inc., *1997 Annual Report*; PepsiCo, Inc., *Annual Report*, 1994, 1995, 1996, 1997.

Exhibit 30.6 KFC Restaurant Count, United States, 1986–97

rather than through franchising and to use strong PepsiCo cash flows to buy back unprofitable franchised restaurants, which could then be converted into company-owned restaurants. In 1986, company-owned restaurants made up 26 percent of KFC's U.S. restaurant base. By 1993, they made up about 40 percent of the total (see Exhibit 30.6).

While company-owned restaurants were relatively easier to control compared to franchises, they also required higher levels of investment. This meant that high levels of cash were diverted from PepsiCo's soft drink and snack food businesses into its restaurant businesses. However, the fast-food industry delivered lower returns than the soft drink and snack foods industries. Consequently, increased investment in KFC, Pizza Hut, and Taco Bell had a negative effect on PepsiCo's consolidated return on assets. By 1993, investors became concerned that PepsiCo's return on assets failed to match returns delivered by Coca-Cola. In order to shore up its return on assets, PepsiCo decided to reduce the number of company-owned restaurants by selling them back to franchisees. This strategy lowered overall company sales, but it lowered the amount of cash tied up in fixed assets, provided PepsiCo with one-time cash flow benefits from initial fees charged to franchisees, and generated an annual stream of franchise royalties. Tricon Global continued this strategy after the spin off in 1997.

Marketing strategy

During the 1980s, consumers began to demand healthier foods, greater variety, and service in a variety of non-traditional locations such as grocery stores, restaurants, airports, and outdoor events. This forced fast-food chains to expand menu offerings and to investigate non-traditional distribution channels and restaurant designs. Families also demanded greater value in the food they bought away from home. This increased pressure on fast-food chains to reduce prices and to lower operating costs in order to maintain profit margins.

Many of KFC's problems during the late 1980s surrounded its limited menu and its inability to quickly bring new products to market. The popularity of its Original Recipe Chicken allowed KFC to expand through the 1980s without significant competition from other chicken competitors. As a result, new product introductions were never an important element of KFC's overall strategy. One of the most serious setbacks suffered by KFC came in 1989 as KFC prepared to add a chicken sandwich to its menu. While KFC was still experimenting with its chicken sandwich, McDonald's test-marketed its McChicken sandwich in the Louisville market. Shortly thereafter, it rolled out the McChicken sandwich nationally. By beating KFC to the market, McDonald's was able to develop strong consumer awareness for its sandwich. This significantly increased KFC's cost of developing awareness for its own sandwich, which KFC introduced several months later. KFC eventually withdrew its sandwich because of low sales.

In 1991, KFC changed its logo in the United States from Kentucky Fried Chicken to KFC, in order to reduce its image as a fried chicken chain. It continued to use the Kentucky Fried Chicken name internationally. It then responded to consumer demands for greater variety by introducing several products that would serve as alternatives to its Original Recipe Chicken. These included Oriental Wings, Popcorn Chicken, and Honey BBQ Chicken. It also introduced a dessert menu that included a variety of pies and cookies. In 1993, it rolled out Rotisserie Chicken and began to promote its lunch and dinner buffet. The buffet, which included 30 items, was introduced into almost 1,600 KFC restaurants in 27 states by year-end. In 1998, KFC sold three types of chicken – Original Recipe and Extra Crispy (fried chicken) and Tender Roast (roasted chicken).

One of KFC's most aggressive strategies was the introduction of its "Neighborhood Program." By mid-1993, almost 500 company-owned restaurants in New York, Chicago, Philadelphia, Washington, D.C., St. Louis, Los Angeles, Houston, and Dallas had been outfitted with special menu offerings to appeal exclusively to the Black community. Menus were beefed up with side dishes such as greens, macaroni and cheese, peach cobbler, sweet-potato pie, and red beans and rice. In addition, restaurant employees wore African-inspired uniforms. The introduction of the Neighborhood Program increased sales by five to 30 percent in restaurants appealing directly to the Black community. KFC followed by testing Hispanic-oriented restaurants in the Miami area, offering side dishes such as fried plantains, flan, and tres leches.

One of KFC's most significant problems in the U.S. market was that overcapacity made expansion of free-standing restaurants difficult. Fewer sites were available for new construction and those sites, because of their increased cost, were driving profit margins down. Therefore, KFC initiated a new, three-pronged distribution strategy. First, it focused on building smaller restaurants in non-traditional outlets such as airports, shopping malls, universities, and hospitals. Second, it experimented with home delivery. Home delivery was introduced in the Nashville and Albuquerque markets in 1994. By 1998, home delivery was offered in 365 U.S. restaurants. Other non-traditional distribution outlets being tested included units offering drive-thru and carry-out service only, snack shops in cafeterias, scaled-down outlets for supermarkets, and mobile units that could be transported to outdoor concerts and fairs.

A third focus of KFC's distribution strategy was restaurant co-branding, primarily with its sister chain, Taco Bell. By 1997, 349 KFC restaurants had added Taco Bell to their menus and displayed both the KFC and Taco Bell logos outside their restaurants. Co-branding gave KFC the opportunity to expand its business dayparts. While about two-thirds KFC's business was dinner, Taco Bell's primary business occurred at lunch. By combining the two concepts in the same unit, sales at individual restaurants could be increased significantly. KFC believed that there were opportunities to sell the Taco Bell concept in over 3,900 of its U.S. restaurants.

Operating efficiencies

As pressure continued to build on fast-food chains to limit price increases, restaurant chains searched for ways to reduce overhead and other operating costs, in order to improve profit margins. In 1989, KFC reorganized its U.S. operations in order to eliminate overhead costs and to increase efficiency. Included in this reorganization was a revision of KFC's crew training programs and operating standards. A renewed emphasis was placed on improving customer service, cleaner restaurants, faster and friendlier service, and continued high-quality products. In 1992, KFC reorganized its middle management ranks, eliminating 250 of the 1,500 management positions at KFC's corporate headquarters. More responsibility was assigned to restaurant franchisees and marketing managers and pay was more closely aligned with customer service and restaurant performance. In 1997, Tricon Global signed a five-year agreement with PepsiCo Food Systems (which was later sold by PepsiCo to AmeriServe Food Distributors) to distribute food and supplies to Tricon's 29,712 KFC, Pizza Hut, and Taco Bell units. This provided KFC with significant opportunities to benefit from economies of scale in distribution.

INTERNATIONAL OPERATIONS

Much of the early success of the top ten fast-food chains was the result of aggressive building strategies. Chains were able to discourage competition by building in low population areas that could only support a single fast-food chain. McDonald's was particularly successful as it was able to quickly expand into small towns across the United States, thereby preempting other fast-food chains. It was equally important to beat a competitor into more largely populated areas where location was of prime importance. KFC's early entry into international markets placed it in a strong position to benefit from international expansion as the U.S. market became saturated. In 1997, 50 percent of KFC's restaurants were located outside of the United States. While 364 new restaurants were opened outside of the United States, only 12 new restaurants were added to the U.S. system in 1997.

Most of KFC's international expansion was through franchises, though some restaurants were licensed to operators or jointly operated with a local partner.

Expansion through franchising was an important strategy for penetrating international markets, because franchises were owned and operated by local entrepreneurs with a deeper understanding of local language, culture, and customs, as well as local law, financial markets, and marketing characteristics. Franchising was particularly important for expansion into smaller countries such as the Dominican Republic, Grenada, Bermuda, and Suriname, which could only support a single restaurant. Costs were prohibitively high for KFC to operate company-owned restaurants in these smaller markets. Of the 5,117 KFC restaurants located outside of the United States in 1997, 68 percent were franchised, while 22 percent were company-owned, and 10 percent were licensed restaurants or joint ventures.

In larger markets such as Japan, China, and Mexico, there was a stronger emphasis on building company-owned restaurants. By coordinating purchasing, recruiting and training, financing, and advertising fixed costs could be spread over a large number of restaurants and lower prices on products and services could be negotiated. KFC was also better able to control product and service quality. In order to take advantage of economies of scale, Tricon Global Restaurants managed all of the international units of its KFC, Pizza Hut, and Taco Bell chains through its Tricon International division located in Dallas, Texas. This enabled Tricon Global Restaurants to leverage its strong advertising expertise, international experience, and restaurant management experience across all its KFC, Pizza Hut, and Taco Bell chains.

Latin American strategy

KFC's primary market presence in Latin America during the 1980s was in Mexico, Puerto Rico, and the Caribbean. KFC established subsidiaries in Mexico and Puerto Rico, from which it coordinated the construction and operation of company-owned restaurants. A third subsidiary in Venezuela was closed because of the high fixed costs associated with running the small subsidiary. Franchises were used to penetrate other countries in the Caribbean whose market size prevented KFC from profitably operating company restaurants. KFC relied exclusively on the operation of company-owned restaurants in Mexico through 1989. While franchising was popular in the United States, it was virtually unknown in Mexico until 1990, mainly because of the absence of a law protecting patents, information, and technology transferred to the Mexican franchise. In addition, royalties were limited. As a result, most fast-food chains opted to invest in Mexico using company-owned units.

In 1990, Mexico enacted a new law that provided for the protection of technology transferred into Mexico. Under the new legislation, the franchisor and franchisee were free to set their own terms. Royalties were also allowed under the new law. Royalties were taxed at a 15 percent rate on technology assistance and know-how and 35 percent for other royalty categories. The advent of the new franchise law resulted in an explosion of franchises in fast-food, services, hotels, and retail outlets. In 1992, franchises had an estimated $750 million in sales in over 1,200 outlets throughout Mexico. Prior to the passage of Mexico's franchise law, KFC limited its Mexican operations primarily to Mexico City, Guadalajara, and Monterrey. This enabled KFC to better coordinate operations and minimize costs of distribution to individual restaurants. The new franchise law gave KFC and other fast-food chains the opportunity to expand their restaurant bases more quickly to more rural regions of Mexico, where responsibility for management could be handled by local franchisees.

After 1990, KFC altered its Latin American strategy in a number of ways. First, it opened 29 franchises in Mexico to complement its company-owned restaurant base. It then expanded its company-owned restaurants into the Virgin Islands and reestablished a subsidiary in Venezuela. Third, it expanded its franchise operations into South America. In 1990, a franchise was opened in Chile and in 1993, a franchise was opened in Brazil. Franchises were subsequently established in Colombia, Ecuador, Panama, and Peru, among other South American countries. A fourth subsidiary was established in Brazil, in order to develop company-owned restaurants. Brazil was Latin America's largest economy and McDonald's primary Latin American investment location. By June 1998, KFC operated 438 restaurants in 32 Latin American countries. By comparison, McDonald's operated 1,091 restaurants in 28 countries.

Exhibit 30.7 shows the Latin American operations of KFC and McDonald's. KFC's early entry into Latin America during the 1970s gave it a leadership position in Mexico and the Caribbean. It had also gained an edge in Ecuador and Peru, countries where McDonald's had not yet developed a strong presence. McDonald's focused its Latin American investment in Brazil, Argentina, and Uruguay, countries where KFC had little or no presence. McDonald's was also strong in Venezuela. Both KFC and McDonald's were strong in Chile, Colombia, Panama, and Puerto Rico.

Economic environment and the Mexican market

Mexico was KFC's strongest market in Latin America. While McDonald's had aggressively established restaurants in Mexico since 1990, KFC retained the leading market share. Because of its close proximity to the United States, Mexico was an attractive location for U.S. trade and investment. Mexico's population of 98 million people was approximately one-third as large as the United States and represented a large market for U.S. companies. In comparison, Canada's population of 30.3 million people was only one-third as large as Mexico's. Mexico's close proximity to the United States meant that transportation costs between the United States to Mexico were significantly lower than to Europe or Asia. This increased the competitiveness of U.S. goods in comparison with European and Asian goods, which had to be transported to Mexico across the Atlantic or Pacific Ocean at substantial cost. The United States was, in fact, Mexico's largest trading partner. Over 75 percent of Mexico's imports came from the United States, while 84 percent of its exports were to the USA (see Exhibit 30.8). Many U.S. firms invested in Mexico in order to take advantage of lower wage rates. By producing goods in Mexico, U.S. goods could be shipped back into the United States for sale or shipped to third markets at lower cost.

While the U.S. market was critically important to Mexico, Mexico still represented a small percentage of overall U.S. trade and investment. Since the early 1900s, the portion of U.S. exports to Latin America has declined. Instead, U.S. exports to Canada and Asia, where economic growth outpaced growth in Mexico, increased more quickly. Canada was the largest importer of U.S. goods. Japan was the largest exporter of goods to the

	KFC Company Restaurants	KFC Franchised Restaurants	KFC Total Restaurants	McDonald's
Argentina	–	–	–	131
Bahamas	–	10	10	3
Barbados	–	7	7	–
Brazil	6	2	8	480
Chile	–	29	29	27
Colombia	–	19	19	18
Costa Rica	–	5	5	19
Ecuador	–	18	18	2
Jamaica	–	17	17	7
Mexico	128	29	157	131
Panama	–	21	21	20
Peru	–	17	17	5
Puerto Rico & Virgin Islands	67	–	67	115
Trinidad & Tobago	–	27	27	3
Uruguay	–	–	–	18
Venezuela	6	–	6	53
Other	–	30	30	59
Total	207	231	438	1,091

Source: Tricon Global Restaurants, Inc.; McDonald's, 1997 Annual Report.

Exhibit 30.7 Latin America Restaurant Count, KFC and McDonald's, as of December 31, 1997

United States, with Canada a close second. U.S. investment in Mexico was also small, mainly because of government restrictions on foreign investment. Most U.S. foreign investment was in Europe, Canada, and Asia.

The lack of U.S. investment in and trade with Mexico during this century was mainly the result of Mexico's long history of restricting trade and foreign direct investment. The Institutional Revolutionary Party (PRI), which came to power in Mexico during the 1930s, had historically pursued protectionist economic policies, in order to shield Mexico's economy from foreign competition. Many industries were government-owned or controlled and many Mexican companies focused on producing goods for the domestic market without much attention to building export markets. High tariffs and other trade barriers restricted imports into Mexico and foreign ownership of assets in Mexico was largely prohibited or heavily restricted.

Additionally, a dictatorial and entrenched government bureaucracy, corrupt labor unions, and a long tradition of anti-Americanism among many government officials and intellectuals reduced the motivation of U.S. firms for investing in Mexico. The nationalization of Mexico's banks in 1982 led to higher real interest rates and lower investor confidence. Afterward, the Mexican government battled high inflation, high interest rates,

	1992		1994		1996	
	Exports	Imports	Exports	Imports	Exports	Imports
USA	81.1	71.3	85.3	71.8	84.0	75.6
Japan	1.7	4.9	1.6	4.8	1.4	4.4
Germany	1.1	4.0	0.6	3.9	0.7	3.5
Canada	2.2	1.7	2.4	2.0	1.2	1.9
Italy	0.3	1.6	0.1	1.3	1.2	1.1
Brazil	0.9	1.8	0.6	1.5	0.9	0.8
Spain	2.7	1.4	1.4	1.7	1.0	0.7
Other	10.0	13.3	8.0	13.0	9.6	12.0
% Total	100.0	100.0	100.0	100.0	100.0	100.0
Value ($m)	46,196	62,129	60,882	79,346	95,991	89,464

Source: International Monetary Fund, *Direction of Trade Statistics Yearbook*, 1997.

Exhibit 30.8 Mexico's Major Trading Partners – % Total Exports and Imports, 1992–6

labor unrest, and lost consumer purchasing power. Investor confidence in Mexico, however, improved after 1988, when Carlos Salinas de Gortari was elected president. Following his election, Salinas embarked on an ambitious restructuring of the Mexican economy. He initiated policies to strengthen the free market components of the economy, lowered top marginal tax rates to 36 percent (down from 60 percent in 1986), and eliminated many restrictions on foreign investment. Foreign firms can now buy up to 100 percent of the equity in many Mexican firms. Foreign ownership of Mexican firms was previously limited to 49 percent.

Privatization

The privatization of government-owned companies came to symbolize the restructuring of Mexico's economy. In 1990, legislation was passed to privatize all government-run banks. By the end of 1992, over 800 of some 1,200 government-owned companies had been sold, including Mexicana and AeroMexico, the two largest airline companies in Mexico, and Mexico's 18 major banks. However, more than 350 companies remained under government ownership. These represented a significant portion of the assets owned by the state at the start of 1988. Therefore, the sale of government-owned companies, in terms of asset value, was moderate. A large percentage of the remaining government-owned assets were controlled by government-run companies in certain strategic industries such as steel, electricity, and petroleum. These industries had long been protected by government ownership. As a result, additional privatization of government-owned enterprises until 1993 was limited. However, in 1993, President Salinas opened up the electricity sector to independent power producers and Petróleos Mexicanos (Pemex), the state-run petrochemical monopoly, initiated a program to sell off many of its non-strategic assets to private and foreign buyers.

North American Free Trade Agreement (NAFTA)

Prior to 1989, Mexico levied high tariffs on most imported goods. In addition, many other goods were subjected to quotas, licensing requirements, and other non-tariff trade barriers. In 1986, Mexico joined the General Agreement on Tariffs and Trade (GATT), a world trade organization designed to eliminate barriers to trade among member nations. As a member of GATT, Mexico was obligated to apply its system of tariffs to all member nations equally. As a result of its membership in GATT, Mexico dropped tariff rates on a variety of imported goods. In addition, import license requirements were dropped for all but 300 imported items. During President Salinas' administration, tariffs were reduced from an average of 100 percent on most items to an average of 11 percent.

On January 1, 1994, the North American Free Trade Agreement (NAFTA) went into effect. The passage of NAFTA, which included Canada, the United States, and Mexico, created a trading bloc with a larger population and gross domestic product than the European Union. All tariffs on goods traded among the three countries were scheduled to be phased out. NAFTA was expected to be particularly beneficial for Mexican exporters, because reduced tariffs made their goods more competitive in the United States compared to goods exported to the United States from other countries. In 1995, one year after NAFTA went into effect, Mexico posted its first balance of trade surplus in six years. Part of this surplus was attributed to reduced tariffs resulting from the NAFTA agreement. However, the peso crisis of 1995, which lowered the value of the peso against the dollar, increased the price of goods imported into Mexico and lowered the price of Mexican products exported to the United States. Therefore, it was still too early to assess the full effects of the NAFTA agreement.

Foreign exchange and the Mexican peso crisis of 1995

Between 1982 and 1991, a two-tiered exchange rate system was in force in Mexico. The system consisted of a controlled rate and a free market rate. A controlled rate was used for imports, foreign debt payments, and conversion of export proceeds. An estimated 70 percent of all foreign transactions were covered by the controlled rate. A free market rate was used for other transactions. In 1989, President Salinas instituted a policy of allowing the peso to depreciate against the dollar by one peso per day. The result was a grossly overvalued peso. This lowered the price of imports and led to an increase in imports of over 23 percent in 1989. At the same time, Mexican exports became less competitive on world markets.

In 1991, the controlled rate was abolished and replaced with an official free rate. In order to limit the range of fluctuations in the value of the peso, the government fixed the rate at which it would buy or sell pesos. A floor (the maximum price at which pesos could be purchased) was established at Ps 3,056.20 and remained fixed. A ceiling (the maximum price at which the peso could be sold) was established at Ps 3,056.40 and allowed to move upward by Ps 0.20 per day. This was later revised to Ps 0.40 per day. In 1993, a new currency, called the new peso, was issued with three fewer zeros. The new currency was designed to simplify transactions and to reduce the cost of printing currency.

When Ernesto Zedillo became Mexico's president in December 1994, one of his objectives was to continue the stability of prices, wages, and exchange rates achieved by ex-president Carlos Salinas de Gortari during his five-year tenure as president. However, Salinas had achieved stability largely on the basis of price, wage, and foreign exchange controls. While giving the appearance of stability, an over-valued peso continued to encourage imports which exacerbated Mexico's balance of trade deficit. Mexico's government continued to use foreign reserve to finance its balance of trade deficits. According to the Banco de Mexico, foreign currency reserves fell from $24 billion in January 1994 to $5.5 billion in January 1995. Anticipating a devaluation of the peso, investors began to move capital into U.S. dollar investments. In order to relieve pressure on the peso, Zedillo announced on December 19, 1994 that the peso would be allowed to depreciate by an additional 15 percent per year against the dollar compared to the maximum allowable depreciation of four percent per year established during the Salinas administration. Within two days, continued pressure on the peso forced Zedillo to allow the peso to float freely against the dollar. By mid-January 1995, the peso had lost 35 percent of its value against the dollar and the Mexican stock market plunged 20 percent. By November 1995, the peso had depreciated from 3.1 pesos per dollar to 7.3 pesos per dollar.

The continued devaluation of the peso resulted in higher import prices, higher inflation, destabilization within the stock market, and higher interest rates. Mexico struggled to pay its dollar-based debts. In order to thwart a possible default by Mexico, the U.S. government, International Monetary Fund, and World Bank pledged $24.9 billion in emergency loans. Zedillo then announced an emergency economic package called the *pacto* that included reduced government spending, increased sales of government-run businesses, and a freeze on wage increases.

Labor problems

One of KFC's primary concerns in Mexico was the stability of labor markets. Labor was relatively plentiful and wages were low. However, much of the work force was relatively unskilled. KFC benefited from lower labor costs, but labor unrest, low job retention, high absenteeism, and poor punctuality were significant problems. Absenteeism and punctuality were partially cultural. However, problems with worker retention and labor unrest were primarily the result of workers' frustration over the loss of their purchasing power due to inflation and government controls on wage increases. Absenteeism remained high at approximately eight to 14 percent of the labor force, though it was declining because of job security fears. Turnover continued to be a problem and ran at between five and 12 percent per month. Therefore, employee screening and internal training were important issues for firms investing in Mexico.

Higher inflation and the government's freeze on wage increases led to a dramatic decline in disposable income after 1994. Further, a slowdown in business activity, brought about by higher interest rates and lower government spending, led many businesses to lay off workers. By the end of 1995, an estimated one million jobs had been lost as a result of the economic crisis sparked by the peso devaluation. As a result, industry groups within Mexico called for new labor laws giving them more freedom to hire and fire employees and increased flexibility to hire part-time rather than full-time workers.

RISKS AND OPPORTUNITIES

The peso crisis of 1995 and resulting recession in Mexico left KFC managers with a great deal of uncertainty regarding Mexico's economic and political future. KFC had benefited from economic stability between 1988 and 1994. Inflation was brought down, the peso was relatively stable, labor unrest was relatively calm, and Mexico's new franchise law had enabled KFC to expand into rural areas using franchises rather than company-owned restaurants. By the end of 1995, KFC had built 29 franchises in Mexico. The foreign exchange crisis of 1995 had severe implications for U.S. firms operating in Mexico. The devaluation of the peso resulted in higher inflation and capital flight out of Mexico. Capital flight reduced the supply of capital and led to higher interest rates. In order to reduce inflation, Mexico's government instituted an austerity program that resulted in lower disposable income, higher unemployment, and lower demand for products and services.

Another problem was Mexico's failure to reduce restrictions on U.S. and Canadian investment in a timely fashion. Many U.S. firms experienced problems getting required approvals for new ventures from the Mexican government. A good example was United Parcel Service (UPS), which sought government approval to use large trucks for deliveries in Mexico. Approvals were delayed, forcing UPS to use smaller trucks. This put UPS at a competitive disadvantage vis-à-vis Mexican companies. In many cases, UPS was forced to subcontract delivery work to Mexican companies that were allowed to use larger, more cost-efficient trucks. Other U.S. companies such as Bell Atlantic and TRW faced similar problems. TRW, which signed a joint venture agreement with a Mexican partner, had to wait 15 months longer than anticipated before the Mexican government released rules on how it could receive credit data from banks. TRW claimed that the Mexican government slowed the approval process in order to placate several large Mexican banks.

A final area of concern for KFC was increased political turmoil in Mexico during the last several years. On January 1, 1994, the day NAFTA went into effect, rebels (descendants of the Mayans) rioted in the southern Mexican province of Chiapas on the Guatemalan border. After four days of fighting, Mexican troops had driven the rebels out of several towns earlier seized by the rebels. Around 150 – mostly rebels – were killed. The uprising symbolized many of the fears of the poor in Mexico. While ex-president Salinas' economic programs had increased economic growth and wealth in Mexico, many of Mexico's poorest felt that they had not benefited. Many of Mexico's farmers, faced with lower tariffs on imported agricultural goods from the United States, felt that they might be driven out of business because of lower priced imports. Therefore, social unrest among Mexico's Indians, farmers, and the poor could potentially unravel much of the economic success achieved in Mexico during the last five years.

Further, ex-president Salinas' hand-picked successor for president was assassinated in early 1994 while campaigning in Tijuana. The assassin was a 23-year-old mechanic and migrant worker believed to be affiliated with a dissident group upset with the PRI's economic reforms. The possible existence of a dissident group raised fears of political violence in the future. The PRI quickly named Ernesto Zedillo, a 42-year-old economist with little political experience, as their new presidential candidate. Zedillo was elected president in December 1994. Political unrest was not limited to Mexican officials and

Annual Change (%)	1993	1994	1995	1996	1997
GDP Growth					
Canada	3.3	4.8	5.5	4.1	–
United States	4.9	5.8	4.8	5.1	5.9
Mexico	21.4	13.3	29.4	38.2	–
Real GDP Growth					
Canada	2.2	4.1	2.3	1.2	–
United States	2.2	3.5	2.0	2.8	3.8
Mexico	2.0	4.5	−6.2	5.1	–
Inflation					
Canada	1.9	0.2	2.2	1.5	1.6
United States	3.0	2.5	2.8	2.9	2.4
Mexico	9.7	6.9	35.0	34.4	20.6
Depreciation Against $U.S.					
Canada (C$)	4.2	6.0	−2.7	0.3	4.3
Mexico (NP)	−0.3	71.4	43.5	2.7	3.6

Source: International Monetary Fund, *International Financial Statistics*, 1998.

Exhibit 30.9   Selected Economic Data for Canada, the United States, and Mexico, 1993–7

companies. In October 1994, between 30 and 40 masked men attacked a McDonald's restaurant in the tourist section of Mexico City to show their opposition to California's Proposition 187, which would have curtailed benefits to illegal aliens (primarily from Mexico). The men threw cash registers to the floor, cracked them open, smashed windows, overturned tables, and spray-painted slogans on the walls such as "No to Fascism" and "Yankee Go Home."

KFC faced a variety of issues in Mexico and Latin America in 1998. Prior to 1995, few restaurants had been opened in South America. However, KFC was now aggressively building new restaurants in the region. KFC halted openings of franchised restaurants in Mexico and all restaurants opened since 1995 were company-owned. KFC was more aggressively building restaurants in South America, which remained largely unpenetrated by KFC through 1995. Of greatest importance was Brazil, where McDonald's had already established a strong market share position. Brazil was Latin America's largest economy and a largely untapped market for KFC. The danger in ignoring Mexico was that a conservative investment strategy could jeopardize its market share lead over McDonald's in a large market where KFC long enjoyed enormous popularity.

Part VI

Issues in Global and Cultural Diversity

31	Put Your Ethics to a Global Test	329
	Charlene Marmer Solomon	
32	Diversity Stress as Morality Stress	336
	Rae André	
33	Remote Control	345
	Neil Merrick	
34	Should HR Survive? A Profession at the Crossroads	348
	Anthony J. Rucci	
35	Cultural Diversity Programs to Prepare for Work Force 2000: What's Gone Wrong?	355
	Norma M. Riccucci	
36	*Case:* Anglo-German Trading Corporation	360
	Kenneth E. Roberts	
37	*Case:* Novell's Global Strategy: "Bytes Are Somewhat Narcotic"	362
	Marjorie McEntire, C. Brooklyn Derr and Chris Meek	

Chapter 31

Put Your Ethics to a Global Test

Charlene Marmer Solomon

Global scandals make headlines daily. There was the Daiwa Bank trading scandal, in which billions of dollars were lost from improper bond trading – and hidden by high banking officials. There was the 1995 U.S. Department of Labor report documenting child labor abuse in 56 countries where children are used to mine gold, among other things. Then there was the Exxon Valdez disaster, the BCCI (Bank of Credit and Commerce International) debacle, and the Bhopal catastrophe. And there were other events that never made the newspapers: piracy of intellectual property, payments to third parties so companies could do business, nepotism and conflict of interest.

All these incidents have one thing in common: they're a matter of ethics – or a lack thereof. The issue of global business ethics is the ultimate dilemma for many U.S. businesses. As companies do more and more business around the globe, their assumptions about ethical codes of conduct are put to the test. Corporate executives may face simple questions regarding the appropriate amount of money to spend on a business gift, or the legitimacy of payments to liaisons to "expedite" business. Or they may encounter out-and-out bribery, child-labor disputes, environmental abuse and unscrupulous business practices. As organizations expand globally, HR managers must play a role in helping to define and achieve ethical behavior from employees throughout the world.

To accomplish this, many international businesses are creating codes of conduct, like the ones such companies as IBM, Xerox and Shell Oil have had for years. These three companies, and others, including Levi Strauss, Honeywell, Digital Equipment and H.B. Fuller, are taking their efforts even further – by incorporating their messages into everyday business practices and making them living documents.

WHAT ARE GLOBAL ETHICS AND HOW DO THEY IMPACT BUSINESS?

Defining ethical behavior in a domestic setting is tricky enough. Not only do people respond differently to moral questions, but individuals – even in the same culture – interpret morality differently. When you add the cultural overlay, business ethics can become a quagmire of moral questions. Some even say the term "global ethics" is an oxymoron. Is it?

"One of the myths about global business ethics is that when you do business in other cultures, they will have a whole set of different ethical values and mores. That simply is blown out of proportion," says W. Michael Hoffman, executive director of the Center for Business Ethics at Bentley College in Waltham, Massachusetts, and co-author of "Emerging Global Business Ethics."

"When you dig deeply enough and scrape away all the trappings, the real ethical solid building blocks or principles of most cultures are the same."

For example, most people agree mistreating children is wrong, but they sometimes disagree about what constitutes mistreatment. For instance, most Americans consider child labor mistreatment. But in countries in which economic conditions warrant child labor, and laws and definitions of the family unit support it, it isn't regarded as cruel, but rather as a fact of life. "You have to understand the full context of the ethical decision-making of each culture. Once you understand it, you might say it's ethically incorrect without believing it's immoral," says Hoffman.

He says it's important for Americans – who sometimes get too moralistic – to walk a moral tightrope between the two extremes of ethical fanaticism and ethical relativism as we venture into other societies. "Ethical fanaticism is the position that says my ethical position is right, and I have the absolute answers. It doesn't recognize legitimate ethical disagreement and has no tolerance or appreciation of different perspectives, including cultural perspectives," Hoffman explains. "Ethical relativism is an equally bad extreme because it's saying there are no absolute values, which eventually leads to a state in which there's nothing right absolutely or wrong absolutely. It's a philosophical position that says I have no way of telling you you're morally wrong if you go out and kill or eat people because there are no absolute values."

Walking the middle road isn't always easy, however. Some global actions clearly lack ethics, such as the actions of Nazi Germany, for example. But there are others that are gray, such as the use of DDT in countries where there are no substitutes and without which the crops would be consumed by insects. Even the use of bribes can be debated on moral grounds. Bribes of hundreds of thousands of dollars to line a military general's pocket, most would agree is wrong, but what about payments to people who take goods off the docks to expedite service? That isn't considered unethical under many circumstances.

ETHICS ARE A MATTER OF BUSINESS

In response to these questions, some groups are taking a leadership role. The Caux Round Table is one such organization. Created in 1986 by Frederik Philips (former president of Philips Electronics) and Olivier Giscard d'Estaing (vice chairman of INSEAD), the Round Table brings together leaders from Europe, Japan and the United States. Their mission: To focus attention on global corporate responsibility, in the belief that the world business community plays a role in improving economic and social conditions.

Including such giants as Siemens AG, the Chase Manhattan Corp., ITT Corp., World Bank (France), Minnesota Mining & Manufacturing Co., Canon Inc. and Matsushita Electric Industrial Co. Ltd., the group has developed world standards to measure ethical behavior. The standards are based on two principles: the concept of human dignity, and the Japanese doctrine of *kyosei* – the idea of living and working together for the common good to enable mutual prosperity. The Round Table is proactive in its commitment to global responsibility. Founders believe business can be a powerful force for good because it's essential to provide employment and products and – more importantly – because it has the capacity to improve the lives of its customers and employees.

The Round Table lays out seven general principles that range from the general edict to protect (and where possible, improve) the environment, to more specific ideas, such as supporting the multilateral trade systems of the world. Underlying these ideals is the assumption that respect for cultural differences requires sensitivity and some flexibility. One of the most astounding aspects of the document is that it's values-driven but steeped in business acumen.

Indeed, Robert MacGregor, president of the Minnesota Center for Corporate Responsibility – the group largely responsible for the language of the *Caux Round Table's Principles for Business* – sees ethical behavior as a business imperative. "The world has shrunk and is so interconnected that behaviors everywhere affect behavior everywhere else."

Contemplating Global Ethics: Where Do You Start?

1. Think about your company's mission statement and values.
2. Clearly articulate those values. Define a code of ethical behavior.
3. Remember that cultural differences dictate flexibility and sensitivity.
4. Develop training in which employees learn – and apply – the company's values.
5. Create appraisal systems that reinforce the ethical behavior the company demands.
6. Communicate company ethics wherever and whenever possible.

—CMS

For example, although a company can save money by laying off expensive American workers and hiring cheap child labor in Bangladesh, these types of actions will backfire financially for a company in the end. "We want companies to move their jobs and capital around the world while making money, [and still] following responsible standards."

H. B. Fuller Company, makers of adhesives and other specialty chemicals, agrees that honesty and trustworthiness – themselves important – translate into dollars and cents. Case in point: The St. Paul, Minnesota-based company pursued buying a subsidiary from a European adhesive manufacturer. It was the only American firm out of a dozen companies interested in the purchase. The European company was interested in H. B. Fuller's bid, but looked a little nervously at the U.S. company because the subsidiary wasn't making money and had too many people in the business. "Their perception of US companies is that they don't think twice about having massive layoffs regardless of what it does to people," says Tony Andersen, chair of H. B. Fuller's board of directors. "We showed them through oral histories – examples within our company – that our corporate culture values people. That really counted to this large European company, which helped us finance the acquisition."

CLEARLY STATING COMPANY VALUES IS THE FIRST STEP

H.B. Fuller's situation demonstrates how ethics stem from corporate values. "You've got to think through very clearly what your company's values are – what you stand for wherever you do business," says John Buckley, ethics officer for Maynard, Massachusetts-based Digital Equipment Corp., which has more than 50 percent of its employees outside the United States. Digital's *Code of Business Conduct* clearly defines practices the company expects its employees to use in their daily activities. This substantial 27-page booklet, which addresses such ethical issues as managing company information and gift giving, provides the wisdom in a specific manner that requires employees to think about their behavior. For instance, in the section on gifts and entertainment, employees are given the following scenarios to think about: "You receive an unsolicited holiday gift from a supplier; you're invited to an annual trade show at a resort by a supplier who offers to pay your airfare and hotel bills; customers are visiting a Digital site for the day and you would like to take them to lunch. Do you know the proper business use of gifts and entertainment?" it asks.

The rest of the chapter details the company's position on gift giving and receiving, its implications and possible misinterpretations. It's straightforward and unambiguous, and offers the chance to question one's own actions.

"Wherever we do business, it's highly dependent on personal relationships between the people conducting the business. By basing our code of conduct on the company's core values, we believe it's more transferable and adaptable internationally," says Buckley.

STEP TWO: COMMUNICATE

Clear principles are one thing, but they're useless unless they're communicated to employees. Digital communicates its values through company newsletters, electronic transmissions and in training programs. Everyone receives a code of conduct booklet, and the company requires all managers to discuss the code with their employees at least once a year.

Honeywell Inc., based in Minneapolis, recently has translated its formal code of ethics into six foreign languages. Senior management regularly communicates the importance of ethics and compliance in newsletters, ethics presentations and other periodic communications. For example, a recent newsletter for the Asia Pacific region included a letter from the president talking about bribery. He reiterated that bribery will not be tolerated at all, and that the company will walk away from business rather than engage in bribery.

Levi Strauss & Co., a recognized leader in corporate social responsibility, encapsulates its values in the company's mission statement, and reiterates them in an *Aspirations* statement and in a printed code of ethics. The San Francisco-based company clearly defines business ethics and commitment to employee respect and fair treatment. Its statements clarify what's important, and what's expected in behavior.

But Levi Strauss doesn't leave the translation of its statement to chance. Since 1988, the company's HR department has conducted global training on different aspects of the aspiration statement. Managers and employees from around the world participate in three- to five-day courses on various aspects of leadership – one of which is ethics. The three-day ethics course gives people the opportunity to understand the company's expectations and definitions, and also gives them the chance to identify their own moral principles to see where they overlap with the company's.

"When people are clear about their own values and can identify the principles that make up ethical behavior, they have the tools for looking at potential decisions and the possible impact on different stakeholders, and whether or not the decision is an ethical one based on these principles," says Richard Woo, currently senior manager for global communications and previously regional manager for community affairs for Asia-Pacific.

An important part of the ethics training is to help people learn a decision-making tool – a process for making ethical decisions – called the *Principled Reasoning Approach*. The Principled Reasoning Approach isn't simply a name; it relies on thoughtful evaluation and a rational process to figure out how ethical principles translate into behavior.

Here's an example: The company went through the process when it considered whether or not to enter the South African marketplace. Levi Strauss convened a cross-functional task force, called the South Africa Policy Group, made up of Levi Strauss' managers worldwide and included people from marketing, operations, finance and community affairs.

The group met over several months for one or two days at a time, and in between, members researched specific issues and reported back to the group. It researched the history of apartheid and the movement of businesses in the country – who decided to leave and who decided to stay. It identified the principal interests and who the different stakeholders were, including the anti-apartheid community that would be affected by Levi Strauss' decision. The task force sent several key members to South Africa to conduct site visits and interviewed the ANC, members of the current government and members of community organizations. Finally, it talked with other multinational corporations already doing business in the country.

All of this took place as South Africa was going through the changes that eventually led to its free elections. The task force was able to make a recommendation to the company: that when certain conditions changed – including free elections – it would be the appropriate time for Levi Strauss to enter South Africa.

Such an inclusive information-gathering process allowed the company to make an informed decision that was based on its principles. It was able to create milestones so the company could judge the most appropriate time.

Since free elections were held, Levi Strauss South Africa opened both marketing and production facilities, including a multiracial, multicultural management team. The business also maintains an active corporate social investment program, which includes charitable contributions to the community – so it can be part of helping the country grow through the transition.

APPRISE YOUR BUSINESS PARTNERS OF YOUR STANDARDS

Levi Strauss also has global sourcing and operating guidelines that address workplace issues. The company uses these guidelines to select business partners who will manufacture its products. Established in 1992, its guidelines were the first created by a multinational company for its business partners. The terms of engagement detail everything from environmental requirements to health and safety issues. Among them: wages, discrimination, child labor and forced- or prison-labor issues. To create these guidelines, the company used the Principled Reasoning Approach. And to launch them, it conducted audits of contractors it was using worldwide.

Implementing the guidelines, Levi Strauss discovered that in Bangladesh, it had two contractors using workers in the factories who appeared to be underage. International standards have set a reasonable working age at 14. When the company brought it to the attention of the factory owners, the owners asked the company what it wanted the factory to do. There were no birth certificates so there was no way to know exactly how old these children were. Also, even if the children were younger than 14, they would very likely be a significant contributor to the family income and probably would be forced into other ways of making a living that would be more inhumane than working in a factory – such as prostitution or begging.

"So, we were faced on the one hand with a set of principles that were very clear, and on the other with the reality of underage workers and severely impacting their family incomes," says Woo. The solution? "The contractor agreed not to hire any more underage workers," he says. They also hired a physician to examine children who seemed to be less than 14 years old using growth charts identified by the World Health Organization. Although not hiring young workers may force them to find work elsewhere, Levi Strauss' position is to be ethically responsible for business issues it can control – such as responsible child labor conditions – as opposed to social conditions in a country that it has no control over.

Levi Strauss also negotiated for the contractors to remove the under-14 workers they already had from the production line and continue to pay them wages as if they were still working. In exchange, Levi Strauss covered the cost of the children's uniforms, tuition and books so they could go to school. When the underage workers reach the age of 14, they will be offered back their original factory jobs. The contractors complied with all this, "to maintain the contracts with us," says Woo.

As a result of the company's guidelines, the organization has made an impact on suppliers around the globe. It has brought about shorter work hours, seen infrastructures reinforced for better health and safety, seen fire extinguishers and fire exits put into workplaces, and seen contractors install equipment to meet environmental guidelines.

TRANSLATE ETHICAL BEHAVIOR INTO PERFORMANCE

Once guidelines such as Levi Strauss' are in place, it's crucial to reinforce principles and ethical actions. Honeywell encourages its business units to use its code as part of their performance evaluations. Levi Strauss includes ethical practices as part of its professional evaluation. In other words, it ties compensation to performance, which includes ethics. Employee's annual performance review includes questions about ethical dilemmas.

Accountability for the company's code of ethics counts at H.B. Fuller, also. The organization identifies people within the business who are in positions that could be subjected to difficult moral decisions. In addition to being sure these employees understand the code of conduct, they receive an "audit" in which they're asked about anyone who has done something that in their view might be questionable. "We communicate that it's really number one in importance," Andersen explains.

Despite its importance, ethics often fall by the wayside because companies aren't clear on what they consider right and wrong. "It's a difficult thing – to understand what's the bedrock that defines your company and the way you operate, while keeping an open mind and trying to learn business practices in other countries," says Buckley. "How do you make the trade off?"

You have to really think about it. Be open-minded. Learn. And be prepared to take the hard stand. "At some point you're going to come up with the decision of not pursuing a piece of business because it violates your values. It could be labor practices or environmental concerns or corrupt payments. It could be that you realize you can't do business while maintaining a diverse work force and that violates your principles."

Hoffman calls it the *child test*. "If the action gives you any pause – and you can't imagine explaining it to your child – then it's probably a good thing to stop, look and listen before crossing the track."

In any case, managers in multinational companies who are confronted with these situations have to think through their own ethics. It's more than a delicate balance; it's a critical balancing act.

Chapter 32

Diversity Stress as Morality Stress

Rae André

- Deciding whom to appoint to a challenging new position in Europe, a manager passes over an Asian employee and gives the job to a white male. He worries that there may be some prejudice in his own judgment.
- Because she wants to see more minorities in visible positions, a manager promotes a slightly less qualified minority candidate over a majority candidate, all the while feeling guilty.
- A male manager hesitates to hug a longtime employee who has just lost her mother.

Worry . . . guilt . . . indecision: These are the symptoms of managers under stress. All of the managers above are facing situations in which their usual modes of coping are not sufficient. Earlier in the careers of these managers, issues concerning multicultural inter-action were pretty much in the background. At one time the manager who today passes over his Asian employee would not have had an Asian – or, in fact, any minority em-ployee – to consider for the position. In that less complicated era, a manager's first concern was to take decisive action, not to spend time puzzling over the subtleties of race relations; a manager was reasonably clear about the goal of promoting the best qualified individual no matter what; a man could touch a woman in a nurturing manner without fear of being inappropriate. However, today the climate in the workplace has changed, and issues of race and gender, indeed of multiculturalism, are in the foreground of many decisions. This new climate at work creates uncertainties and stresses for both managers and employees.

Of course, all of managerial life entails some stress, classically defined as "[the] per-ceived substantial imbalance between demands and response capability, under conditions where failure to meet demands has important perceived consequences" (McGrath, 1970). Time stress, role stress, career stress, and interpersonal stress are all common examples. Today, in addition, people find themselves placed increasingly under a previously uniden-tified form of stress: the discomfort they feel when they face a situation in which, because of the presence of multicultural factors, their usual modes of coping are insufficient. This form of stress can be called "diversity stress."

Diversity stress exists wherever cultures clash: in mixed race settings, in settings where women work alongside men, in companies which employ an international work force. In fact, diversity stress can exist in any situation where beliefs and values differ. Diversity stress can be fleeting and relatively mild. For example, one manager interviewed for this study noted that he was asked to train a Palestinian from Saudi Arabia, and, being Jewish, he was uncomfortable letting on in any way his identity or political beliefs. He got through the week without saying anything, and everything went well. However, diversity stress can also be chronic and severe. As one woman manager put it, "I work in a Japanese company. When I travel to Japan, which is many times a year, the work day extends into the night and the nightclubs. I am terribly uncomfortable with the explicit sex there, but I fear that my job is in jeopardy if I don't socialize."

Diversity stress is a type of morality stress (see Waters and Bird, 1987). Morality stress occurs when managerial decisions are shrouded in ambiguity and competing moral principles, and people are uncertain how to behave. Often, managers are apprehensive about the consequences of their actions. Contemplating their alternatives under a situation in which moral issues are involved and there is no clear path to resolution, they experience morality stress which is exacerbated by the manager's organizational role. "Left largely alone with the burden of making choices and acting in everyday situations which have a moral dimension, a manager must try to achieve the best results for the organization economically while responding to the moral imperative which often calls for a more subtle redefinition of what is the best result for the organization" (Waters and Bird, 1987, p. 17).

Diversity stress frequently results from managerial decision-making under multicultural conditions involving ambiguity and competing moral principles. The Jew asked to train the Palestinian experiences a clash of values – his own personal beliefs and desire to express them, versus the need to maintain a collegial climate in his company – and he must choose which is "right." The woman who faces sex shows in Japan feels that she must choose between her own moral values and her job.

When managing a multicultural work force, managers face several common moral dilemmas that have been detailed by Waters and Bird (1987). One such dilemma is the need to show special consideration for special circumstances while at the same time treating people fairly and impartially. A typical example is the dilemmas which arise because of holding meetings after standard business hours. Often such meetings are business necessities. Yet, people with children may not be able to attend, while other members of their work group do. Inequities of rewards and of opportunities are often the result.

Another moral dilemma is the need to deceive and the need to tell the truth. For instance, under circumstances in which they are required to fill a job with a woman or minority, managers often feel that they must tell the new job holder that they were the best person for the job.

Finally, managers face the moral dilemmas inherent in the need to compete aggressively while competing within standards of fair competition. In the competition to attract the best employees and to meet governmental standards, for example, being racially "correct" is one way to come out ahead. In one company this dilemma surfaced in the following situation: A Spanish-speaking employee from South America was tapped by the company Personnel Manager to do some translating. A few weeks later the company's payroll manager informed the employee that she had been requested to change the employee's race classification in their system from White to Hispanic. The employee questioned whether the company was just trying to make a quota, and was personally uncomfortable with the change: "Just because I am Spanish-speaking does not mean I am Hispanic, does it?"

Certainly, today the culture of business has evolved to the point where many managers now recognize diversity issues in their everyday decisions. Managers working in modern multicultural work environments must weigh competing demands under circumstances in which there is no obvious resolution. They are often uncertain about what behaviors are appropriate in what circumstances. They feel a moral obligation to act in accord with some moral standard, yet are not always clear about what that standard is. In any particular situation, they may not be clear whether their own moral standard or that of the company should take precedence. Furthermore, managers may not be comfortable seeking out others to discuss either the particular situation or the moral standard. In many companies it is difficult to raise moral issues at all.

DIVERSITY AS A STRESSOR

Diversity stress is the experience of ambiguity or uncertainty because one lacks the ability, knowledge or social support to interpret correctly and act properly in a multicultural situation. Diversity stress is similar to culture shock in that experiencing a culture different from one's own is a key factor. If an individual enters a company that has a culture different from his or her own culture, she or he will experience culture shock initially, and continually, until she or he learns the new culture and finds an appropriate alignment of their own cultural values and the new cultural values. However, diversity stress differs from culture shock in important ways (Torbiörn, 1982). First, people do not need to leave their own culture to experience diversity stress: the cultural differences often come to them, in the form of new types of employees, co-workers, or customers. A person who deliberately enters another culture is more likely to anticipate culture shock and to learn how to cope with it, while the person under diversity stress is less likely to be aware of the problem. Furthermore, he or she is less likely to be able to label the problem, and to own it, in part because the concept of diversity stress has not been popularized. Under diversity stress, cultural differences may represent many cultures, too, not just one. A person must adjust not only to one new culture, but to a continuous array of cultures, to multiculturalism itself.

For both research and applied purposes it is useful to think of diversity stress as a social process. Stressors, which are defined as objective social conditions conducive to stress, increase the perception of stress and lead to the short-term and enduring physiological, affective/cognitive, and behavioral responses to stress (House, 1981; Levi 1981). All of these reactions can be affected by conditioning variables (see figure 32.1).

The objective social conditions conducive to diversity stress include exclusion, harassment, role conflict, and role ambiguity.

For instance, exclusion from the normal social and task-oriented functioning of the work group has long been a concern for minorities. As one female engineer interviewed for this study put it, "I was the only female with six middle-aged men. They didn't think I was qualified because I was a woman and they offered me no assistance. I was never included in group discussions or social activities. I had no place in the men's group. I attempted to be friendly but I realized quickly that all I would get is a short answer.

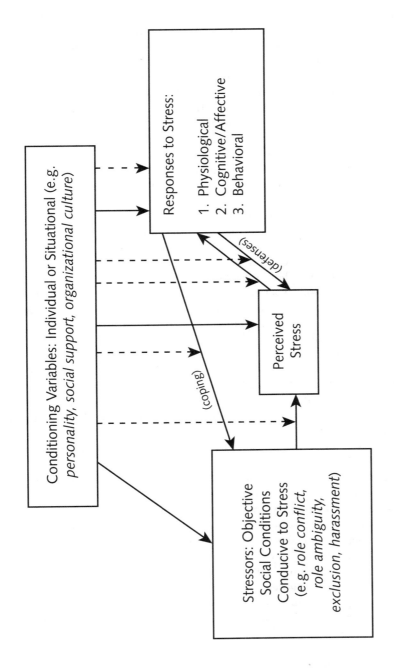

Figure 32.1 A Paradigm of Stress Research

Note. Solid arrows between boxes indicate presumed causal relationships among variables. Dotted arrows from the boxes labeled "conditioning variable" intersect solid arrows, indicating an interaction between the conditioning variables in the box at the beginning of the solid arrow in predicting variables in the box at the head of the solid arrow.

Source. Adapted from House, 1981.

The figure contains the following boxes and labels:

Conditioning Variables: Individual or Situational (e.g. *personality, social support, organizational culture*)

Responses to Stress:

1. Physiological
2. Cognitive/Affective
3. Behavioral

(defenses)

Perceived Stress

(coping)

Stressors: Objective Social Conditions Conducive to Stress (e.g. *role conflict, role ambiguity, exclusion, harassment*)

Integration was impossible and the job became unbearable. I eventually went to another company where women were equals." Harassing actions and statements against an individual because of their differences are also stressors. A man says, "My boss was a woman and was very verbal about the opportunities for women to advance in my company. I have often felt she gave much more attention to the women in the office than the men."

Often diversity stress involves role conflict, the simultaneous occurrence of two or more role expectations such that complying with one would make compliance with the other more difficult (Katz and Kahn, 1978, p. 204). In other words, an individual is torn between acting in one role versus acting in another: "Should I act as a manager in this situation, or as a friend?" "Should I act as a colleague, or as a woman?" Diversity stress may involve making complicated moral judgments which require the weighing of such factors as company culture, one's own status, and loyalty to one's own heritage. As one manager put it, "I am half Jewish on my father's side. Very often someone will make a comment about Jews and I am always faced with the decision of speaking up or not." A related problem is that an individual has trouble deciding how to respond to another person who seems to be acting out of role: "My manager, a woman, broke down several times while we were meeting one on one. It was very difficult for me to figure out what to do. I wanted to hug her (I know her well) but there was still an element of awkwardness. I ended up consoling her without hugging."

At times too a manager will experience the stress of role ambiguity, which is the uncertainty about what the occupant of a particular office is supposed to do (Katz and Kahn, 1978, p. 206): The manager may wonder, "Is managing diversity really my job, or is it a personnel staff and affirmative action issue?" or "Is it the job of the minority individual to try to fit in here? Or is it my job to make it comfortable for them?"

Of course, sometimes stressful situations occur simply because of role misperception: "During my first few months on the job, I was in a meeting with my manager and an operations manager. The operations manager, from Germany, turned to me at the end of the meeting and asked that I distribute the minutes of the meeting. He automatically assumed I was the secretary. It didn't take him too long to find out I was not the secretary, but the group's financial analyst. Now he seeks my financial advice for his $10 million project."

An individual's reaction to these stressors is a function of numerous conditioning variables. An individual's multicultural experiences, for example, would be expected to mitigate their diversity stress. Personality traits such as authoritarianism, dogmatism, and tolerance for ambiguity, are probably related to perceived diversity stress and its outcomes. Patterns of group membership, such as whether one is a member of the dominant coalition (majority) or the minority, and the relative power of these groups, are significant factors as well. Finally, organizational culture is a conditioning variable that is especially pertinent to diversity stress and morality stress.

Diversity stress is a product of the cultural environment in which the individual acts. In diversity stress situations the individual's social context is especially important in part because of the collective nature of moral judgment: To make a "right" or "wrong" decision is qualitatively different from a "go" or "no go" decision. "Am I doing the right thing?" is quite a different question for the individual than "Should I be doing this much work?" because the social context must be considered. A related issue is that often one's own stress is compounded by the fact that one may also be the cause of diversity stress in another person (because one has made the wrong cultural decision). Finally, an additional issue of social context is that one may be punished socially for making the wrong cultural decision.

A key factor in diversity stress is the moral standard by which an individual makes judgments. A moral standard derives in large part from a collective view of what is right. In American society the moral standard is constantly in flux. In particular, in business today moral standards regarding multiculturalism are changing and evolving quite rapidly. For example, managers who have lived by the standard that they should treat employees equally and uniformly are now finding that standard called into question. To understand the diversity stress experienced by managers today, it is important to know how the moral standard has changed during their careers.

UNDERSTANDING THE NEW PARADIGMS

Today's new multicultural paradigms represent profound shifts in the moral standard for human resources management. These paradigms are new moral imperatives for managers. Although certainly these paradigms have not been adopted by every company, they are the norm in companies which seem to be setting the standard of excellence for the future. Several of the most important paradigm changes are described below.

(1) Individual human differences based on diversity characteristics such as race, gender, and sexual preference should be recognized, even valued, in the workplace.

The older paradigm is that the only individual differences that should be recognized in the workplace are differences of skills and abilities. Managers have been encouraged to think of everyone as the same. Indeed, until recently many organizations have endorsed managerial homogeneity as essential to establishing effective teamwork. Many managers have been trained to overlook other differences as not central to the organizational mission. Traditionally they have seen diversity characteristics as of personal rather than managerial concern. The change in this paradigm today is actually visible in the workplace: When first they entered the work force in large numbers in the early Seventies, women wore mannish suits and sported a feminine version of ties. They were advised to blend in with the male culture. Today women wear a greater variety of clothing on the job. They no longer seek to blend in, and indeed often use clothing to distinguish themselves. More substantively, the change is apparent in corporations that value diversity by deliberately pointing it out, by using it as a factor in decision-making, and by celebrating it. Heterogeneity is the new value.

(2) People should be treated equitably but not uniformly.

For many years managers have believed that the best way to treat people equitably is to treat them uniformly. Certainly, uniformity of treatment has had many advantages for management. It has protected them from complaints (both personal and legal), and it has simplified benefits plans and record keeping. Now the paradigm is shifting towards a more ambiguous standard. Managers must ask "How really do you treat people equitably but not uniformly?" Solutions like instituting cafeteria benefits plans are being created and shared.

(3) Rewards for leadership should be reconsidered, given that there are many ways to lead a team, and many ways to contribute to a team, all of which should be valued by the organization.

New theories of multiculturalism encourage managers to reconsider traditional notions of leadership and teamwork. Despite what managers themselves may have been taught, no

longer is the aggressive leader considered necessarily to be the best leader. Now consideration, interpersonal support, team building, and solution-oriented negotiation skills are all
valued. In addition, no longer is the most important contribution to teamwork necessarily
directing the team. Other valued approaches include being a fully participative leader,
being a contributor, sharing the leadership based on differing skills, and developing team
members by encouraging their involvement. The new paradigm challenges the old paradigm of leadership that developed based on male European tradition, and suggests that
other traditions are also valuable.

COUNTERPRODUCTIVE REACTIONS TO DIVERSITY STRESS

Under conditions of morality stress people will exhibit a set of typical counterproductive
reactions (Waters and Bird, 1987). A manager's first instinct is to try to control the
situation, even though they do not really understand it. This is sometimes a form of
avoidance. For example, one counterproductive reaction is that managers adopt current
fads and fashions as a means to solve the problem. Knowing their people are experiencing diversity stress, managers send them for increasingly popular diversity training, yet
they seldom talk about diversity back in the workplace, and they do not set up processes
for discussing real issues.

A second counterproductive approach is to adhere to narrow directives and rules. A
company in which people are experiencing extensive diversity stress may reemphasize
affirmative action guidelines, and point out sexual harassment guidelines, while ignoring
human pain, moral issues, emotions and other ambiguities that managers face in interpersonal relations on a regular basis.

A third reaction is that individuals complain about others to distract potential critics
from their own problems. One racial or gender group may complain about another, or
the victim of cultural mismanagement will be blamed.

Finally, managers may attempt to redefine moral issues into amoral matters of technique or ordinary practice. For example, instead of dealing with the moral issues posed by
having one female staff member in a group of males (whose responsibility is it to assimi-
late her into the group? What do we do if she feels excluded?), a manager might reason:
"We are looking for a team player in this position, and X doesn't fit in," or "We want
aggressive management here; she just doesn't have what it takes."

PRODUCTIVE REACTIONS TO DIVERSITY STRESS

In general, productive reactions to diversity stress can be divided into three categories:
physiological, cognitive/affective, and social support. The physical element has been dealt
with extensively elsewhere (Brown, 1978; Friedman and Rosenman, 1974; Greenberg,
1990). Here we will consider the other approaches.

In terms of the likely cognitive coping reactions that will be useful for dealing with
diversity stress, self-knowledge is key. One implication of this for managers is that discussing the paradigm shifts should be a prerequisite to discussion of particular cases. Unless
some common understandings, if not agreements, exist about basic moral issues, it is
unlikely that specific cases will be handled well.

Individuals also need to know what personality traits they exhibit that are related to diversity stress. Typically stress sufferers are advised to determine whether they have hostile Type A personality traits. Personality traits suggesting high diversity stress could be a tendency towards authoritarianism and dogmatism, and an intolerance for ambiguity. For their part, researchers should investigate whether there is a Type A analog for people who would be particularly susceptible to both morality stress and diversity stress. Another implication along the cognitive/affective dimension is that individuals need to understand whether they are themselves uni-cultural or multicultural. They need to evaluate themselves in terms of their own life experience: Do they, based on their own personal contacts, understand other ethnic groups? Based on their own first hand knowledge, do they recognize gender and other diversity differences? How comfortable are they with such differences? When they lack direct experience with other cultures, individuals can still assess whether they are intellectually predisposed to being multicultural. They can know who they themselves are culturally, and, therefore, what assumptions they are likely to make about other cultures. For example, what would their own cultural upbringing suggest is the right thing to do in a given situation . . . and is this really "right"? Which culture, if any, has the proper moral standard for making a diversity judgment? Can they live with implementation of someone else's moral judgment?

Social support has been extensively researched as a coping mechanism for stress (see House, 1981). However, social support in a multicultural setting suggests some new issues. Typically one seeks social support from a like-minded peer, a person or persons one can trust and feel comfortable with. In a multicultural setting an individual would be likely to turn to someone with whom they typically cluster − a woman would go to a woman, a man to a man, an Asian to an Asian. This has many implications for the diversity climate of the organization. If stress is high and people turn to individuals most like themselves for support, they will exacerbate the diversity conflicts. They will also lose the opportunity to have input from other groups, thus developing a relatively narrow range of solutions. Were the stress merely individual, this variable might be manageable, but where the stress is explicitly diversity stress and has moral overtones, isolating solutions must be detrimental to the organizational culture as a whole. Given the problem, for example, of whether to call an individual "Black" or "African American," one could go to one's own culture, or to a particular individual, or to a multicultural group, and find different answers in each place. Each approach would have its advantages and disadvantages. Certainly when managers seek multicultural rather than uni-cultural approaches to diversity problems, they must manage the interaction of the normal human tendency to cluster and the need for social support.

Related to the need for social support is the need to establish an organizational culture that is skilled in interpersonal processes. In their article on morality stress Waters and Bird suggest ways in which the moral dimension of an organization's culture can be effectively managed. They assert, ". . . Requisite clarity and feelings of obligation with respect to moral standards derive ultimately from public discussion of moral issues within organizations and from shared public agreement about appropriate behavior" (Waters and Bird, 1987, p. 15). This suggests that diversity stress can be reduced in companies where cultural issues have been fully discussed and standards are well understood. At the same time, managers need to recognize that, human psychology being as what it is, the need to continually manage diversity stress within any organizational culture is a given.

Broadly speaking, there are two ways that organizations will deal with diversity stress in their cultures. One is to develop a power culture in which one group dominates and all others are subject to it. In this organization, ambiguities will be ignored. Homogeneity will be the main value. All diverse cultures will be subordinated to one "common" culture.

The alternative mode is to develop a consensual organization based on the diversity of cultures represented. In such an organization, valuing cultural differences is the moral imperative. In this organization the effective individual will be educated about multicultural influences and will be able to monitor their own reactions to diversity stress with some objectivity. Both individuals and management will be sensitive to issues of clustering. The organization itself will strive to resolve ambiguities around values.

Finally, trust is essential to establishing a culture that manages diversity. To cite the most obvious pitfall, many diversity questions fall within the purview of legal constraints. Managers realistically wonder whether they can talk about diversity issues – about prejudice, for example, or about appropriate and inappropriate touching in the workplace, or about the morality of affirmative action – without fear of being sued for insensitive comments. Interventions by managers to create a culture that values diversity will require a significant level of trust.

CONCLUSION

As the workplace becomes more multicultural and more multinational, we can expect diversity stress to increase. It is essential that managers understand the individual and organizational implications of the new stresses that will be placed upon them and upon their employees. These implications have a significant moral component, suggesting the need for improving organizational processes for managing morality stress.

References

Brown, B.: 1978, *Stress and the Art of Biofeedback* (Bantam, New York).

Friedman, M. and Rosenman, R.: 1974, *Type A Behavior and Your Heart* (Fawcett Crest, New York).

Greenberg, J.S.: 1990, *Comprehensive Stress Management* (William C. Brown, New York).

House, J.: 1981, *Work Stress and Social Support* (Addison-Wesley Publishing Co., Reading, MA).

Katz, D. and Kahn R.L.: 1978, *The Social Psychology of Organizations* (John Wiley & Sons, New York).

Levi, L.: 1981, *Preventing Work Stress* (Addison-Wesley Publishing Co., Reading, MA).

McGrath, J.E., ed.: 1970, *Social and Psychological Factors in Stress* (Holt, Rinehard & Winston, New York).

Torbiörn, I.: 1982, *Living Abroad: Personal Adjustment and Personnel Policy in the Overseas Setting* (John Wiley & Sons, New York).

Waters, J.A. and Bird, F.: 1987, "The Moral Dimension of Organizational Culture," *Journal of Business Ethics* **6**, 15–22.

Chapter 33

Remote Control

Neil Merrick

Thanks to information technology, building a team has never been simpler. By using e-mail, video conferencing and satellite links, employees on different sides of the world can communicate with each other and possibly never meet face to face.

There is little doubt that the arrival of the "virtual team", born out of the increasing globalisation of business and more flexible working practices, is an exciting development for many companies. Yet before too many employees settle down in front of their computer screens and relish the chance to work harmoniously without having to look their colleagues in the eye, personnel professionals are being warned about the potential pitfalls of completely eliminating the human touch.

Virtual teams are most likely to exist in multinational companies that need to overcome large geographical barriers. But UK organisations whose employees work from home or are regularly away from the office are also searching for solutions to team-building problems.

Christine Debougnoux, HR development adviser for Arco Chemical Europe, says that the firm's teamworking has changed considerably during the past few years. Whereas members of a team or project group mostly used to work from the same department or office, they are often now spread out across Europe and even the world. "You have to remember to keep [individual members] in the loop or within the team," she says. "There are a large number of ad hoc teams that change during a project."

Digital Equipment encourages its people to make maximum use of the computers and telecommunications products that it makes. Teleworking has become considerably more common within the firm in the past few years, necessitating regular communication via e-mail. Video conferences frequently replace face-to-face meetings.

"Our people are very flexible," says Jill Hearst, Digital's management development consultant. "Virtual teambuilding has been talked about here for several years, and it is something we are getting quite good at."

Wherever people are working, and whatever their role in an organisation, there will always be occasions when they are required to communicate with colleagues. Alison Hardingham, director of consultancy services at Interactive Skills, a firm of business psychologists, says there are certain "shared purposes" that can only be achieved through collaboration and mutual discussion.

Telecommunications may help to overcome the problems caused by distance, but Hardingham warns of the dangers of becoming too reliant upon technology. Discontented employees who communicate mainly by e-mail can sometimes allow their frustrations to run away with them. On one occasion, Interactive Skills was called into a company where two employees had engaged in a bout of "e-mail zapping". Not content with sending rude messages to one another, they copied them to their respective managers as well.

"Just as face-to-face meetings are sensitive situations that require structure, you must have agreed procedures for communicating via e-mail," Hardingham says. "It may appear informal, but it must not be used thoughtlessly. Otherwise, with a single press of a button, a person can wreak organisational havoc."

Roy Harrison, the IPD's training and development policy adviser, believes the main question surrounding virtual teams is how to encourage positive interaction without face-to-face contact. "Technology allows people to keep in touch, but where do you get the 'soul' from?" he says.

Digital tries to recruit employees with good communication skills, and those who are able to establish themselves in teams with a minimum of direction from above. According to Hearst, members of a virtual team must be well educated and require above-average networking skills. The company is experimenting with personal desktop video conferencing facilities in an attempt [to] gauge the importance of face-to-face meetings. But the feeling at Digital is that technology can only ever support virtual team-building and cannot replace human contact.

Language and cultural barriers, which can be problems during traditional meetings, may become a particular headache when virtual team members are in different countries. "People leave the meeting room thinking that they have an agreement and start acting on it; while others will go back home, test it out and come back with feedback," Debougnoux says.

Arco has developed training activities to encourage team-building among employees who may otherwise rarely meet one another. At one workshop, group members had to decide how to prevent an egg, which was hanging from the ceiling, from crashing to the floor. They were given 30 minutes to build an egg-saving construction out of furniture and other materials.

In spite of the firm's regular use of video conferencing, Debougnoux believes that employees still miss the opportunity of face-to-face contact. "You lose the physical vibrations. Sometimes, during a video conference, you feel that people are acting."

There is also the problem of interruptions. For this reason Arco advises its employees to set aside a reasonable amount of time for such meetings and, if possible, to move to a different room from the one that they normally work in.

The British Council, which employs 6,000 people in 109 countries, uses e-mail to maintain contact with its various outposts. But the opportunity to develop 10 technology-based teams overseas only came about after a series of face-to-face workshops based in the UK.

The Council, which is partly government-funded, has responsibility for a range of cultural exchange programmes, language teaching and training consultancy work. Edmund Marsden, its assistant director-general, and his colleagues in the UK must ensure that its staff are working towards corporate goals even though they are based all over the world.

"The problem is: how do you weld together people who have been fiercely independent, and who had a degree of latitude, so that they develop activities in line with the corporate agenda?" he says.

Team-building does not consist solely of directors working with their own staff or counterparts in other countries. They are also required to keep in touch with managers and other professionals in the UK. Three years ago the Council appointed 10 managers to take charge of a series of regional teams. One team, for example, consisted of directors from the tiger economy countries of East Asia. "They welded together their team in whatever way they felt was most appropriate," Marsden says. "We gave them guidelines, but we were not prescriptive."

The Council spent more than £250,000 on a series of week-long workshops in the UK, followed by two-day road shows for employees in each country. Having established initial contact, the objective now is to maintain momentum when many employees will not meet again in the flesh for up to two years – if at all.

According to Marsden, staff had developed strong regional identities. This led to a series of virtual teams being set up across national boundaries to look at issues such as sexual equality, management training and the overseas sale of national vocational qualifications.

Most communication takes place using e-mail, because video conferencing is not available outside the UK. "We are ensuring that we are effectively wired up," Marsden says. "We still use face-to-face encounters for important messages, but technology has made it possible for us to be more selective."

Alison Hardingham agrees that companies should not become too reliant on technology where it is possible for employees to meet in the same place. "The amount of information you can exchange in face-to-face meetings is huge," she says. "They are multidimensional compared with technological communication."

Hardingham does not know of an example where an organisation has built and sustained a team of employees entirely through technology, but speculates whether it might be an exciting experiment waiting to take place.

"It is bound to be harder to manage problems through an information technology environment," she says. "People may be seduced into thinking they can communicate entirely through IT, and that all the nasty little problems and group dynamics won't impinge, but what they will find is that they impinge in spades."

Chapter 34

Should HR Survive? A Profession at the Crossroads

Anthony J. Rucci

INTRODUCTION

Much has been written and heralded over the past few years regarding the Human Resource (HR) profession having achieved strategic partner status in major organizations. If one presses the issue with objective practitioners off-the-record, however, most will admit that the profession is at a perilous crossroads – that the next ten years will spell either the demise or ascendancy of the profession. The formula for demise typically involves a failure to understand business clients, failing to adapt approaches to the new global competitive demands or pursuing an HR agenda rather than an organizational effectiveness agenda. Ascendancy forecasts suggest that HR will not only survive, but will increase its influence by advancing the progress HR has begun to make in many organizations toward creating a competitive advantage through innovative people practices.

"Will HR survive?" It's the wrong question to ask. The more appropriate strategic question is, "Should HR survive?" HR's focus should not be on surviving or strengthening its status. Instead, HR should begin today to take actions which will eventually eliminate itself in major organizations. The issue to consider is not demise versus ascendancy, but rather demise under what circumstances. HR has spent far too much time worrying about how to strengthen itself instead of how to strengthen organizational effectiveness. The clearest illustration is the often repeated reference by HR practitioners on the "need for a strategic plan for HR." The more appropriate focus should be on the "need for a strategic HR plan for the organization."

ELIMINATION OF HR – TWO SCENARIOS

I suggest two scenarios, both leading to the eventual elimination of the HR profession inside organizations over the next ten years. One scenario eliminates HR's role because we as a profession have failed. The second scenario eliminates HR's role because we have been successful in inculcating the profession's skill-set and, more importantly, mindset into our organizations and managers. Under one scenario, HR loses control and influence; under the other scenario HR makes itself obsolete in the best interest of the organization.

The worst-case scenario is obsolescence caused by failure. This scenario involves HR being dismantled by management because the profession is ineffective in adding real value. The predictors of the worst-case scenario involve a profession and practitioners who:

- don't promote change,
- don't identify leaders,
- don't understand business,
- don't know customers,
- don't drive costs, and
- don't emphasize values.

The best-case scenario leading to HR's planned obsolescence involves HR professionals who:

- create change,
- develop principled leaders,
- promote economic literacy,
- center on the customer,
- maximize services and minimize staff, and
- steward values.

Again, the milestone of HR's effectiveness will not be its ability to survive and do these things for the organization, but rather its ability to transfer these into the responsibilities and accountabilities of managers at all levels.

Create change

The greatest competitive challenge faced by United States (US) organizations today is speed. The very survival of entire industries and seemingly solid companies becomes challenged, sometimes overnight, by the introduction of a new technology or a virulent new competitor. Only those organizations who have stayed close to their customer and are constantly vigilant to competitive challenges have weathered a difficult twenty-year period in which most US industries have seen their share of world markets decline.

Even this characterization implies an after-the-fact strategy – wait to see what the customer says or wait to see what the competition does and then react quickly and change appropriately. Organizations in the US have been sporadically effective in reacting with speed and even less effective in initiating change and introducing it with speed. There is an increasing competitive premium on creating change, not just managing change.

What are the implications to the HR profession of the need for organizational speed and creating change? First of all, organizations have historically been based on a management model built as the antithesis of speed. The control and standardization emphasis in manufacturing, which became the competitive hallmark of the US post-Industrial-Revolution period of the early 1900s, crept its way into the people and organizational management practices of organizations. The organizational model of "Plan, Organize, Motivate, and Control" was a management-science mantra as recently as ten years ago. HR was unfortunately too effective in adapting to this model: job descriptions, job grades, policy manuals, and a host of other examples speak to a compliance mentality adopted to promote standardization. Worse still, the one-size-fits-all emphasis in the profession spilled over into the advice and counsel HR provided line management. The standardization of HR prevented the development of an organizational capability of flexibility, speed, and risk-taking.

HR's survival will be threatened to the extent that it insists on retaining the vestiges of the manufacturing era, rather than on meeting the new requirements of a service era. Eventually, HR will be forced to do so by its management and its customers. More proactively, HR should voluntarily reassess its infrastructure and eliminate unnecessary rules and systems thereby emphasizing the need for individual judgment and accountability by managers. This reassessment can be a powerful catalyst toward enabling organizational speed, creating change, and encouraging risk-taking.

HR can provide a constructive influence by creating policy architecture and designs which are consistent with and supportive of the organization's strategic goals, but not being so prescriptive in those designs as to inhibit creativity and business flexibility.

HR can help create powerful change by providing opportunities for the organization to identify its weaknesses, and then facilitate organizational efforts to improve in those areas. Even more proactively, HR can provide leadership in facilitating efforts to help the organization envision a world class future state and organize efforts and measures designed to achieve that standard.

Develop principled leaders

A true limitation in major organizations today is the scarcity of leadership talent. Rarer still are the leaders who ground themselves in a base of moral or ethical principles that are nonnegotiable and which do not "flex" to each new situation. The operative word here is "principled." Principled leaders are those who are role models in behavioral ethics and who demonstrate a courage of conviction regarding values as well as business performance. Such individuals can and do exist at all levels in organizations, not just at top management levels. In fact, depth of principled leadership at all levels is a hallmark of excellent organizations and suggests that senior management has made principled behavior a requirement for selection and promotion decisions.

HR has a key role to play here. Selection, promotion, and performance management techniques must result in the advancement of individuals who display courage of conviction, a willingness to listen and be influenced, and an unwillingness to compromise their principles. To the extent that the profession is successful in identifying these leaders today, they will select in their own likeness in the future. HR's most proactive role here will be to help the organization identify the leadership qualities necessary for success and to create simple, user-friendly ways for managers to implement those criteria in decision making.

Promote economic literacy

As a direct effect of the emphasis on organizational standardization, specialization of functions and professionals has evolved. Accompanying specialization, however, has been a narrowness of focus. As a result, the typical US employee, manager, and executives all too often do not possess a broad understanding of business, their company's competitive environment, or their company's competitive position. This is not an indictment of the US workforce; it's an indictment of managers who have failed to provide information openly to their employees; they are constricted by their own specialization.

HR must be a leader in educating the US workforce. Education and literacy is not training and development, the historic purview of HR functions. Animals are trained, but people are educated.

While HR must play a leadership role in the education process, this is yet another area where we should seek to greatly reduce the profession's direct accountability for coaching and teaching. Skills training can be designed by HR but should be delivered by subject matter experts in an area. Management education can be designed by HR but should be delivered by subject matter experts as well. Those subject matter experts are other managers or outside experts, not HR professionals. HR must think of itself as the administration of an educational institution, the deans and provosts, but not the faculty. HR should proactively move toward minimizing its role in conducting training and development, and focus on creating the necessary conditions and initiatives for self-renewing, learning organizations.

Center on the customer

The service era of today could just as accurately be labeled the era of the customer. Consumers of goods and services are more discriminating, more knowledgeable, and more demanding than ever before. Competitive price and quality have become the cost-of-entry into business. It is those companies who wrap a total customer focus around their products and services who are winning in the market place. A consumer can purchase the same brand product from a myriad of distributors at a comparable price. How convenient, reliable, quick, friendly, and knowledgeable a distributor's service is has become the measure of competitive advantage.

The implication of the era of the customer is that organizations must focus on their target customers and design their infrastructures to help the organizations meet the customer's requirements. HR must help create boundaryless organizations that permit information about and from customers to influence the work of every associate in the enterprise. HR's focus here need not be on eliminating its role, since it historically has not played a pivotal role. HR should, instead, eliminate policies and practices which prevent an external focus on the customer. In addition, HR can introduce the primacy of the customer into every aspect of management practices, by including customer orientation and customer service in performance reviews, promotion criteria, and incentive compensation plans, for example.

Maximize services/minimize staff

Just as organizations must focus on their customers, HR must focus on its customers. HR's internal customers have also become more discriminating purchasers of HR services. As evidence, note the trend toward internal shared service environments and complete outsourcing of functions and subfunctions.

Rather than viewing this trend as a threat to survival, we in HR must actively adopt a continuous "justify-our-existence" mentality. HR must identify where we do add value and eliminate those areas where we do not. We must continually look for ways to drive down costs, just as any business must and eliminate features for which the customer is unwilling to pay. In those HR areas where our skill sets do not represent a core competency of the enterprise, we should also aggressively move those activities outside.

An explicit goal of HR organizations over the next five years should be to eliminate as much of its staffing as possible. A key measure of HR's success should be how few HR professionals are on the payroll of major companies ten years from now as well as the strategic character of those HR roles which remain.

Steward the values

Companies that have excelled over the past twenty years and longer are those with strong cultures, grounded in a common understanding of a few, simple, shared beliefs. Those shared beliefs need not be formal, moralistic statements of values and ethics but rather a simple, shared understanding of what the enterprise views as inviolable principles. Given a choice between earning an expedient profit or sustaining their shared beliefs, premier organizations will safeguard their beliefs. Being profitable can indeed be a legitimate shared belief, so long as it is balanced with the other beliefs of the enterprise.

Too often HR functions and senior management have delegated to HR the role of surrogate values guardian, or worse still, the role of conscience of the organization. HR and HR professionals do not have a corner on the "values market". HR should not be the values police in our organizations nor should we seek out that role to solidify our job security. If managers require a third party such as HR to remind them of the organization's shared beliefs then they aren't "shared" beliefs anyway.

So, what is HR's role in stewarding values? Consistent with the adage of "what gets measured gets done", HR must develop measurement systems that reflect both the values goals and the financial goals of an enterprise. To the extent that HR can create measures, incentives, and rewards on non-financial measures we can further eliminate the need to police those values.

TO THE FUTURE

The implications of the organizational challenges discussed are indeed profound and are equally so for HR. To summarize, we in HR must do the following:

Create change

Eliminate HR systems and policies which inhibit speed in organizations. In the process, eliminate the HR staff necessary to administrate and audit those systems and policies. More proactively, create an opportunity for the organization to envision a world class future state and help mobilize teams to initiate actions to achieve that vision.

Develop principled leaders

Provide leadership in helping organizations define the necessary qualities to ensure the selection and development of principled leaders at all levels of the organization, but HR should not be the decision maker in selection.

Promote economic literacy

Eliminate HR's role in delivering training and education to employees, relinquishing that responsibility to subject experts and line managers. HR's contribution and professional skills should be applied to the design of effective educational techniques and to the creation of virtual universities where coaching and teaching are expected components of each manager's job.

Center on the customer

Eliminate HR policies and practices which inhibit boundaryless organizations and open communication or which promote an internal focus versus a customer-centered culture. Introduce measures into performance reviews, promotion and selection standards, and compensation incentives which evaluate and reward managers on their customer focus.

Maximize services/minimize staff

Eliminate non-value-added HR activities and outsource those HR activities which are not core competencies of the enterprise. Retain those roles which are essential to imparting cultural norms and shared beliefs. Staff HR with people interested in facilitating organizational change, not in perfecting HR competencies.

Steward the values

Extricate HR from the "values police" role and replace itself with measurement systems that incent and reward both non-financial and financial measures.

The goal of eliminating HR in organizations may appear harsh or critical but is actually quite a strategic objective. It is only by taking that perspective that the HR profession can stay ahead of the competitive pressures facing organizations today. If we in HR establish a goal to eliminate our function, our attention will turn toward ways to infuse what the profession has tried to achieve into the daily jobs of leaders and line managers. It's hard to disagree with that as being a healthy outcome for organizations.

Will the goal lead to the literal elimination of HR and its practitioners inside major organizations? Perhaps not completely, but it will certainly lead to more effective HR organizations, and it will at least prevent the eventual elimination of HR due to management frustration with its ineffectiveness.

Some HR professionals may feel threatened by the goal of eliminating or minimizing the role of HR in organizations. The greater threat is in not choosing that course of action. The profession will almost certainly come under continued challenge to its existence unless it changes to meet the new organizational needs.

If we're successful at eliminating the need for HR, what will happen to those in the profession? The business-literate, customer-focused, principled leaders among the profession should find their new roles in line management quite exciting as an opportunity to practice what the profession has preached. Those individuals who were not business-literate, customer-focused, principled leaders probably weren't effective HR professionals and change agents anyway. We in HR should be held to no lesser standard than we require of any other area in our organizations.

Ironically, eliminating the need for the HR profession and its roles may be the most effective way of demonstrating HR's value. On a visit to an outside company recently, I struck up an informal conversation with an administrative employee. She told me what she was doing in her job in checking invoice accuracy and then added that the shareholders of the company shouldn't have to pay for a job to do that function. Her goal, as she stated, was to figure out a way to eliminate the need for her job. In this era of job insecurity you can imagine my surprise at that comment. I asked her if she wasn't a little worried about the possibility of eliminating her own job. She replied quickly, "Not at all. I figure that if I'm creative enough to eliminate the need for my job, then I'm exactly the kind of employee this company will want to find another more important role for."

Should HR survive? No – at least not in its current configuration, but it should cease to exist where appropriate, for the right reasons, not the wrong ones.

Chapter 35

Cultural Diversity Programs to Prepare for Work Force 2000: What's Gone Wrong?

Norma M. Riccucci

"Cultural diversity" has become the buzzword for the 1990s. We hear less and less about equal employment opportunity and affirmative action efforts and programs, but hear more about multiculturalism, managing cultural diversity, and diversity training. The importance of the cultural diversity movement stems in large part from the predicted demographic shifts that are already underway in America's labor force. Those predictions suggested that public and private sector workforces would become more socially diverse because of shifts in the overall population. Although the initial estimates may have been overstated,[1] many public and private organizations nonetheless began to respond to those demographic projections. In particular, organizations developed and implemented an assortment of diversity training programs with the ultimate goal of remaining viable and competitive.

Now, some eight years after the various demographic forecasts were made, human resources specialists, policy makers, and researchers are beginning to look at the effectiveness of those diversity training programs. But, these assessments may be premature, given the problems that exist in the way in that organizations have developed and implemented diversity initiatives. If human resources specialists and researchers try to make definitive conclusions about the effectiveness of cultural diversity programs that are seriously flawed and distorted, they will no doubt draw unfavorable conclusions about the importance of such programs. Before any meaningful conclusions can be drawn about the efficacy of diversity programs, it may be necessary to restructure or "reinvent" those programs.

ORGANIZATIONAL RESPONSES TO CHANGING DEMOGRAPHICS

In 1987, the Hudson Institute published a report, *Work Force 2000*[2] which predicted radical shifts in the demographic make-up of the American labor force. Shortly afterwards, a number of other reports on anticipated demographic shifts in the public sector were released.[3] Organizations were implicitly or explicitly warned by these reports that

Table 35.1   Types and Perceived Effectiveness of Diversity Programs

Program/Policy	In Existence (%)	Perceived Effectiveness (%)
Sexual harassment	92.7	91.1
Physical access for disabled workers	75.8	84.9
Parental leave	56.7	73.1
Literacy training	35.1	58.4
Breaking through the glass ceiling	33.1	48.3
Redesigning jobs for older workers	27.4	43.3
Subsidized daycare	25.6	43.5
English as a second language	23.0	45.5
Mentoring for people of color	21.8	38.0
Fast-tracking for people of color	17.6	27.3
Partner benefits – gay and lesbian workers	14.9	25.9

Source: "1993 SHRM/CCH Survey," Commerce Clearing House, Inc., May 26, 1993, 1–12.

failing to embrace diversity could jeopardize their viability, profitability and competitiveness. And so, many organizations quickly responded by developing "cultural awareness" training programs and/or policies to address problems and concerns such as sexual harassment, illiteracy, and accommodations for disabled workers.

Table 35.1 provides a more detailed account of the various diversity programs that both public and private sector organizations have offered. The list is derived from a survey conducted in 1993 by the Society for Human Resource Management (SHRM) and Commerce Clearing House (CCH). The survey population is comprised of 785 human resources specialists in the public and private sectors.[4] Obviously, the list is not comprehensive, but is intended to provide an idea of the types of programs that have been developed.

The SHRM/CCH survey also found that some diversity programs and policies are perceived to be much more effective than others. For example, as table 35.1 further shows, sexual harassment policies and programs to accommodate the physical needs of disabled workers were seen as the most effective. Other diversity initiatives, such as mentoring programs for people of color, were perceived as being less effective.

While there may be some important information that can be gained from these assessments, they should be considered "mid-term," troubleshooting reports rather than definitive accounts of the efficacy of cultural diversity programs. Shortcomings in the way these programs have been conceptualized and subsequently implemented make any conclusion about the effectiveness of the programs premature.

PROBLEMS IN ORGANIZATIONAL RESPONSES TO CHANGING DEMOGRAPHICS

One of the problems that exists around organizations' efforts to prepare for workforce 2000 is that too much emphasis may be given to diversity initiatives that are driven by federal mandates. For example, as in table 35.1, sexual harassment policy and "reasonable accommodation" of disabled workers were the most popular. While these programs are certainly essential, they address only a fraction of diversity concerns and issues. Moreover, they are motivated or compelled not by a genuine concern for diversity, but rather as measures to avoid liability claims for possible discriminatory practices. In effect, other diversity efforts that are not driven by federal law (e.g., professional development programs aimed at career advancement of people of color) are not adopted. In fact, the SHRM/CCH survey shows that such programs in the form of mentoring and fast-tracking of people of color have been less popular as well as less effective (see table 35.1).

The survey also found that diversity management is a low priority when compared to other issues and concerns such as profitability and market share. Over 50 percent of the survey participants reported that diversity initiatives take a back seat to such measures as revising compensation systems, restructuring, and downsizing. Yet, as the various workforce 2000 reports suggested, diminishing the importance of diversity programs can only negatively affect profitability and market share, in the long run.

Another problem surfaces from the tendency of some organizations to simply substitute the term diversity for affirmative action and equal employment opportunity. That is to say, existing affirmative action programs become the "new" diversity initiatives. This seems to be the case for many organizations, including the federal government. A recent report, *Evolving Workforce Demographics*, conducted by the U.S. Merit Systems Protection Board,[5] said that federal agencies developed very few new diversity programs to address the demographic changes, but rather simply continued with their old affirmative action programs. Moreover, the report stated that the programs are only aimed at the recruitment of people of color, and not their promotion to higher ranks in the federal bureaucracy.[6]

While equal employment opportunity and affirmative action programs are critical to diversity efforts, particularly since they too are driven by legal mandates, successful diversity measures will require much more. In particular, diversity efforts must be integrated into a broader human resources management program aimed at recruiting, hiring, training, promoting, and developing *all* workers. Affirmative action should only be *one* ingredient of this larger program.

Another very critical problem in organizations' efforts to prepare for workforce 2000 is a failure to prepare for the backlash by white males (and their unions). Indeed, we have never progressed beyond the backlash that evolved out of the *Regents v. Bakke*[7] decision, which popularized the concept of "reverse discrimination." Once again, as we are seeing throughout the country, white males are filled with fear and anger. As a recent *Business Week* cover story entitled "White, Male and Worried" pointed out,

> Often for the first time in their lives, [white males] are worrying about their future opportunities because of widespread layoffs and corporate restructuring. Outside the corporation, white men are feeling threatened because of racial and gender tensions that have been intensifying in recent years.[8]

This fear is, in part, a new manifestation of the old backlash against affirmative action. That is, many continue to believe that diversity, just like affirmative action, will lower standards. As the *Business Week* article said, "At the heart of the issue for many white males is the question of merit – that in the rush for a more diverse workplace, they will lose out to less qualified workers."[9] This is an old argument which has little empirical foundation, yet it has been a cogent one for those opposed to affirmative action and now, diversity efforts.

Government and corporate officials did not prepare for this backlash. Perhaps they believed that the driving force behind diversity initiatives is not legal, as it is with affirmative action, but rather economic (i.e., in terms of "competitiveness" and "viability"). This leads to the belief that diversity programs and policies would be accepted unconditionally by white males, unions and even white male managers. But, as we are seeing with the nationwide assault against race- and gender-based employment programs, this has not been the case.

The backlash problem also stems from organizations' failure to address the fears of white men about the *effects* of policies and programs aimed at promoting diversity. Organizations will need to work with white males so that they understand that models of diversity are based on inclusion, not exclusion. That is, diversity programs do not seek to displace white males, but rather to prepare workers and managers to work in a heterogeneous environment, one where *everyone* can compete equally for organizational resources. So, diversity efforts will go beyond race, gender, ability, and age to cover, for example, career planning for everyone. Organizations, however, will be challenged by a dilemma – as they address the needs and concerns of white males, they must not ignore the concerns of white women and people of color who may resent efforts to win over or pamper white males.

Another part of the backlash problem has been failing to educate all workers that diversity initiatives, just like affirmative action, will not lower standards. It is time to correct those misguided assumptions that people of color, white women and other protected-class persons are unqualified for their jobs based on culturally biased indicators of performance and also culturally biased validation scales. As the US Supreme Court stated in its 1987 *Johnson v. Transportation Agency*, Santa Clara County decision, based on a brief submitted by the American Society for Personnel Administration (now SHRM), because of the subjectivity that underlies the hiring process, "there is rarely a single, 'best qualified' person for a job."[10]

Perhaps the most critical shortcoming around organizations' efforts to prepare for workforce 2000 is that many employers have not integrated their diversity initiatives into the broader, long-term goals and missions of the organization. Rather, they tend to be "one-shot" deals. For example, the SHRM/CCH survey of public and private human resources specialists revealed that over 70 percent of diversity training programs are one day or less in length. The survey concluded that this strategy results in failure.

If employers are genuinely interested in developing successful programs, they will need to change the culture of their organizations so that diversity is not just supported but valued. Managing diversity means managing cultural change, which is not just a simple program, but an initiative that will take many years. It requires incorporating diversity efforts into continuous improvement and TQM programs.[11] A key requirement is accountability, where behavior changes on the job are measured and rewarded when set diversity goals have been achieved. In effect, diversity initiatives become a standard way of doing business.

CONCLUSION

Many organizations across the country have been preparing for workforce 2000 by mounting a variety of diversity programs. Some employee populations are already so diverse that such programs are essential. But, there are a host of problems with the way in which diversity programs have been conceptualized and implemented. If organizations are truly interested in remaining competitive and viable, particularly in a global economy, they will need to reconceptualize and overhaul their diversity programs.

Notes

1   Victor Kirk, "Work for Warfare," *National Journal*, September 28, 1991: 2354–6.
2   William B. Johnston and Arnold H. Packer, *Workforce 2000*, Indianapolis, In.: Hudson Institute, June 1987.
3   See, for example, *Civil Service 2000*, Washington, DC: US Office of Personnel Management, June 1988 and *New York State Work Force Plan*, Albany, NY: New York State Department of Civil Service, 1989.
4   It should be noted that governmental agencies represented less than 10 percent of the survey population.
5   US Merit Systems Protection Board (USMSPB), *Evolving Workforce Demographics: Federal Agency Action and Reaction*, Washington, DC: USMSPB, November 1993.
6   Also see, for example, Kristi Cameron, Joan Jorgenson, and Charles Kawecki, "Civil Service 2000 Revisited," *Public Personnel Management*, Winter, 1993: 669–74.
7   *Regents v. Bakke*, 438 US 265 (1978).
8   Michele Galen, "White, Male, and Worried," *Business Week*, January 31, 1994, p. 51.
9   Ibid., p. 52.
10 *Johnson v. Transportation Agency*, Santa Clara County, 480 U.S. 624 (1987).
11 SHRM/CCH (Society for Human Resources Management/Commerce Clearing House), 1993. Commerce Clearing House, Inc., May 26, 1993: 1–12.

Chapter 36

Case: Anglo-German Trading Corporation

Kenneth E. Roberts

Dai Schmidt, General Manager of Associos des Chiles S.A., a subsidiary of the giant multinational conglomerate Anglo-German, reached into a desk drawer and pulled out his bottle of Jack Daniels. Taking a cut-glass tumbler from the same drawer, he carefully poured two fingers of whisky and settled back in his armchair to ponder his dilemma. He had spent the past two hours analyzing papers which contained details of a project with good profit potential for Associos des Chiles. Dai believed that his boss in the Cologne headquarters office would authorise the project if this was Dai's final recommendation.

The project concerned the investment of US$2 million in an old canning factory which the company owned and which was located at the southern tip of Chile, close to an area contested between Chile and Argentina. For some reason the company had not divested itself of this old plant and it continued in operation long after its useful life had expired. A young manager recently assumed responsibility for the factory and the Penguin Project was his first proposal.

Dai could not fault the financial projections. The figures showed that for an investment of US$2 million, largely for refurbishing the existing factory buildings, the company could create a turnover estimated at US$5 million within the first two years, and yielding a profit of 25 percent on turnover.

From every angle but one, the project seemed a winner. It concerned the hunting and capture of large numbers of jackass penguins which inhabited the coastline and islands of southern Chile in numbers which ran into millions. After capture the penguins were to be shipped to the factory for slaughter and processing. The meat would then be frozen and despatched to America and Europe for use in the manufacture of pet food by other companies in the Anglo-German organization. The skins of the penguins would be dried, cured and sold locally for use in the manufacture of waistcoats, handbags and footwear. First year figures suggested sales of around $1.5 million for the skins and $3.5 million for the sales of penguin meat.

Jackass penguins were among the most numerous of all penguins and so named for the noise they made when disturbed, which was like the braying of donkeys, or jackasses. Various estimates existed for the total population of these penguins. For instance, one estimate suggested between 100 to 250 million, with most of these concentrated in two areas around the southern tip of South America and on the islands of the Antarctic sub-continent.[1]

The jackass penguin was a voracious consumer of sild. These fish abound in the coastal waters of the Pacific ocean off Chile. Many of the towns and villages depended upon fishing for their livelihood and existence. In the previous decade or so fishermen had been forced to fish further and further from the coast and catches showed a significant reduction. The fishermen blamed the penguins and it was known that the penguin population had expanded during this period. What was less certain was the relationship between a growing penguin population and the reduced catches of sild.

Another reason for local support for the proposed project was that it would provide employment for about 100 Chilean workers in the refurbished factory. Little alternative work existed and all local parties were in favour of the project.

Dai Schmidt considered the detail provided by his young manager in building up the justification for the proposal. The figures estimated that around 100,000 penguins per week could be processed through the factory and expert opinion suggested that, providing only young males were caught, the overall impact on the total penguin population would be no greater than would occur through losses due to natural depletion and wastage, e.g. through disease, starvation, fighting and other natural causes.

At a recent company conference in the Bahamas, his boss had warned Dai that "he could waste away in South America" unless he came up with projects which impacted on "bottom line performance" in South America. Schmidt believed that the Penguin Project might just do that. However he was also aware that Anglo-German had recently received a bad press on environmental issues, particularly in relation to waste disposal in Europe and a major chemical spillage in Australia.

With these thoughts racing round in his head, Dai drained his second glass of Jack Daniels and began to prepare his overall recommendation on the Penguin Project for headquarters.

Notes

This case study was prepared by Kenneth E. Roberts, Staffordshire University, England, ECCH and EFMD. It is based on a real situation with disguised names and locations. This case was written as a basis for class discussion and is not intended to illustrate either the effective or ineffective handling of a management situation. Copyright K. E. Roberts 1997.

1   Penguins are classified into 18 species and 6 genera. Most are found in Antarctica and on sub-antarctic islands, while others are native to the coasts of Australia, South Africa, South America and to the Galapagos Islands. They feed on fish, cuttlefish, crustaceans and other small sea creatures and range in size from 41 cm (16 in) to the emperor penguin, which reaches 120 cm (48 in) and weighs up to 32 kg (70 lb). Penguins live in colonies or rookeries which often number hundreds of thousands and also tend to live in flocks while at sea. Apart from man, their natural enemies include killer whales, leopard seals and, for the chicks and eggs, the skua and other seabirds.

Chapter 37

Case: Novell's Global Strategy: "Bytes Are Somewhat Narcotic"

Marjorie McEntire, C. Brooklyn Derr, and Chris Meek

BACKGROUND

In less than a decade, a no-name information technology (IT) company became a world-wide presence with offices in 33 countries, employing approximately 8,500 people. From its early years, the president envisioned and directed the company as a global organization. This case describes a 17-year period (1978–1994) during which Novell grew from a small start-up company to one that would define the network computing industry.

Information technology companies are concentrated in several US geographical areas such as the Northeast's Route 128, California's Silicon Valley, Seattle's Eastside, and Utah's Wasatch Front. Examination of a medium-sized Utah-based IT company provides insight into the growth of the industry in the western US and throughout the world.

Novell, Inc., with headquarters in Provo, Utah, was incorporated on January 25, 1983. The company is the leading provider of network server operating system software that integrates desktop computers, servers, and mini-computer and mainframe hosts for business-wide information sharing. The roots of the company go back to 1978 when Novell Data, a venture capital enterprise, sold printers, hardware, and software. The company's leaders established the foundation of an international organization during those early years. According to a manager:

> There were a couple of very visionary people in the early days who saw Novell as a global company . . . They envisioned a franchise program. They went around the world and literally had this idea that they would sell the Novell Data name . . . in 1984, there were people called Novell Data in England and Germany . . . in Saudi Arabia . . . in South America, Mexico, and Venezuela. Even at that point, the company envisioned itself being global.[1]

According to a Novell executive, the company's identity has changed rapidly since its founding. The company has resembled three distinct companies: "the early start-up, where we [Novell] were nobody. And then there was the exciting expansion phase where we were somebody but we were fighting for our lives. Then there is phase three in which we are the dominant Novell networking provider." Novell's explicit mission is to accelerate the growth of the network computing industry.

Novell International Offices	Novell International Subsidiaries
Argentina	Novell de Argentina S.A.
Australia	Novell Pty. Ltd. (Australia)
Austria	Novell Belgium B.V.B.A.
Belgium	Novell do Brasil Software Ltda.
Brazil	Novell Canada, Ltd.
Canada	Novell Europe, Inc.
Chile	Novell S.A.R.L. (France)
People's Republic of China	Novell GmbH (Germany)
Commonwealth of Independent States	Novell International, Ltd.
Czech Republic	Novell Italia S.R.L.
Denmark	Novell Japan, Ltd.
Finland	Novell Korea Co., Ltd.
France	Novell de Mexico, S.A. DE C.V.
Germany	Novell Polska Sp.Zo.o
Hong Kong	Novell Software Development Pvt. Ltd.
India	Novell Spain S.A.
Italy	Novell Svenska A.B. (Sweden)
Japan	Novell Schweiz A.B. (Switzerland)
Korea	Novell U.K., Ltd.
Mexico	Onward Novell Software Pvt., Ltd. (India)
Netherlands	
New Zealand	
Norway	
Poland	
Portugal	
Singapore	
South Africa	
Spain	
Sweden	
Switzerland	
Taiwan	
United Arab Emirates	
United Kingdom	

Exhibit 37.1 Novell International Offices and Subsidiaries

Novell grew from 97 employees in 1984 to 8,457 employees in 1994 (1,951 outside the US; see Exhibit 37.1). Net income increased from $375,000 in 1984 to $206.7 million in 1994 (see Exhibit 37.2). Product development centers are in the US, India, the United Kingdom, Japan, and Belgium. Approximately half of all sales are from non-US markets and expansion into additional countries is fundamental to the business strategy. Novell meets the definition of a global organization: one product is sold throughout the world

Net Sales 1984–1994 ('000s)

Year	Total	Internat'l		Year	Total	Internat'l
1984	10,862	2,450		1990	1,003,444	197,149
1985	45,171	8,694		1991	1,262,073	280,336
1986	95,865	19,768		1992	1,512,488	440,921
1987	182,800	53,613		1993	1,830,411	783,000
1988	347,010	108,169		1994	1,998,077	861,000
1989	421,877	146,644				

Net Sales

1984–1994

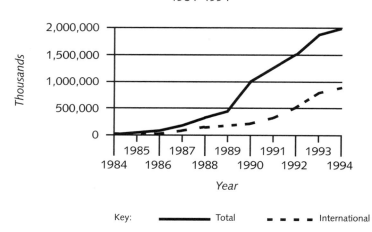

Key: ▬▬▬ Total ■ ■ ■ International

Net Income 1984–1994 ('000s)

Year	Total		Year	Total
1984	375		1990	292,968
1985	5,584		1991	363,316
1986	11,892		1992	321,978
1987	20,338		1993	40,720
1988	35,890		1994	206,731
1989	48,547			

Net Income

1984–1994

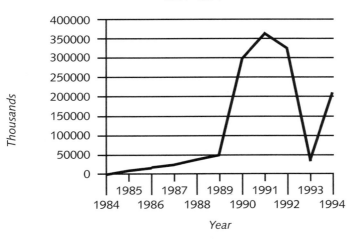

Return on Average Equity 1984–1994

Year	Total
1985	99.4
1986	54.2
1987	29.6
1988	23.3
1989	23.7

Year	Total
1990	63
1991	49
1992	32.4
1993	4
1994	16

Return on Average Equity

1984–1994

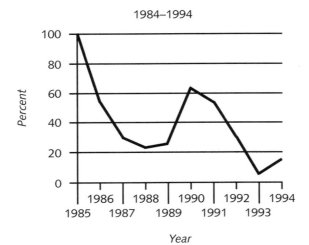

Exhibit 37.2 Novell, Financial Performance, 1984–1994

(Bartlett, 1986; Leavitt, 1992). The company strategy, however, is to be a transnational organization, sensitive to local markets (Bartlett & Ghoshal, 1992; Cook, 1995).

Four themes summarize Novell's international growth: (1) *The Global Product* describes Novell's products that are designed for a worldwide market, (2) *The Entrepreneur* describes the leader who envisioned, designed, and promoted Novell's product and the company, (3) *The Global Business Plan* outlines the company's worldwide strategy, and (4) *The Challenges of Retaining Ownership and Markets* describes the problems facing a growing company in the volatile IT industry.

THE GLOBAL PRODUCT

A Novell vice president's assertion that "bytes are somewhat narcotic when you're growing" describes the attraction that networking products have for expanding business. Companies purchase computer systems that are intended to handle business for years into the future but computer capacity is quickly outgrown. This is the narcotic appeal of bytes – computer users have a compelling need for increasing quantities of bytes and Novell's networking products respond to this demand.

Novell's early products appealed to small organizations in countries that needed improved computer efficiency and used the English language in business. Novell increased computer efficiency by allowing companies to leap-frog or hook lower cost microcomputers together in a network, which enabled them to achieve the computer performance of more expensive mainframe or minicomputers. A manager explains Novell's strategy:

> The strategy of Novell was to put a piece of software in the middle that was compatible with all those existing standards that are out there. We were not really interested in hardware other than that we had to buy hardware – we were primarily focused on software. Hardware was provided to enable the sale of software. Once we got all this rolling, our sales and marketing strategy was to go out and sign up authorized dealers around the country, around the world.

Novell sold both hardware and software until concerns about competition, costs, and logistics created compelling reasons to focus exclusively on software. According to one manager, "In 1988 . . . we limited ourselves to software. Shipping software is very easy. You can put it on an airplane, it is fairly light. You can ship it around the world. It is quite self-contained."

Early users of Novell products were small businesses such as dental offices, but Novell's target market was large organizations. During the early years, Novell sales representatives traveled to large US business centers – Chicago, New York, Dallas, Los Angeles, and San Francisco – to court corporations such as Chase-Manhattan Bank, Coca-Cola, Delta Airlines, American Airlines, and Rockwell. As Novell's reputation grew, these companies became interested in Novell because networking products could make information processing systems more economical. A marketing executive explains:

> Initially, the concept of networking was to share a printer and to share expensive hard disks . . . To put a hard disk in every single computer was very expensive, so people bought a network to share hard drives and to share printers. Over time, what people discovered,

especially with Novell NetWare, is that they could make that system look and act like a minicomputer. That was not the initial reason they bought the thing. They found out that was one of the strengths of our software . . . The bigger companies [and] countries began to look at networking. All of a sudden they realised they could install a network that would do the very same thing that a minicomputer would do for anywhere from 10–50 percent of the value of the other system. A lot of people had thousands of microcomputers already in the shops. So it wasn't a matter of buying new equipment, just a matter of hooking up.

Novell has acquired technology companies, has invested cash in technology companies, and has formed strategic alliances with technology companies in order to promote the growth of the network computing industry and to broaden the company's business as a system software supplier.

THE ENTREPRENEUR

Ray Noorda, Novell's president from 1983 to 1994, directed the company's international expansion through his vision, his business theory, and his ability to motivate employees. In 1983, when Novell Data "went through its venture capital" and got into trouble, Safeguard Scientifics, the major investor, asked Noorda to perform an analysis and provide advice on future investment in Novell Data. A manager explains:

Ray came in as the fix-it guy and said, "Wow, this isn't too bad. I see a software opportunity." He went back to Safeguard and said, "Look, I'll put $100,000 in if you guys will fund the rest. You give me a portion of the stock (he got 10–15 percent of the stock) and I'll make it run. You make me the president and I'll make it run."

Vision

Noorda brought a strategic perspective to Novell. "Noorda had been involved in General Electric and other major companies and had a very global position and attitude," according to a manager. He assembled a team of five specialists – people he knew from previous ventures. This group focused on a new strategic direction and developed a worldwide business model. According to a vice-president, "When I met him [Noorda], he basically told me his vision was to take a software package called NetWare and make it compatible with all the major hardware and software packages out there."

Noorda expected employees to design international applications for every product and service roll-out. He confronted new project designers with "What's the international application of this program?" A manager explains:

He [Noorda] made it clear that from a vision standpoint over time, it had to reach around the world. Whenever we did something that was highly successful, his next statement would be, "Okay, how are we going to get this out there?" He was very, very clear about his expectations. You didn't dare not have your worldwide plan in place when you went to talk to Ray. When you went in with corporate advertising and you said, "We are going to be in the *Wall Street Journal* and the *New York Times*," he would say, "And . . ." And you would say, "The *Financial Times* in London and *Wall Street Journal-Asia*." And he would say, "Okay."

Business theory

Noorda viewed organizational life as a battle for survival. He pinpointed Novell's place in his model of an organization's life cycle and warned employees about the dangers of the latter stages. An executive explains:

> He used to say there are five E's. There was an entrepreneur stage, expansion stage, excitement stage, euphoric stage, and the extinct stage. Novell is in euphoric now [1995] to a certain extent. He used to review those all the time. He said he would never let anyone get euphoric. Even when we were 80 percent of the market, he was saying it was total survival mode for him. He always lived survival mode. He lived constantly in the fear of competition taking over his market.

A member of the executive team explains how *The Noorda theory of how to do business* will benefit any company and should be taught in business schools:

> *The Noorda theory of how to do business* – how to focus on high-volume, high-margin products, and how to conserve money and how to influence markets – is powerful stuff. We will have economical management, we will focus on high-margin products, we will make sure those products are expandable into high-volume markets and we will use leveraged sales. Noorda set the strategy of picking and choosing the pieces of all the products and making sure that we sell the most of the highest profit products.

A manager describes how Noorda implemented company objectives through hedging or planning for multiple contingencies:

> Part of the success of Novell and then part of the genius of Ray Noorda is that you hedged everything. Everything was hedged three different ways . . . Hedging is to go with a plan but have that plan designed so that if it's not accepted one way, it works another . . . Ray doesn't ever do anything without hedging . . . He assumes that his original plans will fail and nobody really knows what they are, except him . . . Novell was bold and moved ahead but it did it in such a way that it made people think that we were being benevolent and partnering.

Noorda and his executives directed the company according to a clearly defined business model. A manager explains Noorda's leadership tactics:

> The driving force was flexibility, hedging, leverage, and aggression but it was always hidden in a marketing campaign so that people always thought we were being nice guys. It was, "Look, here's what we have to do." And everything that was unsaid was, "We're going to do it no matter what." For example, we started out with small dealers because that was all that would work with us . . . We got to a point when they couldn't borrow enough money to sustain our growth, so it was time to move into a different mode. Well, we didn't go in and ask them, "Gee, would you like to do this?" We said, "Here's what we're going to do and here's how you can plan and if you play this way, you'll make money." We never lied to anybody but we bullied. Noorda's a bully and I was a bully. We bullied to do what we had to do to make our company grow, and we let everybody come along if they wanted to play our way. That is how we partnered – we didn't exclude anybody but we called the shots.

Motivation

Noorda governed the day-to-day business through his ability to motivate employees and to control costs. He motivated employees through two methods: the lure of company ownership and fear. Novell salaries were modest when compared with those in other software development companies. A manager explains:

> Noorda's strategy to compensate people and motivate people was not to give them big salaries. His strategy was to give them stock in the company which motivated them to make the company expand and grow. Then they got their money from this growth of the stock value . . . He believed that if you give people too much money they get kind of fat and happy, they slow down, and they get euphoric.

Employees were motivated to avoid punishment. Noorda lived through the depression of the 1930s and he developed a personal ethic of hard work and frugality. He applied this philosophy to his business and expected employees to work long hours and accept assignments wherever requested. His abrasive directives scared people into compliance in order to avoid being targeted for criticism or dismissal.

Employees lived in a fear-charged work environment in which they were closely watched. They projected personal images that were calculated to reassure Noorda that his employees were dedicated to the company and conserved company resources. Customer-orientation was also a high priority. A manager explains repercussions of customer service feedback:

> The best thing you could ever do was have a customer call [Noorda] and say, "Hey, I just got off the phone with so-and-so and boy, did they help me!" The worst thing that could happen: "Hey, I just got off the phone with so-and-so and that person ticked me off." Either of those two people would be in Ray's office within 15 minutes. He would either be patting them on the back and giving them a hug, or they would be threatened – their job would be threatened. It may not be immediate, but over time, he would watch that kind of person.

Noorda prized frugality. The media promoted him as a down-to-earth CEO who advocated cost-saving practices such as working in a small office and flying coach class. An executive reports:

> He watched people and how they spent money. He criticized employees who flew first class (even with free upgrades) and employees who had too much computer software or hardware in their offices. Another thing Ray hated was too many headcount. He was always paring back headcount. And that was a cost saver. Everything was cost savings.

Noorda fired managers who did not meet performance targets and the resulting stress was evident in the personal lives of employees. At one time, 90 percent of the vice-president level personnel had experienced either a divorce or a health failure. An executive explains:

> If there was a pattern of spending too much money, or not working hard enough, or traveling too much, he would get rid of those people – that was part of the business strategy. It was a horribly tough way to live – constant scrutiny on how well you did those things. That

is part of the reason the VPs had so many problems. They didn't last very long. Most people who worked close to Ray didn't last more than a year or two.

Noorda's image as a benevolent grandfather, portrayed by the media, was countered by the inside-industry view of him as the grandfather from hell. Employees criticized his high-stress tactics yet others praised his family-like concern that motivated them to do their best work. In general, upper-level employees describe him as ruthless and lower-level employees claim he showed personal consideration.

The Global Business Plan

Novell markets products through 40 US sales offices and 33 foreign offices in countries in which the infrastructure and socioeconomic conditions are able to support computers. By 1994, Novell had 21 US distributors and approximately 113 foreign distributors.

Partner and leverage model

Novell markets products and support throughout the world through a partner and leverage model. Novell maintains limited personnel and contracts with others to sell and service Novell's products in their respective locations. The NetWare products flow directly to the distribution partners, or commissioned agents, who are liable for taxes and other costs that are included in the selling price. An executive explains how Novell retains control of the distribution channel in the partner and leverage model:

> We called the shots, and they [distributors] learn, after a time, that we were usually right . . . And our dealer councils were war. They loved us because they were making money but they hated us because we were telling them what to do . . . One day in Europe, the European distributors had formed this coalition to tell us what to do. And so I showed up at the Distributor Conference and I stood up to give them a speech and they all had this agenda of what to do that afternoon. And I just came head on and said, "Look guys, this is a world of change and here's what has to be done to compete. You've got all these competitors out here that are trying to kill us. This is what we're going to do and we need people who are willing to change and go forward. If you don't like change, then maybe you should start growing corn because that's the same year after year, and get out of this business."

The corn speech signaled that headquarters is the senior partner in the partner and leverage relationship and solely directs the organizational structure and programs.

From outposts to infrastructures

Novell aims to have wholly owned subsidiaries throughout the world. International expansion evolves from one person outpost operations in widely dispersed geographical areas to regional centers that serve many countries. According to a manager, "because of the way software is developed and is shipped around the world, it's easy to set up representation indirectly, grow the market to the point where you can bring in your own people, and they continue to grow it."

This pattern, not a blueprint, mirrored Novell's method of US expansion: Novell establishes a partner (distributor) in a targeted location who develops the regional market. Novell may recruit local nationals. As an executive explains. "In the early days we would go into a country, hold a seminar, and say, 'Now, this it networking, this is the concept. Anybody want to sell this?' And anybody who raised their hand got to sell it." These commissioned agents distribute Novell products and represent Novell.

One-person outposts do not have extensive contact with headquarters and the people who work in them are typically lower-level employees. As sales increase in an area, formal organizational structures are established to increase the company's visibility and credibility. When the market (a country or a cluster of companies) reaches the $5 million revenue level, Novell establishes a small office. This usually coincides with the time when major accounts say, "I'm not comfortable betting my company's future on a company that is not represented in my own country." When Novell responds by setting up a local office and hiring local people, there is almost a straight-up jump in growth rate because local businesses say, "Okay, Novell is serious about my country, they have local Novell representation. I'm now comfortable with the fact that if there is a major problem, I can go to a local office and resolve it."

As the market grows, Novell elevates the status of employees. For example, when Novell hired the person who is today the vice-president of Novell in Asia, he was a country manager. Eventually, the revenue and growth of Asia justified assigning a vice president to the area and he was promoted to the position.

Novell's international growth evolved from establishing the first non-US office in Germany to a global presence. This growth followed a basic model that was implemented throughout Western Europe, Australia, Japan, Eastern Europe, Asia, and South America. A manager describes the international beginnings:

> In 1984, we already had an office in Dusseldorf, Germany. We had hired a young man right out of college and sent him and his wife to Europe. He had served an LDS [Church of Jesus Christ of Latter-Day Saints] mission there and he worked for another company for a period of time there so he knew the market. He went in, selected Dusseldorf as the headquarters location . . . and that began the early operations. Because of the early work that [Novell Data] had done, we already had some distribution partners in France, Germany, Sweden, and England . . . This young man went in and expanded that role. At the same time, my boss had done some work with some people to push NetWare into South America. We had some people down there that had been promoting NetWare in Mexico and Venezuela. We had picked up a partner very early in Argentina and that company is still with us. We had a very early partner in Japan. So all of this groundwork was in place by February of 1985.

Novell retains control over expansion by refusing to grant exclusive distributorships. An executive explains:

> You have to trust [the distributors] somewhat and give them some flexibility to do what they want to do . . . As soon as you can, you put somebody over there and you say, "Here's the new manager for this country." And the original distributor hates it because now there's somebody there telling him what to do . . . But he brings in two more distributors and they hate it even more because the market's diluted . . . Usually, when a company's starting, the distributors will always tell you they have to have an exclusive . . . and your answer is always

"No." When you add the second one, they don't split the business – it doubles. And we add a third one and it triples or more. Because when you add a second one, the first one starts to work. When they're the only one in town, they don't work. So, no exclusives, ever.

Australia provides an example of how technical support, marketing, and sales are taken closer to the market as an area's sales increase. In the 1980s, there were no Novell employees in Australia, only a representative distributing company. In the late 80s, Novell set up a small office of four or five people. Today [1995], there are 70 people in the Australian region – in Sydney, Canberra, Melbourne, Adelaide, and Auckland, New Zealand. According to a manager, "That's a natural transition for any company that wants to go international . . . they have to determine the threshold points, when there's enough revenue to justify moving in."

International expansion

Novell is centralized into three main regions, each supervised by a vice-president. Novell's early success came in the developing markets that had poorly developed infrastructures and used English as a business language. NetWare works on microcomputers rather than on mainframes and minicomputers, and poorer (or less-automated) countries used micro-computers as a way to become automated. Spain, England, Scandinavia, and several Asian countries were early adopters of the technology because organizations in these countries could not afford to buy more expensive technology. Japan was slower to adopt Novell products because funds were available to buy bigger equipment.

Language was a second factor in adopting Novell products. Technical support products and services were available only in English during the early years. The countries in which English was spoken or used as a business language adopted early – England, Canada, Australia, South Africa, Sweden, Finland, the Belgium–Luxembourg–Netherlands area, Asia, Singapore, Hong Kong, the British colonies, and Malaysia. Countries in which their own language was spoken in business were slow adapters: France, Italy, Spain, Germany, Taiwan, Korea, and Japan.

Several countries use both English and their native language in business. Novell gained initial entry through the English connection, but expanded the market when products were translated into local languages. For example, Latin America adopted early because English is used in the computer divisions of sophisticated companies.

The foreign language skill of Novell's employees enables international expansion. Novell corporate offices are located near three universities in which a large percentage of the students speak foreign languages and have lived in foreign countries while serving missions for the LDS church. At the University of Utah, 53 percent of the MBAs are conversational in another language; at Brigham Young University, 68 percent of the MBAs speak a language other than English. Language ability is beneficial in initial communication with foreign markets and in product translation. According to a manager, "That is a real secret weapon. Because if you're having to modify your product for Japan or Germany, the odds are, one of your engineers speaks that language. The communication is better and the rapport is better."

Technical support centers

The partner and leverage model is also used to provide technical support. When customers learn to use Novell's products, Novell is assured of a future stream of customers. One manager suggests, "Get a lot of people trained because once they're trained on your stuff, they don't like to change to something else."

Partnering and leveraging technical support means that Novell contracts with other business entities that agree to provide technical services to Novell customers. They are trained and prepared to handle the backload or the front-line to help with call-overload control. They are paid per incident. He explains the evolution:

> In 1988, there were 30 support engineers . . . we had 2,000 calls in the queue, a two-week turnaround time. That means when a customer called in, the customer support representative on the phone would tell them the wait time was two weeks. It is impossible to do all the support yourself, so back then . . . the distributors would start doing support and we would leverage them, train them . . . so that they could do the support for us and we would act as a back-up support. That, in a nutshell, is leverage.

This model is projected for future expansion. A manager explains: "Our strategy by the year 2000 is to support a billion customers. The only way we can do that is to leverage our partners. There is no way Novell is going to support a billion customers by itself."

Novell has three major technical support centers: (1) The Germany center provides support for Europe and Africa, (2) The Australia center provides support for India, Asia, and the Pacific Islands, and (3) The US center provides support for Latin America, the US, and Canada.

Designating the location of technical support centers depends on political considerations, illustrated by the decision to create the Dusseldorf, Germany center. In 1987, Novell had three centers in Europe – France, Germany, and the UK – which provided technical support to their own countries. According to an international manager, Novell needed to build a centralized center to improve the situation in Europe and around the world and to obtain critical mass. These small centers did not have the expertise to respond to customer calls. A manager describes the issues that influenced designating a direct reporting line from the Dusseldorf Center to the US:

> We could either build a center in Europe that was located in Paris, Dusseldorf, or the UK, which is a big issue because the Italians don't like the Germans and the Germans don't like the French . . . It created a lot of problems . . . So we put together a proposal . . . of building the center in Dusseldorf, Germany . . . if you put someone in charge who was a native German or a native Italian or a native whatever, that would cause animosity between the other countries. And so basically [the US] stood as a neutral point for all of Europe, which eliminated the cultural issues.

Novell aims to present "one face" in customer service delivery. The company introduced a new support concept to the software industry by bringing people from throughout Europe to Germany to provide support in 14 different languages. Toll-free lines run from the various countries into Dusseldorf, Germany. When customers telephone a local toll-free line, they speak to someone in their native language. This information is recorded in their native language, entered into the computer, and passed on to a native speaking support engineer. This retains the expertise behind the scenes where engineers communicate in English.

Customers should experience "a constant look and feel" when they telephone for technical support. A manager describes the customer interface in Japan to illustrate how this is achieved:

> When the customer calls in, whether they call Novell KK or they call here [US], they get the same feel. Everything in Novell KK is multiplied in difficulty by 100 times because it is all done in kanji . . . Up-front to the customer, it looks like it is in kanji – it is in kanji. But behind the scenes, it is referenced to the English text . . . so that we can figure out where the problems are.

Novell's goal is to provide expert technical support in languages customers from anywhere in the world can understand. The partner and leverage model enables local service to be provided from Novell's central pool of expertise.

Unique markets

Local country laws, customs, and political events require Novell to adapt the partner and leverage model when entering new countries. In Brazil, Japan, and India, Novell altered its business model to accommodate unique markets, with varying results. Novell inadvertently allowed an exclusive distributorship in Brazil and subsequently experienced severe negative financial repercussions. Novell's Japanese entry underscored the importance of social networks and joint ventures. Novell's Indian distributor pirated software from the company as a means to avoid paying tariffs.

National restrictions prohibit Novell from entering several countries. Pakistan and Afghanistan have restrictive import laws. The US government prohibits Novell from selling products in Iran, Iraq, and Cuba. In restricted countries, people typically sneak the product in and pirate it. According to a manager, piracy is difficult to control and when the walls come down in those respective countries, Novell will enter the market with the partner and leverage plan.

THE CHALLENGES OF RETAINING OWNERSHIP AND MARKETS

Novell faces five primary challenges to retaining ownership of its products and expanding its global markets. These include software piracy, creating a unified global organization, fostering cultural sensitivity within the organization, developing international managers, and facing severe competition in the software industry.

Piracy

Artificial barriers to trade imposed by governments complicate Novell's access to markets. Barriers include high tariffs, security regulations, and restrictive ownership requirements. These impositions, however, do not halt the distribution of Novell products. The effect of governmental restrictions is to promote the distribution of illegal software and encourage piracy because legitimate products are not available. One manager explains, "When you've got these artificial barriers that are created by the government, you really set up a major incentive for piracy. So people are motivated. They need the technology and in some cases, they need it desperately."

When Novell acquires access to a country in which pirated copies of NetWare are dispersed, piracy is countered with a strategy that may benefit both Novell and the owners of counterfeit products. An international manager explains:

> When the walls came down and the rules began to change and it became easier to go in with a legal product – the last country we did this was actually Peru . . . We would go in and put in a big ad in the newspaper saying, "Novell's coming in with an amnesty program. We will let you upgrade to real NetWare for upgrade prices if you bring your diskettes in. No questions asked. We don't care how or where you got the stuff. Just bring in your diskettes and for the upgrade price, not full price, we will allow you to get real NetWare." Well, that worked extremely well in Brazil, in eastern Europe, in Russia, in Peru. A lot of people said, "I would love to have real product with real manuals."

Novell's apparent benevolence is a carrot and stick approach to ensure future business. As a manager describes, "Now, it's easy to get NetWare legally. Beyond a certain date, if you don't have NetWare legally, and we find out about it, we will come after you within the bounds of the law."

Piracy may benefit Novell by establishing a market for legitimate products because counterfeit NetWare spreads the demand for products and serves as market promotion. A program of forgiveness allows businesses that use illegal copies of Novell software to acquire legitimate copies and also identifies a future stream of Novell customers. As new products roll out and customers require technical support, newly-registered users work directly with Novell.

Piracy also supplements new product development when the pirates' creative energy can be co-opted by the company. In the Russian market, illegal software was re-directed to Novell's advantage. A manager explains how engineers who stole Novell's products now assist Novell:

> There were two companies in Russia that had reverse-engineered. First, they'd pirated and then reverse-engineered NetWare and they created a Cyrillic version of NetWare. We jokingly said in Novell, "We had Nyetware." We went and talked to the two companies, and one of the companies had done a very good job. So we actually licensed them to be an official partner, basically forgave them of any past sins. They began paying us a royalty on their Cyrillic version of NetWare, and we continued to provide them with new technology and actually assist them in creating the Russian versions.

Software piracy siphons Novell's rightful income yet can be a boon to marketing by preparing a potential stream of future customers and initiating language translation projects.

A united global organization

Novell's worldwide employees should never feel unplugged from corporate offices. Employees from headquarters frequently fly to other countries in order to get to know international employees and to model Novell procedures. An international manager claims that "from 1989 to 1992, all of us put more frequent flyer miles on our systems. We just had to be there. You have to bring them over [to the US] for productive meetings, not just to hang around, but to have productive interchange, so they know what company it is they are representing." She explains company-wide communication:

> Corporate has monthly phone conference communication with each of the [three] regions . . . people from corporate go to the quarterly region meetings . . . And then once a year, we all meet face-to-face in a worldwide communication conference . . . [These are held at headquarters] because everybody wants to come to corporate and see what is here.

Rhetoric promotes a global perspective – a clear understanding among employees that Novell encompasses the world. According to a headquarters manager, "You will see [signs] that say Think globally or Think internationally. [We] have international clocks. [We] have all kinds of different things to remind people." Rhetoric is followed by practice, as a manager describes the NetWorld trade shows held around the world:

> Ray [Noorda] was very, very quick to point out that NetWorld had to be a global initiative. Now there are NetWorlds in Germany, in France, and soon in the UK, in Japan and in Australia, and soon to be in China. You are not really a global company unless you have global marketing initiatives that are spanning all your markets.

US-centric perceptions, however, prevent some employees from developing a multi-cultural perspective. According to an international manager:

> I have been striving for eight years to get people in the US to think internationally, to think globally. I don't think it will ever happen. The reason is because people live here in the States. They don't understand. They don't want to understand. They are in their own environment, their own world. They deal with English day-to-day . . . There are key people, some pockets of people, who really want to get international and to learn and to become a global company . . . If I look back over eight years . . . we have improved significantly . . . but I don't think we will ever reach a point to where everyone is thinking globally and everyone has the right hats on . . . we can continually try to educate people in thinking globally in any decision that they ever make – that one decision that they make here affects the rest of the world.

Cultural sensitivity

Although Novell distributes the same software products throughout the world, technical support must be localized according to language. During the early years, managers harangued engineers to expand their English-only orientation because engineers were not aware of how English-only computer coding limited the transferal of products to other languages. An executive explains:

> The disadvantage of an American company trying to go international versus a European company trying to go international is that American engineers cannot get it through their heads that there's another language spoken anywhere. They always hardwire something into the code that makes it tough to expand it out. And you have to continually be in there saying. "Think of double byte characters. Think of international. Make it so somebody else

can change the language in it." And if you stop doing that for one week, they forget . . . you have to have a zealous person in the company who must make a jerk out of themselves all of the time . . . We begin to think that everyone can communicate if we all speak English if we just speak slow . . . It took eight years to finally get that into development's head, that "Look, we're an international company, would you stop doing those things? Would you stop hard coding the messages?" I don't think it really started to change until . . . [we] started sending the engineers to Europe to sit and deal with their customers that they'd been screwing up.

The most effective way to learn about another culture is to live in that country, according to an international manager:

> It is not easy to tell somebody, "Oh, think global" and make it work magically . . . The only way you can think globally is to live it and experience it. So we have implemented an exchange program. We did that about six years ago, where key support engineers here in the States would provide support to some of those centers . . . We would send them out over there and we would send someone from that center over here and they have their eyes opened to what is going on over there. So when they come back, they are excited and they can help teach others and say, "Hey, it really is different over there and we need to do this differently."

Balancing headquarters control and local autonomy is a challenge when promoting a Novell constant look and feel. Novell establishes company procedures at its US headquarters, and worldwide offices are expected to adopt these standards. A manager describes how local campaigns, however, may resist corporate direction. "I can remember seeing [local European] ad campaigns that were frightening things . . . one in particular had a picture of Ayatollah on it and it had some political joke. We all [in the US] went, 'No! I don't think we had better do that.' "

The interface between Novell headquarters and country offices has vacillated between central and local control. A manager explains how global approaches do not always translate locally:

> One of the first things Novell did after this little incident in Europe . . . the headquarters people became very hard-nosed about usage of the logo in marketing . . . They got to the point where they insisted on exactly the same ads being applied, and that's where the cultural difference comes in because certain things don't translate. We had one ad that was based on American football. Well, that doesn't translate at all . . . And so then the Europeans, the Asian, and other places pushed back hard saying, "Hey, this ad doesn't mean anything over here."

The global approach may also have undesired political overtones. An executive explains:

> Novell put on this big campaign called *Selling Red* in 1986. In '86, when that hit Europe, selling red was connected with the Soviet Union, so it was not a positive thing. People here [US] tried to implement it but our employees there didn't do anything with it because they knew what the effects would be.

Non-US employees may demonstrate different corporate loyalties than US employees, according to a Novell executive:

Your European employees never work for you. They work for their country. So if you think they're working for you, you're really crazy. Now, their objective is to sell your product, but in their own way. They know more than you do, they think, and they probably do . . . But the fact is, they'll never work for you. They say they are. They'll nod their head and then they'll do what they think needs to be done, and that probably saves a lot of companies. But if you don't know that's going on, you could spend a lot of money on a useless campaign. Give them the money and let them do something useful with it.

Novell demonstrated cultural sensitivity in its groundwork for entering the Chinese market. On the day in 1995 when Novell announced a decision that affected the strategy, size, and direction of the entire company, the president was not at headquarters – he was visiting the Vice-Premier of China. This previously scheduled diplomatic mission was not rescheduled, despite Novell's strategic announcement, because changing plans with the Vice-Premier would violate Chinese protocol, create a bad reputation for Novell, and jeopardize an enormous potential market. In Novell's early years, before executives had learned the importance of culture-specific protocol, they may have routinely rescheduled the China appointment, American-style.

Management development

Novell locates distributors who develop markets in their respective areas. Novell also recruits managers from large information technology companies such as IBM and Hewlett-Packard. Management development training programs are designed to increase functional competency and cultural sensitivity.

The German market illustrates the international management development process at Novell. A guitar musician opened Novell's German distributorship. He spoke German, knew the company, and understood the vision of international growth. As the market grew and additional distributors were located, Novell required more personnel and organizational infrastructure to meet the needs of increased headquarters involvement and reporting from the field. Initial distributors were replaced with more sophisticated personnel and a director-level person was replaced by a vice-president. Eventually, Novell's matured German connection became one of Novell's three worldwide technical support centers.

A key management development issue is whether to hire local people to run local country offices or to export US headquarters personnel to run these units. According to an executive, local managers are preferred.

We began trying to integrate [in 1988]. When the country offices were first set up they were incredibly autonomous. Although they were managed quite often at the top management level by someone who had been sent over from the US, there was a real heritage from the very beginning at Novell of hiring local people to run the offices . . . that is a really important success factor . . . the people who were actually running the country organizations – which back in 1988 and 1989 meant 3 or 4 people in an office – were local folks . . . A lot of US companies don't do that when they are small. They send little entourages over to set up offices . . . that is the first misstep a US company can make.

Novell's worst case is to have a regional vice-president or senior executive who is an American but lives in another country. The best case is to have a European senior executive who has worked in the US corporate offices and has returned to the international arena.

International managers must understand cultural traditions. A manager describes several international profiles:

- The Germans . . . want everything in rules and they want everything to be very clear and specific. The more rules there are, the more respect they have for you and the more willing they are to participate.
- The French will never agree with you. The goal cannot be consensus with the French because there is no such thing there. The goal can never be to have them happy because they will never communicate satisfaction, so you just have to know that. You have to know that you do not keep working on them until they are happy, you just do what you have to do. They will never agree that what you have done is good. So the more room you can give them to maneuver, the more they will draw their own conclusions and come to where you want them to come, which is sort of the opposite of the Germans.
- The Japanese use language that makes you think they are agreeing with you, but they never agree in meetings. The culture says that when you say their word for "yes," all it means is that they understand what you have said. They register everything in a meeting, then they leave, they decide, and then they come back. If you want to renegotiate, they re-register the new information and then they leave to decide and then they come back. Everything is done behind closed doors in Japan and you are never invited into the inner sanctum.
- European management always says, "If I have to have a [foreign] boss, it had better be an American, because I will not have an English boss. I will not have a German boss, if I am French. I will not have a French [boss], if I am German. You send me a Canadian, an American, or an Australian [boss] and I can live with that."

These generalizations, based on the experience of Novell employees, suggest differences in national cultures. Selecting and training international managers who can work effectively with people from contrasting cultures is crucial to Novell's successful globalization.

Competition

During the early years when Novell's products included hardware and software, competitors included both small computer companies and giants such as IBM and Hewlett-Packard. Novell's main competitor since 1984 has been Microsoft:

> The market for operating systems software has become problematic due to Microsoft's growing dominance in all sectors of the software business. [Novell] does not have the product breadth and market power of Microsoft. Microsoft's dominant position provides it with enormous competitive advantages, including the ability to unilaterally determine the direction of future operating systems and to . . . achieve a dominant position in new markets. Microsoft's strategy may significantly inhibit Novell's ability to maintain its business . . . [and] impair Novell's competitive position with respect to particular products. (Prospectus, 1994)

Novell implemented a growth strategy of mergers and acquisitions from 1991 to 1994. Competition with Microsoft, which influenced Novell's expansion, appeared to be a personal battle between Noorda and Bill Gates, the president of Microsoft. Criticism of this growth strategy, from within Novell and from outsiders, led to assertions that Noorda had lost focus. Expanding the size of Novell was evidence of a personal goal to beat Gates, rather than a clearly defined organizational strategy.

Expansion through mergers and acquisitions added international offices in countries in which Novell was already established. The largest acquisition, WordPerfect, doubled the size of Novell in 1994 and added four new Latin American countries to the company's market. A challenge presented by new acquisitions is assimilating these newly-acquired companies into the Novell organization.

Summary

The global product. Novell Data, the forerunner of Novell, Inc., was envisioned as an international company from its early years. Novell's software products link together small computers to approximate the performance of larger computers. Novell's products are both global and localized: standard Novell products are distributed worldwide and are run on local computer systems. Technical support materials are provided in local languages.

The entrepreneur. Ray Noorda became the president of the newly-incorporated Novell, Inc. in 1983 and changed the company focus from computer hardware to software products. Noorda's entrepreneurial style, both praised and criticized by employees and the press, is characterized by a strong company vision, a global business plan, and high performance standards.

The global business plan. Novell uses a partner and leverage model to contract with other businesses to distribute products and provide technical support throughout the world. A commissioned agent initially establishes the business and when sales volume reaches $5 million per year, Novell sets up an office to coordinate growth. In three unique country markets – Brazil, Japan, and India – the business model was altered with varying repercussions.

The challenges of retaining product ownership and markets. Novell faces the challenges of software piracy, creating a unified organization of culturally-sensitive employees, and developing international managers. Competition from Microsoft is Novell's most formidable challenge.

Notes

This case was written by Visiting Assistant Professor Marjorie McEntire and Professor C. Brooklyn Derr of the University of Utah, and by Associate Professor Chris Meek of Brigham Young University as a basis for classroom discussion. Grants from the Brigham Young University/University of Utah CIBER and from Novell, Inc. made this case possible. The authors are responsible for the information in the case: neither CIBER nor Novell are liable for statements within the document. The case is part of the CIBER Case Collection, sponsored by the Indiana University CIBER and distributed by the ECCH@ Babson. Copyright 1996 by Marjorie McEntire, C Brooklyn Derr and Chris Meek.

1   All quotations in this case are from transcripts of interviews that were conducted during 1995 and 1996 with Novell employees and former Novell employees.

References

Bartlett, C.A. 1986. Building and Managing the Transnational: The New Organizational Challenge. In M.E. Porter (ed.), *Competition in Global Industries*, pp. 367–401. Boston, MA: Harvard Business School Press.

Bartlett, C.A. & Ghoshal, S. (eds.). 1992. *Transnational Management*. Homewood, IL: Irwin.

Cook, P. 1995. Personal Communication at UITA Conference Speech. November 21.

Leavitt, T. 1992. The Globalization of Markets. In Bartlett, C.A. & Ghoshal, S. (eds.). *Transnational Management*, pp. 225–35. Homewood, IL: Irwin.

McEntire, M., Derr, B., & Meek, C. 1996. *The Global Rise of Novell: Complete Case*. CIBER, Brigham Young University/University of Utah, Salt Lake City, UT.

Novell Annual Reports. 1986–1995.

Novell/WordPerfect Prospectus/Proxy Statement. June 23, 1994.

Index

A&W Restaurants 314
accountability 75, 123, 135, 350–1, 358
  Case: fast-food industry 305
  Case: Inverlat 177–8
  diversity training 184, 189
  pay-for-performance 208
acculturation 246–7, 249, 251–2
achievement 86, 94, 95, 96
Acinder Steel Plant 281
action chains 37–8, 39
adult learning theory 191–4
AeroMexico 322
Aetna Life Insurance 255
AFC Enterprises 311, 312
affirmative action 116, 185, 344, 355, 357,
  358
  multicultural organizations 247, 253, 255,
  258
Afghanistan 374
Africa 72, 152, 154, 157, 193
  Case: Bhiwar Enterprises 234–8, 240–1
  Case: Novell 373
  cultural profile 14–15, 16, 21
  inadequate telephones 82
African National Congress (ANC) 154, 333
age 183, 186–7, 289, 356, 358
  boundaryless organizations 141, 144
  cultural profiles 9, 11
  Hewlett-Packard 108, 113, 114, 115, 117
Albania 289
Amazon.com 199, 205
American Airlines 196, 366
AmericanGraphics 205
American Institute for Foreign Study 150

American Society for Personnel Administration
  358
AmeriServe Food Distributors 318
Amoco 73
Amtrak 256
Anglo-German Trading Corporation 360–1
Anheuser Busch 250
Applebee's 308, 309
apprenticeships 89, 94
Arab-speaking countries 26, 32, 34, 42, 193
  cultural profile 14–15, 16, 21
Arby's 308, 314
Arco Chemical Europe 345, 346
Argentina 193, 271, 274, 277–9, 281, 363
  Case: Anglo-German 360
  Case: fast-food industry 320, 321
  Case: Novell 363, 371
  cultural profile 14–15, 21
Arthur Anderson 256
ascription 86, 97
Asea Brown Boveri (ABB) 46, 81
Asia 55–8, 59–62, 71–2, 152, 157, 197, 347
  Case: fast-food industry 313, 320, 321
  Case: Novell 371, 372, 373
  contingency matrix 85, 86
  cultural profiles 13, 14–15, 16, 20
  ethics 332–3
  European leadership in globalization 41, 48,
  50, 52
  Exercise: WWW 65, 68
  recruitment 41
  training across cultures 190, 194
Associos des Chiles SA 360
AT&T 44, 207, 259

Australia 86, 193
   Case: fast-food industry 301, 302
   Case: Novell 363, 371–3, 376, 379
   cultural profile 14–15, 21
   Motorola 51
Austria 86, 153, 193
   Case: Novell 363
   cultural profile 14–15, 16, 21–2
   Hewlett-Packard 118, 119
Avon 254

Bahamas 321, 360–1
Balkans 42, 288–9
Baltic states 22, 288
Banamex 170
Banca Cremi 179
Banco Bilbao Viscaya (BBV) 179
Banco de Mexico 324
Bangladesh 158, 331, 334
Bank of America 207
Bank of Credit and Commerce International 329
Bank of Nova Scotia (BNS) 169–74, 179
Barbados 321
Barnes and Noble 199
Baskin Robbins 314
Baxter Health Care 256
Bechtel Group Inc. 149–50
Belgium 76, 117–19, 193
   Case: Eurochem 125–8
   Case: fast-food industry 314
   Case: Novell 363, 372
   cultural profile 12, 14–15, 16, 21–2
Bell Atlantic 325
Benetton Company 152
Bennigan's 308
Bentley College 330
Bermuda 319
Bertelsmann Group 199
Bhiwar Enterprises 234–42
bias 11, 49, 51
   Case: Inverlat 175
   multicultrual organizations 247, 249, 253, 257–8
Big Boy 308
biodata 142
Bob Evans 308
Bojangle's 311
Bosnia 21
Boston Chicken, Inc. 312

Boston Market 308, 309–10, 312, 315
boundaryless organizations 133–44, 351, 353
Brazil 193, 197, 205
   Case: fast-food industry 301, 320–2, 326
   Case: Novell 363, 374, 375, 380
   cultural profile 14–15, 21
   new strategy and labour 271, 274, 276–81, 283–4
Brigham Young University 372
British Council 346–7
British Petroleum 73
Buddhism 19, 20, 154
Bulgaria 289
Burger King 307, 308, 312, 314
Burundi 21
business case 177–8
Business Council for International Understanding 42

Cable News Network (CNN) 48, 152
Canada 14–15, 21, 193–4, 252
   Case: Bhiwar Enterprises 237
   Case: fast-food industry 301–2, 320–3, 325–6
   Case: Inverlat 169, 171–8
   Case: Novell 363, 372, 373, 379
Canon Inc. 330
career development 75, 76, 187–8, 357–8
   Case: evaluation 299
   Case: fast-food industry 305
   Central and Eastern Europe 290
   dual-career couples 213, 222–6
   European competencies 161, 162, 165, 166
   global recruitment 151
   Mexico 264, 266
   multicultural organizations 253, 255, 256
   multirater feedback 207
Caribbean 16, 301, 319, 320, 321
Carl's Jr. 308, 312, 314
Casa de Bolsa 170
Caterpillar 207
Caux Round Table 330–1
Center for Creative Leadership 207
change creation 349–50, 352
Chase Manhattan Bank 255
Chase Manhattan Corporation 330, 366
Checker's Drive-In 312
Chemical Bank 257
Chesapeake Bagel Bakery 312
Chick-fil-A 308, 310, 311, 315

Chile 14–15, 21–2, 193, 271, 274, 277
  Case: Anglo-German 360–1
  Case: fast-food industry 301, 320, 321
  Case: Novell 363
Chili's 308, 309
Chimique Helvétique Ltd (CHL) 59, 61,
  295–300
China 55, 72, 97–9, 152, 156–8, 197–8
  Case: Eurochem 125–9
  Case: fast-food industry 301, 319
  Case: Novell 363, 376, 378
  contingency matrix 84, 86–7, 89, 97–9
  Exercise: WWW 67
  Motorola 51
Chinese Academy of Social Science 98
Christianity 19, 56, 152, 155, 157–8, 159
Chrysler 99, 201–2, 207, 250
Chubb & Son 150–1
Chuck E Cheese's 308
Church's Chicken 308, 310–12, 314–15
Cisco Systems 199
Citibank 80
CKE Restaurants 312
Clarke Consulting Group 268
Coca-Cola 10, 198, 250, 256, 366
  Case: fast-food industry 306, 316
Coco's 308
co-determination 95
Colgate-Palmolive 197
collective bargaining 92, 284
collectivism 13, 19, 20–2, 192, 289, 290
  contingency matrix 85–6, 88, 91, 93, 95,
  97–8
Colombia 14–15, 21–2, 193, 198
  Case: fast-food industry 301, 320, 321
Columbia Health Care Systems 208
Columbia University 44–5
Commerce Clearing House (CCH) 356, 357,
  358
Commonwealth of Independent States (CIS)
  86, 288
  Case: Novell 363
Communicaid 287
communism 20, 86, 287–9
compartmentalization 26–8, 30, 36, 37
compensation (including pay and benefits)
  76–7, 164, 357
  boundaryless organizations 134, 144
  Case: evaluation 298–9
  Case: fast-food industry 304, 318

Case: Novell 369
Central and Eastern Europe 290
contingency matrix 84, 87, 89–92, 94–8
developing global leaders 80–2
diversity stress 337, 341
diversity training 184
dual-career couples 214, 227
ethics 333–4
global recruitment 149
Latin America 276, 278, 281, 284
Mexico 89, 95, 96, 261–2, 265, 267–70
multicultural organizations 256, 258
multirater feedback 207
NAFTA 106
plural organizations 250
survival of HR 351, 352, 353–4
see also pay-for-performance
competing on the edge model 200–201, 209
competition and competitiveness 76, 165–6,
  183–9
  Case: Eurochem 127
  Case: fast-food industry 307, 313, 317–18,
    320–3
  Case: Novell 366, 368, 370, 374, 379–80
  contingency matrix 88, 99
  cultural diversity programmes 356, 358–9
  developing global leaders 81–2
  diversity stress 337
  dual-career couples 228
  global recruitment 148
  globalization 43–5, 48, 52, 72, 74
  Hewlett-Packard 109
  Latin America 273, 274, 279, 283
  Mexico 261, 264, 266, 268–9
  multicultural organizations 255
  strategy and initiatives 196–8, 200–2,
    204–6, 209
  survival of HR 348–9, 351, 353
context 26–8, 36–8, 39, 40, 57
  time 31–3, 35
contingency matrix 83–99
contracts 56, 86, 92, 94, 135, 162, 199
  Case: fast-food industry 304, 305–6
  Case: Novell 370
  Latin America 282
core competency model 200–1, 204
Corning Glass 201, 259
corporate culture 11, 163, 190, 207, 247
  boundaryless organizations 139, 140–1, 143,
    144

Case: fast-food industry 304–5
Case: Inverlat 170, 172
diversity stress 339, 340, 343
diversity training 186, 189
dual-career couples 212, 221, 224, 227
ethics 331–2
European leadership in globalization 41, 48, 50, 52–3
Costa Rica 14–15, 16, 21–2, 193, 321
counselling 9, 11, 22–3, 91
CPC Foundation 44
Cracker Barrrel 308
Cray Research 255
creativity 137, 245, 262, 350, 354
Croatia 14–15, 16, 21
cross-culturalism 42–7, 51–2, 58, 75, 80, 293–4
Case: evaluation 296
Case: Inverlat 175
dual-career couples 216
training 190–5
Cuba 374
cultural sensitivity 44, 47, 76, 331, 376–8
Case: Novell 374, 376–8, 380
cultural synergy 47, 50
culture 9–23, 24–40, 71–5, 85–6, 152–9, 355–9
boundaryless organizations 134, 139–41, 143–4
Case: difficult start 59–61
Case: evaluation 296, 299–300
Case: fast-food industry 301, 304–5, 313, 319, 324
Case: Inverlat 171–2, 175–7
Case: Novell 373, 374, 376–80
Central and Eastern Europe 287–90
contingency matrix 83–99
developing global leaders 82
diversity stress 336, 338, 340–1, 343–4
dual-career couples 212–13, 216–26, 228
ethics 329–31
European competencies 160, 163–4, 165–7
European leadership in globalization 41–53
Exercise: WWW 63–8
global recruitment 149–50
Hewlett-Packard 109, 113, 116
IT and teleworking 346
Latin America 273
managing in Asia 55, 57–8
Mexico 261–70

multicultural organizations 245–54, 257–9
NAFTA 103–4
policy basics 76–7
survival of HR 352, 353
"third" 291–4
see also corporate culture
culture shock 42, 47, 59, 338
Case: evaluation 295
dual-career couples 212, 217, 220
customer centralization 349, 351, 353, 354
customs and excise 105
Czech Republic 85, 86, 288, 363

DaimlerChrysler 202
Dairy Queen 308, 314
Daiwa Bank 329
Davos culture 153–4, 155, 156, 158
deference 9, 60, 92
Dell Computer 204, 206
Deloitte and Touche 44
Delta Airlines 366
Denmark 14–15, 16, 21–2, 193–4, 198
Case: Novell 363
Denny's 308, 314
didactic training 193, 194, 195
differentiation skills 161, 162, 163
Digital Equipment (DE) 202, 255, 257, 345–6
ethics 329, 332
disability 186, 356–7
Exercise: WWW 66, 67
Hewlett-Packard 117, 120, 122
diversity 83, 153, 183–9, 190–1, 294
boundaryless organizations 143
cultural programmes 355–9
dual-career couples 213
European competencies 162, 167
European leadership in globalization 41, 46, 48, 53
Exercise: WWW 63–8
Hewlett-Packard 108–24
multicultural organizations 245–8, 251–9
stress 336–44
Dominican Republic 319
Domino's Pizza 308, 309, 314
dual-career couples 211–28, 311
Dunkin' Donuts 314

East Africa 14–15, 21, 193
Eastern Europe 16, 86, 152, 157, 197, 287–90
Case: Novell 371, 375

Eastern Orthodox Christianity 19
Eastman Kodak 255, 258
e-commerce 196, 199, 206, 209
economic literacy promotion 349, 350–1, 353–4
economies of scale 43, 163, 165, 318, 319
Economy Color Card 254
Ecuador 14–15, 21–2, 193
  Case: fast-food industry 301, 320, 321
education 73, 75, 77, 91, 155, 157, 358
  Case: Bhiwar Enterprises 235, 237–8
  Case: Inverlat 171, 176
  Case: Novell 376
  cultural profiles 11
  developing global leaders 79
  diversity stress 344
  diversity training 184, 187–8
  dual-career couples 223, 225
  European leadership in globalization 42, 44, 51
  global recruitment 150–1
  Hewlett-Packard 115, 117, 119–20
  interpreters 39
  IT and teleworking 346
  Latin America 276–80
  multicultural organizations 253, 254, 255
  NAFTA 103–4
  survival of HR 351, 353
Egypt 15, 68
El Pollo Loco 311
e-mail 81, 345–7
Emory University 183
English language 52, 74, 94, 141, 187, 253–4, 356
  Case: difficult start 60
  Case: Eurochem 126
  Case: evaluation 296, 298
  Case: Inverlat 171–2, 175
  Case: Novell 366, 372, 374, 376–7
  Central and Eastern Europe 288, 289
  global culture 152–3, 156, 158–9
  global recruitment 151
  Hewlett-Packard 115, 117
entrepreneurship 200, 203–5, 209
  Case: Bhiwar Enterprises 241
  Case: Novell 366, 367–70, 380
environmental matters 43, 61, 154–5, 158
  Case: Anglo-German 360–1
  ethics 329–31, 333–5
equal opportunities 183–5, 355, 357

multicultural organizations 247, 250, 253, 257
Equitable Life Assurance 254
Esprit De Corp 254
ethics 10–11, 42, 329–35, 350, 352
  managing in Asia 55
  Mexico 269
Ethiopia 15
ethnic minorities 11, 12, 21, 42, 53
  Case: fast-food industry 311, 317
  diversity stress 336–7, 343
  diversity training 184–8
  Hewlett-Packard 109, 113–14, 122
  multicultural organizations 245–59
  see also race and racism
ethnocentrism 47, 49, 249, 294
E*TRADE 199
Eurochem Shanghai 125–9
Europe 152–3, 155, 157, 158, 280, 287–90
  Case: difficult start 60–2
  Case: fast-food industry 301, 313, 320–1, 323
  Case: Novell 370–1, 373, 375–9
  competencies 160–8
  contingency matrix 85, 86
  cultural profiles 13, 14–15, 16–17, 20–2
  diversity stress 336, 342
  ethics 330–1
  Hewlett-Packard 108–24
  IT and teleworking 345
  leadership in globalization 41–53
  strategy and initiatives 197–8
  training across cultures 190, 194
  underlying structure of culture 26–7, 29, 31, 34, 36
European Institute of Business Administration 190
evaluation case 295–300
Expanded Academic Index (EAI) 87
expatriates 42–3, 51, 76–7, 160–4, 166, 213–26
  Case: difficult start 59–62
  Case: Eurochem 125–9
  Central and Eastern Europe 287, 289
  contingency matrix 89, 95, 96
  developing global leaders 79–80
  dual-career couples 211–28
  European leadership in globalization 42–3, 47–8, 51, 53
  global recruitment 148, 151

managing in Asia 55–6
Mexico 263
experiential learning 191–5
externalizers 292–3
Exxon 207, 256
Exxon Valdez 329

Faculty Club culture 154–5, 158
families 77, 79–80, 114–15, 153–4, 256
  boundaryless organizations 141, 144
  Case: Bhiwar Enterprises 234–42
  Case: difficult start 59, 62
  Case: evaluation 296, 300
  Case: fast-food industry 305, 311, 312, 317
  Central and Eastern Europe 289–90
  contingency matrix 85, 86
  cultural profiles 11, 18, 20, 21, 22
  diversity training 186–8
  dual-career couples 211–28
  ethics 330, 334
  European leadership in globalization 41, 51,
    53
  Hewlett-Packard 110, 112, 114–15, 118–19
  Mexican culture 263, 266, 267, 268
  underlying structure of culture 26–7, 31–2,
    35
Federal National Mortgage Association
  (Fannie Mae) 256
feminism 152, 154–5, 158, 250
Finland 14–15, 16, 21–2, 193, 198
  Case: Novell 363, 372
first landing stage 161, 163–4
five-forces model 200–1
FleetGlobal 205
flexibility 72–3, 75, 76, 166, 183, 350
  boundaryless organizations 135–7, 139,
    142–4
  Case: Novell 368, 371
  developing global leaders 80
  ethics 331
  European leadership in globalization 41–2,
    46
  global recruitment 149, 150
  Hewlett-Packard 109
  IT and teleworking 345
  Latin America 272, 273, 281, 282
  managing in Asia 56
  Mexico 262, 324
  multicultural organizations 253, 254, 256
  NAFTA 104, 105

strategy and initiatives 200, 204
flextime 114, 118, 135, 187
focus groups 253, 257, 259
Ford 270, 273–4, 277, 280–3
  Hermosillo 274, 277, 280, 282–3
foreign direct investment (FDI) 197–8, 321, 322
foreign exchange 43, 323–4, 325
formality in Mexican culture 265
France 74, 85, 156, 159, 193, 198
  Case: Novell 363, 371–3, 376, 379
  cultural profile 14–15, 17, 21–2
  underlying structure of culture 26–30, 32–6,
    38–40
franchises 315–16, 362
  fast-food industry 301–2, 304–6, 312–16,
    318–21, 325–6
Friendly's 308
friendship 25–7, 30–2
Frito-Lay 205, 303, 305, 306
Fuddruckers 309
Functional Job Analysis (FJA) 137

gainsharing 87, 91
Gannett Corporation 188–9
gender 42, 183–6, 188, 245–54, 256–9, 356–8
  boundaryless organizations 141, 143, 144
  Case: Inverlat 173
  cultural profiles 11, 21–2
  diversity stress 336–8, 340–3
  dual-career couples 211, 218
  Exercise: WWW 68
  Hewlett-Packard 108–9, 112–22
  managing in Asia 57
  Mexico 262
General Agreement on Tariffs and Trade
  (GATT) 323
General Electric (GE) 199–200, 207, 270
  Case: Novell 367
General Foods 257
General Mills 208, 255
General Motors 250, 270
  Ramos Arizpe 282, 283
Germany 94–5, 152, 193, 197, 291–3, 340
  Case: fast-food industry 312, 313, 322
  Case: Novell 362, 363, 371–3, 376, 378–9
  contingency matrix 84, 86, 87, 89, 94–5
  cultural profile 14–15, 16, 17, 20, 21–2
  Hewlett-Packard 114, 120
  underlying structure of culture 26–31, 33–6,
    38–40

Ghana 15
gifts 42, 172, 329, 332
Global Fleet Graphics 205
globalization 71–5, 76–8, 109, 187, 245
    Case: fast-food industry 301–26
    Case: Novell 362–80
    contingency matrix 99
    development of leaders 79–82
    dual-career couples 211–28
    ethics 329–35
    European leadership 41–53
    four faces of culture 152–9
    IT and teleworking 345
    recruitment 148–51
    strategy and initiatives 197, 198, 209
    survival of HR 348
go native stage 161, 164–5
Godfather's Pizza 308
Golden Corral 308
Grand Metropolitan 312
Grandy's 311
GraphDesign 205
Greece 29, 193, 198, 289
    cultural profile 14–15, 16, 17, 21
Grenada 319
Grupo Financiero Inverlat 169–79
GTE 187–8
Guatemala 14–15, 21, 193, 157

Hallmark Greeting Cards 156
handshaking 42
Hanseatic League 22
Hardee's 308, 312, 314
Hare Krishna movement 152
harmony 267–8, 296
Harry's Farmers Market 312
HB Fuller Company 329, 331, 332, 334
heroes in cultural profiles 9–10, 12
Heublein, Inc. 302, 303, 305
Hewitt Associates 269
Hewlett-Packard 81, 108–24, 252, 254
    Case: Novell 378, 379
hierarchy 265, 266, 296
Highland Superstores 208
Hinayana 19
Hindu 19
Holmes Murphy 208
Honeywell 329, 332, 334
Hong Kong 14–15, 21, 154, 193, 197
    Case: fast-food industry 302

Case: Novell 363, 372
    Motorola 51
Hudson Institute 190, 355
human resource information system (HRIS)
    79–82
human rights 20, 67, 152, 155, 158
Hungary 14–15, 16, 20, 288

IBM 85, 94, 110, 191, 202, 255–6
    Case: Novell 378, 379
    cultural profiles 13, 16, 22
    ethics 329
    Mexico 264
IG Metall 94
imaginization 294
Imasco Ltd 312
immigration 190
India 32, 72, 152, 154, 193, 197–8
    Case: Bhiwar Enterprises 234–5, 241
    Case: Novell 363, 373, 374, 380
    cultural profile 14–15, 21
    Texas Instruments 51
individualism 13, 19, 20–2, 85–6, 94–6, 191
    Mexico 262–3, 266–9, 270
Indonesia 14–15, 19, 21, 42, 55, 72, 193
informal integration 246–7, 249, 251, 253,
    256–8
information flow 27–9, 31–2, 35, 36–7, 39, 72
information overload 36
innovation 44, 45, 50, 75, 99, 165, 245
    Germany 94–5
    Hewlett-Packard 109
    Latin America 271, 273
    survival of HR 348
INSEAD 330
Institute of Management and International
    Studies 44
integration skills 161, 163, 166
integration stage 161–2, 164, 165–6, 167
Intel 199, 205, 254
Interactive Skills 345–6
interfacing 38, 39, 40
intergroup conflict 246–7, 249, 251, 253,
    258–9
internalizers 292
International House of Pancakes 308
International Monetary Fund (IMF) 324
Internet 47, 52, 82, 87, 198, 199, 209
    Exercise: WWW 63–8
interpreters 39, 57, 94, 175

interruptions 29, 30–1, 35
IPD 346
Iran 32, 156, 193
   Case: Novell 374
   cultural profile 14–15, 16, 21
Iraq 15, 374
Ireland 14–15, 16, 19, 21–2, 193, 198
Islam (Muslims) 16, 19, 153, 155, 157, 158
Israel 14–15, 16, 21–2, 154, 193
Italy 27, 29, 85, 193, 322
   Case: Novell 363, 372, 373
   cultural profile 15, 19, 21–2
ITT Corporation 330

Jack in the Box 308, 314
Jamaica 14–15, 21–2, 193, 321
Japan 156–7, 158, 193, 197, 248, 337
   Case: fast-food industry 301–2, 314, 319,
      320, 322
   Case: Novell 363, 371, 372, 374, 376,
      379–80
   contingency matrix 84–7, 88–93, 94, 99
   cultural profile 14–15, 16, 19–20, 21–2
   ethics 330–1
   European leadership in globalization 41, 45,
      50
   Exercise: WWW 68
   methods in Latin America 271, 272–4, 276,
      279–80, 282
   "third culture" 291, 294
   underlying structure of culture 26–8, 33–4,
      36, 39
J.C. Penney 202
Jilin Industries 128
job analysis 133–44
job design 84, 87, 89, 92–3, 95–7, 98–9
Job Element Inventory (JEI) 137, 139, 144
joint ventures 42, 73, 167
   Case: Eurochem 126
   Case: fast-food industry 302, 319, 325
   Case: Novell 374
   Central and Eastern Europe 290
   NAFTA 103
   "third culture" 291, 293–4
Judaism 19, 56, 337, 340
Just-in-Time (JIT) 271, 272–3, 274–80, 282–4

kaizen 272, 274, 279, 280, 282
kanban 275–6, 279
Kenny Rogers Roasters 311

Kentucky Fried Chicken (KFC) 301–26
Kenya 15, 234–8, 240–2
K-Mart 106
knowledge, skills and abilities (KSA) 135–6,
   138–9, 141–2
Kodak 74
Korea 42, 55, 85, 193, 197
   Case: Novell 363, 372
   cultural profile 14–15, 16, 21–2
Korn/Ferry International 45
KPMG Peat Marwick 81, 261
Kuwait 15

labour relations 84, 86, 89, 92, 94–6, 98
   Latin America 271–84
languages 71, 74, 77, 187, 191, 294
   Case: difficult start 60
   Case: evaluation 296
   Case: fast-food industry 301, 313, 319
   Case: Inverlat 171–2, 175–6
   Case: Novell 372–7, 379, 380
   Central and Eastern Europe 288, 290
   contingency matrix 89, 94, 96
   cultural profiles 10, 11, 12, 19
   diversity stress 337–8
   dual-career couples 217
   ethics 332
   European competencies 166
   European leadership in globalization 42,
      45–7, 49–52
   Exercise: WWW 68
   global culture 152–3, 159
   global recruitment 149–51
   Hewlett-Packard 109, 113–15, 117, 120
   IT and teleworking 346
   managing in Asia 57
   Mexico 89, 96, 261
   multicultural organizations 253–4, 258
   underlying structure of culture 24–5, 33, 35,
      39–40
   see also English language
Latin America 16, 32–3, 157–8, 198, 269,
   271–84
   Case: fast-food industry 301, 313, 319–21, 326
   Case: Inverlat 170, 171
   Case: Novell 372, 373, 380
   Motorola 51
   training across cultures 190, 194, 195
laws, rules and regulations 50, 71, 80, 155,
   198, 357–8

Case: fast-food industry 319–20, 324–5
Case: Novell 374, 379
contingency matrix 89, 92, 95–8
cultural profiles 17–18, 20
diversity stress 342
diversity training 183, 185
ethics 330
European competencies 164, 166
Exercise: WWW 68
global recruitment 149
Mexico 265–6, 267, 268–70
NAFTA 105, 106
underlying structure of culture 24, 39–40
lead time 34
Lebanon 15
Lee Way Motor Freight 303
Levi Strauss 256, 329, 332, 333–4
Libya 15
Little Caesar's 308, 309, 314
locus of control 292–3
London University SSEES 287
Lone Star Steakhouse 308, 309
Long John Silver's 314
long term orientation 13
Loterria 314
Lucent 198
Luxembourg 198, 372

Mahayana 19
Malaysia 14–15, 21, 55, 193, 372
maquiladora 95, 106, 279, 282
marketing 45, 71–2, 183, 198, 199, 245, 294
Case: Eurochem 126–8
Case: fast-food industry 317–18
Case: Inverlat 178
Case: Novell 366, 368, 376
Central and Eastern Europe 288
ethics 333
Marriott Corporation 312
masculinity/feminity 12–13, 19, 20–2, 192
contingency matrix 85, 88, 91, 94, 95
Mexico 262–3, 270
Matsushita Electric Industrial 330
Mattel 204
McDonald's 97, 154, 156–7, 255
Case: fast-food industry 307–9, 312–14, 317–21, 326
McDonnell Douglas 252
McWorld 154, 156–7
mediation 259

meditation 19, 20
meetings and appointments 35
Case: Eurochem 125
Case: Inverlat 175
IT and teleworking 345–7
managing in Asia 57
Mexico 268
Saudi Arabia 41
underlying structure of culture 27, 31–5, 37, 39
Men's Wearhouse 209
mental programming 9–11, 12, 15–17, 19–22
"third culture" 292, 294
mentoring 253, 256–7, 356, 357
dual-career couples 211–28
Merck 74, 256
mergers and acquisitions 73, 81, 165, 294
Case: fast-food industry 302, 312
Case: Novell 379–80
Merrill Lynch 199
Mexicana 322
Mexico 51, 95–7, 156–7, 198, 261–70, 320–3
Case: fast-food industry 301–2, 319, 320–6
Case: Inverlat 169–79
Case: Novell 362, 363, 371
contingency matrix 84–7, 89, 95–7
cultural profile 14–15, 21–2
NAFTA 95–6, 103–7, 261, 274, 301, 323, 325
new strategy and labour 271, 274, 277, 278, 280–3
training across cultures 193
Microsoft 198, 379, 380
Middle East 19
Minnesota Mining and Manufacturing 330
Mitsuoishi Shoji Kaisha Ltd 302
mixed economic growth 196, 197–8
Mobil Oil 255
Moldova 289
monochronic time 30–3, 35–8
monolithic organizations 248–50, 251, 259
Monsanto Corporation 150
Montgomery Ward 202
morale 48, 96, 109, 215
Case: fast-food industry 304
morals 11, 42, 336–44, 350
ethics 329–30, 333–4
Mos Burger 314
motivation 51, 56, 76, 142, 165, 357
Case: evaluation 299

Case: fast-food industry 321
Case: Novell 367, 369–70, 375
Central and Eastern Europe 289
contingency matrix 89, 91, 94, 98–9
Hewlett-Packard 114
Latin America 273, 276, 281, 284
Mexican culture 266, 268, 270
pay-for-performance 208
Motorola 44, 51, 74, 96, 200, 254, 270
Mrs Winner's 311
multiculturalism 42, 45–6, 194, 245–59, 355
Case: Novell 376
contingency matrix 96
diversity stress 336–8, 340–1, 343–4
diversity training 183, 187
European competencies 160, 163, 164, 167
global recruitment 151
Hewlett-Packard 116, 121
multinational companies (MNCs) 13, 72–5,
    158, 190, 196–7
Case: Anglo-German 360–1
Case: difficult start 61
Central and Eastern Europe 287
contingency matrix 83–4, 86, 90, 93–6, 98
developing global leaders 79–82
dual-career couples 211, 214–17, 220,
    227–8
ethics 333, 335
European leadership in globalization 45, 49,
    50
global recruitment 148–9
HR policy basics 76–7
IT and teleworking 345
strategy and initiatives 196–8, 203, 205
multirater feedback 206–7, 209
Muslims (Islam) 16, 19, 153, 155, 157, 158
mysticism 19

Nabisco 95, 270, 303, 304
National Academy of Management 254
National Computer Systems (NCS) 103–7
NEC 110
Nestlé 197
Netherlands 86, 193, 198, 291–2
Case: Novell 363, 372
cultural profile 14–15, 16, 19–20, 21–2
neutral/affective 86, 88, 97
New Zealand 14–15, 21, 193, 302
Case: Novell 363, 372
Nigeria 15

Nippo Kasei 127
Nissan 95–6, 280
non-governmental organizations (NGOs) 43,
    155
North American Free Trade Agreement
    (NAFTA) 43, 103–7
Case: fast-food industry 301, 323, 325
Mexico 95–6, 103–7, 261, 274, 301, 323,
    325
North American Van Lines 303
North Carolina National Bank 256
Northern Telecom 258
Norway 14–15, 16, 21–2, 193, 363
Novell, Inc. 362–81

Olive Garden 308, 309
Orange Julius 314
Organizational Effectiveness Change Model 96
organizational identification 247–9, 251, 253
organizational socialization 216–17
Ortho Pharmaceuticals 252
Otis Elevator 74
Outback Steakhouse 308, 309

Pace Foods 254
Pakistan 14–15, 16, 21, 193, 374
Palestine 154, 337
Panama 14–15, 193, 320, 321
Papa John's Pizza 308, 309
particularism 86, 97
paternalism 262, 265, 266, 268–9
pay-for-performance 206, 207–9, 268
contingency matrix 87, 89, 96, 98
penguins 360–1
PepsiCo 198, 255, 303–6, 313, 315–16, 318
Perkins 308
personal space 28, 29, 30
personality 137, 139, 141–2, 150, 208
diversity stress 339, 340, 343
personalization 265–6
Personnel Decisions Inc. 207
Peru 15, 21, 152, 193
Case: fast-food industry 301, 320, 321
Case: Novell 375
Petróleos Mexicanos (Pemex) 322
Philippines 14–15, 19, 21, 157, 193, 291
Philips Electronics 198, 330
Phillip Morris 250, 258
Pillsbury Company 312
piracy 329, 374–5, 380

Pizza Hut 304–9, 313–14, 316, 318–19
plural organizations 248, 249, 250–1, 252, 257, 259
pluralism 157–9, 246, 252–4
    multicultural organizations 249, 251, 252–4, 259
Poland 19, 287, 288, 363
polycentric corporations 50
polychronic time 30–3, 35, 37
Ponderosa 308, 309
Popeye's Chicken 308, 310–12, 314–15
Portugal 14–15, 21–2, 85, 193, 198
    Case: Novell 363
Position Analysis Questionnaire (PAQ) 137, 139, 144
power distance 13–17, 19, 192–4
    contingency matrix 85, 88, 94, 95, 96
    Mexico 262–3, 264–6, 270
PREALC 278, 279
prejudice 246–51, 253, 257, 259
    diversity stress 336, 344
Priceline.com 199
Prim America 255
principled leaders development 349, 350, 353, 354
Principled Reasoning Approach 333–4
Proctor and Gamble 253, 259
productivity 48, 92, 94, 96, 164, 186
    Case: Inverlat 173, 175
    dual-career couples 215, 218, 220
    Hewlett-Packard 109
    Latin America 273, 274, 283
    NAFTA 104
promotion 45, 81, 88, 98, 184–5, 250, 357
    Case: fast-food industry 305
    Case: Inverlat 172
    Case: Novell 371
    dual-career couples 214
    Hewlett-Packard 115, 117, 121
    Latin America 283
    multicultural organizations 255, 256, 259
    multirater feedback 207
    survival of HR 350, 351
protectionism 43, 321
Protestantism 19, 152, 157–8, 159
Pudgie's 311
Puerto Rico 301, 319, 320, 321

Quaker Oats 255
Quality Control Circles 275–6, 284

Quick Restaurants 314
Quincy's 308
quotas 116, 118, 120, 121, 323

race and racism 18, 356–8
    boundaryless organizations 141, 144
    diversity stress 336, 341, 342
    diversity training 183, 184, 186
    Hewlett-Packard 109, 113, 114–16
    multicultural organizations 245–6, 247–51, 254–9
    see also ethnic minorities
Radio Shack 106
Rally's Hamburgers 312
Rand Corporation 44
realistic job preview (RJP) 140, 141
recruitment and selection 75, 88–90, 148–51, 166, 357–8
    boundaryless organizations 133–44
    Case: fast-food industry 319
    Case: Novell 378, 379
    contingency matrix 84, 88–90, 94–5, 97
    developing global leaders 80–2
    diversity training 184, 185, 187, 188
    dual-career couples 227
    European competencies 160, 162–4, 166
    European leadership in globalization 41, 45–6, 49–50
    Hewlett-Packard 117, 118, 121
    IT and teleworking 346
    Latin America 273, 281–2
    Mexico 267, 269, 270
    multicultural organizations 247, 250, 258
    multirater feedback 207
    pay-for-performance 208
    principled leaders 350, 353
Red Lobster 308, 309
Red Robin 309
releasing the right responses 25, 39, 40
religion 42, 154–5, 157–8
    cultural profiles 10–12, 17–20, 22
    diversity stress 337, 340
    diversity training 186–7
    Exercise: WWW 66, 67
    Hewlett-Packard 109, 113
research and development (R&D) 50, 71–2, 95, 205
    European competencies 165
    Hewlett-Packard 120
respect 10, 265, 267–8, 289, 379

return on investment (ROI) 103–4, 205
Revlon Inc. 205
rituals 9–10, 12
R.J. Reynolds (RJR) 303, 304, 305
Rockwell 366
Roman Catholicism 19, 155, 158
Roman Empire 16–17, 19
Romania 19, 289
Romano's Macaroni Grill 308, 309
Rori Company 234, 237–40
Round Table Pizza 308, 309
Roy Rogers Restaurants 312
Ruby Tuesday 308, 309
Russia 85, 86, 198, 288–90
  Case: Novell 375
  cultural profile 14–15, 16, 17, 21–2
Ryan's 308

Safeguard Scientifics 367
Salvador 14–15, 21, 193
SAS 209
Saudi Arabia 15, 41, 66, 337, 362
Sbarros 308
Scandinavia 26, 29, 31, 85, 155, 372
schedules 30–7
Scotland 20
Seagate Technology 202
search engines 63–7
Sears 202
Serbia 14–15, 16, 17, 21
services maximization and staff minimization
  349, 351–3
Servico Nacional de Aprendizagem Industrial
  (SENAI) 276
sexual orientation 183, 186, 341, 356
  Hewlett-Packard 113, 115, 116, 118
Shanghai Batteries 127–8
Shell Oil 329
Shia 19
Shinto 20, 157
Shoney's 308
short term orientation 13
Siam Chemicals Company (SCC) 59–62,
  295–300
Siemens AG 330
Sierra Leone 15
silent language 24, 40
Singapore 51, 55, 85, 86, 158, 193, 197
  Case: evaluation 295, 299–300
  Case: Novell 363, 372

cultural profile 14–15, 21
Single European Market 160, 163–5
Sizzler 308, 309, 314
Skylark 314
Slovakia 288
Slovenia 14–15, 16, 21–2, 288
smoking 155
social support 216, 217–26, 228, 257
  diversity stress 338–9, 343
Society for Human Resource Management
  (SHRM) 356–8
Somalia 21
Sonic Drive-In 308
Sony 198, 202
South Africa 14–15, 21–2, 154, 193, 248, 333
  Case: fast-food industry 302
  Case: Novell 363, 372
Southwest Airlines 209
Soviet Union 12, 86, 156, 198, 288–9
  Case: Novell 377
space 28–30, 36, 39, 86
Spaghetti Factory 312
Spain 27, 29, 35, 36, 42, 86, 193, 198
  Banco Bilbao Viscaya 179
  Case: Novell 363, 372
  cultural profile 14–15, 21–2
  Hewlett-Packard 117, 118, 120
  Mexican trading 322
specific/diffuse 86, 97
speed of messages 25–6, 39
status 10, 86, 340, 348
  Case: Novell 371
  Mexican culture 265–6
  multicultural organizations 247–8, 253, 255
  underlying structure of culture 24, 27–8,
    33–5
Steak'n Shake 308
strategic alliance 42, 73, 104, 198–201, 367
strategic analysis 103–4
stress 213–16, 282, 336–44
  Case: Novell 370
  dual-career couples 211–17, 220, 223, 226,
    228
Stroh Brewery 250
structural integration 246–51, 253, 255–6
subsidiaries 13, 38, 50–2, 85, 86, 331
  Case: Eurochem 125–9
  Case: evaluation 295–300
  Case: fast-food industry 302–3, 311, 319–20
  Case: Novell 363, 370

Case: SCC 59
European competencies 161–2, 164–5,
  167
NAFTA 104–7
Subway Sandwiches 308, 314
succession planning 75, 76–7
Sun Microsystems 209
Sunni 19
Suriname 319
Sweden 46, 148–9, 193
  Case: Novell 363, 371, 372
  cultural profile 14–15, 16, 21–2
Switzerland 26, 31, 36, 38, 46, 86, 193
  ABB Ltd 81
  Case: difficult start 59
  Case: evaluation 295–6
  Case: fast-food industry 312
  Case: Novell 363
  cultural profile 14–15, 16, 21–2
  Hewlett-Packard 115, 118, 119
symbols 9–10, 12

Taco Bell 304–8, 313–14, 316, 318–19
Taco Time 314
Taiwan 14–15, 16, 21, 55, 193
  Case: Novell 363, 372
  Motorola 51
Tanzania 15
Taoism 55–6
taxation 43, 77, 80, 322, 370
  NAFTA 105, 106, 107
TCBY 314
teamwork 208, 341–2
  Central and Eastern Europe 290
  Hewlett-Packard 109
  IT and teleworking 345–7
  Latin America 272–4, 277–80, 282–3
technology 17–18, 72, 77–8, 87, 95, 198–9,
  349
  boundaryless organizations 134–6, 138
  Case: Inverlat 170, 171
  Case: Novell 362–80
  Central and Eastern Europe 288
  developing global leaders 80–1
  European leadership in globalization 43, 45,
    48, 50–1
  strategy and initiatives 198–200, 202–3,
    205–6
  teleworking 345–7
territoriality 28–9, 36

Tetra Pak 149
Texaco 184–5, 186
Texas A&M 95
Texas Instruments 51
TGI Friday's 308, 314
Thailand 14–15, 16, 21–2, 55, 193
  Case: difficult start 59–62
  Case: evaluation 295–300
  Exercise: WWW 66
3M 205
time 30–5, 36–9, 89, 92, 346
  Case: Eurochem 125
  Central and Eastern Europe 288
  dual-career couples 218–19
  NAFTA 104, 105
Time Inc. 258
Total Productive Maintenance (TPM) 272
Total Quality Management (TQM) 274–80,
  358
  Latin America 271–3, 274–80, 282–4
Towers Perrin 95, 183, 264
Toyota 280
training 77, 183–9, 190–5, 207, 355–8
  boundaryless organizations 134, 142, 144
  Case: evaluation 299
  Case: fast-food industry 305, 318, 319,
    324
  Case: Novell 373, 378, 379
  Central and Eastern Europe 287–90
  contingency matrix 83–4, 89–91, 93–8
  developing global leaders 80
  diversity stress 337, 341, 342
  dual-career couples 212, 216, 225, 227
  ethics 331, 332, 333
  European competencies 164, 166–7
  European leadership in globalization 42,
    44–5, 48–51
  global recruitment 150–1
  Hewlett-Packard 114–15, 117, 119, 122
  IT and teleworking 346
  Latin America 273–6, 278–9, 282–4
  managing in Asia 56, 58
  Mexico 261, 269, 270
  multicultural organizations 252–5, 257–9
  plural organizations 250
  survival of HR 351, 353
translators 39, 57, 94, 175
Tricon Global Restaurants 306–7, 316, 318,
  319
Trinidad and Tobago 321

trust 41, 56, 194–5, 217, 290
    Case: Eurochem 126–7
    Case: evaluation 296
    Case: Novell 37
    contingency matrix 88–90, 92
    diversity stress 344
    Hewlett-Packard 109
    Japan 88–90, 92
    Latin America 273
TRW 325
Turkey 14–15, 16, 21, 120, 193, 198

Uganda 241
Ulster 12
uncertainty avoidance 13–20, 192–4, 269
    contingency matrix 85, 88, 90, 93–6
    cultural profiles 9, 13–20, 21, 23
    Mexico 262–3, 269, 270
Unilever 197
unions 49, 81, 357–8
    contingency matrix 87, 89, 92, 94–6, 98
    Latin America 271, 273, 280–4
    Mexico 267, 268–9, 321
United Arab Emirates 15, 363
United Kingdom 29, 31, 86, 93, 158, 193, 287
    Case: fast-food industry 301, 302, 312
    Case: Novell 362–3, 371–3, 376, 379
    cultural profiles 14–15, 16, 17, 19–22
    Exercise: WWW 63–4, 68
    Hewlett-Packard 114–15, 118, 119
    IT and teleworking 345–7
United Nations 63, 154
United Parcel Service (UPS) 207, 325
United States of America (US) 152–9, 193,
        282, 355
    boundaryless organizations 135–6
    Case: Bhiwar Enterprises 234, 237–8, 240,
        242
    Case: Eurochem 127
    Case: fast-food industry 301–26
    Case: Inverlat 171
    Case: Novell 362–3, 366, 370–1, 373–4,
        376–9
    compared with Mexico 261–70
    contingency matrix 83, 85, 86, 91, 93–6
    cultural profile 10, 14–15, 17, 20, 21
    diversity stress 341
    diversity training 183–8
    dual-career couples 211, 227, 228
    ethics 329, 330–2

European leadership in globalization 41–2,
        45, 48–52
    Exercise: WWW 66
    global recruitment 148, 149–51
    Hewlett-Packard 108, 112, 114, 116–18
    managing in Asia 55–8
    multicultural organizations 246–52, 255
    NAFTA 103, 105–7, 261
    strategy and initiatives 197, 205
    survival of HR 349, 350–1
    "third culture" 291, 294
    training across cultures 190, 193–5
    underlying structure of culture 25–40
universalism 86, 94
University of Chicago 44
University of Michigan 254
University of Pennsylvania 44
University of Texas 95
UNUM Life Insurance 185–7
Uruguay 14–15, 21, 193
    Case: fast-food industry 320, 321
US West 254, 259

values 152–6, 158–9, 184, 246, 254, 358
    boundaryless organizations 134, 139–44
    contingency matrix 91, 94, 97
    core concepts of culture 48, 52
    cultural profiles 9–13, 19
    diversity stress 336–8, 341–2, 344
    dual-career couples 216–17, 220
    ethics 330–1, 332, 333, 335
    Hewlett-Packard 109
    Latin America 273
    managing in Asia 57
    Mexican culture 261–4, 269
    survival of HR 349, 350, 352–4
    training across cultures 191, 192, 194,
        195
Venezuela 14–15, 21–2, 86, 193
    Case: fast-food industry 301, 319–21
    Case: Novell 362, 371
venture teams 203–4
Vietnam 55
Village Inn 308
Virgin Islands 320, 321
virtual teams 345–7

W. Edwards Deming 208
Waffle House 308
Wal-Mart 106, 202, 205, 309

Wendy's 308, 314
West Africa 14–15, 21, 193
Western Sizzlin' 308, 309
Wienerwald 312
Wilson Learning 207
Wilson Sporting Goods 303
WordPerfect 380
work analysis 138–9, 144
World Bank 98, 324
World Bank (France) 330

World Health Organization 155, 334
Wuzhou Plastics 128

Xerox 255, 259, 329

Yale University 258
Yugoslavia 12, 16, 193, 289

Zambia 15